ArtScroll Series®

Rabbi Nosson Scherman / Rabbi Meir Zlotowitz

General Editors

SMILING

Published by

Mesorah Publications, ltd

by
Rabbi Abraham J. Twerski, M.D.

FIRST EDITION
First Impression ... June 1993
SECOND EDITION
First Impression ... April 1995
Second Impression ... September 1996
THIRD EDITION
First Impression ... August 1998
Second Impression ... November 2001
FOURTH EDITION
First Impression ... December 2003
Second Impression ... September 2007
Third Impression ... June 2012
Fourth Impression ... February 2018

Published and Distributed by
MESORAH PUBLICATIONS, Ltd.
4401 Second Avenue
Brooklyn, New York 11232

Distributed in Europe by
LEHMANNS
Unit E, Viking Business Park
Rolling Mill Road
Jarrow, Tyne & Wear NE32 3DP
England

Distributed in Australia & New Zealand by
GOLDS WORLD OF JUDAICA
3-13 William Street
Balaclava, Melbourne 3183
Victoria Australia

Distributed in Israel by
SIFRIATI / A. GITLER — BOOKS
POB 2351
Bnei Brak 51122

Distributed in South Africa by
KOLLEL BOOKSHOP
Northfield centre, 17 Northfield Avenue
Glenhazel 2192, Johannesburg, South Africa

THE ARTSCROLL SERIES®
SMILING EACH DAY
© *Copyright 1993, by MESORAH PUBLICATIONS, Ltd.*
4401 Second Avenue / Brooklyn, N.Y. 11232 / (718) 921-9000 / www.artscroll.com

---

ISBN 10: 0-89906-581-3 / ISBN 13: 978-0-89906-581-6

Printed in the United States of America by Noble Book Press Corp.
Bound by Sefercraft Quality Bookbinders, Ltd., Brooklyn, N.Y.

↝§ Introduction

Jewish wit and humor are legendary. Much less appreciated though, is the fact that Torah scholars, who are often thought of as being obelisks of solemnity, make rich use of their latent jocular prowess as a teaching technique.

Wit serves two functions in this context. Like metaphor, which abounds in Torah literature, it can emphasize and help clarify a more obscure message. Secondly, it promotes an attitude of cheer, so vital in Torah study and Torah living.

The Talmud relates that Rabbah, one of the foremost sages, would preface his lectures with witty comments that would give rise to an upbeat mood, following which he would broach the course material at hand with appropriate reverence (*Shabbos* 30b). *Simchah,* or a cheerful attitude, is considered an essential ingredient in achieving a proper mind-set for study.

The Scriptures and Talmud sharply condemn *letzanus*, which is not wit or humor, but derision. Sarcasm, scoffing, and mocking, where not directed at the evil the Torah deems worthy of scorn, are viewed as destructive, in that they discourage people from serious consideration of their behavior. Ironically, other than inducing cheer, *letzanus* is meant to minimize the significance of a person's actions, and thus contributes to a mood of futility and possibly depression. Wit, however, is not *letzanus*.

People who have no direct contact with Torah scholars scarcely suspect that these highly spiritual people who look upon life with a solemnity befitting an acute awareness of its Divinely purposeful nature, might posses a bright smile and a twinkle in the eye which testifys to another aspect of their personalities. In truth, this is not a "lighter side" of them that is separate from their concept of life as serious business, but a well integrated spice which enhances the flavor of a wholesome Torah life.

In the pages ahead, I have compiled some of the wit of Torah personalities, as it has been handed down to us in their writings or by word of mouth. Contained within these gems are often the most sublime teachings, which are simply made more palatable through the vehicle of wit. Or, they may just be mildly humorous remarks that, like the opening lines of Rabbah, can help us attain a more cheerful mind-set. None are intended to produce rollicking laughter. Rather, the hope is to inject a tone of Torah cheer into the morass of routine, so that we can best appreciate the learning and growth experience that life is, and indeed smile each day.

In keeping with the practice of Rabbah, each cheerful message for the day is accompanied by a brief "thought-for-the-day," upon which one may constructively meditate. The thought for meditation and the daily message are not related. Each has an independent purpose. Hopefully, this unique Torah formula of wit and reflection will set the tone for a productive day.

SMILING EACH DAY

*First Day of
Rosh Hashanah*

Wisdom is not to be measured in abstract thought, but in proper action.

SMILING EACH DAY

The Psalmist counsels, "Exult with trembling" (*Psalms* 2:11). This paradoxical concept, while basic to the whole of Jewish experience, manifests itself to no greater degree perhaps, than on Rosh Hashanah and Yom Kippur. The focal points of the "awesome days," during which each person's actions are reviewed for subsequent judgment by the heavenly tribunal, they are nevertheless *Yomim Tovim,* and should be observed with the appropriate festive spirit.

When Ezra chastised the Israelites on Rosh Hashanah they wept in remorse. He then said, "Do not mourn or weep. Eat and drink delicacies and give food to the needy. Do not be sad, for the joy of G-d is your strength" (*Nehemia* 8:10).

Accordingly, the Jerusalem Talmud notes that in contrast to people who approach their trial solely with apprehension, Jews don holiday clothes, and eat and drink in sober rejoicing, secure in the expectation that the Almighty will judge them mercifully (*Rosh Hashanah* 1:3). We thus clearly demonstrate concomitant joy and awe.

❧ ❧ ❧

Rosh Hashanah is the day most Jews perform the *Tashlich* ritual, whereby we symbolically rid ourselves forever of our character defects by casting them into the water.

The Seer of Lublin, returning from *Tashlich*, met his disciple, Rabbi Naftali of Ropschitz, who was known for his wit, going down to the stream. To the master's query as to where he was headed, Rabbi Naftali replied, with playful sincerity, "Why, to retrieve for myself the 'defects' that the master has just thrown away." Indeed just as items very valuable to people of lesser means may be discarded by the wealthy, what we deem to be virtues for ourselves may not meet the extremely high standards that a *tzaddik* demands of himself. What we achieved yesterday may have been satisfactory for yesterday, but we must improve upon that today, so that by comparison, yesterday's achievements will appear deficient by our freshly elevated standards.

Today
I shall smile
because . . .

_____
_____
_____

> If you are not more spiritual today than you were yesterday, you have lost ground, not merely failed to grow. A person does not remain static. If one is not progressing, one is regressing.

Second day of
Rosh Hashanah

SMILING EACH DAY

When Rosh Hashanah occurs on Shabbos, the *shofar* is not sounded on that day. This is due to a Rabbinical decree, to prevent someone from transporting a *shofar* through a public thoroughfare, which is prohibited on Shabbos.

Folklore offers another explanation. The angel assigned to supervise the *mitzvah* of *shofar* is the same one who is sent down to insure that the *cholent* and *kugel* remain hot on Shabbos morning. Since an angel cannot have two simultaneous assignments, whenever the two conflict, the *shofar* is sacrificed. According to this scenario, hot *cholent* and *kugel* on Shabbos transcend *shofar* in importance! Gastronomically correct for sure, but hardly sublime.

In truth however, the custom of hot *cholent* on Shabbos is far more than of gustatory or gastronomical significance. The Talmudic sages interpreted the Biblical verse prohibiting a fire on Shabbos to mean that one may not cook or kindle a flame, but precooked foods may be kept hot on a stove that was lit before Shabbos. The Saducees, on the other hand, who rejected Talmudic interpretations, and translated Scriptures literally, prohibited the use of any manner of fire on Shabbos.

Thus, eating hot foods on Shabbos serves to stress our acknowledgment of the Divine authority of the Talmudic sages, and acceptance of their interpretation of the Torah as singularly authentic. It is that authority which empowers them to dispense with the performance of *shofar* out of concern that it might result in an inadvertent Scriptural transgression. And so, in a sense, hot *cholent* on Shabbos exists on a plane above that of *shofar*.

Cholent may be only a custom, but established Jewish customs *are* Torah (*Mateh Ephraim* 610).

Today
I shall smile
because . . .

Fast of Gedaliah
[When 3 Tishrei
falls on the
Sabbath the fast
is observed
on Sunday.]

Rabbi Yechezkel of Kuzmir said, "Navigating through this world is like walking on a frozen lake. Running may cause the ice to break, while walking too slowly may allow the ice ahead to melt. Either way, you fall through. You must walk gently but quickly."

SMILING EACH DAY

Rabbi Heschel of Cracow, one of the foremost Torah scholars of his day, was a child prodigy. He was once chastised by his father who found him eating goodies on Rosh Hashanah morning, in violation of the accepted practice that one does not eat before the *shofar* is sounded. The bright child was quick to defend himself. "During the entire month of Elul," he pointed out, "the *shofar* is blown daily after the morning prayers. Yet, we do not do so on the day before Rosh Hashanah. Why not? In order to confuse Satan, so that he will not anticipate the *shofar* being sounded on Rosh Hashanah, and will therefore not be in a position to present his incriminations before the Divine tribunal.

"I too," continued the sweet-toothed darling turned smooth-tongued public defender, "wish to confuse Satan. Since he knows that we do not eat before hearing the *shofar*, when he observes me eating, he must then conclude that he was mistaken in his calculations, and that today is not Rosh Hashanah after all. In this way, our people will be spared his evil schemes."

This is superb reasoning for a child, but we must be careful that, as mature adults, we do not similarly rationalize in order to justify gratifying our appetites for the myriad "goodies" life has to offer.

Today
I shall smile
because . . .

_____
_____
_____

Even a peasant, who has a message for the King from a long lost beloved son, is promptly ushered into the throne room. The prayer of a person who does teshuvah is precisely such a message, and is warmly welcomed by G-d (*Maggid of Mezeritch*).

SMILING EACH DAY

In the prayer *Avinu Malkenu* (Our Father Our King), we ask G-d to "Raise high the *keren* (lit. horn; i.e. pride or status) of your people Israel."

The word *keren* has an alternate meaning, though, used in *halachah* to refer to the principle of an investment or a loan as opposed to the dividends, or the interest, which are the profit on the principle.

One of the rabbis cited the Talmudic statement that the purpose of Jews being in exile is to attract non-believers to the light of Judaism. Applying the perspective of investment, these additions to Judaism could be viewed as the "profit" or the income generated by the *keren* or principle, which is the Jewish people proper.

Investment, however, is often fraught with speculation, and surely, if one were to see that his investment is at great risk, to the point where he is in danger of forfeiting the principle, he would certainly pull out and save whatever he could. How much profit is profit when it sacrifices the integrity of the principle?

In this vein do we pray to G-d, "Raise up and pull out the *keren*, the *principle* of your people Israel." You wished us to be in exile in order to accumulate profit, to attract others to Judaism. But the resultant reality of Jewish assimilation is too costly a price to pay. Do not be concerned about profit. Rather, bring us all in from exile, and preserve the principle.

Today
I shall smile
because . . .

How can one ever know if he has achieved Divine forgiveness for his sins? If one never again repeats the sinful act, he can be certain that there has been total forgiveness (*Rabbi Bunim of P'shischa*).

SMILING EACH DAY

After reciting aloud forty-three verses of *Avinu Malkenu* (Our Father Our King), we say the last verse silently, "Our Father our King, be gracious and respond to us, though we have no merits. Be charitable and kind with us and help us." Why is this last verse said silently?

The Maggid (Preacher) of Dubno told of a merchant who ordered goods from his supplier. He loudly specified how much of each item he wanted delivered. After the entire order was taken and the sales person asked for payment, the merchant requested to speak with the proprietor. Taking him aside, he then whispered, "Listen, I have fallen on bad times, and I cannot pay for the merchandise now, but if you will just extend me some credit, I will surely be able to sell the merchandise at a profit and pay you." Self-pity or masochism notwithstanding, this is hardly a statement which he would allow others to hear.

"Similarly," said the Maggid, "when aroused to ponder His eternal beneficence, we boldly ask for many things from G-d as though we had earned them. When we finish the list and come to our senses, however, we must silently entreat, 'Dear G-d, we know we do not deserve what we have asked for because we have no merits, but please extend us credit. If You grant us life, health, a livelihood, and peace, we will certainly be able to do Your bidding and be deserving of Your gifts.' "

Pleading for an extension of credit because we are devoid of merits is something we only whisper. Yet, we can be certain that the merciful G-d responds to whispers as he does to resonant prayer, with love and graciousness for his children/customers.

Today I shall smile because . . .

_____

_____

_____

Chassidim of Tomashav noted with constructive scorn, "It is not the hand that should beat on the heart when repenting one's sins, but to the contrary, the heart should beat the hand."

SMILING EACH DAY

In our high holiday prayers we note that during these awesome days of judgment, even the angels tremble. וּמַלְאָכִים יֵחָפֵזוּן, the angels hurry past the Divine tribunal. Why the haste?

The Talmud informs us that with each *mitzvah* a person performs, he creates a benign angel (*Ethics of the Fathers* 4:13). One can perform a *mitzvah* with proper preparation and appropriate *kavannah* (concentration and intent), fulfilling it in all its minutest details. The angel who is born from such performance is accordingly handsome and well formed, certain to make a strongly favorable impression on that most supreme court. However, when one performs a *mitzvah* perfunctorily, as so often is the case when we rush through our prayers or the Grace after Meals because we must make an appointment, the angels created from such *mitzvah* performances are understandably defective. They may be deformed, and/or lacking in parts of their being, corresponding to the flaws in the performance of the *mitzvah*. Despite their lacking the all-important, but uniquely human, quality of vanity, these angels are ashamed of their less than flattering appearance, and when they appear for review by the Heavenly tribunal that evaluates our deeds, they go by rather hurriedly to avoid the embarrassment and inherent criminal implication that accompanies this sorry state.

Let us then perform *mitzvos* properly, so that we create angels who will proudly display themselves and eloquently plead our cause before the Heavenly bench.

Today
I shall smile
because . . .

Rabbi Chaim of Sanz would record in a notebook every single moment of his that was not devoted to Torah or *mitzvos*. One year, prior to Yom Kippur, he added up the figures and the sum was three hours. He then wept for three hours, asking for Divine forgiveness. We must train ourselves to appreciate that time, however short, is precious, not to be wasted.

SMILING EACH DAY

Rabbi Naftali of Ropschitz revealed, much to our naive relief, that there is a simple way of assuring oneself a favorable judgment on Rosh Hashanah and Yom Kippur.

The Talmud (as if we didn't already know on our own) states that Satan and the *yetzer hara* (the evil inclination) are one and the same. Furthermore, the Talmud defines an enemy as someone with whom one has avoided, out of ill-will, all communication for three consecutive days (*Sanhedrin* 27b). Since the Divine tribunal will not accept testimony from one's outspoken enemy, all that is necessary to disqualify Satan from delivering any testimony for the prosecution is to avoid any contact with the *yetzer hara* for three consecutive days before Rosh Hashanah and Yom Kippur. Satan will thus be designated as one's enemy, and his testimony, however intriguing, will not be admitted.

Of course, in order for this stratagem to be effective, the break must be absolute. This is by no means a simple task, since a person may have to deny himself many formerly rewarding pursuits (including the comfort of one of life's truly close relationships — the one we all maintain with the *yetzer hara*). Still, the prize being so great, it is a feat well worth an effort — at least for three days.

Today
I shall smile
because . . .

_____
_____
_____

Every person has the capacity for doing *teshuvah,* except a liar, who because he comes to believe his own lies, does not realize that what he is doing is wrong. Thus, it is a sin to deceive another person, but pure folly to deceive oneself (*Rabbi Bunim of P'shischa*).

SMILING EACH DAY

One Yom Kippur eve, when everyone had gathered for *Kol Nidrei*, and it was still before sunset, Rabbi Levi Yitzchak of Berdichev took a candle and searched under all the benches in the synagogue. When asked what he was trying to find, he looked up incredulously, "Why, an intoxicated Jew of course!"

After completing his futile search, Rabbi Levi Yitzchak approached the open Ark while the crowd looked on, trembling. "Master of the Universe," he cried. "You made it mandatory that on the day before Yom Kippur, we eat and drink as if it were a holiday.

"Suppose you had given this *mitzvah* to other nations of the world, what would have been the result? They would surely have eaten like gluttons, drunk to excess, and by now, been thoroughly inebriated.

"But look down upon your holy people, merciful Father," he continued, sobbing. "They faithfully fulfilled Your commandment, and ate and drank in a festive manner as You instructed. Yet, they have all gathered here now in utter solemnity, ready to approach You in prayer. Is a single one of them drunk? Is one of them nodding off? Is any one of them tottering?"

Arms outstretched, and with a wail that pried open the hearts of all assembled, he concluded, "You must appreci-'ate Your people, dear G-d. They are a spiritual people, and indeed merit forgiveness. They truly deserve Your blessing for a year of life and prosperity." And with that, he began *Kol Nidrei*.

Today
I shall smile
because . . .

The Midrash states that G-d caused Adam to pass before all the trees in Eden and said, "See how beautiful are My works, and I have created them all for your sake. Take heed not to follow a destructive spiritual path and thereby damage My world." This challenge/warning to Adam is intended for every human being (*Path of the Just*).

SMILING EACH DAY

"Blessed are You, Almighty G-d, who forgives our sins and the sins of His entire people, Israel." We recite this benediction in the Yom Kippur service, as though we were absolutely certain that we have merited Divine forgiveness. How can we be so sure of this?

Rabbi Levi Yitzchak of Berdichev told of a child whose mother gave him some cookies for a snack at *cheder* (Hebrew school). When another child saw his bag and asked him for a cookie, he refused to share his goodies, whereupon the second child took the initiative and immediately recited the *berachah* for pastries, ending with an outstretched hand and the emphatic plea, "Nu, uhh!" The first child, knowing that it is a grave sin to pronounce G-d's name in vain, felt morally obligated to save the other child from sin. And of course, the only way to save his friend from having said a purposeless *berachah*, was to give him a cookie, which he promptly though reluctantly did.

"This is exactly what we have in mind on Yom Kippur," Rabbi Levi Yitzchak said, "with one crucial distinction. We pronounce the *berachah* stating that G-d forgives our sins. If He would not then do so, we would be guilty of having made a purposeless *berachah*, of having said G-d's name in vain. Like the child who yielded his cookie, G-d therefore forgives our sins so that our *berachah* will be a valid one. But in this case, G-d is only too happy to accede to our request/ploy (provided we have repented properly), for we are His beloved children upon whom He so desires to bestow His blessings."

**Today
I shall smile
because . . .**

_____
_____
_____

The final prayer of *Neilah* on Yom Kippur is the culmination of the period of *teshuvah* of the month of Elul, the Ten Days of Repentance beginning with Rosh Ha-shanah, and the intensive day of Yom Kippur itself. As such, every word is doubly significant. We close the day by saying, "You gave us this day of forgiveness so that we may refrain from being guilty of theft." Alas, all the *teshuvah* in the world is of no avail if we have unjust possession of the belongings of others.

Yom Kippur
[Yizkor]

SMILING EACH DAY

As the *Neilah* service of Yom Kippur was drawing to a close, Rabbi Levi Yitzchak of Berdichev appeared distressed. Apparently the prayers of Israel had not been adequate to earn a favorable judgment for the new year.

As he paced to and fro in the synagogue, searching in his heart for some merit to arouse the Divine attribute of mercy, he overheard a conversation between two women in the *ezras nashim* (ladies section). "This year will surely be a happy one for us," one woman remarked.

"How do you know that?" the other asked.

"Didn't you hear the heartrending cries of the worshipers?" the first replied. "Why, they were enough to appease the most merciless highway robber! Just think how the all-merciful G-d is going to respond!"

Rabbi Levi Yitzchak's ran to the Ark and lifted his eyes to heaven. "Merciful Father, did You not hear? The plainest of people recognizes that even the most calloused scoundrel could not reject the sincere pleadings of people at his mercy. With Your infinite love and kindness, surely our prayers will effect Your blessings."

Rabbi Levi Yitzchak stressed that the sincere prayers of simple folk are of utmost efficacy.

Today
I shall smile
because . . .

תשרי

If someone in need asks you for a loan and you are in a position to assist him, do so cheerfully, as if you were making an investment with a guaranteed profit. G-d himself has promised to amply reward you (*Chafetz Chaim*).

SMILING EACH DAY

There was once a discussion as to why the *Al Chet*, the prayer in which we enumerate all the sins we have committed, proceeds according to the *Aleph-Beis*. Rabbi Bunim of P'shischa offered a characteristically sharp, yet deceivingly simple explanation: "How else would one know when to stop?"

Is our list of sins really endless? In *The Path of the Just*, Luzzato points out the importance of reflecting on everything we do, as to whether the action we are about to take contributes to our ultimate goal or not. He insists that many of our improper acts are not as much a result of distorted thinking as of failure to think at all. A wise business person whose goal is to further his gains deliberates over everything he embarks upon, examining whether it will result in a profit, and if not, avoiding the endeavor even if it does not clearly result in a loss.

If we would give similar consideration to everything we do, in light of our goal which is to fulfill the Divine will, we would probably find too many things that simply deserve no space in our spiritual baggage. At the very least, the amount of talking we do would be sharply curtailed. Indeed, if we had to confess all our actions that were not goal directed, the entire day of Yom Kippur might not suffice to list them, let alone express remorse. Mercifully, we focus on the gamut of sin expressed so succinctly in the *Aleph-Beis* formulation, with the hope perhaps being that we will take to heart the *Aleph-Beis* of proper Jewish living — thoughtful approach to all our actions.

Today
I shall smile
because . . .

_____
_____
_____

Anger and sadness are both derivatives of vanity. A truly humble person is not easily provoked to either, because he does not live life feeling he deserves more than he has. Humility brings with it satisfaction and inner tranquility (*Rabbi of Karlin*).

SMILING EACH DAY

We conclude the Yom Kippur service with a familiar declaration/supplication, "Next year in Jerusalem!"

A man had a non-Jewish friend who was curious to witness a Passover Seder, and so was invited to his friend's home. At the close of the Seder he heard everyone proclaim, "Next year in Jerusalem!"

The following year he again attended the Seder, and when the "Next year in Jerusalem" slogan was invoked once more, the guest asked, "I thought you said last year that you would be in Jerusalem this year."

The host explained, "Yes, we always pray to G-d to bring us back to Jerusalem, and even though He did not do so this year, we faithfully expect that He will return us there by next year."

When the next Passover approached, the man decided he wasn't taking any chances and offered the following prayer. "Look, dear G-d, for whatever reasons, You have not yet redeemed us. But please understand one thing. Passover is approaching, and I am again going to entertain my non-Jewish guest. It will be most embarrassing if I have to explain why we are still not in Jerusalem! So, please redeem us and spare me the humiliation."

We would do well to pray intensely for the redemption, if only because of the disgrace of such a lengthy exile. Perhaps we will take the shame to heart and then truly merit immediate redemption.

Today
I shall smile
because . . .

Sometimes a person ties a string around his finger, but then forgets what it was supposed to remind him of. The *tzitzis* (fringes) are meant to maintain an atmosphere of awareness towards *mitzvos*. Looking at them and failing to be alert to *mitzvos* is missing the entire point (*Chafetz Chaim*).

SMILING EACH DAY

A man who built his *succah* adjacent to his home was served a warrant on the basis of a complaint by a cantankerous neighbor, that he had erected a structure without first obtaining a building permit, and that this thatched hut was in violation of the building code.

The judge before whom the case was brought was familiar with the Succos festival and so, though he sharply reprimanded the defendant, gave him a *period of ten days* by the end of which the hut must be completely dismantled. Of course, by that time the festival would be over, and the *succah* would anyway be taken down. However, the plaintiff was elated that he had been triumphant in getting a verdict in his favor.

Borrowing from our judge's insight, perhaps this is a good way to deal with the *yetzer hara* (evil inclination): Give the *yetzer tov* (good inclination) a period of ten days during which time he can have *his* way, while reassuring the *yetzer hara* that when that time is up, the stage will be his. When the eleventh day arrives, you can probably succeed in placating the *yetzer hara* further, even granting a ten day extension. In fact, as long as he is led to believe that it's just a matter of time before he gets his way, you should be able to set the amount of that time according to *your* schedule, pushing him off for days, weeks or even months at a time, and you can live each day of your life by the biddings of the *yetzer tov*.

Today
I shall smile
because . . .

_____
_____
_____

> "Naftali is deeply satisfied and is full of the blessings of G-d" (*Deuteronomy* 33:23). To one who is content, G-d's gifts and blessings are perceived as such. A person who is chronically dissatisfied, however, will not appreciate anything G-d gives him (*Rabbi Tzvi Elimelech*).

SMILING EACH DAY

One year there was a dearth of *esrogim* (citrons) and the Gaon of Vilna was greatly distressed that he might miss the opportunity to fulfill the *mitzvah* of *esrog* and *lulav*. He let it be known that he was willing to pay the highest amount for an *esrog*, but alas, there was none to be had at any price.

One day before Succos a friend of the Gaon heard of a wealthy man who had somehow acquired an *esrog*. He pleaded with the man to sell it to him at twice the price he had paid, but the fellow was not in need of money, and insisted on keeping the *esrog*. After imploring the owner in vain for some time, he resorted to impressing upon him the great *z'chus* (merit) of supplying the Gaon with his coveted *esrog*. Finally the man conceded to part with the *esrog*, but only on the condition that the reward for performance of the *mitzvah* will not go to the Gaon, but will revert to him.

When the Gaon received the *esrog* he was ecstatic and could not thank his friend enough for his efforts. Nevertheless, when he was informed, in meek tones, that he had acquired the *esrog* only by surrendering his reward for the *mitzvah*, his elation took on an even greater dimension. "I have never been able to perform a *mitzvah* purely without ulterior motive, always knowing that I stand to gain a Divine reward for it. Now, however, I have the unique opportunity to perform a *mitzvah* solely because it is the will of G-d, without self-serving motivation, without self-interest, since the reward will not be mine. How wonderful!"

Today
I shall smile
because . . .

How great is the *mitzvah* of *succah*. One can enter into the *mitzvah* with one's entire self, even with one's boots.

SMILING EACH DAY

The Torah commands us to perform the *mitzvah* of *esrog* and *lulav* on the first day (of the Succos festival). The Talmud comments that this is also the first day on which sins are counted. The obvious question is, What does Succos have to do with a counting of sins, which relates to judgment, and belongs in fact to the period of days just concluded?

The Rabbi of Radomsk explains that when Satan brings our sins before the heavenly tribunal on Rosh Hashanah, the archangel Michael defends Israel, claiming that they are not at fault, because Satan duped them into believing that these sinful acts were not sins at all. "Not so," counters Satan. "Jews are clever people, and they cannot be deceived. Anything they did was carried out with complete awareness of the terms involved."

"I insist that they *can* be deceived," argues Michael, whereupon the tribunal decrees that the trial must be suspended until it can be determined whether Jews can easily be duped or not.

On the first day of Succos, Jews bring their *esrogim* to the synagogue. "Look at this beauty," one says, proudly passing it around. "It is without blemish, and I paid $150 for it." Another person pipes up, "This *esrog* is 100% pure *esrog*, not a hybrid. It costs $250!" The angel Michael then triumphantly returns to the court. Didn't I tell you! he beams. Look how easily Jews can be duped."

At that point, the trial is allowed to proceed. Hence, the counting of sins on the first day of Succos.

Today I shall smile because . . .

_____
_____
_____

The Talmud states that a person's *parnassah* (livelihood) is similar to the dividing of the Red Sea. In that context, it is noteworthy that the Israelites prayed for *salvation*, but no one expected the sea to split. *Parnassah* can come from a totally unexpected source (*Rabbi Simcha Bunim*).

Second Day of Succos

[In the Land of Israel this is the first day of Chol Hamoed, the Intermediate Days.]

SMILING EACH DAY

Rabbi Levi Yitzchak of Berdichev made a special effort to bring into his *succah* the social outcasts of the city, whose behavior, one way or another, had resulted in their being rejected by everyone else. When asked why he did this, he explained, with a hint of glee.

"The *Midrash* states that in the World to Come G-d will invite all the *tzaddikim* to a great feast in a huge *succah* made out of the hide of the legendary *Leviathan*. I so crave to be in the company of these great *tzaddikim*! But how can I possibly aspire to this? Surely the angel who stands guard at the door will refuse me entrance. 'Go away, Levi Yitzchak,' he will say. 'You don't belong among these honorable people.' "

Rabbi Levi Yitzchak's tone changed from one of pained reflection to the confidence of sure triumph. "Then I will plead my cause," he continued. "The Divine system of justice follows the principle of measure for measure, I will point out. In my *succah*, all the social outcasts were welcomed and treated with dignity. I therefore deserve to be admitted to *this succah* even though my stature does not warrant it. Measure for measure!, I will demand. Do you imagine I won't be welcomed then?" he ended playfully.

Rabbi Levi Yitzchak would smile and say, "You must be very clever to get things when you know you don't deserve them."

Today
I shall smile
because . . .

Chol Hamoed
Succos

Rabbi Nachman of Breslov said, "The *yetzer hara* functions like the man who convinces people that he has something valuable in his fist, but here too, when he opens his hand, it turns out to be empty."

SMILING EACH DAY

Rabbi Mordechai of Neschiz was hardly a man of means, so he would put away pennies every day in order to be able to buy an *esrog* for Succos, which was often quite costly. Several days before the holiday, he joyously made his way to purchase the coveted *esrog*, for which he had saved all year with great anticipation.

On the way he came across a man sitting at the roadside, weeping. When Rabbi Mordechai inquired as to the reason for his grief, the man replied that he made his living by peddling or hauling loads with his horse and wagon. The day before, his nag had died. "I have no way to earn anything, and I have a large family to feed," he wailed.

With a great *mitzvah* clearly at hand, Rabbi Mordechai asked him how much money he needed to buy another horse, and the sum turned out to be just what he had saved for his precious *esrog*. Without a second thought, and with all the enthusiasm he had reserved for his *esrog*, he handed the man the bag of coins he had collected, saying, "Here, go buy yourself a horse." The stunned man could hardly believe his ears, and after heaping blessings on Rabbi Mordechai, ran off excitedly to the horse dealer.

Rabbi Mordechai watched the man take off with his year's savings. "Well," he mused. "Tomorrow all Jews will rejoice over an *esrog*. As for myself, I will rejoice over a horse!"

Truly, can we compare anyone else's *mitzvah* to Rabbi Mordechai's?

Today I shall smile because . . .

_____
_____
_____

Overcoming anger does not mean suppressing it, but dissipating it. Every person has done things he regrets, but which he thought were right at the time. If we could empathize with the person arousing our anger, adopting his/her current perspective of right and wrong, we might defuse explosive situations, and avoid much unnecessary anger.

Chol Hamoed
Succos

SMILING EACH DAY

It has been traditional to acquire a most perfect *esrog* (citron) for Succos. Since many people are not connoisseurs on an *esrog,* they may take it to a *maven* for an opinion. In Slonim the practice was to take the *esrog* to Rabbi Eizel to determine if it was really a *hadar,* the fruit of beauty the Torah requires.

One year the entire crop of *esrogim* was extremely poor, and a steady stream of disappointed people left Rabbi Eizel's home after invariably being told their particular purchase was not a *hadar.* Soon, the *esrog* merchant came to Rabbi Eizel in desperation. "What are you doing to me?" he exclaimed. "Everyone is returning his *esrog.* I will be left with my entire stock unsold, and become impoverished."

Rabbi Eizel responded with facetious, yet soothing sagacity. "My dear man, I am unable to say that an *esrog* is *hadar* when it is not. But let me suggest something. When customers come for an *esrog,* give them three, and tell them to bring them to me to choose which is the nicest of all three. That I can do in good conscience."

Today
I shall smile
because . . .

The Rabbi of Talna observed, "The Midrash states that there is one angel that has a thousands mouths, each one with a thousand tongues, whereby he sings incomparable hymns of praise to G-d. But what of it? He cannot give even one cent of *tzedakah* to the poor. Every person can surpass him in merit."

SMILING EACH DAY

One *Succos* the Baal Shem Tov was sitting with his disciples and appeared to go into a trance. After a few moments of profound concentration, he emerged from his exalted state with a bright smile adorning his already holy countenance.

"In the celestial spheres" he announced, "there had been a great expression of joy, and I was curious as to what had brought this about.

"It seems that a simple Jew had been traveling on foot, and in order to reach home for *Succos*, he took a shortcut through the forest. Unfortunately he became lost in the thicket, and soon realized, to his great dismay, that not only would he not be home with his family for the holiday, but, even more distressing to him, he would not fulfill the *mitzvah* of *Succah!* This last circumstance he simply could not bear, and as the sun began to set, he was suddenly inspired to rip off the top of his hat and cover it with branches and leaves. Being a person of little learning, he thought this would constitute a *succah*, and so, danced with joy that he had thought of a way to fulfill this precious *mitzvah*."

The holy master concluded, "Although he of course did not fulfill the *mitzvah*, his intent was so pure and sincere that it caused great joy among the Heavenly host."

While we must know how to perform *mitzvos* properly with all the conditions required by *halachah*, we must never overlook or underestimate the essential nature of sincerity and purity of heart in their fulfillment.

Today
I shall smile
because . . .

_____
_____
_____

> Many people search at length for an *esrog* (citron) that is without blemish. They would do well to make equally certain that the hands that hold the *esrog* are without spiritual blemish.

Chol Hamoed
Succos

SMILING EACH DAY

Rabbi Jacob of Kozlow was a private citizen, and because of his great Talmudic scholarship, he was offered the position of rabbi in his community. He refused the offer, claiming that community responsibilities would distract him from his studies. His wife pressured him to accept the position, however, pointing out that he would receive a decent salary and they would no longer have to live in abject poverty. As *Succos* was approaching, he proposed to her, "If you will buy me a beautiful *esrog* that is perfect and without a blemish, I will consider the offer."

Not anticipating the thrust of his offer, she promptly borrowed the money and purchased a perfect *esrog*, which her husband duly praised for its beauty. As word spread in the community that the rabbi had a real *"hadar,"* everyone came to use his *esrog* for the *berachah*. Sure enough, after being handled every day by so many people, the *esrog* soon lost its luster and began to deteriorate, its canary yellow turning to a rusty brown.

The rabbi then showed it to his wife. "Just a few days ago," he reminded her "this was a perfect, beautiful *esrog*. After being handled by the public though, it has quickly degenerated. What do you think will become of me if I assume the official position as rabbi of the community, and will be continuously in the hands of the public? Will I not also deteriorate?"

Some people seek public office as a matter of pride. Rabbi Jacob's wise words should alert one to the inherent risks of such pursuit, even when wholesome.

Today
I shall smile
because . . .

Hoshana Rabbah

The Gaon of Vilna said, "If you have tried your utmost to secure forgiveness from someone for offending him but you cannot locate him, you can be assured that G-d will put the idea in his mind to forgive you. It is only dependent on the sincerity of your intentions and efforts."

SMILING EACH DAY

During the *Hoshana Rabba* service, the willow branch, which is an essential element of the four species, is taken by itself, beaten on the ground, and cast aside. What point might we be making with this bizarre custom?

Let us remember that the four species must be taken together in order for the *mitzvah* to be fulfilled, and absence of even the lowly willow renders the entire *mitzvah* null and void, just as though the succulent *esrog* were missing.

The four species depict four types of Jews. The *esrog*, which has both fragrance and flavor, represents a person who has both scholarship and good works. The palm, whose fruit has flavor but no fragrance, symbolizes a person of learning but without good works. The myrtle branch is fragrant but tasteless, and bespeaks a person with good works, but no learning. The willow, with neither flavor nor fragrance, stands for a person who has neither learning nor good works.

The insipid willow is of great value when it remains together with the other species and is equal to them as a component of the whole. If it separates itself from the other three species though, it sacrifices its worthwhile identity.

A person's circumstances may result in his not having an opportunity to become a scholar, and he might be lacking in good works, but if he remains together with his people and shares in their purpose, he not only has integral worth, but he may actually emit a fragrance of his own when left in contact with them long enough. If, however, such a person isolates himself, rejecting people of learning and good works, his value and effect are demonstrated by the status of the willow on *Hoshana Rabba*.

Today
I shall smile
because . . .

_____
_____
_____

Abraham said, "Now I know that you are beautiful" (*Genesis* 12:11). Did Abraham not know of Sarah's beauty heretofore? Of course he did. But physical beauty may be lost in times of distress. Only spiritual beauty remains even in the presence of suffering (*Rabbi Yisrael of Rhizin*).

Shemini Atzeres
[Yizkor —
in the Land of Israel
this day is also
celebrated as
Simchas Torah.]

SMILING EACH DAY

This day is celebrated in Israel as *Simchas Torah.* It is only in the Diaspora that Simchas Torah is celebrated on the following day.

A rabbi observed a man on *Simchas Torah,* rejoicing exuberantly, dancing with the Torah. He asked the man, "Have you studied the Torah so well that you exult in it?"

The man replied, "No, not at all, but the Torah has been very good to me. I sold a property to someone at an inflated price, far above its real worth. When the buyer discovered that he had overpaid, he tried to void the sale, and threatened to take me to court to enforce such action. I remembered once listening to the rabbi discussing some of the *halachic* laws of commerce, and he said that in a sale of personal property one can void a sale if one was overcharged more than 20%, but that with real property, the sale cannot be voided unless the inflated price was twice the real value. I then convinced the buyer not to go to a secular court, but to a *Beth-Din* (Rabbinic court). He agreed, and since the inflated price was less than 200% of its value, the judgment was in my favor, and I made a handsome profit, thanks to the law of the Torah. That's why I celebrate with the Torah."

The rabbi sadly shook his head "You're missing the whole point. *Simchas Torah,* " he admonished, "is not a one way affair. It is not enough for you to be happy with the Torah, but the Torah must also be happy with you. If you exploited the Torah to take unfair advantage of someone, the Torah is not at all pleased with you and certainly does not rejoice with you while the fellow cries out to G-d in anguish over having been duped. So for you, it is not really *Simchas Torah.* "

Today
I shall smile
because . . .

In the *Amidah* we pray, "Protect my tongue from speaking evil." Is it not a person's own duty to do this? Rabbi Simcha Bunim answered, "Sometimes we may think that degrading a bad person is a *mitzvah*. We pray that G-d protect us from such distorted thinking."

SMILING EACH DAY

At the *Simchas Torah* celebration, with people singing and dancing joyously with the Torah, one of the people who was particularly lively was a person who had virtually no contact with Torah study. Someone couldn't resist, and asked him, "Do you have any idea of what is contained in that Torah with which you are dancing? In what way does celebration of the Torah concern you?"

The man's answer was enlightening. "Suppose my brother were marrying off his child. Would I not rejoice in my brother's *simcha*, even though it was not my child that was being married?

"I know nothing of Torah, but the Torah scholars are my brothers, and their *simcha* is my *simcha*."

This man was so right. The *simcha* of one Jew with the Torah should be a *simcha* for all Jews. In this respect especially, we are all one family.

We should all rejoice in *Simchas Torah*, because the scholars who celebrate are indeed our brothers. But then we must preserve this kinship all year round. When one family member is in need, all other family members should come to the rescue. Institutions that foster Torah study and growth should be supported, and sincere scholars who devote themselves entirely to Torah and who will eventually serve as our teachers and Torah guides should be afforded every possibility to continue their studies without distraction.

Simchas Torah should be a *simcha* for everyone, provided, as was noted yesterday, that the Torah is as happy with us as we are with it, and we can rightfully identify with it.

Today
I shall smile
because . . .

_____

_____

_____

A chassid brought his child to a Rebbe and asked that he bless him to be a devout, G-d-fearing, scholarly Jew. The Rabbi smile benignly. "Devoutness, fearing G-d, and Torah knowledge" he said, "are not the result of blessing, but of hard work, training, and studying. I will bless you instead with good health and *parnassah* (livelihood) so that you can devote yourself to teaching your child to learn, to be devout, and to be G-d-fearing."

SMILING EACH DAY

Rabbi Yosef Dov of Brisk was walking with some of his students on the road when they passed three horse-drawn wagons of hay proceeding one behind another.

Rabbi Yosef Dov turned to his students. "If you will note, the horse with the third wagon is eating the hay of the wagon in front of him. The lead horse has nothing to eat from, but his burden gets lighter as the second horse eats from his load. The middle horse benefits the most from this arrangement because he gets to eat from the wagon in front, and his burden is lessened as the third horse eats from his load.

"This scene should serve as a vivid reminder" he went on, "that being at either extreme of anything is rarely beneficial, or proper, for that matter. Maimonides extols the 'mean of virtue,' pointing out that with specific exceptions, moderation is spiritually superior to extremism."

The import of the "mean of virtue" and the preference of moderation over extremism is routinely relevant. Perhaps of even greater significance though, in infusing our routine with enhanced substance is the realization that some people can read and reread ethical works and learn nothing from them, whereas someone like Rabbi Yosef Dov can take a momentary look at a procession of horse-drawn wagons and derive valuable guidelines for living from that scene.

Today
I shall smile
because . . .

It is customary to observe people polishing gold and silver items or their jewelry, to bring out their true luster. These are often no less valuable before they are made to shine, yet one wishes to reveal their splendor. That should be our attitude toward *mitzvos:* perform them in a manner that their beauty should be manifest (*Chafetz Chaim*).

SMILING EACH DAY

A rabbi who collected for a yeshiva called upon a wealthy man who was known to be a miser. "There is no point in your appealing to me" the man advised. "I do not give donations to yeshivos."

"I did not come here for a donation," the rabbi shot back. "I came to fulfill the *mitzvah* of *bikur cholim*, visiting the sick."

"But I am perfectly healthy," the miser asserted, not comprehending the rabbi's assessment.

"No, you are not," the rabbi insisted, rather calmly. "Solomon teaches in *Ecclesiastes* (5:12), 'There is a bad disease that I have seen: wealth that is kept to its owner's detriment.' Since you hoard your wealth, you indeed suffer from a disease, so I came to see you."

"But are there not many other sick people," the miser asked, puzzled. "Why do you single me out for a visit?"

"Because," the rabbi grinned in satisfaction, "the Talmud says that whoever visits a sick person takes away one sixtieth of his disease. What can I expect if I walk away with one sixtieth of someone's malaria? Nothing, but 'tzoros.' Ah, but if I walk away with one sixtieth of *your* disease, I will do very well indeed!"

Today
I shall smile
because . . .

_____
_____
_____

The seismograph has taught us that a tremor in any part of the world can be felt by a sufficiently sensitive instrument everywhere else in the world. The same is true of a person's deeds. One should not think that his actions do not affect others. Everything one does in some way affects everyone else in the world (*Rabbi Yerucham of Mir*).

SMILING EACH DAY

Someone complained to a rabbi about the deterioration that has occurred in observance of Judaism, and the fact that sinful people are unfortunately in the majority.

"Actually, it all depends on how you look at it," the rabbi replied, and related the following incident.

"A man once consulted me claiming that he was a *kohen* (from the priestly tribe) and that he wished to marry a divorcee, which is forbidden by the Torah (*Leviticus* 21:7). When I tried to explain the *halachic* impossibility of such a union, he began to plead with me: "I know that the Talmud states that a *tzaddik* can avert a harsh Divine judgment. Inasmuch as the prohibition of a *kohen* marrying a divorcee is a Divine decree, and the rabbi is certainly a great *tzaddik*, why can't he just annul this prohibition for me?"

"You see," the rabbi continued, smiling broadly, "what has happened in today's generation is that people have become such great *tzaddikim*, that many have simply overridden the Divine prohibitions contained in the Torah by virtue of their own superior decree! We dare not call these lofty souls sinners."

All jest aside, the problem of laxity and decadence in observance of the Torah may be precisely because some people have set themselves up as authorities, and believe that they have the prerogative of fashioning a Divine doctrine more closely reflecting their particular emotional, intellectual, or even spiritual outlook.

Today
I shall smile
because . . .

Someone asked Rabbi Jacob of Radzimin how one can satisfactorily explain the repeated troubles that have plagued Israel throughout its history. He wisely pointed out, "For a believer there are no questions, and for a non-believer there are no answers."

SMILING EACH DAY

At a get-together of rabbis, someone complained of the extremely cold weather that had prevailed that winter. The Rabbi of Chortkov, who was a guest at this conference, remarked, "If all we do is complain, then we are pointing a guilty finger in the wrong direction. Extremes in weather are the fault of rabbis who do not function with integrity." Noting everyone's quizzical look, he explained.

"The Talmud states that a rabbinic judge who decides a case with utmost honesty and sincerity, becomes a partner to G-d in the work of creation (*Shabbos* 10a). The Talmud also declares that 'A pot belonging to two partners is neither hot nor cold' " (*Eruvin* 3a, which is a metaphor the Talmud uses to point out that if one tries to satisfy everyone, one ends up satisfying no one). The illustration is that where one partner prefers the pot to be hot and the other prefers it to be cold, their conflicting goals prevent the realization of either one's desires. The Rabbi of Chortkov took the metaphor literally to make his point.

"If we put these two Talmudic statements together," the rabbi reasoned, "we may conclude that as long as rabbis rule with truth as their guide, they are partners with G-d in ownership of the world, and like a pot belonging to two partners, it is neither too hot nor too cold. If there are extremes in weather, it can only be because the partnership no longer exists, and unfortunately, that is because the rabbis have failed to qualify as co-creators of the world.

"So do not complain" he reiterated. "Let us be the kind of rabbis we are supposed to be, and the weather will be more moderate."

Today
I shall smile
because . . .

_____
_____
_____

Rabbi Meir of Premishlan gave away everything he earned to the poor. "Everyday I thank G-d that it is not a *mitzvah* to have money. If it were, I don't believe I could sleep a single night knowing that I have means while the unfortunate are going hungry.

SMILING EACH DAY

Several townsfolk petitioned their rabbi to dismiss the cantor from his position, inasmuch as there were some rumors of his indecent behavior.

The rabbi refused the request, citing the portion of the Torah relating that the patriarch Abraham was tested with a Divine commandment to bring his son Isaac as a sacrificial offering. Abraham received this instruction from G-d Himself," the Rabbi noted. "But after he had proven his loyalty to G-d, an angel was sent to stop the procedure: An angel called to him from heaven, 'Do not touch the lad,' (*Genesis* 22:12). Why was the original command given by G-d Himself, and the second by an angel?

"This is to teach us," the rabbi cautioned, "that to save a person's life, one may follow the instructions of an angel. However to take someone's life, the word of an angel does not suffice, and one can do so only if one hears it directly from G-d Himself."

The Rabbi stared intently into the group; "You wish me to discharge the cantor and deprive him of his livelihood on the basis of a rumor? That is tantamount to taking his life, and none of you is G-d."

Tragically, we may sometimes do things that impinge on a person's livelihood or dignity in life. Do we give such actions the serious deliberation which is their due?

Today
I shall smile
because . . .

Erev
Rosh Chodesh
*[Eve of the
New Month]*

We say the prayer *Adon Olam* both at the beginning and the end of morning services. Why? So that when we think we have finished, we should realize that we have only begun.

SMILING EACH DAY

One of the leaders of assimilation appeared one day in the synagogue of Slutzk. The *gabbai* (synagogue official), not recognizing him as someone who mocked all Jewish traditions, called him up to the reading of the Torah.

Surprisingly, the man recited the blessing for the Torah with great fervor: "Blessed is G-d who chose us from all nations and has given us His Torah." Those people who did recognize him and knew of his derisive attitude toward Torah commented curiously on the intensity with which he had recited the blessing.

The rabbi saw this and smiled. "Don't you understand?" he began elucidating. "He is extremely happy that G-d gave the Torah to the Jews. This man has discarded everything that smacks of Judaism, and in his effort to deny his Jewishness, has adopted all the practices of the non-Jewish environment. Now just think, if the Torah had been given to other peoples instead of to the Jews, then *they* would be observing all the restrictions of Shabbos and eating kosher, and *they* would have all the prohibitions and duties of the Torah. Then, in his effort to identify with non-Jews, he would have had to observe Shabbos and eat kosher, and although that would have imposed much hardship and inconvenience upon him, he would surely have done so lest he be recognized as Jewish! Truly a horrendous fate for someone of his outlook!

"But now that G-d gave the Torah to us," the Rabbi chuckled, "behaving like a non-Jew is quite appealing and convenient. Little wonder then that he recited the *berachah* with such *kavannah* (intent and concentration). He is really delighted that the Torah was given to the Jews!"

**Today
I shall smile
because . . .**

_____

_____

_____

When the *Tzemach Tzedek* (Rabbi Menachem Mendel of Lubavitch) was a child, he and his playmates once climbed a tall pole. He reached the top, while his friends slipped and fell. "When climbing up," he philosophized beyond his years, "you must look towards the sky. Never look below yourself." This was a major theme of his later chassidic teachings.

First Day of Rosh Chodesh Cheshvan

SMILING EACH DAY

A chassid complained to the Rabbi of Rhizin that his source of livelihood had dried up and that he was impoverished. The Rabbi gave him a blessing that he should succeed in *parnassah* (a livelihood).

"But that is not enough, Rabbi," the man persisted, hoping to elicit immediate salvation. "I have no money to buy food."

"Then do you go hungry?" the Rabbi asked.

"Of course," the man answered.

"How fortunate you are!" the Rabbi exclaimed, ignoring the man's puzzled frown. "Yesterday I was consulted by a man whose wife has a serious illness which has caused her to lose her appetite, and she cannot even tolerate the sight of food. He has spent large sums of money, and taken her to many specialists to try and restore her appetite, but to no avail. She is slowly withering away.

"Just think how fortunate you are," the Rabbi repeated, his tone softly critical, "that you can be hungry and have a desire for food."

It is true that we sometimes undergo various deprivations and are unhappy because of what we are missing. We should remember, however, that sometimes the very awareness of lack can indicate a blessing of a deeper nature.

Today
I shall smile
because . . .

CHESHVAN

חשון

*Second Day of
Rosh Chodesh
Cheshvan*

The Rabbi of Kotzk said, "If a person were busy doing what he should be doing, when would he have time to sin? Sin should be avoided not only because it is wrong, but more practically, because one is too preoccupied with doing what is right to have occasion to do anything wrong.

SMILING EACH DAY

A man complained to the Rabbi of Ostrovtza that his father had left him a store as an inheritance, but whereas the business had yielded a handsome profit for his father, it was performing very poorly for him. Hours could go by without a single customer entering the store.

"What do you do with all that idle time?" the rabbi queried.

"Sometimes I just sit around doing nothing, or perhaps I'll read a newspaper," the man answered, with a shrug that suggested complacency.

"There is your solution" the rabbi nodded understandingly. "You see, Satan has been given extensive powers. When your father had a free moment, he would learn a portion of the Talmud or the Scriptures, or perhaps read the *Tehillim* (Psalms). This greatly irritated Satan, who would direct customers to the store, to interrupt your father's Torah study or prayer. With you, however, Satan is perfectly satisfied to allow you to go without customers, since you only waste away your time anyway. When you abuse the gift of time, you are doing exactly what he wishes. Not only does he not direct people to your store, but he uses his vast authority over circumstances to prevent would-be customers from going there, so that you will continue to misuse your time. Unfortunately, as long as you are content with following his path, he will be comfortable with yours and will try not to disturb you."

We may think we know how to earn money, but we are often way off course.

Today
I shall smile
because . . .

_____
_____
_____

Rabbi Chaim Vital warned, "Sadness results in failure to do *mitzvos,* study Torah, and pray with *kavannah* (concentration). It is an entry point for the *yetzer hara* (evil inclination) to seduce a person to sin."

SMILING EACH DAY

One of the followers of Rabbi Yitzchak of Vorki was very wealthy. On one occasion the rabbi asked him about his lifestyle. He assured his Rebbe that he was not led astray by his riches, and that in fact, he was following the dictates of the sages, leading a very austere life (*Ethics of the Fathers* 6:4), and getting along on a simple diet. He did not wear lavish clothes, nor did he have servants.

"No, No!" the rabbi protested. "You are doing it all wrong. You must follow my instructions and leave the teachings of the sages to my discretion. I want you to hire servants and to buy yourself several changes of the finest suits available, along with expensive dresses for your wife. You are to hire a gourmet cook, and have delicacies at every meal. You must also take lavish vacations, and use your great wealth for maximum enjoyment. Then you will merit the Divine blessing for continued wealth."

When the astonished chassid left, some of the bystanders expressed surprise at these unusual instructions. The rabbi revealed the insight behind his charge.

"If he will indulge in luxurious food and clothes, then when a needy person asks for help, he will understand that this poor fellow requires at least enough for bread and simple clothes. However, if he himself lives an ascetic life and eats simple food and wears inexpensive clothes, how will he view the needy? He will probably think that the poor can eat rocks and wear rags! I say, let the wealthy enjoy their wealth, then the less fortunate will have at least enough for a meager existence. If the rich train themselves to survive on the bare minimum, they will let the poor starve."

Today
I shall smile
because . . .

The Talmud states that one reason Jerusalem was destroyed was because the Israelites lived according to the letter of the law, never yielding what was due them. Mercy and forgiveness are beyond the letter of the law, and when we conduct ourselves with mercy and forgiveness to others, G-d behaves similarly toward us.

SMILING EACH DAY

The Gaon of Vilna did not function as the city's official rabbi, and begged not to be distracted from his Torah studies. He did consent, however, that if any new ordinance binding on the community was to be enacted, he would attend the community council as a consultant.

One time the town was inundated with people from outside Vilna who sought *tzedakah* (charity), and the populace was annoyed by this, particularly since the city had its own share of poor people to support. A suggestion was made to restrict anyone other than Vilna residents from collecting *tzedakah* in the city, and the Gaon was requested to attend a community meeting where this idea would be reviewed and voted upon. He agreed to attend.

After listening patiently to the proceedings he remarked with feigned dismay, "I thought we had agreed that I was not to be disturbed unless a *new* ordinance was to be passed." The community leaders, taken aback, assured him that this was indeed a new decree they were considering.

"Not at all," asserted the Gaon, exposing their oversight. "The *Midrash* states that restricting strangers from receiving *tzedakah* was an established practice in the sinful city of Sodom. This shameful law is thus not new at all, but an ancient one of Biblical origins," and with that he arose and left the meeting.

Today
I shall smile
because . . .

_____
_____
_____

> Our thoughts acquire their precise meaning only when we try to express them. It is at that time that they gain their exact structure and are tested by the standard of truth (*Rabbi Samson Raphael Hirsch*).

SMILING EACH DAY

Someone once suggested to one of the Torah authorities that modifications in *halachah* (Jewish law) are needed because the Torah was given thousands of years ago and is not relevant to modern times.

The rabbi replied calmly, "A while back I had to litigate a case. A merchant had ordered goods from a supplier, and specified that he wanted them delivered by November 1, in time for a special sale. That fall there were very heavy rains, and the roads were impassable, with the result that the order was not delivered when it should have been. The merchant sued the supplier, claiming that he had lost a great deal of money due to his failure to deliver on time. After studying all the facts, I ruled in favor of the merchant.

"The supplier protested, but I told him that I must apply the rules of the Torah, according to which the judgment was in favor of the merchant. Realizing the case was about to be closed, he made one final attempt to sway me.

" 'The Torah was given on Shavuos, wasn't it?' he pointed out. 'Yes, of course' I responded, eager to hear what argument he could have contrived.

'There you have it!' he exulted. 'Shavuos does not occur in autumn, and that's why the Torah law favors my opponent. If the Torah would have been given during the rainy season, the *halachah* would have favored my side.' "

After allowing the message to sink in for a second, the Rabbi added, "Don't you recognize the simple truth that it is as absurd to restrict the Torah to any one era as it is to make it seasonal?!"

Today
I shall smile
because . . .

The Talmud states that the last verses of the Torah which read, "Moses, the servant of G-d, died," and contain his praises (*Deuteronomy* 34:5-12) were written by Moses, who wept as he wrote. Dare we then equate him with the rest of humanity? "Moses did not weep over his imminent death," claimed the Rabbi of Kotzk, "but rather, because this paragon of humility was compelled to write flattering comments about himself."

SMILING EACH DAY

A rabbi was told about the plight of a particular individual who had no income, and was asked to help raise funds for him. "The man is literally dying of hunger," he was told.

The rabbi was suspicious, "I don't understand. He is a healthy and capable person. Surely he could find a job to earn enough to sustain himself."

"But none of the jobs to be had are suitable for him," the applicant countered. "He is a very proud person, and the jobs that are available are menial and he feels they are beneath his dignity."

"Well then," the rabbi said, dismissing the cause, "in that case, it is not true that he is dying of hunger. He is really dying of pride."

Some people are unable to distinguish between the two. Their sense of personal status so dominates them that they can not consider many viable options.

The Talmud requires that one should take even the most menial job rather than resort to living off others. "Skin hides in the market place if you must, but don't descend to accepting charity because of your (often imagined sense of) dignity (*Pesachim* 113b)."

Today
I shall smile
because . . .

_____
_____
_____

"A wise person who argues with a silly person (specifically, a foolishly wicked person) may become angry or laugh, but draws no satisfaction" (*Proverbs* 29:9). One may be provoked to amusement over idiocy, or be irritated by it, but there is never any ultimate gain in facing off with a fool (*Rabbi Samson Raphael Hirsch*).

SMILING EACH DAY

In Frankfurt there was a wealthy man who was a miser, refusing to contribute to *tzedakah*. Rabbi Pinchas Horowitz, who was Rabbi of Frankfurt, chastised the man for his tight-fistedness.

"It is not that I am stingy," the man rationalized, "just that my worst fear is that I will grow old and not be in a position to earn money. I must put away enough to assure my sustenance in my old age."

Shortly afterward, a woman complained to the rabbi that her husband gave everything away to *tzedakah*, hardly keeping enough to pay for household expenses. Rabbi Pinchas sent for the man who explained, "How do I know I have performed enough *mitzvos* to warrant entry into *Gan Eden* (Paradise)? Many *mitzvos* are not available for me until later in the year, such as *shofar*, *succah*, *matzah*, and others. How can I be certain I will get to fulfill them? I may die tomorrow and come before the Heavenly tribunal empty handed. The only *mitzvah* I can do immediately is *tzedakah*!"

Rabbi Pinchas called both people together and cleverly spelled out the prospects for their respective dilemmas. "Both of you are nervous. You," he said, pointing to the miser, "are afraid that you may grow very old, and you are afraid that you may die very young." He smiled and said almost casually, "I suppose that it is my obligation as rabbi to pray that G-d protect you both from your fears coming true!"

Today
I shall smile
because . . .

A person is judged according to the way he relates to others. If you cannot overlook minor infractions that others have done to you, how can you expect G-d to forgive major infractions that you have committed in front of Him?

SMILING EACH DAY

When Rabbi Meir Shapiro of Lublin built his famous yeshiva, with comfortable lodging and abundant food for the students instead of the usual, meager subsistence that was available at other yeshivas, he sought support from wealthy donors. One such person was very critical of the project. "The Mishna maintains that the way of Torah is to eat bread with salt and sleep on the ground (*Ethics of the Fathers* 6:4)," he argued "There is no place for luxurious accommodations in a yeshiva."

Rabbi Meir responded, "We often find contradictory statements in the Torah. In *Exodus* we read, "Do not retain the bedclothes of a poor borrower as a pledge" (*Exodus* 22:25), whereas Solomon contends that a debtor must consider himself a servant to the lender (*Proverbs* 22:7). The way these opposite statements are reconciled is that the first injunction is directed at the lender, while the second quote is addressed to the borrower. Each one must behave appropriately for his role.

"It is the same here" the great rabbi made clear. "The Mishna which you quoted is directed toward the yeshiva student, who is instructed to learn to content himself with minimum subsistence and not make demands. As far as the donors are concerned, their proper approach is the verse, 'It is a tree of life for those who hold fast to it (Torah), and those who support Torah will be fortunate' (*Proverbs* 3:18). You must follow the course that is appropriate for you and not the one specifically prescribed for the aspiring scholar. Advocating such a lifestyle," he concluded with a grin, "is really not your business."

Today
I shall smile
because . . .

_____
_____
_____

In the lowest realms of my depression, I remembered the words of the psalmist, "In the depths of Hell, You are there too" (*Psalms* 139:8). I knew that I was not alone, because G-d was with me, and I so needed that comfort! The worst of all feelings is abandonment (*Rabbi Nachman of Breslov*).

SMILING EACH DAY

Rabbi Chaim Soloveitchik once noticed a man praying, shouting the words at the top of his voice. Indeed, sometimes a person's fervor and emotion in prayer become so intense that one is overwhelmed and the words emerge with a loudness characteristic of someone who screams in pain or emits a shout of joy. In this instance, however, Rabbi Chaim detected that this performance was nothing more than much noise with little *kavannah* (concentration).

He felt it necessary to rescue the man from his own intentions, so he gently approached him with the following question. "The Torah states that on the vestments of the High Priest there were bells, so that when he entered and left the Sanctuary, his movement would be heard (*Exodus* 28:35). What need was there for that? Would it not have been sufficient for the High Priest to pray loudly, and then it would be obvious that he was there?!"

"But I could not contain myself," the man blurted defensively, not daring to miss the point "I cried in my prayer."

Rabbi Chaim smiled. "The Torah tells us that when Pharoah's daughter found Moses in the little box on the Nile, she 'saw an infant crying' (*Exodus* 2:6). Would it not be more properly to say she *heard* the infant cry rather than *saw*?

"What the Torah is telling us," he said, as he softly took hold of the man's arm, "is that we must learn how to cry in silence."

Today
I shall smile
because . . .

Rabbi Ahron of Karlin was asked what he had learned from his teacher, the Maggid of Mezeritch. "Nothing" he answered, to everyone's amazement. "Then why did you travel to him and spend much time there?" they further questioned. He opened their eyes; "I learned how a great *tzaddik* and Torah scholar can humble himself to the point where he is, in his own eyes, a mere 'nothing'."

SMILING EACH DAY

Rabbi Michel of Zlotchow said that when the *yetzer hara* (evil inclination) would try and distract him from concentrating during prayer, he would say to him, "How come you only show up when I am *davening* (praying)? I don't have time for dialogue with you now. Go away, and come back when I am eating, and then I will have some time for you."

Inasmuch as a person's innermost thoughts are known only to G-d, the *yetzer hara* can judge a person only by his manifest behavior. When he came to Rabbi Michel during mealtime and saw him indulging himself with food, he saw no reason to disturb him. Yielding to one's physical desires is precisely what the *yetzer hara* prefers. What he could not know was that Rabbi Michel's true thoughts at mealtime were entirely on a different plane; that he was giving his body its necessary nutrition so that it would be strong, healthy, and in optimal condition to perform *mitzvos*.

We can all use Rabbi Michel's strategy to outwit the *yetzer hara*. Whenever we provide the body with its needs, let us do so with a higher purpose in mind. As we are not being ascetic and denying the body its wishes, but indeed, satisfying them in a permissible manner, we should make an effort to sublimate these actions.

The *yetzer hara* is described as sly and cunning. However, with the Torah's guidance, and the example of our sages, we can beat him at his own game.

Today
I shall smile
because . . .

_____
_____
_____

"The wisdom of the wise is understanding his path, but the silliness of fools is trickery" (*Proverbs* 14:8). When someone talks in circles, one is either trying to deceive others, or doesn't understand the meaning and purpose of his own words. The wise person makes himself easily understood (*Rabbi Samson Raphael Hirsch*).

SMILING EACH DAY

The Rabbi of Rhizin was a child prodigy, and when his teacher taught him the *Chumash* (The Five Books of Moses), the child would anticipate every question raised by the *Rashi* commentary.

When they came to the portion of the Scriptures which relates Jacob's dream of a ladder that reached the sky, upon which angels were "ascending and descending" (*Genesis* 28:12), the teacher readily expected the child to raise the obvious question mentioned by *Rashi*, that the phrase should read "descending and ascending," because the angels would first have to descend from heaven before they could ascend. But the child said nothing.

After a bit of fruitless prodding, the teacher resolved to ask directly, "Isn't there something strange about this verse?"

"Not at all," replied the child, coolly.

The teacher was now fully aroused. "But it reads 'ascending and descending' " he cried, his voice a combination of impatience and curiosity. "Isn't it obvious that the order should be reversed?"

"No," said the child once again revealing the clarity and depth of his intellect. "You must remember that the Torah is describing a dream. Dreams are rarely logical, and patent absurdities occur frequently. Why should this one be logical?"

Today
I shall smile
because . . .

We generally assume that prejudice is a product of discrimination whereas it is in reality most often indiscriminate. Like a simpleton guard at the door who refuses entry to friend and foe alike, prejudice causes one to lose as many potential friends as it does enemies.

SMILING EACH DAY

One morning after services, a man approached the rabbi with a problem.

"I sold some supplies to the government," he said, "and I realized that I overcharged them. This doesn't disturb me ethically, because I did so inadvertently, while many people do this regularly and intentionally. However, what I am concerned about is that if this should be discovered, I could be indicted for defrauding the government. What do you think I should do?"

The rabbi surprised him, "You are *not* correct ethically. Just because other people are crooks does not make it permissible for you to engage in similar activities, and you are morally obligated to notify the government of the mistake. However, your concern about indictment is groundless, because your error will never be discovered."

"How can you be so sure?" the man asked, wanting to believe that his rabbi was gifted with *Ruach HaKodesh* (Divine intuition).

The rabbi indeed read his thoughts, and smiled. "The fact that you overcharged the government occurred to you while you were thinking about your business transactions as you were praying the *amidah*, instead of concentrating on the prayer. Since government agents do not recite the *amidah*, there is very little likelihood that they will ever take note of this transaction!"

Today
I shall smile
because . . .

_____

_____

_____

> "And there shall not be a plague among the Israelites when they approach the sanctuary" (*Numbers* 8:19). Rabbi Meir of Zhikov advised, "Do not delay your visiting the sanctuary until troubles move you to prayer. Frequent the synagogue even when you are not in distress."

SMILING EACH DAY

An itinerant rabbi came to a town, where he delivered a long sermon, following which the townspeople took up a collection for him. However, his honorarium turned out to be meager, and he was duly disappointed. When he later came to the local rabbi to bid farewell, he noted that the townsfolk had given the rabbi much larger donations than he had received, and he could not conceal his vexation. "After the beautiful sermon I delivered, I should have been rewarded more handsomely," he commented bitterly.

The rabbi responded with annoying insight. "Whenever you deliver a sermon, what impacts upon the people are not the words you use, but the feelings you convey, and your true beliefs are thus actually transmitted to them.

"The people must have sensed" he continued, without a smirk, "that you value money very highly, and this impressed them so, that they too began to cherish their monetary assets, which is why they refused to part with any of them. To me though, money is of no significance, and when I speak to them, that attitude is clearly conveyed. As a result of my influence, they part with what they have very easily."

The truth is, whether it is a spiritual leader guiding a congregation or a parent who is training family members, we would all do well to keep in mind the words of this rabbi. It is our true feelings rather than our verbal messages that have the most impact.

Today
I shall smile
because . . .

Moses charged, "You were defiant with G-d" (*Deuteronomy* 9:24). He did not say toward or against G-d, but with G-d. Some people may distort religion and actually use it to disobey the will of G-d hence they are defiant with His word (*Rabbi Asher of Rimanov*).

SMILING EACH DAY

Rabbi Jacob of Lisa and Rabbi Aryeh Leib HaCohen were Talmudic scholars of great renown who wrote intricate commentaries on Jewish law. Whereas the works of both are of undisputed scholarship, the books of Rabbi Aryeh Leib achieved much more popularity than those of Rabbi Jacob.

One time the two met, and Rabbi Jacob remarked that he had tried to make his discussion of the law lucid enough to be understood by all students. "I do my writing first thing in the morning," he said. "My mind is rested, my thought processes are keen. I am then at my very best. Yet, I haven't succeeded in gaining acceptance of my works the way you have."

Rabbi Aryeh Leib replied with *his* formula for success. "When I arise in the morning and my mind is rested and my thought processes are keen, I review whatever I wrote the previous day and that is when I do my editing. Perhaps that is why my commentaries may be more pleasing than yours."

For us, it is vital that both made valid points, just that Rabbi Aryeh Leib's method seems to be superior. When one arises in the morning, one may plan what he wishes to accomplish that day. But it would be even more profitable if one would review what he did the day before, and with the mind at its optimum, weed out the things that should not be repeated.

Today
I shall smile
because . . .

_____
_____
_____

Kindness and consideration for others is an inborn trait of human maturity. Someone who is utterly selfish must have actually extirpated or suppressed this natural quality. That is one reason why selfishness is a sin: it is against the law of nature (*Rabbi Yerucham of Mir*).

SMILING EACH DAY

A man who had written a commentary on the Scriptures brought his book to one of the prominent rabbis for an endorsement. As the rabbi read the commentary, he noted that it was a very poor work, which totally distorted the meaning of the Scriptures. He continued to leaf through the book, pausing at various passages and each time remarking, "How brilliant of you to think of this!" or "This is a great idea." The author smiled from ear to ear, assuming that the rabbi's comments indicated approval of his works. He was therefore taken aback when, after completion of the review, the rabbi refused to endorse the book.

"But I heard you say that my ideas were great and brilliant," he protested.

"They certainly were," the rabbi confirmed. "What you did was indeed marvelous. You see, you printed your book with the text of the Torah at the top of the page and the commentary at the bottom, rather than just printing your comments in the book by themselves. Had you done the latter, anyone reading your absurd distortions of the Scriptures would undoubtedly have cast it aside. Now that you have portions of the Torah on each page however, the book must be treated with respect, and it cannot be thrown away. That is what I meant when I said it was a brilliant idea!"

Today
I shall smile
because . . .

A person takes pleasure in viewing a work of art, even though it does not belong to him. Why? Because it is natural for perception of beauty to arouse a good feeling. Alas, if people would only perceive the beauty of G-dliness, they would be truly happy (*Rabbi Simcha Zissel of Kelm*).

SMILING EACH DAY

The prayer *Ein K'elokenu* ("There is no G-d like our G-d, there is no master like our Master, there is no king like our King, and there is no savior like our Savior") is said at the conclusion of the morning service. Someone asked Rabbi Naftali of Ropschitz why this declaration of the unity of G-d was not rather placed at the beginning of the services where it would appear to be more appropriate, just as the *Adon Olam* is. "You are right," Rabbi Naftali agree, observing dryly, "but if it were placed at the beginning, everyone might think the service was over already and go home."

Rabbi Naftali's witticism is more than jest. Merely declaring that one believes in the unity of G-d is not enough. It is easy to pay lip service to this concept without really contemplating and accepting it.

The text of the morning service, if said with the proper *kavannah* (concentration), develops the concept of the unity of G-d so that one can have a firm grasp and a profound belief in it. Verbalizing the words alone is of questionable value at best.

What Rabbi Naftali meant is deeply instructive. Reciting the prayer at the beginning of the service might mislead people to think that they are truly professing *Ein K'elokenu*, whereas in reality it would be only empty poetry, as it takes much meditation to achieve a sincere belief.

Today
I shall smile
because . . .

_____
_____
_____

Science defines man as *homo sapiens*, a hominid with intellect. However, intellect is not the only feature distinguishing man from animal. More crucial is the capacity to apply that intellect to higher purposes than the mundane, such as refining one's character, thinking about ultimate goals in life, and making free-willed moral decisions. Together with intellect, these pursuits define man.

SMILING EACH DAY

A *tzaddik* was once approached to pray for a sick person who was in critical condition. The *tzaddik* secluded himself, and after a while emerged and asked that they send for the person who was known to be the captain of the thieves in the city.

The man was brought to the *tzaddik* who told him, "There is a person in desperate need of Divine mercy, and I want you to pray for him." He gave the name of the sick person to the bandit chief and also instructions as to which prayers to say. Although mystified and somewhat amused by the strange request, the gangster did as he was told.

Lo and behold! After a while a messenger came with the happy news that the patient had abruptly shown remarkable signs of recovery, and doctors were now optimistic that he would recover.

To the surprised bystanders the *tzaddik* explained, "I tried to intercede in heaven for this man, but I found all the doors closed to me and my prayers could not enter. I therefore sent for someone who knows how to pick locks and break through barriers. Once he removed those obstacles with his prayers, mine were able to enter and be received."

Who amongst us has not attempted, as a child, to open or pick some sort of lock, often successfully. Perhaps we all harbor within us a potential skill for breaking down doors and would do well to put it to use in the form of deep and heartfelt prayer.

Today
I shall smile
because . . .

The Talmud warns that if two Torah scholars residing in the same city are at odds with each other in matters other than Torah and do not rectify the situation, one will die and the other will be exiled (*Sotah* 49a). If Torah has not refined their characters so that they could overlook their differences and live in harmony, then they have debased, and therefore forfeited, the merit of their Torah studies (*Rabbi Chaim Shmulevitz*).

SMILING EACH DAY

A grain merchant complained to the Rabbi of Talna that he was at risk of losing a great deal of money. He had withheld much grain from the market the previous year, assuming the price would go up, but this year there was a bumper crop and the price fell sharply.

"Why did you not sell last year's grain then?" the rabbi questioned him.

"Because last year was a drought," he answered ruefully, "and the price of grain was high. There was a prediction of another drought, so I kept the grain, hoping to sell it at an even higher price. However, this year there was much rain and the price of grain is down. I could have sold the grain at a much higher price last year," he lamented.

"You have no need to worry," the rabbi comforted him, observing his remorse. "In the Shabbos prayer we say, 'You nurtured us through famine and You provided for us in satisfaction.' In other words, the same G-d that looks after the poor in the years of drought will also take care of the wealthy in a year of plenty."

Today
I shall smile
because . . .

_____
_____
_____

> "Remove your shoes from your feet, because the place on which you stand is sacred soil" (*Exodus* 3:6). A person has the capacity to make the very place he occupies sacred, and that in fact, is man's mission on earth.

SMILING EACH DAY

When the Israelites committed the sin of worshiping the Golden Calf and G-d threatened to turn them over to the custody of an angel, Moses pleaded, "Please G-d, You go among us Yourself, because they are a stubborn people, and You will forgive our sins (*Exodus* 34:9)." What kind of plea is that?

The Maggid (Preacher) of Dubno explained with a parable. Several peddlers got together at the end of the day, and one complained that he had a very poor day. He had no customers at all for the cheap wooden forks and spoons which, ridiculously, he had been trying to sell in the wealthiest section of town.

"You fool!" the other peddlers chastised him. "Nobody in that section will buy wooden utensils. Those people use only gold and silver for their needs. You should peddle cheap utensils in the poor sections of town."

"Similarly," the Maggid observed, "G-d had just told Moses that He was merciful and forgiving. Seizing the opportunity to effect total reconciliation, Moses pointed out, 'What will You do with Your mercy and forgiveness? The angels in heaven have no use for them. They are never disobedient nor sinful and, you will never see actualization of these exalted qualities. It is more befitting Your glory to come down and accompany the Israelites. They are a stubborn and defiant people, and here You will have many customers for Your mercy and forgiveness.' "

Today
I shall smile
because . . .

The Sages state that Torah and decent behavior are interrelated (*Ethics of the Fathers* 3:17). Just as one cannot learn, and/or observe Torah properly in the absence of decency, so too, one cannot rightfully conclude what constitutes decency without a knowledge of Torah. Given selfish motivation, one's distorted thinking can even consider blatant corruption as being decent.

SMILING EACH DAY

When Rabbi Shimon Schrieber assumed the position as Rabbi of Cracow, he found that there were about one hundred synagogues and *shteibles* (small chapels) in the city. Rather than being united in larger congregations, each little group had a *minyan* (worship group) of its own.

"Now I understand" he criticized, "why the Talmud says that although G-d foiled Bilaam's curses and converted them into blessings, (*Deuteronomy* 23:6) all nevertheless reverted to curses, except for 'How good are your tents, O Jacob,' (*Numbers* 24:5) which remained as a blessing (*Sanhedrin* 105b). The 'tents of Jacob' refer, of course, to Jewish synagogues."

"G-d thwarted Bilaam's evil intentions," Rabbi Shimon continued wryly, "and those blessings that turned back to curses were rendered harmless. The only one that remained intact and operative was the one about multiplicity of places of worship, because that is a "blessing" which we bring upon ourselves quite willingly. However, this may turn out to be not a blessing at all, but a curse."

There is no need for the splintering and factionalism that prevails among us. We would do better with more people and fewer buildings.

Today
I shall smile
because . . .

_____
_____
_____

A true spiritual leader erects a ladder upon which his followers should ascend to spiritual heights on their own. It is foolish of them to expect that the leader will pull them up (*Rabbi Joseph of Izbiz*).

SMILING EACH DAY

During the summer months, Rabbi Moshe Schrieber, Rabbi of Pressburg and Dean of its yeshiva, would take some of his students to a village in the countryside. There was but one Jew in this village, and he insisted that it was only proper that the rabbi should be his guest. Although this Jew was totally ignorant of Torah, the rabbi complied.

After the first Shabbos spent at his home, the man went to Pressburg in an agitated state, and declared that he had personally seen the rabbi violate Shabbos. The Jewish community was understandably stunned, and when word got back to the rabbi, he requested that the man come before him and testify to the incident, which he promptly did.

"My father was a truly observant Jew," the man began earnestly, evoking sacred memories, "and I knew that everything he did was proper. Every Shabbos morning, after the first part of the services, my father would immediately make *kiddush*, taking some schnapps and refreshments. Rabbi Schrieber, I noticed, failed to do so, waiting until the services were entirely over. Since he did things differently than my father, he was surely in violation of the Shabbos!"

Everyone present had a good laugh at this poor fellow's expense, but Rabbi Schrieber, rather than being irritated by his unwarranted accusation, was most impressed by the man's sincerity. "I greatly respect this man," he confided. "Our survival throughout the Diaspora has always been a direct result of the commitment to preserving our tradition, and this man's assertion that anyone who does things differently than his father did must be guilty of a violation of Shabbos, is a most welcome perspective. Let us all adhere to practices that our ancestors followed, and acknowledge that any deviation, regardless how minor it may appear, constitutes a violation of the Torah."

Today
I shall smile
because . . .

People who are strangers in a foreign country seek out one another, and since they share a common origin and a mutual identity, they naturally form a bond. So it is with man. If he would reflect on his having been created in the image of G-d, and the fact that in this physical world, he enjoys the enviable opportunity to proclaim that identity for all of humanity to see and hear, he would bond with G-d.

SMILING EACH DAY

The Torah wails, "They are a perverse generation" (*Deuteronomy* 32:20). In what way are people perverse?

One of the rabbis suggested, "If a person who has a great deal of money wishes to buy something on credit, he can do so very easily. However, if a poor person tries to do the same, he will be refused. Isn't that perverse? The one who has money readily available should be made to pay, while the one who does not currently have the means is the one who should be extended credit."

"But people will argue," the rabbi continued, "that if someone grants credit to a person who is lacking, and the latter is not able to pay his bill, the merchant will go broke. That should not be a worry, though, because with the proper system in place, he will then be able to buy on credit himself!"

"Moses was right," the rabbi shook his head. "Society is indeed perverse."

Is it not unfortunate that good, simple logic does not always prevail?

Today
I shall smile
because . . .

_____
_____
_____

How topsy-turvy the world is! The Talmud cautions (*Pesachim* 50a), "Even if everybody considers you to be a *tzaddik*, you should view yourself as grossly negligent in your duties." The fact is that many people who are utterly derelict in their responsibilities fancy themselves to be *tzaddikim* (*Rabbi David Bleicher of Novardok*).

SMILING EACH DAY

Many of the chassidic masters were opposed to imposing fast days other than those designated as such in *halachah*.

The Rabbi of Apt once came to a town and was told that the local rabbis had decreed that particular day as a fast, due to a severe drought which threatened local crops, and they were going to offer special prayers for rain. He immediately called the local rabbis and community leaders together, and recommended that they cancel the fast, and instead prepare a lavish community banquet. He promised them that before the feast he would join them in special prayers for rain.

The rabbis were dumbfounded at this suggestion, but out of deference to the great chassidic master, they complied with his wishes. After the special prayers they sat down to a hearty meal.

During the repast, the Rabbi of Apt revealed the superiority of his reasoning. "You must apply logic," he virtually gushed, between mouthfuls. "If you are threatened with a drought that would result in a scarcity of food, what sense does it make to fast and demonstrate to G-d that you can survive without it? To the contrary, by eating heartily and emphasizing that you cannot possibly exist without food, your prayers are much more consistent with your behavior, and G-d will certainly respond favorably to them."

Extraordinary! Under the guidance of the Master, and with proper intent, what appears to be self-indulgence is not only akin to ascetic devotion, but perhaps more effective in approaching the Heavenly throne!

Today
I shall smile
because . . .

"If one steals from a thief, one is nevertheless a thief oneself" (*Berachos* 5a). Some people justify cheating someone out of his ill begotten wealth. Dishonesty does not become honest however, just by addressing it towards an evil entity.

SMILING EACH DAY

When Rabbi Eizel of Slonim (known as "Reb Eizel, the sharp" because of his keen mind) published one of his scholarly works, he sent a copy to one of the wealthy citizens of his community. The latter rejected the book and returned it to him.

Some time later Rabbi Eizel met the wealthy man and said, "You have no idea how grateful I am to you."

"Why would you be grateful?" the man asked, not sensing he was being set up. "After all, I scorned your book."

"Precisely," shot back Rabbi Eizel, with his finger pointed directly at the man. "When my book was published, I was thrilled at the warm reception it received from all Torah scholars. Then I began to think, is it possible, perhaps, that my Torah writings are really not the truth? After all, the Midrash states that when G-d offered the Torah to all the nations of the world, they rejected it, and only after that was it given to the Israelites, who accepted it. Perhaps something that is readily accepted is not truly Torah! This idea tormented me night and day.

"However," he broke into a broad smile, "when you rejected my book, I felt vindicated. Now I know that my writings, like the Torah itself are indeed true, because just like the Torah, my book was rejected by those ignorant of its content and worth."

Today
I shall smile
because . . .

_____
_____
_____

Animals instinctively avoid eating plants that are poisonous, but a human being must use his intellect to shun things that are harmful. A person who fails to exercise his intelligence and indulges in self-destructive behavior is thus beneath a brute beast (*Path of the Just*).

SMILING EACH DAY

The Talmud tells us that when Rabbi Yochanan was told that there are people in Babylon who live to an old age, he said, "That is strange! The Torah stipulates, 'Therefore your days will increase on the land that G-d promised to your ancestors' (*Deuteronomy* 11:21). On what basis do people who live in other countries merit longevity?" But when he heard that they arise early in the morning to study Torah and continue to do so late into the night, he then understood how they earned this blessing (*Berachos* 8a).

The Rabbi of Rodzin interpreted this passage as follows. The number of years that a person lives is not at all in his own hands, but whether one's *active* or actually lived life is long or not is very much a product of his own discretion. A lazy person who rises late in the morning and retires early in the evening, sleeping away most of his life, has very few days of actual living to his credit, regardless of how many years he occupied space on this planet. On the other hand, one who arises early and is productive until very late into the night is actually *lengthening* his days. This is the kind of longevity we are discussing.

No matter where one lives, a person has the ability to extend or shorten his days not only qualitatively but also quantitatively, as one increases the number of hours of actual living.

We all pray for long life. To ask to be so blessed and then to squander that gift by being unproductive, is the height of foolishness. Through diligence, we can simultaneously earn and actually bestow that blessing ourselves.

Today
I shall smile
because . . .

A slave is someone who toils for others, but does not enjoy the fruits of his labor. Someone who works only for worldly goods ultimately leaves the product of his efforts to others, and has therefore led a life essentially of slavery. The person who achieves for himself in the eternal world is a truly free person (*Rabbi Eliyahu Dessler*).

SMILING EACH DAY

The Talmud states that if a person feigns blindness in order to receive charity, his punishment will be that he will actually go blind. Similarly, if one makes himself out to be lame so that people will feel sympathy for him and give him money, he will eventually become lame.

"If so," questioned one of the chassidic masters, half jokingly, "what if one masquerades as a Rebbe in order that people will give him money? Does that mean that he will eventually become a genuine Rebbe? What kind of punishment would that be?"

The master asked, and the master clarified. "People pay much more for the imitation of the natural than for the original itself. A real bird may not be worth much, but a carefully crafted ceramic likeness of a bird can be expensive. And of course, no one pays to hear an animal make its noises, but an entertainer who can mimic animal sounds is rewarded handsomely for his performance.

"So too," he laughed, "real Rebbes are not given much money, but imitation Rebbes can be wealthy. The punishment for someone who accumulates wealth by masquerading as a Rebbe is that he will one day become a genuine Rebbe, and then he will no longer have any money."

Today
I shall smile
because . . .

_____
_____
_____

In the *Book of Proverbs,* Solomon is very harsh with scoffers. You can have a purposeful dialogue with someone you sharply disagree with, but you cannot reason with someone who dismisses everything with ridicule. "A scoffer does not like to be reproved" (*Proverbs* 15:12), and these people are best avoided.

SMILING EACH DAY

When Rabbi Levi Yitzchak assumed the position as Rabbi of Berdichev, he was honored with an elaborate welcoming celebration.

In his inaugural address, Rabbi Levi Yitzchak quoted the Mishnah: " 'When one comes into a city, he should recite two prayers; one for entering and one for leaving (*Berachos* 54a).' Why," he asked, "does the Mishnah already discuss the prayer upon *leaving* when it is talking about someone who is first *entering* the city?"

Rabbi Levi Yitzchak injected a little humor into the affair. "The Mishnah is referring to someone who enters the city as its new rabbi. When he is welcomed, he should recite a blessing of gratitude to G-d for this kindness. However, he should also pray right there and then, that when the time comes for him to leave the city, his departure should be as honorable as his installation. Too often a rabbi is warmly greeted, but his stay is later made intolerable and he is dismissed from the city in disgrace." (This indeed occurred to Rabbi Levi Yitzchak in another community).

And so he prayed, "May my departure from this city be as gracious and dignified as this lovely welcome."

Today
I shall smile
because . . .

Rabbi Simcha Bunim wondered, "A person who has no firm *parnassah* (livelihood) lives by virtue of his faith in G-d, but the person who has wealth and thinks he does not have to trust in G-d for *parnassah,* what keeps him alive?"

SMILING EACH DAY

A man who was known to be a miser pleaded with his rabbi for help. His wife had been tormenting him for years, and he simply could not tolerate living with her any longer. However, she refused to accept a divorce.

"I have a solution for you," the rabbi advised. "The Talmud warns that if a person fails to honor his pledges, he will be punished with the death of his spouse (*Shabbos* 32b). So the next time there is an appeal for funds, make a commitment and refuse to pay it."

The man followed instructions, and pledged a huge sum, but then threw the collectors out the door. Weeks later he complained to the rabbi that his advice was not working, because his wife was as healthy as ever.

"Oy, don't you see," the rabbi chuckled, "this is supposed to be a punishment, not a reward! Do this. Buy your wife a gift each day, speak lovingly to her, try to soothe her, and then when she becomes compatible, the curse will certainly take effect."

Again the man did as he was told, and wouldn't you know it; gradually his wife began to be kind and caring, and their relationship improved day by day. Weeks later the man was able to report, "Rabbi, it is a miracle! We are in love now as though we were newlyweds."

The Rabbi donned a look of terror. "Hurry then and fulfill your pledge!" he exhorted, "because the punishment can now take effect any moment!"

Today
I shall smile
because . . .

_____
_____
_____

Rabbi Aaron of Koznitz remarked, "A person can act only according to what he sees. But what good is it if one sees the young as old, the old as young, the poor as wealthy, the wealthy as poor, the slaves as free, and the free as slaves? What good is faulty vision?"

SMILING EACH DAY

Rabbi Aryeh Leib, better known as the *Sha'agas Aryeh* from the title of his monumental halachic work, undertook a voluntary exile as part of compensation for his "sins." Many great *tzaddikim* whose demands of themselves were exceedingly rigid underwent self-imposed penance for what they felt were their spiritual shortcomings.

In one community, while not recognized as the great man that he was, Rabbi Aryeh Leib was invited as a Shabbos guest by the local rabbi, who was an accomplished scholar. The two entered into a discussion of Talmudic law, and this eventually escalated from a lively dialogue to a heated exchange, with the two defending opposite sides of the issue. Each tried to bolster his line of reasoning by recourse to opinions of accepted Talmudic authorities. As may happen in an argument where one feels one's position to be challenged, one may take it personally and strike out against the opponent. The local rabbi was carried away by the fervor of his argument and made some insulting remarks to Rabbi Aryeh Leib, calling him among other things, a boor and an ignoramus. Rabbi Aryeh Leib, though, stood his ground and was not shaken.

"I'll prove to you that I am right," the local rabbi then exclaimed with an air of finality. He then went to his bookcase and withdrew a book. "Here! The *Sha'agas Aryeh* supports my position."

"How strange," Rabbi Aryeh Leib quipped. "When the *Sha'agas Aryeh* stands in the bookcase he is respected, but when he stands on his own two feet he is insulted!"

Today
I shall smile
because . . .

CHESHVAN

חשון

Erev
Rosh Chodesh
[Eve of the
New Month]

"The voice is that of Jacob, but the hands are those of Esau" (*Genesis* 27:22). Although Jacob acceded to his mother's wish that he masquerade as Esau by wearing the latter's clothes, he refused to lower himself to mimic Esau's vulgar speech. Speech is sacrosanct, and should never be profaned.

SMILING EACH DAY

One Yom Kippur in Sanz a man who was known as a miser began to feel very faint in *shul,* and said that he must have some water. Although he was not apparently ill, the *halachah* states that if a person feels he cannot survive without water, and says so, he may be given something to drink.

The *tzaddik* of Sanz, Rabbi Chaim, was consulted and he instructed that the man be given water by the spoonful, so that this would not constitute the severe Biblical violation of drinking on Yom Kippur, which occurs only when one swallows a minimum of several ounces within a few moments. But after being fed a little water, the man protested that these tiny amounts were not enough, and that unless he is allowed to drink in abundance he will surely die, and his innocent blood will be on the hands of those who refused him water.

The *tzaddik* was again approached, and this time he ruled the man be offered as much as he feels necessary to save his life, but with one stipulation: For each ounce of water he drinks he must donate one hundred dollars to charity after the holy day has passed.

Needless to say, the man's thirst promptly abated.

Today
I shall smile
because . . .

_____
_____
_____

A chassid confided to the *Maggid of Mezeritch* that he wished to discard all worldliness. "Does the world belong to you that you have the right to dispose of it?" the *Maggid* rebuked him.

First Day of Rosh Chodesh Kislev

[Most years Cheshvan has only 29 days and Kislev has only one day of Rosh Chodesh.]

SMILING EACH DAY

The humility of the Chafetz Chaim is legendary. Although he was an outstanding Torah scholar and his *magnum opus*, the *Mishnah Berura,* has been widely accepted as the final authoritative work on issues pertaining to that section of Torah law, he was nevertheless not thought of as being in the same ranks of great Talmudic geniuses of his generation, as for example, Rabbi Chaim of Brisk. On the other hand, he was universally revered as a great *tzaddik*.

It is said that this was so because in his profound humility, the Chofetz Chaim endeavored to keep his extraordinary scholarship as concealed as practicality would allow. Obviously, the person who felt qualified to write the authoritative *Mishnah Berura* was well aware of his encyclopedic Torah knowledge, and righfully feared that exposure of this would bring him great acclaim which he genuinely despised. He therefore prayed fervently to G-d, and did whatever he could to insure that people should not become aware of his immense Torah resources.

But if he was recognized as a *tzaddik*, why did he not pray that his saintliness remain hidden from the world? Simple. Since he never considered himself to be a *tzaddik*, it never even occurred to him that he was in any danger of being regarded as such by others! He could not deny his scholarly knowledge, but he did manage to remain unaware of his saintliness; at least to the degree that others saw in him.

True humility is not simulated. It is the product of an acute awareness of G-d and oneself, and the relationship between the two. The humble person may be cognizant of his great capacities and achievements, yet can retain a perspective of total self-effacement, for he is living in the presence of a higher entity.

Today
I shall smile
because . . .

[Second Day of]
Rosh Chodesh

The Rabbi of Kotzk commented, "The *yetzer hara* found it was too much work getting people to sin. He therefore decided to concentrate on establishing only one framework for activity — falsehood. In that context, he lets you do as you wish."

SMILING EACH DAY

Rabbi Yosef Rosen of Rogachov was more than a Torah genius. He was a phenomenon.

At a conclave of the great leaders of European Jewry, a photographer circulated to take pictures of these awesome men. This was in the days prior to the candid camera, and in order to take a picture, one had to set up the apparatus on a tripod. Anyone who did not wish his picture taken could easily avoid it. Rabbi Rosen was one such person, and he repeatedly turned away from the camera.

Rabbi Meir Shapiro of Lublin, although many years his junior, disapproved of this behavior, and boldly approached the sage. "Permit me to suggest that the great gaon (Torah luminary) has overlooked a *Midrash,*" he pointed out with reverence.

"What *Midrash*?" Rabbi Rosen asked, startled at the notion that his renowned, breathtaking erudition was in question.

"The *Midrash* states that G-d engraved the features of the patriarch Jacob on the Divine throne. Why? Because G-d knew that one day there will be no one left who will have a true Jewish appearance, and when He would long to see what a Jew looks like, he would look at Jacob's image.

"Listen to me, Rogachover Gaon," Rabbi Meir pleaded, sincerely. "There will come at time when no one will remember what a true Jew should look like. Allow them to record your image for posterity."

Rabbi Rosen yielded to the younger rabbi's wisdom, and this is why we have his photograph today.

Today
I shall smile
because . . .

_____
_____
_____

> Rabbi Mendel of Vorki recalled, "I was always thrilled to discover *seforim* (texts) which gave instructions on how to combat the tactics of the *yetzer hara,* until I realized that the *yetzer hara* also read these books and would simply develop new tactics."

SMILING EACH DAY

Following a convention of prominent leaders of European Jewry, some of them returned home by train, and at each stop, a crowd of people gathered at the station to greet the rabbis, who accommodated them by appearing outside for a few moments. Only the revered Chafetz Chaim remained in the coach, refusing to step out onto the platform.

Rabbi Meir Shapiro of Lublin, many years younger than the venerated sage, but not lacking in religious spunk, thought it improper, and approached him. "Why does the great Sage of Radin not join the other rabbis on the platform? Many people out there are clamoring to see him."

The Chafetz Chaim responded, characteristically. "What is there to see? I am no different than any other human being. I have no horns on my head. They only want to gaze at me because they think I am some kind of *tzaddik*, and my going out to them would not only confirm this mistake, it would constitute vanity on my part."

"I concede that this is vanity," Rabbi Meir argued. "So what?"

"Vanity is a sin, and for sin one is severely punished by being whipped in *Gehinnom* (Hell)," replied the Chafetz Chaim, visibly shaken at the notion.

"So you will suffer whipping in *Gehinnom*," the youthful sage/lawyer persisted. "Can't you endure some suffering willingly in order to afford Jews the pleasure of seeing you?"

At this suggestion, the Chafetz Chaim was shocked into action, and thereafter was the first to appear on the platform.

Today
I shall smile
because . . .

Rabbi Naftali of Ropschitz cautioned, "Be on the alert. The *yetzer hara* can be found where you least expect him to be."

SMILING EACH DAY

A case came before Rabbi Yitzchak Nathan Berlin, involving two men who were disputing ownership of a small plot of land. Neither of them had adequate proof that the land was his, so Rabbi Berlin sought to arrive at an equitable compromise. However, neither party wished to yield to arbitration, insisting instead that he apply the letter of the law.

The rabbi was upset by their intransigence and pettiness, and tried to impress upon them that earthly possessions are after all only temporary, and that a small plot of land is hardly worth the enmity they were generating. However, the two turned a deaf ear to his pleas.

The rabbi then related the *Midrash* that when the Israelites occupied Canaan and it was portioned among the twelve tribes, the division was accomplished by casting lots, and the validity of the lot was confirmed by a Heavenly voice which announced, "I belong to this tribe." The rabbi suggested that since there was not enough evidence to rule on, the two parties should rely on a Divine revelation. "Let the land speak for itself," he said with as much Biblical inflection as he could. The intrigued litigants agreed.

The rabbi and the two parties then went to the site. Very impressively, the rabbi bent over and spoke to the earth, "I command you to tell me to which of these two people you really belong." He put his ear to the ground and listened, then arose slowly. With a somber look and a foreboding tone, he relayed what he heard. "The earth says it belongs to neither of you, but that you belong to it, because it will eventually claim both of you."

The two, of course, got the message, and with shivers, agreed to a compromise.

Today
I shall smile
because . . .

_____

_____

_____

Rabbi Yisrael of Rhizin taught, "We are told, 'Turn away from evil and do good' (*Psalms* 34:15). But what if temptation remains in our way? Then one should do so much of what is proper, that the evil will be drowned in a sea of good."

SMILING EACH DAY

Rabbi Shimon Schreiber exhorted his congregants to be certain that their children choose appropriate companions, because even if their teachers are G-d fearing and scholarly, children can be harmfully influenced by friends who do not behave properly.

To emphasize his point, he quoted the *Midrash* which sheds light on the verse that describes how when the matriarch Rivka was pregnant with twins, the two were constantly moving about and causing her great pain (*Genesis* 25:22). The *Midrash* explains that whenever Rivka passed a place of idol worship, Esau tried to exit, and whenever she passed the study house of Shem and Eber, Jacob sought to leave.

"Now why would Jacob wish to exit to the house of study?" Rabbi Shimon asked. "After all, the Talmud informs us that the unborn infant is taught Torah by a heavenly angel. Certainly, that Divine messenger was more saintly than Shem and Eber, and his knowledge far surpassed theirs. Jacob could not possibly have had a better tutor.

"It can only be," Rabbi Shimon concluded, his finger raised, "that Jacob understood that even if the teacher is a heavenly angel, being in the same classroom with Esau is destructive. He was ready to learn from someone of lesser status, in order not to be exposed to the companionship and influence of Esau. And surely, we are no better equipped to withstand such a challenge than our father Jacob."

Today
I shall smile
because . . .

If a deaf person views the gyrations of an orchestra conductor, without having ever been exposed to the concept of symphony music, he may think him to be somewhat crazy. Unless you understand what is going on, it is possible you will assume that others are mad.

SMILING EACH DAY

The two chassidic masters, the brothers Rabbi Elimelech and Rabbi Zusya, used to travel from village to village in their early years to arouse people to spirituality and proper devotion to G-d. On Friday night they would wait after services for someone to invite them to the Shabbos meal. Since they were shabbily clad and gave the appearance of ordinary beggars, the nobility of the community never invited them, and they shared the table of the simple folk.

As time went by and they became established as chassidic masters with large followings, their fame spread. They continued to make the rounds of the villages, only now they were dressed in dignified garments and would arrive in a fine horse-drawn carriage. They were always warmly received in the community, and the wealthiest citizen of the town would invite them to be his guest for Shabbos.

To these offers however, the brothers would respond with rebuke. "Each time we came here previously you did not invite us, because we came on foot and were poorly dressed. You never really cared who we were. But now that we come in an impressive horse-drawn carriage, you wish us to be your guests. In truth though, we have not changed at all, and the only difference is the beautiful coach. That has caught your attention. We will therefore spend the Shabbos with the simple townsfolk who always welcomed us, and you may gladly have our horses at your table. But remember, feed them well, or they will not honor you again with their presence."

Today
I shall smile
because . . .

_____
_____
_____

Rabbi Simcha Bunim observed, "The difference between a fool and a wise person is that a fool says everything he knows, while the wise person knows everything he says."

SMILING EACH DAY

A rabbi in a European village who received a meager salary petitioned the community for an increase, stating that his wage was below the subsistence level. When the community leaders turned him down, he called them together and announced, "I am most grateful for your refusing my request for a raise."

Puzzled, the group waited for an explanation. "All these years that I have served as your rabbi," he began, "I have repeatedly preached to you to mend your ways, to spend more time in prayer and Torah study, and to develop better character traits.

"When I saw that my words were falling on deaf ears, I felt guilty that perhaps I was somehow remiss in my duties. The Talmud assures us that words that emanate from the heart will enter the heart of the listener. Since my lectures were not having any impact upon you, I concluded that I must be lacking in sincerity, and that is why my moralizing was ineffective. This bothered me greatly.

"However," he consoled himself at their expense, "when I asked for a raise, there was no doubt in my mind that this was from the depth of my heart. My inability to put enough food on the table for my family made my request absolutely sincere. When you refused, it proved to me that it was not my lack of proper motivation that was at fault for my unsuccessful efforts, but simply your obstinacy. And so," he concluded, "I thank you, with all sincerity of course."

Today
I shall smile
because . . .

Rabbi Mordechai of Rakov noted with irony, "A poor man is of superior stature than the czar. The poor man begs politely for the money of others, whereas the czar seizes it by brute force."

SMILING EACH DAY

A chassid en route to his Rebbe was met by a Talmudic scholar who was opposed to chassidic practices. "What is it about this person that attracts you so?" he probed, jealously. "I am certainly as great a Talmudic scholar as he is, yet you do not make pilgrimages to me!"

The chassid responded patiently, "Torah scholarship is indeed most important, but it does not, by itself, encompass all that a Jew must achieve. My Rebbe is a very saintly person who is even known to read other people's thoughts."

"That is impossible," the scholar scoffed. "Only G-d can know what a person is thinking. No human is capable of that, not even your Rebbe."

"Of course he is," the chassid persevered, cleverly laying the groundwork for victory. "In fact, I can also do that."

"Oh really?" the scholar was incredulous. "Then tell me, what are my thoughts now?"

"The chassid pondered for several seconds, then said, You are thinking what the *Shulchan Aruch* (Code of Jewish Law) requires — namely, 'I constantly see G-d before me.' "

"Wrong!" the scholar shouted triumphantly. "I am not thinking that at all."

The chassid smiled. "Well then, now you know exactly why I go to see my Rebbe and do not come to you."

Today
I shall smile
because . . .

_____
_____
_____
_____

The eyes have lids that cover it, the mouth has lips that can close, the nostrils and ears are easily plugged. But the brain is without a covering that can block its action. Obviously G-d intended for a person to be open-minded (*Rabbi Yissachar of Zlobotov*).

SMILING EACH DAY

Rabbi Naftali of Ropschitz had no tolerance whatsoever for fools. He once said that if he were to see one of them being escorted into heaven, he would shout after him, "a fool is still a fool."

Someone asked him why he was so intolerant. After all, the Talmud claims that before a person is born, it is decreed whether he will be bright or foolish. It is therefore not anyone's fault if he was predestined to be a fool.

"Yes it is," Rabbi Naftali retorted, barely containing his disdain. "There is a Divine decree that one must eat *matzah* on Passover, right? Yet there is a minimum quantity whereby one can fully satisfy the requirement. One need only eat a piece of *matzah* equivalent to the size of an olive. Of course, if one wishes, he may be *machmir* (take extra care) and eat more, but there is no halachic need to do so.

"Nu, what's different here?" he railed. "If a person merely wishes to comply with the Divine decree that he be a fool, it is surely sufficient to be a small one, barely the minimum necessary to satisfy the heavenly ordained calling. Why though, do people have to be *machmir* and be greater fools than is required?

"It is the stupidity of trying to perfect oneself as a fool that I cannot tolerate" he seethed.

Today
I shall smile
because . . .

The mouth serves two functions: eating and speaking. People brush their teeth to make sure that the eating mechanism is clean. But oy, how important it is to see that the speaking mechanism remains clean. (*Rabbi Yitzchak of Sokolow*).

SMILING EACH DAY

In Europe, most Jewish communities had a book of chronicles, in which were recorded not only important historic events, but also traditions which had been established by the town's earlier citizens.

When the *Sha'agas Aryeh* was Rabbi in Metz, he was often consulted by people regarding a particular practice which might be in violation of a community tradition. People regarded these with the greatest respect, and violation of an inherited custom was considered a grave transgression.

One time, the *Sha'agas Aryeh* demanded that as rabbi, he should have the authority to add to the community chronicles. The townspeople readily agreed, whereupon he casually entered the full text of the Ten Commandments into the book.

The community leaders were of course shocked, and begged the rabbi to explain this action. He told them, "I am frequently approached regarding the permissibility of something which may impinge on a community tradition. At the same time however, I often see flagrant violation of the Ten Commandments, as when people do not respect their parents or are derelict in observing the Shabbos properly." At this point, he revealed a sardonic smile. "It simply occurred to me that perhaps if the Ten Commandments were entered into the community chronicles rather than just being the direct word of G-d, people would take them more seriously!"

Today
I shall smile
because . . .

_____
_____
_____

Rabbi Levi Yitzchak of Berdichev expounded, " 'The superiority of wisdom over folly is like that of light over darkness' (*Ecclesiastes* 2:13). While an intense light might be blinding, the proper degree illuminates, but darkness is just plain dark. A wise man may outsmart himself, but a fool is always nothing more or less than foolish."

SMILING EACH DAY

In the village of Premishlan, the *mikveh* was located at the top of a hill. One bitter, winter day the hill was frozen over, but Rabbi Meir of Premishlan ascended the steep, icy slope as though it were flat, dry land. Others who tried to climb the hill slipped and fell.

"What is your secret?" people asked Rabbi Meir, amazed. "How could you reach the *mikveh* without falling?"

"Secret?" he echoed, feigning ignorance "what secret?" Then he looked them in the eye and asserted, "there is no secret. If you are firmly secured to something above, you don't slip!"

It is common practice to hold onto a ceiling strap in the subway to avoid falling. One can even cross a river via rope by going hand over hand. Rabbi Meir's spiritual grip on the world above him was so tight that it prevented his slipping.

There are times in all our lives when we are in danger of "slipping and tumbling downhill." If we can just reach up and get a firm grasp on the truth above, we can spare ourselves a nasty spill.

Today
I shall smile
because . . .

The Talmud teaches that hospitality to travelers takes priority over receiving the Divine Presence (*Shabbos* 127a). Why is this? Because the Divine Presence is always there, whereas the opportunity to be kind to wayfarers is not (*Rabbi Moshe Leib of Sasov*).

SMILING EACH DAY

Two litigants presented their case before Rabbi Benjamin Diskin, and together placed 5,000 rubles in escrow with the rabbi pending resolution of their dispute.

Several days later one of the parties approached the rabbi, asking him to release 3,000 rubles for just a few days. He was in a tight squeeze for cash, and he assured the rabbi that he was an honorable person who would return the money shortly.

"I'm so sorry I can't help you," the rabbi responded, shrewdly, "You see, just two days ago the other claimant was here and also requested 3,000 rubles, but don't worry; he promised me he would have it back within a few days."

At this news, the man pounded his fist angrily on the table. "What! You released escrow money that was entrusted to you? You have no right to do that!"

"Oh, I did not give it to him, of course," the Rabbi said calmly. I just told you that he had asked for it. But now you yourself have effectively ruled out my giving you any money either."

The embarrassed man left without another word.

Today
I shall smile
because . . .

_____
_____
_____

> Rabbi Yerucham says, " 'I was mightily pushed to fall, but G-d saved me' (*Psalms* 118:13). Within every person's world there is a force that acts to crush him, and he must pray to G-d for salvation."

SMILING EACH DAY

Rabbi Naftali of Ropschitz was once a candidate for the position of rabbi of a community, but there were some people who opposed his selection.

At a community meeting, Rabbi Naftali presented himself thusly. "The *Midrash* relates that G-d revealed the entire course of world history to Adam, showing him each generation and its leaders, each generation and its elders, etc.

"Inasmuch as what G-d wanted to do" he asked, "was to let Adam see who would be the great men among his descendants, what need was there to display before him the people of each generation too?"

Rabbi Naftali let the question sink in before proceeding. "The reason is that if G-d had only shown Adam the leaders, when he came to me, Adam would have exclaimed, 'What! Naftali too is a rabbi!' Therefore G-d showed him the people of each generation before displaying its leader, so that Adam could see that these otherwise unworthy men were commensurate with their generation.

"I know this community well," Rabbi Naftali sized up his listeners, "and without a doubt, I am more than adequate to be its rabbi."

Today
I shall smile
because . . .

Rabbi Yehudah Leib Chasman said, remarkably, that true piety is when a person is aware that everything he does in fulfilling the Divine Will is ultimately to his own benefit.

SMILING EACH DAY

Rabbi Naftali Berlin (the *N'tziv*) was once asked, "Why is it that in bygone days rabbis were paid very low wages, whereas today rabbis receive relatively generous salaries?"

Nodding his head, he answered, "It is very simple. You see, the Talmud actually forbids a rabbi to accept payment for his primary function, which is to teach Torah to the people. However, he is allowed to collect money as *s'char bittul*, i.e., for being kept idle, because he could have been otherwise gainfully employed.

"Time was" the *N'tziv* continued, "when rabbis spent most of their day and much of the night studying Torah, and had very little idle time on their hands, hence the *s'char bittul* they received was minimal. Today's rabbis unfortunately spend much less time involved in Torah study, therefore they have much more potentially lucrative opportunity, and they must be better compensated."

It should be remembered that the *N'tziv* lived in Europe over one hundred years ago. What might he say of some modern day rabbi, whose function as performer of ceremonies and community coordinator generally leaves him precious little time for actual Torah study?

Today
I shall smile
because . . .

_____
_____
_____

> Every positive *mitzvah* dictates, "Be wise."
> Every prohibitive *mitzvah* shouts, "Do not
> be a fool" (*Rabbi Mendel of Kotzk*).

SMILING EACH DAY

A man once complained to a chassidic master that he had fasted for forty consecutive days, and according to the reading he had done, this should have merited him Divine inspiration. However, he felt no different than before.

The master dutifully illustrated his pitiful error. "It is legendary that the Baal Shem Tov traveled at miraculous speed. A trip that should have taken days was completed in hours or even minutes.

He continued, "It was the practice of people who traveled by horse and buggy to stop at every inn to feed and water the horses. When the Baal Shem Tov's horses flew by the first inn at great speed, they thought, 'Maybe we are not horses after all. Maybe we are really human beings, who only stop to eat every few hours.'

"As they continued to pass more and more inns without stopping for food and water, these thoughts escalated; 'Even human beings would have stopped to eat by now. Since we are still not being fed at all, maybe we are actually angels, who require no food and water at all!'

"When they finally arrived at their destination however, and pounced on the hay they were given with animal relish, they realized, 'You know, we must be horses after all.' "

The master summed up, instructively, "Forty days of fasting can not earn you Divine inspiration if after all that, you go back to eating with the same level of indulgence you maintained before."

_____

_____

_____

Today
I shall smile
because . . .

KISLEV

כסלו

A truly pious person can essentially fast even while eating, can be seclusive even among many people, and can feel the chills of the homeless while lying in his warm bed.

SMILING EACH DAY

The *tzaddik* of Sanz was once visited by an old man who was his first teacher, and had taught him the *Aleph-Beis*. The *tzaddik* accorded the simple man great honor, thoroughly humbling himself before him.

Word of this unusual event spread quickly, and reached the ears of the obscure teacher who had taught the *tzaddik* Talmud in his youth. This poor man reasoned, "Why should I not take advantage of such behavior on his part. I will undoubtedly be received with even greater honor, since I taught the *tzaddik* much more than just *Aleph-Beis*." That decided, the teacher made haste to Sanz.

Much to his surprise, although the *tzaddik* greeted him warmly, the man did not receive any of the distinction accorded his predecessor. He could not restrain himself, and asked the *tzaddik* for an explanation.

"It is very simple," the *tzaddik* said. "That man taught me that an *Aleph* is an *Aleph* and a *Beis* is *Beis*. That is absolutely as true today as it was then, and what he taught me was 100% correct. For this, he deserves my utmost respect.

"In your case though, when I grew older and studied the Talmud on my own, I realized that the version you had taught me was erroneous, and I had to unlearn it all and relearn it the correct way. What you taught me did not remain with me. While I appreciate your efforts, I feel no obligation to honor such distortion." The *tzaddik* then blessed the man and sent him on his way."

Today
I shall smile
because . . .

_____
_____
_____

If one has aspirations to be a saint, he could no doubt achieve being an average person. However, if one aspires to nothing other than an ordinary level, he may very well remain a little more than an animal.

SMILING EACH DAY

Rabbi Yosef Dov of Brisk received a complaint that a wealthy man refused to contribute to the community charities. The next time they met in his home, the Rabbi steered the conversation to the subject of the Egyptian sorcerers described in the Scriptures, who were able to mimic some of Moses's miracles. The rich man revealed that he was cynical about all of this, and doubted that anyone could perform either magic or miracles.

"Why do you say that?" Rabbi Yosef Dov asked casually, ignoring the affront to the Torah. "Even I can perform miracles. I will gladly do so right now, but only if you donate one-hundred rubles to charity." The skeptical man accepted the challenge.

"Very well," the rabbi said, adjusting his tone to the event. "I will now show you that if you place four twenty-five ruble notes on the corners of this table, I will utter only one word, and the money will find its way into the bowl at the center." The man was veritably trembling with anticipation as he placed the four notes on the four corners of the table. "Chaim!" Rabbi Yosef then called to his little son, who promptly picked up the four bank notes and deposited them into the bowl. "Well, there you have it! It is just as I said," the rabbi declared.

"That is not fair!" the man howled in protest. "There was no miracle involved in this."

"No miracle?" the rabbi mocked, good-naturedly. "You think that getting one-hundred rubles for charity out of you is not a miracle?"

Everyone had a hearty laugh, and the wealthy man left without ill feelings.

Today
I shall smile
because . . .

A person should learn how to bow while standing upright, how to cry out in silence, and how to dance without moving a limb.

SMILING EACH DAY

A Talmudic scholar was solicited to assume the position as rabbi in a town in Europe but was reluctant to do so because the community had very few learned people, and he felt there would be no stimulus for him to advance in his Torah studies. A committee visited him and told him that their town had a special distinction which should warrant his consideration — the fact that several of the greatest Talmudic authorities and commentaries were buried there, e.g., Rashi, Rabbeinu Tam, MaHarsha, Marshal, and others. The rabbi was surprised to hear this, and was so impressed that he enthusiastically accepted the post.

It wasn't long though, before the rabbi called the community leaders together because he discovered they had lied to him; all these Talmudic greats were buried elsewhere, far away from that community.

"We did not lie at all," the people vigorously, if facetiously, defended themselves. "In other cities Rashi, Rabbeinu Tam, and all the others are very much alive, because everyone studies their writings, and they live on through their great works. In this town they are dead and buried because no one pays any attention to them here!"

Only G-d can literally resurrect the dead, but everyone has the capacity and meritorious responsibility to keep our great scholars alive by studying their writings and implementing their teachings in his daily life.

Today
I shall smile
because . . .

_____
_____
_____

> A person is supposed to advance himself by moving his legs, not by pushing with his elbows.

SMILING EACH DAY

A famous rabbi was asked why he was so passive and did not openly dispute his opponents. He replied with the following story.

A *shochet* once consulted one of the rabbis about a lesion found on the lung of an animal he had slaughtered. Although there was controversy among the *halachic* authorities about this defect, the prevailing opinion was that it rendered the animal non-kosher, and this was based on the decision of the *Shach* (Rabbi Shachna HaCohen) who was generally accepted as the final word on the subject. The rabbi researched the question laboriously, and ultimately ruled, much to the *shochet's* delight, that the animal was kosher.

When the news spread that the rabbi had overridden the accepted opinion of the *Shach*, he was summoned by one of the leading Torah authorities to account for his audacity. The rabbi explained himself:

"We are taught that departed souls may require an act of rectification before being admitted to their eternal rest in heaven. Sometimes this is brought about by the particular soul being reincarnated in an animal. When that animal is eaten, and people pronounce *berachos* (blessings) at the meal, and then use the nutritional energy supplied by the food in order to do *mitzvos*, the poor soul locked within may then be redeemed, and can find its eternal peace. This would not happen if the animal is found to be *treifa* (non-kosher) and cannot be eaten."

Feeling he had vindicated himself, he concluded, "On Judgment Day, if the *Shach* will take me to task before the Heavenly Tribunal for overruling him, I am ready and eager to dispute the fine points of the law with him. But if the animal were to indict me for rendering it *treifa*, I do not wish to become involved in an argument with an animal." Finishing his tale, the prominent rabbi smiled knowingly, and left it at that.

Today
I shall smile
because . . .

If you cannot find your way out of a forest, retrace your steps and mark the paths that led nowhere, so that you should not try them again.

SMILING EACH DAY

Rabbi Abli of Vilna was once conducting a class in Talmud when a young woman abruptly burst into the room and pleaded, "Rabbi, what should I cook for dinner tonight?"

The students' bewilderment at this bizarre interruption was only intensified when Rabbi Abli responded calmly, "Give me a moment to think, please." He closed his eyes as if deeply concentrating, and then said, "I think you should cook a vegetable soup with mushrooms." The girl thanked him profusely and left.

Rabbi Abli knew that his students were desperately curious about this strange interchange. "I can only speculate as to what happened," he began. "This young woman must be employed as a cook and she probably asked her mistress as always, what to prepare for dinner tonight. That lady was no doubt in a bad mood, and must have shouted, 'Why do you bother me with that question? Go ask the rabbi!' The poor girl did not understand this to be a sarcastic brush-off, and took her employer literally.

"If I would have dismissed the issue," he observed wisely, "and sent her back, warning, 'Don't bother me with such foolish questions,' the result might have been that when a real question arises about whether something is kosher or not, and the young woman is told to ask the rabbi, she would be reluctant to come, fearing more rebuke. Since she appears to be unable to distinguish between sarcasm and straight talk, an important *kashrus* question might go unanswered. I therefore had to react as I did so that she should not hesitate to come when a real question occurs."

If only we would all view our actions with such responsible forethought.

Today
I shall smile
because . . .

_____

_____

_____

> If you travel along the main road, you will constantly see signs to guide you to your destination. If you choose to use an isolated path, you are on your own.

SMILING EACH DAY

Rabbi Heschel of Cracow, who was a child prodigy, was once asked, "The biblical city of Sodom was known for its topsy-turvy laws: evil was rewarded, and good was punished. The Torah relates that when Lot refused the demands of the Sodomites to turn his guests over to the mob, they complained, 'A foreigner has moved into our midst and wishes to act as a judge' (*Genesis* 19:9).

"Inasmuch as it is logical that a judge should be someone who is an established citizen of the community, well-acquainted with the prevailing sense of justice, rather than a newcomer, the warped system of Sodom should then have required just the reverse; i.e., that the judge *should* be a stranger to the land and its customs. Why, then, did the Sdomites object to Lot?"

The young genius thought only a brief moment and then replied, "Yes, it was indeed the law of Sodom that the judge be unfamiliar with them. However, you must keep in mind that the people who rejected Lot were themselves Sodomites, and they were so perverse that they did whatever was the opposite of their own laws. Thus, while the law itself was crooked; i.e., that only newcomers should pass judgment, these thoroughly wicked people acted contrary to their own understanding, and therefore reverted to the traditional assumption that strangers should not rule!"

Not historically accurate but how's that for the reasoning of a small child?

Today
I shall smile
because . . .

Rabbi Moshe of Mekarov noted, "The earth normally absorbs water, but when you add a lot to saturate the soil, it turns into mud. The poor use their money to live, whereas for the wealthy, additional money creates a swamp into which they sink."

SMILING EACH DAY

Some of the *chassidim* of Rabbi Mendel of Kotzk pleaded with him to write a book containing his teachings, so that they could study it during the time they were not in his presence to learn from his direct instruction.

The Kotzker, renowned for his biting insight, dismissed the suggestion, pointing out, "Most people are too busy with their work all week, and whatever time they can spare for study is appropriately spent on the Talmud. When would they have a chance to study my book?

"The only time available" he continued, painting his scenario, "would be on Shabbos. They would arise in the morning, go to the *mikveh*, and recite the *Tehillim* (Psalms) until the morning prayers. After the services they would come home, make *kiddush* on wine or schnapps, partake heartily of the fish, *kugel*, and *cholent*, and with their stomachs full from all these delicacies they would lie down for siesta. That is when they would have the time to read my book — before falling asleep.

"In that particular state though, they would undoubtedly doze off before finishing even one paragraph, and the book would fall from their hand, ending up under the bed.

"For that I should invest my time and effort to write a book?"

Today
I shall smile
because . . .

_____
_____
_____

> There are many elaborate explanations of the commandment, "Thou shalt not steal." The most correct one is, "Do not steal!"

SMILING EACH DAY

Rabbi Yosef Dov of Brisk was once asked by some of his congregants what time the *molad* (appearance of the new moon) was to be that month. The mind of this great sage was occupied by matters of far greater significance, but he knew that to these simple townsfolk this information was just as important, and he did not wish to trivialize it to them.

Rabbi Yosef Dov therefore responded, "There are some things that one is not permitted to rule from memory without consulting a written authority. Please bring me a calendar, and I will tell you when it is." (The *molad* is usually included in each Jewish calendar.)

The people promptly searched for a calendar but returned empty-handed. No calendar could be located.

Rabbi Yosef Dov maintained a serious demeanor. "In the event that there is no calendar available, the law then permits one to pronounce the *molad* from memory." Certain that in the absence of a calendar he could not be contradicted, he then quoted a time for the *molad*, and the people went away satisfied.

Knowing when the first day of the new month was, Rabbi Yosef Dov was able to give them an approximate time based on a quick calculation, and since the precise time does not in any way affect *halachah* or practice, there was no danger or impropriety in giving an approximate rather than exact time.

There are things that may appear to us to be trivial, but one should always respect the perception of others. To dismiss something as insignificant might result in the unlearned taking liberties and ignoring issues that are of much actual substance.

Today
I shall smile
because . . .

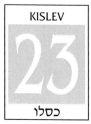

We need faith in order to know that G-d is concealed within the Universe. But once we know that He is hidden there, he is no longer disguised (*Rabbi Pinchas of Koritz*).

SMILING EACH DAY

The Maggid of Mezeritch taught that there are three things one can learn from an infant and seven things one can learn from a thief, all of which one can apply to the Divine service.

From the infant:

1. It never is idle, regardless of how much time it has on its hands.
2. It is almost always happy.
3. If it wants something it cries for it without hesitation or embarrassment.

From a thief:

1. He does his most important work at night, when no one sees him.
2. If he fails one time, he goes back to try again, because it's worth it.
3. There is a strong bond of loyalty among them.
4. A thief is ready to exert great effort even for minimal gain.
5. Once he acquires something, he may give away an expensive item for a song.
6. He will not admit to others what he possesses.
7. He will not relinquish his line of work, regardless what others may think of him. After all, he knows he's being smarter and more efficient at providing for himself than everyone else.

If we analyze these traits, we should see how they can be constructively utilized by one who dedicates himself to serve G-d and do His bidding.

Today
I shall smile
because . . .

_____
_____
_____

> Why worry? If there is something you can do about a problem, then by all means, do it! If there is nothing you can do, what good will worrying do?

SMILING EACH DAY

One Purim a student of Rabbi Chaim of Brisk had too much to drink, and in his intoxicated state made insulting comments about his teacher. When he sobered up, he apologized profusely and since his Rebbe was as much a tzaddik as he was a world renowned Talmudic genius, he was forgiven.

A colleague of Rabbi Chaim opposed his granting forgiveness, citing the Proverb "A drunk has on his tongue what the sober person has on his lung"; i.e., thoughts that are verbalized while intoxicated reveal the feelings the person has while sober, hence he must be harboring attitudes of disrespect.

Rabbi Chaim disagreed, with recourse to brilliance. "If that observation would be universally true, then butchers would be able to avoid major losses. Most animals that become *treifa* (non-kosher) are so because inspection of the lungs reveals a problematic lesion. But wait! There is a simple solution to prevent this dreaded occurrence. Get the animal drunk and inspect its tongue! If no defect appears on the tongue, that should mean there is nothing on the lung either. Just think how much money could be saved if animals known to have lesions would not be butchered for kosher use!

"Why is this not done?" he drew his desired conclusion. "Apparently, the saying applies only to human beings, but does not hold true for oxen. There is therefore no reason for me to apply it in this case."

Rabbi Chaim may have been a *tzaddik*, but he was nobody's fool.

Erev Chanukah
[Eve of Chanukah] —

[The first candle is lit tonight.]

Today
I shall smile
because . . .

Chanukah

[The second candle is lit tonight.]

May I come to love the greatest *tzaddik* as much as G-d loves the greatest *rasha* (*Rabbi Shlomo of Karlin*).

SMILING EACH DAY

When Rabbi Chaim of Brisk was a young child, he and his friends were once asked why the sockets of the chandeliers face upwards. All the children answered the obvious, that if the sockets were to face downward, the candles would fall out. The young Chaim, whose mind abhored the simplistic, instead searching out the *purely* simple, shook his head in disagreement. "It's not that they would fall out, but that they could not be made to stay in to begin with."

This mental attitude characterized Rabbi Chaim in study of the Talmud throughout his entire life. Difficulties did not require answers, but rather precise and so complete a clarification of a subject that there would no longer be any questions.

Ideally, this should be as recognized in all aspects of life as in understanding of the Talmud. People are always looking for solutions to their problems and various possibilities are considered, usually none of which are completely satisfactory. But if they would only analyze the alleged obstacle with an open mind, without bias or prejudice, they might be surprised to discover (and for some, that could be a rather annoying discovery) that there is no need for any solutions, because the problem was an illusion to begin with!

Some Talmudic students unfortunately prefer answers to questions rather than elimination of the source of difficulty. Similarly, there are people who need problems to exist for which they can claim solutions. Life could be much simpler if we would just stare for a moment at the chandelier.

Today
I shall smile
because . . .

_____
_____
_____

> "I will not leave you, [I will be with you] until I will have fulfilled My promise to you" (*Genesis* 28:15). G-d does not abandon us even before He actually helps us.

Chanukah

SMILING EACH DAY

An itinerant *maggid* (preacher) came into a village and requested permission to speak. He also asked that the rabbi accord him the honor of attending his sermon.

The well-meaning fellow carried on with a lengthy discourse which, for all its emotional energy, was unfortunately, totally devoid of substance. When he finally finished, he eagerly approached the rabbi for his opinion of the talk. "I must tell you, you have done me a great favor," the rabbi began, choosing his words for maximum effect, "because you have answered a perplexing question for me.

[The third candle is lit tonight.]

"In *Ecclesiastes*, King Solomon states that there are different times for everything: 'A time to cry and a time to laugh . . . a time to construct and a time to dismantle,' etc. (*Ecclesiastes* 3:1-8).

"For each pair of extremes," he went on, "there is also a point of neutrality, i.e., a time neither to laugh nor to cry, neither to construct nor to demolish. The exception is, 'there is a time to speak and a time to remain silent.' Where is the place in between? One is either talking or holding his voice. Correct?"

The *maggid* affirmed that this was indeed a difficult verse, and couldn't wait to hear how the rabbi had resolved the problem.

"I was bothered by this question for years," the rabbi swooped down upon his unsuspecting prey, "but your sermon just provided the solution. You spoke for two whole hours, but said absolutely nothing at all!"

Today
I shall smile
because . . .

Chanukah

[The fourth candle
is lit tonight.]

It is worthwhile to learn *mussar* an entire lifetime, even if it only accomplishes avoiding speaking *lashon hara* once (*Rabbi Yisrael Salanter*).

SMILING EACH DAY

Chassidic masters had differing concepts about the appropriate time for prayer. A number of them delayed their prayers, explaining (perhaps to themselves as much as to the *misnagdim*, opponents of chassidus), that in an advancing army there is always a patrol at the rear assigned to pick up stragglers that have fallen along the wayside. Similarly, these masters waited until everyone else had finished their prayers, so that they could gather up those that had failed to make it up to heaven and renew their trip skyward.

Another explained that while a king may have a designated period of time during which he accepts petitions from his subjects, this applies only to those who make personal requests. If a minister wishes to talk to the king about something that pertains to the welfare of the kingdom, however, he may enter at any time.

Yet another master claimed that when he began saying the prayer of gratitude upon arising in the morning, *Modeh Ani Lefanecha* (I thank You) and "When I reflect on who is *ani* (I) and who is *lefanecha* (You, G-d), I am paralyzed with awe, and it takes me time to free myself of this condition to be able to proceed with prayer."

All valid. But on the other hand, we have the master who prayed at the break of dawn. He poignantly observed, "When you have inferior merchandise to offer, your only hope is to be the earliest at the marketplace, before other vendors get there." Take your choice.

Today
I shall smile
because . . .

_____
_____
_____

> There is something so unique that it has never existed in the past and will never be here again: Today.

Chanukah

[The fifth candle is lit tonight.]

SMILING EACH DAY

During the height of the *haskala* ("Enlightenment") movement, a number of Hebrew schools were opened under the auspices of people who sought to solve the "Jewish problem" (whatever that is) by assimilation. While they could not hope to uproot Judaism entirely, their strategy was to disparage traditional teachings and make it more palatable for young people to break away from Torah observance and adopt practices of their non-Jewish environment. These schools were thus full of heretical instruction.

In one city, a teacher at such a school was befriended by the local rabbi, a man of considerable intellectual and social acumen, who carried on long conversations and disputes with him. This fellow then began to bring his colleagues with him, and the rabbi would spend hours in discussions with them. A *melamed* (Hebrew teacher), who taught at the traditional *cheder*, was unable to get much time from the rabbi, and asked him, "Why do you invest so much of your resources in these lost souls? Do you really think you can change their attitude? I have been trying to talk over an important issue with you, and I cannot get more than a few minutes of your time, whereas you readily donate many hours to these people."

The rabbi embraced the *melamed* in conciliation. "My dear child, you don't understand. Every minute that I keep these people occupied in my study, I am preventing them from spouting their obscene philosophies to their students. I wish I could detain them here all day! But you teach true Torah to your charges, and I don't want to keep you from them for one extra moment!"

Today
I shall smile
because . . .

*Chanukah —
Erev Rosh
Chodesh*

*[The sixth candle
is lit tonight.]*

"You shall eat, be satisfied, and thank G-d" (*Deuteronomy* 8:10). This may well mean that one should gain more satiety from praising G-d than from eating.

SMILING EACH DAY

Rabbi Naftali of Ropschitz once visited a village which had been drenched by uninterrupted rain for days. The townsfolk complained to the rabbi that their fields were being flooded and that unless the deluge came to an end, they would lose all their produce. Rabbi Naftali told them that inasmuch as rain is essentially a blessing, it is improper to pray for its cessation.

Upon entering the local synagogue for services, Rabbi Naftali noticed that the roof was leaking in several places, and he sharply reprimanded the townsfolk for neglecting the repair of the holy place. "Not only is this a lack of respect for the Divine presence," he claimed, "but this is actually why the rain is persisting so long."

The people's incomprehension lasted but a moment.

"The Talmud states that whereas the Torah promises long life to those who live in the Holy Land (*Deuteronomy* 11:21), it can also be earned by those who live elsewhere by virtue of their coming daily to the synagogue" (*Berachos* 8a).

His audience captivated, he made his point.

"By your failure to fix the roof, you have allowed the water to enter the synagogue on a regular basis. As a consequence, it has merited the Divine promise of longevity. If you repair the structure and keep the rain from continuing its worthy habit, it will soon stop!"

Today
I shall smile
because . . .

_____
_____
_____

> A lower position of someone who is ascending is better than a higher position of someone who is descending. That is how one is viewed on Judgment Day (*Rabbi Jacob Joseph*).

Chanukah — First Day of Rosh Chodesh Teves
[Some years Kislev has only 29 days and Teves has only one day of Rosh Chodesh. During those years the 7th and 8th candles are lit on the nights following 1 and 2 Teves, and the last day of Chanukah is 3 Teves.]

SMILING EACH DAY

Sometimes we try to conceal some of our behavior, and while this may succeed for an isolated act, it proves futile for deeds that are repeated.

One of the residents of Nickolsburg was a wealthy person who was known to be a miser. None of the local charities benefited from him, and collectors for out-of-town causes were invariably dismissed with nothing. Rabbi Mordechai Benet once sharply reprimanded the man for his unwholesome conduct.

The man attempted to defend himself. "Rabbi, I have often heard you preach about the great virtue of giving *tzedakah* in secrecy, so that one does not do so for public acclaim. I do indeed give *tzedakah,* but I wish to do so in its purest form, and so I perform this great *mitzvah* behind closed doors to avoid honor."

Rabbi Mordechai chose not to slap the man across the face for his audacity, and actually graced him with a rebuttal. "There are many sins you have committed over the years, and although you have tried to hide them from the public eye, word has gotten around." The rabbi then went on to enumerate some of the evil activities the man had engaged in, ostensibly in private.

[The seventh candle is lit tonight.]

When he saw the shock of revelation having the desired effect, the rabbi continued.

"No matter how much you try to conceal something, a repetitive act will eventually be exposed. If you contributed to *tzedakah* secretly, you would surely have been caught in the act just as you were in the other things you thought you could cover up. Since no one has ever witnessed you giving *tzedakah,* it is obvious that you have never done so. So give up, if not yourself, then at least some of your money."

Today
I shall smile
because . . .

*Chanukah —
[Second Day of]
Rosh Chodesh
Teves*

*[The eighth (in some
years the seventh)
candle is lit tonight.]*

A servant of G-d is not only someone who willingly serves Him, but also someone who *wishes* to willingly serve Him.

SMILING EACH DAY

A chassid told a friend that he had consulted his Rebbe about a business venture, and that by following the Rebbe's recommendations, he had succeeded beyond his wildest dreams. This friend, who also had several business opportunities, sought an audience with the Rebbe and asked his advice as to what would be best. The Rebbe shrugged his shoulders and said, "I am not a financial consultant."

"But you gave my friend such excellent advice," the man said.

The Rebbe explained. "A merchant once came to a jobber and purchased a large amount of merchandise. After it was all loaded on the wagon, he told the jobber that he could not get the wagon to move, and perhaps he had some grease with which he could lubricate the wheels. The jobber soon appeared with a bucket of grease.

"Another person, who observed this, told the jobber that he, too, was stuck with his wagon, and asked whether he could supply him with grease. 'No,' the jobber said. 'This man is an old customer of mine, and he regularly takes my merchandise. Since he happened to get stuck this once, I fetched him some grease. But I don't know you, and you never buy from me. I am not in the business of supplying grease.' "

The Rebbe continued, "Your friend is my chassid, who regularly seeks my Torah teachings and advice on how to conduct himself spiritually. One time he had a financial question, so I answered him. But you have never come to me for spiritual advice, and you seek only advice on business matters. Well, I am not a financial consultant."

Today
I shall smile
because . . .

_____

_____

_____

> Whatever is forbidden is absolutely prohibited, but not all that is permissible is necessary (*Rabbi Shneur Zalman*).

Chanukah

SMILING EACH DAY

Many of the *tzaddikim* used to act as advocates, pleading the cause of Israel before G-d. Some did not hesitate to challenge Divine justice. Although this might appear to be audacious and irreverent, they believed that G-d wished them to do so, just as a loving Father would appreciate anyone who pleaded for mercy for an errant child.

The Chassidic master, the *Shpoler Zeide,* once addressed G-d, "You are displeased with us because we sin, because we should have chosen right over wrong, good over evil.

"Fair and free choice can exist only when there is an equality between two options. It is not free choice when the scales are tipped in one direction.

"You have placed temptation toward physical pleasures in front of our very eyes, as clear as day, and within easy reach. On the other hand, the torments of hell are an abstraction, concealed somewhere with the works of *mussar* (*ethics*).

"Why didn't You place the torment of hell before our eyes, and conceal temptation within the books? I assure You, dear G-d, that had You done so, not one single person would have sinned!

"You must forgive us, because the system is not a fair one."

[In some years the eighth candle is lit tonight.]

Today
I shall smile
because . . .

[Last day of Chanukah in some years.]
Chanukah

Rabbi Yerucham said, "We think of the Biblical miracles as great wonders. It is a much greater wonder when a person makes a change in one's character."

SMILING EACH DAY

A poor man who was in desperate need of money to marry off his daughter appealed for help to a wealthy relative, who gave him a mere pittance. The man then turned to the local rabbi to intercede for him. The rabbi told the wealthy relative that the Scripture states, "Do not turn away from your own kin" (*Isaiah* 58:7).

"But he is a very distant relative," the wealthy man protested. "I have no greater obligation toward him than toward a stranger."

The rabbi said, "Tell me, my dear friend, do you pray daily?"

"Of course," the man answered. "I pray three times every day."

"Then you do say in the *amidah* (silent prayer) 'The G-d of our ancestors, Abraham, Isaac, and Jacob,' and you ask for the Divine blessing by virtue of the good deeds of the Patriarchs?"

"Yes," the man responded.

"These ancestors, whose memories you invoke, lived hundreds of generations ago, and are far more removed from you than this relative is. If you wish to be the beneficiary of the Patriarchs by virtue of being their descendant even though they are so far removed from you, then you must honor a kinship even though it is distant. G-d judges you according to the standards you adopt in your own life."

Today
I shall smile
because . . .

_____

_____

_____

Rabbi Pinchas of Koritz said, "One who tries to correct the corruption of the world is like a chimney cleaner. Try as one might, one cannot avoid becoming soiled."

TEVES

4

טבת

SMILING EACH DAY

Some people pride themselves because of their *yichus* (ancestry), as though it had an intrinsic value. They may expect others to respect them by virtue of their *yichus*, even though they may not have merits of their own.

A young man visited the Rabbi of Rhizhin and boasted of his genealogy, asserting that his ancestors were great Torah scholars and *tzaddikim*. He expected that the rabbi would accord him a special place of honor at the table. The rabbi noted that the young man himself, however, was devoid of the fine qualities of his ancestors.

"There was once a king," the rabbi said, "who built a new palace, and commissioned four artists to each paint a mural on one of the four walls of his throne chamber. One artist waited until the other three completed their masterpieces, then he placed a huge mirror on the fourth wall, which reflected the beautiful art work of the other three walls. The king was thrilled with this brilliant idea.

"Much the same is true with a person's ancestry. If one perfects himself in Torah and good deeds, he becomes like a highly polished surface, so that he can reflect the beauty of his ancestry, and then his genealogy manifests itself in him. But if he lacks the luster and polish of his own personality, he reflects nothing, so what good is his *yichus*?"

Today
I shall smile
because . . .

Decency is a prerequisite for Torah. It is possible for a person to run to a *mussar* lecture and push elderly people out of his way because he is so hungry to hear mussar (*Rabbi Yisrael of Salant*).

SMILING EACH DAY

The great *chassidic* master known as the Seer of Lublin was once confronted by the great local Torah scholar, Rabbi Azriel Horowitz, who was an opponent of chassidim. "Why do you attract so large a following?" Rabbi Azriel asked. "You are not a particularly great Torah scholar. You should discourage people from coming to you."

The Seer was in full agreement, and the following Shabbos he addressed his followers: "You must stop coming to me," he said. "I am not deserving of being a Rebbe. I am not adequately learned and I lack the qualifications to be your leader." The chassidim, impressed with the Seer's profound humility, flocked to him in even greater numbers.

Rabbi Azriel reprimanded the Seer. "Of course you will attract more people. They took your statement as an indication of humility, and have even greater admiration for you. In order to discourage them you must do the opposite. Tell them that you are a great *tzaddik* and an outstanding Torah scholar, and that you deserve to be their leader and you have earned their respect. Then they will avoid you."

The Seer shook his head. "That I cannot do," he said. "As much as I would like to comply with your wishes, I cannot get myself to lie."

Today
I shall smile
because . . .

_____
_____
_____

> Rabbi Simcha Bunim said, "A person who is not owned by another person is not yet free. A truly free person is one who is not a slave to anyone, including himself."

SMILING EACH DAY

The rabbi of Belz once took his son along to the *mikveh*, which happened to be unheated that day. When the young boy put his foot into the cold water he said, "Oy, Oy! It's too cold." After immersing himself and coming out into the warm room, the boy said, "Ah, ah! That was good."

The rabbi seized the opportunity to make a point. "There you have the difference between a *mitzvah* and a sin," he said. "Doing a *mitzvah* may sometimes cause inconvenience or discomfort, and you may initially say 'Oy, Oy!', but afterwards you will feel good about it, and the pleasant feeling of 'Ah' will be long lasting.

"Doing a sin, on the other hand, may give you momentary pleasure, and you may say 'Ah!', but soon afterwards you will say 'Oy, Oy!', and this time it will be the 'Oy' that will be long lasting."

In modern times, when our plastic credit cards represent a way of life characterized by "Get what you want now and pay for it later," we need to be reminded of the rabbi of Belz's teaching to his son, and not trade in a momentary "Ah!" for a terribly long "Oy!"

Today
I shall smile
because . . .

The *yetzer hara* often disguises himself as the *yetzer tov*. If the *yetzer hara* was unable to present some sins as being *mitzvos*, many improper acts would have been avoided (*Rabbi Tzvi Elimelech*).

SMILING EACH DAY

There are arguments today to legitimize drugs as well as various practices that are immoral. While those who advocate this may have good intentions, it should be realized that there are things that are inherently evil and cannot be pronounced to be legitimate.

A rabbi had a daughter who was very pious, and she developed a serious disease for which the only cure was eating hog liver. The young woman protested that she would not eat *treifa* (non-kosher), and when her father told her that she was required by the Torah to do whatever necessary to save her life, she acquiesced on the condition that the hog be ritually slaughtered by a *shochet* (ritual slaughterer). To appease the sick girl, this was done, and she then insisted that the hog viscera be inspected to determine whether there might not be a *treifa* lesion.

No amount of logic could dissuade the girl from this foolishness. When the viscera was examined, a lesion in the lungs was indeed found, and she then insisted that it be submitted to a rabbi for an opinion on whether this was a permissible lesion.

The rabbi who examined the lung explained, "This particular lesion in a cow's lung would be kosher. But how can you expect me to declare a *chazzer* (hog) to be kosher?"

Today I shall smile because . . .

_____
_____
_____

Rabbi Naftali of Ropschitz said to a chassid, "If you are not achieving your goal in this world in spite of your extensive efforts, how do you plan to achieve anything in the Eternal World in which you invest so little effort?"

SMILING EACH DAY

When the great Talmudist, Rabbi Yechezkel Landau (The *Noda B'Yehudah*) became Rabbi of Prague, a dispute arose in the congregation whether the *chazan* (reader) should recite the *kaddish* before the Torah scroll is returned to the Ark or afterwards. It was decided to consult the rabbi, who ruled that the *kaddish* should be recited afterwards. The rabbi then called the *shammes* (sexton) and instructed him to enter the ruling into the chronicles of the community.

Several weeks later another dispute arose about the order of the services, and again the rabbi instructed that his ruling be recorded in the chronicles. A committee of community leaders met with the rabbi and explained that the chronicles were for recording momentous historic events, and not for every minor rabbinical ruling.

The rabbi explained, "If someone will consult me today on a question of *halachah*, I will give him an answer. If someone raises the same question ten years later, I will give him the same answer, because there is *halachah* on this. On these matters of sequence of the services there is no *halachah*. I might rule differently on the same question two weeks from now, and someone will then criticize me for being inconsistent. Therefore I want these rulings recorded, so that I can refer to them for the sake of consistency."

Today
I shall smile
because . . .

TEVES

טבת

Rabbi Meshulam of Zbarz said, "The *yetzer hara* was unsuccessful in getting me to sin, so he tried another tactic. He urged me to learn much Torah and perform many *mitzvos,* so that I would consider myself a *tzaddik* and a scholar. This way I would be vain, which is the worst of all sins. One must be alert to his wily tactics."

SMILING EACH DAY

The *Midrash Shocher Tov* relates that when Noah brought all living things into the ark before the flood, *sheker* (falsehood) also wished to enter. Noah explained that only couples were allowed to enter the ark, and *sheker* would have to find himself a mate. However, no one wished to unite with *sheker*.

In his wanderings, *sheker* came across *schlimazel* (ne'er-do-well), who appeared dejected. *Schlimazel*, too, had sought entrance into the ark, and had also been rejected because he lacked a mate. *Sheker* then suggested the obvious, that the two of them form a union. As a condition of this liaison, it was agreed that everything that would be gained by *sheker* would be turned over to *schlimazel*.

This union has thus existed since ancient times. *Sheker* and *schlimazel* always accompany one another, and the terms are strictly observed: Whatever is gained by falsehood ultimately goes down the drain with *schlimazel*.

Today
I shall smile
because . . .

_____
_____
_____

> Rabbi Mordechai of Lechovitz said, "The battle against the *yetzer hara* is no different than any other battle between two adversaries, where victories and defeats may alternate. The important thing is that you get the final triumph."

Fast of
Asarah B'Teves

SMILING EACH DAY

Rashi states that when Jacob sent messengers to Esau, he sent heavenly angels (*Genesis* 32:4).

Rabbi Boruch of Medziboz was a grandson of the Baal Shem Tov, and was very critical of many of the Baal Shem Tov's disciples, who had established themselves as chassidic masters in their own right. One time, when several of them visited him, he quoted the above *Rashi*, and asked, "Why would Jacob have sent heavenly angels to someone as non-spiritual as Esau?

"The Torah relates," he said, "that when the heavenly angels appeared to Abraham, they took the form of ordinary humans. (Ibid. 18:2). However, when they came to Jacob, they presented themselves as Divine angels (Ibid. 32:2).

"This irritated Jacob," Rabbi Boruch said. Then, addressing his visitors who had been his grandfather's students, he continued, " 'When you came to my grandfather,' Jacob said to the angels, 'you presented yourselves as ordinary human beings, but now you come to me appearing to be holy angels! I will have no part of you. Off with you! You may go to Esau.' "

Today
I shall smile
because . . .

Laziness is not necessarily slowness. A lazy person may sometimes act quickly because he is too lazy to think about what he is doing.

SMILING EACH DAY

A *tzaddik* who was meticulous in his caution never to utter even a single false word, once called upon one of the community members, and happened to find the family in the midst of a meal. The man welcomed the *tzaddik* and his *shammes* (attendant) and asked them to please join in the meal.

A glance at the sparse food on the table indicated to the *tzaddik* that there was hardly enough for the family, and that his partaking of any food would impinge upon their rations. Yet, he did not wish to refuse in a manner that would betray the reason for his reluctance and possibly embarrass the host.

"I'm sorry I cannot join you," the *tzaddik* said, "but I am under strict orders from a physician not to eat."

The *shammes* was surprised at this, knowing that the *tzaddik* would rather die than say an untruth. After they left, he asked the *tzaddik* why he had lied.

"I did not lie at all," the *tzaddik* said. "It is well known that the *Rambam* (Maimonides) was a great physician. The *Rambam* rules that one should not partake of a meal that is inadequate for the host. Hence I was under physician's orders not to eat."

Today
I shall smile
because . . .

_____
_____
_____

Rabbi Wolf of Strikov said to a chassid, "You are not as good as you think, and the world is not as bad as you think. Get to know yourself better, and you will get to know the world better."

SMILING EACH DAY

There have unfortunately been episodes in our history when communities were brought to ruin as a result of disputes between several of its rabbis. Generally it was the adherents of each leader who became zealous in their loyalty, and a factionalism developed which was to the detriment of everyone.

In one such community where a dispute had developed into a conflagration, an outside rabbi was brought in as an arbiter and peacemaker but — alas! — try as he might, he could not bring about a peaceful resolution. He pointed out to both sides that if peace was not restored, everyone would lose, but this had no impact.

Before leaving the community, the rabbi called both sides together. "Now I understand," he said, "why the Patriarch Abraham pleaded to G-d to spare Sodom from destruction (*Genesis* 18:23-32). Abraham said, 'If there are fifty *tzaddikim* in its midst, will You not spare the city?'

"Abraham's reasoning was simple," the rabbi concluded. "If there are fifty *tzaddikim* in the city, they will take care of bringing it to ruin by themselves, and there is no need for You to intervene."

Today
I shall smile
because . . .

Those who think too quickly may find that they lose their thought due to its very speed.

SMILING EACH DAY

Among chassidim the practice of the Shabbos meal of late afternoon (*seudah shelishis*) is regularly observed. In some circles this meal is omitted, and in its place a discussion of Torah is held. One of the chassidic masters argued that a discussion of Torah cannot be a substitute for the meal.

"The Torah relates that Abraham sent his servant Eliezer to find a wife for Isaac," he said. "Abraham was adamant that Isaac not take a wife from the pagan population in his immediate environment. But why was all this necessary? The Torah states that G-d blessed Abraham with everything, and the *Midrash* explains that 'everything' means that he also had a daughter. Inasmuch as in pre-Biblical days marriage between a brother and sister was permitted, why did Abraham go to all the trouble of bringing a wife from Aram, when Isaac could simply have married his sister?

"Apparently," the rabbi continued, "Isaac wanted to have a real, factual wife, rather than one that is not explicit cited in the Torah but is derived by the *Midrash* from the word 'everything.' Why did Isaac have this preference? Because if someone were to refute the *Midrash* he would remain without a wife.

"Similarly," the rabbi said, "a meal that consists of real food is a factual meal. One that consists of a discussion of *Midrash* is unreliable, because if someone refutes the explanation of the *Midrash*, the entire 'meal' is refuted."

Today
I shall smile
because . . .

_____

_____

_____

Jacob dreamt of a ladder standing on the ground reaching into the sky (*Genesis* 28:12). When one lives a life of G-dliness, one produces Torah even when asleep (*Rabbi Baruch of Medziboz*).

SMILING EACH DAY

One of the chassidic masters who had been widowed was interested in remarrying. His fame as a great *tzaddik* and scholar had spread far and wide. When he met one of the women who was interested in marrying him, he said to her: "The *halachah* states that a marriage that is entered into on false pretenses is fraudulent. I know that my chassidim say things about me that are not true. They say that I am a great scholar, which I am not. They say that I am a *tzaddik,* which I am not. They say that I can perform miracles, which I cannot do. They say that I am Divinely inspired, which I am not. And in case you may think that someone who has so many devoted followers is wealthy, then you are mistaken. I don't have any money either."

The woman was greatly impressed with the chassidic master's humility. "You have told me all your defects," she said. "A person like yourself must certainly have some virtues as well. Tell me some of them."

"Oh, yes," the master replied. "My only virtue is that I always tell the truth."

Today
I shall smile
because . . .

A truly pious person can be happy even when things do not go his way.

SMILING EACH DAY

It is not unusual to find that at the morning *minyan* (services in the shul) disputes may arise among some worshipers who are observing the *Kaddish* either during the year of mourning or on a *yahrzeit* (annual memorial service) for a relative. They may argue over priority to lead the services, to be called to the *maftir* (the final portion of the Torah reading) or to recite a special *Kaddish*. These disputes can become quite violent, and it is tragic to see how some people think that they are thereby honoring their departed relative and contributing to his eternal repose.

In Brisk one such dispute resulted in fisticuffs, and when Rabbi Yosef Dov entered the shul, the dispute was brought before him. Rabbi Yosef Dov responded:

"I now understand a previously enigmatic verse of the Torah. Esau was furious with Jacob for his deceptive acquisition of Isaac's blessings (*Genesis* 27:41) and said, 'Wait until my father dies, then I will kill Jacob.' Why the delay?

"But inasmuch as Esau masqueraded as a pious person (*Rashi, Genesis* 25:27), he could not jeopardize his reputation by committing a flagrant crime. Therefore he said, 'Just wait until father dies. Then there will be an opportunity for me to dispute priority rights for *Kaddish* with Jacob, and in that context, my killing him will appear as having occurred in the course of defending my father's honor!'

"We do not honor the memories of our loved ones by causing disputes."

Today
I shall smile
because . . .

_____
_____
_____

> Perhaps ignorance is bliss, yet is better to be wise, even if this means suffering pain (*Rabbi Mendel of Kotzk*).

SMILING EACH DAY

The *Midrash* states that Moses was born when his mother, Yocheved, was 137 years old. Why, then, is much ado made about the Matriarch Sarah's pregnancy at ninety, and so little heard about Yocheved's miraculous pregnancy?

The *Maggid* of Dubno answered with a parable. A group of beggars gathered to discuss their respective successes and failures. It was their practice to share information with one another, so that they might solicit from more generous donors.

One beggar maintained that he had received a handsome donation from a certain wealthy man. "Impossible!" the others said. "He is a tightwad. He never gives more than a trifle." Yet, the first beggar insisted that his account was true.

"When did you receive this donation?" one of them asked. "On Purim," the first replied.

"Oh, well, that explains it. On Purim everyone is more generous. That is why he gave more. All year round, however, he is a tightwad."

The *Maggid* then explained, "The episode of the Jews in Egypt was replete with so many miraculous events, that an unusual pregnancy at an advanced age was hardly worth mentioning. Sarah's miracle occurred at a time when things were proceeding according to the laws of nature, and that is why her pregnancy was such an outstanding event."

Today
I shall smile
because . . .

A tightrope walker may be paid for his performance, but if he concentrates on his pay while walking on the high wire, he is certain to fall.

SMILING EACH DAY

Rabbi Chaim of Brisk once solicited the community for funds for a worthy cause. He knew that one wealthy man was reluctant to part with his money, and he sought some method to obtain a reasonable donation. He therefore sent a messenger to the man, asking him to promptly appear in his study.

The wealthy man, anxious because of the urgent tone of Rabbi Chaim's request, dropped everything and responded immediately, whereupon Rabbi Chaim told him of the need for funds for this particular project.

The wealthy man became quite agitated. "Was that any reason for you to send for me? Is it not simple courtesy that when you want something from me you come to me rather than calling me to come to you?"

"You are right," Rabbi Chaim said. "But if I had come to you and you had refused, I would have wasted my time."

"Well, isn't my time valuable too?" the man asked. "Why didn't you consider that you would be wasting my time by calling me here?"

Rabbi Chaim responded, "Because if you donate properly, your time will not have been wasted. You have the option to make your time well spent. Had I come to you, I would not have had such an option."

The man appreciated Rabbi Chaim's reasoning and contributed appropriately.

Today
I shall smile
because . . .

_____
_____
_____

> How do you know if you love G-d? "Those who love G-d despise evil" (*Psalms* 97:10). If you despise evil, then you love G-d.

SMILING EACH DAY

The citizens of a village once complained to Rabbi Eizel of Slonim, an authoritative regional rabbi, that the integrity of the rabbi of their community was less than perfect, and that he could be convinced to grant unjustified leniencies in *halachah*. Rabbi Eizel, who knew the composition of this particular community quite well, felt that the community had gotten what they had asked for, because he had recommended far superior candidates for that position.

Rabbi Eizel called the attention of the community leaders to the comment of *Rashi* that although Lot was a newcomer to Sodom, the people appointed him as their judge (*Genesis* 19:1).

The Torah relates previously that there had been a dispute between Abraham's shepherds and Lot's shepherds. Abraham refused to allow his herds to graze in other people's fields, whereas Lot said, "G-d promised this entire land to Abraham, and I am his sole heir. The entire land therefore belongs to me, and my herds may graze anywhere they wish" (*Rashi,* ibid., 13:7).

"When the people of Sodom heard that Lot was so adept at rationalizing, that he could argue to legitimize theft, they promptly appointed him as their judge," Rabbi Eizel said.

"When you interviewed candidates for the community, I suggested several people whom you rejected. You were obviously looking for someone who would accommodate your wishes. Stop complaining, You got what you asked for."

Today
I shall smile
because . . .

If you are finding fault with others, you are wasting your time. You could be searching out your own defects.

SMILING EACH DAY

The ineptitude of bureaucracy is hardly a new phenomenon.

During one year of drought in Russia, food supplies became quite scarce. One community responded by doing what many governmental bodies do in order to solve a problem, i.e. appoint committees to see that whatever food is available should reach the consumers and be distributed fairly. Needless to say, these committees did as most committees do, taking a difficult problem and making it infinitely worse.

Rabbi Yosef Dov of Brisk stated that this occurred even in Biblical times. "When Yosef interpreted Pharaoh's dream that seven years of plenty would be followed by seven years of famine, he suggested that Pharaoh appoint officials in each community to see that the produce of the years of plenty be stored for the years of famine (*Genesis* 41:34).

"Joseph made this recommendation in order to protect his reputation. He reasoned that if G-d would mercifully revoke His decree, and the seven years of famine would never come about, his predictions would then turn out to have been false. To insure that there would never be enough grain to go around, Joseph cleverly recommended that committees be appointed everywhere to distribute the grain, and that way, he could rest assured that even if grain were to be available in abundance, the committees would see to it that it was somehow sequestered and squandered and never reach the consumer, and his prediction of a food shortage would be secure!"

Solomon wisely said, "There is nothing new under the sun" (*Ecclesiastes* 1:6).

Today
I shall smile
because . . .

_____
_____
_____

> If a person does not criticize what G-d does, G-d may not be too critical of that which he does either.

TEVES

20

טבת

SMILING EACH DAY

On Shabbos after completion of the morning services, as the chassidim of the Rabbi of Gur left the synagogue in Jerusalem, a car drove by, and the driver called to the worshipers asking for directions. No one bothered to answer him, considering it the height of *chutzpah* for a person to drive on Shabbos in an ultra-Orthodox neighborhood, and an even greater *chutzpah* to expect observant Jews to give him directions where to drive.

Just then the Rabbi walked out of the synagogue, and when the man continued to call out for directions, the chassidim were astonished to see the Rabbi walk over to the car and give the man precise directions to his destination.

Noting the bewilderment of the chassidim, the Rabbi explained, "True, this man was violating Shabbos by driving his car. However, if you did not give him directions, do you think that that would eliminate his violation of the Shabbos? Do you really believe he would have parked the car and walked the rest of the way? To the contrary, not knowing where to go, he would have to do even more driving until he found the correct way, and he would thus accumulate even greater violations of Shabbos. By telling him precisely how to get to his destination, I minimized the amount of driving he would have to do, and actually decreased his violation of Shabbos."

While zealousness has its place, the Rabbi's reasoning indicates that discretion rather than zeal may be more effective in reducing Torah violation.

Today
I shall smile
because . . .

SMILING EACH DAY / 111

G-d's wisdom is unfathomable. I would not worship a god whose mind is within my grasp to understand.

SMILING EACH DAY

The practice among chassidim is to present a Rebbe with a "*kvittel*," which is a slip of paper on which one has enumerated all one's problems, and whereby one asks the Rebbe's blessing to be relieved of these distresses.

One chassidic master explained this custom as follows: "It is really the responsibility of every Jew to spend the greater portion of his day in prayer, Torah study, and performance of *mitzvos*, by which one would then merit the Divine blessings of good health, *parnassah* (livelihood) and *nachas* (pleasure in one's children).

"Since most people must devote so much of their time to earning a living, they delegate the duties of prayer, Torah study and performance of *mitzvos* to the rabbi, and they support him so that he can be their agent in accomplishing these duties. If they are distressed by poor health, lack of *parnassah*, and problems with their children, this indicates to them that the rabbi, as their agent, must have been derelict in his duties.

"Perhaps they would be justified in frankly rebuking the rabbi for his neglect and dereliction. But Jews are too polite and considerate to do this. Instead, they list all their distresses and problems on a slip of paper, which they give to the rabbi in private, thereby essentially stating, 'Look how many problems we are suffering because you are not doing your job adequately.' "

Today
I shall smile
because . . .

_____
_____
_____

Rabbi Asher of Stolin said that even if only one of many dollars which one gave to *tzedakah* reaches a worthy recipient, it is more than worthwhile to have given all the others just so that single dollar reaches a proper goal.

SMILING EACH DAY

In one community, one of the citizens became very wealthy, and several congregations sought to enlist him as a member in order to benefit from his philanthropy. Soon the rabbis of the congregation became involved in a dispute, each trying to outdo the other in bringing him into their particular circle. The subject of this dispute was quite confused, unable to decide where he belonged.

When one of the chassidic masters visited the community, the wealthy man sought his advice. The master listened, then commented:

"How tragic it is that times have changed so radically. The Torah relates that when Jacob was en route to Laban, he made himself a pillow from some of the rocks (*Genesis* 28:11). The *Midrash* states that the rocks then began to argue with one another, each one demanding, 'I want the *tzaddik* to rest his head upon me.' G-d therefore fused all the rocks into one unit, to satisfy all their wishes.

"In bygone days," the master continued, "rocks would argue over a *tzaddik*. Today, it appears, *tzaddikim* argue over a rock."

"Unfortunately," he continued, "it is easier to fuse hard rocks into a single unit than to unite some erstwhile *tzaddikim*."

Today
I shall smile
because . . .

Rabbi Baruch of Medziboz said, "How pleasant the world is if we do not subjugate ourselves to it, and how difficult it is if we do."

SMILING EACH DAY

On *Simchas Torah,* when the annual reading of the Torah is completed, it is customary to call a scholar to the reading of the final portion. This honor is referred to as *choson Torah,* i.e., the "bridegroom" of the Torah, indicating a loving relationship between the person who is engaged in the study of Torah (as though he were the husband) and the Torah, the latter being the *kallah* (bride).

In one community, a wealthy man who was totally unlearned wished to receive this distinct honor, and he paid the *gabbai* (officer of the synagogue) to accord him the honor of *choson Torah.* The rabbi, suspecting that this was done for financial gain, confronted the *gabbai*, who reluctantly admitted that he was paid to give this honor to someone totally ignorant of Torah.

The rabbi quipped, "I can understand this very well. You see, *choson Torah* is a bridegroom-bride relationship. When a young man and a young woman are acquainted with one another and are mutually attracted, there is no need to have a *shadchan* (matchmaker) involved, and no payment is necessary. However, if the two are total strangers and are brought together by a matchmaker, the latter receives a fee for his services.

"When a Torah scholar receives the honor of *choson Torah,* it is a loving relationship, because he and the Torah have known each other for a long time and have developed a mutual fondness. In a situation where the person receiving *choson Torah* is a total stranger to the Torah, there obviously had to be a matchmaker, who had to be given his fee."

Today
I shall smile
because . . .

_____
_____
_____

Rabbi Levi Yitzchak of Berdichev said, "Of course the world is good. Can't you see? It tolerates even someone like myself."

SMILING EACH DAY

Rabbi Bunim of P'shische, when advising people about a *shiduch* (matrimonial match) stated what we generally know to be true — that the degree of spirituality that prevails in a home is usually determined by the wife rather than the husband.

Rabbi Bunim supported his position by referring to the episode in the Torah where the Patriarch Jacob asked Laban for the hand of his daughter, Rachel, in marriage. Laban responded, "I'd rather give her to you than to any other man" (*Genesis* 29:19). Inasmuch as Laban has come down in history as a sly, wicked person, why would he favor his daughter marrying a *tzaddik*?

But Laban must have been disappointed that his daughter Rachel deviated from the family pagan beliefs and despised his idolatrous practices (*Genesis* 31:19). He knew that she was a true, G-d fearing person. Laban therefore reasoned that if Rachel were to marry anyone else, she would certainly influence that person and convert him into a *tzaddik*. Being the wicked person he was, he wished to minimize the number of just people in the world.

Laban therefore decided to cut his losses, and concluded that it would be better if Rachel married Jacob, who was already a *tzaddik*, rather than anyone else. In that way, there would be one less *tzaddik* in the world. This, then, is the way the Torah indicates the importance of the woman's role in setting the spiritual tone in the family.

Today
I shall smile
because . . .

Rabbi Itzel of Petersburg said, "In business your profit may exceed the effort invested, or may be less. In spiritual matters the yield is exactly equal to the effort expended."

SMILING EACH DAY

"*Yud*" (or *Yid* in some Jewish dialects) is a word that means "A Jew" (probably a colloquialism of the Hebrew *Yehudi*). Yud is also the name of the tenth letter of the Hebrew alphabet, which is essentially a dot (י).

One child, in practicing the writing of the *Aleph-Beis*, wrote the *Yud* with a stem (ו) or with a head (ר) which thus converted it into another letter (*vav* or *resh*). The teacher corrected him, "If you make the *Yud* bigger than it is supposed to be, it is no longer a *Yud*."

Someone who overheard this comment realized its significance. The *letter Yud* represents the *person Yud*. A person is a true *Yud* only if he does not make himself greater than he is. Vanity attacks the very essence of being a *Yud* (person) just as enlarging the letter *Yud* destroys its identity.

The Talmud states, "A vain person is equivalent to an idolator" (*Sotah* 4b). The simple comment of the teacher in *cheder* shows how the *Aleph-Beis* demonstrates this point.

Today I shall smile because . . .

_____

_____

_____

We may not be as learned as our fore-bears, but each generation is a step in the process of purification. The ultimate drop of the distillate is the most concentrated and the purest.

SMILING EACH DAY

Rabbi Baruch of Medziboz commented on the verse in *Proverbs* (13:25), "A *tzaddik* eats to his satiation, while the stomach of the wicked person is lacking." Since a *tzaddik* usually eats very sparingly, and it is the hedonist that is indulgent, shouldn't the verse read just the opposite, that the non-spiritual person has a full stomach, whereas the *tzaddik* is apt to be hungry?

Rabbi Boruch stated that the verse refers to a host and guest. The *tzaddik*, being desirous of fulfilling the *mitzvah* of *hachnasas orchim* (hospitality) will join his guest at a meal even though he has already eaten, because his guest will feel more at ease in eating when the host eats along with him. The wicked person, however, who begrudges others, may refrain from eating along with his guests even though he may be hungry, hoping that by abstaining from eating his guests will follow suit and eat very little.

Mitzvos such as hospitality, charity, and other acts of benevolence are enhanced or flawed by the attitude with which they are performed. The Torah states, "(Give to the poor) and do not have a bad heart in doing so" (*Deuteronomy* 15:10).

Today
I shall smile
because . . .

The chassidim of Ostrova said, "There are few people who flee from their pursuers. Most people run away from themselves, and leave even no shadow behind."

SMILING EACH DAY

Rabbi Levi Yitzchak of Berdichev once noted a man moving about frenetically in the marketplace. He asked the man, "Pardon me, but what are you doing?"

The man continued hurrying about, saying, "I'm sorry, rabbi, but I am very busy and I don't have time to talk with you now."

Rabbi Levi Yitzchak kept pace with the man, and again asked, "Please tell me what it is that you are doing."

The man responded rudely, "Can't you see? I'm trying to make a living, that's what I'm doing."

Rabbi Levi Yitzchak said calmly, "No, my friend. That is what G-d is doing. Whatever it is that you are supposed to earn has been pre-ordained, and your frenetic actions will not affect it. Your earning is what G-d is doing for you. What G-d does not do for you and what is *your* obligation is the study of Torah, prayer, and the performance of *mitzvos*. That is why I asked, 'What is it that *you* are doing?' "

Today
I shall smile
because . . .

_____

_____

_____

Rabbi Chaim of Sanz said, "People get off one train and run to catch another, in pursuit of the good they seek. Perhaps if they stood still for a while, the good would overtake them."

SMILING EACH DAY

A chassid complained to Rabbi Elimelech of Lizensk that he was suffering from forgetfulness. Rabbi Elimelech said, "Do *teshuvah* and your memory will improve."

The chassid was bewildered. "What is the relationship of *teshuvah* to memory?" he asked.

"It is very simple," Rabbi Elimelech responded. "The Talmud states that *teshuvah* is so great that it reaches the very throne of the Almighty (*Yoma* 86a). We also say in the prayer of Rosh Hashanah that 'there is no forgetfulness before the throne of the Almighty.' All you must do is to

put the two together. If you do *teshuvah*, you will reach the throne of the Almighty. In that status, you will have no forgetfulness."

Rabbi Elimelech's wit is more than supported psychologically. If we can free ourselves of the burden of our mistakes by proper *teshuvah*, the acuity of our minds is certain to improve.

Today
I shall smile
because . . .

Erev
Rosh Chodesh
*[Eve of the
New Month]*

Rabbi Nosson Tzvi Finkel said, "The Torah is not too little for even the greatest person, and is not too great for even the least person."

SMILING EACH DAY

Rabbi Chaim of Volozhin was a true disciple of the High Priest, Aaron, as stated in *Ethics of the Fathers* (1:12) "To love peace and pursue peace." Whenever he heard of a dispute between two people, he would invest a great deal of effort to make peace between them. Often these disputes were amongst simple folk and involved petty matters, and Rabbi Chaim's students thought it was beneath his dignity to engage in such affairs. One student was bold enough to tell Rabbi Chaim that he was humiliating himself by this practice.

Rabbi Chaim said, "Have you ever wondered why it is that when we conclude the *amidah* (silent prayer) we take three steps backward? It is because the last verse of the *amidah* is 'May He Who makes peace above make peace among us and among all of Israel.' We step back to indicate that in order to make peace we must be ready to retreat from our position.

"When we genuflect and bow during the *amidah*, we humble ourselves before G-d. When we take three steps back at the conclusion of the *amidah*, we indicate that even with other humans it is often necessary to retreat from a lofty position."

**Today
I shall smile
because . . .**

_____
_____
_____

> The Talmud relates that Rabbi Judah wept, "One can acquire eternity in one brief moment of *teshuvah.*" Why the weeping? It is for all those precious moments that we do not utilize for *teshuvah.* (Rabbi Tzvi of Zidachov).

SHEVAT

שבט

Rosh Chodesh

SMILING EACH DAY

Years ago, the religious population of Eastern Europe knew America as a place where Jews threw off the yoke of Torah observance. Because professional schools in Europe were essentially closed to them, and there were so many restrictions on doing business, many young people emigrated to America to improve their lot in life. Grieving parents considered them lost to the faith forever.

One man consulted his rabbi, stating that his son who had emigrated to America, had become successful in business, and was now sending him money. He was certain that the boy was not observing Shabbos, and his question was whether he was allowed to accept the *treifa* (non-kosher) funds.

The rabbi clearly blended his advice with solace. "You are concerned that your child has cast aside his heritage. However, there is one *mitzvah* that he is still observing, which is to show respect for his parents. Now you wish to deprive him of that also?"

In a more objective sense, before we do anything to reject someone, we would be wise to give serious consideration as to what the consequences of such action might be.

Today
I shall smile
because . . .

Rabbi Moshe of Rozvadov confided, instructively, "Dying does not frighten me, because I was placed in this world with that in mind. What concerns me is that I should not die like an animal, because for that I was not created."

SMILING EACH DAY

A man once complained to the Rabbi of Ostrovtza that his children were neglecting him. He was especially angry and disappointed because he had been a very devoted father, but his family was not repaying his kindness. He cited the aphorism that a father can provide for ten children, but ten children seem unable to provide for one father. "It is grossly unfair," the man lamented bitterly.

The rabbi agreed that this state of affairs was indeed unpleasant, "but it is not unfair," he corrected, without compromising his sympathetic stance.

"You see, the pattern of parent-child relationships is one that has been handed down through the generations," the rabbi expounded. "Adam cared for his children, and they in turn cared for theirs. However, Adam did not have to provide for his father," he pointed out. "Hence the precedent of solicitude towards a parent was never similarly established."

While there are many things in life that we wish would be different, we generally adjust quite well to experiences that are perceived as the norm. The Rabbi of Ostrovtza's observation may help us accept that some of the unpleasantness we face, while inexcusable from a strictly intellectual point of view, just happens to be "normal."

Today
I shall smile
because . . .

_____
_____
_____

Rabbi Joseph Leib Bloch said, "It is the pettiness of our generation and its accompanying imagined superiority that stand in the way of our appreciating the greatness of the previous generations."

SMILING EACH DAY

In the Biblical saga of Joseph, it is related that when the brothers returned to Canaan and told Jacob that Joseph was still alive, and then began describing his exalted position as a viceroy of the Egyptian empire, Jacob exclaimed, "Enough! My son Joseph yet lives" (*Genesis* 25:28).

A woman was walking along the beach with her little son when a violent storm broke out. Without warning, a huge wave came ashore and swept the child out into the sea. The distraught, helpless mother fell to her knees and began screaming to G-d, "Please give me back my baby!" Moments later, another wave arrived and deposited the tot, unharmed, at her feet.

The grateful woman, at first overwhelmed, embraced the child for a few moments, unable to utter a word. Then, regaining her composure, she turned her tearful eyes toward heaven and cried, "Oh, thank You G-d, thank You for Your kindness. My gratitude to You is eternal." Suddenly, she took a good look at the child, then lifted her eyes again upward, and in a demanding tone called out, "But G-d, he was wearing a hat!"

When the brothers wished to tell of Joseph's greatness, Jacob interrupted, "Stop! It is enough for me that my son Joseph is alive. Everything else is superfluous."

We are often the beneficiaries of profound goodness, and may even express some degree of thanks, yet we still remain dissatisfied, because things are not *exactly* the way we would like them to be. We could all use a lesson in true gratitude.

Today
I shall smile
because . . .

The Talmud compares this world to a wedding hall. There is always a celebration going on, but each day someone else is partying (*A disciple of the Baal Shem Tov*).

SMILING EACH DAY

Before one Rosh Hoshona, Rabbi Levi Yitzchak of Berdichev was looking for someone to blow the *shofar*, and let it be known that he wished to interview prospective candidates. Many learned and experienced people responded, hoping to be accorded the honor, some of whom were well versed not only in the intricate *halachic* regulations of the *shofar*, but also in the esoteric kabbalistic implications of the various sounds. Strangely, Rabbi Levi Yitzchak was not satisfied with any of these.

Nearing the holy day, one rather simple person presented himself before the *tzaddik*. When Rabbi Levi Yitzchak asked him if he was skilled in the proper *kavannah* (meditation) for blowing the *shofar*, the man replied tearfully:

"Rabbi, the truth is that I know nothing about the secret meanings. I am very poor, and do not even have the money necessary to provide a dowry for my daughter, who therefore cannot find a husband. When I blow the *shofar*, I concentrate on one thought: 'Dear G-d, I am doing Your will by performing this *mitzvah*. Please do my will, and provide me with the means to marry off my child.' "

Rabbi Levi Yitzchok jumped up, impressed. "You are my man!" he declared triumphantly.

Today
I shall smile
because . . .

_____
_____
_____

Rabbi Gershon Henoch remarked, "I am delighted when I hear a wise person speak, but even more appreciative when a fool remains silent."

SMILING EACH DAY

It is told about one great Torah scholar (some attribute this story to Rabbi Heschel of Cracow) who was a child prodigy, that when the position of rabbi of the community was vacated and various applicants vied for it, this boy of ten or eleven mounted the pulpit one Shabbos and delivered a Torah discourse that kept the audience spellbound for hours. They had rarely heard such scholarship and brilliance, and certainly nothing of the sort from any of the other candidates. The young child sensation then proposed that based on his proven qualification, he should be engaged as the new rabbi.

The elders of the community were taken aback, and hurriedly tried to explain to him that although there was no denying his superior talent, it was unthinkable to appoint a mere youth as rabbi of a community. But this kid, who was really no kid at all, was one step ahead of them.

He argued, "No human being is perfect, right? Everyone has shortcomings, some of which may not even be evident to you during an interview, but could later cause you much distress.

"You know me well," he went on, "because I grew up among you. Thus far, you have found only one defect in me, which is my young age.

"Well then, I can promise you something that no other candidate can. Without reservation, I guarantee you that every day of my life I will progressively improve on my one fault!"

Today
I shall smile
because . . .

Rabbi Simcha Bunim claimed that miserliness ruins performance of all *mitzvos*, and is a contributing factor to committing sins.

SMILING EACH DAY

In the *Malbim's* commentary on the *Book of Daniel,* he tries to unravel the cryptic verses at the end predicting the "end of days." His contemporaries were very critical, citing that the Talmud pronounces a curse on those who attempt to compute the day of the redemption.

The *Malbim,* however, would counter with a story. "A merchant in Poland once took along his small boy on a journey to the commercial center in Leipzig. In those days, the trip by horse and buggy took many days, and when at first, the child would ask, 'Papa, how far is it to Leipzig?' the father indicated he was displeased with the question and changed the subject. The youth soon understood he was not to press the issue.

"After several days' travel the boy heard his father ask the driver, 'Do we still have much to go till Leipzig?' Puzzled, he then questioned why he had been rebuked when he had posed the same question.

"The father responded, 'Earlier in the trip, when I knew we were still very far from our destination, I did not wish to tell you how distant we were, because I knew you would become impatient and cause me problems. Now that I sense we are approaching the area, I feel free to ask just how close we are.'

"The Talmud," continued the *Malbim,* "was written two-thousand years ago, and the sages knew we were destined for a long stay in exile. Now that we are obviously so close to the redemption, however, it is permissible and even natural to ask, 'How far is it to Leipzig?' "

Today
I shall smile
because . . .

_____
_____
_____

Rabbi Moshe of Savran pointed out, "It is generally accepted that if a person recites the entire *Psalms* without interruption, his prayers will surely be answered. What people fail to understand, though, is that 'without interruption' means between the mouth and the heart."

SMILING EACH DAY

In one city, there was a Jewish hospital whose survival was threatened because of lack of support by local philanthropists. When the Maggid (preacher) of Kelm came to the community and took in the situation, he delivered a powerful sermon which included the following message:

"The Talmud states that a Divine angel stands at the head of the bed of every sick person.

"One time this angel complained to G-d that he was tired of going to the homes of the sick poor, where conditions were so terribly deteriorated, with the house in ruins, the children hungry, and everyone in the family depressed. To appease him, G-d made some wealthy people sick, so that the angel could do his duty in more comfortable, luxurious surroundings.

"When the people realized what was happening, they quickly built a hospital to cater to the impoverished, with bright rooms and attractive furniture, so that the angel would not resent being sent there, and G-d would no longer need to bring disease upon the rich in order to accommodate his servant.

"But if the hospital should be forced to close, sick people will have to remain in their homes, and the angel isn't likely to suddenly be happy in such shabby surroundings. He will again complain to G-d, who will have no choice but to once again make the wealthy sick.

"If you wish to protect yourself from headaches and heartaches," the Maggid advised the well-to-do of the congregation, "make sure that the hospital remains open and is well cared for."

Today
I shall smile
because . . .

If you really appreciate and value independence, remain silent. Speech serves no end unless someone is listening, hence you are dependent on others when you speak. If you keep quiet, you need no one (*The Holy Yehudi*).

SMILING EACH DAY

In one city there was desperate need for a certain community project, but while there was universal agreement on this point, nothing seemed to materialize. Week after week saw lengthy meetings, with impressive speeches by community leaders and much discussion, but alas, no action.

At one such gathering, the rabbi arose and mildly took his people to task. "The Torah tells us," he began, "that when Moses was commanded by G-d to deliver the Israelites from their Egyptian bondage, he initially refused, claiming that he was tongue-tied and could not communicate effectively with Pharaoh or with the Israelites. G-d reminded him, 'Who is it that gives man the power to speak or renders him mute? It is I, G-d. Now then, do as I told you and go to Pharaoh, and your brother Aaron will be your interpreter' (*Exodus* 4:10-16).

"What's amazing is, having stated that it was He that can make a person speak, why didn't G-d just do the obvious and cure Moses' speech defect?

"The reason is that G-d was afraid that if Moses would be an orator, he might come to enjoy making speeches about the beauty and value of liberty, and get so carried away with his prowess, that he would hold endless community meetings to provide a forum for his lectures. But of course, the Israelites would then never get out of Egypt."

The rabbi ended with a heartfelt plea. "Our community needs are not being met through speeches. Let us instead take a lesson from the experience of Moses and focus on getting things done."

Today
I shall smile
because . . .

_____

_____

_____

Rabbi Chanoch of Alexander taught, "An Englishman speaks English, a Frenchman speaks French, and a Russian speaks Russian. The heart, too, has a language of its own."

SMILING EACH DAY

In one synagogue, there were several worshipers who regularly left the chapel during the Torah reading. Apparently, they felt that the essence of the service was the prayer, and the reading of the Torah was optional. And since they imagined themselves to be fluent in the content of the weekly portion, they would dispense with hearing it read, particularly since this time could well be used catching up on the latest gossip. Their weekly meeting in the vestibule was most distressing to the rabbi, whose reprimand to each individual in private proved futile.

He therefore decided he had no choice but to go public, and even humiliate the offenders. He reasoned that an act of disrespect towards the Torah that was committed in plain view of all justified such fierce rebuke. Unfortunately, this too was to no avail, and even after exhortation from the pulpit, the regularly scheduled exodus continued.

The rabbi's patience with his "recess crew" was exhausted. Prior to the reading of the Torah on Shabbos, he interrupted the service and announced, "I must publicly apologize to those people whom I had criticized for leaving the chapel by the Torah reading." The congregation could hardly believe their ears, and waited anxiously for him to continue.

"It is certainly not their fault," the rabbi rationalized on their behalf. "They are merely following the instructions of the congregation. When we take the Torah out of the Ark, we invoke the plea, 'Arise O G-d, and let Your foes scatter. Let Your enemies flee before You,' and these people are simply doing precisely what they are told. May we all learn from their sense of obedience."

Today
I shall smile
because . . .

The Talmud states that a person's *yetzer hara* (evil inclination) renews itself every day. Why? "Because," noted Rabbi Avraham Zalmans, dryly, "even the *yetzer hara* realizes that yesterday's indulgences are without any substance."

SMILING EACH DAY

Rabbi Levi Yitzchak of Berdichev was famous for his moving dialogues with G-d. He was the advocate *par excellence* for Israel, and the *tzaddikim* of his generation would jokingly marvel that according to his judgment, G-d had not dealt justly with even a single Jew.

Rabbi Levi Yitzchak once pointed out that when a *shiduch* (matrimonial match) is arranged, the family tree is most important. If one family lacks impressive ancestry as compared to the other, but is wealthy, this may compensate for the genealogy deficiency, depending of course on the sensitivities of those involved. If, however, one side boasts illustrious lineage, but the other has neither roots nor wealth, what then is the basis for joining these two families together?

Rabbi Levi Yitzchak cast his gaze heavenward and spoke compellingly of our spiritual union with the Almighty. "Dear G-d, we have a proud past. We are the children of the Patriarchs, Abraham, Isaac, and Jacob, and of the Matriarchs, Sarah, Rivka, Rachel, and Leah. But You, G-d, have no father, no mother, no roots to brag of. What did You bring to the marriage then? Only the means to support us, as You have stated 'I have the silver and mine is the gold, is the word of G-d' (*Haggai* 2:8).

"Okay. that's fine. But, dear G-d," here Rabbi Levi Yitzchak broke into sobs, "if You do not provide adequate *parnassah* (livelihood) for all Jews, then You are derelict in Your commitment to the relationship. Please, don't ruin this otherwise historically beautiful *shiduch*!"

Today
I shall smile
because . . .

_____
_____
_____

The only moment of true unity our people ever knew was at Sinai. After that every experience was characterized by divisiveness (*Rashi, Exodus* 19:12). Apparently, even then, everybody claimed that his version of the Torah was the only correct one (*Rabbi Naftali of Ropschitz*).

SMILING EACH DAY

A European rabbi who was visiting the United States was invited to attend a modern bar-itzvah celebration. The star of the event had received a bare minimum of Jewish education in an after-school Talmud Torah, and knew little more than the ritual he had been taught to recite. When the local rabbi presented the young man with a pair of *tefillin*, the boy was bewildered. He turned to his father and asked in a hushed tone, "Hey dad, what am I supposed to do with these?" Unfortunately, he too had been reared by a generation that failed to safeguard and transmit its precious heritage, and responded, "I don't know, but it looks religious. You had better ask grandpa."

The guest rabbi took in this tragic spectacle and remarked painfully, "Well, Moses predicted this would happen."

Confronted with blank stares, he went on to explain. "In his last address to the Israelites, Moses told them to, 'Ask your father and he will tell you; your grandparents and they will say it to you' (*Deuteronomy* 32:7).

"In reality, though, this was more a prediction than a command. This was what Moses envisioned would eventually transpire where Torah education would be allowed to deteriorate to such pitiful levels as are currently in practice. 'You will ask your father and he will tell you.' Tell you what? 'Go ask your grandfather, he will know what this is all about.'"

Today
I shall smile
because . . .

Rabbi Shimon mused, "I once thought it would have been better to have two mouths, so that one could be devoted exclusively to prayer and Torah, uncontaminated by improper talk. Then I realized, if a person abuses the gift of speech with one mouth, how much more would he do so if he had two!"

SMILING EACH DAY

A rabbi who unfortunately had outspoken opponents within his own congregation, arrived at morning services early one day to find one of his adversaries eagerly waiting for him. The latter verbally attacked him without any consideration for his position, but the rabbi kept his silence until the man had completed his diatribe.

Instead of responding directly to the man's insults, however, the rabbi then said, "I am most grateful to you for helping me understand a portion of the prayers that has always been an enigma.

"In the introductory section of the morning services, we pray, 'May it be Your will to guard me today and every day from insolent people.' I had always wondered, why it is necessary to include 'today and every day.' Why is it not enough to ask each day for protection for that particular day?

"However," he smiled knowingly, "I now understand the reason. We must pray to be spared from those people whose impudence so burns within them, that against their character, they will rise early to confront us in the morning before services, when we have not yet had the opportunity to plead for Divine assistance that day."

Today
I shall smile
because . . .

_____
_____
_____

"How ironic," observed the ever-astute Rabbi Heschel of Warsaw, "that a liar must perforce rely on the quality of truth. If people would not believe his words to be true, what purpose would there be in his lying?"

SMILING EACH DAY

In one community, there was a dire need for funds to provide relief for several poor families. One wealthy but very stingy citizen ignored the sense of urgency involved and contributed a mere pittance. The rabbi of the community personally appealed to him, with little success.

The rabbi then tried this angle. "The Talmud relates that when the Gibeonites who had come over to Judaism behaved in a barbaric manner, King David renounced their conversion, relying on the absolute fact that kindness and compassion are innate Jewish character traits, and that cruelty is incompatible with a Jewish identity. Thus, anyone who does not manifest these attributes is raising doubts about the authenticity of his roots. For you to refuse to be of help when the needs of the poor are so desperate makes us wonder as to whether you indeed belong to our great nation."

The rich man was foolishly indignant. "How dare you say that! I am as Jewish as anyone else. I am extremely open-hearted and my soul is as steeped in nobility of spirit as yours."

While loath to respond to that ridiculous and insulting defense, the rabbi nevertheless focused on his mission and persisted. "Have you ever observed how a doctor examines someone who complains of pain in the heart? The first thing he does is take the patient's hand to check his pulse. Why? Because it is a scientific fact that the status of the heart can be determined by checking the hand."

He then declared with finality, "If your hand remains closed, you cannot claim that you have an open heart."

Today
I shall smile
because . . .

Rabbi Levi Yitzchak of Berditchev once saw a simple man wearing his *tallis* and *tefillin* and greasing his axle. "Master of the universe," he cried out, seemingly oblivious to the impropriety, "even when a Jew greases his wagon wheels he insists on wearing *tallis* and *tefillin*."

SMILING EACH DAY

The profound humility of great Torah scholars is manifested in their utter self-effacement. Although they are well aware of their exalted status and their capacity as authorities, they never allow this to go to their heads, and they do not see any reason why they should be singled out for undue honors.

The two outstanding Torah luminaries, Rabbi Akiva Eiger and Rabbi Jacob of Lisa, were once passengers in a coach. When they approached their destination, many of the community citizens who anticipated their arrival came out to form an honor guard to accompany these great men into the city.

When Rabbi Jacob saw the crowd that had gathered to escort the wagon, he decided that this could only be a tribute to his fellow sage, and he therefore secretly descended from the coach to join the throngs who marched alongside it. Rabbi Akiva Eiger, who was sitting on the other side of the coach, similarly concluded that this whole tumult must be for Rabbi Jacob, and he quietly alighted from the other side to participate in the *mitzvah*.

The empty wagon thus entered the city with its two prominent passengers lost in the crowd. Neither had accepted the possibility that he might be the intended recipient of the honor. Who can compare to these giants?

Today
I shall smile
because . . .

_____
_____
_____

> To a chassid who felt that G-d was treating him unjustly, Rabbi Yehoshua of Ostrova pointed out, "The Torah requires that we judge every person favorably. Shouldn't we extend the same courtesy to G-d?"

SMILING EACH DAY

Tu BiShvat
[Rosh Hashanah la'eelan — New Year for the trees]

About two hundred years ago, a dispute arose among leading Torah scholars regarding proper methodology of Talmud study. Some championed the path of *pilpul*, which consists of comparing, relating, and combining different portions of the logic behind any *halachah*, much as one would view and mix the various ingredients that produce a cake. Others opposed this approach, saying that the complexity involved would result in failure to clarify each point, ultimately confusing the issues.

Rabbi Chaim of Slutzk once visited Rabbi Yehoshua of Kutna, and in their discussion, Rabbi Chaim told over an hour long, intricate *pilpul* of his. Rabbi Yehoshua, who vehemently opposed that school of thought, refuted the entire argument, and pointed out to his honored, if defeated, guest how flawed the method was.

Rabbi Chaim responded without flinching. "When I come before the Almighty on Judgment Day, He will ask me, 'Chaim'ke, did you study Torah?' and I will reply by delivering a *pilpul*. If G-d will then refute my creation, I will say, 'Look, dear G-d, I did the best I could with the intellect You gave me. What more could you ask of me.'

"But what will you do," he noted with a pained expression, "when G-d asks you, Rabbi Yehoshua, whether you labored in Torah? All you will be able to answer is, 'Just try and deliver your best *pilpul*, G-d, and I will show You that I can demolish it.' "

Without involving ourselves in the argument, we should at least derive from this one point. It is always easier to criticize than to innovate.

Today
I shall smile
because . . .

Why do we pray in the *Amidah* for "a good reward for the righteous?" Is there a reward that is bad? A chassidic master explained, "We ask that the blessings we receive be obvious and not in disguise."

SMILING EACH DAY

A litigant in a *din-Torah* (rabbinic trial) rightly suspected that his opponent had bribed the *dayan* (judge), and when he lost the case, he insisted that they submit the decision to one of the authoritative Torah scholars for concurrence. The latter reviewed the case and concluded that the *dayan* had indeed ruled wrongly, instructing him to reverse his opinion immediately.

The *dayan*, however, refused to retreat. "My judgment is correct," he argued brazenly, "and is supported by the opinion of the Chasam Sofer," he continued, citing the particular source in the responsa. The scholar then proceeded to show him that he had completely distorted the renowned sage's position to favor his "client."

Then he added, mockingly. "Now I understand why the Torah says that 'A bribe will blind the eyes of the wise and distort the words of *tzaddikim*' (*Deuteronomy* 16:19). How can a judge who accepts a payoff be called a *tzaddik*?

"What the Torah is stressing is that such a judge will himself distort the words of the *tzaddikim*, twisting their holy wisdom to the benefit of the one whom he favors. You deliberately misconstrued the words of the great *tzaddik*, the Chasam Sofer, in order to suit your own interests. How dare you not recoil in shame!"

Today
I shall smile
because . . .

_____
_____
_____

Rabbi Wolf of Strikov observed, "A person can master a foreign language in only a couple of years, but some people live an entire lifetime without ever truly understanding what they themselves are talking about."

SMILING EACH DAY

A rabbi visited one of the "progressive" Jewish schools, where the students were taught an abridged version of the Torah, one that deleted the more demanding sections and stressed the "stories" and "ethically inspiring codes of behavior." When asked his opinion of the curriculum, the rabbi responded with a parable:

"A king once went hunting and was separated from the rest of his party. He became hopelessly lost in the woods, and as it grew dark, he took shelter in the hut of a woodsman he had miraculously come upon. The latter did not know the identity of his guest, but treated him very cordially, giving him ample food and a comfortable place to sleep.

"The following morning, after receiving thorough directions for returning home, the king revealed who he was and said, 'I would like to reward you for your hospitality. Ask for any wish and you will have it.'

"His host replied, 'Everyday I take my bundle of wood into the city to sell. The path is a long and exhausting one. I ask Your Highness only to shorten the road to the city.'

" 'But I cannot do that,' the king protested, startled at such a request. 'That is not within my powers.'

" 'Of course it is,' the woodsman asserted. 'At various points along the way, there are signs indicating how many miles it is to the city. Have your officials change the numbers to lesser ones.'

" 'You foolish man,' the king now shouted. 'Changing the numbers will not shorten the trip one drop.' "

Here, the rabbi made his point with emphasis. "Neither will abridging the Torah alleviate its dictates one single bit."

Today
I shall smile
because . . .

The Talmud promises that someone who prays for another person with similar needs has his personal needs answered first. If someone can set his own problems aside and consider the deficiencies in others' blessings, he surely deserves to have his requests honored.

SMILING EACH DAY

During the era of the *maskilim*, an eighteenth century movement which sought to secularize Judaism and reduce Torah authority, there were numerous meetings where those on the forefront offered up a variety of plans, all seeking to change the educational system to one where the secular teachings of the sciences and the humanities would dominate, diluting Torah study and relegating it to a minor role.

At one such gathering, a leader of the movement delivered a vitriolic attack on traditional Torah teaching, claiming that children were being imbued with absurdities, such as the occurrence of supernatural events, which is in defiance of all logical and scientific thinking. He argued that rational minds will immediately reject such stories, and will therefore also discount the authority of the morals of the Torah. "To salvage the ethical instruction of Torah," he ranted, his face livid with misguided passion, "we must purge it of all such myths."

He continued to attack the Biblical accounts as being legends, and to prove his case, cited the story of Balaam, wherein the Torah relates that G-d gave his donkey the power of speech. "How can you expect any sensible person to believe that an ass could speak?"

One of the rabbis in attendance could not resist the opportunity. "What is the problem?" he called out with relish. "At this very moment, we are all living witnesses to such a phenomenon."

Today
I shall smile
because . . .

_____
_____
_____

No one person can possibly perform all the *mitzvos*; e.g., an Israelite cannot fulfill the requirements of a *Kohen*, and one whose first child is a daughter is not obligated by the ritual of redemption. Only when we are united as one body, is the *mitzvah* of every person shared by everyone else.

SMILING EACH DAY

Rabbi Akiva Eiger was once told about some young people who had deviated from strict Shabbos observance and would go to the theater on Friday evening. When confronted, they rationalized to the rabbi that they were actually not in violation of Shabbos because they arranged to pay their admission fee beforehand. The great sage patiently tried to impress upon them that at the very least, attending the theater was not compatible with the spirit and sanctity of Shabbos, but this did not appear to dissuade them.

Not at a loss, Rabbi Akiva then suggested, "Since you pay for your entrance before Shabbos, you are obviously interested in avoiding an open transgression. You would certainly not do anything which was in clear violation of any of the Ten Commandments, would you?"

"Of course not," these otherwise saintly souls virtually shouted at him.

"Well then, the Talmud states," Rabbi Akiva pressed his case, "that on Friday night two angels accompany every person. So first of all, you are dragging these spirits to a place they do not wish to be. Secondly, while you may have taken care of yourselves, you are each sneaking two angels in without permission. Isn't that dishonest? Bringing someone in without payment directly contravenes the Commandment, 'Thou shalt not steal!' How do you excuse yourselves for that?"

Today
I shall smile
because . . .

SHEVAT

שבט

G-d spoke to Moses from amidst a thick, dark cloud (*Exodus* 19:9). The words of G-d may reach us only when we are immersed in a sublime darkness, removed from and not distracted by all the things we see and crave.

SMILING EACH DAY

Rabbi Chaim of Volozhin once elaborated on the *Midrash* which states that the Patriarch Jacob advised his children that if they would stay united they would remain unconquerable.

Rabbi Chaim told of a wealthy man who was traveling in a luxurious coach drawn by four beautiful horses, which strayed from the main road and soon sank into a swamp. The driver was unable to get the animals to extricate the wagon, no matter how heavily he applied the whip.

Just then, a farmer drove by with a team of horses and offered his help, suggesting that he would hitch his animals to the coach. The wealthy man, though appreciative, was skeptical. "What makes you think your two horses can do what my four cannot?" he asked.

The farmer replied with his own question. "Where did you get your horses from?"

"Why, I bought them from the best dealers," the man answered, suspicious of his savior's intent. "Each one was the choice of the lot."

"There you have it, then," the farmer snapped. "None of these animals ever learned to work in unison. Whenever you whip one, the other three rejoice. My two horses, however, have long worked as a team. When one is down, the other makes a greater effort to help him."

"That is what unity is all about," Rabbi Chaim concluded. "The hostile nations of the world each tug their own way, but we who pull together are indeed invincible."

Today
I shall smile
because . . .

_____
_____
_____

Shabbos is an eternal "sign between G-d and Israel" (*Exodus* 31:17). In everyday life, even if a shop appears closed, as long as the sign remains, there is hope it will one day be reopened. When the sign disappears, it indicates that the store has been abandoned forever (*Chafetz Chaim*).

SMILING EACH DAY

The *tzaddik* of Sanz would often go into states of profound meditation, during which he appeared to lose all contact with the physical world. For example, he had a congenital weakness of one leg, yet during prayer, he would sometimes get carried away with such fervor that he would stamp repeatedly with this leg until it would begin to bleed. His wife pleaded with the *shammes* (attendant) to protect his weak leg, but he always replied, "It is pointless. I assure you our master has no idea with which leg he is stomping."

One time, at a public gathering, the *tzaddik* was in a state of spiritual ecstacy, and was seized by a sudden severe coughing spasm. With great difficulty his son aroused him from his trance, and urged him to drink some hot tea in order to relieve himself.

"Why did you interrupt me?" the *tzaddik* turned to him, annoyed. "I was in the highest of celestial spheres, and in those conditions of spirit, one has no need for hot tea."

"True, father," the son countered, "but in those exalted states, one does not cough either."

"You win," the master admitted with a smile, "you win." And he gladly drank of the tea.

Today
I shall smile
because . . .

"In the heavens above and on the earth below. . ." (*Exodus* 20:4). When it pertains to spirituality, look above you to emulate those who have achieved greater heights. When it comes to earthly possessions, cast your gaze downward, and see how much more fortunate you are than those who have less.

SMILING EACH DAY

It is traditional to eat fish at the Shabbos meals, and various reasons have been given for this custom. Perhaps we may add one perspective to the list.

Someone once mocked a Jew who was performing the *Tashlich* ritual, whereby one symbolically casts his transgressions into the water. "If you throw your sins into the ocean," the scoffer contended, "they will no doubt be eaten by the fish. When you then eat the fish on Shabbos, you will end up ingesting the very items you had tried to get rid of."

"Not quite," the man replied, without a moment's thought. "You seem to have forgotten (or maybe you never knew) that when a person does *teshuvah* (repentance) out of deep love and devotion for G-d, the sins at issue are converted into merits. By the time the fish consume what we have thrown to them, it has all been granted a new identity, and it is with relish that we partake of our watery catch."

The message inherent in fish at the Shabbos meal is thus that we should be aware that by correcting the mistakes of the past, and learning not to repeat them, they have themselves become valuable lessons, and useful, positive experiences. What extraordinary powers we possess!

Today
I shall smile
because . . .

_____
_____
_____

"Do not make an idol of silver or gold" (*Exodus* 20:20). This refers not only to an idol's physical makeup, but to worshiping riches. To some people, money and possessions have become their god.

SMILING EACH DAY

In the community where Rabbi Akiva Eiger lived, there was a money lender who bled the people poor with his usury, and grew wealthy at their expense. When he died, the burial society decided to return some of his ill-begotten riches to the community, and demanded a very large sum for a grave, refusing to have him interred until the estate paid in full. The heirs, knowing they could not elicit a favorable ruling from a rabbinical court, brazenly took their complaint to the governmental officials.

The appointed judge sent for Rabbi Akiva Eiger to present the community's case as to why such an outlandish price was being demanded. The *gaon* complied by offering the following reasoning:

"We Jews have a firm belief in the ultimate resurrection of the dead. Hence, every grave site is essentially a short-term sale, since we expect it soon to be vacated. However, the Talmud claims that the sin of usury is so serious an offense, that one who has practiced it will not return to life when all others do.

"Therefore, since this man made his living by such behavior, he will not enjoy the privilege of restored life, and his grave is therefore not a temporary sale. Since it is a permanent investment, the price is justifiably much higher."

Today
I shall smile
because . . .

"Decency is a preface to Torah" (*Vayikra Rabbah* 9:3). From the introduction of a book, one can judge its content. From a person's behavior, one can tell how serious is his regard for Torah.

SMILING EACH DAY

When Rabbi Yoel Sirkas served as the Rabbi of Belz, he was paid a starvation wage. One night he did not have any oil for his lamp, so he studied Torah by reviewing what he remembered by heart.

The townsfolk who passed the rabbi's house at night and found it to be dark, assumed that he was asleep. The following day they called a community assembly, and voted to oust him from his position, claiming that "a dedicated rabbi studies Torah at night, and does not retire early."

When Rabbi Yoel left the city, he remarked with chagrin, "The Torah relates that the city of Sodom was destroyed when G-d turned it *upside down* (*Genesis* 19:25). Isn't this a rather unusual manner of retribution?

"However, our sages tell us that G-d judges people according to their own behavior and by their own standards. We know of course that Sodom was a city of profound distortion: good was punished and evil was rewarded. The consequence of this was that the city was eliminated by being turned 'upside down.'

"The rabbi's responsibility is always to be concerned about his Torah learning. The citizens of a community, on the other hand, must insure that the rabbi has an adequate livelihood. These duties are not to be alternated. This community, however, functions in reverse: It is not worried about support for its rabbi, but only whether he learns what they consider to be enough Torah. May the Lord protect them from their own devices."

Today
I shall smile
because . . .

_____

_____

_____

"Honor you father and mother so that your days may be long" (*Exodus* 20:12). As a practical suggestion, since you too will someday grow old, you had better set an example for your children of how to behave towards elderly parents.

SMILING EACH DAY

As a young man, Rabbi Yosef Dov Soloveitchik longed to meet the great Torah scholar, Rabbi Shlomo Kluger of Brody, but he could not afford the fare for the trip. In desperation, he hired himself out as an assistant to a coach driver who drove passengers to Brody.

Not having the slightest inkling how to handle the reins or feed and water the horses at the rest stops, he proved inept at his new undertaking and the coachman scolded him for his clumsiness, even beating him mercilessly several times.

When they finally arrived in Brody, one of the students who had studied with Rabbi Yosef Dov in the yeshivah of Volozhin recognized him and they embraced. The coachman, realizing that he had been so disrespectful to a Torah scholar, apologized profusely.

Rabbi Yosef Dov, however, smiled with a benign warmth only a giant of spirit could have radiated at that moment. "There is no need for regret," he assured the distraught man. "Had you reprimanded or beaten me because I erred in Talmud, that would have been wrong, but I apprenticed myself to you in order to help with the horses, and for that function, as my legitimate teacher you had every right to discipline me for my awkwardness."

Today
I shall smile
because . . .

The Talmud states that the reason a sneak-thief is penalized more than a bold robber, is that the latter at least equated G-d with man, fearing neither; whereas the late night worker endeavors to hide from humans, but either denies or does not care that G-d sees him. The extra fine is for placing man above G-d.

SMILING EACH DAY

The wife of one of the chassidic masters became angry with a young woman whom she had hired to help in the kitchen. The poor girl had apparently been negligent and had broken several dishes. At the end of the day, her mistress refused to pay the agreed upon sum, claiming that she had been derelict in her responsibility and therefore deserved to have deducted from her wages the value of the dishes. The young woman protested and had her employer summoned to the *Beth Din* (rabbinic court).

As the mistress prepared to go to court, she noticed that her husband was putting on his Shabbos garments. "Where are you going?" she asked, puzzled.

"I'm coming with you to the *Beth Din*," the master answered, quite casually.

"Oh, there is no need for you to come along," the wife quickly assured him, certain he had her interest in mind. "I can handle my claim adequately on my own."

"I am sure you can," the master agreed, then corrected her. "And that is why I am not going to assist you. I am trying to support the young woman. She is an orphan, totally alone, and has no one to speak up on her behalf. It may end up costing me money, but I absolutely must come to her defense!"

Today
I shall smile
because . . .

_____

_____

_____

"Do not oppress an alien, because you were yourselves strangers in Egypt" (*Exodus* 22:20). The Torah foresaw the psychological defense of "identifying with the aggressor" and warned against it. A liberated slave has the potential to evolve into the worst tyrant.

SMILING EACH DAY

The Gaon of Vilna held no official position in the community, and all *halachic* questions where directed to Rabbi Shmuel, the city's official rabbi. One Friday, shortly before sunset, a next door neighbor of the Gaon discovered that there had been a mix up of some kitchen utensils, and therefore had a question whether the food she prepared for *Shabbos* was kosher or not. Because of the late hour, instead of consulting the Rav, her husband sent their son to ask the Gaon, who ruled that the food was *treifa*. The wife, unaware of this, hurriedly sent another child to ask Rabbi Shmuel, who ruled that the food was kosher. When the conflicting opinions were revealed, Rabbi Shmuel was quickly notified, but he reassured the family that the food was indeed kosher.

Rabbi Shmuel then went to the Gaon. "You are the greatest Torah authority in the world," he announced, humbly, "and I am not worthy to be the dust that you tread on. Still, I am the recognized authority on *halachah* in this community, and it is not proper to have my rulings undermined.

"I therefore beg of you to accompany me to your neighbor's home and partake of the food that you declared to be *treifa*. This will plainly establish unquestionable respect for Torah authority."

Amazingly, the Gaon deferred to Rabbi Shmuel and agreed to eat of the food that he himself ruled *treifa*, submitting to the authority of the local Rav in order to make a point. Can we begin to fathom the greatness of our leaders?

(One version has it that before he could eat of the food, drippings from a tallow candle fell into the Gaon's plate, sparing him from this ordeal.)

Today
I shall smile
because . . .

_____
_____
_____

"A bribe will blind the eyes of the wise" (*Exodus* 23:8). But more so, a blind person sees nothing and is neutral, whereas one who is bribed or in any way biased is much worse, because he sees false as being true (*Rabbi Abraham of Sochochov*).

SMILING EACH DAY

One Erev Yom Kippur, Rabbi Yonasan Eibeschitz overheard a man reciting the *amidah*, and after completing the *al-chet* (confession), concluded with the verse "I am mere dust even when I live, let alone after I die." He was moved by the man's profound self-effacement which came across in this prayer.

In the evening service, when the man was not accorded the honor of holding one of the Torah scrolls at *Kol Nidre*, he was deeply offended, and raised a furor for having been overlooked and not appropriately recognized as he felt was his due.

Curious, Rabbi Yonasan asked him, "Are you sure you went to the *mikveh* before Yom Kippur?"

"Of course," the man answered, even further wounded.

Rabbi Yonasan shrugged. "This is a mystery to me. I heard you say this afternoon that you are nothing but dust. If so, why would you insist on receiving a lofty honor? Then it occurred to me that loose dust is sometimes blown high into the air, and perhaps you were like the dust that is raised high. But then, when you sprinkle water on dust, it remains on the floor and does not rise.

"That is why I thought," he concluded, dropping his innocent tone, "that perhaps you had failed to go to the *mikveh*, because the holy waters would surely have prevented your dust from flying so high."

Today
I shall smile
because . . .

_____
_____
_____

Rabbi Wolf of Zbaroz would not allow a coachman to whip the horses. He would say, "If you knew how to talk to them, you would not need to whip them, right? Is it fair to punish them because of your ignorance?"

SMILING EACH DAY

When Rabbi Yisrael Salanter came to Kovno, he accepted service employment in the community. However, when he realized that this job was greatly distracting him from the study of Torah, and particularly from his mission to disseminate the learning of *mussar* (ethics), he resigned his post. His sole support then came from a dole meted out by several of the wealthier citizens.

One time, a scholar visited Rabbi Yisrael, and at mealtime, he noted that Rabbi Yisrael hardly ate, yet urged his guest to partake heartily of the food. "Please eat," Rabbi Yisrael prodded, "because for you everything is kosher."

The visitor was bewildered. "How can it be permissible for me and not for you?" he asked.

Rabbi Yisrael explained, with classic humility, "People support me because they think I am a scholar and a *tzaddik*. Personally I know this to be untrue, hence the money I am accepting from them has really been given to me on false pretenses and is dishonest. I should not be benefiting from anything obtained in this fashion, and therefore for me this food is not too kosher. However, you are probably as deluded about me as they are, so for you it is not the product of deceit, and everything is therefore perfectly kosher. In that case, 'bon appetit'!"

Today
I shall smile
because . . .

First Day of
Rosh Chodesh
Adar

Rabbi Eizik of Komarno observed, "Miserliness is the worst character trait. A glutton is a slave to his appetite only before he indulges, whereas a miser clings to his wealth even in his dreams."

SMILING EACH DAY

Rabbi Eliyahu Chaim Meisel was rabbi of Lodz, and despite an adequate salary, seemed to be always in debt. He used to borrow huge sums of money to distribute to the poor or to support merchants whose businesses were failing. When the prominent community of Warsaw sought to recruit him as their rabbi, he graciously refused their offer. When asked why he was reluctant to accept the most coveted rabbinical position in Europe. Rabbi Eliyahu answered:

"Initially I was rabbi in the village of Prozhin. There I would borrow much money to give to impoverished people, and although it was well known that my salary was insufficient for repayment of the loans, I was nevertheless trusted because it was assumed that I would eventually be offered the position of rabbi in the city of Lomza, and my earnings there would enable me to settle my accounts.

"When I became rabbi of Lomza, people there lent me money, sure that I would one day become rabbi in the even bigger city of Lodz, and have enough to cover my affairs. In Lodz, people only trust me because they imagine I will yet become rabbi of Warsaw.

"Now, if I accept the position of Warsaw, people will no longer have any reason to believe that I can advance myself, and they will refuse to lend me money. How then will I be able to help the poor?" Such were the dilemmas troubling great men of yesteryear.

Today
I shall smile
because . . .

_____
_____
_____

Rabbi Yehoshua of Ostrova taught, "A vain person is worse than a liar. A liar knows he is lying, whereas someone who is absorbed in his self-image of greatness, firmly believes in his delusions."

SMILING EACH DAY

Second Day of Rosh Chodesh Adar

[During Hebrew leap years a thirteenth month called Adar Sheni (the second Adar) is added to the calendar. For those years, two sets of corresponding dates are given below, the first for Adar, and the second for Adar Sheni.]

In Lodz, one of the community officials whose duty it was to collect and distribute money for the poor submitted his resignation to Rabbi Eliyahu Chaim Meisel. He complained that he could no longer stand the abuse he was taking from both sides. When he solicits money, he claimed, the donors are angry with him for imposing so heavily upon them, and then when he distributes the money to the poor, the latter are always dissatisfied with what they receive and are angry at him for not effecting more generous donations.

"You have no right to resign," Rabbi Eliyahu Chaim admonished him upon hearing his woes. "The Torah forbids it."

"Where does the Torah say that?" the man asked, skeptically.

The rabbi then pointed out, "When Eldad and Medad prophesied that Moses would die in the desert and not lead the Israelites into the Promised Land, Joshua, his chief disciple, pleaded, 'Master, destroy them!' (*Numbers* 11:28). *Rashi* explains that this means, 'Place the burden of public duty upon them, and this will do away with them.'

"But why would such service ruin them?" Rabbi Eliyahu asked. "If they felt the job too burdensome, they could just give it up, couldn't they?

"Apparently," the rabbi concluded, "it isn't that simple. The Torah indicates here that people who are appointed to public duty do not have the option of resigning regardless of how frustrating their job may be. The great reward awaiting those who sacrifice themselves for the larger, common good is not earned by way of a here today-gone tomorrow attitude. Rather, it is the result of a commitment, one not to be taken lightly."

Today
I shall smile
because . . .

ADAR

אדר

The Torah calls for majority rule where there is a difference of opinion among the judges of the high court (*Exodus* 23:2). Of course, this is a method to be employed only when there is doubt. The laws of the Torah themselves are never in doubt, and are not subject to majority opinion.

SMILING EACH DAY

A student who applied for *semicha* (ordination) was turned down because he was not adequately versed in *halachah*. Naively, he begged to be certified anyway, promising, "You have no reason to fear that I will err to permit what is prohibited. I will never approve anything of even questionable *kashrus*. If there is even the slightest doubt, I will rule that it is *treifa*."

The examining rabbi took pity on the desperate candidate and attempted to illustrate his folly. "Let me tell you a story. A villager would periodically bring chickens on which there were questions about their being kosher into the city to obtain a decision from his rabbi.

"One day someone suggested to him that there is a much easier way to get a ruling on the matter of *kashrus*. The Torah commands, 'Do not eat *treifa* meat. Throw it to the dogs' (*Exodus* 22:30). All you need to do then if you have any uncertainty about whether meat is kosher or not, is to offer it to a dog. If it is *treifa*, the dog will eat it, and if not, he won't.

"After a while the villager again began bringing his problems to the rabbi in the city. He explained, 'I had to discontinue relying on the dog for an opinion. Everything I offered him he ate. Apparently a dog rules that everything is *treifa*.' "

Today
I shall smile
because . . .

_____
_____
_____

Rabbi Meir of Apt noted, "Love is not a one-way street. Therefore, a person cannot have love of money, because money cannot reciprocate. He can only have a lust for money. What is the difference, you ask? Ah, unfortunately, love can be satisfied, whereas lust is a never-ending, unfulfilling chase."

SMILING EACH DAY

The Talmud states that a wise man is superior to a prophet. The ability of Torah scholars to foresee things through their sheer wisdom is often tantamount to prophecy.

King Juan of Portugal had a Jewish advisor, Abraham Zacuta. One day the King called Zacuta in and told him that he was about to travel to one of the provinces, and wished to know, according to Zacuta's astrological divinations, through which gate of the province would it be most propitious for him to enter.

The Jew sensed that the King was setting a trap for him. "Of what use is it, Your Majesty?" he asked. "I will tell you one gate, but you may will to enter another."

"No, no," the King protested. "Let me assure you that I will do no such thing. Put your recommendation into a sealed envelope and give it to one of my officers. I promise that I will not open it until I have chosen the gate I wish to enter."

Zacuta chose his words carefully. "The King will enter through a totally new gate," he wrote, and sealed it in an envelope. Indeed, in order to frustrate his Jewish "friend," the King ordered that the wall around the city be breached, and he marched through this new opening in order to prove that Zacuta was incapable of predicting the future course of events. The wise man, however, had foreseen this, and the King, who hadn't realized he was dealing with something beyond a "mere prophet" was forced to concede that Zacuta had outwitted him.

Today
I shall smile
because . . .

The Torah commands, "You shall love G-d" (*Deuteronomy* 6:5) and elsewhere, "You shall love your fellow man" (*Leviticus* 19:18). In reality, each of these is contingent on the other.

SMILING EACH DAY

Rabbi Yitzchak Elchanan of Kovno was once approached by a student who complained that he had come across a very difficult piece in the Talmud, and that in his view, this particular *halachah* was simply irreconcilable with everything else he had ever learned. He said he had been working for days to solve the problem, but to no avail. He pleaded with the rabbi to search for a possible solution, because until this conflict was satisfactorily resolved, he was unable to go on with his studies.

Rabbi Yitzchak Elchanan listened to the question, and after a few moments of thought, referred the young man to a particular *Tosafos* (a commentary on the Talmud), citing page and verse.

The student eagerly looked up what he had been told, expecting to delight in a sure path out of his difficulty. It wasn't long, however, before he returned, very annoyed. He had not found anything in that particular *Tosafos* that was in any way related to the subject at hand.

"Oy, vey, you have missed the point entirely," Rabbi Yitzchok Elchanan told the discouraged fellow. "That *Tosafos* raises a very difficult problem regarding a particular *halachah*, and provides no solution to the problem. Yet, he continues on to deal with other portions of the Talmud and is not paralyzed by being at a loss to properly answer his question."

At this point, he put an arm around the student and exhorted, "You do a terrible injustice to your obvious skill at perceiving the underlying rationale of the Talmud and raising deep questions if you allow that very talent to keep you from moving on and using it further. Don't ever fall victim to your own outstanding qualities."

Today I shall smile because . . .

_____
_____
_____

What is so unique about *tzedakah* that it can ward off death? (see *Proverbs* 10:2). It is that even if a person is so feeble that he cannot accomplish anything in the world, and his existence appears useless, he is always able to give something to *tzedakah*, and that places his life in a different perspective of purpose.

SMILING EACH DAY

Rabbi Emmanuel Gottlieb of Hanover was known for his cleverness.

One day he encountered some children who had been reared in an atmosphere of anti-semitism, and who shouted mockingly at him, "Itzik Jew! Itzik Jew!" Rabbi Gottlieb immediately took some candy from his pocket and threw it to the children. "If you will shout 'Itzik Jew' real loud tomorrow," he coaxed them, "I will give you more candy."

Sure enough, the following day, the children were there, shouting, "Itzik Jew" at the top of their lungs. "Wonderful!" exclaimed the Rabbi, and threw them some more goodies. This daily ritual continued for a while.

One day Rabbi Emmanuel walked by, showing the children that his pockets were empty. "I have no more candy to give you," he said solemnly. The disappointed children responded, "Then we will never shout 'Itzik Jew' for you again."

"Too bad," Rabbi Emmanuel said, shrugging his shoulders, "it can't be helped." And with a barely perceptible grin, he continued on his way.

Today
I shall smile
because . . .

Rabbi Yaakov Dov of Rodoshitz used to bless people with wealth. He would reason, "as long as people are poor, they think that money would solve all their problems. Once they have money, they at least stand a chance of realizing that what they are really lacking in life is spirituality, and strive for it."

SMILING EACH DAY

The Chafetz Chaim was once summoned to testify as a character witness for a Jew who was the victim of a conspiracy. The holy sage asked to be excused from being sworn to tell the truth, since he had never taken an oath in his life.

The well-known Jewish lawyer Oskar Grosenberg pleaded with the judge, describing the Chafetz Chaim's piety and saintliness, and assuring him that it was absolutely impossible for him to ever utter a lie, even to save his life.

"Let me tell you an incident about this man," the attorney went further. "As he came into his home one day, he found it being ransacked by thieves. Caught in the act, they began to flee, whereupon this rabbi, whose word you question, called out to them, 'Come back! Maybe you need these things more than I do.' "

Needless to say, the judge was incredulous. "And you expect me to believe that story?" he mocked.

"Look, does it really make a difference whether it is factual or not?" Grosenberg replied candidly. "Has anyone ever told a story like that about you?"

Taken with the realization, the judge gladly accepted the Chafetz Chaim's unsworn testimony.

Today
I shall smile
because . . .

_____
_____
_____

"The naked truth" is a familiar expression. In reality, truth is always naked, because if it is dressed up, it is no longer truth. That is probably why so many people avoid the truth. They are sorely embarrassed by its nudity (*Rabbi Eizel of Slonim*).

SMILING EACH DAY

The *Maggid* (preacher) of Kelm came to the town of Wasville, and the local rabbi complained bitterly to him that the townspeople were very disobedient. Various disputes had been brought before him, but although he excelled at equitable rulings and the litigants had promised to abide by his decisions, they never kept their word.

When the community gathered on Shabbos to hear the famous *Maggid,* he began ascending to the pulpit, then abruptly stopped. The bewildered people could only look on as he appeared to be engaged in a conversation with an invisible being. Suddenly he shouted, "But I am in Wasville!" and proceeded to the pulpit.

Of course, after an outburst like that, the Maggid couldn't just launch right into his prepared sermon. "Let me explain to you what happened," he said. "When I set out to come here, Satan confronted me and declared, 'You have no right to enter Wasville. That town is totally under my domain.' He refused to let me continue on my way until I promised I would not speak in this town.

"When I began walking up here, Satan appeared and protested, 'Hey, you cannot preach here. Remember, you guaranteed me that you wouldn't.'

"We argued back and forth, until finally I pointed out, "But I am in Wasville, and inasmuch as it is local practice not to keep one's promises, I am exempt from doing so here!"

He let that line sink in and then began his speech.

Today
I shall smile
because . . .

The Talmud states that wisdom is like wine. It improves if stored in an earthenware cask, but spoils in silver or gold vessels.

SMILING EACH DAY

Two partners in a munitions factory had a dispute over the division of their profit from the sales of arms. Each claimed that he had put extra effort into the deals and therefore deserved a larger share of the earnings. The judge before whom the case was being tried had a reputation for being less than honest, and it was widely rumored that he was easily bribed.

Someone then suggested to the litigants that they have the case settled by a *Beis Din* (rabbinic court) rather than by a secular court. Agreeing, they brought their arguments before a rabbi, who said:

"If it were up to me, I would recommend that the judge should get the entire amount of the gains. The Talmud says that wars break out as a Divine punishment for distortion of the law by judges who take bribes (*Shabbos* 33a). If it would not be for these corrupt individuals, there would be no wars and thus, no need for ammunition. Neither of you would then have had any sales at all, let alone profit. Therefore, if you really seek an honest settlement, all the money in question should go to the judge, whose disgraceful behavior stands at the root of your business.

Today
I shall smile
because . . .

_____

_____

_____

A chassid complained to the Rabbi of Kotzk that he suffered from severe headaches and could not concentrate properly on his prayers. The Rabbi noted sharply, "Who told you to pray with your head? You should be praying with your heart."

SMILING EACH DAY

At an important gathering of community leaders from around the country that was convened to deal with new restrictive anti-Semitic regulations by the Czarist government, some of the representatives exploited this opportunity to boast of their own achievements back home. Rabbi Yitzchak Blazer of Peterburg was understandably upset by this preoccupation with self-aggrandizement when the focus should have been on finding ways to revoke the oppressive regulations. When it came his turn to speak, he decided to send a resounding message:

"The donkeys once came before the Almighty's throne with a complaint: Why had He assigned them the role of being beasts of burden? Couldn't He have allotted them a better role in life? Why not give them the power of speech so that they could accomplish things with their thoughts just as humans do, instead of being limited to physical labor?

"G-d agreed that they had a legitimate point, and told them that He would experiment by giving the wisest of them the capacity to talk, which He did with Bilaam's pet. But lo and behold! As soon as the creature was empowered to speak, what did it announce? 'I am your ass upon whom you have ridden from always until now!' (*Numbers* 22:30).

"G-d therefore decided, 'If all a donkey can talk about is his own great achievements, he is better off being silent.' "

Today
I shall smile
because . . .

ADAR

אדר

Someone who is uncertain whether or not he sinned is required to perform a greater atonement than someone who knows for sure that he has done wrong (*Leviticus* 5:17-19). This is because the latter is fully aware he is a sinner, whereas the former thinks he might really be a *tzaddik.*

SMILING EACH DAY

In the structure of *davening* (prayer services), there are a variety of customs, few of which are really substantive, but are usually merely a matter of local practice. Yet, those people who subscribe to a particular opinion often become overly defensive if anyone wishes to introduce another format, as though the latter was some type of cardinal sin.

In one synagogue, on the Shabbos on which we bless the new month of Iyar, a dispute arose among the worshipers as to whether the prayer "*Av Harachamim*" (Merciful Father) is recited or omitted. Each side had its proponents, and no one seemed to remember what the established practice had been. After loud arguments that ruined the tranquil spirit of the day, it was finally decided to consult the oldest citizen of the community, who, being one of the synagogue's original founders, would certainly know which was the accepted manner. This elderly man was too weak to attend services, so someone was dispatched to his home to ask him.

When the messenger placed the question before him, the elderly man quickly sized up the situation back at the synagogue, and assumed the role of preacher. He wiped off his silver-rimmed glasses, took a sip of hot tea, and said:

"The established practice in our synagogue since its founding, my child, is that on the Shabbos that we bless the new month of Iyar, there is always a dispute as to whether or not to say '*Av Harachamim*.'" And then the old fellow just broke into hearty laughter.

Today
I shall smile
because . . .

_____

_____

_____

"Love your neighbor as yourself" (*Leviticus* 19:18). It is only natural to respect someone who is perceived as far superior, and as a rule, one has little difficulty in dealing warmly with someone upon whom one can justifiably look down. The greatest challenge is in relating well to peers. The verse then might better be read, "Love your neighbor who *is* as yourself," i.e., a peer.

SMILING EACH DAY

A respected scholar was once insulted by a vulgar and ignorant person, but he voiced no opposition to this assault, and went on with his studies as though nothing had occurred.

Onlookers were quick to praise him for his remarkable restraint. The scholar, however, attributed his control to a higher course than his own inner strength, explaining:

"Our Sages teach that silence acts as a 'protective zone' for wisdom. They are referring here to keeping quiet when unjustly attacked, as they state that 'one who hears himself insulted and does not retaliate, is considered beloved by G-d' (*Shabbos* 88b).

"But if such behavior is merely a 'protective zone' for wisdom," the scholar continued, "then what does wisdom itself consist of?

"It must be," he finished off, half-jokingly, "that wisdom itself is not to consider oneself slighted in the least when the assailant is someone who is not qualified to make such critical remarks."

It wouldn't hurt for all of us to maintain such wisdom, and to protect it with a sprinkle of silence.

Today
I shall smile
because . . .

ADAR

אדר

"Sin begets sin" (*Ethics of the Fathers* 4:2). This idea constitutes an effective deterrent for some. How, though, would a person who has not advanced to the notion of reeling from sin, and who indulges in the pleasure derived through sin, be discouraged by this warning? Only because the second and subsequent sins are done out of compulsion, and the poor transgressor can no longer enjoy them.

SMILING EACH DAY

In Pressburg it was once discovered that a large sum of money was missing from the community coffers. No one was able to explain how it had disappeared, and so, they consulted Rabbi Moshe Schreiber, the *Chasam Sofer*, for advice. The renowned sage asked to be given a list of all those who had access to the community funds.

After studying it for but a moment, he sent for one of those listed, and accused him of embezzlement, stating that he had absolute evidence of the fellow's guilt. Faced with this assertion, the man broke down and admitted his crime.

When the community leaders asked why the rabbi had suspected that this man was the thief, he responded:

"I remember him as a young lad in the yeshivah. When we studied the *halachah* that a custodian who claimed that an article entrusted to him for safekeeping was lost must swear that he does not have it in his possession, this boy piped up, 'Hey, wait a minute. 'How will such an oath force an admission? The man might give the item to a friend to hold for him, and then truthfully swear that it is not in his domain.'

"I knew right then and there," the Chasam Sofer reminisced, nodding his head, "that someone with a devious mind such as that would one day become a thief."

Today
I shall smile
because . . .

_____
_____
_____

In the *Amidah* we say, "You have given us a Torah of life." Too often, people may not have contact with a *shul,* or Jewishness in general, except when they must say *Kaddish* and observe *yahrzeit,* both unfortunately related to services for the dead. The Torah should be primarily a Torah of life, a living Torah.

Fast of Esther
[During Hebrew leap years the fast is observed in Adar Sheni. When 13 Adar falls on the Sabbath the fast is observed on the preceding Thursday.]

SMILING EACH DAY

A *maggid* (preacher) once (or perhaps more than once) observed that during his sermon, a number of the listeners in the audience fell asleep. In order to make light of it, the *maggid* announced, "This tendency to doze off when hearing words of *mussar* (ethics) is not a new phenomenon. The Talmud tells us that when the great Rabbi Akiva preached, the people also slumbered.

"The Talmud goes on to relate that in order to arouse the crowd, Rabbi Akiva would begin talking about the *Megillah (Book of Esther)*. Why did Rabbi Akiva choose that particular subject for this purpose?

"I guess it was because there is evidence in the *Megillah* that there were once no *maggidim* (preachers). How so? The *Megillah* reveals that one night King Ahasveros was unable to fall asleep, and he therefore had his servants read to him from the Book of Chronicles.

"Now had there been any preachers around at that time, he would certainly not have had to do so. He could simply have called the *maggid* to deliver a brilliantly moving and relevant sermon, which would promptly have sent him into the bliss of dreamland."

Today
I shall smile
because . . .

ADAR

אדר

Purim

[During Hebrew leap years Purim is celebrated in Adar Sheni.]

Biblical miracles were patent, supernatural occurrences. The experience of Purim was not openly miraculous, but one can clearly see the hand of G-d weaving a series of events that brought about the salvation of Israel. These hidden acts of G-d are, in truth, no less miraculous than the overt ones (*Rabbi Levi Yitzchak of Berdichev*).

SMILING EACH DAY

In one village there was a man who indulged in eating and imbibing during the entire month of Adar. When asked why he did so, he explained:

"Everyone celebrates Haman's downfall on Purim with food and drink, right?

"But just think. Haman decreed that all the Jews in the one hundred and twenty-seven provinces of the empire be annihilated on one single day, the fourteenth of Adar. How on earth is it feasible to kill all the men, women, and children spread out over such a vast empire in a single day?

"The truth of the matter is that Haman originally planned to designate the entire month of Adar for the destruction of the Jews. However, aware of their history, and the fact that G-d intervenes to save the Jews, as He did in Egypt, Haman reasoned that if G-d saved them from his scheme, they would celebrate their salvation by establishing a holiday such as Passover. If the month of Adar were set aside for their extinction, and then they were miraculously saved, the Jews would of course turn the whole month into one of rejoicing.

"Haman was so wicked that he wished to prevent such a possibility. He therefore decreed only one day for the realization of his plot, so that in the event of a miracle, the Jews would have only that one day for their partying."

Here, the villager licked his lips, raised his eyebrows, and said, "But I know what his evil plans really were, so I celebrate the entire month."

Today
I shall smile
because . . .

_____
_____
_____

> "Reprimand your brother, and you will not carry a sin over him" (*Leviticus* 19:17). If you properly rebuke someone, he will explain his actions to you, and once you understand his behavior, you will not hold a grudge against him.

Shushan Purim
[During Hebrew leap years Shushan Purim is celebrated in Adar Sheni.]

SMILING EACH DAY

On Purim, after completing the reading of the *Megillah* (Book of Esther), the reader in a certain town recited the blessing, "Thank you, O G-d, for having performed a miracle for me here!" The congregation immediately asked him why he had substituted this *berachah* (blessing), which is recited only for a personal rather than a national miracle.

The man responded: "The *Shulchan Aruch* (Code of Jewish Law) requires that the names of the ten children of Haman who were executed be read in one breath.

"The Talmud states that Haman boasted about his great wealth and his many children and concludes that Haman had many more than ten children.

"Just think," the man continued, "if they had executed all Haman's children, and I had to read all their names in one breath, I would surely have died of asphyxiation.

"For me, therefore," he smiled triumphantly, "it is a personal miracle that only ten of Haman's children were executed, and I can therefore make a personal *berachah*."

Today
I shall smile
because . . .

A learned man once complained that in a crowded room he was allowed to remain at the door and was not called up to a seat of honor. Rabbi Shmuel of Volozhin laughed, and said, "Tell him that the sacred *mezuzah* is never insulted by being left standing at the door."

SMILING EACH DAY

In one community, the proprietor of the dairy was suspected of diluting the milk with water, but no one was ever able to clearly prove the accusation.

The rabbi of the town thought it prudent to bide his time. When the dairyman married off his daughter, he made a lavish banquet for hundreds of guests.

Shortly before the wedding ceremony, after all the food had been prepared, the rabbi sent for the father of the bride.

"A terrible thing has happened," he revealed with a look of dismay. "The cook just reported to me that by accident one of the kitchen help added milk to the pots instead of water, thus rendering all the meat for the entire meal *treifa*, having been cooked with milk."

The man's face turned as white as his milk. Seeing that his words had produced the desired effect, the rabbi offered hope. "Now it is still possible that the food may be kosher if the proportion of meat to milk is sufficiently great. That depends, of course, on whether the milk is pure, or if it has been diluted with water, and to what extent. If it is absolutely pure milk, then I'm afraid all the food for the wedding feast is inedible."

The distraught man then quickly admitted that he routinely tampered with the quality of the milk, and after the rabbi made him repent and take an oath that he would never do so again, the celebration was allowed to proceed.

Today
I shall smile
because . . .

> As a rule, people who dominate others do not possess much self-mastery. They are too concerned with steering everyone else and have little resolve to exert control over themselves (*Rabbi of Rodzin*).

SMILING EACH DAY

In the Austria-Hungary empire, it was customary to display a picture of Emperor Franz Joseph in the vestibule of the synagogue. One time, when the mighty ruler visited Cracow, which at that time was part of his domain, an anti-semitic troublemaker removed the portrait prior to the emperor's visit to the great synagogue there. When he angrily demanded to know why his likeness was not displayed, Rabbi Shimon Schreiber, the illustrious community rabbi, had to think quickly. He knew that telling the truth — that it was removed by a no-goodnik — would not be readily accepted, and that the emperor would suspect the Jews of being disloyal.

"Your Highness," the rabbi attempted to explain, "we Jews have a precious *mitzvah* of *tefillin*, which we wear every day as a sign of the bond between G-d and ourselves. On Shabbos, however, we do not wear the *tefillin*, because Shabbos itself is a sign of our covenant with G-d, and proof that the Divine Presence is among us. To put on *tefillin* on Shabbos would therefore be a denial of the significance of the day.

"Therefore, Your Majesty," the rabbi swallowed hard and continued, "we keep the picture hanging only in your absence, to remind us that we are your loyal subjects. However, when Your Majesty is present in person, we believe it would be improper to display a mere likeness, just as we do not utilize the *tefillin* as a symbol of the Divine Presence when the observance of Shabbos attests to His being among us.

Indeed, there was no cause for alarm. The emperor was thrilled with the rabbi's explanation.

Today
I shall smile
because . . .

Of Ishmael it is written, "G-d was with the lad," but still, he became a robber (*Rashi, Genesis* 21:20). Of Joseph it is said, "G-d was with Joseph, and he was in all his ways successful" (*Genesis* 39:2). G-d gives each person potential, but one may use or misuse this gift.

SMILING EACH DAY

The following story is attributed to Rabbi Yisrael of Salant or Rabbi David of Lelov. It is equally compatible with the character of both.

One Yom Kippur eve, the worshipers were all gathered for *Kol Nidre,* ready to usher in the holiest day of the year. The rabbi, however, who was usually the first to arrive, was nowhere to be seen. As the sun began its descent, and the time for reciting *Kol Nidre* drew near, the congregants concluded that something terrible must have befallen the rabbi, who was otherwise never tardy. A group of them therefore fanned out to locate him.

Passing a small hut, one of them was amazed to find the saintly rabbi standing beside an infant's crib, rocking the baby to sleep.

When he realized he was being watched, the rabbi quickly put his finger to his lips, then tiptoed outside and explained.

"As I passed this home on my way to the synagogue, I heard a baby crying incessantly. I looked through the window and saw no one inside the house. Obviously the parents had put the child to bed and gone to *Kol Nidre,* assuming the child would sleep until they returned from services.

"It was unthinkable to allow the child to wail and remain unattended. He is now dozing off again, and when he is sound asleep I will come to *shul* and ask one of the parents to go back home."

It needn't be emphasized how crucial being at *Kol Nidre* was for the rabbi, but obviously, relieving the distress of the child was even more important. We should then, totally rethink our sense of religious priorities.

Today
I shall smile
because . . .

_____

_____

_____

The Midrash reveals that when Miriam and Aaron were openly critically of Moses (*Numbers* 12:1), they also spoke against G-d. Why, then, did Moses remain silent and not defend the Divine honor? Because, since he was personally involved, he was afraid he would not distinguish between G-d's honor and his own.

SMILING EACH DAY

Rabbi Eizel was known as *charif* (the sharp) because of his biting wit. He was an outstanding Torah scholar, and did not think well of rabbis who were lacking in scholarship yet assumed positions of leadership and authority anyway. When he was rabbi in his first position, he did not wear a silk kaftan as most rabbis did. When asked why he departed from the norm, Rabbi Eizel replied:

"Do you know why many rabbis wear such clothing? It is because they are rather vain, and so they are concerned that when they recite the verse, 'I am but a worm and not even a man' (*Psalms* 22:7), they would be saying a falsehood, since they do not at all consider themselves to be as lowly as a worm. They therefore don silk robes, since this fabric is produced by the silkworm. That way, when they compare themselves to a worm, there is at least some truth to their words. After all, clothes do 'make the man.'

"I, however, do not have that problem. I know myself to be as unworthy as a worm, hence I do not need silk robes to avoid speaking a falsehood."

Today
I shall smile
because . . .

Sometimes we forgive a person his wrongdoing, but at a later time something arouses our memory of the offense, and we are again resentful. That is like demanding payment for a loan that was nullified, or insisting someone return a gift. You have no right to do so (*Rabbi Yisrael of Salant*).

SMILING EACH DAY

At speaking engagements, I am often asked whether I wish to be introduced as Rabbi or Doctor. This question was already posed to a rabbi-physician that preceded me, who had responded:

"The Talmud insists that a person must have great respect for his spiritual teachers, and in some ways, this obligation may surpass even parental honor, because whereas parents assure the child physical life in this world, the spiritual mentor brings him to the life of the eternal world.

"Apparently, then, bringing one to the life of the eternal world is a great achievement. But of course, this is so only when it is one's teacher who accomplishes this. However, if one's physician brings him to eternal life, this is hardly something a doctor would boast about, because this would mean that treatment for whatever ailed him had failed, and the patient went to his final resting place.

"I therefore prefer being introduced as a rabbi rather than a physician, because if I do help people approach the life of eternity, in this capacity it is indeed meritorious, whereas it would be a disaster if I did so as a physician."

What a unique and humble (not to mention amusing) outlook on one's profession!

Today
I shall smile
because . . .

Vanity is a grievous sin. A person may clandestinely learn, fast, and do *mitzvos,* but think to himself: "How clever of me. I have kept everyone from discovering how great a *tzaddik* I am." A new, profound *Gehinnom* (Hell) will be created for that person (*Rabbi Simchah Bunim*).

SMILING EACH DAY

A person's dignity commands the highest priority in Torah law. The Talmud warns that even a Torah scholar, possessing many *mitzvos,* who humiliates someone publicly, forfeits his entire share in the eternal world. It would therefore appear that if one can prevent someone from embarrassment, he has fulfilled the greatest of *mitzvos.*

Rabbi Akiva Eiger once had a number of guests at his Pesach *seder.* At some point, one of them accidentally tipped over his cup of wine. Very quickly, the host tilted the table with his knee, so that several of the cups likewise spilled, whereupon he apologized, "This table has been wobbly for a while, and I had intended to have it fixed before *yom tov.*"

The greatness of the action appears to be in tilting the table, causing the other cups to topple over so that the person who originally tipped his cup would not be embarrassed. But there is more to it than that. If several moments had elapsed before Rabbi Akiva Eger made his move, the first person would have already been humiliated by his clumsiness, and the subsequent tilt recognized as a ruse. What was crucial here was his instantaneous response, so that the spilling of the other cups appeared simultaneous. This constant state of alertness and sensitivity to other people's dignity is part of what *tzaddikim* are made of. If this were all we could emulate of their exalted behavior, we would deserve congratulations.

Today
I shall smile
because . . .

Ben Zoma teaches: "A wise person is someone who learns from everyone" (*Ethics of the Fathers* 4:1). It does not say, one who learns from only his *teachers*. A truly wise person can find something of value to learn from anyone, great or small.

SMILING EACH DAY

Tzaddikim were always extremely thorough in examining all their actions, lest they might have inadvertently done something wrong for which they must atone or make amends. Since they knew that they were highly respected and no one was likely to reprimand them, some went so far as to engage a person whose job it was to rebuke them. They were particularly concerned about speaking *lashon hara* (slander or gossip) since the Talmud declares that *lashon hara* is a grievous sin, and that furthermore, one may not realize that in the process of normal conversation, he has said something improper. On that score, virtually no one is completely free of *lashon hara*.

One *tzaddik* fell sick, and began to do some soul-searching to determine in what way, if at all, he had sinned. Unable to recognize anything that constituted a transgression, he concluded that he must have said something that he could not recall which constituted *lashon hara*.

The *tzaddik* then consulted a physician who began the examination by asking him to stick out his tongue (in prior days this was the first step in a physical checkup). The doctor remarked, "Hm! That tongue does not look clean to me." Whereupon the *tzaddik's* eyes lit up as he exclaimed to his wife, "See! I was right! Even he can tell!"

Today
I shall smile
because . . .

_____

_____

_____

Someone who has a mind of his own is a fool. The Talmud teaches that a wise person is someone who learns from any and all people, thus, he has a piece of everyone else's thinking. A fool learns from no one, so he truly possesses a mind all his own (*Rabbi Baruch of Medziboz*).

SMILING EACH DAY

It is the practice among chassidim, when consulting the Rebbe, to write their requests on a slip of paper and submit it to him. This little petition is referred to as a *kvittel,* and is usually written by the chassid or by the Rebbe's *shammes* (attendant).

One of the followers of the Rebbe of Talna was a villager who was illiterate and whose son-in-law did all the necessary writing for the household. On one occasion, before he left to consult the Rebbe, the chassid had his son-in-law write the *kvittel* for him.

Prior to this, the son-in-law had also put together a laundry list for the family, which he accidentally handed to his father-in-law along with the other piece of paper. Upon entering the Rebbe's study, the chassid mistakenly handed the Rebbe the laundry list instead of the *kvittel.*

The Rebbe took one look at it, and without batting an eyelash, remarked, "My dear man, a laundry list of this size should certainly contain a larger number of *talleisim ketanim!*"

(A *tallis katan* is a diminutive *tallis,* which is worn under the shirt. Proper observance of the *mitzvah* would have surely resulted in there being a larger number of them in the wash.)

Who but one of the masters could read spirituality into a laundry list!

Today
I shall smile
because . . .

Willfully harboring indecent thoughts is a grave sin, even though one does not act on them. A person's mind is his essence and should be regarded as a sanctuary. Contaminating it with improprieties is like putting an idol into the Holy of Holies (*Rabbi Levi Yitzchak of Berdichev*).

SMILING EACH DAY

A chassid once visited the *Tzaddik* of Sanz, and when the latter inquired as to his well being, the chassid complained that he was a victim of chronic insomnia.

"Do you have any serious problems that keep you awake?" the *Tzaddik* asked warmly. "Any money or family worries?"

The chassid replied negatively.

"Then the solution is simple," the *Tzaddik* advised. "When you cannot doze off, take a *sefer* (a book of Torah) and learn. This way you utilize the time constructively by studying Torah, and eventually you will fall asleep."

The chassid shook his head. "I have no capacity for Torah study," he mourned. "I never had the opportunity to receive a proper education."

"*Oy vey iz mir*" (woe unto me), the *tzaddik* wailed. "Then when I asked you if you had any serious problems, why did you answer, 'No'? If you are incapable of Torah study, then you suffer from a much more worrisome condition than just inability to sleep."

Today
I shall smile
because . . .

_____
_____
_____

"The rabble amongst them craved a craving" (*Numbers* 11:4). It is understandable that a person should have desires, but some people are always dissatisfied. When they have all they want, they remain unhappy because they miss the excitement of lust. Thus, they crave to have cravings, and that is truly sinful (*Damesek Eliezer*).

SMILING EACH DAY

Rabbi Abraham of Sochochov was a child prodigy and also rather mischievous. One day he upset a peddler's fruit-stand, scattering the fruit all over the street. The poor man complained to the boy's father, who promptly paid for the loss.

Although the father knew that his son was given to playfulness, he was also well aware of his Torah knowledge, and that it was not characteristic of the lad to harm anyone with his actions. Instead of delivering a reprimand, the father asked for an explanation of his behavior.

"I watched the man arrange the fruit on his cart," the future leader of thousands defended himself. "He put spoiled and inferior fruit on the bottom, then covered it all with a thin layer of good-looking fruit. He was attempting to cheat the customers, who would assume that their entire purchase was of quality. It was my duty to protect unwitting buyers from being robbed by a dishonest person."

Already in his childhood, Rabbi Abraham manifested both the genius and sense of fairness that later earned him great renown in the Torah world.

Today
I shall smile
because . . .

A vain person is always angry at the world, because people rarely accord him the honor he feels is his due. A humble soul, however, is generally at peace with the world, because he feels he has received more than his fair share.

SMILING EACH DAY

The Baal Shem Tov made a point of displaying great love for simple, G-d-fearing people, even though they had never labored to attain scholarship in Torah.

Similarly, Rabbi Isaiah of Prague was known to become upset at learned people who looked down at sincerely pious but unlearned people. He would quote the *Midrash* saying, "at Sinai G-d lifted the mountain above the heads of the Israelites and threatened to destroy them if they refused to accept the Torah. Why was this necessary? Was their outer joy masking an inner reluctance?

"Having heard from Moses that the Almighty was going to reveal Himself and present the Israelites with the Torah, the scholars amongst the people prepared themselves for a profound discourse on the most esoteric and difficult *halachic* intricacies. Imagine their disappointment then when G-d announced his will as follows: 'Keep Shabbos! Do not steal! Respect your parents!' These people cried foul! 'This is an insult to our intelligence,' they complained. 'This is for lay people who know nothing of intellectual depth, not for scholars such as we are.' It was most evident that they were ready to return their tents.

"For these people, then, G-d had to raise the mountain over their heads, in order to coerce them to appreciate the simple facade of the commandments in the Torah."

Today
I shall smile
because . . .

_____
_____
_____

"Let the G-d of all human spirits appoint a leader over the community" (*Numbers* 27:16). Just as G-d is accessible to all people, the wicked no less than the just, so must a leader tune his eyes, ears and heart to all of the nation, and not discriminate between a good person and a bad person (*Rabbi Levi Yitzchak of Berdichev*).

SMILING EACH DAY

In *The Path of the Just*, Luzzato is critical of people who think that piety consists of self-flagellation and mortification of the flesh. The chassidic masters similarly disapproved of that perception, and Rabbi Naftali of Ropschitz used to mock practitioners of such behavior.

One time Rabbi Naftali saw a person wearing sackcloth under his shirt. The very fact that the sackcloth was visible indicated that this was merely a show of piety. "It seems that Satan has caught this person in his sack," he quipped to those around him, shaking his head in pity.

Another time, he observed someone beating his head against the wall while praying, as if he were so carried away by the intensity of his prayer that he lost control of his actions. Rabbi Naftali suspected that this gesticulation was meant to attract attention and commented wryly, "Now there is someone I approve of! If he is praying with such fervor that his banging his head is sincere, then all is well and good. And if he is doing so only to impress others with his devotion, then he deserves a headache!"

Today
I shall smile
because . . .

The real test of a person is how he reacts to minor challenges. Most people are capable of withstanding major stress, but their resolve to strive for any degree of greatness dwindles in the face of trivia, which they dismiss as insignificant. It is when dealing with such ostensibly petty matters that a person reveals his true character (*Rabbi Yerucham of Mir*).

SMILING EACH DAY

The Rabbi of Belz regularly had hundreds of followers from all parts of the country congregating in his synagogue on Shabbos. One time, after Shabbos, a chassid complained to him that his *shtreimel* (fur hat worn by many chassidim on festive occasions) had been taken.

"Go quickly to the train station," the Rebbe advised, "and look for a man with this particular description. Tell him that the Rebbe ordered him to promptly return the hat or he will suffer grave consequences."

The flabbergasted chassid did as he was told, and behold, the man indeed admitted the theft and willingly surrendered the stolen property. The chassid quickly spread word of the *tzaddik's* prophetic powers. When he heard of it, the Rebbe dismissed this talk as nonsense.

"It was not anything prophetic," he insisted. "Every other chassid who submitted a *kvittel* to me asked for a blessing towards greater spirituality and fear of G-d along with his other requests. This man only wished to be blessed with success in business. It was simple reasoning that anyone who pleads strictly for material good and is not in the least concerned with improving his spiritual life is prone to thievery."

Today
I shall smile
because . . .

_____
_____
_____

The Gaon of Vilna, in a letter to his family, instructs his daughters that in the event they overhear gossip when attending *shul*, they should better adjust to remaining at home to pray, rather than expose themselves to the grievous sin of listening to *lashon hara*.

Erev
Rosh Chodesh
[Eve of the
New Month]

SMILING EACH DAY

My grandfather, Rabbi Benzion Halberstam of Bobov, had a great affection for young people, many of whom became his devoted followers. It was not unusual for him to ignore older chassidim in favor of the youths. He reasoned that the former were already secure in their beliefs and practices, and that it was the next generation that required the greatest attention in order to strengthen their Jewishness. He used to boast of having chassidim who did not put on *tefillin* and did not fast on Yom Kippur: they were not yet *bar mitzvah*.

Chassidim have a way of becoming ecstatic in their adoration of the Rebbe. One time Rabbi Benzion came to a town where a throng of his admirers came out to welcome him. In their fervor, they unhitched the horses from the coach and put the harness over themselves, drawing the wagon to town.

The great rabbi protested vehemently. "No, no!" he pleaded. "You are missing the point. My life's work has been to convert animals into *mentschen* (people of integrity) and instead, you are making *mentschen* into horses!"

Today
I shall smile
because . . .

ADAR

אדר

*First Day of
Rosh Chodesh
Adar Sheni*

[During most years
Adar has 29 days.
During Hebrew
leap years Adar has
30 days, while
Adar Sheni has 29.]

"Theft of money is theft, and so is theft of time, theft" (*Path of the Just*). There are people who would not touch a cent that is not theirs, yet have no qualms about keeping someone waiting unnecessarily. Robbing someone's time may be more severe a sin than taking his money, because the latter can easily be returned, while lost time can never be restored.

SMILING EACH DAY

The Rabbi of Ostrovtza, one of the leading Talmudic scholars of the pre-Holocaust generation, was an ascetic who fasted frequently (to forestall the impending disaster, it was said), many times going forty consecutive days without food. At one point, he even began fasting on Shabbos. Although *halachah* requires that one eat three meals on Shabbos, this is because Shabbos is supposed to be a day of enjoyment as well as rest and sanctity. Therefore, under certain criteria, if an individual derives greater pleasure from fasting than from eating, he may be permitted to do so.

One time the Rabbi reprimanded someone for publicly violating the Shabbos. The man responded brashly, "You have no right to criticize me. You, too, violate the Shabbos when you fast. If taking pleasure in what you do renders a forbidden act permissible, then I too may do whatever it is that satisfies my needs."

The Rabbi was not shaken for a moment. With a glowing smile, he pointed out, "You are correct, my dear man, but there is one major difference between me and you. Many people are liable to emulate you in your violation of Shabbos, whereas no one is likely to mimic my unorthodox behavior."

Today
I shall smile
because . . .

_____

_____

_____

> One Chassidic master said, "I know that on Judgment Day I will be sent to *Gehinnom* (Hell), but I will cite the *halachah* that if the student is in exile, his Rebbe must accompany him. So my Rebbe will be brought down to me, and that will convert *Gehinnom* into *Gan Eden* (Paradise).

SMILING EACH DAY

Whereas *tzedakah* is a *mitzvah* that must be observed all year long, it assumes special significance prior to Passover, when people who live in poverty would be unable to supply themselves with the more costly food for Passover. Therefore, a special drive for *tzedakah* called *maos chittim* (literally: money for wheat) is conducted in all Jewish communities to provide the poor with their holiday needs. Although people generally respond well, rabbis are sometimes not satisfied with the level of support provided for the poor.

As the month of *Nissan* was ushered in, Rabbi Naftali of Ropschitz tried to stimulate his community to give *maos chittim* more generously. He delivered a particularly passionate sermon on the importance of enabling every person to celebrate the Festival of Liberation as a truly free person. It was not sufficient, he said, to provide just the basic needs of the poor. The *seder* table should be adorned with fine dishes, so that each person should feel himself to be a prince.

When Rabbi Naftali returned home, his wife asked him how he had fared with his sermon. "I am absolutely certain that I was at least fifty per cent successful," he said. "The poor have fully agreed to accept more generous donations. As to whether the rich have agreed to give more, I don't know for sure."

Today
I shall smile
because . . .

A Chassidic master who visited Israel said, "I saw camels there. It was obvious that each camel could see the humps on other camels' backs but could never see its own."

SMILING EACH DAY

Special prayers are recited and fast days may even be decreed, in the event of a serious drought. It is particularly important to encourage people who are lax in observance of the Divine Will to participate in these services, in the hope that they will be moved by the precarious position of the community and correct their errant ways. Indeed, the Talmud states that a fast day in which transgressors do not participate is not much of a fast day.

In one community which was in a drought area, the rabbis proclaimed a fast day. One of the rabbis tried to urge a non-observant person to join in the services, but the latter refused. "You certainly do *not* think that the prayers of someone like myself will placate G-d," he said.

The rabbi tried to impress upon him that the prayers of every person are important, and that on the contrary, when someone who is distant from religious observance turns to G-d, his prayer is particularly effective.

"I take it from this," the man said, "that you are insinuating that it is my sinfulness that has evoked the Divine wrath and caused the drought. I resent that!"

"No need to worry about that," the rabbi said. "I could not possibly think that you caused the drought. In fact, we know that it was people like yourself who once caused it to rain for forty days and forty nights consecutively."

Today
I shall smile
because . . .

_____
_____
_____

Rabbi Pinchas of Koritz said, "A newborn ox is an ox, and a mature ox is an ox, having changed essentially in size and strength only. A human being should be different."

SMILING EACH DAY

It is expected that a person have an occupation with which to earn his livelihood. However, he should work in order to live rather than the converse. If one has a life's goal that transcends work, then he would work only as much as is necessary to provide himself with the essentials of life, and his free time would be directed towards his ultimate goal. Unfortunately, this is rarely the case, and if we may judge people's goals in life by what they do after they have acquired their essentials, we must conclude that for many of them, either work or money or fame has become an end in itself.

The Rabbi of Kotzk said that the Psalmist praises one who partakes of the works of his hands (*Psalms* 128:2). "Yes," the Rabbi said, "but let it be the work of his *hands* and not the total preoccupation of his mind." The works of *Mussar* note that the need to work for a livelihood was part of Adam's punishment, and why should an individual wish to assume more punishment than is absolutely necessary?

On one occasion a chassid who manufactured shoes came to the Rabbi of Kotzk for a blessing for success in his ventures. Noting that this person was directing all his thinking and energies into his business, the Rabbi said, "You are truly an unusual person. Most people put their feet into shoes, whereas you have put your head into shoes!"

Today
I shall smile
because . . .

Moses took a census by having each person contribute a half *shekel*. Why not a whole *shekel*? Because he wished each person to realize that if one stands alone, one is incomplete.

SMILING EACH DAY

The *Tzaddik* of Sanz reprimanded someone for having encroached upon another person's livelihood, something which is explicitly forbidden in the Torah. The man defended his actions, saying, "Why, that so-and-so is an evil person. Why does the Rabbi seek to protect him? He does not deserve consideration. It is a *mitzvah* to bury him!"

"That cannot possibly be the case," the *Tzaddik* said. "The Talmud states that prior to the Exodus from Egypt, G-d required the Israelites to perform two *mitzvos*, the Paschal offering and circumcision. This was because they had become so assimilated with the Egyptians that they lacked any merits by virtue of which they could be redeemed, and by performing these two *mitzvos* they earned their redemption.

"But how could it be that they were totally bereft of *mitzvos*? The *Midrash* states that there were many assimilated Israelites who refused to follow Moses and preferred to remain in Egypt, and that because of their defiance and their rejection of liberation, they died during the three days of darkness. They must have been buried by the other Israelites, and if burying a sinful person is such a great *mitzvah*, then surely they must have had an abundance of *mitzvos*!

"We can only conclude from that," the *Tzaddik* said, "that contrary to what you said, burying a sinful Jew is not a *mitzvah*."

Today
I shall smile
because . . .

_____

_____

_____

> We commemorate the Exodus each day in our prayers, because each day we should liberate ourselves from the tyrannical enslavement of our passions.

SMILING EACH DAY

It is customary that on *Shabbos HaGadol* (the Great Shabbos), the Shabbos before Passover, the rabbi delivers a Talmudic discourse. To enable the scholars in the community to have maximum benefit from the discourse, the rabbi in past times would announce in advance the various passages of the Talmud and commentaries that he intended to discuss.

A favorite topic was reconciling conflicting *halachic* rulings by the *Rambam* (Maimonides). A study of *Rambam* may often reveal two rulings that appear to be contradictory, and the task of the discussant is then to demonstrate that the conflict is only apparent, and that a more thorough understanding of the rulings shows them to be compatible.

Prior to one *Shabbos HaGadol*, Rabbi Mendel of Linsk posted two rulings of the *Rambam* that he was planning to discuss in his lecture. The scholars looked these up, but were perplexed because they could not see any relationship whatever between the two.

On *Shabbos HaGadol* the audience waited eagerly for the lecture. Rabbi Mendel began, "The *Rambam* rules that it is mandatory for every person to have *matzah* and the four cups of wine, and that no one is exempt, even a poor person. Elsewhere, however, the *Rambam* rules that stealing is absolutely forbidden. This poses a conflict between the two rulings, because what can the poor do if they have no money for *matzah* and wine, yet are not permitted to steal?

"In order to reconcile these two rulings, it is incumbent upon us to give enough money to charity before Passover so that the poor can purchase all their Passover needs, without resorting to any unlawful methods to get money."

Today
I shall smile
because . . .

Rabbi Abraham of Porisov said that a person who is born with a defect will try to conceal it with cosmetics or a prosthesis. "Why, then, does a fool display his fallacy instead of concealing it by keeping silent? That is why I cannot tolerate a fool," he said.

SMILING EACH DAY

Scholarship is better achieved by teaching others than by any other means. The Talmud states that we learn much from our teachers, more from our colleagues, and most from our students. Great scholars have always sought an environment in which they would be challenged by students. Indeed, the Talmud reports a tragic event: when the great Sage Rabbi Eliezer left the academy to live in an area of cleaner air and water, he eventually forgot all his vast learning.

Rabbi Tzvi Hirsch left Berlin to become Rabbi of London. He was highly respected and loved in the new community, but at that time there were few people in London who were interested in the services of a rabbi as a teacher of Torah and as a *posek* (one who decides (on) *halachic* questions). When his attempts to make the community more Torah-conscious failed, he decided to resign his position and return to Berlin.

The leaders of the London community met with Rabbi Tzvi Hirsch and asked, "Why are you leaving us? Did we not provide well for you?"

"I have no complaints about my salary," Rabbi Tzvi Hirsch said. "The problem is that since I have been rabbi here, the question you have just posed is the first question I have ever been asked."

Today
I shall smile
because . . .

_____

_____

_____

One descendant of a proud line of great *tzaddikim* boasted of his impressive genealogy and belittled scholars who were of humble origin. A Chassidic master said to him, "Some people are the beginning of a *yichus* (lineage), whereas with others the *yichus* ends."

SMILING EACH DAY

There were numerous occasions in history when prominent Jewish leaders were in contact with church leaders. Whenever possible, dialogues were avoided because they were felt to be useless. They were invariably sought by the church, however, which wished to prove the validity of the Christian faith on the basis of the Scriptures. However, all recorded dialogues showed that just the reverse occurred, with Jewish scholars demonstrating gross errors in translation from the original texts and other distortions in interpretation. Dialogues were not initiated by Jews, who had no desire to prove others wrong and were content to be left alone, free of the threat of inquisitions or pogroms.

Many times, however, looking after the interests of the Jewish community necessitated meeting with church leaders. Rabbi Yonasan Eibeschitz, a Talmudic scholar whose extraordinary genius is legendary, was held in high esteem by the local church clergy. At one of these meetings, the priest had wine served, and when Rabbi Yonasan explained that he could not drink it, the priest said, "Your laws are too restrictive, rabbi. Will there never be a time when you can drink with us?"

Rabbi Yonasan replied smilingly, "Of course there will be. At your wedding feast."

Today
I shall smile
because . . .

Chassidim once asked the Rabbi of Lechovitz how one can achieve humility. "You need a way to *achieve* humility?" he asked. "You have nerve! Just look at the difference between what you are and what you are supposed to be."

SMILING EACH DAY

On the eve of Yom Kippur, Rabbi Yitzchak Elchanan would come to the synagogue, remove his shoes, and remain in the synagogue until Yom Kippur was over, reciting *Tehillim* (Psalms) or studying Torah all night. One time, at the close of Yom Kippur, he looked for his shoes but wasn't able to find them. One of the worshipers saw the rabbi searching and asked if he could be of help. The rabbi explained that he was looking for his shoes and was confident that he would eventually find them.

"You are weak from the fast and from being awake all night," the man said. "Please sit down and rest, and I will look for your shoes."

Rabbi Yitzchak Elchanan politely declined the offer, whereupon the man said, "Why are you depriving me of the opportunity to serve a *talmid chacham* (a Torah scholar), especially of the chance to do a *mitzvah* the first thing after Yom Kippur?"

"You consider me a *talmid chacham*?" the rabbi asked.

"Of course," the man said.

Rabbi Yitzchak Elchanan smiled. "Then I, too, wish to have the opportunity of serving a *talmid chacham* and doing a *mitzvah* the first thing after Yom Kippur," he said, and continued to look for his shoes.

Today
I shall smile
because . . .

_____

_____

_____

> Rabbi Yechezkel of Shiniva said, "Displaying one's silver items is *ga'avah* (vanity). Displaying *silver-plated* items is both *ga'avah* and *sheker* (falsehood)."

SMILING EACH DAY

A young scholar who often associated with freethinkers used to circulate occasionally among the chassidim of Rabbi Shneur Zalman. One time the rabbi sent for him and reprimanded him, telling him that by associating with non-believers he was placing his *neshamah* (soul) in jeopardy, since he was likely to be influenced by their heresies.

The young man brushed off the rabbi's comments. "You need not have any fear of that," he said somewhat defiantly. "Look how often I have associated with your chassidim, but none of their practices have rubbed off on me. Neither will those of my other friends."

"That is not an accurate comparison," the rabbi said. "You see, the *halachah* is that when something *tamei* (unclean) comes into contact with something clean, it contaminates the clean object. On the other hand, if regular meat is touched by sacrificial meat, its status is not affected, and it becomes sacred only if it *absorbs* from the sacrificial meat.

"We see from this that contamination can be transferred by superficial conduct, whereas sanctity must be absorbed. Your conduct with my chassidim has not affected you because you do not wish to absorb from them, but even superficial contact with heretics will affect your thinking and behavior."

Today
I shall smile
because . . .

Among your acquaintances there are some who criticize you and others who praise you. You should love the former, who may stimulate your character growth, and avoid the latter, whose flattery can result in your character deterioration (*Avos De R'Nosson*).

SMILING EACH DAY

Some of our finest rabbis were often the victims of people who were dissatisfied with everything and would find fault with their leaders. The precedent was set by the greatest of our leaders, Moses, who was also unjustly criticized by rabble-rousers (*Numbers* 11:1-15). Unfortunately, opposition to great leaders often emanated from people who were know-nothings.

One rabbi was told that he was being vilified by some of the least-respectable members of the community. "Too bad," he said. "I wish it were more decent people who were doing this."

To his bewildered listeners he explained, "King David complained that he was being vilified by drunkards (*Psalms* 69:13). What difference did it make to him who the slanderers were?

"The Talmud states that if a person speaks badly about another person, he loses the merits of the *mitzvos* he has achieved, and these merits are transferred to the person whom he vilified. Thus, if a decent person were to slander me, I would at least benefit by acquiring whatever *mitzvos* he had. But if people who have no *mitzvos* to their credit vilify me, what can I possibly gain from their slander?"

Today
I shall smile
because . . .

_____

_____

_____

How insatiable is the craving for honor! Haman had the entire population of one hundred and twenty-seven nations prostrating themselves before him, but the refusal of one Jew to recognize him gave him no peace and ultimately led to his destruction.

SMILING EACH DAY

Rabbi Elimelech of Lizensk, who was one of the foremost Chassidic masters and was revered by all chassidim as a great Torah scholar and *tzaddik,* used to say that he felt quite secure that he would merit admission to *Gan Eden* (Paradise). He pointed out that there is nothing as dear to G-d as truth, and that the Talmud states that truth is the Divine seal. Each day in the *Shema* we say, "G-d is a G-d of truth."

"When I appear before the eternal tribunal, they will ask me, 'Elimelech, did you study Torah adequately?' I will say, 'No.'

" 'Elimelech, did you pray with the proper *kavannah* (concentration)?' I will say, 'No.'

" 'Elimelech, did you perform the *mitzvos* with the requisite devotion and intensity of will?' Again, I will say, 'No.'

"The tribunal will then condemn me to *Gehinnom* (Hell) for my dereliction. But then A-lmighty G-d will intervene and say, 'Elimelech speaks the truth, and for speaking the truth, he deserves *Gan Eden.*' "

Today
I shall smile
because . . .

Self esteem is not vanity. The vain person demands to be honored for his achievements, whereas a person with self-esteem, who knows his own potentials, feels that he has not achieved enough.

SMILING EACH DAY

The Chafetz Chaim devoted his entire life to the battle against *lashon hara* (slander or gossip). He pointed out that it is as great a transgression to hear *lashon hara* as it is to speak it, and he made every attempt to avoid inadvertently overhearing *lashon hara*. When his hearing began to fail, he rejoiced, because now he would not have to make as great an effort to avoid overhearing *lashon hara*. What would be a disaster to others was a windfall for him! Every moment free of *lashon hara* he considered a triumph.

One time a *maggid* (preacher) came to town and asked for permission to deliver a sermon on *lashon hara*. The Chafetz Chaim readily approved and attended the sermon himself. The *maggid* spoke for a full two hours, drawing upon every possible source to impress his listeners with the evil effects of *lashon hara*.

After the sermon was over, the Chafetz Chaim thanked the *maggid* heartily. The *maggid* confided to him that he did not feel good about the sermon, because he had felt less-than-passionate vibrations from the audience.

"No matter," said the Chafetz Chaim. "Don't you realize that for the two hours that you preached no one spoke a single word of *lashon hara*? Two hours free of *lashon hara*! What a marvelous achievement!"

Today
I shall smile
because . . .

_____
_____
_____

Some people may love the truth when it is to their advantage, and may love falsehood when it is to their advantage. Both really love only themselves, and may be incapable of loving anything other than themselves.

SMILING EACH DAY

The wise Solomon warned against writing a limitless number of books (*Ecclesiastes* 12:12), a warning which has unfortunately not been well heeded. Maimonides said that one should speak only one-tenth of what he thinks, write only one-tenth of what he says, and publish only one-tenth of what he writes.

[The search for chametz takes place tonight.]

Because of the plethora of books available, authors have always sought to obtain impressive endorsements. Many *sefarim* (books of Torah literature) therefore carry endorsements from acknowledged authorities, which help readers avoid wasting their time on books that are without merit.

Rabbis have often been besieged by authors seeking their endorsements. One author kept on bothering Rabbi Yitzchak of Volozhin for an endorsement on two commentaries he had written, one on the *Book of Job* and the other on *Song of Songs*. Rabbi Yitzchak, who had reviewed the works and found them to be without merit, told the man that he would write an endorsement for *Job*, but not for *Song of Songs*.

"Why the difference?" the author asked.

"Simple," Rabbi Yitzchak said. "Job was subjected to so many *tzoros* (miseries) that adding your commentary to the list would be just one of the many and not make much difference. But King Solomon had no *tzoros*, so why inflict one on him?"

Today
I shall smile
because . . .

For the Succos festival, the Torah mentions the *mitzvah* of *simchah* (joy) three times. For Passover, the Festival of Liberation, the Torah does not mention *simchah* even once. Why? Because on Passover the oppressive Egyptians were destroyed, and the Scripture states, "Do not rejoice when your enemy falls" (*Proverbs* 24:17).

SMILING EACH DAY

In the olden days the walls of houses were very thick, and large hollows in the wall were used for storage purposes. Since people sometimes stored food items there, the hollows had to be cleaned before Passover, because pieces of items containing *chametz* (leavened dough) might have remained there. The *halachah* states that when the pre-Passover search for *chametz* is conducted, it is only necessary to check as far as one's hand can reach. If there should happen to be a morsel of *chametz* beyond that depth, it can be abandoned.

Some people are more particular about ritual observances than about their obligatory social responsibilities. This was the case of one wealthy man, who was ritually pious but extremely tight-fisted when it came to giving *tzedakah*.

One day before Passover the rabbi passed this miser's house and found that he was cleaning his clothes for Passover. He had turned the pockets of the garments inside out and was shaking them to remove any possible crumbs.

"There is no need for that," the rabbi said to him. "The *halachah* requires that you must check only as far as your hand can reach. Your hand has never yet reached into your pocket."

Today
I shall smile
because . . .

_____

_____

_____

A scholar was asked, "Which is more important, Torah or prayer?" He answered, "Torah is G-d speaking to man, while prayer is man speaking to G-d. Both are equally essential for a dialogue to take place."

First Day of Pesach

SMILING EACH DAY

A man once asked Rabbi Yosef Dov of Brisk whether it is permissible to fulfill the *mitzvah* of the four cups at the *Seder* by drinking milk instead of wine. Rabbi Yosef Dov asked if this was for health reasons, and the man stated that he simply could not afford wine. Rabbi Yosef Dov told him that milk was not satisfactory, and gave him a large sum of money for his Passover needs.

Rabbi Yosef Dov's wife, who had witnessed this exchange, asked him why he had given the man so large a sum. "He does not need all that money just to buy wine," she said.

Rabbi Yosef Dov responded, "Knowing the four volumes of the Code of Law is not sufficient. The fifth volume, that of common sense, is most important.

"Since the Passover meals are usually *fleishig* (containing meat), how could this man possibly have considered using milk for the four cups? The only reasonable conclusion is that he could not afford to buy meat for the festival either. It is therefore not enough to give him money just for wine for the *Seder*. He needs enough money to buy meat for his entire family for all of Passover!"

Today
I shall smile
because . . .

_____
_____
_____

Second Day of Pesach

[In the Land of Israel this is the first day of Chol Hamoed, the Intermediate Days.]

The Talmud says, "If someone says 'I have tried, but I have not achieved anything,' do not believe him" (*Megilla* 6b). Why? Because trying *is* achieving. It is the effort one puts forth that counts, rather than the result (*Rabbi of Kotzk*).

SMILING EACH DAY

The laws of Passover are indeed very strict, but Jewish housewives have added precautions of their own, all to avoid the possibility, G-d forbid, of any contamination of the Passover food by the minutest crumb of *chametz*. Many of their practices have been adopted within families as the correct way to observe Passover, and inasmuch as Solomon says, "Do not forsake the teachings of your mother" (*Proverbs* 1:18), these customs have taken on the authority of law within the family.

The kitchen, of course, is the area which requires the greatest attention, since this is the area where *chametz* is concentrated all year long. Whereas many utensils — dishes, pots, cutlery — are set aside only for Passover use, other kitchen items, such as the stove, oven, tables, and cabinets, must be thoroughly cleaned, and in some cases *kashered* (sterilized).

The wife of Rabbi Yehoshua Kutner was extremely meticulous in preparing the kitchen for Passover. One time Rabbi Yehoshua found her scrubbing a table so vigorously that she was dripping with perspiration.

"You may stop scrubbing," he said, "because you have exceeded the necessary cleaning. According to the *Shulchan Aruch* (Code of Jewish Law), that table has been more than adequately cleaned."

His wife continued her scrubbing. "You and your *Shulchan Aruch*!" she said. "If we followed you and the *Shulchan Aruch*, we would all be eating *chametz* on Passover!"

Today
I shall smile
because . . .

_____

_____

_____

Rabbi Sholom Dov of Lubavitch observed someone at the *Seder* carefully measuring the broken *matzah* to see which was the larger part to be put away for the *afikomen*. "Greatness that has to be discerned by millimeters," he said, "is hardly greatness at all."

SMILING EACH DAY

Chametz on Passover differs from other forbidden foods in that if a tiny morsel of non-kosher food is accidentally mixed into kosher food and the proportion of kosher to non-kosher is at least sixty to one, it may be ruled permissible. Not so with *chametz*, where the minutest crumb of *chametz* admixture, even one to a million, can render the entire batch of food forbidden.

Once flour has been baked into *matzah*, it can no longer become *chametz*; hence, *matzah* can be ground to make *matzah* meal. However, if a speck of flour happened to escape saturation in the kneading, it never became *matzah*, and therefore, if it subsequently comes into contact with liquid, it may turn into *chametz*. Therefore, some have a practice not to allow *matzah* to become moist, and these people, of course, cannot eat *knaidlach* (*matzah* balls). Understandably, some consider this practice overkill.

A very concerned man consulted Rabbi Yitzchak Meir of Gur. "A piece of *matzah* fell into my bowl of soup. May I still use the bowl on Passover?"

The rabbi shrugged. "I haven't the faintest idea," he said. "The *Shulchan Aruch* only gives instructions if a piece of *chametz* falls into food. It says nothing about a piece of *matzah*."

Today
I shall smile
because . . .

Is a person permitted to borrow money if he has no prospect of any resource to repay the loan, other than his trust that G-d will help him? "Yes," said one ethicist, "but only if he would also be willing to lend money to someone who had no other visible resources, on the basis of his trust that G-d would help him repay the loan."

SMILING EACH DAY

It is customary for children to steal the *afikomen* (hidden) *matzah,* and to hold it for ransom until the father grants whatever they may request, within reasonable limits. This practice was instituted in order to keep children awake during the Seder, so that they may hear the story of the Exodus in the Haggadah. When Rabbi Heschel of Cracow was a child, he followed this tradition. One time he did not return the stolen *matzah* until his father promised to buy him a new suit.

After Heschel returned the *afikomen matzah,* his father distributed portions of the *matzah* to all at the Seder except him. "You will not get *afikomen matzah,* Heschele," the father said, "until you release me from the promise to buy you a suit."

The young Heschele responded, "I foresaw such a possibility. Before returning the *matzah* to you, I took off a piece for myself," and triumphantly showed his father the piece of *matzah* that he had retained. "I still get the suit."

Today
I shall smile
because . . .

_____
_____
_____

A man who had once been a student of the Chafetz Chaim complained to the sage that he had failed in business. The Chafetz Chaim said, "I taught you to be perfect in your trust in G-d, because G-d will never cheat you. However, when you deal with *people* in business, you must keep on the alert, because people may be deceptive."

SMILING EACH DAY

Rabbi Naftali of Ropschitz was known for his wit. He had very little tolerance for fools and said that the author of the Haggadah agreed with him.

"The four sons in the Haggadah are named the wise son, the wicked son, the simple son, and the son who does not know enough to ask. Why did the author of the Haggadah place the wicked son second rather than last, which is where he belongs? It can only be because the wicked son is not stupid, and there is still hope that he may correct his errant ways. A simpleton, however, is beyond hope, for a fool cannot become wise."

Today it has become fashionable for criminals to become wealthy by writing a best seller. Rabbi Naftali had something to say about villains who become heroes. "Do you know why every year there are new editions of the Haggadah?" he asked. "It is because the *rasha* (wicked son) of last year's Haggadah has become the *chacham* (wise son) of this year."

Today
I shall smile
because . . .

NISSAN

20

ניסן

*Chol Hamoed
Pesach*

The *Midrash* states that Bilaam's ass died immediately after her miraculous speech (*Numbers* 22:28), so that people should not say, "There is the ass that rebuked its master." G-d was protective of the honor of even as wicked a person as Bilaam (*Rabbi Chaim Shmulevitz*).

SMILING EACH DAY

In Berdichev there was a town drunkard who, knowing he would not be able to have any whiskey for the eight days of Passover, tried to make up for it on the day before the holiday. On Passover night he was in a stupor, and his wife tried to arouse him to conduct the *Seder,* but to no avail. It was almost dawn when she finally awoke him and said, "It is Passover night! You must make a *Seder* and say the Haggadah."

The man sat up, poured a cup of wine, and mumbled the *kiddush,* then took a second cup of wine. "I don't know much about the Haggadah," he said. "All I know is that our ancestors were slaves in Egypt, and that G-d miraculously took them out. Now we are in exile and slaves again under domination of wicked *pritzim* (medieval lords of estates), but the same G-d that took us out of Egypt will redeem us again. That's all I know, and that's good enough for me." He then drank two more cups of wine and went back to sleep.

The following day Rabbi Levi Yitzchak of Berdichev sent for the wife and asked her how her husband had conducted the *Seder.* She ashamedly related the sorry state of affairs.

"Too bad he is a drunkard," Rabbi Levi Yitzchak said. "His simple and sincere expression of faith — that the G-d Who took us out of Egypt will redeem us again — caused great joy in Heaven."

Today
I shall smile
because . . .

_____
_____
_____

People sometimes dismiss other people's questions as foolish or trivial. The great sage Hillel reacted to someone who tried to provoke him with silly questions by saying, "My child, you have asked very wisely" (*Shabbos* 31a). How cautious we must be of people's honor!

Seventh Day of Pesach
[In the Land of Israel this is the last day of Pesach.]

SMILING EACH DAY

One influential member of the Jewish community in Slonim caused a great deal of harm to many people under the pretext that he was championing the cause of truth. Rabbi Eizel of Slonim reprimanded him, but the man defended his action on the basis of his noble intention to see justice done.

On Passover, Rabbi Eizel called the man and asked him whether he had recited the ballad *Chad Gadya* (One Little Kid) in the Haggadah. The man responded that of course he had.

Rabbi Eizel then pointed out that in *Chad Gadya* there is a chain of events where a hero-victim is punished by a villain. The one who then punishes the villain now becomes a hero. If we follow this sequence, the little kid is the innocent victim who is eaten by a cat (villain), which is bitten by the dog (hero), who is beaten by the stick (villain), which is burnt by the fire (hero), which is doused by the water (villain), which is drunk by the ox (hero), which is slaughtered by the *shochet* (ritual slaughterer — villain), who is killed by the Angel of Death (hero), who is then destroyed by G-d.

Since it turns out that the Angel of Death in this chain of events is a hero, why does G-d destroy him?

"It is because," said Rabbi Eizel, "no one has the authority to enforce what he believes is justice by killing people."

Others explained, "The cat in fact is a villain; but who asked the dog to get involved?"

Today
I shall smile
because . . .

*Eighth Day
of Pesach*
[Yizkor]

Rabbi Yerachmiel of Koznitz said that entering a shul should be like crossing the border to another country. One must rid himself of all contraband, which in this case consists of vanity, greed, *lashon hara*, hostility, etc.

SMILING EACH DAY

The Talmud cautions us not to convert the Torah into an instrument for earning a livelihood. "Do not make it into a shovel to dig with" (*Ethics of the Fathers* 4:7).

Rabbi Zanvil of Warsaw used to conduct the sale of *chametz* annually for a wealthy man. One year the man sent him a message that another rabbi had offered to come to his home to transact the sale of *chametz*, and that if Rabbi Zanvil would not come to his home, he would engage this other rabbi for the service. Rabbi Zanvil was insulted by the man's arrogance and sent the messenger back with an appropriate reply.

Several days later Rabbi Zanvil met with the other rabbi, who for a few kreuzers had degraded the dignity of the rabbinate to make house calls on the wealthy. "I now understand why the sages, in warning us not to exploit the Torah for our livelihood, said, 'Do not make the Torah into a shovel to dig with.'

"With every other craft the artisan works in his shop — for example, the tailor, shoemaker, and watchmaker. It is only the person who earns his living by digging who must go to the place of his employer, because he is obviously not going to be hired to dig in his own home.

"Our sages were therefore telling us not to exploit our rabbinical status to make house calls just for profit."

Today
I shall smile
because . . .

_____

_____

_____

Rabbi Nosson Tzvi Finkel cited the *Midrash* that Moses' reluctance to become the deliverer of the Jewish people (*Exodus* 4:13) was because he was concerned that his older brother, Aaron, might be offended by his appointment. "Think of it! The fate of all Israel hangs in the balance, and he is concerned that one person's feelings might be hurt. That is the greatness of Moses."

SMILING EACH DAY

When Rabbi Heschel of Cracow was a small child, he once helped himself to the drumstick of a chicken without first getting his mother's permission. When his mother discovered that one drumstick was missing, she accused Heschele, but he denied any knowledge of it. His mother then pointed out that he was the only person who had access to the chicken, but Heschele said that the chicken must have had only one leg. His mother said that this was absurd, but he told her that he would show her a one-legged chicken.

Heschele then took his mother down the road where a farmer had some chickens and showed her that there was a chicken standing on one leg. "See," he said, "there is a one-legged chicken."

"Ridiculous!" his mother said, and stamped her foot firmly on the ground, frightening the chicken and causing it to lower its second leg and run off. "There you see its second leg."

Heschele was not to be bested. "Yes, mother," he said. "If you had stamped your foot hard on the ground in the kitchen, the second leg would have appeared there, too!"

Today
I shall smile
because . . .

A person who has been insulted and remains silent appears to be the vanquished victim of a triumphant assailant. However, the offender's triumph is over a mere mortal, whereas the one who restrained himself has overcome a powerful temptation to retaliate, and thereby vanquished his *yetzer hara* (evil inclination). Who is greater?

SMILING EACH DAY

Rabbi Raphael of Bershed used to say that he can well understand why the Talmud considers vanity to be the worst of all sins.

"Take my case," he said. "How will I ever defend myself before the Heavenly tribunal on Judgment Day, when they indict me for having been vain?

"They will ask me, 'Raphael, did you study Torah properly as you should have?' and I will say that I did not do so because of my limited intellect. They will then ask me if I prayed with sufficient *kavannah* (concentration), and I will say that I could not muster enough energy to pray properly. They will ask me whether I gave adequate *tzedakah,* and I will explain that I was not a person of means, and I could not give *tzedakah* appropriately.

"Then they will say, 'Raphael, if you did not study Torah adequately, nor pray properly, nor give *tzedakah,* what right did you have to be vain?' How can I answer that? I will be totally defenseless. That is why vanity is so great a sin. It can often not be defended."

Today
I shall smile
because . . .

_____
_____
_____

Things that are forbidden do not require any thought; but before doing something that is permissible, one should take time to contemplate whether it is really necessary (*Rabbi Sholom of Lubavitch*).

SMILING EACH DAY

It is probably true that some people hear only that which they wish to hear. We seem to have a capability of "selective perception," which makes us oblivious to things we do not wish to be aware of.

Rabbi Meir Shapiro of Lublin revolutionized Torah study when he built the famed Yeshiva of Lublin. Instead of the makeshift and sometimes dilapidated quarters that often served as study halls, Torah study would now be given respectability and dignified physical surroundings. This project was very costly, and Rabbi Shapiro traveled the world over to raise the necessary funds.

People are not always receptive to being asked for donations. In one community Rabbi Shapiro delivered an impassioned sermon on the need to support Torah study, claiming that his academy would make learning Torah more attractive to young people by providing a comfortable environment conducive to Torah study.

Rabbi Shapiro had serious doubts that his message was on target. It seemed to him that the audience received his sermon as a philosophical discussion on the value of Torah study. He stopped a child and asked, "Did you understand my speech?"

"Not really," said the child. "It was too hard for me to understand, but I think it was something about money."

"Then you understood the speech better than all the adults in the congregation," Rabbi Meir said.

Today
I shall smile
because . . .

When David fled from his rebellious son Avshalom, Shimi cursed him violently. Defying the king in such a manner is a capital crime, yet David did not execute Shimi, but instructed Solomon to do so. Why? Because he was personally offended, and he did not consider himself objective enough to pronounce sentence upon him.

SMILING EACH DAY

Joining together with others for a meal is considered desirable, because eating together tends to bring people closer in friendship. For this reason, some food restrictions (e.g., the prohibition of drinking wine with a non-Jew) were introduced in order to minimize the kind of fraternization with non-Jews that could lead to emotional ties, assimilation, and intermarriage. Since close ties among Jews, however, is considered vital, inviting a fellow Jew to share a meal is considered commendable. Rabbi Yisrael of Salant states that the *halachah* supports this concept.

In order to repeat the *Amidah* (silent prayer) aloud, it is not enough to have a *minyan* (quorum of ten). Among these there must be six people who said the silent *Amidah* together.

On the other hand, in leading the Blessing after Meals, for which it is necessary to have a *minyan* in order to pronounce the name of G-d in the introductory prayer, it is necessary to have *seven* participants in the meal. Why only six for prayer, while seven are needed for a meal?

Rabbi Yisrael of Salant pointed out that these regulations were formulated by the rabbis, who wished to provide additional incentive for inviting another person to a meal. For prayers, six are enough, but let there be a need for a seventh person to eat with the others in order to invoke the Divine Name.

Today
I shall smile
because . . .

_____
_____
_____

"It was not because you are more numerous of all nations that G-d has chosen you, because you are the least populous of all nations" (*Deuteronomy* 7:7). G-d is not interested in quantity. A small amount which is pure is far superior to an abundance which is not pure (*Rabbi Yerucham of Mir*).

SMILING EACH DAY

The *Maggid* of Slutzk was once in a group of people where one incessant talker monopolized the entire conversation and did not allow anyone else to get a word in edgewise. The man prattled much foolishness, but the *Maggid* sat by silently and said nothing, until the man related an episode involving Rabbi Yonasan Eibeschitz. The incident he described was a frank insult to the great Rabbi Yonasan.

At this point the *Maggid* could not contain himself and, to defend the honor of the great Torah scholar announced, "Do not believe a word of this. It is a story that he fabricated. I am certain that it never occurred."

The people were bewildered. How could anyone know for certain that a given incident did not occur?

"Very simple," the *Maggid* said. "Obviously the man has no firsthand knowledge of such an incident, as it is one hundred and fifty years since Rabbi Yonasan died. He also could not have read it, because I am familiar with all the literature about Rabbi Yonasan, and this story does not appear anywhere. The only possibility is that he heard it from someone. But how could someone who talks incessantly and never stops long enough to listen possibly have heard anything from anyone?"

Today
I shall smile
because . . .

The Maggid of Koznitz said, "Ben Azai's soul left his body when he reached a spiritual level incompatible with an earthly existence. And what did this angelic person teach? 'Never embarrass anyone, even the lowest of all people'" (*Ethics of the Fathers* 4:3).

SMILING EACH DAY

It is not unusual that children who are particularly active grow up to be very stable and outstanding Torah scholars. One young prodigy justified his boisterous behavior, saying, "If I do not discharge this (energy) now, it will remain with me in my adult life."

Rabbi Shlomo Schreiber, son of Rabbi Shimon Schreiber, also had his share of juvenile wildness. One time Rabbi Shimon was delivering a *derashah* (sermon), in which he bewailed his own shortcomings and that of the populace in the study of Torah and observance of *mitzvos*. He became very emotional and wept openly about his dereliction in serving G-d. During the sermon, his little son Shlomo was romping around in the courtyard of the shul, singing and playing with characteristic childhood abandon.

One of the worshipers approached him. "Do you think this is really proper?" he asked. "Your father is in the *shul*, broken-hearted and weeping, while you are out here, joyous and carefree."

The young man responded, "Why shouldn't he cry? After all, he has a son like me. But I have every reason to be joyous because look what kind of great father I have!"

Today
I shall smile
because . . .

_____

_____

_____

> Rabbi Yisrael of Salant said, "A child stands on his tiptoes or on a chair to try to show how tall he is." When someone tries to impress everyone with his greatness, that indicates how little he thinks of himself and how small he really feels.

Erev
Rosh Chodesh
[Eve of the
New Month]

SMILING EACH DAY

Although there were some people in the old country who did not observe *kashrus,* they were nevertheless reluctant to be exposed. In those days transgressing the Torah was something people felt ashamed of.

A proprietor of a non-kosher restaurant in Lemberg complained to Rabbi Jacob Orenstein that several Jewish customers had left the restaurant without paying their bills. Rabbi Orenstein felt that this reflected badly on Jews as a whole, who might be considered to be condoning thievery. In order to soften this perception, he therefore suggested that the next Jewish customer be given a bill that would include the unpaid bill of the others. In the event the customer protested, the proprietor was to suggest taking the matter to the local rabbi for adjudication.

The proprietor followed the recommendation, and the next Jewish customer was outraged at the enormity of his bill. The proprietor suggested taking the case before the rabbi. Knowing that to do so would be exposing himself before the rabbi as someone who had eaten in a non-kosher restaurant, the man paid the entire bill.

Today
I shall smile
because . . .

First Day of Rosh Chodesh Iyar

In Kelm, everyone was called to the Torah simply by his name, without any title. The only exceptions were people who had been benefactors to the community, who were called with an honorary title.

SMILING EACH DAY

A man rushed into a rabbi's study, irate with rage because of having being offended by another person. He demanded that the rabbi publicly rebuke this person from the pulpit. When the rabbi explained that this is not the way things are handled, but that he would speak privately to the person, the man objected. "Then I will handle it my own way!" he said. When the rabbi pointed out that it is a sin to seek revenge, the man protested, "A sin! It is the greatest *mitzvah* to punish that scoundrel."

Seeing that the man's rage precluded being discouraged from seeking revenge, the rabbi said, "Well if it is really a *mitzvah*, then it should be done properly as befits a *mitzvah*. It is wrong to do *mitzvos* without adequate preparation." The rabbi withdrew is *gartel* (sash worn by chassidim during prayer) from his *tallis* bag and said, "You must wear this so that you have the proper *kavannah* (meditation) for a *mitzvah*." He then led the man to the water basin and had him conduct the ritual handwashing. Then the rabbi said, "Now we must think of what the proper *berachah* (blessing) is for such a fine *mitzvah*. Hm! How about 'He has sanctified us with His Commandments and instructed us to punish those who offend us'?"

The angry man began to realize that his proposed action was not quite as worthy a deed as he had assumed, and agreed to place the matter in the rabbi's hands.

Today
I shall smile
because . . .

_____

_____

_____

We observe Shabbos because G-d rested on the seventh day of creation. If one observes Shabbos in order to rest up for the next week, one makes the Shabbos subordinate to the work week. G-d did not rest because of weariness. He made the Shabbos holy, and we should work the entire week to be able to have Shabbos as a day of spirituality and holiness.

Rosh Chodesh

SMILING EACH DAY

The Rebbe of Rhizin was an ascetic, eating barely enough to sustain life. One day he was visited by his *mechutan* (his son's father-in-law), the Rebbe of Kossov, who ate normally. When the Rebbe of Rhizin pushed his dish away after eating a mere morsel, the Rebbe of Kossov commented on this. The Rhiziner said that his *neshamah* (soul) had agreed to come down to this earth only if it were assured that it would not be bothered by earthly appetites. The Kossover then stopped eating, whereupon the Rhiziner asked him to please continue eating as usual.

The Kossover explained, "Friday night we recite *Shalom Aleichem*, welcoming the angels into our home, and after asking their blessing, we bid them farewell. Why do we send the heavenly angels on their way? Would it not be better if we asked them to remain with us throughout the Shabbos meal?

"Apparently," continued the Rebbe of Kossov, "it is most difficult for someone to eat when in the presence of angels who do not eat."

Today
I shall smile
because . . .

"You shall be complete with your G-d" (*Deuteronomy* 18:13). You must turn yourself over completely to G-d. If you think there are some things, other than those involving moral free choice, that you control and that are not in the hands of G-d, you are detached from Him (*Rabbi of Kotzk*).

SMILING EACH DAY

Imagine a research physicist having his work interrupted by people seeking advice on how to repair a malfunctioning motor. That is how one Talmudic scholar felt when people besieged him with various problems. He complained to Rabbi Yechezkel Landau of Prague (the *Noda B'Yehuda)* that it was not his position to serve as counselor to the community, and that his studies were suffering. He asked for advice on how to discourage people from bothering him.

Rabbi Landau said, "It is really quite simple. Some people who come for advice are well-to-do and are asking for your blessing on some new business venture, while others come because they are poor, and are looking for guidance on how to escape from poverty.

"If the people who consult you seem to be people of some means, ask them to lend you money. I assure you they will not come back very soon. On the other hand, if they are needy people, lend them some money. In the fear that you may ask them to return the money, they will avoid you.

"You will see that you will hardly be bothered at all."

Today
I shall smile
because . . .

_____

_____

_____

The animals asked the snake, "We kill for our food, because that is how we survive. Why do you kill, when you derive no benefit therefrom?" The snake answered, "Some sinners benefit from their sin. What does the slanderer gain from his sin?"

SMILING EACH DAY

In Slonim there was a wealthy man was tight-fisted and who gave very little to *tzedakah,* which resulted in his being unanimously disliked in the community. On the other hand, he would try to impose himself as the *chazan* (reader) at prayer services, and in addition to his miserliness, he had a raspy voice which irritated the worshipers. They complained to Rabbi Eizel.

Rabbi Eizel said, "Why, this man is equivalent to the Holy of Holies!"

To the bewildered worshipers Rabbi Eizel explained, "The Talmud states that Israelites are all holy. There is a person who gives of himself even though he is impoverished, and he is certainly holy. Then there is the person of wealth who refuses to give, yet he too is holy (*Chulin* 7b).

"This man fits both categories. As far as money is concerned, he has much and refuses to give, yet the Talmud says he is holy. But he is one who insists on leading the services and giving of his musical talents, of which he has none. Since he is musically impoverished but still wishes to give, that makes him holy. When you put both together, he is the 'Holy of Holies.' "

Today
I shall smile
because . . .

The *Maggid* of Trisk said, "Speech is the faculty which defines the human being (*Onkelos, Genesis* 2:7). If a person guards his speech to avoid all falsehood and *lashon hara,* he is the ultimate jewel of creation."

SMILING EACH DAY

There are many folk tales about the legendary prankster, Hershel of Ostropol. He was not a mythical figure, but a real person who was in attendance at the courtyard of Rabbi Baruch of Medziboz. Rabbi Baruch was prone to depressive moods, and it was Hershel's duty to cheer him up.

One time the chassidim sent for Hershel because the Rebbe was very dejected. Hershel asked him, "What is bothering the Rebbe so?"

Rabbi Baruch sighed. "What will be with me, Hershel, when I come before the Heavenly Tribunal on Judgment Day? I have no Torah, no *mitzvos,* and no good deeds to show for myself."

Hershel shrugged. "I don't know what the Rebbe will do, but I know what I will do.

"At the end of the *Amidah*, we say the verses that will enable us to remember our names on Judgment Day. Well, when the Tribunal asks me for my name, I will say, 'Moshe.' They will say, 'Not true. Your name is Hershel.' I will say, 'If you know, then why did you ask? Obviously, you are just trying to pick on me.' They will have to admit that I am right, and they will let me go."

Rabbi Baruch cracked a smile. Hershel had again done his job well.

Today I shall smile because . . .

_____

_____

_____

The Talmud says, "The pain of envy is more intense than that of a sharp thorn." 63). *Yet people will avoid being pricked by a thorn, but do not take precautions to avoid envy.*

SMILING EACH DAY

The Chassidic master Rabbi Meir of Premishlan once received a letter accompanied by a large sum of money. It was addressed to "The Great *Tzaddik* Rabbi Meir," with an expression of gratitude from a couple who had been childless and who felt that they had been blessed with a child as a result of Rabbi Meir's *berachah* (blessing). Rabbi Meir's children, who had often gone without food because of their poverty, rejoiced in this windfall, but Rabbi Meir said he must return the money because (1) it was intended for a *tzaddik*, which he was not, and (2) it was in payment for an effective *berachah*. He said, "I don't have such powers; hence, the money was sent under false pretenses, and to keep it would be dishonest."

The children pleaded with him to keep the money, and he finally consented to ask for a *halachic* ruling. The outcome of the ruling was that he was entitled to the money.

Rabbi Meir then said that he must ask his wife's opinion. She responded, "Whenever a *shaila* (a question about whether something has become non-kosher) occurs, you always say that even if it is ruled kosher, you do not wish to eat something whose *kashrus* had been questioned. If you have a question about this money, then you should not use it, even if the ruling declared it permissible."

Rabbi Meir returned the money.

Today
I shall smile
because . . .

A thief steals under the cloak of darkness, while a robber robs in broad daylight, but only from one who is alone and defenseless. A liar lies during daytime and nighttime, both privately and in front of throngs of people. He is the worst sinner of all.

SMILING EACH DAY

A rabbi who traveled from town to town collecting *tzedakah* for a charitable institution would visit the rabbi of each community and present his credentials and documents testifying as to the legitimacy of his institution and its need for support. The local rabbi would then provide an endorsement for him to collect money in the community.

In one city where the rabbi was of a rather new breed, his secretary told the man that the rabbi was available only on Wednesdays and Thursdays between 2 and 4 p.m. Since this was Sunday, the collector would have to wait three days and would not be able to make any solicitations in the meantime.

When the itinerant collector finally met with the community rabbi, he said, "Now I understand the wording we say in the Blessing After Meals. We express our gratitude to G-d for nurturing us and providing us, 'always, each day, at any time, and at every hour.' We may ask: once we have said 'always,' what need is there to further specify 'each day, at any time, and at every hour'?

"It must be that the Sages who formulated the *berachah* (blessing) wished to emphasize that when people are in need, G-d does not have specified office hours. He is available to them, 'each day, at any time, and at every hour.' "

We should emulate G-d.

Today
I shall smile
because . . .

_____
_____
_____

Think of your prayers as ascending all the way to heaven. If a space missile is launched only a few millimeters off course, it will deviate thousands of miles in its long journey and completely miss its target. Do not allow your thoughts and prayers to deviate the least bit, because they have a long course to traverse.

SMILING EACH DAY

It is often said that a specialist is likely to be a doctor from out of town. Various idioms attest to the phenomenon that people are not likely to accept the authority of someone whom they watched grow up from childhood on, and they may be more willing to accept someone of lesser competence who is unknown to them.

The famed Talmudic scholar Rabbi Meir Simchah of Dvinsk was born in Bialystok. When the position of rabbi of Bialystok was vacated, Rabbi Meir Simchah applied for it but was turned down. The community of Bialystok therefore lost the opportunity to have one of the generation's leading Torah authorities as its rabbi.

Rabbi Meir Simchah reacted to his rejection by commenting, "Why did the Israelites in the desert make the Golden Calf? If they had erroneously assumed that Moses had died, why did they not appoint Aaron to be their leader? Apparently, some people prefer to have an inanimate cow as their leader rather than someone who is competent but who grew up in their midst. They rejected Aaron, but were able to accept the Golden Calf."

Today
I shall smile
because . . .

It is said of the manna, "I will shower upon you bread from the Heavens" (*Exodus* 16:4). A person must know that even if he derives his bread by tilling the soil and planting seed, his food comes not from the earth, but is ordained from Heaven (*Rabbi Moshe of Kobrin*).

SMILING EACH DAY

The Talmud relates that one person began his budget by tithing for *tzedakah*. Some people relegate *tzedakah* only to the amount that remains after they have deducted expenses for all their "necessities." Of course, what constitutes a necessity is highly relative.

Rabbi Yisrael of Salant once solicited a prospective donor for an important charity. He was pleased to see that since his last visit, the man's economic condition had improved, for his home was lavishly furnished and richly decorated. Rabbi Yisrael was certain that he would appreciably increase his donation over that of the previous year, and was disappointed when the donation remained unchanged. The donor apologized for not being able to give more, claiming that his financial state did not permit it.

Rabbi Yisrael said, "Now I understand the meaning of the verse in *Psalms* (112:3): 'Wealth and riches are in his home, and his *tzedakah* remains forever.' This describes a person who fills his home with wealth, but whose *tzedakah* disbursements remain forever unchanged."

Today
I shall smile
because . . .

_____
_____
_____

If you see people speaking quietly among themselves, do not inquire about the subject of their conversation. Had they wished you to know, they would have spoken loudly. Thus, you will be causing them to lie to you (*Book of the Pious*).

SMILING EACH DAY

Some people may do the strangest things under the banner of piety. Rabbi Yisrael of Salant said that this is apt to be a most stubborn self-deception. He said that it is possible for someone to run to listen to a lecture on *mussar* (ethics), and on his way push others aside and be disrespectful of older people. One may not be aware of the irony in a situation where one violates basic ethics in the process of a passionate desire to listen to a lecture on ethics.

The Rabbi of Blendov knew that sermonizing has a limited impact, and he wished to impress his chassidim with the folly of such behavior. Once, while his chassidim were gathered in *shul*, he began running up and down the aisle and between the benches with his hands outstretched, as if in pursuit of someone. Finally, he ran to the huge bookcase which contained many volumes of Torah writings and slumped against it, sighing and out of breath.

The Rebbe then explained to the bewildered chassidim: "I saw the *yetzer hara* (evil inclination) here, and I tried to seize him. I ran after him up and down the aisles, but then he eluded me by jumping into the bookcase and hiding among the Torah volumes, where I can't find him."

One must be aware that the *yetzer hara* is very cunning and may try to conceal himself among Torah volumes.

Today
I shall smile
because . . .

If Jews all over the world would join hands, they would form a long chain that would reach all the way to the Divine throne, and they could then bring down abundant good for everyone (*The Maggid of Koznitz*).

SMILING EACH DAY

In the Yeshiva of Volozhin there was a time when the two great Talmudic scholars, Rabbi Yosef Dov of Brisk and the N'tziv, shared teaching duties. Their methodologies differed markedly, and disputes among their students gradually turned into hostility, which eventually led to a personal rift between these two great men. A panel of Torah authorities was convened to restore peace.

One of the authorities was the Maggid of Vilna, who stated, "This week's portion of the Torah, which relates the episode of Joseph and his brothers, is the most difficult for me to discuss.

"The first portions of *Genesis* contain the polar opposites of good and evil, personified by Adam versus the serpent, and Abel versus Cain. Then there is Noah versus his sinful generation, Abraham versus Pharaoh, and Abraham versus the Sodomites. These kinds of relationships make it easy for me to exalt the protagonist of good and condemn the protagonist of evil.

"This week's portion, however, relates the dispute of Joseph and his brothers, and we know from the *Midrash* that in spite of their actions, the fathers of the Tribes were all great *tzaddikim*. When two *tzaddikim* are in disagreement, I am left speechless."

Today
I shall smile
because . . .

_____
_____
_____

The Psalmist says, "I have chosen the path of faith" (*Psalms* 119:30). Faith is not an isolated act, but a path, a way through life. Faith that is not manifested in everything one does is not really faith (*Rabbi Yerucham of Mir*).

SMILING EACH DAY

In 1927 my father visited Montreal, and a man who hailed from Chernobyl and knew many of my father's relatives came to see him. Although this man was eighty-six years old, he claimed that he had a father who was residing in the home for the aged, and asked my father to please visit him.

"How old is your father?" my father asked.

"He lies about his age," the man said. "He claims he is only one hundred and twelve. We know he is one hundred and fourteen."

When my father visited the centenarian, he told my father that he remembered the *Maggid* of Chernobyl, who died in 1837. He then asked, "Was my *boychick'l* in to see you?" At age eighty-six, his son was still a "*boychik'l.*"

The Rabbi of Gur explained a *Midrash* with this phenomenon. The *Midrash* asks why the Torah refers to Joseph as a "boy" when he was seventeen (*Genesis* 37:2). Yet, the *Midrash* does not make a similar comment when Abraham refers to Isaac as a "boy," even though the latter was thirty-seven (*ibid.* 22:5).

"That is because," said the Rabbi of Gur, "a father always considers his son 'a boy' regardless of how old he is."

Today
I shall smile
because . . .

IYAR

אייר

"Each person should remain in his place, and a person should not leave his place" (on Shabbos) (*Exodus* 16:29). The Shabbos should teach one to remain humbly in his place, and not seek to elevate himself over others (*Rabbi Yisrael of Rhizin*).

SMILING EACH DAY

In the days of Rabbi Nachum of Grodno, the regional administrator was an ardent anti-Semite, thoroughly despised by all the Jews. Nevertheless, he respected Rabbi Nachum, knowing that he was a person of impeccable honesty and integrity.

On the civil New Year's day a committee of the community leaders, including Rabbi Nachum, came to wish the administrator a year of prosperity and success. He listened politely and then dismissed them, asking Rabbi Nachum to remain behind.

"I am surprised at you," he said. "I know that the Jews hate me. I know that they wish me nothing but evil and that their good wishes are nothing but window-dressing to cover up their hatred of me. But you, who are a man of uncompromising truth, how can you participate in such a sham?"

Rabbi Nachum responded, "I beg your excellency's pardon, but I was every bit sincere in my wishes. What would constitute success for you? Obviously, a promotion in the administrative hierarchy. You could be elevated to the government ministry, in which case you would be transferred to the capitol, and the Jews in Grodno would not be subject to your rule anymore. Your success will be our good fortune."

Today
I shall smile
because . . .

_____

_____

_____

If you know that your debtor does not have the money to repay his debt, do not press him. Think of how you would feel if you were in his position (*Rashi, Exodus* 22:24). Acts of benevolence require that one identify with the recipient of one's kindnesses (*Rabbi Chaim Shmulevitz*).

SMILING EACH DAY

Rabbi Yechezkel Landau of Prague (the *Noda B'Yehuda*) reprimanded his congregation for not being more diligent in charity and others benevolent acts. When his words did not appear to bear fruit, he put a lock on the yeshiva door and paraded around aimlessly in the street.

The amazed Jews of Prague approached Rabbi Yechezkel, asking for the meaning of this strange behavior.

"The Talmud tells us that the world rests on three pillars: Torah, the Divine service, and acts of benevolence (*Ethics of the Fathers* 1:2).

"If one of the three legs of a table is broken, the table can be propped up and used. If a second leg is broken, the only way the table can be used is by removing the remaining leg and putting the table on the ground.

"When the Sanctuary in Jerusalem was destroyed, we lost the pillar of Divine service. But Torah and acts of benevolence remained, and the world could be propped up on two of the three bases. However, since you are not performing any acts of kindness, the only remaining pillar is Torah. But one leg out of three is totally useless, and it is much better to do away with it entirely. That's why I decided to close the yeshiva and give up the study of Torah."

Today
I shall smile
because . . .

"The fragrant myrtle may grow among thorns, but it is still myrtle" (*Sanhedrin* 44a). Do not project blame for your defects onto your environment. You can be whatever you should be regardless of where you are.

SMILING EACH DAY

There is more to Torah than meets the eye.

The Gaon of Rogachov was once asked by a distraught mother for a *berachah* for her infant. Although the child was pleasant all week, Shabbos was just terrible! He was cranky all Shabbos and refused to eat. She had consulted doctors, but could get no help. She thought that perhaps the child was possessed by a *dybbuk* that resented Shabbos.

The Gaon railed, "How can you expect doctors to help when they are totally ignorant of Torah!

"The Talmus states that if someone owns an ox that habitually gores, he is liable for full damages it causes. If the ox gores only on Shabbos, he is liable for full damages only on Shabbos. Why? Because there must be something different about the way people dress on Shabbos that provokes the animal, who is otherwise docile during the rest of the week.

"Your child is very sensitive. On Shabbos you dress differently than all week, and the child is just not accustomed to this, and the strangeness irritates him. This Shabbos, just wear your weekday clothes. Next Shabbos wear your Shabbos clothes for one hour, and increase it every week. Let me know what happens."

The results were exactly as the Gaon predicted, and a few weeks later the woman reported that the child had adjusted to Shabbos beautifully.

It's all in the Torah, but it may take the Gaon of Rogachov to point it out.

Today
I shall smile
because . . .

_____

_____

_____

"How good are your tents, O Jacob, your dwelling places, O Israel" (*Numbers* 24:5). The tents of Jacob are the synagogues, and they are good only when they are regularly inhabited, rather than being empty buildings of architectural value only (*Rabbi Yaakov Yosef of Polnoah*).

SMILING EACH DAY

Rabbi David of Dinov once visited a hot springs spa and was shocked to discover that people who lived decent and modest lives at home had thrown off restraints and engaged in improper levity at the spa. This indicated to him that their proper behavior at home was due only to social pressure which kept them in line, and that in the absence of such control, they were morally defective at the core.

Rabbi David said, "Now I understand why the Talmud says that the hot springs are the residue of the boiling waters that spewed forth from the earth in the great Flood that destroyed the sinful population (*Sanhedrin* 108b).

"Someone learning the saga of Noah and the Flood might conclude that G-d was unduly severe and unjust in meting out so terrible a punishment to an entire generation. G-d therefore allowed these few hot springs to remain, so that anyone who observes the levity with which people behave there will understand that G-d was just and correct in His judgment."

Today
I shall smile
because . . .

A child had a nightmare in which he envisioned his family in a small boat on a stormy sea, and he was able to save either his father or his mother, but not both. His solution was to wake up. Even in real life, some problems which present unbearable stresses might go away if we just woke up (*Rabbi Ephraim Rosenblum*).

SMILING EACH DAY

We have previously referred to Rabbi Heschel of Cracow who was a child prodigy. Once he failed to get up in time for his early morning study session, and his father reprimanded him for his laziness.

The child apologized. "I couldn't help it," he said. "I awoke very early, and as I was about to get out of bed, the *yetzer hara* (evil inclination) said, 'It's too early, Heschel. You can still go back to sleep for a few minutes more.' I did, but then I overslept."

The father did not accept this excuse. "But why did you allow yourself to be duped by the *yetzer hara?*" he asked. "Obviously the *yetzer hara* was up much earlier than you in order to do his job! You should have reasoned that if it was not too early for the *yetzer hara* to be up, than it was not too early for you to be up either."

"There is no comparison," the young Heschel replied. "The *yetzer hara* could get up early because he doesn't have a *yetzer hara* who tells him to stay in bed. I do!"

Today
I shall smile
because . . .

_____
_____
_____

Joseph said to his father and brothers, "You shall dwell in Goshen and be close to me" (*Genesis* 45:10). When family members live too near one another, envy and bickering may separate them. Sometimes physical distance allows the family to stay together (*Rabbi Meir of Premishlan*).

SMILING EACH DAY

Our ethical works give the highest ratings to humility. In those situations where the dignity of the office required that the rabbis be distinct in their appearance, the rabbis complied. Where this was not essential, their dress was simple and their demeanor such that they could not be distinguished from anyone else.

Rabbi Yosef Zundel of Salant was the epitome of humility, and there are countless tales about his self-effacement. No less an authority than his star disciple, Rabbi Yisrael of Salant attests to this great man's humility.

In the days before indoor plumbing was common, water was fetched by water carriers. One day a woman, seeking the water carrier in the marketplace, approached Rabbi Yosef Zundel, and asked him if he was perhaps the water carrier. Rabbi Yosef Zundel replied that he would be glad to fetch water for her, and made several trips to the well for the woman. When she offered to pay him the regular fee, he told her that she could pay him next time.

Several days later she sought out the "water carrier" to pay him, and the townspeople then informed her that this was none other than the saintly sage. The woman apologized profusely to Rabbi Yosef Zundel for her ignorance. He laughed heartily, assuring the woman that no forgiveness was necessary, since he thoroughly enjoyed doing an act of *chesed* (kindness) for someone, and indeed thanked her for giving him the opportunity to do so. He explained that because of his academic position in the community, he did not have such opportunities, and was truly grateful that he was accorded the privilege of doing such a *mitzvah*.

Today
I shall smile
because . . .

Lag B'Omer

When Joseph advised Pharaoh to store grain during the years of plenty for the ensuing famine, Pharaoh exclaimed, "He has Divine spirit!" (*Genesis* 41:38). True wisdom can come only from a person blessed with Divine inspiration, as Job said, "Reverence of G-d is true wisdom" (*Job* 28:28), (*Rabbi Simchah Zissel of Kelm*).

SMILING EACH DAY

Rabbi Shimon Schreiber was a member of the parliament of the Austrian empire. He participated in various governmental meetings and used whatever influence he had to mitigate conditions for the Jews, who were often subject to oppressive discriminatory regulations. Great caution had to be taken not to offend the powers-that-be.

On one occasion a meeting with the emperor was scheduled for Shabbos. Since Rabbi Shimon's presence there was vital to the protection of Jewish interests and involved no infraction of Shabbos restrictions, he attended the meeting. He was unprepared for what transpired, however, because the emperor distributed complimentary cigars to all present. To refuse to accept the cigar could be interpreted as an affront to the emperor.

While everyone lit their cigars, Rabbi Shimon let his lie before him untouched. The emperor noted this, and asked for an explanation.

"Your highness," Rabbi Shimon responded, "it is not always that I am privileged to receive a gift from the emperor himself. Should I take something so precious and let it go up in smoke? I will keep this forever as a remembrance of this moment!"

Today
I shall smile
because . . .

_____

_____

_____

Fulfillment of the *mitzvos* is the only means to bridge the chasm between finite man and infinite G-d. Failure to perform any *mitzvah* at hand causes an insurmountable gap between man and G-d (*Path of the Just*).

SMILING EACH DAY

The wife of Rabbi Naftali of Ropschitz was a very irritable person, and there are many stories of how careful Rabbi Naftali was in not allowing himself to be provoked. His wife was an extremely devout person, however, and when she prayed she was oblivious to the world.

One time Rabbi Naftali removed the keys to the cupboard from her apron while she was deep in prayer, and added some *schmaltz* (chicken fat) to the *kugel*. That Shabbos the *kugel* was delicious. "See," she said, "you criticize me for being stingy. Look how fat the *kugel* is!"

"Yes," Rabbi Naftali said, "that is indeed a blessing, resulting from your profound prayers and my good deeds."

Another time, the kitchen help allowed the food to burn, and after eating the spoiled food she rebuked them sharply with some unpleasant words. Rabbi Naftali said to her softly, "My dear wife, I know how careful you are not to transgress a single word of the Torah, G-d forbid,. The Torah tells us, 'You shall eat and be satisfied and bless' (*Deuteronomy* 8:10). It is totally improper to eat and then curse!"

Today
I shall smile
because . . .

IYAR

אייר

"You shall eat and be satisfied and give thanks to G-d" (*Deuteronomy* 8:10). A person who learns to thank G-d for everything can be satisfied with whatever he has to eat. One who does not thank G-d will remain unsatiated even with a full stomach (*Rabbi Shlomo of Karlin*).

SMILING EACH DAY

The Talmud says that silence is an introduction to and a protector of wisdom (*Ethics of the Fathers* 3:17). Rabbi Raphael of Volozhin rarely spoke, and it was said of him: "Rabbi Raphael keeps his silence so long that it exhausts him; then he rests up a bit, and is again silent."

When the Rabbi of Gur returned from his first visit to Israel, the Rabbi of Kalisch greeted him, asking, "The Talmud says that the very air of the Holy Land makes one wise. Do you feel you acquired additional wisdom in the Holy Land?"

The Rabbi of Gur knew what direction this questioning was taking. He had visited with Chief Rabbi Kook, who was criticized by right-wing orthodoxy for sympathizing with non-religious Zionists. As a founder of Agudah, the Rabbi of Gur was an ardent supporter of the rebuilding of *Eretz Yisrael*, and he did not wish to be pulled into a controversial discussion about the settling of the land by non-observant people.

The Rabbi of Gur replied smilingly, "Of course I acquired wisdom in the Holy Land. As the Talmud says, silence is the protector of wisdom. What I learned in the Holy Land was to remain silent."

Today
I shall smile
because . . .

_____
_____
_____

"Let these words. . .rest upon your heart" (*Deuteronomy* 6:6). Why on the heart rather than in it? Because even if the Divine message is not immediately absorbed, a person's stubbornness and resistance may momentarily give way, and his heart is then open to teaching and discipline. The words that are on the heart can then enter (*Rabbi of Kotzk*).

SMILING EACH DAY

Public officials have always been suspected of tampering with public funds. This may be considered an occupational hazard, as the adage "power corrupts" indicates. Some other occupations are similarly suspect, and merchants of *esrogim* (citrons for Succos) have traditionally come under fire. My great-grandfather, the first Rebbe of Bobov, used to say, "If I should turn to selling *esrogim,* don't trust me either."

The townspeople of Sanz accused their community official of dipping into the public coffers for his personal use, and they complained to the *Tzaddik* of Sanz, demanding to have this man dismissed. The *Tzaddik* remarked: "Since the creation of the world, there has been a special seat of honor designated in *Gan Eden* (Paradise) for a public official who is scrupulously honest. Thus far that seat has been vacant. Do you really think that after thousands of years, the public official of the tiny village of Sanz should be the first one to occupy it?"

Isn't it sad that we must find ways to rationalize corruption in government?

Today
I shall smile
because . . .

"Bundle up the money in your hand" (*Deuteronomy* 14:25). Make sure that your money remains in your hand; i.e., that you have control over it. Some people lose control, and they are then in the hands of their money, since it controls them. Do not let money become your master (*Rabbi Meir of Premishlan*).

SMILING EACH DAY

Rabbi Joseph of Ostraha used to discourage people from taking upon themselves extra fast days as an atonement. He said that fasting to atone for a sin is similar to a taxation system: the wealthy members of the community who wield the power impose the taxes on the backs of the middle class and the poor. Those who have the wealth make those who have little or nothing pay.

That's how it is with fasting. Who is it that does the sinning? It is not the stomach. It is the eyes that look at things that they should not see, arousing a desire for forbidden things. It is the ears that listen to things they should not hear. It is the mouth that speaks gossip and slander. And how does one atone? By penalizing the stomach, which had nothing to do with the majority of the transgressions. Thus one emulates the unjust system of taxation.

If you wish to atone, place the burden where it belongs, just like taxation should rest more heavily on the wealthy. Restrain your eyes from looking at things that can arouse lust, restrain your ears from listening to obscenities and gossip, and restrain your tongue from speaking evil. In that way, the atonement corrects the defects.

Today
I shall smile
because . . .

_____
_____
_____

"Justice, justice, shall you pursue" (*Deuteronomy* 16:20). Why does the Torah repeat the word "justice"? To tell us that justice must be pursued by just methods. Even an end as noble as justice may not be implemented by unjust means (*Rabbi Bunim of P'shischa*).

SMILING EACH DAY

The Torah relates that Moses asked his father-in-law Jethro, who was a convert to Judaism, to remain with the Israelites and enter the Promised Land. He virtually pleaded with him, "Do not forsake us . . . you will be as eyes for us" (*Numbers* 10:31). This implies that he desired Jethro to be Israel's guide. Inasmuch as G-d was guiding Israel both physically and spiritually, why was Jethro's guidance necessary?

One of the rabbis explained that if one enters a shul on an average Shabbos, one is likely to see some people conversing, others pacing up and down, and little children running around unattended. The decorum in many synagogues is far from proper, and many Torah authorities have bewailed this state of affairs. In some synagogues a special blessing is recited for those who refrain from talking during services.

However, if for some reason a non-Jew is in attendance — for a bar mitzvah, perhaps, or some other occasion — things change radically. Everyone prays, everyone is silent, and children sit with their parents. "Let's not give non-Jews the impression that we have no respect for our place of worship."

That is what Moses meant when he asked Jethro to remain. "As a convert, Jews will behave better in your presence. Please stay with us and 'be all eyes,' just look at us. That's all we need."

Today
I shall smile
because . . .

IYAR

אייר

Whenever you see someone performing any *mitzvah.* stand up for him as a sign of reverence (*Book of the Pious,* 580).

SMILING EACH DAY

Following World War I, the negotiations regarding redrawing national boundaries were very complicated. As usual, various nations claimed hegemony over certain areas, and each side set forth what it considered to be its legitimate claims. These were invariably conflicting, and were often resolved in a manner that was unsatisfactory to everyone.

The border negotiations between Russia and Lithuania were conducted by two Jews, Adolph Jaffa representing Russia and Shimon Rosenbaum representing Lithuania. The two met to discuss reasonable guidelines on resolving the border disputes between these two countries.

Shimon Rosenbaum said, "Adolph, everyone else may have difficult problems with claims and counter-claims. We have a criterion that is infallible and can quickly resolve the problem.

"We simply go from village to village and ask Jews to read the first verse from *Song of Songs*. Wherever they say, '*Sir Hasirim Aser LeSlomo*,' that is Lithuania, and where they begin saying, '*Shir Hashirim Asher LeShlomo*,' that is where Russia begins!" (Lithuanian Jews were unable to pronounce the sound "sh" and said "s" instead.)

Today
I shall smile
because . . .

_____
_____
_____

"Eat it (the manna) because today is the Divine Shabbos" (*Exodus* 16:25). Perhaps "it" refers to the word Shabbos rather than to the *manna*. In other words, engulf the Shabbos as if it were food, and incorporate it so that it becomes part of your very person (*Rabbi Hirsh of Rimanov*).

SMILING EACH DAY

Rabbi Aryeh Leib, author of the *Ketzos HaChoshen*, engaged in *halachic* polemics with Rabbi Jacob of Lisa, and this resulted in a degree of personal antagonism between the two. When Rabbi Aryeh Leib was widowed, he asked a matchmaker to approach Rabbi Jacob and ask for his daughter's hand in marriage. The matchmaker exclaimed, "Why would you wish to marry the daughter of your sharpest adversary?"

Rabbi Aryeh Leib responded, "We learn everything from the Torah. Pharaoh gave Joseph the daughter of Potiphar as a wife (*Genesis* 41:45). But Potiphar had been Joseph's master and had thrown him into the dungeon for alleged indecent behavior. Why would Joseph wish to marry his daughter?

"This is because Joseph knew that Potiphar, as his father-in-law, would certainly never bring up his past as a slave and a prisoner, information which would be harmful to his daughter.

"The best way to disarm an adversary," Rabbi Aryeh Leib concluded, "is to marry his daughter."

Today
I shall smile
because . . .

"The Israelites walked on dry land through the Sea" (*Exodus* 15:19). They came to the realization that walking on dry land is no less a miracle than walking through the sea. All of nature is one huge Divine miracle (*Rabbi Elimelech of Lizensk*).

SMILING EACH DAY

Rabbis in the old country did not get lifetime contracts. In the town of Mohilev, there was a prominent citizen who dominated the community by virtue of his wealth. Having had some training in the Talmud when attending yeshiva in his youth, he fancied himself a Talmudic scholar and *halachic* authority, and entered into *halachic* disputes with the community rabbi. Many rabbis, including the famous *Malbim,* had to leave the position because they could not carry out what they felt were their rabbinical duties in the face of this man's opposition. Solomon's observation that wealthy people are prone to have a great deal of *chutzpah* was more than justified.

For a long time the rabbinic position in Mohilev remained vacant. Every candidate was rejected by this powerful person.

The community then appealed to Rabbi Yosef Dov of Brisk to help them find a rabbi. Rabbi Yosef Dov responded, "Mohilev will never have a rabbi. You have an influential community member who has veto power and who wishes to feel superior to the rabbi. In order to achieve this, he will approve only of a rabbi who is less learned in Talmud than he is. You will never find a rabbi with such qualifications."

Today
I shall smile
because . . .

_____
_____
_____

"You shall love your neighbor as yourself" (*Leviticus* 19:18). Although there are parts of yourself that you value more than others — the eyes more than the toes, for example — you nevertheless protect the latter, too, from harm. That is how you must care for all people, even if some are less worthy than others (*The Holy Yehudi*).

SMILING EACH DAY

A man once approached Rabbi Shlomo of Radomsk, complaining that the local *shochet* (ritual slaughterer) was not sufficiently diligent in the study of Torah, as befits a person who has the responsibility of ritual slaughter. "He is my next-door neighbor," he said, "and I have been observing him every Shabbos. No sooner does he finish a meal than he goes directly to bed. I have never once seen him pick up a *sefer* (Torah volume) and study."

Rabbi Shlomo's eyes brightened. "How wonderful! Thank you for this good news. I have always harbored misgivings," he continued, "about eating from food that was slaughtered on Saturday night or early Sunday. You see, the most important thing about a *shochet* is that his hand must be firm and steady. If the *shochet* spends all of Shabbos studying, he may not have sufficient rest, and would therefore be weary right after Shabbos. In a state of exhaustion, his hand might be unsteady, and he might not function properly.

"Now that you have assured me that he rests on Shabbos, I will be able to eat from Sunday's *shechitah* with peace of mind."

Today
I shall smile
because . . .

Ideally, one should avoid doing wrong simply because it is wrong. But if one avoids doing wrong purely for selfish reasons, realizing that wrong acts will ultimately hurt him, although he may not have the purest of motivations, that too is praiseworthy (*Rabbi of Karlin*).

SMILING EACH DAY

Chassidic masters often warned against self-deception. The Rabbi of Kotzk cited the verse in the Scriptures which states that one may not deceive another person (*Leviticus* 25:17) and commented, "That is the letter of the law. The next step one must take is that one should not deceive oneself."

Rabbi Naftali of Ropschitz said that if a person leads others to believe he is fasting while he eats in secret, he is deceiving others who may think him to be a *tzaddik*. However, if he really does fast, he may be deceiving himself that he is a *tzaddik,* and that is even worse.

Rabbi Wolf of Strikov cited the verse in *Proverbs* (17:28), "A fool who keeps his silence may be thought to be wise," and asked, "Why does Solomon recommend this? Is it not wrong to mislead others and make them think one is wise when one is really a fool?"

He answered, "A fool who speaks a great deal undoubtedly thinks he is wise, and wishes to impress others with his wisdom. It is far better that he be silent and deceive others rather than speak and deceive himself."

Today
I shall smile
because . . .

_____
_____
_____

People go early to the market to take advantage of bargains before they are sold to others. That is the kind of zeal one should have in performing *mitzvos,* seizing every possible opportunity (*Rabbi of Karlin*).

SMILING EACH DAY

Chassidic teachings emphasize joy, vigor, and youthfulness. Advanced age is no excuse for being old. Sincere belief in G-d and dedication to the Divine will should renew and restore energy, and serve as a spiritual fountain of youth, as the Scripture states, "Those who have hope in G-d *exchange* their energies" (*Isaiah* 40:31); i.e., their weariness is replaced by vigor.

Rabbi Baruch of Medziboz quoted the verse referring to the attack of Amalek on the Israelites, "You were weary and exhausted and did not fear G-d" (*Deuteronomy* 25:18). He commented that the lack of fear of G-d can refer to the Israelites as well as to Amalek. One who is truly G-d-fearing does not become weary and exhausted.

A group of young chassidim had congregated to listen to their Rebbe's teachings. Suddenly a spry oldster pushed himself through the crowd, shoved aside the younger people, and seated himself on the bench closest to the Rebbe. As the others marveled at his physical prowess, he triumphantly exclaimed, "You think I am an old man of 96. Well, that is where you are mistaken. I am three young men of 32!"

Today
I shall smile
because . . .

"You shall seek G-d and you shall find Him, but you must search for Him wholeheartedly" (*Deuteronomy* 4:29). Even after you have found G-d, you must continue to search for Him wholeheartedly. G-d is infinite, and you should not be so complacent as to think that you have already found Him. Keep searching, because there is so much more (*Rabbi of Kotzk*).

SMILING EACH DAY

A chassid came to the Rabbi of Kuzmir, presented him with a list of sins he had committed, and informed him that to atone for these, he had done penance by fasting frequently and tormenting himself by sleeping on the ground and putting pebbles inside his shoes. He wondered whether all of this self-flagellation was sufficient to achieve forgiveness for his sins.

The Rabbi listened intently and studied the list of sins carefully. Then he remarked, "Yes, you have done a complete job. Truly a complete job."

The chassid was pleased that the rabbi appeared to have approved of his penance. "Then I am forgiven?" he asked.

"Not quite," the rabbi said. "You began by committing sins to ruin your *neshamah* (soul). Having done that, you then directed your attention toward ruining your body as well. That is a complete job."

According to Luzatto and other ethicists, atonement does not require self-torment and flagellation. Rather, one should understand the gravity of transgressing the Divine will, appreciate how injurious this is to oneself, and make a concerted effort to refine his character so that he is no longer likely to repeat the improper behavior. Self-flagellation can mislead one to think that he has achieved atonement, whereas nothing in his character may have changed.

Today
I shall smile
because . . .

"G-d made man just, but they have sought complicated calculations" (*Ecclesiastes* 7:29). Justice is simplicity. Man's cunning and calculations are deviant in that he tries to circumvent the simplicity of justice with complicated arguments (*Rabbi Simchah Zissel of Kelm*).

SMILING EACH DAY

Rabbi Yosef Dov of Brisk was once called to a community where the position vacated by the rabbi had been filled by two opponents, each a candidate of dissenting parties. The town could not afford to support two rabbis, and neither group wished to yield. The heated dispute soon obscured all other concerns, and people neglected their jobs and businesses to turn all their energies into the escalating quarrel.

Rabbi Yosef Dov addressed the community, saying, "I have now come to understand why, when the Israelites in the desert grumbled about having nothing to eat but the *manna*, G-d's response to Moses was, 'Assemble seventy of the nation's elders, and I will install them as leaders to share the burden with you' (*Numbers* 11:16). What relevance did this have to the Israelites' dissatisfaction with the *manna*? How would this quell their grumbling?

"But," continued Rabbi Joseph Dov, "we can now see that this strategy was an excellent one. Just imagine trying to nominate six elders from each tribe to become the leaders. A dispute will immediately arise as to which six should be chosen. Support groups for each will form. Within a short time the argument will become so intense that people will become totally distracted from their dissatisfaction with the *manna*."

Today
I shall smile
because . . .

When someone is in rage, turn your eyes away from him. Even observing rage is harmful to one's character (*Book of the Pious,* 1126).

SMILING EACH DAY

It is customary on Shavuos night to recite the *Tikkun*, which is a compendium of excerpts from each portion of the Torah, Scripture, Talmud, etc.

One time the *Maggid* of Dubno spent Shavuos with the Gaon of Vilna. While the Gaon of Vilna said the *Tikkun*, the *Maggid* studied the Talmud. "Why are you not saying the *Tikkun*?" the Gaon asked.

The *Maggid* answered, "A merchant places samples of his merchandise in his store window, to inform the customers of what he has to sell. When customers request one of these displayed items, he then sells it out of stock.

"It only makes sense to display samples if you have stock to back them up. What *Tikkun* consists of is small excerpts or 'samples' of various portions of the Torah. You, Gaon, have abundant stock, so you can say the *Tikkun* and display the samples. Unfortunately, I do not have such stock, so I have no right to display samples."

Today I shall smile because . . .

_____
_____
_____

Sometimes it appears to me that if I pray in solitude, I can meditate much more profoundly. Nevertheless, prayer with a *minyan* (communal prayer) with less meditation is superior to prayer in solitude with greater meditation (*Rabbi of Karlin*).

SMILING EACH DAY

Chassidic masters did not approve of people who tried to "uproot" their undesirable character traits. Said one, "That is like standing in a dark room with a big stick and trying to drive the darkness out the window. All one needs to do is light a candle, and the darkness will leave by itself. Bad traits are darkness, while Torah and *mitzvos* are light. Bring a little light into your life, and the darkness will disappear."

Some schools of thought supported this position by quoting the verse in *Psalms,* "Avoid evil and do good" (*Psalms* 34:15), which appears to mean that one must first divest oneself of bad traits in order to be able to do good. Chassidim, however, interpreted the verse thus: Avoid evil. How? By doing good.

A chassid of Lublin once confronted a young man who claimed that he was trying to break his *yetzer hara* (evil inclination).

"Did it ever occur to you, young man," he asked, "that if you succeed in breaking your *yetzer hara* in half, you will then have two *yetzer haras* instead of one?"

Today
I shall smile
because . . .

"Moses was a most humble person" (*Numbers* 12:3). *Rashi* comments, "Humble and tolerant." Some people affect humility, but they are sorely vexed by this adopted attitude. Moses was truly humble, because he tolerated his humility well (*Rabbi of Kotzk*).

SMILING EACH DAY

In czarist Russia, the *poritz* (feudal lord) had unlimited powers over his vassals. These *pritzim* had little to do with their time, and sometimes they would make sport by tormenting their Jewish vassals, pressuring them to convert to their faith.

One *poritz* repeatedly urged one of his Jewish vassals to convert. When his efforts proved futile, he tried to exploit the Jew's poverty by offering him a sum of money as an incentive. "If you will accept my religion," he said, "I will give you a handsome reward."

The Jew shrugged his shoulders. "Your excellency," he said, "I am but a simple man. I never had any formal education, and I know only what my father taught me.

"My father was a porter and earned his livelihood by delivering packages with a horse and wagon. He told me, 'If someone wishes to trade horses with you and offers you a sum of money along with the trade, you can be sure he is giving you an old nag.' "

Today
I shall smile
because . . .

_____
_____
_____

> "Know G-d in all your ways, and He will lead you in a just path" (*Proverbs* 3:6). The world is so confusing and complicated that one can never be sure what is just by relying solely on one's own reasoning. If one sincerely seeks to do the will of G-d, He will guide one in a just path (*Rabbi Yerucham of Mir*).

First Day of Shavuos
[In the Land of Israel Shavuos is only celebrated one day.]

SMILING EACH DAY

When the Chafetz Chaim reached the age of eighty, he gathered his family and disciples to celebrate his birthday.

"It is not my custom," the sage said, "to celebrate birthdays. However, this is a special occasion for which I am grateful to G-d.

"When I was thirty-six, I wrote a book on the evils of *lashon hara* (slander or gossip). I based my book on the verses in *Psalms* which read, 'Who is a man who desires life, who loves long life in order to see the good? Guard your tongue from evil, and your lips from speaking evil' (*Psalms* 34:13-14). The implication is that if one refrains from *lashon hara*, one will merit long life.

"I was always worried that if I were to die young, there would be those who would mock and say, 'See what championing the restraint of speech has achieved for him? Nothing!' And in this way there would be, G-d forbid, a *chilul Hashem* (desecration of the Divine Name) and people would not take the sin of *lashon hara* seriously. Now that I have reached a respectable old age, I need no longer have this worry. On the contrary, G-d's gift to me of an advanced age supports my thesis, and that is reason to celebrate."

Today
I shall smile
because . . .

Second Day of Shavuos
[Yizkor]

The sages of *mussar* (ethics) say, "Do not ask a person a question if you think he is unlikely to give you a truthful answer, because you are then an accessory to his sin of lying."

SMILING EACH DAY

Knowledge of the physical sciences was never considered to be a deterrent from Torah study. Some of our greatest sages, from the Talmudic era to our own generation, were extremely well versed in mathematics and physics. Works on these subjects by Ibn Ezra and the Gaon of Vilna are extant and demonstrate their extensive knowledge. Indeed, the Gaon said, to the degree that one is lacking in knowledge of mathematics, one lacks tenfold in knowledge of Torah.

The *haskalah* (Enlightenment) movement tried to undermine traditional Judaism and the study of Torah by introducing secular studies in all Jewish educational institutions, and they tried to use mathematics as a way of getting a foot in the door. To this the rabbinic leaders objected. While they had no problem with the study of mathematics, they knew this was only a ruse to gain influence over the *cheder* (classroom).

One member of the *haskalah* movement argued with the rabbis, saying that the knowledge of mathematics would not affect anyone's Jewishness in the least. One of the rabbis challenged him: "Then let me ask you a simple arithmetic question. How many days is it today in the counting of the *Omer* (days between Pesach and Shavuos)?"

When the *maskil* was unable to answer, the rabbi said, "See, with all your enlightenment, you don't even know simple Jewish arithmetic."

Today
I shall smile
because . . .

_____
_____
_____

When we were infants, we cried and fought over things we now recognize as trivia. As we mature and acquire more knowledge, we recognize that things we thought to be important even as adults were also really trivia. We would be wise to recognize this in the present rather than to see it only in retrospect.

SIVAN

8

סיון

SMILING EACH DAY

Some of our greatest rabbis suffered *tzoros* (troubles) in their respective communities, and many had to change positions when conditions became intolerable.

Rabbi David Eibeschitz, author of major *halachic* and homiletic works, was rabbi of the town of Soroka. Not only was he not paid a living wage, but he also met severe opposition in implementing the Torah regulations regarding commerce and education.

When the position of rabbi in Yasi, Romania, was vacated, Rabbi Eibeschitz applied and was accepted. When he left Soroka, even those who had been his most ardent adversaries gathered for the send-off.

When the procession reached the outskirts of town, Rabbi Eibeschitz dismounted from the coach, turned towards the city, and said, "Soroka, you are one of the most beautiful cities of the world."

The community officials asked him, "Why, then, were you always so critical of our town?"

"You don't understand," he said. "Now that you are all out here, Soroka is a beautiful town. It is while you are in the city that it becomes an impossible place."

Today
I shall smile
because . . .

If a person saw someone hauling trash in a Rolls Royce, he would certainly say, "How foolish to use such a precious car for such a coarse purpose." The power of speech is a precious Divine gift to man, to be used for prayer and Torah study. How foolish to use it for gossip and profane talk (*Rabbi Simchah Zissel of Kelm*).

SMILING EACH DAY

Jewish history is replete with Torah scholars who are also well versed in other fields of knowledge. Torah and science are not incompatible, and the opposition to secular studies arose only when the latter was introduced with the intent of diminishing Torah study and imposing a secular way of life on Jewish youth.

One *maskil* (representative of the "Enlightenment" movement that sought to infiltrate the *cheders* and yeshivos) once argued with one of the rabbis about the need for secular studies. "Why are you so opposed to the teaching of science? Why do we not find people like Saadia Gaon, the Rambam, the Ralbag, the Ramban, and others who were knowledgeable in the sciences, among today's Torah personages?"

The rabbi responded, "I too have been bothered by that. Why are you so opposed to the intensive study of Torah? Why do we not find people like Saadia Gaon, the Rambam, the Ralbag, the Ramban, and others who were great Torah scholars among today's scientists?"

Today
I shall smile
because . . .

_____
_____
_____

People in the last days of life often say, "My one regret is that I did not spend more time with my family," or "My one regret is that I did not spend more time studying Torah." No one has ever regretted not having spent more time at the office. Why postpone getting wise until the end?

SMILING EACH DAY

After delivering a fiery sermon in one of the cities he visited, the *Maggid* (preacher) of Kelm, was confronted by the head of the community, a clean-shaven man who not only refused to give the *Maggid* an honorarium for his sermon, but also sharply criticized him for the content. The *maggid* had rebuked the people for their laxity in observance of Torah and *mitzvos*; he now realized that his sermon had been on target and that this man's insolence was defensive.

The *Maggid* replied, "As I came into this village, I was greeted by an ox. 'What reason do you have to greet me?' I asked. 'I have no reason to relate to you.' The ox answered, 'Yes, you do, you eat of my meat.'

"I was subsequently greeted by a cow, and when I asked what relationship she had to me, the cow said, 'You drink my milk.' I was then greeted by a goat, who said, 'We share a common feature, because you have a beard and I too have a beard.'

"But then I was greeted by a hog. 'This is too much,' I said. 'You give me nothing. I don't eat your meat and I don't drink your milk. You don't have a beard like I do. Why should I relate to you?' "

Today
I shall smile
because . . .

SIVAN

11

סיון

It is not enough to do *teshuva* on the sins we know we have committed. We must pray to G-d to help us realize the wrongs we have done of which we are unaware, so that we can do teshuva for them as well (*Rabbi Nachman of Breslov*).

SMILING EACH DAY

There are divergent opinions about prayer. Some people pray very slowly, concentrating on every single word, while others pray very rapidly.

One person was asked why he prayed so hurriedly, and he said, "If you drive your wagon slowly through the streets, dogs may jump into it, whereas if it goes fast, they can't. Similarly, if I pray slowly and meditate, the chances of improper thoughts creeping into my mind are greater. When I pray fast, there is no time for improper thoughts to intrude."

Someone who advocated slow prayer rebutted, "But what do you do if the dog is already in the wagon before you start?"

One chassid was asked by his Rebbe for an account of his daily schedule. He proudly related that he regularly awoke at dawn, and before *Shacharis* (morning service) recited the entire *Tehillim* (Psalms).

The Rebbe was not impressed and shrugged his shoulders in wonderment. "Amazing," he said. "It took King David seventy years to compose the *Tehillim*, and you can go through the entire *Tehillim* in just one hour!"

Today
I shall smile
because . . .

_____
_____
_____

The Torah states, "Do not steal, murder, or commit adultery." Clearly G-d knows how base a person can be, yet from that same person He demands, "You shall be holy." We cannot rationalize our behavior as due simply to our physical cravings, because we can be their master (*Rabbi Yerucham of Mir*).

SMILING EACH DAY

Many *tzaddikim* used to devote their precious time to collecting money for needy families or to ransoming anyone who had been imprisoned in a dungeon by a *poritz* (feudal lord) for being unable to pay his rent. *Tzedakah* was given such highest priority that it superseded other *mitzvos*.

Collecting funds is not a thankful task. Some people resent being asked to contribute and may slam the door in the collector's face. The *Tzaddik* of Sanz, whose *tzedakah* efforts are legendary, once said to his son, "When you ask someone for a donation and you are refused, you must judge the person favorably. He may be in serious financial straits and is reacting out of his distress. If you harbor resentment against him, you are counteracting the *mitzvah* of collecting *tzedakah* by having feelings of hostility towards a fellow Jew, which is sinful."

One *tzaddik* met with a diatribe of insults and curses when he asked someone for a donation. He listened calmly, then very quietly said, "Thank you. The insults and curses I will accept for myself, but what are you going to give for the poor?"

Today
I shall smile
because . . .

Wherever there is strife, there is an open invitation to Satan to cause trouble. Where peace prevails, no harm can occur. G-d so loves peace that He will forgive all sins if only people will live in true harmony (*Rabbi Chaim Shmulevitz*).

SMILING EACH DAY

When the chassidic movement began to blossom, there were many scholars who feared that it would be a populist movement, which, in order to attract adherents, might be lax in demanding rigid observance of *halachah*. The movement had begun not long after the Shabbtai Tzvi (false messiah) debacle, and the scholars were also afraid that the chassidic emphasis on Kabbalah might lead to similar defections. The early *Misnagdim* (opponents of Chassidim) were absolutely sincere in their opposition. When Chassidus proved itself to be faithful to *halachah*, the differences between the two groups took on the flavor of feud for the sake of feuding, and people who enjoyed fighting found a banner under which to do battle.

In the *beis medrash* of the Chassdic master, Rabbi Mordechai of Lechovitz, a group of young *Misnagdim* entered, and it was clear that they had not come with benign motivations, but rather to see what chassidic practices they could observe to provide fuel for their mockery. Some of the chassidim wished to usher them out.

Rabbi Mordechai held them back. "Every creature was created to give pleasure to some other creature. I was also created to provide joy to others. If these people can rejoice by poking fun at me, why should I deny them this source of happiness? Who knows but that they may have little else to be cheerful about."

Today I shall smile because . . .

_____

_____

_____

Only a person with a great mind can harbor opinions that are opposed to his own. A small mind has no room for dissenting opinions. If you see someone who cannot tolerate a dissenting opinion, you know how limited his intellect is (*Chabad*).

SMILING EACH DAY

One of the practices thoroughly condemned by Jewish ethics is cursing. The Biblical villain, Bilaam, is maligned in the Scriptures because of his proclivity toward cursing.

Rabbi Naftali of Ropschitz did not receive a huge wage from his community, and when there was not enough food for the children, his angry wife told him to curse the people who were indifferent to their plight. Rabbi Naftali opened the door and shouted, "My dear brethren! May G-d bless you with long life, good health, and much *nachas*."

To his wife, Rabbi Naftali explained, "Our teacher, Moses, was tormented by the Israelites for forty years, and his only wish — to be allowed to enter the Promised Land — was denied him because of their sins. While he did rebuke them and discipline them for their misbehavior, he lovingly blessed them before his death, on the threshold of their entry into the Promised Land."

My father told me that in his home no malediction was ever allowed to be uttered. When my grandmother was overcome with anger and was so provoked that she wished to curse someone, she would say, "May he have fresh, soft bread and hard butter!"

Well, everyone has a boiling point.

Today
I shall smile
because . . .

"Who is wise? He who learns from every-one" (*Ethics of the Fathers* 4:1). A person is always in contact with other people, and if he learns from everyone, he is always learning. Someone who is constantly learning is truly wise (*Rabbi Bunim of P'shischa*).

SMILING EACH DAY

One of the most common psychological defenses is to project blame or fault on everything and everyone else, rather than to examine the corrections one needs to make in himself. This concept is similar to the story of Izak Reb Yekelas', who dreamt that there was a huge treasure buried in a distant city. When he got there and began digging, someone told him of a dream that there was a treasure buried beneath the floor of the hut of Isak Reb Yekelas'. He then returned home to find the treasure under his own floor.

Just as we may have great resources within ourselves yet look for them elsewhere, so too the reason for one's problems may lie within himself, but he may look for them elsewhere.

A young man came to P'shischa, and when the Rebbe asked him why he had come, he said that he needed to do *teshuvah*. "Good," the Rebbe said, "but you can do *teshuvah* back at home."

"I came to find the reason for my misbehavior," the young man said.

"So what makes you think the reason for your misbehavior is here in P'shischa?" the Rebbe asked.

Today
I shall smile
because . . .

_____
_____
_____

The prescribed prayers in the *Siddur* are mandatory, but it is extremely helpful that in addition a person have a dialogue with G-d just as one would converse with a trusted friend, baring one's soul and expressing one's needs (*Rabbi Nachman of Breslov*).

SMILING EACH DAY

While Solomon's wisdom is legendary, that of Rabbi Yechezkel Landau (the *Noda B'Yehudah*) was not far behind.

Two people entered Rabbi Landau's study, one dressed as a merchant and the other as a porter. The latter claimed he was really the merchant and had hired the other man, a porter, to drive him with his merchandise to Prague. On the way, he claimed, the porter had robbed him at knifepoint and forced him to exchange clothes. The man dressed as the merchant said, "Rabbi, this man is crazy. I hired him as a porter, and he thought up this absurd story." Both men stuck to their stories.

Rabbi Landau told them to return very early the next morning. Then he instructed the *shammes* (attendant) to keep them waiting and to tell them repeatedly, "Just a few minutes more." In this way they were kept waiting several hours, and while the man dressed as the porter paced up and down impatiently, the one dressed as the merchant sat quietly, nodding off.

Suddenly Rabbi Landau opened his study door and shouted, "Hey, porter, over here!" The one dressed as the merchant, who had been nodding off, abruptly jumped up and responded.

The case was solved.

Today
I shall smile
because . . .

If someone loses money and then has a windfall, he may still be sad, because without the loss he would have had still more money. But if someone is stimulated by a spiritual setback to increase his efforts to gain spiritually, the loss itself is converted into something positive (*Rabbi Simchah Zissel of Kelm*).

SMILING EACH DAY

While anyone who was not exposed to Torah education in his youth cannot be held responsible for his parents' dereliction, when he reaches the age of reason, he should avail himself of learning. The search for truth should be an adequate stimulus, said the Rabbi of Kotzk, and neglecting it is due to laziness.

The Rabbi related the following story. The Prophet Elijah encountered a fisherman and asked him how he was faring in the pursuit of Torah and service of G-d.

"I know nothing about those things," the fisherman said. "I was never taught them in my childhood."

"I see you have a fine net for fishing," Elijah said. "Who taught you how to make one?"

"I had no choice," the fisherman said. "I had to find a way to earn a living, so I watched other fisherman until I learned how."

"If you had realized that spiritual life is as vital as physical life," Elijah said, "you would have found a way to learn that too."

Today
I shall smile
because . . .

_____

_____

_____

If both a friend and an enemy give you advice, you can be sure that the enemy wishes to mislead you. When an idea comes into one's mind, one should ask, "What is the source of this idea, the yetzer tov (good inclination) or the yetzer hara (evil inclination)?" (*Chabad*).

SMILING EACH DAY

The Gaon of Vilna had great respect for Rabbi Jacob Kranz, the famed *Maggid* (preacher) of Dubno, who was never lacking for a parable. With some of his parables, he was able to resolve difficult passages in the Talmud. His genius was that he never had to prepare, but was able to produce parables spontaneously.

One time Rabbi Jacob came directly to the Gaon after arriving in Vilna. The Gaon welcomed him warmly. "Please tell me a parable," he said.

Rabbi Jacob, who was weary from the long trip, responded, "A man once went to the market to buy a goat. On his return home his wife tried to milk the goat, but no milk was forthcoming. 'What kind of freak did you let them sell you? It may look like a goat, but it certainly does not act like a goat.'

" 'Don't worry,' the husband said. 'It is a very fine goat. However, she was not fed and watered in the marketplace, and she is very weary from the long trip. Give her something to eat and drink, and let her rest up a bit, and she will give you all the milk you want.' "

Today
I shall smile
because . . .

"A conceited fool has no desire for understanding, but only wants to express his own view" (*Proverbs* 18:2). By refusing to listen to another person's opinion, one makes a very uncomplimentary statement about himself.

SMILING EACH DAY

The Talmud demands that a person judge everyone in a favorable light, giving everyone the benefit of the doubt. Some of the *tzaddikim* carried this principle to extremes, such as the rabbi whose clock was stolen.

"Where is the clock?" his wife asked.

The rabbi shrugged his shoulders. "Some *tzaddik* came and took it."

"What!" she exclaimed. "A thief, and you call him a *tzaddik*!"

The rabbi responded, "Who knows? He probably needs it to wake up in the morning in time for *davening* (services)."

Rabbi Zalman, who was a disciple of the Gaon of Vilna, once returned from the bathhouse minus his shirt. "Where is your shirt?" his wife asked.

"Someone in the bath house accidentally mistook my shirt for his," Rabbi Zalman said.

"Well, if he exchanged shirts, then why don't you have his?" she asked.

"I guess that in his hurry to get home, he must have forgotten to leave it behind," Rabbi Zalman said.

Today
I shall smile
because . . .

_____
_____
_____

Should you meet a person who, having sipped from the wells of wisdom, already believes himself to be wise, you may conclude from his arrogance that he has not drawn from the right well, or has not done so in the right way (*Rabbi Samson Raphael Hirsch*).

SMILING EACH DAY

The chassidic works of *Chabad* contain a great deal of Torah philosophy, with many intricacies and abstract concepts. The philosophical arguments are most enchanting, and the logical progression from concept to concept is convincing. One Friday night, a group of *Chabad* chassidim sat in a *beis medrash* illuminated by candlelight, discussing the *Tanya* teaching that the only true reality in the universe is G-d, and that without the nucleus of G-dliness in all created things, nothing could exist. Since everything pales into insignificance in comparison to the Divine spark within, there is essentially only one true existence in the world, and that is Divinity.

The discussion went into great depth, and when the candles burned out, it continued in the dark. When the chassidim finally got up to go home, one of them left singing a merry tune to the words, "Only G-d exists; nothing else exists." In the absolute darkness, he bumped his head against the tall iron stove that heated the *beis medrash*.

Rubbing his painful forehead, he said, "Nothing else exists, except for the iron stove in the *beis medrash*."

Today
I shall smile
because . . .

Rabbi Samson Raphael Hirsch spoke prophetically when he said, "Whatever position a wise man may occupy, he brings honor even to the highest, but a fool can meet with no worse fate than to be called to public office, where his ineptness becomes exposed to all."

SMILING EACH DAY

Another example of Rabbi Yechezkel Landau's Solomonic wisdom was manifested when a well-to-do merchant consulted him. The merchant related that several months earlier he had put away a large sum of cash in a hiding place in the cellar, and that it had been stolen. One of his tenants was a person of meager means who had recently begun to live a luxurious life, claiming that a rich uncle had left him an inheritance. The merchant suspected that this tenant had found the money, but he had no evidence to confront him. Could the Rabbi help him?

Rabbi Landau stationed witnesses to listen behind the door and then sent for the tenant. He congratulated him on the news that he had inherited a small fortune.

"I must tell you why I sent for you," he said. "It is for your own welfare. You see, when you began spending money, the local police became suspicious and made an investigation. The money you inherited is counterfeit. Spending counterfeit money may result in your facing very serious charges."

"Rabbi!" the man said. "I am not a counterfeiter! It is the merchant, my landlord — this money is his. He is the counterfeiter. I am innocent!"

Confronted with his admission, the man had no option but to make restitution.

Today
I shall smile
because . . .

_____

_____

_____

> "They shall make Me a sanctuary and I shall dwell in their midst" (*Exodus* 25:8). The Divine spirit is within every person, and it is only fitting that one make oneself into a dwelling suitable for the Divine presence. Every person can fulfill the *mitzvah* of building a sanctuary for G-d: oneself.

SIVAN

סיון

SMILING EACH DAY

The Talmud states that marriages are indeed made in Heaven. Incidentally, one may ask, why there are incompatible marriages that result in divorce. It is because the Divine decree is that A *should* marry B, not that A *will* marry B.

Rabbi Nachum of Sadogura married his first cousin, the daughter of Rabbi Avraham Yaakov. Although he had been addressing him as "uncle" for many years, he now began addressing him as "father-in-law." Someone asked him the reason for this change, particularly since Rabbi Avraham Yaakov had been his uncle long before he became his father-in-law.

"Not true," Rabbi Nachum said. "The Talmud says that forty days before the formation of the fetus, it is decreed in Heaven, 'The daughter of this person should become the wife of that person.' Rabbi Avraham Yaakov did not become my uncle until after I came into being, whereas he was destined to become my father-in-law long before that."

Today
I shall smile
because . . .

SIVAN

סיון

"G-d fulfills the wishes of those who revere Him" (*Psalms* 144:19). There are many stories about people who squandered their wishes foolishly. Someone once said, "Be careful what you pray for, because you might get it." It is unfortunate that one may be so foolish as to not to know what is really important to pray for (*Chafetz Chaim*).

SMILING EACH DAY

One Shabbos night, when Rabbi Heschel of Cracow was a child, his father sent him to buy wine for *havdalah* (prayer marking the end of Shabbos), but did not give him any money. "How can I get wine without money?" the child asked.

"Anyone can buy wine with money," the father said. "But you are a very bright child, Heschele, and you should be able to find a way to buy wine without money."

The child dutifully left. A bit later he returned and handed the father an empty bottle.

"What is this?" the father asked. "How do you expect me to make *havdalah* when the bottle is empty?"

Heschele responded, "You are a bright man, Father. Anyone can make *havdalah* with a full bottle of wine. You should be able to make *havdalah* with an empty bottle."

Today
I shall smile
because . . .

_____
_____
_____

The Talmud says that it is appropriate to beautify the *mitzvos* and perform them in splendor (*Shabbos* 133b). This means not only an external, aesthetic splendor, but also an inner beauty — i.e., to perform *mitzvos* with the purest of motivations (*Chafetz Chaim*).

SMILING EACH DAY

Many stories are told of Herschel of Ostropol, who was the "court jester" of Rabbi Baruch of Medziboz, and was able with his wit to lift Rabbi Baruch from moods of dejection.

One time Rabbi Baruch was away, and a woman came to ask that the rabbi pray for her daughter, who had been in labor for many hours. The doctors were doubtful that she would be able to deliver. (This was before Caesarean delivery was a safe procedure).

Herschel did not have the heart to send the woman away empty-handed, so he told her that there was a foolproof tactic to help her daughter deliver the child promptly: to gather a *minyan* (quorum of ten) in the labor room and say *yizkor* (the memorial prayer).

After Rabbi Baruch returned from his trip, the woman came to thank Herschel with the good news that his recommendation had worked a miracle.

Rabbi Baruch asked Herschel, "What in the world made you recommend saying *yizkor*?"

Herschel replied, "Simple. When they say *yizkor* in shul, the *shammes* announces, 'All children must now exit,' and they do."

Today
I shall smile
because . . .

SIVAN

סיון

We recite the *Shema* upon arising in order to dedicate the day to the service of G-d. We recite it again upon retiring, not only in gratitude for another day of life, but to prepare ourselves for the following day. If one goes to bed with a spiritual attitude, one will arise with a spiritual attitude.

SMILING EACH DAY

That wit was valued even by the authors of the Talmud is evident in the stories related in its pages about the wit of the Jewish children of Jerusalem. For example, one visitor who saw a child carrying a pot of food asked him what he was carrying. The child responded, "If my mother would have wanted people to know what was inside the pot, she would not have covered it."

But Jerusalem did not have an exclusive claim on witty children. It is related that when Rabbi Chaim of Brisk was a child, his mother once scolded him for not washing his hands. "Have you ever seen me with dirty hands?" she asked.

"Of course not," the little Chaim said, "but I'm sure your mother did."

Today
I shall smile
because . . .

_____

_____

_____

We pray, "Inspire our heart to understand and perceive all the words of the Torah." Our prayers are often answered, and G-d does indeed give us the ability to understand and perceive, but we may foolishly neglect to use it (*Chafetz Chaim*).

SMILING EACH DAY

In the days when the Karaite movement had a large following, the king once called the Jews and the Karaites to debate and establish which of their faiths was the original. The Karaites were represented by their elder, whereas the Jews sent one of the lesser luminaries of the community.

Upon entering the throne room, the Jew removed his shoes and put them under his arm. "Respect your king!" the king thundered.

"Your majesty," the Jew said, "when approaching our G-d we remove our shoes, as was told to Moses. This is our greatest sign of reverence."

"Well and good," the king said. "But why are you holding them under your arm?"

"Because," the Jew replied, "when G-d gave the Torah at Sinai and we removed our shoes to approach the sacred site, we found on our return that the Karaite thieves had stolen them."

The Karaite elder interrupted. "Ridiculous and absurd," he said. "There were no Karaites at Sinai."

The Jew bowed before the king. "Your majesty," he said, "the Karaites have just conceded our primacy."

Today
I shall smile
because . . .

There is a folk saying, "A worm that infests a horseradish root must think that it is in the sweetest place in the world." Sometimes a person is in a rut and does not realize that life can be so much more meaningful if only he would make the effort to investigate other options.

SMILING EACH DAY

A young man who was a chassid invited his rebbe to be the *sandek* (one who holds the baby during the circumcision) at the *bris* (circumcision) of his newborn son. The young man's father-in-law was not exactly an ardent lover of chassidim and their Rebbes, and when the Rebbe did not arrive at the precise time set for the *bris,* the father-in-law gave the honor of *sandek* to someone else.

When the Rebbe arrived after the *bris,* the young man apologized. The Rebbe smiled and said, "No apology is necessary. In fact, I am grateful for what happened.

"When I do a *mitzvah* myself," he continued, "I undoubtedly am derelict in performing it to its perfection. The Talmud says that if a person intends to do a *mitzvah* but circumstances beyond his control preclude it, G-d considers the *mitzvah* as having been done. When G-d Himself considers the *mitzvah* done, it is certainly 'done' with a much higher perfection than I could have achieved if I had done it myself."

Today
I shall smile
because . . .

_____

_____

_____

The *Midrash* states that to love G-d means to make Him beloved by all people. If a person behaves in a manner that demonstrates how the observance of Torah refines a person's character, he is glorifying G-d and making Him respected and beloved by others.

SMILING EACH DAY

Our great ethicists, exemplified by the *Chafetz Chaim*, waged an all-out battle against *lashon hara* (slander or gossip). "There should be no need even to talk about anyone else," one said. "If you wish to praise someone, praise G-d. If you wish to find fault with someone, you would do better to look for faults within yourself."

Some *tzaddikim* did not have this problem, because they were simply unable to see faults in anyone. They always judged people favorably and followed in the footsteps of the Talmud, which cited the prayer of one *tzaddik*: "May I always be able to see people's virtues and not their faults."

The chassidic master, Rabbi David of Lelov, once overheard a son arguing with his father, saying, "If I did not fear G-d, I would kill you!" Rabbi David remarked, "See! There goes a G-d-fearing person."

Rabbi Shmuel of Sasov used to offer daily prayers of gratitude, thanking G-d for all His kindnesses. He would say, "I thank you, G-d, for making *lashon hara* a sin and not a *mitzvah*. If it were a *mitzvah*, how could I possibly fulfill it, when I do not see any faults in other people?"

Today
I shall smile
because . . .

SIVAN

29

סיון

Erev
Rosh Chodesh
[Eve of the
New Month]

Sins of omission can be every bit as serious as sins of commission. One may repent a sin and have it erased by forgiveness, but nothing can compensate for a lost opportunity. Take advantage of every opportunity to do an act of kindness.

SMILING EACH DAY

It was the practice of some *maggidim* (preachers) to circulate among the towns and villages and preach, often severely reprimanding the populace for being derelict in observance of Torah and *mitzvos*. The chassidic masters were very critical of this approach. Most of the Jews in the villages lived in a hostile environment and were severely oppressed, and their observance of Torah could be considered to be *mesiras nefesh* (self-sacrifice). To the *maggidim* they said, "Instead of berating people for their sins, why don't you appeal to G-d and cite their many virtues?"

One *maggid* delivered a classic *mussar* sermon, with threats of fire and brimstone for people's sinfulness.

The Baal Shem Tov, who happened to be in attendance, asked him, "How can you address and relate to people's sinfulness if you have never tasted sin yourself?"

"What makes you think that I have never sinned?" asked the *maggid*.

"Then if you have sinned, you should be occupied with rectifying your own behavior, rather than being self-righteous and reprimanding others! And if you are confident that you have already completely rectified your own behavior, then you are really in trouble."

Today
I shall smile
because . . .

_____
_____
_____

> There is no wealth like being content with what one has; no wisdom like good behavior; no piety like reverence of G-d; and no charm like a calm personality.

First Day of Rosh Chodesh Tammuz

SMILING EACH DAY

It is known that some of the chassidic masters were prone to moods of depression. A number of them stated that they foresaw the enormous sufferings that Jews would experience before the coming of *Mashiach,* and they were unable to make peace with this knowledge. Many of their predictions, recorded more than a hundred and fifty years ago, unfortunately have come true.

Yet, because they were ardent advocates of *simchah* (joy), they appointed people to try to bring them out of such low moods. One such person was a chassid by the name of Chaim, who once found his Rebbe in a dejected state and said: "The Rebbe has many times been critical of *lashon hara* (slander and gossip) and has cautioned us to maintain silence and speak the very bare minimum. Well, I disagree with this. Last week, my life could have been changed for the better with only two words, but the man who could have said them listened to the Rebbe's advice and kept his silence.

"I walked into the bank last week, and there were many officials sitting at their desks. One official had millions of dollars piled up on his desk. If he had only said, 'Chaim, take!' those two words could have changed my entire life!"

Today
I shall smile
because . . .

There was a man who was privileged to attend the king. However, upon leaving the palace he was employed to haul garbage. The king rebuked him, "It is an indignity to me when you do not behave as a royal servant upon leaving the palace." We should think of this when we leave the synagogue (*Chafetz Chaim*).

SMILING EACH DAY

There are countless reports of sightings of Elijah the Prophet. There are various stories of how a tenth person was needed for a *minyan* (quorum), for a *bris* (circumcision), or for some other important function, and abruptly a stranger appeared out of nowhere, and after the event no trace of him could be found. This is how the *"Shul* of Elijah the Prophet" in the Old City of Jerusalem got its name. *Tzaddikim* occasionally revealed that a particular person was Elijah, who appeared in various disguises.

One time a man came breathlessly to Rabbi Moshe Teitelbaum (the *Yismach Moshe*), reporting that he had seen Elijah. "Was he very tall and dark-complected?" the Rebbe asked.

"Yes, yes!" the man answered.

"And was he carrying a shovel and pail?"

"Yes, yes!" the man answered excitedly. "That was him."

"And was his face covered with soot?"

"Oh, yes, yes!" the man answered.

"Too bad," Rabbi Moshe said. "All you saw was the chimney cleaner."

Today
I shall smile
because . . .

_____
_____
_____

Berachos (blessings) at the wedding ceremony should actually be recited by the bridegroom. The custom of the rabbi reciting the *berachos* was instituted to avoid public embarrassment of a *choson* (bridegroom) who might not be fluent in reciting the *berachos*. This is but one of many precautions which protect a person's dignity.

SMILING EACH DAY

The chassidim of the Rebbe of Stolin have a practice of *davening* (praying) at the tops of their voices. One time, when the chassidic *shteibel* (small synagogue) was closed for remodeling, the Stoliner chassidim *davened* in the local *shul*, and their mega-decibels were annoying to the worshipers.

The *gabbai* (officer) of the *shul* told the chassidim that unless they lowered their voices, he would forbid them to enter the *shul*. Inasmuch as he was the agent of the community and the *shul* was community property, he had the authority to restrict the use of the property as he saw fit.

The matter ultimately came before the local rabbi for a judgment. The rabbi, who was sympathetic to chassidim, said to the *gabbai*, "Your authority over property is on the building, and extends only up to the ceiling. The prayers of these people penetrate the ceiling and reach up to Heaven. You do not have the authority to restrict anything that goes beyond the ceiling of the *shul*!"

Today
I shall smile
because . . .

When someone does something that you consider wrong, think about how many rationalizations you would have devised to justify yourself had you done that very thing, and use these rationalizations to give the other person the benefit of the doubt (*Rabbi Moshe Leib of Sasov*).

SMILING EACH DAY

Anivus (humility) is the cornerstone of character development. Without *anivus,* all other traits, regardless of how spiritual they may seem, are grossly defective.

The Rabbi of Chernobyl and the Rabbi of Rhizin were close friends, and the chassidim of one very often visited the court of the other.

One time the Rabbi of Chernobyl said to a chassid of the Rabbi of Rhizin, "I am a greater Rebbe than your Rebbe is."

The chassid was taken aback. This was certainly not the way any of the *tzaddikim* spoke of themselves. However, he did not have the audacity to ask for an explanation.

The Rabbi of Chernobyl, noting the chassid's perplexity, said, "The last time I met with the Rabbi of Rhizin, we exchanged blessings. Each of us wished the other to become a true *yirei Shamayim* (person fearful of and revering G-d). Your rabbi has already achieved that, whereas I have not. Therefore, my blessing to him has been realized, whereas his has not." He smiled and added, "I can only conclude that my blessings are more potent than his."

Today
I shall smile
because . . .

_____
_____
_____

If your only option in choosing a friend is between a foolish person who is humble and a bright person who is arrogant, choose the fool. Folly may indeed be harmful, but arrogance is lethal (*Maalos Hamidos*).

SMILING EACH DAY

On Shabbos morning, my mother would serve two *kugels:* a *challah kugel,* containing honey, raisins, and slices of apple, and a *lokshen* (noodle) *kugel,* rather tangy with pepper. These were both gustatory delights.

We always had Shabbos guests, usually several itinerant rabbis who were soliciting for their respective institutions. One Shabbos morning a discussion arose among the group as to the origin of the custom of eating *kugel* on Shabbos. One rabbi said that the reason we eat *kugel* is because it represents the *manna*, which the Israelites in the desert baked into cakes. Another took a philosophic-philologic approach, saying that the word *kugel* is from the Hebrew *k'egul*, meaning circular, and he tried somehow to associate the fact that a circle has no beginning and no end with the phenomenon of creation, a connection which I found difficult to understand.

After listening politely, my father asked, "Gentlemen, was there anything wrong with the *kugels* today?"

"Of course not!" they said. "They were exquisite, absolutely delicious."

"Then why are you searching for reasons for eating *kugel?* If there were a practice that one must eat rocks, then you would have to search for a reason. But why are you racking your brains to discover a reason for eating *kugel?* We eat it because it is delicious, and Shabbos is supposed to be celebrated with tasty dishes."

Today
I shall smile
because . . .

"Fortunate is the person who is considerate of the poor" (*Psalms* 41:2). It is not enough to be charitable to the poor. One must also be considerate, and give charity in such a manner as to avoid embarrassing the person in need (*Vayikra Rabbah* 34:1).

SMILING EACH DAY

Too often we make judgments about other people based on skimpy evidence. We tend to take things out of context and may believe the worst about someone when noted by the media, whose sensationalist writers thrive on such practices. We may overhear something and jump to unwarranted conclusions. How true are the teachings of the Talmud: "Judge everyone favorably," and "Do not judge another until you have stood in his position."

A rabbi was once visiting one of the great *halachic* authorities when the door to his study opened, and a man hurried in, saying, "Rabbi, I am a *Kohen* (of the priestly tribe). Is it true that I am not permitted to take a divorcee?"

The rabbi replied, "Have no fear. You may take a divorcee."

The visiting rabbi jumped up in amazement. "What! And you are looked up to as a *halachic* authority? Why, every child in *cheder* (school) knows that a *Kohen* may not marry a divorcee."

"My dear man," the rabbi said. "This man is happily married. He is a simple but very pious man, and he earns his livelihood as a cab driver. He must have heard that a *Kohen* may not 'take' (i.e., marry) a divorcee, and he understood the word 'take' literally — to take on as a passenger!"

Today I shall smile because . . .

_____
_____
_____

The Talmud says, "Be certain to keep a promise you have made to a child, because otherwise you are instilling within him a propensity to lie, at an early, impressionable age (*Succah* 46b).

SMILING EACH DAY

Chassidim tend to be chauvinistic. In their world, loyalty to their Rebbe may be fierce. They may see themselves as similar to someone who fell overboard and whose only hope for survival is to cling to the lifeline that is thrown him. In the stormy sea of life, where there are infinite possibilities of doing the wrong thing, the chassid may cling to his Rebbe for dear life.

However, this loyalty may sometimes result in exclusivity, with the chassid insisting that his Rebbe is the only authentic Rebbe. Although the chassidic masters condemned this attitude, it often persisted.

Two chassidim who were traveling together saw another chassid in the coach. "Where are you headed?" they asked.

"To Kopost," he answered.

"Kopost? Why Kopost?" they asked.

"I have my reasons," he answered.

"Our Rebbe is a greater scholar than the Rebbe of Kopost," they said. "You should come with us."

The man shook his head. "I have my reasons."

"Our Rebbe is a great *tzaddik*. His *berachos* (blessings) never fail. You would be wise to come with us."

"No," the man said. "I am going to Kopost."

"With all due respect to the Rebbe of Kopost," they said, "you are making a mistake. Why not come with us and see for yourself? What is it that is drawing you to Kopost?"

"Very simple," the man said. "I live in Kopost. My wife and children are there. That is a very good reason."

Today
I shall smile
because . . .

One can tell the true mettle of a hero when he is in battle, of a true friend in time of need, and of a humble person when he is provoked to anger (*Sefer Chassidim*).

SMILING EACH DAY

The six hundred and thirteen *mitzvos* of the Torah are not to be tampered with. We are forbidden either to add a six hundred and fourteenth *mitzvah* or to delete a *mitzvah*. But what could be wrong with adding to the *mitzvos*?

The *Maggid* (preacher) of Dubno explained the answer with a parable. A man borrowed a silver spoon from a neighbor and several days later returned two silver spoons, explaining that the first spoon had given birth to the second; hence, the latter was therefore the lender's rightful property. The neighbor accepted the bonus, and when the man asked to borrow other things, he gladly complied. Each time the borrower returned two of the item, explaining that the first had given birth to a second. The lender was overjoyed with this windfall, and was ecstatic when the borrower asked for a loan of his silver candelabra.

When the candelabra was not returned after several weeks, the lender asked for it, and the borrower said, "I must tell you the terrible news. Your candelabra died."

"What! Are you insane? A candelabra cannot die," the lender said.

"You certainly had no problem accepting that the other items you lent me gave birth. If they could give birth, a candelabra can die."

The *Maggid* continued, "If one can tamper with the Torah by adding to the *mitzvos*, one will assume that one can detract from the *mitzvos* as well."

Today I shall smile because . . .

_____

_____

_____

A wise man was asked, "Is there anything a person can do to alleviate his desire for revenge, since the Torah forbids acting vengefully?" He answered, "Do something to improve yourself. When you become a better person, it will torment your enemies to no end."

SMILING EACH DAY

It is well known that a sick person's attitude can have a major effect on the course of his illness. Cheerfulness enhances recovery, whereas dejection contributes to deterioration. Indeed, there are numerous reports of cases where patients who had been diagnosed with a malignancy astonished their doctors by essentially laughing their way into recovery.

Rabbi Yechezkel Landau (the *Noda B'Yehudah*) knew this well. Rabbi Landau did not believe in amulets, and although other *tzaddikim* would write amulets whose esoteric content was considered therapeutic, he would not accept the practice.

One time a father pleaded with him to give his daughter an amulet because she had been diagnosed as having an incurable disease. Unable to refuse the distraught father, Rabbi Landau took a blank piece of parchment, sealed it in a leather container, and told the father that his daughter should wear the amulet continually for one week and then open it. If the letters had disappeared, that would be a sign that she would recover.

How thrilled everyone was to see the parchment blank at the end of the week! Convinced that she would recover, the young woman indeed did.

Today
I shall smile
because . . .

A person should recite the full *Shema* on retiring, for it contains the words, "I forgive anyone who has in any way offended me, and may no one be punished on my account." One should then realize that if he retains ill feelings toward another person, he has been lying in prayer.

SMILING EACH DAY

The Talmud and all Jewish ethical works denounce vanity as being the worst character trait a person can have.

One of the chassidic masters explained that in order to commit a sin, some action or object is usually necessary. For example, if a person wishes to eat *treifah* (non-kosher), he cannot really commit this sin unless he has something *treifah* to eat. Vanity, however, requires no external object and no action. A person can be lying in bed in a totally dark room, hidden under the covers, and yet be thinking, "I am the greatest."

Rabbi Naftali of Ropschitz used to relate that when he was a student in Lublin, there was a young man who worked in the *mikveh*, known as the "boot remover."

"Because of the frequently muddy streets in Lublin," Rabbi Naftali said, "we all wore high boots, and they were somewhat difficult to take off. This young man's job was to help people remove their boots, for which we gave him a few coins.

"One time he pulled so hard on my boots that I felt my leg would come off, and I told him so. He responded, 'Don't tell me what to do. I'm the greatest boot-remover in the world.'

"That is why vanity is so grave a sin. No one is immune to it."

Today
I shall smile
because . . .

_____
_____
_____

The *Zohar* states that G-d is distressed when people are sinful. If one forgives another person, he thereby eliminates that person's sin against him and minimizes the Divine distress. It is the finest manifestation of one's love for G-d to alleviate the Divine distress (*Ohr HaChaim*).

SMILING EACH DAY

Although the Torah relates the prophetic nature of Joseph's dreams, the Talmud downplays dreams as a whole, saying that they are often nonsensical. In keeping with authoritative psychological theories, the Talmud states that a person's dreams are usually the result of the kinds of thoughts one harbored during the day.

A man once came to Rabbi Bunim of P'shischa, dressed in robes that befit a Rebbe of chassidim. Feigning humility, he told the rabbi that he was a humble and very private person who shunned acclaim and had no intention of becoming a Rebbe. However, he felt compelled to become a Rebbe of chassidim because his late father had been appearing to him repeatedly in his dreams, instructing him to become a Rebbe. He therefore felt obligated to suppress his humility and accept the role ordained for him by Heaven which his father had revealed to him.

Rabbi Bunim responded, "You don't have to accept this awesome responsibility and suffer the pangs of being publicly revered, which is so alien to your natural humility.

"As far as the dreams are concerned, you should wait until the chassidim begin to dream that you are their Rebbe and force the position on you. Your own dreams may be somewhat misleading."

Today
I shall smile
because . . .

A person of true substance is humble and self-effacing. Empty branches do not have anything to weigh them down, whereas the branch that is heaviest with fruit is the lowest of all.

SMILING EACH DAY

One chassid, a rather simple person, kept the practice of assuming absolute silence once he put on his *tallis* for prayer. Until he removed his *tallis*, one could not extract a single word from him.

Others asked him for the origin of this practice. The *Shulchan Aruch* (code of law) indeed states that one should not engage in conversation while one is wearing the *tefillin*, but it says nothing about restricting conversation while wearing the *tallis*.

The man responded, "I heard a rabbi say that on Judgment Day the Heavenly Tribunal asks a person to relate everything he did during his lifetime. If he omits anything, he is confronted with evidence about what he did, and final judgment is not meted out until he admits that he did all these things. Faced with incontrovertible evidence, a person must admit everything.

"But since I will be buried in a *tallis*, I will simply indicate to the judges that I am unable to speak at all, and since it was my practice throughout my lifetime never to talk while wearing a *tallis*, I sincerely doubt that they will force me to violate my *minhag* (custom). In this way, I will not have to admit to anything, and I will be spared from the punishment of *Gehinnom* (hell)."

A short time after this man died, the Rebbe whom he had followed was once sitting with his chassidim, when he went into a deep meditative trance. He then awoke with a smile and said, "His strategy was successful. He got away with it!"

Today
I shall smile
because . . .

_____

_____

_____

"Sarah denied laughing . . . and the angels arose (to leave)" (*Genesis* 18:15-16). When the angels heard that Sarah had deviated from the truth, they left. The Divine spirit cannot tolerate even the slightest inkling of falsehood (*Chofetz Chaim*).

SMILING EACH DAY

In one town there was a wealthy miser who refused to give *tzedakah* (charity). Representatives who came to town to collect for their respective institutions knew not to waste their time appealing to him for a donation, because not only did he refuse to give, but he would also let loose with a diatribe of insults.

One time a rabbi came to town who claimed that he would succeed in extracting a donation from the miser. He knocked on the man's door and was greeted with vulgarity.

"Just listen to me one minute," the rabbi said. "I have something for you. I know that you hoard your money because you are afraid of losing it and becoming impoverished. I can guarantee you that G-d will never take your wealth from you."

"How so?" asked the miser.

"I will gladly tell you," the rabbi said. "But since I'm going to give you something so valuable, you must first donate to my institution." The miser gave him some money.

The rabbi said, "If a poor man sees a penny lying in the garbage, he might reach for it because he is so desperate that he is willing to soil himself even for a penny. Someone who is better off would not reach into the garbage for a penny, but might do so for a dollar. A rich person would not do so for a dollar, but might reach for a hundred-dollar bill, and a billionaire might even overlook a large sum of money, in order not to soil himself.

"Since G-d has all the wealth in the world, He would never reach into your garbage to take away your money, regardless of how much you have."

Today
I shall smile
because . . .

Gold dust and silver dust may have great monetary value, but nothing can ever grow in them. It is the lowly earth that provides life-sustaining food. So it is with people: It is not the "glittery" people but rather the humble that sustain the world.

SMILING EACH DAY

Humility is a most important character trait. With all Moses' greatness, the only feature the Torah lists in praise of him is that he was the most humble man on earth (*Numbers* 12:3). Given its enormous importance, why does the Torah not include humility among the *mitzvos*?

Various Torah commentaries give essentially the same answer in a variety of ways. A *mitzvah* should be done with the awareness that one is doing a *mitzvah* and with the proper *kavannah* (concentration). This is impossible with humility, because if a person thinks of himself as having achieved humility, he is actually vain. To think, "In spite of how wise and virtuous I am, I am going to remain humble," is vanity.

A person who is offended because he is not accorded what he feels is his due is obviously being vain. The person who thinks, "It doesn't bother me that I was not given the honor due me," is not only being vain but also self-deceptive.

The Rabbi of Kotzk said that if humility were a *mitzvah*, pious people might first go to the *mikveh*, put on their finest clothes, and go on to say, "I am hereby about to fulfill the *mitzvah* of being humble."

Today
I shall smile
because . . .

_____

_____

_____

A person who lies loses the merits of many *mitzvos.* For example, when he says *Shema Yisrael,* professing his belief in G-d, Satan says, "Of what value is his declaration that G-d is one? He always lies." In this way he loses the *mitzvah* of *Shema* (*Rabbi Levi Yitzchak of Berdichev*).

SMILING EACH DAY

People are prone to the most absurd rationalizations and projections to protect their egos.

Rabbi Bunim of P'shischa told of a man who shared a room in an inn with a priest. In the darkness of early morning, the man mistakenly put on the priest's clothes and reached for the latter's bag. Later on he passed a mirror and was stunned to discover himself in priestly vestments.

"How could I possibly be a priest when I am a Jew?" he thought. Initially he thought that there must be some mistake, but when he opened his bag and instead of his *tallis* and *tefillin* found paraphernalia of the mass, his belief that he was indeed a priest was reinforced.

Yet the awareness that he had a wife and children challenged this identity. He decided to settle the matter by opening the Latin Bible. If he did not understand it, then there must be some mistake. Yet even his inability to understand a word of Latin was not enough to make him aware of the truth, and he could not deny the image he saw in the mirror.

"I am indeed a priest," he concluded. "But why, if I am a priest, do I not understand the Latin Bible? It must be that none of the other priests understand it either!"

There is no limit to the extent that a person can adhere to self-deception.

Today
I shall smile
because . . .

Rabbi Jose said, "I never said anything that would require my looking behind me to see who might overhear it" (*Shabbos* 118b). This is an excellent guideline to proper speech. If you must check who might overhear you, you would be better off to keep your silence.

SMILING EACH DAY

In the introduction to the *Zohar*, Rabbi Shimon bar Yochai states that he heard a voice calling, "Shimon! Shimon!" and he knew it was G-d calling to him. Someone asked the Rabbi of Rhizin, "Isn't that a bit presumptuous? Shouldn't a *tzaddik* have more humility than to think himself worthy of being addressed by the Almighty Himself?"

"Not at all," the Rebbe answered. "A great and famous Torah scholar said that when he receives letters from faraway places, the salutation contains several lines of honorary titles. When he visits a strange town, he is introduced as 'the great and famous Gaon.' 'In my hometown,' he said, 'people address me as just rabbi. My wife, who knows me best, calls me plain "Baruch." The better people get to know me, the more they know I do not deserve honorary titles.'

"The very same thing happened with Rabbi Shimon," the Rebbe continued. "As the outstanding scholar and *tzaddik* of his generation, everyone addressed him with great reverence, and no one would dare call him by name. When he heard himself being called 'Shimon,' without any title, he felt that the only one who knew that he was just plain Shimon and did not merit any title was the One Who knew the truth about him. This could only be the Almighty Himself."

Today
I shall smile
because . . .

_____

_____

_____

Do not say, "I don't have the time to study Torah." The Talmud states that there is always room for a delicacy even with a full stomach (*Eruvin* 82b). If you really desire something, you will find time for it even on your busiest day.

SMILING EACH DAY

Reality demands that institutions, whether synagogues or yeshivos, must pay the bills for their staff, maintenance, buildings, and other expenses. In any city there are various community projects that require funding. While many people participate in supporting these causes, there are often several major donors whose wealth allows them to make significant contributions.

Not infrequently, people who are aware of the vital importance of their gift and who know that withdrawal of their support would bankrupt the institution may flex their muscles to determine policy. They may wish to decide who should be the rabbi of the *shul,* what the school should teach, whether it should be co-ed, etc. They suddenly feel qualified as Torah scholars, educators, and sociologists, fields in which they have little expertise.

One rabbi was particularly vexed with one wealthy contributor's *chutzpah* in asserting himself on *halachic* questions. He pointed out that the Talmud says, "Who is a wealthy man? One who is satisfied with his portion" (*Ethics of the Fathers* 4:1).

"The portion given to you by G-d is wealth, not necessarily wisdom or Torah knowledge," he said to the man. "Be satisfied with your portion. Be satisfied with having wealth, and do not expect to be recognized as a scholar or an expert in other fields. Just as your wealth does not qualify you to dictate a surgical procedure or operate a jet plane, neither does it qualify you in any other field."

Today
I shall smile
because . . .

Fast of
Shivah Asar
B'Tammuz
[When 17 Tammuz
falls on the
Sabbath the fast is
observed on Sun-
day.]

A wise man said, "Whoever relies solely on his own intelligence is prone to error; whoever trusts only his own judgment is apt to fail; and whoever considers himself superior to others will eventually degrade himself before others."

SMILING EACH DAY

The Seventeenth of Tammuz ushers in a period of three weeks of mourning, commemorating the fall of Jerusalem and the destruction of the Sanctuary. This poses a problem in writing a book which encourages cheer for every day. Obviously, cheer and grief are mutually exclusive.

Or are they? The seventy-ninth *Psalm* begins with, "A song of Asaph. Almighty G-d, heathens have come into Your inheritance and have desecrated the Sanctuary of Your Glory." The Talmud asks the obvious question: Why is this *Psalm* called a song? It should more appropriately read, "A lamentation of Asaph," a dirge rather than a song.

The Talmud goes on to find the silver lining in the national calamity. By discharging His wrath on the wood and stones of the Sanctuary, G-d spared the people of Israel themselves. This silver lining not only reduces the intensity of the grief, but is reason enough to sing.

We, too, must learn never to abandon cheer, even in the most difficult moments of life. Just as a nation must learn how to sing while licking its wounds, so we must use our faith in G-d to be able to find cheer even amongst ruin.

For the next three weeks we will say. "A *song* of Asaph," and continue to find something to smile about every day.

Today
I shall smile
because . . .

_____
_____
_____

One must be very sensitive to the feelings of a blind person. Rabbi Eliezer took utmost caution to protect the dignity of the blind, who blessed him saying, "You are kind to those who can be seen but cannot see. May you be blessed from the One who sees all but remains unseen" (Jerusalem Talmud, *Peah* 8:8).

SMILING EACH DAY

There are conflicting attitudes about giving *tzedakah* in order to receive honor. One wealthy man boasted to a *tzaddik* that he had given a large sum of money to build a new synagogue, and that his name had been engraved in the cornerstone. "My charity has a permanent testimony. My deeds are recorded in stone."

"How unfortunate," the rabbi responded. "The Prophet said, 'I will remove your stone hearts and give you a heart of flesh' (*Ezekiel* 36:21). The Torah wishes to convert stone into life, and you have taken a living act and converted it into stone."

On the other hand, the Talmud states that a person who gives money to *tzedakah* and prays to be deserving of reward for it is a *tzaddik* (*Pesachim* 8a). One man told the *Tzaddik* of Sanz, who was famous for his lavish *tzedakah*, that he too gave *tzedakah*, but didn't want it known.

"Stop with the humility" the *Tzaddik* said. "Let it be known! The important thing about *tzedakah* is that the poor have food to eat and clothes to wear, and as long as that goal is accomplished, it makes no real difference whom you tell about it."

Today
I shall smile
because . . .

The psalmist describes a person who is beloved by G-d as one who "speaks truth in his heart" (*Psalms* 15:2). It is not enough to refrain from *speaking* falsehood. One should also train oneself not to *think* falsehood.

SMILING EACH DAY

In all the Torah's ethical works, vanity is condemned as the worst of all character traits, regardless of how much a person may feel justified in his pride. Humility, on the other hand, is exalted as the finest trait, even in a person who has nothing objectively to be proud of. One *tzaddik* said that he loved the ignorant poor, because although they might be humble only because of their ignorance and poverty, they are more virtuous than someone with wealth and knowledge who thinks highly of himself.

The Rabbi of Apt once came to a town and was invited to stay in one of two places. The first was the home of a very wealthy, *frum* (pious) person who was known to be vain, and who wished to boast that he was host to the Rabbi of Apt. The other was the home of a person of modest means whose quarters were not as comfortable, and who furthermore was considered in the community to be less than fully observant. To everyone's surprise, the rabbi chose the latter.

The rabbi said, "G-d says, 'I will rest among them [the Israelites] even in their state of contamination' (*Leviticus* 16:17), so that the Divine Presence does not abandon the sinner. In addition, G-d so despises vanity that He says, 'The vain person and I cannot share one abode' (*Arachin* 15b). Why should I wish to be somewhere where G-d does not wish to be?"

Today
I shall smile
because . . .

_____

_____

_____

A wealthy person once accidentally dropped a *siddur,* and promptly picked it up and kissed it. Rabbi Moshe of Bayan said to him, "A *siddur* has no feelings. When you see another person who has come upon bad times and has fallen, lift him up and embrace him with love."

SMILING EACH DAY

When we talk about a family living below poverty level today, we may refer to a family that is indeed living below the median standard but may still have a television and an automobile. In the older Jewish communities in Europe, poverty was poverty. There was no welfare system and the poor had no food or clothes.

Many *tzaddikim* went from village to village collecting money for the poor. They also collected money to ransom debtors from the dungeons where the feudal lord had thrown them for failure to pay rent.

When Reb Baruch of Rike was well into his eighties, he still dragged himself from town to town to raise money for the poor. His friends said to him, "Enough! You have reached the age when you should retire and relax a bit. You really are too old to be making all these trips."

Rabbi Baruch responded, "You are not the first to give me such advice. The *yetzer hara* (evil inclination) preceded you, and I said to him, 'You are much older than I am, and yet you have not retired. When you give up doing your work, I will then give up mine.' "

Today
I shall smile
because . . .

The Talmud states that the blade of the ax that cuts down trees would be impotent if it did not have a wooden handle (*Sanhedrin* 39:2). No one else can harm us unless we somehow contribute to our own harm.

SMILING EACH DAY

The chassidic masters had absolutely no use for people who sought to be their followers but who thought very highly of themselves. Any chassid who had *yichus* (an impressive lineage) had to prove that his distinguished ancestry had not caused him to become vain. Rabbi Naftali of Ropschitz had to plead with Rabbi Elimelech of Lizensk to accept him as a disciple, because he had too great a *yichus*. "It is not my fault who my parents were!" Rabbi Naftali cried.

To one chassid who boasted of his *yichus*, the Rebbe said, "When G-d gave Bilaam's donkey the power of speech, his first words were of self-praise."

One time a chassid who fancied himself to be a Rebbe in his own right came to the Rabbi of Tolna, accompanied by no less than three *gabbaim* (attendants), obviously trying to impress everyone with his importance.

The Rabbi of Tolna said, "I know you to be a truthful person, and I would never accuse you of lying. If you had come here with only one *gabbai* and told me that you had two more at home, I would certainly have believed you. What an unnecessary waste of effort and money to have *shlepped* two more people along with you!"

Today
I shall smile
because . . .

_____
_____
_____

"Raise your voice like the *shofar*" (*Isaiah* 58:1). Just like the sound of the shofar is not its own but represents the force that is blown into it, so you must realize that your voice does not represent your own wisdom, but expresses the soul which God has given to you.

SMILING EACH DAY

My mother used to say that the problem that has plagued humanity throughout history is that everyone is concerned with his own material welfare and everyone else's spiritual welfare. How much harm has been done by those who try to impose their own beliefs on others!

Rabbi Joseph Engel said that this trend can be noted in the prayer for the new month, where we ask וְתִתֶּן לָנוּ, that G-d give *us* long life, peace, blessing, a livelihood, good health and all else that is good. Then we say, חַיִּים שֶׁיֵּשׁ בָּהֶם יִרְאַת שָׁמַיִם וְיִרְאַת חֵטְא, "Lives which (shall) have *in them* fear of Heaven and fear of sin." Although "in them" refers to the antecedent "lives," it can also mean *"in others."*

"That is quite characteristic," Rabbi Joseph Engel said. "For all material goods we say לָנוּ, unto *us,* but for spiritual values, we pray that they be given בָּהֶם, to *others.* People are always aware of how many more material things they need, but they believe that they are already perfect spiritually. Others, however, are assumed to have all that they need materially and are lacking only in spirituality."

Today
I shall smile
because . . .

A person blessed with cheerful serenity has only one concern: Not to fall short of accomplishing one's duty. This is a concern which is meant to accompany us throughout life, and is one that can relieve us of all other worries (*Rabbi Samson Raphael Hirsch*).

SMILING EACH DAY

The Talmud states that on Rosh Hashanah everything is preordained for the entire year, with the exception of matters that relate to free will. In the latter area, an individual retains total freedom to act as he desires. However, how much he will earn and other things that will occur during the year are all preordained.

A physician in Belz came to the Belzer Rebbe, Rabbi Yissachar Dov, with a complaint. He said that when people came to the Rebbe with a health problem, he would tell the wealthy people to go to the professors in Lemberg or Vienna, whereas those without money he always sent to the local physician in Belz. "Am I to be a physician only for the poor?" the doctor asked.

The Rebbe answered: "We believe everything to be preordained on Rosh Hashanah, which includes how much a person is destined to spend for medical expenses. G-d does not tax the poor with a huge medical bill, but he may decree a large medical expense for the wealthy.

"If the wealthy were to go to you when they are sick, they would have to have a prolonged illness in order to spend the preordained sum for medical expenses. That is why I tell them to go to London or Vienna, so that the cost of the trip, lodgings, and the doctor's fee will add up to the preordained sum, and they can get well quickly. The designated amount for the poor is very small, and they can quickly spend this small amount right here in Belz and get better fast."

Today
I shall smile
because . . .

_____

_____

_____

In the prayer for the New Month, we ask for "wealth with honor." Sometimes a person uses his wealth to boast that he is superior to other people. He thus shames others with his wealth. Benign wealth is one which brings not only honor to its owner, but to others as well.

SMILING EACH DAY

What practices and ideas are honorable and respectable? These may vary. For example, in one culture, removing one's hat is a sign of respect, whereas for Jews, putting on the hat is a sign of reverence. Individuals' ethical concepts may also vary, and some people's values may be very different from Torah values.

One of the finest concepts of *tzedakah* is *matan beseiser*, giving money secretly, so that one does not receive public recognition, which could detract from the purity of the *mitzvah*. However, it is common practice for the needy to apply for help to any of the resources that distribute funds.

One wealthy person who claimed to champion the cause of the poor wished to establish absolute secrecy in receiving *tzedakah*. He proposed that communal distribution of *tzedakah* be abolished and replaced by private giving. He claimed that would save the poor from the embarrassment involved in public charity. This was *his* understanding of *matan beseiser*. Unfortunately, this would have seriously curtailed the availability of *tzedakah* for those who might not know where to turn.

Rabbi Wolf of Strikov opposed this proposition. "Many of the wealthy came by their riches through deceit, exploitation, and corrupt business practices, yet none of these people seem to be embarrassed, and they do not keep their wealth a closely guarded secret. The poor person came by his poverty honestly. If the rich are not ashamed of being rich, why should the poor be ashamed of being poor?"

Thus, applying *matan beseiser* in this way is not the Torah attitude.

Today
I shall smile
because . . .

If you ask someone for a favor and you are refused, you may harbor resentments against that person. The Torah forbids acting on such resentments, and logic tells you that just retaining such resentments even without acting on them is foolish, because it results in nothing but aggravation.

SMILING EACH DAY

Rabbi Levi Yitzchak of Berdichev was famous for his ingeniousness in pleading the cause of the people before G-d. For all his saintliness and absolute devotion to G-d, he never justified anyone's suffering. He constantly argued that G-d should be more merciful to His children.

One Tisha B'Av he encountered a man who was eating on this fast day. "My dear man," Rabbi Levi Yitzchak said, "I am certain you have totally forgotten that today is Tisha B'Av."

"No," the man answered. "I know it is Tisha B'Av."

"Ah, then you must not be in the best of health, and you are under doctor's orders not to fast," Rabbi Levi Yitzchak said.

"No," the man said. "I am perfectly healthy, and it would not harm me to fast."

Rabbi Levi Yitzchak turned his eyes to Heaven. "Look at Your people, dear G-d," he said. "I have given this man several options to explain away his eating on Tisha B'Av, but in his love for truth he does not allow himself to take advantage of these excuses. Tell me, then, do Your people not deserve better than You have given them?"

Today
I shall smile
because . . .

_____
_____
_____

Rabbi Akiva told his wife, Rachel, that he was about to be appointed as director of the community's charity disbursement. Rachel said, "You may accept that position only if you feel you are able to absorb curses and insults without incurring resentments" (Jerusalem Talmud *Peah* 8:6).

SMILING EACH DAY

The chassidic master, Rabbi Meir of Premishlan, used to spend much time collecting *tzedakah*. Someone asked him how he could justify taking so much time away from Torah study and prayer in order to collect *tzedakah*.

Rabbi Meir replied: "One time I dreamt that I was at the doors of *Gan Eden* (Paradise). A Torah scholar was requesting entrance to *Gan Eden* by virtue of his study of Torah, and the angel at the door said, 'We must first see whether you studied Torah with proper intent, and not in order to receive acclaim for your scholarship.' A bit later another person came asking for admission by virtue of his prayer. The angel told him that they must first investigate whether his prayers had been said with the proper *kavannah* (concentration).

"Then another man came along who said that he had collected money for *tzedakah* and distributed it to the needy. He was promptly given entrance to *Gan Eden*, because regardless of what intent or *kavannah* he had, the needs of the poor had been met.

"Upon awakening, I decided that I would spend much time on a sure thing rather than on uncertainties. That is why I spend so much time collecting *tzedakah*."

Today
I shall smile
because . . .

Some scientists claim that man evolved from animals and was not specially created with a Divine soul. These scientists are not to be blamed, because they never saw a person like Rabbi Yisrael of Salant or the Chafetz Chaim. How are they to realize that true man is qualitatively different?

SMILING EACH DAY

The *mitzvah* of *hachnasas orchim* (hospitality to travelers) is given high rank in the Talmud. One of the first things we are told about the Patriarch Abraham is that he excelled in *hachnasas orchim*.

Hachnasas orchim is more than just supplying a room and meals for the traveler. It means trying to make him comfortable in whatever way possible.

Rabbi David of Lelov generally ate very sparsely, just enough to keep his body functioning. However, when he had guests at the table, he ate along with them, so that they should not feel uncomfortable in satisfying their appetites while their host barely touched the food.

One time there was a guest who ate ravenously, and Rabbi David followed suit. Someone asked him how he could do so, since his stomach was not accustomed to holding more than a few morsels.

"If several guests come to my small home," Rabbi David said, "they are nevertheless accommodated, because somehow the house makes enough place for all of them. If my house can expand in order to accommodate guests, why should my stomach not expand in favor of the guests?"

Today
I shall smile
because . . .

_____
_____
_____

> The perfection of a person is in controlling one's anger, as is indicated in *Proverbs*, "Wisdom consists of being difficult to anger" (*Proverbs* 19:11).

SMILING EACH DAY

Most people would be less than perfectly honest if they denied that they are sometimes irritated when they are constantly put upon to give *tzedakah*. One person complained to his rabbi that a certain collector had asked for money for three different institutions.

"In your business you sell appliances, don't you?" the rabbi replied. "You don't sell only one brand. You have the same appliance made by five or more different companies. If you can be an agent for multiple firms why can't a collector do the same?"

One man complained that on one day more than twenty people had knocked on his door for *tzedakah*. "Twenty times in one day is a bit much," he said. "We must do something to relieve this pressure on people."

"Not necessarily," the rabbi said. "On the average day you breathe about 25,000 times, and that doesn't seem to be too much."

"That's different," the man said. "How can a person live without air?"

"The Torah says that *tzedakah* can save one from death. I don't understand how a person can live without giving *tzedakah*," the rabbi said. "Even thousands of times a day is not too much."

Today
I shall smile
because . . .

TAMMUZ

תמוז

Erev
Rosh Chodesh
*[Eve of the
New Month]*

People avoid exposure to the cold or to contagious diseases in order to protect their bodies from harm, even if the risk is remote. If we value our spirits, we will avoid exposing ourselves to scenes of violence and indecency, and not consider ourselves immune to these harmful influences.

SMILING EACH DAY

Our ideas of prayer are sometimes distorted. Some people consider prayer to be an order to G-d to do what they want, and they are disappointed when their wishes are not granted.

One man told the *Maggid* (preacher) of Trisk that he had heard him quote the *Midrash* that states, "Prayer accomplishes half" (*Vayikra Rabbah* 10:5), meaning that G-d will grant only half of what a person requests.

"I don't understand that," the man said. "G-d's resources are unlimited. If He is going to respond to a person's request, why not give him everything he asks for?"

The *Maggid* responded, "You misunderstood the *Midrash*. What the *Midrash* is telling us is that a person's desires are often far greater than his needs, but he fails to see that his desires are excessive.

"If one prays properly and meditates on the words of the prayer, he should come to an awareness of what is really important in life, and he will realize that many things he had thought necessary are really superfluous. 'Prayer accomplishes half' means that it reduces a person's requests by half."

Today
I shall smile
because . . .

_____
_____
_____

"Influence your child by education, for there is always hope, and do not be overwhelmed by his crying (*Proverbs* 19:18). A child must be taught right from wrong, and parents should not retreat from just guidance and discipline because of the child's crying (*Rabbi Samson Raphael Hirsch*).

AV

אב

Rosh Chodesh

SMILING EACH DAY

The First of Av begins the Nine Days of more intensive mourning for the fall of Jerusalem that began with the Seventeenth of Tammuz.

As we have said, *tzaddikim* were able to find solace even among the ruins. The Talmud states that when the Sages saw the ruins of the Sanctuary, they wept, whereas Rabbi Akiva rejoiced. He explained that the certainty that the prophecy of the ultimate Redemption would be fulfilled was reinforced by the fulfillment of the prophecy that Jerusalem would first be destroyed. The worst had already happened, and therefore we could now anticipate the best with joy.

The yeshivos of Europe had no dormitories or dining rooms. Students were farmed out to people in the community, who obligated themselves to provide meals for a certain number of days for one or more students. This system was referred to as "eating days"; that is, ten days at this home and fifteen days at another, etc.

On the first day of Av, Rabbi Naftali of Ropschitz asked his student, "Do you eat days?"

"Of course," the student replied.

"Then please eat up the Nine Days. We really don't need them."

Today
I shall smile
because . . .

"Give me neither riches nor poverty . . . lest I become vain and say 'who is G-d,' or desperate and become a thief" (*Proverbs* 30:7-9). A wise man asks only for his daily bread, recognizing that his spiritual and moral health are safest in moderation, and at risk at either extreme (*Rabbi Samson Raphael Hirsch*).

SMILING EACH DAY

The reason we must find some cheer even during the period of mourning is because unmitigated grief may result in despair. A hopeless person is likely to resign himself to a loss rather than take the necessary steps to emerge from the ruins and rebuild.

It is related that during the Three Weeks of Mourning, Rabbi Naftali of Ropschitz would repeatedly sing a tune to the words of the prayer, "And You will restore the *Kohanim* (priests) to their service, the Levites to their chants, and Israel to its place of beauty."

A Torah scholar was once walking along the edge of a river when a cry of "Help!" drew his attention to a person who was struggling to stay afloat in the water. Unable to swim, the scholar found a long rope and threw it out to the man, saying, "Better catch hold of this. If you miss it, give my greetings to the *Levyasan* (the legendary whale at the bottom of the sea)."

The scholar explained that this was not gallows humor, but an attempt to minimize the person's anxiety somewhat so that he would be more capable of seizing the rope and saving his life. In a state of panic one may fail to see the way out of disaster.

This is why we must find cheer even in these difficult Nine Days.

Today I shall smile because . . .

_____
_____
_____

> "Do not exert yourself to gather riches, desist from your understanding" (*Proverbs* 23:4). Do not make your main aim in life to be wealthy, and do not think that by your own intelligence, without Divine blessing, you can acquire or protect your possessions (*Rabbi Samson Raphael Hirsch*).

AV

3

אב

SMILING EACH DAY

We say in our prayers, "[Following the loss of our national sovereignty and of the Sanctuary] Now we have nothing left except for the Torah."

A wealthy man stood by helplessly as his beautiful home went up in flames. He cried bitterly over this tragedy, but after the ashes had cooled, he found the metal safe where he kept his money and valuables unharmed by the fire. He rejoiced, because he now had the means to rebuild his beautiful home.

That is how we should relate to the loss of our homeland and Sanctuary. The Torah is indestructible and has remained intact. With the strength of the Torah we can again rebuild our land and our Sanctuary.

Medical research concentrates on finding the cause of a disease. Once the virus or bacteria is discovered, efforts can be directed toward finding a cure. That is how tuberculosis, a disease which killed millions, was overcome.

On each Shabbos of the Three Weeks, we read a portion of the Scriptures that reprimands Israel for its negligence in observance of the Torah. The words of the prophets tell us the cause of our national misfortune, and since we know the cause, correcting our dereliction in Torah observance will enable us to be restored to the glory of old.

Today
I shall smile
because . . .

AV

אב

Sometimes a visitor is an imposition, yet you must receive him politely and pleasantly in order not to offend him. However, when he gets up to leave and you are thrilled that he is departing, do not say, "Must you leave so soon? Can't you stay a bit longer?" That is being totally dishonest (*Beis Yechezkel*).

SMILING EACH DAY

The origins of some established customs are not always known. For example, in the old country there was a practice that on Tisha B'Av (Ninth Day of Av), children would throw thistles that would stick to people's clothes. Perhaps this was someone's idea to add to the misery of the day by causing people to have to remove the annoying thorns from their clothes.

But if this practice made the day more unpleasant for grownups, it certainly had the reverse effect on children, who would collect bags full of thistles to throw on people's clothes and watch with glee as they tried to dislodge the sticky thorns. The children would have contests to see who could get the most thistles to hit their targets. One observer remarked, "Whoever has not seen the *simchah* of children on Tisha B'Av has never seen a *simchah*."

The Rabbi of Rhizin, noting the totally inappropriate atmosphere of the children's glee on Tisha B'Av, raised his eyes to Heaven. "Master of the Universe," he said. "It is obvious that Your children do not observe this special day. Therefore, I think You should take it from them. Let there be no more cause for observing Tisha B'Av."

Today
I shall smile
because . . .

_____
_____
_____

It is a mistake to think that a "harmless" lie is permissible. If a person cheats or deceives by lying, he is transgressing the prohibition against cheating or deceiving. Telling a lie which has no apparent harmful consequences is nevertheless a violation of the Biblical injunction against lying (*Chafetz Chaim*).

SMILING EACH DAY

For so many hundreds of years we have been praying for our Redemption, yet our prayers have not been answered.

It is told that there was a simple pious Jew who had worked hard to secure a piece of land from the *poritz* (feudal lord). He supported himself by a bit of farming and by selling the milk from his cow and the eggs from his chickens. From time to time he would feel the wrath of the local cossacks, who would often get drunk and torment the Jews.

One day the man came home from *shul* with the good news that the rabbi had given a *drashah* (sermon) in which he stated that G-d promised to gather all the Jews from exile and resettle them in Israel under the reign of *Mashiach*. He was somewhat surprised at his wife's cool reception of the good tidings.

"What will become of our farm and cow and chickens if we have to go to Israel?" she asked. The husband tried to convey to her the idea of the Divine promise, but all in vain. "Let *Mashiach* take the cossacks to Israel," she said, "and we will stay here on our farm."

Perhaps our prayers have not been answered because we are too content with where we are.

Today
I shall smile
because . . .

Rabbi Shmuel Greineman was the tenth for a *minyan,* but told the Chazon Ish that he promised to meet someone at one o'clock, and if he remained for the *minyan,* he would be late for his appointment. The Chazon Ish responded, "Keeping your promise overrides the *minyan,*" and instructed him to leave.

SMILING EACH DAY

Rabbi Nachman of Breslov told the story of a Jew who had a non-Jewish friend. The friend asked to be allowed to experience a Seder. Although the table was beautifully set, the guest was disappointed that he was not given anything to eat. Instead, a big book was put into his hands, and he sat patiently while the host recited some unintelligible words in a sonorous tone.

When the books were finally put aside, the guest assumed that the food would now be served. Instead he was given a generous helping of horseradish, which caused him to cough so severely that he felt he would die of choking. He arose and ran out of the house.

The following day he met his friend and complained about the torment of the Seder. "You fool," the friend said. "It is after the bitter horseradish that the delicious meal is served!"

"We, too," said Rabbi Nachman, "have swallowed much bitterness, but it is a prelude to a feast."

Today
I shall smile
because . . .

_____
_____
_____

A rabbi reprimanded someone for addressing a person with a derogatory nickname. "But everyone calls him that!" the man said. "So what?" the rabbi said. "Isn't there room enough in Hell for everyone who does something improper?"

SMILING EACH DAY

Nothing in Jewish life is coincidental. Everything that happens is for a purpose, but we must be alert to it.

The day of the week on which Tisha B'Av occurs is always, without exception, the same day of the week on which the first day of Passover occurs that year. Thus, the night that we read the *Book of Lamentations,* bewailing our exile, is the same night we read about our deliverance from the *golus* (exile) and enslavement of Egypt, and proclaim, *"leshanah haba'ah biYerushalayim —* Next year in Jerusalem!"

It is beyond our understanding why the Redemption must be preceded by so much distress. We are very much like the infant who cannot understand why the mother who obviously loves him with her entire being would allow a doctor to afflict him with a painful injection, and the infant fights to free himself of his mother's grasp as she holds him tightly to assist the doctor. When the infant reaches the age of reason, he is grateful that his mother acted on his behalf to prevent him from getting dreaded diseases.

In our *golus* we are in severe distress, and we ask G-d, "Why are You doing this to us?" One day we will understand, but until then we must have faith that a loving G-d would not harm us.

Today
I shall smile
because . . .

The reader's introductory prayer to the *Amidah* on the high holidays begins with, "I stand here trembling with awe before the majesty of the Almighty." Rabbi Eliyahu Lopian omitted this phrase. "I wish it were true," he said, "but I am not going to lie before G-d."

SMILING EACH DAY

One hundred and fifty years ago the Rabbi of Chordkov said:

"The Talmud refers to the generation of the Exodus as the *dor de'ah*, the generation of knowledge.

"But let us see. The people of that generation had Moses as their leader. They witnessed extraordinary miracles in Egypt and the dividing of the Red Sea. They saw the pillars of cloud and fire guiding them through the wilderness. They were nourished by the *manna* that fell from the sky each day and the well of Miriam that traveled along with them in the desert. Yet the Torah tells us that their faith was not perfect.

"Our generation," the rabbi continued, "is a generation devoid of miracles and prophecy. Jews are oppressed everywhere and suffer bitter persecution. Yet our generation maintains its belief in the G-d of Abraham, Isaac, and Jacob. Are we not a greater generation, truly deserving of Redemption?"

Since the days of the Rabbi of Chordkov, Jews have experienced unprecedented challenges to our faith, yet we maintain our trust in the G-d of our fathers.

By virtue of this unshakable trust we will indeed merit the Redemption.

Today
I shall smile
because . . .

_____
_____
_____

> "A false balance-scale is an abomination to G-d" (*Proverbs* 11:1). Not only is deceiving someone by false weights sinful, but the mere possession of a dishonest scale is a sin. One should divest oneself of instruments of sin even if one does not use them (*Rabbi Samson Raphael Hirsch*).

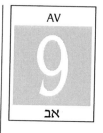

AV

9

אב

Fast of Tishah B'Av
[When 9 Av falls on the Sabbath the fast is observed on Sunday.]

SMILING EACH DAY

Our faith in the Redemption never falters, and the mourning of Tisha B'Av does not go into effect until Tisha B'Av actually arrives.

In the late afternoon before Tisha B'Av, Rabbi Levi Yitzchak of Berdichev stood at the window, and even when he was told that people were gathering at the synagogue to read the *Book of Lamentations,* he nevertheless remained at the window. Only when it was fully dark did he leave the window, saying, "*Mashiach* has not come. We have no choice but to observe the fast of Tisha B'Av."

One chassidic master could not be distracted from his incessant weeping on the night of Tisha B'Av, and chassidim were fearful that his profound mourning would cause his soul to depart from his body. They therefore called a very resourceful member of the group to try and draw the Rabbi out of his deep mourning.

The chassid entered the Rabbi's study and said, "I see the Rabbi is crying because the Sanctuary was burnt to the ground. Well, you can stop right now. True, the building is gone, but the real estate is worth every cent!"

The Rabbi stopped crying. True, the Sanctuary that was once there is gone, but the sacred site is intact, waiting for the ultimate Sanctuary to be rebuilt.

Today
I shall smile
because . . .

We pray to G-d that He fulfill His promises to the patriarchs to bless their children, promises that were unconditional. We must remember, however, that G-d relates to us as we relate to others. If we will love unconditionally, we will be loved unconditionally.

SMILING EACH DAY

As was mentioned earlier (27 Tammuz), the *mitzvah* of *hachnasas orchim* (hospitality to guests) is given high priority. The Talmud states that the patriarch Abraham was in the midst of a dialogue with G-d when he saw the three travelers from afar (*Genesis* 18:1-2), and that he took leave of G-d in order to welcome them. The Talmud concludes that *hachnasas orchim* even supersedes speaking with G-d.

Rabbi Chanoch of Bendin once rushed breathlessly into the kitchen and said to his wife, "Quick! We have a special guest coming! Prepare the table appropriately." The wife quickly set the table with the tablecloth and dishes usually reserved for use on Shabbos or festivals.

When the guest came, Rabbi Chanoch helped him off with his coat and behaved toward him with great respect. After the man left, his wife asked, "Who was the man that you treated so regally?"

Rabbi Chanoch said, "I don't know. He is just a stranger passing through town."

"Then why did we have to make such a fuss over him?" she asked.

"Because the Talmud says that receiving a stranger is greater than receiving the Divine Presence," he said. "What would we do to greet the *Shechinah* (Divine Presence) if it were coming into our home?"

Today
I shall smile
because . . .

_____

_____

_____

We say in our prayers, "You have given us a Torah of life." When an accident victim is brought into the emergency room, the first concern is to see that he is able to breathe, because otherwise all other treatment is futile. The Torah is our breath of life, for without it nothing else is of value.

SMILING EACH DAY

The *yetzer hara* does his job well. No sooner does a person begin to pray and meditate than the *yetzer hara* introduces a variety of thoughts to distract him.

Rabbi Shmuel of Lubavitch told a chassid that a person should never lose sight of the fact that he is always in the service of G-d. "Even when you are involved in purchasing grain from the peasants, you should always be thinking of your devotion to G-d."

"But how can I do that when I am engaged in trade?" the chassid asked.

"That should be no problem. You seem to have no difficulty thinking of trade while you are praying," the Rabbi answered.

Rabbi Levi Yitzchak of Berdichev once said to a chassid after the *Amidah*, "*Shalom aleichem!* Welcome home."

The astonished chassid said that he did not understand the greeting. "Very simple," Rabbi Levi Yitzchak said. "During the *Amidah* you were in Leipzig and in various other marketplaces, so I greeted you on your return!"

Today
I shall smile
because . . .

"The unwise disparage wisdom and ethics" (*Proverbs* 1:7). Some people respect knowledge, but think that it can be of value even if detached from proper behavior. Knowledge and ethics must go together, because otherwise knowledge may be disgraceful.

SMILING EACH DAY

A man once consulted a rabbi. "I bought an item from a merchant, and I discovered that he had overcharged me. However, since the excess is less than the amount for which I can claim a refund [in Jewish law there is no recourse for an overcharge of less than one-sixth above the price], I cannot get my money back. I know the rabbi has taught us that the Torah forbids us to take revenge, but this gives me no peace. I must do something to get back at that scoundrel."

The rabbi tried to explain to the man that one must overcome the desire for vengeance even when he has been cheated, but to no avail. The man insisted that he must draw blood.

Seeing that there was no reasoning with him, the rabbi said, "Then listen to me and do exactly as I say. Go into his store and pick up an item. Ask him the price, and without any haggling pay the specified amount immediately. Then say, 'Thank you so much. This is just what I needed and could not find elsewhere.' Then return to me."

The man did as he was told and returned with an item for which he had paid two rubles. "Now what am I to do?" he asked.

"Now you are to think about how that merchant is eating his heart out because he did not quote you a price of five rubles!"

Today
I shall smile
because . . .

_____

_____

_____

"One who restrains himself when in anger will never have cause for regret" (*Book of the Just*). How often do we regret having said things in the heat of anger. If one can maintain a calm attitude, one will have no reason to regret words that cannot be retrieved.

SMILING EACH DAY

The Rabbi of Ovrutch, a town in the Ukraine, had an intense longing to live in Israel, an objective which was not easily achieved in the early 1800's. Occasionally a visitor from Israel would travel through Ovrutch on his rounds to raise funds for the poor, and the Rabbi would question him about every detail of the land and its people. One visitor told him, "Every stone, every rock in the Holy Land is a jewel."

After much effort the Rabbi made *aliyah* and settled in Tzefas. Although living conditions were very difficult, he was overjoyed. In his book, *Bas Eyin*, which is full of praise for the Holy Land, he writes that there is a level of spirituality that is impossible to achieve unless one's body is nourished by fruits and grains that grow in the sacred soil.

One time the aforementioned visitor came to Tzefas, and the Rabbi shared with him his joy about being in Israel. "However," he said, "I still see the rocks as being merely rocks."

"Then you have not advanced sufficiently in your spirituality," the man said.

Time went by, and one day the Rabbi prepared a feast and called all his friends together for a celebration. To his surprised guests, who had no idea why they were assembled, the Rabbi said, "Today I finally came to see that every rock in the Holy Land is a precious jewel!"

Today
I shall smile
because . . .

"If a person becomes furious, all forces of Hell dominate over him" (*Nedarim* 22a). Each individual temptation can lead to only one sin, whereas loss of self-control in fury can lead to a multiplicity of sins, hence all forces of Hell can become dominant (*Chafetz Chaim*).

SMILING EACH DAY

The Torah relates that when Pharaoh's daughter saw the little basket in which Moses had been hidden floating down the river, "She sent forth her maid to fetch it" (*Exodus* 2:5). The Hebrew word for "maid" can also be translated as "arm," in which case the verse reads, "She stretched out her arm." The Midrash says that the box was beyond her reach, but that when she tried to retrieve it, her hand miraculously stretched.

The brothers Rabbi Elimelech and Rabbi Zusya were once walking in the countryside when a man called to them, "Hey, you Jews, come help me load my wagon." Because they were in a hurry to reach their destination, Rabbi Zusya said, "Sorry, we can't."

"Yes, you can," the man said. "You just don't want to."

The brothers looked at one another, understanding this as a Divine message for them. There is much that one *can* do, and if we think we cannot, it is often because we don't really want to.

You may think something is beyond your reach, but if you really want to do it, go ahead and try. Like Pharaoh's daughter, your capacity to achieve it may increase.

Today
I shall smile
because . . .

_____
_____
_____

The person who smokes poisons himself, and others who inhale and absorb the smoke subject themselves to the poison. Similarly, a person who is furious destroys himself, but those who absorb the fury subject themselves to its destructive effects.

SMILING EACH DAY

Someone once asked a rabbi, "Since Shabbos is supposed to be a totally spiritual day, one characterized by prayer and Torah study, why is there so much emphasis on delicacies — *gefilte* fish, *kugel*, roast chicken, and all the other trimmings? Doesn't this detract from the spirituality of the day?"

The rabbi answered: "A king once had to exile his wayward son to a far-off land, where the young prince paid dearly for his misbehavior.

"After several years passed, the king sent a messenger to see whether his son had repented, and if so, to convey a pardon and invite him back. The messenger found that the son had indeed repented, and told him that he could return to the palace.

"The prince was overjoyed and wished to express his great joy in song and dance. But he knew that if he did this, people who did not understand what had happened would think he had gone crazy. He therefore went into a tavern and bought rounds of drinks for everyone there. Soon all the people began to sing and dance, and he sang and danced along with them. They danced because of their inebriation, while the prince danced from the joy of his imminent return home.

"The *neshamah* (soul) wishes to rejoice in the holiness of Shabbos, but the physical body gets in the way. We therefore give the body something to enjoy so that it too celebrates, and the *neshamah* can then enjoy the spirit of Shabbos without impediment."

Today
I shall smile
because . . .

AV

אב

Fury knows no limits. A person who is furious will be so with G-d, with other people, and even with himself. Fury will therefore deprive a person of the companionship of G-d, of other people, and will also alienate a person from himself.

SMILING EACH DAY

Rabbi Yaakov Kranz, the famed *Maggid* (preacher) of Dubno, was traveling in a coach where several *maskilim* ("enlightened" Jews who had deviated from Orthodox tradition) were mocking him, ridiculing his beard and traditional garb. Their behavior was so offensive that one of the other travelers, who recognized Rabbi Yaakov, told them to stop. He informed them that the person they were ridiculing was the famous *Maggid*.

One of the *maskilim* approached Rabbi Yaakov and said, "If you are indeed so famous for your parables, let us see you think up a parable promptly for us, but don't quote Scripture to us."

Rabbi Yaakov responded: "A teacher once told his students that if they were ever attacked by a dog, they were to say the verse, 'To all the Jews not even a dog barked at them' (*Exodus* 11:7), and this would subdue and silence the dog.

"As the teacher left the school, a dog jumped at him, and he picked up his heels and ran. The following day the students asked him why he had fled without invoking the defensive tactic he had taught them.

" 'I couldn't,' he said. 'The dog did not give me a chance to quote the Scripture.' "

Today
I shall smile
because . . .

_____
_____
_____

The blessings preceding the *Shema,* both in the morning and in the evening, refer to the great phenomena of nature. "How great are Your doings, Oh G-d, You have fashioned them all with wisdom" (*Psalms* 104:24). The appreciation of G-d through the wonders of nature is an introduction to attesting to His unity.

SMILING EACH DAY

A man once came to one of the chassidic masters and said that he had been suffering tremendous anxiety because he was sure that some evil would befall him. He said that he was happily married and that his children were all well, his business was prospering, he had many friends, and that he lacked for nothing. He felt this state of contentment was unnatural and was terrified that something dreadful was certain to happen. The only other possibility was that he belonged to the category of people who are so evil that G-d rewards them in this world for the few *mitzvos* that they have done so that they will not have any portion in Paradise. However, the man did not think he was that bad.

The rabbi took out a book with some small print and asked the man to read it. The man said he could not see the fine print. "Then you do not wear eyeglasses?" the rabbi asked.

The man explained that he did not want to be bothered with eyeglasses, since he could get along well enough without them.

"No," the rabbi said. "You must get eyeglasses in order to read. You will then frequently misplace your glasses and be frustrated when you can't find them. That will suffice as a source of distress for you, so that you will not have to anticipate any misfortune."

Today
I shall smile
because . . .

We pray, "Do not cast us away from Your presence." The truth is that G-d never detaches Himself from us. If there is ever any separation, it is because we detach ourselves from Him. "Let there not be any indecency among you, so that G-d will not depart from you" (*Deuteronomy* 23:15).

SMILING EACH DAY

The adage "Strike while the iron is hot" applies to *mitzvos* as well, and the Talmud states that if one has the opportunity to perform a *mitzvah*, he should promptly take advantage of it.

Shimon Rothschild of Frankfurt was once walking in the street when he was approached by a man who told him of his sad plight. Rothschild was very touched by the man's distress, but at the moment he did not happen to have any money with him. He removed the gold chain from his watch and said, "Here, my dear man, sell this; and may G-d bless you!"

The man was taken aback. "Please," he said, "there is no need for that. I will be glad to come to your office at your convenience."

"No," Rothschild said. "You see, right now your story has deeply touched me. By the time you see me tomorrow, I might not feel for you as profoundly as I do now, and I might give you less."

While there is nothing humorous or even witty about this anecdote, it is uplifting to know how intensely a person can feel about helping another, and also that it is possible for one to know enough about himself to realize that he should act before his enthusiasm wanes.

Today
I shall smile
because . . .

_____

_____

_____

It is customary to recite the thirteen principles of faith every morning after services. Some things expire after passage of time, and require renewal. So it is with faith. Unless it is frequently renewed, it may deteriorate without our being aware of it (*Chafetz Chaim*).

SMILING EACH DAY

The great Talmudist Rabbi Pinchas Horowitz (the *Hafla'ah*) told the story of how he became a follower of the chassidic master, the *Maggid* of Mezeritch. Rabbi Pinchas was an accomplished scholar, and on his initial visit to Mezeritch he was disappointed at the level of scholarship among the *Maggid*'s disciples.

Before he left, the *Maggid* told him to discuss Talmud with Rabbi Zusya. The latter claimed to be ignorant of Talmud, but stated that he did have a question which bothered him.

"One authority in the Talmud states that if there are only nine people assembled for *davening,* one can count the Ark as the tenth person to complete the *minyan* (quorum of ten). This is challenged by someone who asks, 'But is the Ark really a *mentsch* (person)?' What kind of challenge is this? Obviously the one who gave the first opinion also knew that the Ark is an inanimate object."

Rabbi Pinchas could not answer the question.

"Perhaps," Rabbi Zusya said, "the first proponent felt that because it contains the Torah, the Ark should be counted for a *minyan*. The challenger then said, 'What good is something that is full of Torah if it is not a *mentsch*?' "

Rabbi Pinchas got the point. It is possible to be full of "book-knowledge" of Torah and yet not be a *mentsch*.

He remained in Mezeritch.

Today
I shall smile
because . . .

A person who overcomes the propensity to be easily aroused to anger will develop humility and sensitivity to others. Harboring anger and resentments leads to arrogance and cruelty (*The Ways of the Righteous*).

SMILING EACH DAY

A rabbi once pointed out that in the past, people would tell their rabbi about their shortcomings and character defects so that he could guide them to *teshuvah*, whereas today people tell him about how much *tzedakah* they give, how much they learn, etc.

The rabbi told the following story. "Two patients who both had broken legs shared a room in a hospital. The doctor examined the first patient, who cried with pain every time the doctor manipulated the leg.

"When the doctor finished with the first patient, he examined the second patient, who did not utter a sound during the entire procedure. After the doctor left the room, the first patient said, 'I have the greatest admiration for you for being able to withstand so much pain without uttering a single sound.'

"The second patient said, 'Do you think I'm crazy? After watching what he did to you, I showed him the good leg.' "

Not revealing one's defects to a rabbi is as helpful as not showing a doctor the diseased leg.

Today
I shall smile
because . . .

_____
_____
_____

> When people behave decently and pleasantly to one another, G-d is pleased and forgives their transgressions (*Maalos Hamidos*).

SMILING EACH DAY

When the Empress Maria Theresa came to Prague for a state visit, she was honored with a reception at which young Jewish girls entertained her with colorful dancing. The rabbi of Prague, Rabbi Yechezkel Landau (the *Noda B'Yehudah*), as head of the Jewish community, had to attend the reception to honor the Empress.

One of the officers in attendance was a General Brockman, a high official in the government who was an ardent anti-Semite. It was rumored that he had once lost an important battle because instead of being at his command post, he was indulging in drunken revelry.

When the Empress applauded the performance of the Jewish girls, Brockman was irritated and said, "It is little wonder that they dance so well. After all, they learned how to dance in front of the Golden Calf" (*Exodus* 32:6).

Rabbi Landau promptly responded, "The episode of the Golden Calf is indeed a shameful mark in our history. It occurred because Moses had not returned from Sinai (ibid. 32:1). Such calamities can happen only when the general who is supposed to be responsible is away from the people."

Today
I shall smile
because . . .

Even when a person is championing the cause of justice, he should be cautious that righteous indignation should not deteriorate into fury. Our great leader Moses was justly upset by the Israelites' lack of trust in G-d, yet was reprimanded for becoming furious with them.

SMILING EACH DAY

Rabbi Levi Yitzchak of Berdichev overheard a man relating a tale of woe to a *maggid* (preacher). The man said that he had been doing his best to live according to the Torah but had suffered enormous *tzoros* (misery); he was sick, financially destitute, and distressed by problems with his children. "Where is G-d's justice?" he asked. "Is this my reward for doing His will?"

The *maggid* responded that G-d's judgment is always perfect, and that the reward for *mitzvos* is a spiritual reward, to be received in the Eternal World.

Rabbi Levi Yitzchak, who was an advocate *par excellence* for the Jews, interrupted, saying to the *maggid*, "You have no right to say that! This man came to you with a complaint against G-d. If you are going to act as the judge in the case, you must be unbiased. A judge who receives gifts from one of the litigants is disqualified. G-d has given you life, health, and everything you own. You are therefore disqualified from hearing this case, particularly from deciding in favor of the One to whom you are indebted. This man's claims remain unanswered. My opinion is that if he has suffered physical *tzoros*, he is entitled to physical relief and reward."

Today
I shall smile
because . . .

_____
_____
_____

"If you see someone losing control because of anger, you can be certain that his sins outnumber his good deeds" (*Nedarim* 22b). A public display of anger is thus a public admission of one's lack of spirituality. How foolish to make such a public declaration!

SMILING EACH DAY

The two chassidic masters, the brothers Rabbi Elimelech and Rabbi Zusya, took upon themselves several years of voluntary exile and wandered from hamlet to hamlet, trying to pick up the spirits of their oppressed Jewish brethren.

One time they came to a village and entered the shul where the rabbi was giving a Torah lecture. They sat by quietly, listening to his talk. This went on for several days, and no one, including the rabbi, greeted them or paid any attention to them.

On Friday night it was customary for the townsfolk to invite any strangers in shul to the Shabbos meal. After the services the rabbi approached the two brothers and asked them who they were.

Rabbi Elimelech said, "Now I understand why Moses said, 'They are a perverse generation' (*Deuteronomy* 32:20).

"The *Midrash* states that when Moses came up to Heaven to receive the Torah, the angels asked, 'What is a mortal doing here?' On the other hand, when Abraham saw the three angels, he invited them to eat promptly and did not ask them who they were.

"All week when we came to your Torah lectures, you did not ask us who we were. But now that we are to be invited for a meal, you wish to know who we are. That is just the reverse of the order that the Torah teaches us."

Today
I shall smile
because . . .

A person's heart should be a dwelling place for the Divine presence. Since harboring anger is equivalent to idolatry, one who harbors resentments is placing an idol in one's heart, and thereby banishing the Divine presence from there.

SMILING EACH DAY

There has been a long-standing controversy about pictures of *tzaddikim*. Although the Ten Commandments explicitly forbids making images, the *halachah* explains that this refers only to a statue and not to a picture. In days prior to the candid camera, taking a picture required the laborious process of setting up a tripod, and those who did not wish to be photographed could easily avoid it.

Some *tzaddikim* were concerned that although picture-taking was halachically permissible, their students or followers might inadvertently or subconsciously come to adore their pictures, which would be remotely akin to the worship of an image. Others who took an opposite position quoted the verse, "Let your eyes behold your teacher," claiming that a visual reminder of the *tzaddik* could serve as an inspiration to spiritual progress. Of course, since the introduction of the candid camera there is no longer a choice, because anyone can be photographed without his awareness.

Rabbi Abraham of Sochochov visited the home of a chassid where a picture of Rabbi Shneur Zalman was displayed. "Anyone who learns the *Tanya* and the *Shulchan Aruch* of Rabbi Shneur Zalman," he said, "has a far better grasp of what he was like than one who looks at his picture. If you are really interested in knowing the Rebbe, learn his works."

Today
I shall smile
because . . .

"One who publicly embarrasses another person forfeits one's share in the eternal world" (*Ethics of our Fathers* 3:15). Losing one's demeanor in fury may result in such embarrassment, and all the merits of a lifetime may be lost by a single thoughtless comment made in the heat of anger.

SMILING EACH DAY

A rabbi solicited a donation for a worthy cause from a very wealthy man and was refused. He politely said goodbye and then added, "You will certainly merit entering *Gan Eden* (Paradise)."

"That is strange," the miser said. "You give me a blessing even though I refused you."

"Well, it's like this," the rabbi said. "Many years ago a miser died and instructed that all his money be buried along with him. When he came before the Heavenly Tribunal and they asked whether he had given *tzedakah*, he said that there were too many cheats who fraudulently collected for charity, and he therefore had to take his money to distribute in the Eternal World, where truth prevails.

"The Heavenly Tribunal could not decide what to do with this man, because they had never heard such an argument. On the one hand, the reasoning was bizarre, but on the other hand it had some merit. They therefore told the man to wait outside the gates of *Gan Eden*. If another person came along with a similar argument, that would prove its validity, and he would be permitted entry.

"It is obvious that you, too, intend to take your wealth with you," the rabbi said in conclusion to the miser. "You will be that second person, and both of you will enter *Gan Eden*."

Today
I shall smile
because . . .

Anger may so blind a person to reality that one may even swear falsely under the impression that one is telling the truth. Thus, anger may result in the violation of one of the most serious offenses of the Torah: Taking G-d's name in vain.

SMILING EACH DAY

Truth and humility are like Siamese twins. Wherever you find one, the other is always there.

Someone asked the *Maggid* of Mezeritch: "Inasmuch as it is written,' Truth springs forth from the ground,' truth should certainly be available in great abundance. Why is it that falsehood seems to prevail, and truth is such a rarity?"

The *Maggid* answered, "It is because when truth springs forth from the ground, it remains at a low height, and in order to pick it up, one must stoop down. But no one wishes to humble himself to pick up the truth."

Truth is G-dliness, and if one is aware of the infinity of his duties towards G-d, he cannot but be humble. One of the chassidic masters said, "I am so grateful that *ga'avah* (vanity) is not a *mitzvah*. If it were, what could I possibly be vain about?"

The Rabbi of Kotzk, referring to the above verse that "Truth springs forth from the ground," said that growth from the ground first requires planting. "If you bury falsehood, truth will grow."

Today
I shall smile
because . . .

_____
_____
_____

A wise man said, "I could walk on hot coals without being burned, and I could walk through a flame without being scorched. But I cannot avoid being completely consumed by the flame of anger if I do not promptly extinguish it (*The Lamp of Illumination*).

SMILING EACH DAY

A chassid once complained to his Rebbe about his many miseries.

The Rebbe replied, "A man was once accused of stealing something valuable, but he protested his innocence. The judge believed the accuser and sentenced the man to lashings. Each time he was lashed, he cried out in pain, 'But I am innocent!'

"Some time later, the real thief was apprehended. The judge then told the accuser that he must compensate the man whom he had unjustly accused by paying a gold coin for each lash the man had received.

"As the accuser was counting out the gold coins, the man turned to the judge and said angrily, 'Why did you order so few lashings? Had you ordered more, I would be richer yet!'

"Believe me," concluded the Rebbe, "when you come to the Eternal World and see that the distress you experienced in this world atoned for so many of your misdeeds, you will bewail the fact that you had so few miseries rather than so many."

Today
I shall smile
because . . .

If a person who felt offended by not being duly honored in *shul* reacted by deserting the faith, he would be soundly condemned. One who becomes furious when his ego becomes offended is doing no less, because the Talmud says that becoming furious is equivalent to idol worship.

SMILING EACH DAY

Rabbi Abraham of Sochochov was a child prodigy who was fluent in the entire Talmud even before his Bar Mitzvah. His father, Rabbi Nachum Ze'ev, was an accomplished scholar. One time when the young Abraham related to his father an intricate *halachah* he had developed, Rabbi Nachum Ze'ev told his son that he was in error, and rebutted his entire argument.

Several years passed. Rabbi Nachum Ze'ev was studying a particular commentary on the Talmud one day when he realized that his rebuttal of his son's argument had been in error. He contacted his son and asked him if he remembered their discussion of several years earlier. "I remember every word," the young man answered.

"Well, I just discovered that you were right and I was wrong," Rabbi Nachum Ze'ev said.

The young man smiled. "I knew that," he said.

"Then why didn't you correct me?" Rabbi Nachum Ze'ev asked.

"Just because I was right does not absolve me of the *mitzvah* of *kibbud av* (respecting one's father)," Rabbi Abraham said.

Today
I shall smile
because . . .

> A saintly person is one who is difficult to anger but easy to appease (*Ethics of the Fathers* 5:14). If he is difficult to anger, then he must have been intensely provoked before becoming angry, yet even then he is easy to appease.

SMILING EACH DAY

A man came to Rabbi Yitzchak of Vorki and asked him to speak on his behalf to a relative of his, who had refused his request for financial help. Rabbi Yitzchak visited the wealthy man, who gave abundant reasons why he could not give his relative the requested amount of money.

Rabbi Yitzchak made no further comments, but just sat silently.

The wealthy man became impatient. "I'm sorry, Rabbi, but you are wasting your time if you think I will change my mind. There is no reason for you to wait."

"Of course there is," Rabbi Yitzchak said. "You see, the *yetzer hara* (evil inclination) is present in a person at birth. The *yetzer tov* (the good inclination) does not come until much later.

"What you have just told me is the opinion of the *yetzer hara*. If I wait a bit, the *yetzer tov* will catch up, and he will give you another opinion which will be altogether different."

After a few moments, the wealthy man took out his checkbook and wrote a check for the desired amount.

Today
I shall smile
because . . .

AV

אב

First Day of
Rosh Chodesh
Elul

Is it not strange that a person who seeks honor and recognition may think himself to be independent and self-sufficient? But where would he be without others to supply his ego needs? This poor soul is the most dependent person in the world (*Rabbi Yisrael of Salant*)!

SMILING EACH DAY

A wealthy man once complained to Rabbi Hillel of Rodoshitz about the poor who came to him for alms. "When someone asks politely for alms and is satisfied with whatever he receives, that is fine with me. What I cannot tolerate is those who have *chutzpah* and demand more money as though it is their due, and who are never satisfied with what they get."

Rabbi Hillel responded, "I share your tolerances and intolerances, with just a slight modification.

"If a wealthy person is a miser and refuses to give charity, claiming that G-d entrusted the money to him for safekeeping and that he is not permitted to squander it, I strongly disagree with him — but I can tolerate that.

"But a wealthy person who thinks that the money he has is all his, that he gathered it by his own effort and cunning and has the right to make decisions about whom to give to and how much to give, as though he were the rightful master of his own wealth rather than someone to whom it has been entrusted — that is someone whom I cannot tolerate."

Today
I shall smile
because . . .

_____
_____
_____

> A vain person is very aware of himself. One is generally not aware of one's eyes, ears, or throat until they are diseased and cause discomfort. One is generally not aware of one's "self" unless it is diseased. Vanity is a disease of the "self."

SMILING EACH DAY

Today begins the month before the High Holidays, a month designated as particularly propitious for *teshuvah*. As with the Three Weeks of Mourning, we might appear hard pressed to arouse cheerfulness during such solemn days, when conducting a personal inventory reveals the unfortunate, sinful mistakes we have made in the past year.

The Talmud states that in the imminent presence of G-d there is always *simchah* (joy) (*Chronicles I* 16:27). It also states that *teshuvah* reaches all the way to the Divine throne. Thus, doing *teshuvah* brings one before the Divine presence, where *simchah* prevails.

A child who must have a splinter removed cries bitterly as the needle painfully probes his hand. Once he hears the remark, "There, it's out!" the tears are immediately wiped away and he smiles from ear to ear, apparently forgetting his suffering of just a moment ago.

Sin is a foreign body which does not belong in our systems. We may hurt and cry as we try to eliminate it, but once we have done so, we can happily exclaim, "There, it's out!" and the pain quickly falls into the oblivion of the past.

Today
I shall smile
because . . .

Why be vain? One cannot impress G-d, and can only impress others until they begin to see through one's exterior. The only one who can be consistently deceived is oneself. What kind of triumph is it to deceive a fool?

SMILING EACH DAY

Not far from the home of Rabbi Isaiah of Prague, there was a blind man who would put up a stand daily to sell cookies. On winter days he would stand in the cold until the cookies were sold, continuously in fear that he would be penalized for peddling without a license. One day he was indeed arrested and fined, and he poured out his aching heart before Rabbi Isaiah.

Rabbi Isaiah promptly paid the fine, and every day after that, as soon as the man set up his stand, the Rabbi would buy the entire stock of cookies and distribute them to the school children. Some people asked him why he went through this charade. Would it not be simpler if he just gave the man the money?

"In no way," the Rabbi said. "This man feels he is doing something useful, performing a service by supplying me with cookies and thereby earning an honorable living. If he were to get the money as charity, he would be deprived of his pride.

"He has already lost his vision. Shall we take his pride from him, too?"

Today
I shall smile
because . . .

_____

_____

_____

One who is self-effacing because he is unaware of his talents and strengths is not a humble person at all, but rather a fool. A humble person knows his capabilities, but is aware that they are Divine gifts for which he cannot take credit.

SMILING EACH DAY

A man asked Rabbi Michel of Zlotchow what he must do to atone for having accidentally violated the Shabbos. Rabbi Michel prescribed a stringent program of penance.

When the man related this incident to the Baal Shem Tov, the latter told him that the penance was unnecessary, and that all he needed to do was to supply the synagogue with candles for a month. He then sent a message to Rabbi Michel, inviting him for Shabbos.

Rabbi Michel left home on Thursday with ample time to arrive in Medziboz, where the Baal Shem Tov lived. However, while he was en route there were heavy rains, and his wagon got stuck in the mud. After he extricated it, an axle broke, followed by several other freakish happenings that delayed his arrival in Medziboz until late Friday afternoon, thirty minutes before sunset. He rushed to the Baal Shem Tov's home, only to discover that his host was already reciting the *kiddush*. Concluding that he had been riding on Shabbos, Rabbi Michel fainted.

The Baal Shem Tov helped to revive him, and then said, "I made *kiddush* before sunset today, so you did not violate the Shabbos at all. But now you know the deep regret a person feels when he thinks he has accidentally violated the Shabbos. This regret constitutes the true *teshuvah*, and no severe penance is necessary."

Today
I shall smile
because . . .

Rabbi Avraham the *Malach* (the "angel") was once visited by a man in whom he detected vanity. Rabbi Avraham pointed to a tall mountain and said, "Is it not amazing that the mountain considers itself tall and majestic, when it is only really a mere clump of earth?"

SMILING EACH DAY

Someone asked the *Maggid* (preacher) of Dubno why the order of the Ten Plagues is different in the *Psalms* than in the Torah. In *Exodus* (8:13) the plague of lice precedes the invasion by wild animals, whereas in *Psalms* (105:31) lice comes after the invasion by animals.

The *Maggid* answered, "A wealthy man married off his daughter, and the wedding celebration was held for the traditional seven days. He wished to invite all the townsfolk, and in order to accommodate everyone, he designated one day for all his relatives, one day for business people, one day for scholars, one day for the poor, etc. He told his servants that no one should be allowed to attend more than one celebration.

"A poor man came for a second time, and the servants refused him entry. 'You were already here once,' they said.

"The man replied, 'Yes, I was here on the day for the poor. But I am also a distant relative, and today I come as a family member. I am doubly qualified.'

"This," the *Maggid* said, "is precisely what happened in Egypt. First the lice came as a distinct plague. But when G-d sent in all the various animals, the lice came along as members of the animal kingdom, because they were doubly qualified. The versions in the Torah and in the *Psalms* are both correct."

Today
I shall smile
because . . .

_____

_____

_____

"Without Divine assistance, a person cannot withstand temptation" (*Succah* 52b). "Arrogance drives the Divine presence away" (*Arachin* 15b). It follows that an arrogant person is totally at the mercy of his temptation, and that arrogance can lead to total dissolution.

SMILING EACH DAY

Rabbi Levi Yitzchak of Berdichev once met a man who was known in the community to be totally non-observant. In his characteristically boundless love for everyone, Rabbi Levi Yitzchak embraced him and inquired after his welfare. Then he said, "I truly envy you. You can reach a place in *Gan Eden* (Paradise) that I cannot aspire to."

"Why do you mock me, rabbi?" the man asked. "You know I have nothing to do with *Gan Eden.*"

Rabbi Levi Yitzchak answered, "The Talmud says that when a person does sincere *teshuvah*, all his sins are converted into merits. Of course you will one day do *teshuvah*, because at the core of your *neshamah* (soul) you wish to do the will of G-d. It is just that so far temptation has been overwhelming, and you are unable to resist it. The nature of temptation is that it grows weaker with time, and when your temptations are exhausted, you will then do sincere *teshuvah*.

"Just think of how many merits you will then acquire. When all of the things you have done are converted into merits, you will have more than anyone else could ever aspire to."

Today
I shall smile
because . . .

If someone tells you something of Torah that you already know, just listen patiently. It is arrogance to interrupt and say, "I already know that." Furthermore, words of wisdom are worth hearing many times (*Sefer Chassidim*).

SMILING EACH DAY

Several hundred years ago, the *pilpul* method of Talmud study was introduced. Instead of analyzing each *halachah* on its own, as had been the practice, *pilpul* compares various *halachos* or statements of Talmudic authorities, finds contradictions between them, and devises ingenious methods to reconcile them, resulting in a very complex discussion. Many Talmudic authorities disapproved of the *pilpul* method, claiming it to be intellectually dishonest, and they openly ridiculed it.

One of them jokingly paraphrased a *pilpul.* "A man returned to his studies and could not locate his eyeglasses. He reasoned, 'Who could possibly have taken them? Certainly not someone who has no need for them. Yet someone who does need them would have his own glasses. If a thief stole them, who could he possibly sell them to? Anyone who needs them would already have a pair.

" 'The only possibility is that someone moved his glasses up unto his forehead and forgot that he did so. As this person walked by and saw my eyeglasses, he took them by mistake. But by the same token, I too might have moved my eyeglasses onto my forehead and forgotten that they were there.' The man then reached up to his forehead, and lo and behold! There they were."

That is how the *pilpul* method arrives at a conclusion.

Today
I shall smile
because . . .

_____
_____
_____

Rabbi Chaim Cheskia Medini, author of the classic halachic work *Sede Chemed,* would enter the synagogue at a time when the congregation was reciting one of the prayers that are said in a standing posture, so that no one would rise in his honor.

SMILING EACH DAY

Although changing one's character might appear to be a major task, and sometimes quite a formidable one, Rabbi Levi Yitzchak of Berdichev reduced it to a simple formula.

"Not much has changed in the world," Rabbi Levi Yitzchak said. "People have always told the truth, and people have always lied. The only difference is one of place.

"In past days, people used to be pious and observant. They dealt honestly in business and were truthful in relating to others. When they came into *shul* and confessed, 'I have sinned, I have cheated, I have stolen,' they were lying. In other words, they were truthful in the street, and they lied in *shul*.

"Today people are dishonest in business and lie to one another. When they say the confession in prayer, they are therefore telling the truth. Thus they lie in the street and are truthful in *shul*.

"All that is necessary is simply to restore truth and lying to their original locations," Rabbi Levi Yitzchak concluded. "That should not be too difficult."

Today
I shall smile
because . . .

Man shares many appetites with animals, and like animals, he seeks to gratify them. But man should also have a hunger for knowledge, which distinguishes him from animals. If man fails to pursue acquisition of knowledge, he is very much like an animal (*Rabbi Simcha Zissel of Kelm*).

SMILING EACH DAY

At a *bris milah* (covenant of circumcision) the child's father is wished, "Just as he (the baby) was entered into the *bris*, so shall he be introduced to Torah, *chupah* (marriage), and good deeds." The obvious question is that since a person has the opportunity to do good deeds long before marriage, shouldn't the order rather be, "introduced to Torah, good deeds, and *chupah*"?

Rabbi Bezalel, the *posek* of Vilna, was a child prodigy. At age eleven his knowledge of Talmud was astounding, and since most marriages in those days were arranged, many people sought to obtain this future Torah luminary as a son-in-law. The competition was fierce, and a *shidduch* (marriage match) was completed when Bezalel was about twelve.

At the engagement celebration, one rabbi said, "Now I understand the sequence of the blessing at the *bris*. We wish the father that his son should so excel in Torah that at a very young age everyone will seek to take him as a son-in-law. In that way, the *chupah* may actually occur before the young man has had an opportunity to do many good deeds."

Today
I shall smile
because . . .

_____

_____

_____

When Rabbi Shneur Zalman was asked why he did not include Shabbos *zemiros* (songs) in his *siddur,* he said, "Song must come from the heart, not from the *siddur.* If you sing only because it is written in the *siddur,* it is not true *zemiros.*"

SMILING EACH DAY

Yichus (genealogy) has occupied an important place in Jewish culture. People have taken great pride in their ancestry, and *yichus* has often been a critical factor in the arrangement of marriages between families.

Rabbi Naftali of Ropschitz once recounted the luminaries in his family tree. One of those present said, "Rabbi, my *yichus* is greater than yours. I am the only one in my entire family who puts on *tefillin* and observes Shabbos." Rabbi Naftali smiled and conceded the point.

When the grandchildren of the Rebbe of Rhizin and Rabbi Hirsh of Rimanov married, the Rhiziner listed his impressive *yichus,* mentioning that he was a grandson of Rabbi Abraham "the *Malach*" (the angel), and the great *Maggid* of Mezeritch, as well as other prominent *tzaddikim.*

Rabbi Hirsh responded: "I was orphaned at an early age, and the townspeople made me an apprentice to a tailor so that I would learn a trade and be able to support myself.

"The tailor was an honest, simple, and G-d-fearing person. He taught me, 'Be careful to repair the old material, and be careful not to spoil any new material.' My only *yichus* is that I was a student of someone who told me to repair the old and see that the new does not become spoiled."

"You have triumphed," the Rabbi of Rhizin said.

Today
I shall smile
because . . .

Joshua was chosen to succeed Moses, not because of his scholarship and knowledge, for in fact there were greater scholars than he. Joshua was chosen because he had been Moses' constant attendant. Observing how *tzaddikim* conduct their lives and emulating them is superior to book learning.

SMILING EACH DAY

The great *tzaddikim* did not dissimulate. On the one hand they knew that they were very learned in both the revealed and esoteric aspects of Torah; yet it was precisely their awareness of how much there is to know, as well as their awareness of their own potential to learn and do *mitzvos* more intensively, that caused them to feel grossly derelict in their duties.

Rabbi Tzadok of Lublin refused a gift a chassid had brought him. "Please accept it," the chassid said. "The Talmud says that giving a gift to a *talmid chacham* is a *mitzvah*."

At the next opportunity where many chassidim were assembled, Rabbi Tzadok arose and tearfully said, "Have I deceived you, that you think of me as a *talmid chacham*? I cannot deny that I have learned Torah, but perhaps I am the one of whom the Psalmist says, 'To the wicked G-d says, "What right do you have to study My law?" ' (*Psalms* 50:16). This is not the *talmid chacham* the Talmud is referring to."

A close friend of Rabbi Tzadok's later said to him, "Why do you make such statements about yourself publicly?"

Rabbi Tzadok answered with every bit of sincerity, "Do you really expect me to confess to every person individually?"

Today
I shall smile
because . . .

_____

_____

_____

A person should be promptly repulsed by immorality and corruption, and should maintain this attitude. Condoning impropriety, for whatever reason, may result in a loss of sensitivity. One may then become calloused and tolerant of degenerate behavior.

SMILING EACH DAY

A major goal of our great Torah personalities was to try to attract people to Torah observance. The sincerity with which they did so can be seen from Rabbi Yisrael of Salant, who dedicated himself to this cause even in the last moments of his life.

During his last days, Rabbi Yisrael called in his many acquaintances to say a few last words to each of them. In the city there was one man who had remained defiant, refusing to accept Rabbi Yisrael's teachings. Rabbi Yisrael sent for this man and engaged him in long conversation.

The man, seeing how difficult it was for Rabbi Yisrael to speak, tried to cut the conversation short. "Do not exert yourself, Rabbi," he said. "You have graciously given me much more time than anyone else."

"There is a reason for that," Rabbi Yisrael said. "You see, I look forward to meeting all these other people again in the next world, so I can finish my conversation with them there. You, however, I do not anticipate meeting ever again, so I have to bid my final farewell to you now."

Today
I shall smile
because . . .

ELUL

אלול

Sometimes a person who is thoroughly evil is better than one in whom good and evil co-exist. The former is more apt to recognize he is wrong when made aware of it, whereas the latter may delude himself that he is a righteous person and not correct his ways (*Rabbi Chaim Shmulevitz*).

SMILING EACH DAY

Throughout history there have been numerous attempts by anti-Semitic leaders to defame the Talmud. The cryptic nature of some Talmudic statements has often made them subject to distortion and derision.

One time someone mocked at the Talmudic statement that if someone dreams of a pot, it is a sign that there will be peace (*Berachos* 56b). "How nonsensical a statement," he said.

Rabbi Mordechai Banet responded, "It makes perfect sense, if one only uses his brain. The two proverbial antagonists of history are fire and water, which can never coexist since each tries to extinguish the other. However, if you insert a pot between the two, they not only coexist peacefully, but actually cooperate to cook food."

Someone who overheard the Rabbi's wise explanation added, "Yes, and it is typically the case that after the peacemaker has spent his efforts to bring opponents to an agreement, he ends up being scorched himself."

Today
I shall smile
because . . .

"You shall be holy, because I, your G-d, am holy" (*Leviticus* 19:2). How does G-d's holiness obligate humans to be holy? Because within every human being there resides a Divine spirit which as it were is part of G-d himself. Hence every person is comprised of holiness.

SMILING EACH DAY

Rabbi Abraham of Sochochov was a child prodigy. When he was six years old, his father sent him home from *shul* on Yom Kippur morning to eat. Upon his return, his father asked him if he had made *kiddush*. "Yom Kippur is a festival, just like all other festivals. Since there are no meals, there is no *kiddush,* but a child who is permitted to eat should make *kiddush.*"

The young child responded, "I gave that some thought on my way home. Then I reasoned that a child is not required to perform *mitzvos* at all, and the only reason he does so is for *chinuch* (training), so that when he becomes of age, he will already be familiar with the performance of the *mitzvos*.

"However, since I will not be making *kiddush* on Yom Kippur when I grow up, there is no reason for me to train myself now to do something that I will never do later."

Anyone who studies the monumental Talmudic works of Rabbi Abraham can see the keen wisdom and clarity of thought which had begun to bud when he was but six.

Today
I shall smile
because . . .

"You shall proclaim freedom throughout the land to *all* its inhabitants" (*Leviticus* 25:10). When slaves are emancipated, their owners become free as well. Anyone who controls another person is himself a slave. A truly free person seeks mastery over himself rather than over others.

SMILING EACH DAY

The problem of caring for the elderly is not a new one in society. It is as old as history itself.

Rabbi Yehoshua Kutner explained that when an elderly father needs care, the son may say, "I would love to have you live with me, but what can I do? My wife feels it is an imposition upon her, and after all, she is not your daughter."

When the father turns to the daughter, she may say, "For my part, I would love to have you stay with us, but I cannot get my husband to agree. After all, he is only a son-in-law, not your son." The only recourse thus left to the elderly father is an institution for the aged.

Rashi states that the Israelites in the desert wept over the Torah prohibition of marriage between close relatives (*Numbers* 11:10).

Had brothers and sisters been permitted to marry, neither would have had grounds for rejecting the elderly parents, who would have found homes with their children. It was for this reason that they wept in the desert.

Today
I shall smile
because . . .

_____
_____
_____

"Those that seek G-d shall rejoice" (*Psalms* 105:3). Treasure hunters are happy only if they find treasure, otherwise their efforts are futile. With the search for G-d it is otherwise. One grows in character and stature as one searches for G-d, and therein lies happiness.

SMILING EACH DAY

Rabbi Levi Yitzchak of Berdichev was known for his unceasing advocacy on behalf of Israel, and he frequently complained to G-d that He was not dealing fairly with His children. Rabbi Levi Yitzchak emulated Moses, who complained to G-d when the plight of the Israelites in Egypt worsened. Someone once asked the Rabbi, "Is it not *lashon hara* (slander) to say such things about G-d?"

Rabbi Levi Yitzchak explained, "The spies sent by Moses spoke derogatorily about the Land of Israel, and they also spoke against G-d (*Rashi, Numbers* 13:31). When Moses pleaded for forgiveness, G-d forgave the insult to His own honor but did not forgive their evil talk about the Holy Land. Why? Because it is not considered *lashon hara* when one speaks negatively directly *to* someone, but only when one speaks *about* someone in his absence (*Arachin* 15b). Therefore, since G-d is present everywhere, speaking about G-d is not considered *lashon hara*.

"When I say that G-d is not treating Israel with enough kindness, I am not speaking *about* Him, but *to* Him. He is present everywhere, and speaking in His presence is not *lashon hara*."

Today
I shall smile
because . . .

ELUL

אלול

"Three people's lives are unlivable: those who are overly compassionate, overly irritable, or overly sensitive" (*Pesachim* 113b). The finest character traits can become troublesome if carried to an extreme. A wise person is one who knows the proper proportions of all traits.

SMILING EACH DAY

When the Israelites received the report from the spies about the Holy Land, they said, "Let us go back to Egypt, where food was plentiful." After Moses rebuked them, they decided to invade and conquer the Land, but they were defeated. Why was their *teshuvah* not accepted?

The *Maggid* of Dubno explained. A *nouveau riche* man had a daughter for whom he sought a *shiduch* (matrimonial match). Two young men were suggested: the first was a scholar from a poor family, while the second was unlearned but from a wealthy family. The father said he preferred the scholar, but only if the boy could buy his daughter a diamond ring. Since the scholar could not afford a ring, he chose the second young man.

The family was very critical of the father for not choosing the scholar, and he finally relented, saying he would forgo the diamond ring. But the scholar's father now refused the match. "Any family who would turn down my son because of his inability to purchase a diamond ring is not the family I wish him to marry into."

This is what happened to the Israelites. Having rejected the Holy Land in favor of Egypt, their repentance was no longer acceptable. G-d said, "Anyone who could reject Israel in favor of a pot of meat in Egypt is not someone who should have the privilege of being in the Holy Land."

Today
I shall smile
because . . .

Rabbi Yechiel Meir of Gostinin refused to learn how to play chess. "They told me I could not retract a wrong move. I believe that *teshuvah* can undo every wrong move."

SMILING EACH DAY

Some of our great leaders were experts on "the perfect squelch."

In Czarist Russia there were "official" rabbis, who were governmental appointees. These were invariably people of little learning who sought to appease their superiors by advocating the secularization of Judaism. One of these rabbis was a Dr. Lillienthal, a known assimilationist.

At one rabbinical gathering, the Russian minister of education challenged Rabbi Yitzchak of Volozhin: "Why is it necessary for you to display your *tzitzis* so prominently? After all, Dr. Lillienthal is a fine rabbi, and his *tzitzis* are concealed."

Rabbi Yitzchak responded, "Your excellency, the Torah states that the *tzitzis* are to remind us of the Divine commandments and of our constant servitude to G-d. Dr. Lillienthal is a highly educated person, and given his prodigious mind and great scholarship, it is sufficient for him to have a token reminder. For simple people like myself, a token reminder is not adequate. I need a very prominent reminder to keep me aware of my obligation to G-d, and I must therefore wear large *tzitzis* and display them prominently where I can see them at all times."

Today
I shall smile
because . . .

A *chassid* once complained to Rabbi Yisrael of Rhizin, "I sinned, then I did *teshuvah,* but have sinned again." The Rabbi responded, "Just as it is characteristic for a human being to relapse and sin, it is characteristic of G-d to repeatedly forgive."

SMILING EACH DAY

When Rabbi Avraham Mordechai of Gur came to Israel, which was then under the British mandate, he was greeted by a committee. The British official gave a moving speech, expressing his pleasure in welcoming a prominent European Jewish leader to the Holy Land, a place which has been so important to the Jewish people historically, and stating how appropriate it is for Jews to live in the Holy Land.

After the lengthy speech, the Rabbi was asked to respond. He simply shrugged his shoulders and said, "Nu!"

A member of the Rabbi's entourage, who was embarrassed by the Rabbi's less-than-enthusiastic response to the British official's long address, acted as a spokesman. He expressed the Rabbi's appreciation of the official welcome, as well as the government's recognition of the importance of Israel as the Jewish homeland.

When the Rabbi was later asked why he had responded in a monosyllable, he said, "In the Torah, G-d repeatedly tells us that Israel is the Jewish homeland, and that all Jews should live there. This man says he concurs with what G-d says — so I said, 'Nu!' "

Today
I shall smile
because . . .

_____

_____

_____

A man once said to a rabbi, "I would do *teshuvah* if I were sure that this would relieve me of all my misery." The rabbi responded, "Did you make your sins conditional too?"

SMILING EACH DAY

Doing *teshuvah* requires a bit of sagacity, because the *yetzer hara* (evil inclination) is a cunning adversary. Under the guise of piety, the *yetzer hara* may tell a person, "You have sinned too much to have your *teshuvah* accepted."

A customer once asked a bartender for a drink, but the bartender refused to serve him. "You have never paid the bill for your previous drinks," he said. The drinker replied, "I owe you so much, what difference does it make if I have one more drink? I'll just owe you a bit more." The bartender then said, "Look, I forgive your debt. You don't owe me anything. Now go away!"

It is important for a person to believe that *teshuvah* results in his slate being wiped clean, because as long as he feels that he is still carrying the burden of sins, he may be discouraged and think, "What difference does it make? I owe so much, I'll just owe a bit more." One must say to the *yetzer hara*, "G-d has forgiven me. I have no sins anymore, so it is foolish to commit new ones now."

Today
I shall smile
because . . .

"What worries me," said Rabbi Shmelke of Nickolsburg, "is what kind of bliss there can possibly be in the Eternal World where there is no Yom Kippur. What kind of existence is it if one cannot do *teshuvah?*"

SMILING EACH DAY

The Talmud states that the reward for a *mitzvah* is so vast that it cannot be paid in earthly terms; only in Heaven are there adequate means of compensation. Yet we are told that people who reject the Torah are rewarded in this world for the few *mitzvos* they may have done. But if *mitzvos* cannot be paid in earthly terms, how is such a reward possible?

In Czarist Russia there was a governmental official who issued anti-Semitic decrees. It was rumored that Baron Ginzberg (a wealthy, well-connected Jewish advocate) was collecting money to bribe this official to revoke his harsh decrees. On one occasion the official met Ginzberg and asked, "How much do you want to offer me?" Baron Ginzberg answered, "Your excellency, what Jews are worth to me I can never pay. However, what they are worth to you I am ready to pay at any time."

A person who dispenses with *mitzvos* on the slightest pretext has obviously placed a very small value on them. It is only just, therefore, that for those *mitzvos* that he has performed he should receive the value he has placed on them. Someone who observes *mitzvos* even at considerable cost to himself, however, obviously values them greatly, and for such an individual there is not adequate compensation in this world.

Today
I shall smile
because . . .

_____
_____
_____

Do not behave like a housefly, which seeks out diseased parts of a person on which to alight. Look for the healthy among your acquaintances and do not focus on their defects (From the *Last Will of Rabbi Eliezer the Great*).

SMILING EACH DAY

It is the duty of a *tzaddik* to intercede on behalf of his people and to ask forgiveness for them. The Talmud is critical of Noah, who was informed of the forthcoming destructive deluge and was advised that he and his family alone would be saved. There is no mention of Noah praying for his generation, and the prophet therefore refers to the Flood as "the waters of Noah" (*Isaiah* 54:9), as if Noah bears partial responsibility.

The Patriarch Abraham did intercede to save Sodom, but he sought forgiveness on the condition that there were enough meritorious people in whose virtue G-d could spare the entire city (*Genesis* 18:24). This approach was not successful.

Moses made no conditions. The Israelites sinned grievously, and Moses pleaded for forgiveness for them without trying to find merits: unconditional forgiveness. Indeed, if forgiveness were impossible, Moses said that he did not wish to survive (*Exodus* 32:32).

The Torah tells us that Abraham improved upon Noah's behavior, and that Moses improved upon Abraham's. Moses is called "Rabbeinu," our teacher, whom we must emulate not only by praying for forgiveness, but also by forgiving those who have offended us — unconditionally.

Today
I shall smile
because . . .

If one's primary goal in life is only to "feel good," one may indulge in very transitory pleasures, which may often produce long-term misery. If one's primary goal is to "do good," one may be rewarded by long-term pleasures.

SMILING EACH DAY

Whereas the early ethical works advocated various types of self-deprivation as penance for sins, the chassidic masters did not emphasize this practice. Although they themselves indulged in fasting, they discouraged it among their followers. Instead they emphasized sincere regret for having done wrong and a firm commitment not to repeat the mistake.

Rabbi Shlomo of Karlin, explaining why self-flagellation was discouraged, said, "I don't understand what it is supposed to accomplish. If one has not sincerely regretted one's sin and has not determined never to repeat it, what good will fasting and other acts of penance do? On the other hand, if one has sincerely regretted one's mistakes and has made the necessary commitment not to repeat them, what need is there for anything more?"

In these *teshuvah* days of Elul, we should realize that *teshuvah* is not as complicated as it may seem. Every person should be making a commitment to live properly, which is the essence of *teshuvah*. One can approach the New Year with a clean slate, with the certainty that one has been forgiven, and thus even the solemn days of Rosh Hashanah and Yom Kippur can be greeted with an attitude of *simchah*.

Today
I shall smile
because . . .

_____
_____
_____

"He who justifies a lawless man, and he who condemns a righteous man, both are an abomination to G-d" (*Proverbs* 17:15). The wisest of all men has taught us that keeping peace by condoning evil actually promotes violence.

SMILING EACH DAY

Rabbi Abish of Frankfurt was known for his total self-effacement. When he was appointed as the rabbi of Frankfurt, Rabbi Abish said that three questions bothered him:

(1) Was the community of Frankfurt really so foolish as to accept Abish as their rabbi?

(2) How did Abish have the *chutzpah* to accept the leadership of such a large Jewish community?

(3) How could G-d allow such an unreasonable match to occur?

Rabbi Abish continued, "Perhaps each question provides the answer to another. If the community of Frankfurt is foolish enough to want Abish as its leader, then it really is not a *chutzpah* for him to accept the position. And if the community and Abish are both of the opinion that they belong with one another, what reason is there for G-d to intervene?"

Today
I shall smile
because . . .

ELUL

אלול

"Like an open, unwalled city, is a man who cannot restrain his desire" (*Proverbs* 25:28). Many pleasures have a saturation point, whereas greed is never satisfied.

SMILING EACH DAY

The word "*es*" (אֶת) is a definite article, a grammatical word which precedes a noun but has no meaning of its own. The Talmud states that Shimon HaAmsoni (one of the sages of the *Mishnah*) said that each "*es*" is an inclusionary device legally equating something else with the noun which it precedes. However, when he came to the verse, "Have reverence for G-d," in which the word "G-d" is preceded by the word "*es*," he decided he must be wrong, because there is nothing that could possibly be equated with G-d as an object of reverence. Rabbi Akiva disagreed and said that the Torah indicates that one must have reverence for a Torah scholar just as for G-d Himself.

When the *Tzaddik* of Sanz assumed his first rabbinical position, he said in his inaugural address, "Why did Shimon HaAmsoni not explain the verse as Rabbi Akiva did?

"Shimon is not referred to as Rabbi Shimon, because he was not ordained. He therefore feared that if he equated reverence for a scholar with reverence for G-d, people would say that he was self-serving. Rabbi Akiva, a recognized authority, was much bolder. He said, 'You must revere a scholar as you do G-d Himself — and yes, I am even referring to myself.'

"I am now your rabbi," the *Tzaddik* concluded, "and I will expect you to respect my authority."

Today
I shall smile
because . . .

_____
_____
_____

"When a man's ways please G-d, even his enemies shall be at peace with him" (*Proverbs* 16:7). Instead of seeking revenge, seek to improve yourself. The best way to get back at enemies is to convert them into friends.

SMILING EACH DAY

The Torah states that if one is so far away from the Sanctuary that bringing the tithes of his produce to Jerusalem is burdensome, he can redeem these for money and bring the money to Jerusalem. The Alshich interprets this verse to mean that if one feels that bringing the tithes is too burdensome, it is because he has distanced himself from G-d.

The *Maggid* of Dubno explained this idea with a parable. A diamond dealer once sent a porter to pick up a parcel for him. When he saw the porter carrying a large, heavy load on his back and sweating under the burden, he knew that he must have picked up the wrong parcel. The package with precious stones was compact and light, and could be carried without any exertion.

"The *mitzvos*," said the *Maggid*, "are like precious stones. They are compact and light, and can be fulfilled with minimal effort. If one feels the *mitzvos* to be burdensome, he must somehow have picked up the wrong package.

"If one is close to G-d, bringing the tithes to Jerusalem is not a burden. The more removed one is from G-d, the heavier the package becomes."

Today
I shall smile
because . . .

Some people seem to be addicted to quarreling, and argue simply for the sake of arguing. Solomon calls them sinners: "One who loves strife loves sin" (*Proverbs* 17:19).

SMILING EACH DAY

After the Sanctuary was built, Moses gave an accurate accounting of what had been done with the silver and copper that was donated by the Israelites (*Exodus* 38:27-31), but not of the gold. Rabbi Yonasan Eibeschitz explained that all the Israelites had donated silver because this was obligatory (*Exodus* 30:13). Among such a huge number of people, there were likely to be some who might have been mistrustful of the way the silver was used, and to avoid any suspicion, Moses gave a precise accounting of the silver. However, since the donation of gold was not obligatory and those who donated gold did so of their own free will, they were not likely to suspect Moses of corruption.

But, one may ask, why was it then necessary for Moses to give an accounting of the copper, since that too was given of the people's own free will?

"Because," said Rabbi Yonasan, "there were some who donated only copper, but who did not wish to part with their gold. These people, because of the guilt resulting from their miserliness, were likely to project their greed onto Moses and accuse *him* of greed. Those who readily parted with their gold would not have had such feelings. This is why it was necessary to account for the copper but not for the gold."

That appears to be human nature. Those who donate more generously are more trusting. It is the more miserly donor who is likely to cause trouble.

Today
I shall smile
because . . .

_____

_____

_____

_____

> "The ear that harkens to the admonition of life, abides among the wise" (*Proverbs* 15:31). If you enter a perfumery, you will carry away a fragrance with you. To be wise, keep company with the wise.

SMILING EACH DAY

One Succos the Gaon of Vilna sat in his *succah*, so immersed in his Torah study that he did not notice a person entering. The latter, thinking that the Gaon was intentionally ignoring him, felt deeply hurt and later expressed his resentment.

The Gaon embraced him. "Why would I intentionally ignore you? If you came to my *succah* to share the spirit of the festival with me, I am deeply honored. I am very grateful that you did so. May you live to be one hundred years old."

This man indeed lived to an old age, and when he fell sick at ninety-eight the family sent for the doctor. The man refused to be examined, saying, "I do not need a doctor. I have an assurance from the great Gaon that I will live to be one hundred years old, so I know I will get well now. I still have two more years to live. I will not allow even one day to be deducted from the blessing of the *tzaddik*."

On his hundredth birthday the man died, and all the notables of Vilna attended the funeral. Everyone knew that the words of the Gaon had not been in the least bit compromised.

Today
I shall smile
because . . .

Impatience in listening is presumptuous. "He who answers before he hears, causes himself folly and shame" (*Proverbs* 18:13). Patient listening is not only courteous, but also wise.

SMILING EACH DAY

A very respectable citizen of the community invited Rabbi Yisrael of Salant to be his guest on Friday night. Knowing how meticulous Rabbi Yisrael was in his observance of *halachah*, the man assured him that the *kashrus* in his home was of the highest caliber, and that his wife personally supervised the kitchen help to make certain that everything was in order. "Between courses we have long discussions of Torah subjects," the man added, "so that the Friday night meal extends long into the night, abundant with Shabbos *zemiros* (songs) and Torah discussions."

Rabbi Yisrael accepted the invitation, but with one condition: the Torah discussions must be brief, and the meal must be concluded a full two hours earlier than usual. The host was surprised at this request but agreed, and on that Friday night the meal was hurried, with only brief words of Torah exchanged.

After the meal Rabbi Yisrael apologized to the kitchen help for having caused them to hurry. One of the workers, a widow, said, "May a thousand blessings come your way, Rabbi. Every Friday night, after a full day's work, I have to remain here until late in the night, and I can hardly stand on my feet. Tonight I will be able to get a much-needed rest."

Only then did the family appreciate Rabbi Yisrael's brilliant insight. He understood not only what goes on in the Talmud, but also what goes on in the kitchen.

Today I shall smile because . . .

_____
_____
_____

Savings institutions may fail, and invest-ments may be lost. "One who gives to the poor lends to G-d, and He repays him with ample reward" (*Proverbs* 19:17). G-d never goes bankrupt, hence giving to the poor is the soundest investment.

SMILING EACH DAY

Although we study the scholarly works of the great Torah luminaries, the Talmud states that observing their conduct in everyday life is even superior to studying their profound Torah works (*Rashi, Genesis* 24:42), because by viewing the Sages one can see how these great people put their Torah knowledge into practice.

One Friday night, the Chafetz Chaim had several wayfarers as guests at his table. To everyone's surprise, when he returned home from *shul,* the Chafetz Chaim omitted the traditional chant *Shalom Aleichem*, whereby one welcomes the heavenly angels into his home on Shabbos, and immediately recited the *kiddush.* Then the Chafetz Chaim began the meal, and only after the first course was completed, did he arise and chant the *Shalom Aleichem*. A disciple of his, Rabbi Yehuda Leib Chasman, who witnessed this strange happening, could not contain his curiosity and asked for an explanation.

"It is very simple," the Chafetz Chaim said. "The guests had traveled all day, and I am sure that they did not have the opportunity to eat, especially since they were in a hurry to arrive before Shabbos. Angels are not hungry, and they can wait until after the first course. People who are hungry should not be made to wait."

Today
I shall smile
because . . .

This volume is part of
THE ARTSCROLL SERIES®
an ongoing project of
translations, commentaries and expositions on
Scripture, Mishnah, Talmud, Midrash, Halachah,
liturgy, history, the classic Rabbinic writings,
biographies and thought.

For a brochure of current publications
visit your local Hebrew bookseller
or contact the publisher:

Mesorah Publications, ltd

4401 Second Avenue
Brooklyn, New York 11232
(718) 921-9000
www.artscroll.com

Ripley's Believe It or Not!

Executive Vice President, Intellectual Property Norm Deska
Senior Director of Publishing Amanda Joiner

Editorial Manager Carrie Bolin
Editors Jessica Firpi, Jordie R. Orlando
Creative Content Manager Sabrina Sieck

Designer Luis Fuentes

ISBN 978-1-60991-250-5

For more information regarding permission, contact:
VP Intellectual Property
Ripley Entertainment Inc.
7576 Kingspointe Parkway, Suite 188
Orlando, Florida 32819
publishing@ripleys.com
www.ripleys.com/books

Manufactured in China in May 2018
First Printing

PUBLISHER'S NOTE
While every effort has been made to verify the accuracy of the entries in this book, the Publisher cannot be held responsible for any errors contained in the work. They would be glad to
receive any information from readers.

WARNING
Some of the stunts and activities are undertaken by experts and should not be attempted by
anyone without adequate training and supervision.

THE BEST OF

Ripley's
Believe *It or Not!*®
100
YEARS

TWISTS EDITION

VOLUME 1

PUBLISHING

a Jim Pattison Company

Ripley's

SNAKES AND REPTILES

Believe It or Not!®

TWISTS

RIPLEY
PUBLISHING

a Jim Pattison Company

Written by Kezia Endsley
Cover Concept by Joshua Surprenant

PUBLISHING

PAGE 37

Executive Vice President, Intellectual Property Norm Deska

Vice President, Archives and Exhibits Edward Meyer

Director, Publishing Operations Amanda Joiner

Managing Editor Dean Miller

Editor Jessica Firpi

Designer Michelle Foster

Researcher Sabrina Sieck

Additional Research Jessica Firpi

Fact Checker, Anglicisation James Proud

Production Coordinator Amy Webb

Reprographics Juice Creative Ltd

www.ripleys.com/books

Published by Ripley Publishing 2015

Ripley Publishing 7576 Kingspointe Parkway, Suite 188
Orlando, Florida 32819 USA

10 9 8 7 6 5 4 3 2 1

Random House Books 20 Vauxhall Bridge Road London SW1V 2SA
www.randomhouse.co.uk

Random House Books is part of the Penguin Random House group of
companies whose addresses can be found at
global.penguinrandomhouse.com

 Penguin
Random House
UK

ISBN 978-1-60991-233-8 (USA) | ISBN 978-1-78475-313-9 (UK)

For information regarding permission, write to VP Intellectual Property,
Ripley Entertainment Inc., Suite 188, 7576 Kingspointe Parkway,
Orlando, Florida 32819
email: publishing@ripleys.com
www.ripleys.com/books

A CIP catalogue record for this book is available from the British Library.

Manufactured in China in January 2018.
2nd Printing

WARNING

Some of the stunts and activities in this book are undertaken by experts and
should not be attempted by anyone without adequate training and supervision.

PUBLISHER'S NOTE

While every effort has been made to verify the accuracy of the entries in this
book, the Publishers cannot be held responsible for any errors contained in
the work. They would be glad to receive any information from readers.

CONTENTS

WHAT'S INSIDE

TWISTS

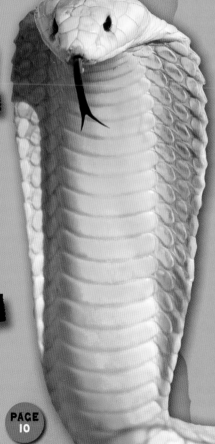

WILD WORLD

MARVELOUS CREATURES

WHAT'S INSIDE YOUR BOOK?

Green tree boas from the Amazon River Basin grow 2 to 3 m long in length.

Emerald green tree boas have been known to grab birds that are in mid-flight.

If you just take a minute to pause, you'll find exceptional reptiles flourishing all around, even in your own backyard. But how much do you really know about them?

Join us on a trip around the world, where you'll discover the kingdom of the reptiles, cold-blooded creatures that cover the planet and have been thriving on Earth since the time of the dinosaurs. Reptiles have a diverse and adaptable way of life, and you won't believe the extremes they endure to survive and thrive!

TWISTS

These books are about 'Believe It or Not!' – amazing facts, feats and things that make you go 'Wow!'

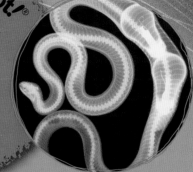

Ripley's Believe It or Not!®

Zoologists at the University of Florida operated on a pine snake that had swallowed two light bulbs! Doctors were successful in removing the bulbs, and the snake actually survived to be re-released into the wild!

BIG WORD ALERT
CLUTCH
A group of eggs hatched at the same time.

Found a new word? Big word alerts will explain it for you.

Look out for the 'Twist It' column on some pages. Twist the book to find out more amazing facts about snakes and other reptiles!

HH! THEY ARE EVERYWHERE!

REPTILES RULE THE ROOST

eptiles make their homes in so ny amazing places. Check out eir exotic habitats across the world!

Reptiles live on every continent except Antarctica. Reptiles are found in deserts, rain forests, wooded forests, lakes, rivers, salty oceans, and even underground!

TWIST IT!

In 1968, the Soviet Union launched the Zond 5 spacecraft carrying a pair of tortoises that became the first animals to ever enter deep space!

A runway at John F. Kennedy International Airport in New York City was shut down briefly in 2009 after about 80 turtles crawled onto the tarmac!

Most reptiles can't tolerate the cold, but the Blanding's turtle is sometimes found swimming under the ice in the Great Lakes region of the United States!

Small garter snakes can live in parts of northern Canada, where it's so cold that the snakes hibernate for eight months of the year!

The web-footed gecko lives in the African desert and drinks dew from its eyeballs every morning to keep cool and hydrated.

SCALY SKIN

WHITE-LIPPED PIT VIPER
Snakes live everywhere but Ireland, New Zealand, and the North and South Poles. These bright green pit vipers live in tropical forests and scrublands all throughout Asia.

FACINATING FACTS
You're in lizard territory.

The bigger the lizard, the bigger its territory. Small lizards might have a territory no bigger than your bedroom, whereas the Komodo dragon, which can grow as big as 10 feet long, might roam a much larger territory. Territory size also depends on food availability—the more scarce food is, the larger a lizard's territory must be.

BLUNT-NOSED LEOPARD LIZARD

Desert reptiles use the morning sun to warm up after a cold desert night but then spend the rest of the day hiding in burrows and under rocks to avoid the scorching daylight.

PANTHER CHAMELEON
The island of Madagascar is home to these beautiful chameleons made up of 11 different species! The color patterns of panther chameleons depend on their geographical location, and the males usually have more vibrant colors.

EASTERN COLLARED LIZARD

Ripley Explains...
See the 'Ripley explains' panels for extra info from our snakes and reptiles experts.

Turn over to find out more about snakes and reptiles.

REPTILES

THE REAL DEAL

Scaly but not slimy, and only sometimes venomous!

Most reptiles are harmless and shy, but they still freak some people out. Oddly enough, they aren't slimy, don't want to hurt you and are incredible relics from an ancient time!

Living on Earth at least 300 million years, reptiles include snakes, crocodiles and alligators, lizards and turtles and tortoises. They are ectotherms, meaning they must use the air temperature to stay comfortable – not too hot nor too cold.

Sturdy Sea Turtle

Reptiles lay their watertight, leathery eggs on land. This sea turtle has to work hard to break free from her egg's sturdy shell.

Did you know that there are over 9,000 types of reptiles on Earth?

Hairy Bush Viper

Reptile scales are dry and watertight. They come in a variety of colours, and some can even change colour depending on their mood and environment.

TWIST IT!

Reptiles are extremely versatile and can live in many different types of climates.

SCALY SCOOP

Research shows that humans can detect images of snakes more quickly among other non-threatening images, furthering the idea that humans have developed the ability to sense snakes and fear them.

In Illinois, there is a law requiring any person selling a reptile to give written notice to the buyer stating, 'Don't nuzzle or kiss your pet reptile'.

1 February is National Serpent Day!

In 1987, the American alligator became Florida's official state reptile.

More Americans die each year from wasp and bee stings than from snake bites.

Reptiles need the sun's heat to survive, so they are most common in hotter areas.

Marine Lizards

Marine iguanas are found exclusively in the Galápagos Islands and are the world's only seafaring lizards!

7

LEGS, SCALES AND SHELLS, OH MY!

Reptiles are an ancient group of animals sharing common characteristics. Although they share ancestors and millions of years of evolution, they differ in many ways from each other.

Reptiles have dry, waterproof skin, and all reptile skin is covered in scales (made from keratin) that vary in form depending on the animal.

DISGUSTING OR DELIGHTFUL?

You decide...

Fierce and powerful, crocodiles and alligators have horny scales and hard plates that cover their bodies.

Thorny Devil Defence

The scales of a thorny devil lizard consist of hard sharp spines, making it hard to swallow.

This snake was discovered in China in 2009 with a rare mutation: a single clawed foot growing out from its body. The 40-cm-long mutant reptile was found by Duan Qiongxiu clinging to the wall of her bedroom with its talons. Terrified, Mrs. Duan killed the snake with her shoe.

Ripley Explains...

Evolved from legged lizards, legless lizards are not snakes at all. Similar to snakes in behaviour and appearance, legless lizards have fixed jaws, moveable eyelids, ear openings and the ability to detach their tail in an emergency.

BIG WORD ALERT
KERATIN
Reptile scales, like our hair and fingernails, are made of keratin (a fibrous protein).

TURTLE SHELL SHOCK

Turtles and tortoises carry their homes around on their backs. A turtle's shell is covered in scales called scutes, which strengthen the shell bone.

Well, what do you think — are reptiles terrific or terrible?

Eye Lash Viper

Snakes have no legs and have scales of various shapes and sizes. Some scales have been modified over time, such as the rattle on rattlesnakes or the 'eye lashes' on certain snakes.

WHAT'S IN A SHAPE?

Reptiles have evolved fantastic shapes, body parts and defences to help ensure their survival.

Some reptiles have shells, fangs or even colour-changing scales to help protect them from predators. However, for other reptiles, it's what they DON'T have (like eyelids, ears or even legs) that helps keep them safe. When it comes to survival of the fittest, reptiles have almost every angle covered!

FUNCTIONAL AND FANTASTIC FORMS

Located in the middle of Kakadu National Park in Australia, the Gagudju Crocodile Holiday Inn is shaped to look just like the saltwater crocodile, which is native to the region!

Fierce Front

When threatened, cobras spread out their neck ribs to form a flattened, widened hood around their head.

TWIST IT!

A blindworm is neither blind nor a worm – it is actually a legless lizard!

Egg-eating snakes have sharp spines along their backbones that extend into the oesophagus and break the eggshell. The snake regurgitates the crushed shell after swallowing the egg's contents.

Baby rattlesnakes are born without rattles!

Alligators and crocodiles have flaps of skin that seal their ears, nose and throat from water, while a double pair of eyelids protects their eyes.

SHAPE CENTRAL

Supple Skin

Instead of having horny scutes (scales) on their shells, softshell turtles simply have thickened skin. Their light and flexible shells allow for easier movement in open water or muddy lake bottoms as well as faster movement on land.

Master of Disguise

The satanic leaf-tailed gecko from Madagascar takes camouflage to the extreme! It can change colours — including purple, orange, tan, yellow, brown and black — blending perfectly into their forest habitat.

When faced with predators, bearded lizards flare out their throats to look intimidating.

AHH! THEY ARE EVERYWHERE!

REPTILES RULE THE ROOST

Reptiles make their homes in so many amazing places. Check out their exotic habitats across the world!

Reptiles live on every continent except Antarctica. Reptiles are found in deserts, rain forests, wooded forests, lakes, rivers, salty oceans and even underground!

PANTHER CHAMELEON

The island of Madagascar is home to these beautiful chameleons made up of 11 different species! The colour patterns of panther chameleons depend on their geographical location, and the males usually have more vibrant colours.

TWIST IT!

In 1968, the Soviet Union launched the *Zond 5* spacecraft carrying a pair of tortoises that became the first animals to ever enter deep space!

A runway at John F. Kennedy International Airport in New York City was shut down briefly in 2009 after about 80 turtles crawled onto the tarmac!

Most reptiles can't tolerate the cold, but the Blanding's turtle is sometimes found swimming under the ice in the Great Lakes region of the United States!

Small garter snakes can live in parts of northern Canada, where it's so cold that the snakes hibernate for eight months of the year!

The web-footed gecko lives in the African desert and drinks dew from its eyeballs every morning to keep cool and hydrated.

WHITE-LIPPED PIT VIPER

Snakes live everywhere but Ireland, New Zealand and the North and South Poles. These bright green pit vipers live in tropical forests and scrublands all throughout Asia.

SCALY SKIN

BLUNT-NOSED LEOPARD LIZARD

FACINATING FACTS
You're in lizard territory.

The bigger the lizard, the bigger its territory. Small lizards might have a territory no bigger than your bedroom, whereas the Komodo dragon, which can grow as big as 3 metres long, might roam a much larger territory. Territory size also depends on food availability — the more scarce food is, the larger a lizard's territory must be.

Desert reptiles use the morning sun to warm up after a cold desert night but then spend the rest of the day hiding in burrows and under rocks to avoid the scorching daylight.

EASTERN COLLARED LIZARD

WHAT'S FOR DINNER?

THE MEALTIME MENU

Most lizards and snakes are carnivores and snack on small animals, insects, birds and even other reptiles. Only a small handful, like very large iguanas, are herbivores and eat only plants.

From sticky tongues and venomous bites, to hiding in plain sight for a surprise attack, reptiles have special ways of hunting for a meal. Reptiles also use camouflage to hunt, not just to hide from predators.

Some chameleons have tongues longer than their bodies!

Ripley's Believe It or Not!

Reggie, a 1-metre-long kingsnake, swallowed his own tail after he mistook it for another snake and was unable to regurgitate it because of his rear-facing teeth. Luckily, a veterinary surgeon removed the tail before it had been digested.

Snakes can swallow animals larger than their head with their flexible jaws.

BIG WORD ALERT

CARNIVORE

An animal whose diet consists mainly of meat.

HERBIVORE

An animal whose diet consists mainly of plants.

In 2011, on the Greek island of Corfu, a lucky Dahl's whip snake wriggled its way to freedom after being eaten by a four-lined snake, which was in turn killed by a pet cat!

Temperature affects how fast a meal is digested — the warmer the snake, the faster the digestion.

The Subtropical Teahouse is a 'reptile café' in Japan where customers can observe and pet dozens of species.

The smallest of all snakes, the Barbados threadsnake, is so small it can only eat the pupae (or eggs) of insects like ants, termites and centipedes.

READY REPTILES

Ripley Explains... Chomp Chomp

Alligator Snapping Turtle

The alligator snapping turtle rests on the riverbed with its mouth open to trick fish into coming near to eat the 'worm' – a bright-red, worm-shaped piece of flesh on its tongue. When the fish try to attack the worm, the turtle clamps its jaws shut and enjoys its meal.

VS.

Alligators and Crocodiles

Alligators and crocodiles hide in the water and ambush other animals coming for a drink. Although almost completely under water, they can still hear, see and breathe. They eat fish, rabbits, turtles, snakes and even large mammals like deer and buffalo!

FANGS AND JAWS GALORE!

ARMED TO THE TEETH!

From bites and venom to spikes and poison, the fangs and jaws of certain reptiles should not be underestimated!

When hiding or running doesn't work, reptiles might just strike back! Only after giving plenty of warnings will they attack in self-defence. Of course, reptiles use their powerful jaws and fangs to attack and devour their dinner.

KOMODO KILLER!

The Komodo dragon, found only on a few Indonesian islands, is the biggest lizard on Earth and is extremely venomous. The venom ducts in its lower jaw release venom into the blood that hastens death by decreasing blood pressure, sending the victim into shock.

MONSTER MOUTHFUL!

The Indian Gharial crocodile has an extra long snout with over 100 razor-sharp teeth that developed so they can catch and eat small fish easily.

Ripley's Believe It or Not!®

For more than 50 years, Bill Haast survived being bitten more than 170 times by injecting himself with deadly snake venom. He built up such a tolerance that his blood was used as a snakebite antidote!

Although most snakes have teeth, not all snakes have fangs – only the venomous ones do.

ATROCIOUS CHOPS!

Boa constrictor jaws are lined with small, hooked teeth for grabbing and holding prey, which helps as they squeeze their victims.

17

DEFENCE: THE BEST ATTACK

FIGHTING FOR SURVIVAL

Reptiles live in a dangerous world where many animals would love to have them for lunch – they are both predators and prey. Reptiles have various ways to protect themselves against attack.

Some reptiles use camouflage to hide, whereas others confuse or fool attackers by using clever tricks: looking bigger than they really are, dropping their tails when attacked, and using warnings like rattles or blood to caution predators. Other reptiles have thorns and shells to protect themselves.

When under attack, many lizards can detach their tails and escape. Their tails will grow back without much harm to the lizard.

Armadillo Lizard

Armadillo lizards are so named because of the armadillo-like tactic they use to avoid predators. When in danger, armadillo lizards curl into a ball that is inedible for most animals because of the spines on the neck and tail.

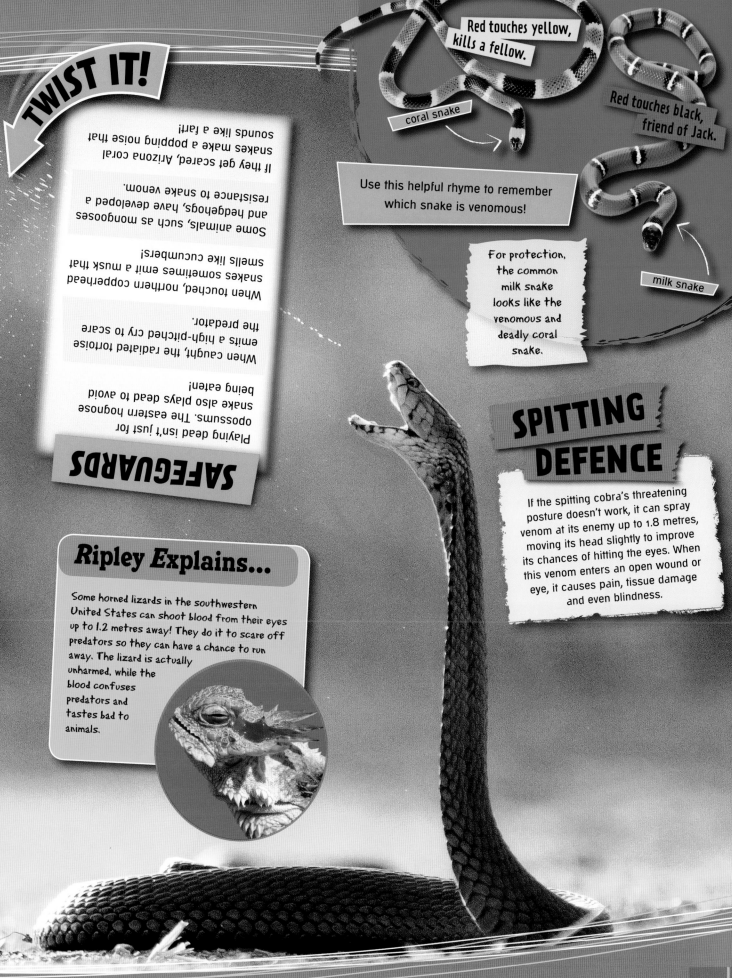

TWIST IT!

Red touches yellow, kills a fellow.

coral snake

Red touches black, friend of Jack.

milk snake

Use this helpful rhyme to remember which snake is venomous!

For protection, the common milk snake looks like the venomous and deadly coral snake.

If they get scared, Arizona coral snakes make a popping noise that sounds like a fart!

Some animals, such as mongooses and hedgehogs, have developed a resistance to snake venom.

When touched, northern copperhead snakes sometimes emit a musk that smells like cucumbers!

When caught, the radiated tortoise emits a high-pitched cry to scare the predator.

SAFEGUARDS

Playing dead isn't just for opossums. The eastern hognose snake also plays dead to avoid being eaten!

SPITTING DEFENCE

If the spitting cobra's threatening posture doesn't work, it can spray venom at its enemy up to 1.8 metres, moving its head slightly to improve its chances of hitting the eyes. When this venom enters an open wound or eye, it causes pain, tissue damage and even blindness.

Ripley Explains...

Some horned lizards in the southwestern United States can shoot blood from their eyes up to 1.2 metres away! They do it to scare off predators so they can have a chance to run away. The lizard is actually unharmed, while the blood confuses predators and tastes bad to animals.

EGGS-ACTLY!

LAYING EGGS IS THEIR BUSINESS!

Nearly all reptiles lay eggs, but the process and results differ greatly depending on the animal.

Most reptiles are born on land, not in water. They lay their eggs in underground burrows, which keeps the eggs warm and protects them from other animals. Reptiles that have fewer young at a time and give birth to live babies are usually more caring and supportive parents.

Greater short-horned lizards are one of the few lizards that give birth to live babies and care for their young after birth. It carries its babies on its back to keep them safe.

Unlike many reptiles, alligators and crocodiles nurture their young for up to a year, carrying them around in their mouths and keeping them safe from predators.

Laying their eggs in one basket?

* Tortoises and crocodiles lay eggs with hard shells, whereas most turtles, lizards and snakes lay eggs with soft, leathery shells (although some turtles do lay hard shells).

* Developing reptile babies get their food from inside the wet, yolky egg. The outer layer of the egg keeps it from drying out on land.

* Some snakes (e.g. adders) and lizards (e.g. blue-tongued skinks) give birth to live young. Reptile babies that hatch inside the mother usually have a better chance of surviving.

THE BIG HATCH

To lay their eggs, female sea turtles swim as far as 1,609 kilometres or more back to the same beach where they were born.

Collecting leaves, sticks and other vegetation, the King Cobra is the only snake in the world that builds a nest like a bird!

Reptile babies have a special 'egg' tooth that they use to break open their shell at the time of birth.

Egg-eating snakes do not lay their own eggs all in one place — instead, they scatter the eggs in multiple locations.

The smallest known snake, the Barbados thread snake, is so small it can only lay one egg at a time.

TWIST IT!

For many reptiles, the temperature of the nest determines the gender of the baby.

FANG-TASTIC!

VENOMOUS SNAKES

Like all animals, snakes face danger when they are hunting for food. Their prey doesn't want to be eaten and will fight back to survive! Venomous snakes have a natural advantage that makes them more successful hunters.

Venomous snakes inject their prey using fangs – special sharp hollow teeth – that poke holes in the victim before the venom flows into the body, overpowering the prey so the snake can safely eat.

Ways to tell if a snake might be venomous:

* **Shape of its head.** If the head is triangular or heart shaped, stay away!
* **Eye/pupil shape.** When the pupil is a slit, instead of round, back off!

BOOMSLANG

Boomslangs are rear-fanged snakes. The fangs near the back of their mouths allow the venom to seep into the bite wounds.

sea snakes

Sea snakes are some of the most venomous of all snakes, but they don't bite humans very often, since humans are not their prey.

There are some 50 different species of sea snakes, and all of them are venomous.

SNAKE BITE

Snakes retain biting reflexes for some time after death. A chef in China preparing cobra soup, a rare delicacy, was fatally bitten by the decapitated head of the meal's main ingredient!

Some snakes, like the *Rhabdophis tigrinus*, can actually steal poison from their prey, collecting it in glands to use for defence.

In the town of Ban Kok Sa-Nga (aka Cobra Village) in Thailand's northeast province, nearly every home has a pet snake.

A new snake species found in Panama in 2013 was named Sibon noalamina, or 'No to the mine' in English, because its habitat is under threat from mining.

TWIST IT!

Ripley Explains...

How does venom work?

Different types of chemicals called 'toxins', exist in venom. The purpose of the toxin is to conquer or kill the victim, which can be done in different ways:

* Some toxins attack the blood or muscles, possibly paralysing the animal or causing internal bleeding.

* Some toxins attack the nervous system so the victim suffocates.

* Some toxins attack the heart muscles causing direct damage to the heart.

Toxins flow quickly through the blood so their effects are felt instantly. Scientists have created antivenoms that reduce the effects of snakebites, and they work well if the victim is treated quickly.

Venomous snake fangs allow the venom to flow from the gland behind the fangs into the victim, like a needle.

MODERN ARCHOSAURS

ALL ABOUT CROCS AND GATORS

With ancestors living alongside dinosaurs, crocodiles and alligators are directly related to a group of extinct creatures called *Archosaurs*. Today's crocodiles and alligators are more closely related to birds than to other reptiles.

Crocs and gators belong to the *Crocodilian* group of reptiles and are the world's largest (but not the longest) reptiles. With powerful jaws and tails, they take down and feast on animals as large as deer and buffalo! Although fierce meat-eating predators, they are also very attentive parents and live in social packs.

Crocodiles and alligators have over 70 sharp, pointy teeth. When they lose teeth, new ones grow in.

Chinese alligator

There are only two types of alligators: the American Alligator, which resides in the southeastern United States, and the Chinese alligator, which is now very rare.

Close Cousins

What's the difference between crocs and gators?

Crocodiles...

* have a longer, narrower, more v-shaped snout
* live in the wild all over the world
* can live in freshwater and salty oceans
* generally have lighter-coloured scales
* are more aggressive
* have visible upper and lower teeth when their mouth is closed

Alligators...

* have a wider, more u-shaped snout
* live only in the United States and China
* live in freshwater
* generally have darker-coloured scales
* are less aggressive
* have hidden lower teeth but visible upper teeth when their mouth is closed

TWIST IT!

BIG BRUTES

When alligators close their mouths, every fourth tooth fits into a socket in the top jaw.

Crocodiles release heat through sweat glands, which is why they sunbathe mouths rather than through their with their mouths open.

Palaeontologists discovered ancient, galloping, dinosaur-eating crocodiles in the Sahara Desert of Africa.

A crocodile in a Ukrainian park accidentally ate a visitor — and it continued dropped by a visitor — and it continued to ring inside the animal's stomach!

Saltwater crocs, the largest Crocodilian group, can grow to over 7 metres long. That's as long as about four grown men lying head to toe!

LIVING FOSSILS

ALL ABOUT TURTLES AND TORTOISES

Turtles and tortoises have been on Earth since the time of the dinosaurs. They have changed very little since those ancient times – other than generally getting smaller – thus many people call them 'living fossils'. There are more than 250 different species living on Earth today.

They are the only *vertebrates* (animals with backbones) with hard shells. Covered with scaly plates called scutes, their shells grow and expand as they age, and the animals can never leave their shells. When threatened, many species pull their heads and legs completely into their shell for protection.

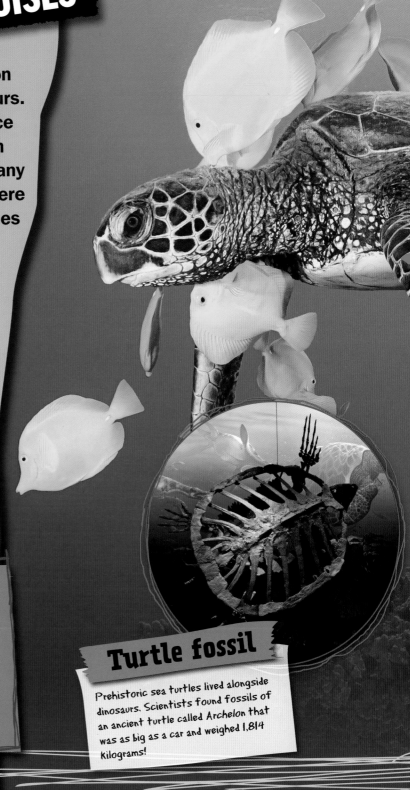

KEY FACTS

* All turtles and tortoises lay their eggs on land, which is the only time sea turtles leave their ocean home.
* The first turtles lived on Earth about 200 million years ago.
* Tortoises use their strong front limbs to dig burrows.

Turtle fossil

Prehistoric sea turtles lived alongside dinosaurs. Scientists found fossils of an ancient turtle called Archelon that was as big as a car and weighed 1,814 kilograms!

Brothers in Armour

What's the difference between turtles and tortoises?

Turtles...

* live mostly in water (and at times on land)

* are found in every ocean except for the Arctic

* have flippers, webbed feet and streamlined bodies for swimming

* eat fish and other marine creatures

Tortoises...

* live on land, usually in hot, dry places

* are native to every continent except Australia and Antarctica

* have round, stumpy feet for walking on sand, gravel and dirt

* eat low-growing shrubs, grasses, fruits, vegetables and flowers

TWIST IT!

An international team of scientists have successfully trained four red-footed tortoises to use a touchscreen computer.

23 May is World Turtle Day.

Like their amphibian cousins, terrapins spend equal amounts of time in the water and on land and are always found near water.

Terrapins are a kind of hybrid between turtles and tortoises. They might not move for two to three months!

Turtles and tortoises can hibernate during the cold winter months by burying themselves in mud and living off their body fat.

TURTLE TIME

BIG WORD ALERT

CARAPACE
The top part of a turtle's shell.

PLASTRON
The bottom part of a turtle's shell.

sea turtle

Unlike land-bound turtles, sea turtles have flatter, more flexible carapaces and plastrons and flipper-like feet for navigating the oceans. Since they cannot pull their bodies into their shells, they must swim away quickly to avoid predators.

Galápagos tortoise

The Galápagos giant tortoise is the largest living species of tortoise and one of the heaviest living reptiles. They are found in the wild on a few Pacific Ocean islands, can weigh over 227 kilograms and live for more than 100 years.

LEGLESS LURKERS

ALL ABOUT SNAKES!

Snakes evolved from lizards, and some snakes, such as pythons and boas, still have tiny traces of back legs. However, they are not simply 'legless lizards' – snakes are different in many ways.

Snakes are adaptable, living in trees, deserts, lakes and oceans and even underground. They are dedicated hunters, yet only a small percentage of snakes are venomous. They differ from other reptiles in that they don't have ears or eyelids. Instead, snakes have other sophisticated ways of finding food and sensing danger.

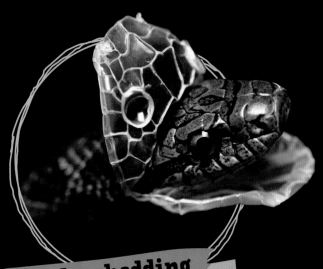

snake jawbone

The snake's lower jaw is hinged to its skull, which allows it to open its mouth incredibly wide. This is important since all snakes swallow their prey whole.

Snakes use their forked tongues to 'smell' and 'taste' what is near them, which is why they often flick their tongues in and out.

Snake shedding

When a snake outgrows its skin, the inner skin layer makes an oily fluid that removes the outer layer, allowing the snake to slip it off in one piece.

KEY FACTS

* Snakes don't have eyelids and therefore never blink. Instead, they have a moist, clear scale that protects their eyes and sheds with the rest of their skin.

* Snakes don't have ears — instead, their jawbones are linked to sensors that sense vibrations on the ground.

* Some snakes have a hole at the bottom of their mouths called the glottis that allows them to breathe even when their mouth is chock-full of prey!

Leg spurs

Boas and pythons have 'leg spurs', which are likely left over from their lizard ancestors. This tiny bit of leftover leg is called a vestigial limb.

TWIST IT!

Burmese pythons enlarge their own hearts by up to 40% when eating!

The largest snake fossil species ever discovered is called Titanoboa: a monster 15-metre-long snake that lived 60 million years ago.

Many snakes hibernate together in clusters in underground caves during the cooler months. This is one way that snakes living in colder habitats stay warm and survive.

The word cobra comes from the Portuguese cobra de capello, which means 'snake with a hood'.

Venomous snakes can accidentally bite themselves and die from their own venom! It's not common, but it can happen when snakes are under a lot of stress.

FORKED TONGUES

Pit viper

Pit vipers have special pits (holes) under their eyes that contain infrared heat sensors that allow them to 'see' warm-blooded prey (such as mice) in total darkness!

BIG WORD ALERT

GLOTTIS

The hole at the bottom of a snake's mouth that allows it to breathe even when its mouth is chock full of prey.

MOVERS AND SHAKERS

Snakes move quickly and in ways that other animals cannot. Because they have strong muscles and hundreds of bones in their spines, they can move sideways and vertically, creep along in an 's' movement, burrow and climb, quickly strike, swim and stand tall – all without feet!

Snakes can bend and coil their bodies to move quickly across loose or hot surfaces. Traveling in wavelike movements called undulations, they use their muscles to push off from the ground and other obstacles in their path. Snakes also move by gripping the ground with the curves of their bodies and then stretching out.

Snake skeleton

Snakes can bend in several directions at once, and their long backbones are the key to their movement.

Some snakes have more than 400 bones in their bodies and tails!

MOVING WITHOUT LEGS!

Sea snakes are the best swimmers because their tails are flattened like a paddle. They can dive deep and stay underwater for over an hour!

Snake swimming

All snakes are good swimmers. They use the serpentine method to move through the water, which works well because water is dense and gives snakes something strong

BIG WORD ALERT

VERTEBRA

A fancy word for a small bone in the back. We have about 30 of them, and snakes have them too.

The more vertebrae an animal has, the more agile and flexible it is!

Believe It or Not!®

Researchers have successfully created various snake robots, or 'snakebots'! These snakebots can climb, crawl, and even scale trees. Snakebots can one day be used in search-and-rescue missions and possibly help NASA explore other worlds, like Mars!

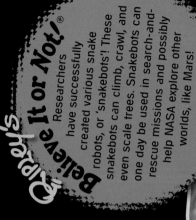

Flying snake

As seen in this multiple exposure image, some Southeast Asian snakes even seem to fly! They hide high up in trees, and when they see prey such as lizards, they launch themselves into the air, flattening their bodies into a long ribbon. The air and wind under its ribbon-shaped body keep it afloat, and it uses its tail to steer.

Ripley Explains...

Snake Movement

Snakes have four main ways of moving:

Concertina
Gripping the ground with the front half of their body, they pull their tail forward, creating an 's' shape.

Serpentine
Snakes use their muscles to push against obstacles. As they wriggle, waves pass down their bodies from head to tail.

Sidewinding
Sidewinders 'throw' the front part of their body sideways, and a wave passing along its body enables the back to follow the front.

Rectilinear
Heavier snakes raise their bodies off the ground, head first, and then lower it so the underbelly scales grip the ground.

REMARKABLE REPTILES

ALL ABOUT LIZARDS

Lizards are the most common and numerous reptile on the planet. Scientists have found almost 6,000 species of lizards – more than all other reptiles combined!

Most lizards are carnivores and eat insects, spiders, scorpions, centipedes and even other lizards. Larger lizards (like iguanas) are sometimes herbivores, eating flowers, fruits and leaves. Since lizards are typically hunted and eaten by other animals, many use camouflage to hide.

ACTUAL SIZE

2.5 cm long!

Tiny Lizard

Lizards vary greatly in size. This tiny dwarf leaf chameleon is about 2.5 centimetres long.

The Gecko lizard can walk up walls and on ceilings. Special tiny hairs on its feet help it stick to all kinds of surfaces.

LIZARD LUCK

An iguana can stay under water comfortably for up to 30 minutes.

A protein in the western fence lizard's blood can kill the bacterium that causes Lyme disease (fever, headache, skin rash), fatigue and a 'bull's-eye' skin rash! So when disease-carrying ticks feed on the lizard's blood, the ticks leave no longer carrying the disease!

The tuatara lizard of New Zealand has three eyes — two on either side of its head and one on top.

Flying lizard

Draco lizards are able to glide through the air because of skin flaps that spread out from their ribs to catch the air while the smaller neck flaps help them steer.

Basilisk lizards
('Jesus Christ' lizard)

Green basilisk lizards can run across the surface of water to catch insects. They do this thanks to their long toes with fringes of skin that unfurl in the water. By quickly slapping their feet hard against the water, they can travel across the water's surface at up to 1.5 metres per second.

Ripley Explains...

How can they change colour like that?

Lizard skin is covered with layers of special cells called chromatophores. These cells contain tiny sacs of colour and respond to chemicals that the lizard releases. They have only four colours to work with (yellow, red, blue and brown) but they can mix colours (like mixing red and yellow to produce orange).

A lizard's own paint by numbers set!

Ripley's Believe It or Not!®
Photographer Aditya Permana captured this once-in-a-lifetime photo of a forest dragon lizard lazily playing a leaf guitar in Yogyakarta, Indonesia.

Many lizards live in underground burrows. These burrows are used for shelter from predators and midday desert heat.

CHARMING CHAMPS

ALL CREATURES, GREAT AND SMALL

Sporting some impressive members, the reptile family comes in all shapes and sizes. Find out how the biggest and the smallest contenders stack up against each other!

LIZARDS

CROCODILIAN

1 ST

For the largest overall size and weight, the winner is the saltwater crocodile.

LARGEST

Giant Saltwater Croc

These crocs live near the salty shores surrounding much of Australia and the Indian Ocean and are known to occasionally eat humans, so watch out!

SIZE: Can grow to over 7 m long

WEIGHT: Over 1,000 kg

Cuvier's Dwarf Caiman

Found in northern and central South America, dwarf caiman live alone or in pairs and eat fish, crab, molluscs, shrimp and terrestrial invertebrates.

SIZE: Typically 1.2–1.5 m long

WEIGHT: 6–7 kg

SMALLEST

Komodo Dragon

The name comes from rumours that a dragon-like creature lived on the Indonesian island of Komodo. Komodo dragons are fierce hunters and eat large prey, like water buffalo, deer, carrion, pigs, other smaller dragons and even humans!

SIZE: Up to 3 m long

WEIGHT: Up to 166 kg

Leatherback Sea Turtle

Leatherbacks can dive to depths of 1,280 metres — deeper than any other turtle — and can stay down for up to 85 minutes. Leatherbacks are also able to maintain warm body temperatures in cold water by using a unique set of adaptations, so they have the widest global distribution of all reptile species.

SIZE: Up to 2 m long
WEIGHT: Up to 907 kg

LARGEST

The Komodo dragon is the largest lizard in the world!

LARGEST

This dwarf gecko is about the size of a dime!

SMALLEST

SMALLEST

Dwarf Geckos

There are several tiny lizards and geckos fighting for smallest reptile, but the Jaragua Sphaero (*Sphaerodactylus ariasae*) dwarf gecko is the tiniest! It lives on the remote Caribbean island of Beata, part of the Dominican Republic.

SIZE: 1.6–1.8 cm long

Speckled Tortoise

Found in South Africa, their speckles help to keep them camouflaged in rocky areas, where they spend a great deal of their time hiding.

SIZE: 6–10 cm long

RADICAL REPTILES

Reptiles often develop extreme traits because these traits help them survive in a very specific habitat. These traits might seem 'extreme' to us, but they provide reptiles with their best chances for survival and reproduction.

FRILLED LIZARD

When faced with predators, frilled lizards flare out their neck frills in an intimidating threat display.

Whether it's all about the looks or more about function, these reptiles are really radical!

MATA MATA TURTLE

Called by many 'the weirdest-looking turtle ever', this Amazonian turtle has a very long, snake-like neck and an odd mouth filled with two sharp plates resembling human teeth that are stuck together. It eats fish, water birds and other reptiles.

SPIDER-TAILED HORNED VIPER

The spider-tailed horned viper uses its unique tail as a lure, shaking and wiggling it to mimic the movement of a spider. When birds approach and peck the tail, the snake makes its lightning-fast move.

TWIST IT!

Adwaita, an Aldabra Giant Tortoise from India, lived to be about 255 years old — which means he was born around 1750. That made him an entire generation older than the United States!

In the early 1990s, India tried to solve its problem of corpses in the Ganges River by releasing 25,000 flesh-eating turtles into the river, spending £21 million on the unsuccessful endeavor.

Box turtles can be dangerous to eat — at times they consume poisonous mushrooms and the toxins may linger in their flesh.

Desert-dwelling toadhead agama lizards communicate by curling and uncurling their tails.

VITAL BUSINESS

FACINATING FACTS
A Snappy Sting

Snapping turtles have a powerful beak-like jaw that really packs a punch! They are known for being fierce and grumpy, particularly when out of water. Unlike other turtles, they can't hide fully inside their shells, which is why they have developed a snapping defence.

MALAGASY LEAF-NOSED SNAKE

As their name implies, leaf-nosed snakes have bizarre nasal appendages. These snakes are often seen hanging from branches with their heads pointing toward the ground, although researchers have not figured out why.

GECKO VISION

A SIGHT FOR SORE EYES

Gecko eyes don't just come in various colours and sizes, they are also incredibly powerful. They can see in the dark, and their night vision is so acute they can even see various shades of colour!

Just like snakes, most geckos don't have eyelids, but instead have clear scales over their eyes that they actually lick with their tongues to keep clean. Geckos can also focus sharply on objects at two different depths at the same time. These amazing eyes are colourful and impressive indeed.

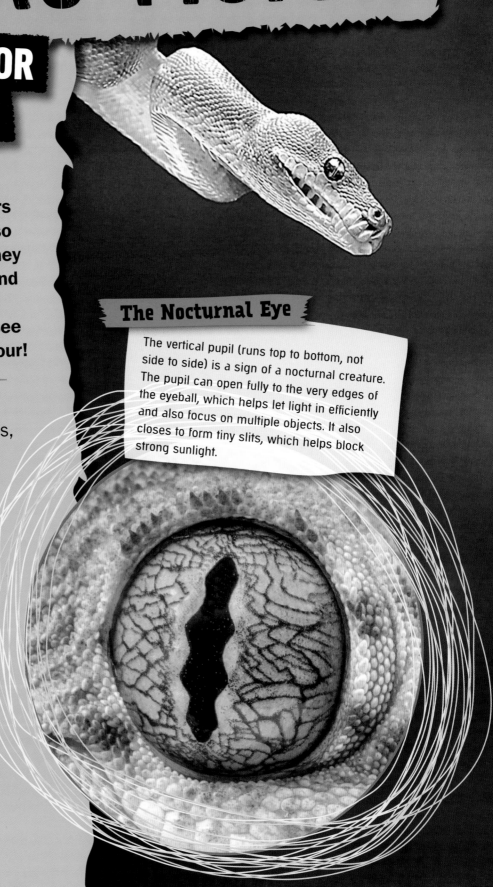

The Nocturnal Eye

The vertical pupil (runs top to bottom, not side to side) is a sign of a nocturnal creature. The pupil can open fully to the very edges of the eyeball, which helps let light in efficiently and also focus on multiple objects. It also closes to form tiny slits, which helps block strong sunlight.

TWIST IT!

FIELD OF VISION

Geckos, like other reptiles, even shed their eye scales (called spectacles), and their eyes might temporarily look milky or grey/blue during this process.

With eyesight comparable to a cat's, geckos can see better than any other lizard whose vision has been studied.

The sensitivity of most gecko eyes to light is estimated to be about 350 times stronger than human eyes!

In parts of Southeast Asia, tokay geckos are regarded as harbingers of luck and good fortune!

The name gecko comes from the Indonesian Malay language's gekoq, which isn't actually a real word but an imitation of the sound geckos make.

Madagascar Velvet Gecko

The Madagascar velvet gecko — including its eyes — is patterned to blend with logs and rocks.

BIG WORD ALERT

NOCTURNAL

Awake and active at night and asleep during the day.

SAVVY SQUEEZERS!

SNAKES THAT LEAVE YOU BREATHLESS

This class of snakes includes pythons, boas and the giant anaconda. Before swallowing their prey whole, constrictor snakes wrap around their prey and use their extremely strong muscles to squeeze them to death.

When the unfortunate victim breathes out, the snake coils even more tightly so it can't breathe in again. These long, heavy-bodied snakes are built to handle digesting a gigantic meal over several days or even weeks.

Boa constrictor

Snakes like this boa constrictor ambush their prey, using their teeth to grab and force the meal down its throat. While digesting a large meal, the snake is vulnerable because it can't move or defend itself easily.

Anacondas can grow to between 7.6 and 9 metres and weigh over 250 kilograms.

Giant anaconda

Anacondas, the largest of the constrictors, can easily kill and eat something as large as an antelope. After a meal that big, they often go into hiding while the super-sized meal is digested.

True or false?

	TRUE	FALSE
A constrictor snake can swallow prey much bigger than its own head.	✓	
Snakes can't breathe while they are swallowing prey.		✓
Some constrictors can weigh over 180 kilograms.	✓	
Anacondas can go months between meals.	✓	
Constrictor snakes can 'unhinge' their jaws to swallow giant meals.		✓

Python X-ray

Using a special scanning technique, scientists from Denmark took X-rays of a python digesting a rat. After being swallowed by the snake, the rat gradually disappeared during the course of 132 hours – five and a half days!

Rat

MORTAL COMBAT

REPTILES THAT KILL

Certain reptiles can pose a real threat to humans – but only when humans first threaten their space or safety.

Even the most venomous snakes, hazardous lizards and aggressive crocodiles have an important place in the ecosystem. Remember, these animals might seem like they are out to get you, but like all living things, they are just trying to survive.

Taipan

The taipan, found in Asia and Australia, is a large, fast-moving snake. Its venom is very toxic, and it's considered one of the deadliest known snakes in the world. Luckily, it doesn't live near humans, so bites are rare.

Saw-scaled viper

This highly venomous snake is found in Africa and the Middle East, and it takes the title of deadliest snake because of its nasty, aggressive temper — it often strikes at anything that disturbs it. Interestingly, it is also known for the 'sizzling' warning sound it makes before it bites down on its victims.

During the Vietnam War, American soldiers referred to the many-banded krait as the 'two-step snake' in the mistaken belief that its venom is so lethal, if bitten, you will die after taking just two steps.

In March 2014, wildlife officials finally apprehended a young Nile crocodile in Florida's Everglades National Park. The juvenile croc had escaped from a Miami-Dade facility and was on the run for two years!

Hefty, aggressive monsters, Nile crocodiles kill up to 200 people every year.

The puff adder's venom can kill a human in about 30 minutes. In 2009, a 23-year-old British woman was bit by a puff adder while hiking in Africa and survived without antivenom after more than two hours en route to the hospital.

FIERCE FOES

Green iguana

These iguanas might look friendly, but if they become agitated, they will bite down with their razor-sharp teeth or use their tail as a powerful, painful whip. It's not a good idea to keep these guys as pets!

Gaboon viper

This venomous viper is found in the rainforests and woodlands of Africa. Generally unaggressive and tolerant, these snakes have the longest fangs and deliver the biggest dose of venom of any snake.

Ripley's Believe It or Not!®

While walking around Australia in a *Star Wars* stormtrooper costume to raise money for Monash Children's Hospital, Scott Loxley was attacked by a deadly King Brown snake. The snake tried to bite Loxley on his shin — but was stopped by the plastic costume!

Gila monster

The Gila monster (pronounced HEE-lah) is the largest lizard native to the southwestern United States and northern Mexico — and one of the world's only venomous lizards. A Gila monster will latch on to a victim and chew, allowing neurotoxins to move through the venom glands in its lower jaw and into the open wound.

REPTILES AT RISK

HOW CAN WE SAVE THEM?

Critically Endangered Turtles

The critically endangered list includes several turtles, like the hawksbill sea turtle and the leatherback sea turtle. Many conservation groups help save turtles by encouraging fishermen to use different hooks and nets that don't ensnare turtles, passing laws that make it illegal to sell turtle eggs, and creating safe nesting sites where turtle eggs are protected from humans and other predators.

Every year, more than 250,000 sea turtles are accidentally caught in fishing nets and then drown because they can't get to the surface to breathe.

More fisherman are moving to 'turtle excluder devices', which have trap doors that allow smaller trapped turtles to escape, but they don't work as well with large species like the leatherback.

This safe hatchery created by conservationists in Costa Rica protects the leatherback sea turtle eggs from poachers and other predators. Their efforts are working because the number of female turtles returning each year to lay eggs is slowly rising.

Whether it's habitat destruction and pollution, over-hunting and overfishing or environmental changes, many reptiles are now on the endangered list, meaning they are in danger of becoming extinct.

Although there are natural changes to a reptile's habitat that can endanger it, man-made problems – like poaching – cause the most damage and increase the risk of extinction. We need to make changes before they are gone forever!

More than one-third of all reptile species are threatened, which means they could be endangered in the near future unless they are fully protected.

Many types of Crocodilians are endangered, like this Chinese alligator. Their homes are being turned into rice paddies, and farmers consider them pests and kill them. They are also being eaten as part of traditional Chinese medicine.

BIG WORD ALERT

POACHING

The illegal hunting, killing or capturing of wild animals.

What You Can Do

Visit your local zoo or animal sanctuary to learn more about the reptiles in your area. You can also visit websites such as the Sea Turtle Conservancy (www.conserveturtles.org) to find out what you can do to help turtles in danger. Finally, don't buy any reptile products unless you know they come from a legal supplier.

Many lizards and tortoises are at risk due to loss of habitat, poaching and the active wildlife trade, especially the critically endangered day gecko and the beautiful radiated tortoise.

ACKNOWLEDGEMENTS

COVER (sp) Kevin Horan/Getty Images, (b/l) © Nick Garbutt/naturepl.com; **2** (t) © Dennis van de Water - Shutterstock.com; **3** (t) Dave Beaudette, (b/r) © EcoView/Fotolia.com; **4** (sp) Kevin Horan/Getty Images; **6** (t/r) Jason Edwards/National Geographic Creative; **6–7** (dp) © Daniel Heuclin/naturepl.com, (bgd) Mattias Klum/National Geographic Creative; **7** (b) Andy Rouse/Getty Images; **8** (b/l) © JanelleLugge/iStock.com, (b/r) © EuroPics[CEN]; **8–9** (dp) © Elliotte Rusty Harold/Shutterstock.com; **9** (t/c) © Edwin Giesbers/naturepl.com, (b) © Daniel Heuclin/naturepl.com, (b/r) © Teerapun/Shutterstock.com; **10** (l) © EcoView/Fotolia.com, (c/r) Geoeye Satellite Image; **10–11** (dp) © Jurgen Freund/naturepl.com; **11** (t) © hadkhanong/Fotolia.com, (r) Piotr Naskrecki/Minden Pictures/National Geographic Creative; **12** (b) © Cathy Keifer/Fotolia.com; **12–13** (dp) © mgkuijpers/Fotolia.com; **13** (t) © LightRecords/Shutterstock.com, (b) © James DeBoer/Shutterstock.com; **14** (b/r) Seers Croft Vet Surgery; **14–15** (dp) © Stephen Dalton/naturepl.com; **15** (b/l) Linda Davidson / The Washington Post via Getty Images, (b/r) Rob Brookes / Barcroft Media; **16–17** (dp) Mauricio Handler/National Geographic Creative; **17** (t) © Anup Shah/naturepl.com, (b/r) © Pete Oxford/naturepl.com, (c/l) State Archives of Florida, Florida Memory, http://floridamemory.com/items/show/82911; **18** (b/l) © reptiles4all/Shutterstock.com, (b/r) Joel Sartore/National Geographic Creative; **18–19** (dp) © Stuart G Porter - Shutterstock.com; **19** (t/l) Joel Sartore/National Geographic Creative, (t/r) © amwu/iStock.com, (b/l) Dave Beaudette; **20** (b/l) © Anup Shah/naturepl.com, (t/r) R. D. Bartlett; **20–21** (dp) © Daniel Heuclin/naturepl.com; **22** (t) © Sprocky/Shutterstock.com; **22–23** (dp) © Alex Mustard/naturepl.com; **23** (c/r) © Millard H. Sharp / Science Source, (b) © Stephen Dalton/naturepl.com; **24** (b) © Andrea Izzotti/Fotolia.com; **24–25** (dp) Jim Abernethy/National Geographic Creative; **25** (t/l) © atosan/iStock.com, (t/r) © Kitch Bain/Shutterstock.com; **26** (b/r) Jason Edwards/National Geographic Creative; **26–27** (dp) © Doug Perrine/naturepl.com; **27** (b/r) © Pete Oxford/naturepl.com; **28** (t/r) © Renphoto/iStock.com, (b/l) HEIDI AND HANS-JURGEN KOCH/ MINDEN PICTURES/National Geographic Creative; **29** (sp) © Michael D. Kern/naturepl.com, (t/l) Simon D. Pollard / Science Source, (t/r) Courtesy of Sunshine Serpents; **30** (b/r) © Ethan Daniels/Shutterstock.com; **30–31** (dp) © Peter B. Kaplan / Science Source; **31** (t/r) Carnegie Mellon University/Rex/REX USA, (b/l) © Tim MacMillan / John Downer Pr/naturepl.com; **32** (t/r) © Bernard Castelein/naturepl.com, (b/l) © Dimitris Poursanidis / terrasolutions / www.terrasolutions.eu,MY/naturepl.com; **32–33** (dp) © Bence Mate/naturepl.com; **33** (t/r) © Tim MacMillan /John Downer Pro/naturepl.com, (b/r) ADITYA PERMANA / MERCURY PRESS / CATERS NEWS; **34** (c/l) © Jamie Robertson/naturepl.com, (b) © Eric Gevaert - Shutterstock.com; **34–35** (c) © Pedro Narra/naturepl.com, © albund - Shutterstock.com; **35** (t/r) Frans Lanting / MINT Images / Science Source, (c/l) Jason Edwards/National Geographic Creative, (c/r) Joel Sartore/National Geographic Creative; **36** (c/r) Steve Cooper / Science Source, (b/l) © Rosa Jay - Shutterstock.com; **36–37** (bgd) © juan sanchez - Shutterstock.com; **37** (t) Omid Mozaffari, (c) © Michiel de Wit - Shutterstock.com, (b/r) © Dennis van de Water - Shutterstock.com; **38** (b) © reptiles4all - Shutterstock.com; **38–39** (dp) MANG DAY / MERCURY PRESS / CATERS NEWS; **39** (r) Thomas Marent/ MINDEN PICTURES/National Geographic Creative; **40** (b) © Christophe Courteau/naturepl.com; **40–41** (dp) © Nick Garbutt/naturepl.com; **41** (r) Henrik Lauridsen, Kasper Hansen, Michael Pederson, and Tobias Wang; **42** (t) © reptiles4all - Shutterstock.com, (b) © Tony Phelps/naturepl.com; **42–43** (bgd) © DVARG - Shutterstock.com; **43** (t/r) © John Cancalosi/naturepl.com, (c/l) Philip Blackman/Monash Health, (c/r) Joel Sartore/National Geographic Creative, (b/r) © reptiles4all/iStock.com; **44** (c) © Jordi Chias/naturepl.com, (b/l) Jason Edwards/National Geographic Creative, (b/r) © italiansight/iStock.com; **44–45** (bgd) © rangizzz - Shutterstock.com, © Picsfive - Shutterstock.com, © PeterPhoto123 - Shutterstock.com; **45** (t/l) Brian J. Skerry/National Geographic Creative, (t/r) © Laures/iStock.com, (c) © Ryan M. Bolton - Shutterstock.com, (b) © hakoar/iStock.com

Key: t = top, b = bottom, c = center, l = left, r = right, sp = single page, dp = double page, bgd = background

All other photos and artwork are from Ripley's Entertainment Inc.

Every attempt has been made to acknowledge correctly and contact copyright holders and we apologise in advance for any unintentional errors or omissions, which will be corrected in future editions.

TWISTS

a Jim Pattison Company

Written by Camilla de la Bedoyere
Illustrations by John Graziano

RIPLEY PUBLISHING

Executive Vice President, Intellectual Property Norm Deska
Vice President, Archives and Exhibits Edward Meyer
Director, Publishing Operations Amanda Joiner
Managing Editor Dean Miller

Editor Wendy A. Reynolds, M.S.Ed.
Designers Sam South, Joshua Surprenant
Researcher Sabrina Sieck
Additional Research Jessica Firpi
Fact Checker, Anglicisation James Proud
Production Coordinator Amy Webb
Reprographics Juice Creative Ltd
Cover Concept Joshua Surprenant
Cover Art John Graziano

www.ripleys.com/books

Random House Books
20 Vauxhall Bridge Road
London SW1V 2SA
www.randomhouse.co.uk

Random House Books is part of the Penguin Random
House group of companies whose addresses can be found
at global.penguinrandomhouse.com

Penguin Random House UK

ISBN 978-1-60991-225-3 (USA) | ISBN 978-178475-314-6 (UK)

CONTENTS

Scimitar

Axe

TWISTS

Fire Bomb

PAGES 30-31

PAGE 32

Pirates *of* the World

THE HAIR-RAISING TRUTH!

You're standing on the deck of a huge wooden ship. The smell of gunpowder is thick in the air. Everywhere you look men are fighting for their lives, and the clashing sound of swords and cutlasses is cut only by their screams. Your captain signals for you to join them – all for your share of the treasure that lies in the ship's hold. Do you have what it takes to be a pirate?

If you do, then prepare for an exciting pirate adventure! You'll learn lots of important pirate lingo, hints for designing your own pirate flag, and tips for creating your personal pirate "look". You'll also find unbelievable facts about some of the most famous pirates in history, including their evil raids, hidden treasures, and terrible ends.

Found a new word? Big Word Alert will explain it for you.

BIG WORD ALERT

— *RIGGING* —
The ropes and chains used to attach sails to the masts and yards.

When a petrified passenger refused to hand over a diamond ring, Blackbeard simply sliced off his finger!

TWISTS

KEY FACTS
Learn a fast fact
about the picture!

Don't forget to look out for
the 'Twist It!' column on some
pages. Twist the book to find
out more unbelievable facts
about pirates.

AAAARG! Practice the
pirate lingo on the scrolls
throughout this book and on
September 19, you'll be ready
to celebrate 'International
Talk Like a Pirate Day'!

te Ships

ARD AND HEAVE-HO!

the Go... len Age of Piracy
of woo... and many broke
the stra... of a heavy storm.

...am...ed, ...irty, smelly places,
...ny pir... a ship was the
...ly home ...hey had.

Today, the world's largest cruise ship
MS *Allure of the Seas* is nearly four
football fields long and 16 decks
high. That's more than 90 metres
longer and more than four times
heavier than the *Titanic*!

England's
Willard Wigan works
under a microscope to
create tiny sculptures
such as this pirate ship
– which stem to stern
is even smaller than
the eye of a sewing
needle!

SHIPPING OUT

Discovered in 1996 off the North
Carolina shore, a 300-year-old
shipwreck is believed to be none
other than Blackbeard's ship, the
Queen Anne's Revenge!

TWIST IT!

Pirates arranged rat hunts to get rid
of the rodents — on just one journey,
a Spanish captain reported that
4,000 rats were killed!

The poop deck is a small, raised
deck in the back of the ship. When
the seas got so rough that a
wave broke over the stern
of the ship, sailors would
cry, 'Avast, we're pooped!'

THE LINGO!
FAMOUS
PIRATE SHIPS

Blackbeard
Queen Anne's Revenge
~
Henry Avery
The Fancy
~
Francis Drake
The Pelican, later renamed
The Golden Hind
~
Calico Jack
The William
~
Black Bart
Royal Fortune
~
Christopher Moody
The Rising Sun
~
William Kidd
Adventure Galley

FACTS

...ships did not have
...ams. When pirates
...d to relieve themselves,
...at on a platform called
...eakhead bulkhead' near
...ront of the ship and hung
... bottoms over the edge!

Crow's Nest

Rigging

Galley

Foremast

Gun Deck

Water and Beer Barrel Store

Anchor

Jolly Roger

Quarter Deck

Main Deck

Poop Deck

Captain's Cabin

Sleeping
Quarters

Food Stores

Keel

Bilge

Ripley's Explains...

Types of Sailing Ships

- **BRIGANTINE:** A large ship used by
  the navy or as a merchant vessel.
- **FRIGATE:** A warship (man o' war)
  with three masts, two decks, and as
  many as 90 guns.
- **GALLEON:** A large European sailing
  ship with three or four masts.
- **SCHOONER:** A large ship that
  was light, fast, and easy to sail.
- **SLOOP:** A small sailing boat
  with one mast.

These books are
all about amazing
'Believe It or Not!
facts, feats, and
items that will make
you say, 'WOW!'

Ripley's Believe It or Not!®
By completing
courses in pistol
use, archery, sailing, and
fencing, Jacob Hurwitz
earned a pirate certificate at
the Massachusetts Institute
of Technology, U.S.A.!

LABELS
Love the picture?
Learn even more
about it here!

Ripley's Explains...
See the 'Ripley's
Explains' panels for
extra info from our
pirate experts.

The Golden Age of Pirates

A TIMELINE OF TERROR...

Pirates have troubled sea travellers for many centuries. There was one brief time in history – the Golden Age of Piracy – when pirates actually controlled the seas.

From 1650 to 1730, fleets of pirate ships wreaked havoc around the Mediterranean Sea, across the Atlantic, in the China Sea and the Bay of Bengal, and throughout the Caribbean.

Pirate ship crews could range between two and 300 members.

The sloop was a popular choice for a pirate ship.

PIRATES' LOG BOOK:

~

Key Events in History

Ripley's Explains...

BCE

BCE is short for Before Common Era. If a date says 250 BCE, and the current year is 2016, add the two numbers to work out when the event happened: 2016 + 250 = 2,266 years ago. (Sometimes BC is used instead of BCE).

GASPARILLA PIRATE FESTIVAL

Every year, pirates and pirate wannabees gather in Tampa, Florida, for the Gasparilla Pirate Festival – named after a famous local pirate.

Timeline

1200 BCE Earliest piracy in history is recorded

230 BCE Queen Teuta terrorises Roman and Greek ships

75 BCE Julius Caesar is captured by pirates

220 Chinese piracy grows in the Far East

793 Vikings terrorise northern Europe

1536 England's King Henry VIII passes laws against piracy

1550s Privateers serve European royalty

1600 Spanish explorers plunder treasure in the Americas

1615 Barbary corsairs operate in the Mediterranean

1650s The first buccaneers begin their reign of terror

1678 The first Pirate Code is created

1721 Maratha pirates evade capture by the British Navy

1729 The British Navy drives pirates from their Caribbean lairs

1816 A huge fleet of ships puts an end to the Barbary corsairs

1883 *Treasure Island* is published

1998 Piracy in parts of the world becomes a major problem again

2009 Combined Task Force 151 is formed to fight piracy

SWORD FIGHTING!

Would-be pirates – including Kate and Adam Driscoll – practise sword fighting and other skills at gatherings like Captain Redbeard's Feast in Honeyoe Lake, New York.

TWIST IT!

TARNISHED GOLDEN AGE

Over 98 per cent of buccaneers led law-abiding lives as sailors on merchant ships or in the navy before turning to a life of crime!

Pirate ships were plagued by rats, mice, lice, and fleas, and while many pirates died in battle, most died from the diseases these vermin spread onboard!

Cats helped control the rats and mice on board – black cats were considered especially lucky.

Ancient Mariners

If you were a pirate in the Middle Ages, you were made to suffer before your execution – including being dragged to your death behind a horse!

PIRATES OF THE FAR PAST

Pirating goes back to ancient Greece around 1200 BCE, when the Greeks invented the word *peiratēs*, which evolved into the word 'pirate'.

In 67 BCE, Pompey the Great gave captured pirates plots of land and helped them become farmers instead!

KEY FACTS

Roman captains often paid pirates 'wages' so they wouldn't attack their ships!

KIDNAP!

In 75 BCE, Julius Caesar was captured by pirates who demanded money for his release. Once free, Caesar returned to their lair – and had their throats cut.

TWIST IT!

The streets in the ancient town of Mykonos, Greece, were arranged in a maze pattern to foil invading pirates!

Fenrir Greyback, the werewolf in the Harry Potter books, was named after a ferocious giant wolf in ancient Viking mythology.

The pirates who captured Julius Caesar at first demanded a ransom of 20 talents of silver, but Caesar allegedly laughed and suggested he was worth at least 50!

MARAUDERS' MAYHEM

8

The skogkatt, or Norwegian Forest cat, was used by Vikings to keep their ships clear of rodents.

Ripley's Explains...

Ship Spoils

The Golden Age of Piracy thrived as pirates targeted the large amounts of treasure, money, and slaves being transported by ship between the Americas, Europe, and Africa.

TEUTA THE TERROR

Queen Teuta of Illyria terrorised the Adriatic Sea around 230 BCE. However, when more than 200 Roman ships intercepted her fleet, Teuta quickly gave up piracy!

VICIOUS VIKINGS

From 800 to 1100 AD, the Vikings ruled the northern seas, sailing their longboats in search of ships to raid.

Ripley's Believe It or Not!®

In 2008, Robert McDonald built a 90-metre Viking ship from 15 million ice cream sticks and sailed it from the Netherlands to England!

Privateers

...AND OTHER SCARY SEA DOGS

A special type of piracy known as privateering allowed certain sailors to attack foreign ships – but only if they shared the booty with their king or queen!

Privateers were still pirates at heart, however. If they were licensed to take only a certain type of vessel but couldn't find one, they would usually just attack the next ship they saw!

Although he was hanged for being a pirate, Captain Kidd was actually a privateer!

THE LINGO!

Barbary corsair
A pirate from the Barbary (North African) coast.

~

Buccaneer
A pirate of the Caribbean – named after the French word *boucanier* (a person who barbecues) because they cooked meat on a frame over a fire.

~

Corsair
A French pirate – the word means 'chaser'.

~

Filibuster or Fiibustier
A pirate in the 1600s, often English, Spanish, Dutch, or French.

~

Freebooter
A Dutch word for thieves in search of treasure, which was known as booty.

~

Marooner
A Spanish runaway slave or sailor.

~

Sea dog
An old or experienced sailor.

~

Sea king
A Viking pirate chief.

~

Sea rover
Another word for pirate.

BUCCANEER KING

Born in 1635, Henry Morgan was called the 'King of the Buccaneers'. King Charles II was so pleased with the piles of treasure Morgan collected for him that he made him governor of Jamaica.

WARRIORS AT SEA

England's Queen Elizabeth I gave Francis Drake permission to plunder Spanish ports and ships. In return, Drake helped her defeat the Spanish Armada fleet sent to invade England in 1588.

TWIST IT!

BAD BOYS

Jean Bart, a French corsair who captured about 80 ships in the English Channel, was honoured by the King of France in 1694 – much to the frustration of the English!

Francis Drake's privateering took him far and wide – in the 1570s, he became the first Englishman to circumnavigate, or travel completely around, the world!

CRUEL CORSAIRS

When North African pirates known as Barbary corsairs captured 493 English ships between 1609 and 1625, the luckiest English sailors were sold as slaves – the unlucky ones had their throats slit.

Jamaica's Port Royal was known as 'the most wicked and sinful city in the world', and was the favourite hideaway of Henry Morgan and other bad-to-the-bone buccaneers.

KEY FACTS

Kings and queens provided privateers with a Letter of Marque and Reprisal, which protected them from arrest if they were caught.

Pirate Ships

ALL ABOARD AND HEAVE-HO!

Ships during the Golden Age of Piracy were made of wood, and many broke apart under the strain of a heavy storm.

They were cramped, dirty, smelly places, but for many pirates, a ship was the only home they had.

KEY FACTS

Wooden ships did not have bathrooms. When pirates needed to relieve themselves, they sat on a platform called the 'beakhead bulkhead' near the front of the ship and hung their bottoms over the edge!

Crow's Nest

Rigging

Galley

Foremast

Gun Deck

Water and Beer Barrel Store

Anchor

Bi

THE LINGO! FAMOUS PIRATE SHIPS

Blackbeard
Queen Anne's Revenge

~

Henry Avery
The Fancy

~

Francis Drake
The Pelican, later renamed The Golden Hind

~

Calico Jack
The William

~

Black Bart
Royal Fortune

~

Christopher Moody
The Rising Sun

~

William Kidd
Adventure Galley

SHIPPING OUT

Discovered in 1996 off the North Carolina shore, a 300-year-old shipwreck is believed to be none other than Blackbeard's ship, the *Queen Anne's Revenge!*

Pirates arranged rat hunts to get rid of the rodents – on just one journey, a Spanish captain reported that 4,000 rats were killed!

TWIST IT!

The poop deck is a small, raised deck in the back of the ship. When the seas got so rough that a wave broke over the stern of the ship, sailors would cry, 'Avast, we're pooped!'

Jolly Roger

Quarter Deck

Poop Deck

Main Deck

Captain's Cabin

Sleeping Quarters

Food Stores

Keel

Ripley's Explains...

Types of Sailing Ships

- **BRIGANTINE:** A large ship used by the navy or as a merchant vessel.

- **FRIGATE:** A warship (man o' war) with three masts, two decks, and as many as 90 guns.

- **GALLEON:** A large European sailing ship with three or four masts.

- **SCHOONER:** A large ship that was light, fast, and easy to sail.

- **SLOOP:** A small sailing boat with one mast.

Blackbeard

TOP PIRATE OF THE CARIBBEAN

Few pirates are as infamous as Blackbeard, who terrorised the Atlantic Ocean and Caribbean Sea from 1716 to 1718.

Probably an Englishman called Edward Teach or Thatch, Blackbeard was a privateer in the Caribbean before taking over a ship and pursuing a pirate's life.

KEY FACTS

Blackbeard and his crew pretended to be friendly until they got close enough to attack.

Blackbeard's Jolly Roger!

When nine-year-old Beatrice Delap wrote to Captain Jack Sparrow – Johnny Depp's character in the *Pirates of the Caribbean* movies – he responded by turning up at her Greenwich, London, school in full pirate costume!

PIRATE KING

Blackbeard's crew always covered his ships' decks with sand to soak up all the blood that would be spilled in a sea battle.

Blackbeard was said to have had 14 wives. His last wife, Mary Ormond, is said to haunt the North Carolina coast, still waiting for her husband to return!

Blackbeard had no sense of honour. Legend has it he even shot members of his own crew for fun!

Pirates enjoyed a good party, and Blackbeard threw some of the best in the Caribbean. There was drinking, eating, dancing, and bonfires, and all the local pirates were invited!

TWIST IT!

Ripley's Believe It or Not!®

This might look like a pirate's treasure chest, but it's even better – it's made entirely of cake!

A Picture of Evil

To make himself look fierce, Blackbeard carried six pistols in slings over his shoulders, shoved extra pistols down his trousers, and stuck lit matches under his hat!

Ransom

Blackbeard once captured a ship full of passengers and locked them all, including the children, in the ship's dark, dirty hold. He demanded a chest of medicine as a ransom, and it was delivered just in time to save their lives.

Missing Treasure

No one knows what Blackbeard did with his treasure – it might still be hidden somewhere!

THE PIRATE CHRONICLES

LOCAL MARAUDER

TWO CENTS
2¢ EACH

NO. 11   SATURDAY, OCTOBER 11, 1721   TWO CENT EDITION

HEADLESS HAUNTING

Facing his executioner on 20 October 1401, German pirate Klaus Störtebeker struck a last-minute deal: if his headless body managed to walk past a member of his crew, he would be freed.

According to legend, Störtebeker's corpse got up and walked past eleven of his men – before the executioner tripped him. All 70 of his crew were also beheaded, despite the deal.

THIS WEEK

PIRATES

~ PIRATES' WORLD OF WORK ~

Corsair Classifieds

Do you desire a life on the open sea?
Do you know your knots from your knickerbockers?
We have vacancies for keen, young, strong men who are looking for a life of adventure!

POSITIONS AVAILABLE:

• A **bosun** to organise supplies and check the ship and its sails.

• A **shipmaster** for choosing routes, navigation, and map maintenance.

• A **master gunner** to take control of all guns and ammunition.

• A **sail-maker** to oversee the stitching and care of all sails.

• A **striker** to replenish ship supplies – excellent fishing and hunting skills essential!

• A **swabbie** to wash all blood, gore, and gross body parts off the deck after battles. Must have own mop.

Applicants must have:

• *Great teamwork skills*
• *A strong stomach and sea legs*
• *No nasty diseases*

Previous experience in murder, menace, and mayhem are not necessary. We will provide all training necessary.

Minimum contract:
Six months. No pension, no health benefits, no other perks – but you'll receive a daily tot of rum and all the treasure you can plunder.

Apply to: Captain D'eath, *The Marauder*, moored at Portsmouth Harbour.

TWIST IT!

Captured by pirates, carpenter Richard Luntly was marooned on a desert island when they overheard him planning to escape. Luntly was eventually rescued – and hanged for being a pirate anyway!

SEA-FARING FACTS

Anyone who could sing or play an instrument helped to pass the time, so pirates were always on the lookout for musicians to capture.

Gunpowder was carried to the cannons by younger boys in the crew known as 'powder monkeys'.

Sailor? Try Being a Sea Dog!

~

Are you a navy sailor considering a life of crime? Well-known pirate captain has immediate openings for a first mate to be his second in command, and a quartermaster to guard treasure and take over in the event of his untimely demise.

APPLY IN PERSON, WITH REFERENCES, TO CAPTAIN H., *THE FURY*, MOORED IN LONDON HARBOUR.

The Pirate Code

HOW TO BE A PIRATE: PART 1

Every pirate crew created and followed their own special set of rules called the Pirate Code, or the Articles.

First mentioned in a book called *Buccaneers of America* over 330 years ago, the Pirate Code is an important part of the story of piracy.

STEP ONE

MAKE SOME RULES

THE PIRATE CODE

1. Everyone should have a fair share of the plunder. A surgeon will receive twice as much as a carpenter.

2. Everyone should have a vote on what the crew does, where the ship goes, and who the captain will be.

3. Food and drink should be shared out equally.

4. If anyone steals from the ship's booty, he will be marooned. If he robs another pirate, he shall have his nose and ears slit before being set ashore.

5. Everyone shall keep his or her weapons clean and ready for action.

6. If anyone is injured, he or she shall be given some money. 600 pieces of eight for the loss of a right arm and 100 pieces of eight for the loss of an eye.

TWIST IT!

The Pirate Code set a strict bedtime for the pirates: candles had to be put out by 8 pm if anyone wanted to carry on partying, they had to go on deck so they didn't disturb everyone else!

CODE CLUES

To prevent his pirates from fighting aboard ship, Black Bart stated in his Code that crewmembers could not play cards for money.

Anyone have
any sun cream?

KEY FACTS

Red Legs Greaves had
fair Scottish skin that
was always sunburned.
That's how he got his
strange name!

SPOOKY SHIP

In 1872, the *Mary Celeste* was found
in the Atlantic
Ocean ten days
after she set sail.
Her cargo and
valuables were
completely
untouched, but all
the passengers
and crewmembers
had vanished!

Red Legs Greaves

Few pirates could
be described as
honourable, despite
their Code.
Red Legs Greaves,
however, was a
better man than
most.

Originally a Scottish slave in Barbados, Red Legs
was forced into piracy, became a captain, and
captured both a Spanish fleet and the island of
Margarita, off Venezuela.

Captured and thrown into prison, Red Legs
managed to escape during an earthquake and
became a pirate hunter to stay out of jail.

Unlike most pirates, Red Legs never tortured
his prisoners, and he refused to rob the poor.

19

Sailing the High Seas

ALL HANDS ON DECK!*

Keeping a sailing ship afloat was a huge task that took teamwork. Sails needed to be constantly repaired, and weapons needed to be cleaned or sharpened, ready for action!

Riggers controlled the many sails on a ship. It was an incredibly dangerous job, as the ropes and wood were constantly wet with sea spray, making it easy to slip and fall into the ocean.

BRICK BOAT

Peter Lange's two-tonne, six-metre-long brick boat made its maiden voyage around Auckland Harbor, New Zealand on April Fool's Day, 2002. It took three months and 676 bricks to make the boat!

Caskets of rum were often called 'Nelson's blood'. When Admiral Nelson died in the Battle of Trafalgar, his body was immersed in a casket full of brandy to preserve it on the voyage back to England.

KEY FACTS

*A 'hand' is a crewmember, so this call was used in an emergency to get everyone on the deck.

THE LINGO!

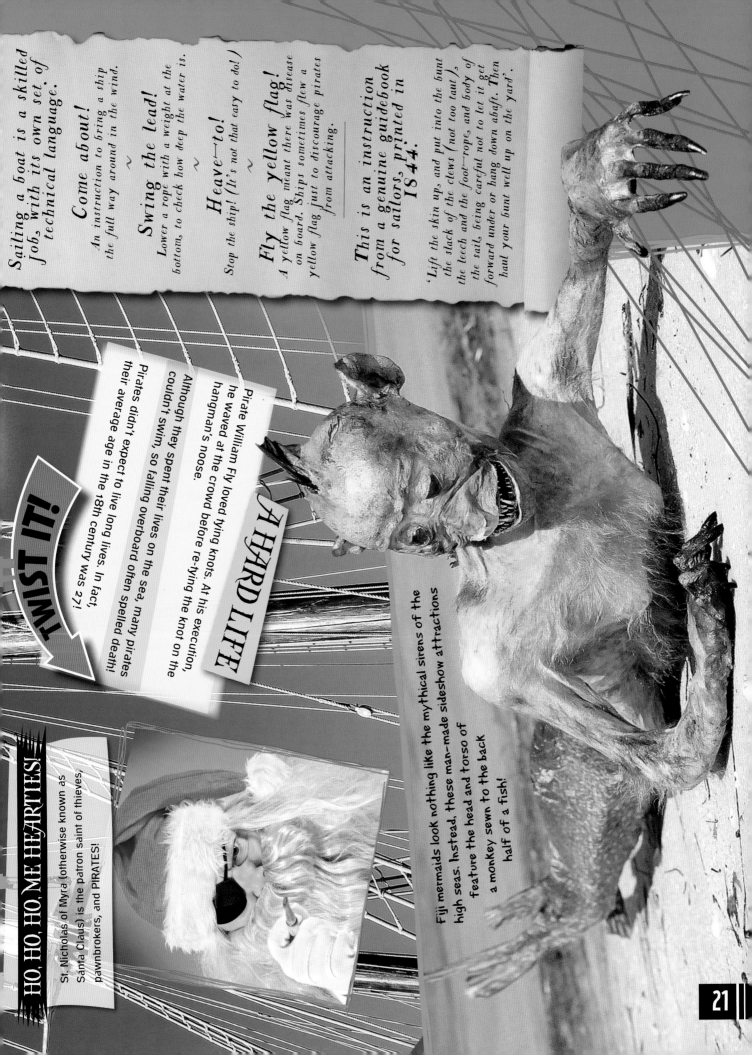

Sailing a boat is a skilled job, with its own set of technical language.

Come about!
An instruction to bring a ship the full way around (to bring a ship around).

Swing the lead!
Lower a rope with a weight at the bottom, to check how deep the water is.

Heave-to!
Stop the ship! (It's not that easy to do!)

Fly the yellow flag!
A yellow flag meant there was disease on board. Ships sometimes flew a yellow flag just to discourage pirates from attacking.

This is an instruction from a genuine guidebook for sailors, printed in 1844:

'Lift the skin up, and put into the bunt the slack of the clews (not too taut), the leech and the foot—rope, and body of the sail, being careful not to let it get forward under or hang down abaft. Then haul your bunt well up on the yard'.

A HARD LIFE

Pirate William Fly loved tying knots. At his execution, he waved at the crowd before re-tying the knot on the hangman's noose.

Although they spent their lives on the sea, many pirates couldn't swim, so falling overboard often spelled death!

Pirates didn't expect to live long lives. In fact, their average age in the 18th century was 27!

TWIST IT!

HO, HO, HO, ME HEARTIES!

St. Nicholas of Myra (otherwise known as Santa Claus) is the patron saint of thieves, pawnbrokers, and PIRATES!

Fiji mermaids look nothing like the mythical sirens of the high seas. Instead, these man-made sideshow attractions feature the head and torso of a monkey sewn to the back half of a fish!

Pirates of the East

SPINE-CHILLING SEA THIEVES

The ruthless pirates of Asia spread terror far and wide, especially across the South China Sea.

They sought power as well as treasure in this rich, thriving region.

The underwater cave system of England's Hodge Close Quarry, Cumbria, has claimed the lives of several divers, and when Peter Bardsley took this photo, he discovered a skull-shaped face was created by the reflection on the water.

Cunning Coxinga

Raiders of the Far East

From 1752 to 1832, over 200 Lanun pirate ships swarmed the merchant ships and coastal towns of Borneo, the Philippines, and New Guinea.

KEY FACTS

According to legend, Chinese pirate Cheung Po Tsai hid a vast treasure trove in a cave on Cheung Chau Island. No one has found the treasure yet!

Coxinga raised a huge army of 250,000 men and a navy of 3,000 ships to help his friend, Prince Tang, become emperor. After the emperor was defeated in battle, Coxinga turned to piracy, and successfully drove the Dutch settlers out of Taiwan (then known as Dutch Formosa) in 1661.

TWIST IT!

Lanun pirates carried huge swords that were decorated with long tresses of human hair.

Captured corsairs' ships were converted to floating prisons. Life on these diseased, rat-infested hulks was a sentence considered second only to death.

Coxinga went mad with malaria fever, and ordered his soldiers to kill his son. They refused, and Coxinga died soon after at the age of 37.

FAST FACTS

Costing a pirate lover in Florida an impressive booty of **£1.6 million**, this ship-styled home cinema features a tavern to serve snacks!

Zheng Zhilong

Held on the Isle of Sheppey, Kent, participants in the Annual World Plank Walking Championship are judged on their use of pirate language and costumes as well as their jumping style!

Chinese pirate Zheng Zhilong (1604–1661) was persuaded by the Chinese government to defend the Taiwan Strait from other pirates, and he soon became rich and powerful. Zheng's son Coxinga, however, also turned to a life of piracy and crime – and when Coxinga wouldn't surrender, his father was executed.

23

Ching Shih

THE TERROR OF
THE SOUTH CHINA SEA

When Ching Shih married the pirate Cheng I, in 1801, they ransacked towns along the Chinese coastline, captured ships, and collected large hoards of treasure together.

It was just the beginning of a long pirate career for one of the world's most dangerous women.

Going Solo

When Cheng I died in 1807, his widow controlled their fleet of 300 ships and up to 40,000 pirates, including men, women, and children.

Smart Tactics

Instead of attacking local villagers, Ching Shih made sure they were paid for any rice and wine the pirates consumed.

The Cruel Queen of the Sea

Ching Shih used cruelty to keep her pirate crew in line – including cutting off pirates' ears, flogging them, nailing their feet to the deck of a ship, or throwing them overboard!

SHE-DEVIL OF THE SEA

Pirate captains who worked for Ching Shih often gave themselves scary or strange names, such as 'Scourge of the Eastern Sea', 'Frog's Meal', and 'Jewel of the Whole Crew'.

Ching Shih didn't consider herself a smuggler, and preferred to say she 'transshipped goods' instead.

The Chinese government offered to let Ching Shih go free if she promised to give up pirating, which she did. She died of old age in 1844.

TWIST IT!

Keeping It in the Family

Cheung Po Tsai, a fisherman's son, was kidnapped and adopted by Cheng I and Ching Shih. According to legend, when Cheng I died, Cheung Po married his adoptive mother, and together they carried on the family business of piracy.

STINKPOT

Chinese pirates were infamous for their creation of the stinkpot. Filled with gunpowder and sulphur, stinkpots were thrown onto the deck of their victims' ship, where they released such a foul smell most sailors would jump overboard to avoid it!

KEY FACTS

The first rule in Ching Shih's Pirate Code was that anyone who disobeyed her would be beheaded on the spot!

BIG WORD ALERT

┤ SMUGGLER ├

A person who moves goods in and out of the country, against the laws of the land.

MERMAID SCULPTURE

Ripley's Believe It or Not!®

Greg Lewis of Chesterfield, Virginia, created this mermaid sculpture from 67,000 toothpicks!

Flying _the_ Jolly Roger

HOW TO BE A PIRATE: PART 2

STEP ONE
CHOOSE YOUR FLAG

Imagine you are a sailor who has decided to turn to a life of crime. You've staged a mutiny, thrown your annoying captain overboard, and persuaded your crewmates to join you in a new life of maritime mugging.

Now, you need to choose a flag, dress like a pirate, and practice speaking like an old sea dog.

Some believe the French name 'Jolie Rouge' (pretty red) gave us the name 'Jolly Roger' for a pirate's flag. You'll need to design your own flag, just as the pirates of old did. Here are some samples to help:

▶ A red skeleton on the front of the flag.

Edward Low

▶ A red flag (!), a golden winged hourglass, a white arm holding a dagger, and a golden skull and crossbones all in a row.

Christopher Moody

Walter Kennedy

Edward England

◀ The typical skull and crossbones, along with a figure holding a sword and an hourglass.

Christopher Condent

◀ The classic skull and crossbones design, with the crossbones below the skull.

◀ A long black banner with three of the classic skull and crossbones in a row.

26

You'll need to look menacing, brutal, and swashbuckling. As the captain, you can go overboard (not literally!) on your fashion statement, with flouncy fabrics and lots of flashy jewellery.

Need supplies for your pirate crew? San Francisco's 826 Valencia Pirate Supply Store and website offer everything from captain's logs to mermaid bait!

PIRATE PETS

Cats, monkeys, and even lizards were popular pets aboard ship. To pirates in Madagascar, the panther chameleon must have seemed like a mythical monster with independently roving eyes. This predator's lightning-fast, insect-snatching tongue can extend nearly the length of its body!

Who's a pretty boy then?

Will I need a parrot?

Definitely. Parrots are super intelligent, and can learn to mimic things you say. Once you catch one in a tropical forest, you can sell it for lots of money when you sail to Europe or North America.

Ripley's Explains...

BIG WORD ALERT

— MUTINY —
When a crew disobeys the captain and takes control of their ship.

THE LINGO!

You'll need to learn how to speak like a pirate, so here are some useful phrases:

Aye-aye!
A pirate's way of saying 'yes', 'OK', or 'I'll get right on it!'

~

Aaargh!
A deep growling sound that makes every pirate seem even scarier.

~

You filthy bilge rat!
The 'bilge' was the lowest part of the ship, so it was dark, dank, and smelly. Calling someone a bilge rat was a terrible insult.

~

Shiver me timbers!
The 'timbers' were the masts, and they might shake if struck by a cannonball. The phrase means 'What a surprise!'

~

Avast ye, me swashbuckler mates!
'Avast ye' means 'Hey, stop that!' It came from a Dutch phrase used to tell sailors to stop pulling the ropes. 'Swashbuckler' is a term used to describe a daring adventurer, including a pirate.

Pirates on Parade

'Calico' Jack Rackham's Jolly Roger was a skull above crossed swords.

Pirates often dressed flamboyantly in fine clothes for special occasions and when they went on land.

CHIC, NOT CHEAP!

They adopted a more relaxed look for everyday work, wearing a uniform that was practical for sailing a ship or fighting.

NO SKIRTS? NO PROBLEM!

While in Nassau, Bahamas, Rackham fell in love with a sailor's wife named Anne Bonny. She and another woman named Mary Read joined Rackham's pirate crew. Women pirates often dressed as men, as men's clothes were far more practical for life aboard a ship than a woman's corsets and long skirts.

'Calico' Jack Rackham

Mary Read dressed as a man long before she became a pirate to make it easier to find a job.

Captain 'Calico' Jack Rackham, a British sailor who turned pirate in 1718, became famous for his fancy outfits – the word 'calico' is used to describe fabrics that are printed with colourful, flowery patterns as well as plain, cream – coloured cottons.

A genetic mutation has given Whipper, a parakeet in New Zealand, fancy feathers to grace any dandy pirate's shoulders!

Simple styles

Sumptuous silks and satins, gold buttons, and black lacy shirts made a pirate look glamorous, but they were not practical for a pirate seaman who had chores to do.

PATCH SWITCH

Many pirates wore a patch over one eye to keep it adapted to the light outside. If a battle broke out and a pirate had to shimmy below, he would cover his 'outdoor' eye with the patch, allowing him to see better in the dark.

KEY FACTS

Pirates often wore gold hoop earrings because it was believed they helped reduce seasickness.

The unique stripe over this insect's eye gives the impression of an eye patch, so the scientists who discovered it in 2013 named it the pirate ant!

Eye-eye, Cap'n!

Tri-cornered hats were often made of leather so they weren't ruined by salty sea spray.

A pirate's clothes might not fit very well if he had stolen them.

A fine silk necktie or bandana was useful to catch sweat as it poured off the pirate's head.

Woollen or canvas shirts and trousers were warm and sturdy. Trousers often ended at the knee (breeches) or above the ankle.

Jackets were often blue, waistcoats were red, and shirts were often checked.

Clothes needed to be short but tight fitting so they didn't get caught on the rigging.

Belts were often worn across the shoulder – they were too heavy for the waist when laden with pistols.

Pirates and sailors usually went barefoot at sea. This made climbing the ropes easier.

Cutlass, Pistol and Cannon

Pirates chose from a large armoury of weapons during a mission to plunder, smash, and grab.

PIRATE WEAPONRY

The type and variety of weapons differed across the world – and through the centuries.

Treasury Street in St. Augustine, Florida, is the narrowest street in the United States. It was purposely built to be 2 metres wide – just enough room for two men to carry a chest of gold to the Royal Spanish Treasury from ships docked on the bay, but not wide enough for a horse and carriage to drive by and snatch the loot!

BAY ST.

AUGUSTINE, Fla. Treasury Street, the Narrowest Street in the U.S.

TWIST IT!

Guns were named after the weight of the iron round shot they fired. 'Four-pounders' were the most common size, while smaller grape shot was used to hit sailors on deck without causing damage to the ship.

BANG, BANG, BOOM!

Captain Kidd's 34-gun warship, *Adventure Galley*, lost its final battle not to the navy, but to shipworms – pesky underwater molluscs that love to munch on wood!

Except for warning shots, pirates avoided firing their guns. Their goal was to rob and steal ships, not destroy them!

Ripley's Explains...

Gunpowder

This is a fine powder explosive that was invented in China and was used in early guns and cannons – and it makes fireworks explode. Pirates used lots of gunpowder, but they had to keep it dry or it wouldn't work.

Granado

Pirates threw granado shells, which were an early type of hand grenade, a small bomb that is thrown at the enemy. The word 'granado' came from *granada*, the Spanish word for pomegranate.

30

WEAPONRY

Flintlock Pistol
A noisy gun that is fired by a spark created from a flint.

Thumbs up:
Guns can kill lots of people quite quickly.

Thumbs down:
If pistols get damp – which they often do at sea – they don't work. They are difficult to aim, too.

Cutlass
A short sword, often curved.

Thumbs up:
Great for fighting in cramped spaces and for slashing ropes.

Thumbs down:
Hard work to kill people, and you can only kill one person at a time.

Scimitar
A heavy, curved sword commonly used by Muslims and Indian pirates.

Thumbs up:
This sword can slice and slash, so it does a lot of damage.

Thumbs down:
It is heavy and more difficult to control than European cutlasses.

Axe
A sharp blade and a hammer on one wooden handle.

Thumbs up:
Great for attacking people, smashing open doors, cutting ropes, and digging out fire bombs from a ship's timbers.

Thumbs down:
Heavy, so it needs a pirate with big muscles to use it.

Fire Bomb
Anything that can be thrown at a wooden ship to set it on fire.

Thumbs up:
Tar bombs are easy to make using a rope dipped in a burning lump of tar.

Thumbs down:
You need to be close enough to the enemy ship to throw it on board.

Cannon
A huge, heavy gun that fires cannonballs.

Thumbs up:
A perfect weapon for knocking down sails and masts, bombing a town from the sea, or putting a hole in the side of a ship.

Thumbs down:
Heavy, expensive, and hard to reload.

Black Bart

WICKED, BUT BRAVE

In just four years, Bartholomew Roberts, or Black Bart, captured more than 400 ships and terrorised the Caribbean and North American coasts.

He and his pirate crew were so powerful they almost put an end to all trade between Europe and the Americas!

Reign of Terror

From 1720 to 1721, Black Bart attacked English, Dutch, French, and Spanish ships around the Caribbean and along the eastern coast to Newfoundland in Canada.

From Sailor to Slave

Born in Wales in 1682, Roberts joined the British Navy. Enslaved when pirates captured his ship, he soon earned his freedom and rose to the rank of captain.

A Cutthroat Killer

In just one action, Bart ambushed 14 French ships, torturing and killing the sailors aboard. He took over a huge brigantine that he named Good Fortune to celebrate his success.

Bart Meets His End

Bart eventually sailed to Africa, where a pirate hunter named Chaloner Ogle fired at his flagship. When the smoke from their battle cleared, Black Bart was found slumped dead over a cannon.

SKULL AND CROSS-BULB

Black Bart's Jolly Roger was a drawing of himself holding an hourglass with a skeleton!

Ripley's Believe It or Not!®

Dutch artist Hans van Bentem makes beautiful crystal chandeliers in the most unique and unusual designs—including this stunning skull and crossbones chandelier, which took about two months to create and is worth more than £10,500!

SCHOOL AND CROSSBONES

Ripley's Believe It or Not!®

Dale Price of American Fork, Utah, has waved his teenage son Rain off to high school every morning wearing over 170 different costumes. He received thunderous applause from the entire school bus for his pirate garb, complete with a peg leg!

BART'S BOTTOM LINE

Although he did terrible things, Black Bart didn't approve of drinking alcohol or swearing!

Black Bart once burned a ship knowing there were 80 slaves aboard and that they would all die.

Black Bart Roberts lives on in popular culture. In the movie *The Princess Bride*, the character Dread Pirate Roberts was named in honour of him!

TWIST IT!

Black Bart's death in 1722 marked the beginning of the end of the Golden Age of Piracy.

33

Pillage *and* Plunder

HOW TO BE A PIRATE: PART 3

Successful pirates have a few tricks up their sleeves when it comes to catching a ship.

Follow these top tips to become a fearsome, plundering pirate and ruthless scallywag.

TWIST IT!

BAD ATTITUDE

Pirates of the 16th century proved they were 'macho', by drinking a mixture of rum and gunpowder!

Anne Bonny was said to have a fierce temper. Before she became a pirate, she once became so angry that she stabbed her maid to death.

Sneaky Thieves

On a summer's night in 1720, 'Calico' Jack Rackham, Anne Bonny, Mary Read, and a few members of their pirate crew rowed across Nassau Harbor in the Bahamas. Silently, they climbed aboard a British sloop called The William and sailed it away!

Anne Bonny

ALL ABOARD!

Once a pirate crew got close to their target, there was no time to lose. The first task was to send the ship's captain over to their pirate ship in a small boat. He would be kept hostage there while the pirates ransacked his vessel.

DEADLY BATTLES

If there was a battle, the air would become thick with gunpowder smoke and the sound of blades clashing as sailors and pirates fought hand-to-hand.

BIG WORD ALERT

PILLAGE & PLUNDER

Both of these words mean stealing while using violence at the same time.

Pirates didn't have a bank or cash machine onboard, so some made a secret stash to hide their cash.

Ripley's Explains...

How to Capture a Ship

Many ships during the Golden Age of Piracy were equipped with rows of cannons, and plundering pirates put them to good use. A common tactic was to sail alongside (broadside) the enemy and blast them with all their cannons – perhaps as many as ten cannons firing at once – while the men fired with muskets and pistols at very close range.

CAVE-INGS ACCOUNT

The cave through Dungeon Rock in Lynn, Massachusetts, was dug in 1852 by Hiram Marble, who believed the ghost of pirate Thomas Veale was directing him to his treasure. Marble dug until his death, but he never found the loot.

STEP TWO

WORK HARD, PLAY HARDER!

Ripley's Believe It or Not!®
Redemption Part I by artist Peter Riss is a children's jungle gym on display at Heilig-Kreuz Church in Munich, Germany – in their former cemetery!

SKELETONS OF FUN!

KEY FACTS

Pirates did not make their prisoners walk the plank. That's a popular myth!

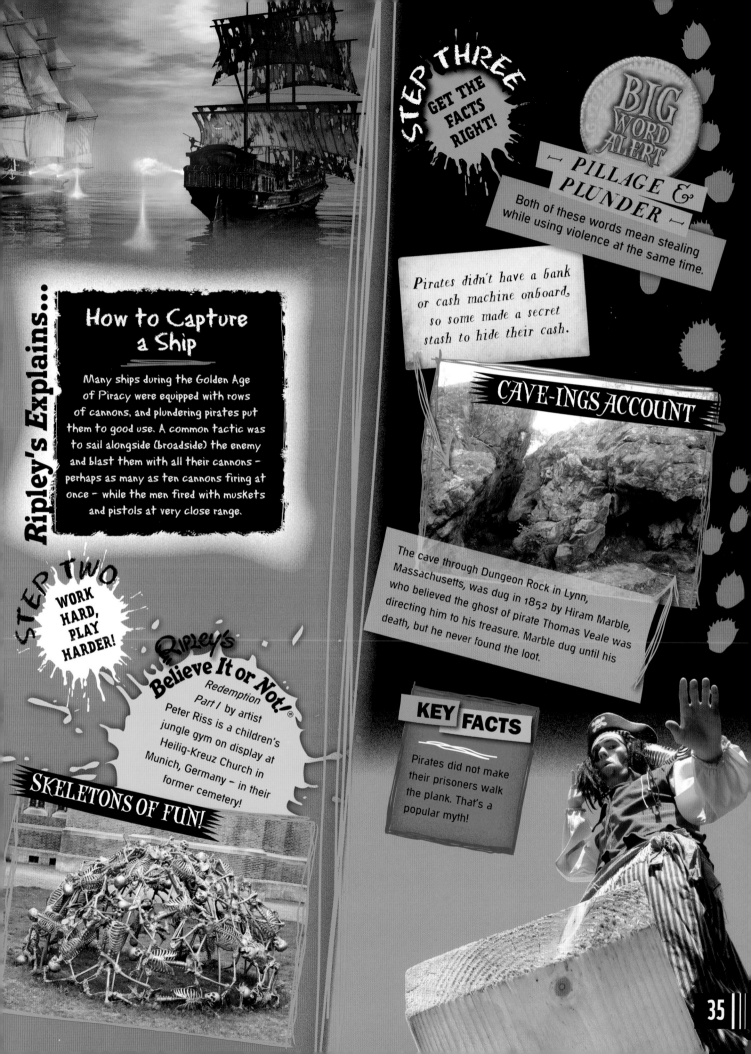

Pirate Treasure

It is difficult to say exactly what a pirate's treasure trove might be worth today.

However, there is no doubt that a life of crime did pay – unless the hangman got them before they had a chance to spend all their gold!

According to legend, when a pirate buried treasure, he would kill someone and bury his or her body on top of it. This way, the murdered person's ghost would protect the booty!

TREASURE MAPS

Historians aren't sure if pirates really buried their treasure on islands, recording the location with an X on a map. In fact, the idea seems to have come from Robert Louis Stevenson's famous novel, *Treasure Island*, published in 1883.

X marks the spot!

Ripley's Explains...

Precious Swag

If you found a casket full of doubloons, ducats, and pieces of eight, would you be happy – or confused?

Ripley explains the perplexing subject of old currencies:

Reale = a small silver Spanish coin
Piece of Eight = a coin worth 8 reales
Dollar/Peso = alternative names for a piece of eight
Escudo = a coin worth 2 pieces of eight
Doubloon = a gold coin worth 4 pieces of eight
Ducats = gold and silver coins used in the Mediterranean region

Today, a piece of eight is worth about £50!

Florida's Annual Lower Keys Underwater Music Festival combines a pirate's love for music and the sea. Hundreds dive 9 metres beneath the waves to hear musicians play on the ocean floor.

LOVELY LOOT!

Pirates didn't just want gold. They needed everyday items, too.

~

Cloth such as silk, canvas, and cotton

Maps and charts

Navigational equipment

Medicine

Weapons

Tobacco for their pipes

Anchor chains

Cattle, chicken, fish

Ropes

Spare sails

Carpentry tools

Sugar

Wine and rum

This ancient chest was once used to store pirate booty – and Robert Ripley himself stored some of his most valuable treasures in it!

TWIST IT!

In 2015, while studying a shipwreck off the coast of Madagascar that is thought to be the pirate ship *Adventure Galley*, archaeologists discovered a 50-kilogram slab of silver that may have belonged to Captain Kidd!

TREASURE TALES

While every pirate dreamed of treasure chests filled with gold and jewels, sugar and tobacco shipped from the Americas to Europe were also popular booty – they could be sold for a king's ransom.

BIG WORD ALERT

— CURRENCY —
The coins and notes used as money in a country.

KEY FACTS

Pieces of eight were used as currency in the United States until 1857.

Pirate Hunters

Governments hired pirate hunters to give the sea robbers a taste of their own medicine.

One of them, British Navy Lieutenant Robert Maynard, is most famous for capturing the notorious Captain Blackbeard at Ocracoke Island in North Carolina.

Blackbeard's Death

One of Maynard's ships was badly damaged after Blackbeard bombarded it with cannon fire. The pirates clambered on board, not realizing Maynard's crew were hiding below with their pistols ready, and were slaughtered.

Maynard shot Blackbeard, who still had the strength to raise his cutlass – before a sailor slashed his throat. After the battle, Blackbeard's head was hung from the bow of Maynard's sloop as a gruesome warning to other pirates.

SHORT ROPE, LONG DANCE

Using a short rope ensured that hanging victims would die by strangulation, slowly turning purple as they 'danced the hempen jig'.

PARDON THE PIRATES

Privateer Woodes Rogers (1679–1732) was made governor of the Bahamas and told to destroy the pirate fleets around the islands. He first offered them amnesty, which meant the king would pardon their misdeeds. Eager to avoid a date with the gallows, almost 300 pirates turned in their swords!

THE GENTLEMAN PIRATE

Stede Bonnet was a wealthy Barbados landowner who met Blackbeard, and was so impressed with his tales of adventure that he decided to become a buccaneer himself. After a long and bloody fight with a pirate hunter, Bonnet surrendered, but managed to escape!

TWIST IT!

In 1696, Captain Kidd was hired to be a pirate hunter, but became a pirate himself. During his execution the rope broke, so he had to be hanged twice!

Pirates rarely betrayed one another, but Cyril Hood offered to tell pirate hunters where to find buccaneer Abraham Cooke in exchange for just a single bottle of rum!

HUNTER TURNED HUNTED

Stede Bonnet was pardoned in 1718 and became a privateer. However, he decided that he preferred being a pirate and returned to his life of crime!

They Got Away...

...AND LIVED TO TELL THE TALE!

A few lucky pirates managed to escape capture and retired to enjoy a quiet life spending their vast amounts of treasure.

Some were even honoured by their governments and given important jobs!

MARY KILL-THE-CREW

Lady Mary Killigrew (1530–1580) had everyone aboard a Spanish ship murdered while she plundered two barrels full of pieces of eight. Her pirate crew were captured and sentenced to hang, but Queen Elizabeth I took pity on her, and she served a short jail sentence instead.

Ripley's Explains...

SECRETS OF SUCCESS

Many pirates got away with a life of crime because they shared their booty with powerful people who turned a blind eye to the evil events off the coast. Even pirate hunters could be bribed this way.

Avery's Jolly Roger is recorded as having the same skull and crossbones design on both a red or black background.

AN UNSURE END

Known as the 'King of Pirates,' Captain Henry Avery attacked the Ganj-i-Sawai, a huge ship laden with treasure, in 1695. No one knows what happened to Avery afterward – some people said he retired to a life of great luxury on a tropical island, while others claimed he lost all his money and died in poverty in England.

Ripley's Believe It or Not!

This model of Captain Jack Sparrow, created by Thailand-based company Art From Steel, measures over 2 metres high, weighs several hundred kilograms, and is made completely of recycled car parts!

TWIST IT!

Barbarossa – also known as Redbeard – was one of the most feared corsairs in the 16th century. The ruthless pirate was so unafraid of ever being punished, he wrote and published his memoirs when he retired, confessing to everything!

When captured after plundering a Spanish treasure ship, pirate Bartolomeu Portugues jumped overboard and escaped, using pottery jars he'd stolen from the hold as buoys to stay afloat until he reached shore.

Privateer Francis Drake ransacked Spanish colonies and plundered merchant ships. When he was knighted for his efforts by Queen Elizabeth I, the Spanish king was furious!

ESCAPE

When Jack, the Capuchin monkey who stars in the *Pirates of the Caribbean* films, arrived in Queensland to begin filming the sequel, *Pirates of the Caribbean: Dead Men Tell No Tales*, both he and his primate understudy were placed in 30-day pest quarantine in accordance with the law Down Under!

The Black Spot

...AND OTHER GRUESOME ENDS

A captured pirate usually faced a brief trial, followed by hanging.

However, a pirate who betrayed his own crew, or disobeyed the Pirate Code, could face a far worse fate!

THE BLACK SPOT

In the novel *Treasure Island*, pirates considered traitors to their ship were given a 'black spot' on a piece of paper... and a death sentence.

Pirates in Jamaica were put in a narrow metal cage called a gibbet and hung in the sun. They would die a slow and painful death from the burning heat.

Brutal Buccaneers

Buccaneers and other pirates had a nasty array of punishments they used against traitors, unpopular captains, and any poor prisoners they captured.

Keel hauling

The unfortunate victim was tied to a rope and dragged the length of the boat along the keel, from front to back. Apart from the high chance of drowning, his body would be ripped to shreds by the many rough shellfish attached to the keel.

Marooning

Prisoners and pirates were sometimes simply left on a deserted island, perhaps with a bottle of rum for company.

Cat-o'-nine-tails

This was a whip with nine leather strips that were knotted with pieces of metal at the end. A severe whipping with one of these instruments of torture could be enough to kill a person.

This customised pirate bedroom in Minnesota features a rope bridge, a steering wheel, and a slide from the ship-shaped bed. There is even a small jail cell for mutiny-minded brothers and sisters!

THE LINGO!

Blow the Man Down
This was a popular sea shanty, or song. It means, 'knock a man to the ground'.

~

Feed the Fish
If a pirate was thrown overboard, he would become food for the fish.

~

Sharkbait
If a pirate was told he was 'sharkbait', he knew he was about to be thrown overboard.

~

Davy Jones's Locker
This is the pirate's term for the bottom of the sea - so a pirate who was going to Davy Jones's Locker was about to die. No one knows who Davy Jones really was!

TWIST IT!

GRUESOME FATES

One evil pirate made a ship's captain cut off his own ears and eat them.

When a captured sailor once complained about his treatment aboard a pirate ship, the pirate captain took a needle and thread and sewed up his mouth!

NO FOND FAREWELLS

Sea robbers often attacked coastal towns and villages, and put the lives of honest sailors in danger. It's no wonder that when a pirate was caught, he was often executed while being jeered and spat at by onlookers.

Pirates *in* Today's World

MODERN PIRATES, MYTHS AND LEGENDS

Many myths and legends have arisen around piracy in the past. However, some cutthroat criminals still operate today, both at sea and at home.

DANGER AT SEA

Modern Somali pirates attack cargo ships or tankers carrying valuable loads of oil. Often they simply steal the crew's belongings and cargo, but sometimes they hold the ship for ransom – or worse.

SPEARS AS AMMO

Tra-la-la!

Ripley's Believe It or Not!

Songs by pop star Britney Spears are blasted by British naval officers in an attempt to scare off pirates along the east coast of Africa!

DIGITAL PIRACY

Stealing digital media is illegal – always check that you have permission to swap downloaded music with friends, rip CDs, or share software, or you might find yourself being accused of being an Internet pirate!

PIRATIN' APP

People using pirated versions of the Today Calendar Pro app virtually walk the plank! A 'Walk the Plank' event appears onscreen with the message, 'That's what ye get fer piratin' matey!'

TWIST IT!

The modern-day pirate hunters in Combined Task Force 151 use high-tech equipment and surveillance to combat today's tech-savvy buccaneers.

The modern-day pirate hunters in Combined Task Force 151 use high-tech equipment and surveillance to combat today's tech-savvy buccaneers.

PIRATE TECH 101

Unlike pirates of old, modern pirates usually operate from shore, and use speedboats to reach their targets.

Cruise ships are attractive targets for today's pirates. They defend themselves by blasting sonic cannons — the concentrated sound can permanently affect the attacker's hearing from over 275 metres away.

KEY FACT

As many as 400 ships are attacked by pirates every year, mainly around Indonesia, Panama, Somalia, and Bangladesh.

POP CULTURE PIRATES

Sao Feng, a character in *Pirates of the Caribbean: At the World's End*, is based on the 18th-century Chinese pirate Cheung Po Tsai.

The fictional character Captain Jack Sparrow is believed to be based in part on another fictional pirate — Long John Silver, a trickster in *Treasure Island*.

ACKNOWLEDGEMENTS

Cover Illustrations by John Graziano; **2** (c) Illustration by John Graziano, (t) © XiaImages–iStock.com; **2–3** (bgd) © XiaImages–iStock.com, © daksun–Shutterstock.com, © photocell–Shutterstock.com, (t) © sharpner–Shutterstock.com; **3** (t) © mj007–Shutterstock.com, (b) Illustration by John Graziano; **4** (b) Illustration by John Graziano; **4–5** (bgd) © Fedor Selivanov–Shutterstock.com; **5** (c) Illustration by John Graziano; **6** © 1971yes–iStock.com; **7** (t/r) © ZUMA Press, Inc./Alamy, (t/l) © Dennis MacDonald/Alamy, (b) Lorie (O'Donnell) Finger; **8** (t) *William Marsh being dragged to his execution in 1240* (vellum), Paris, Matthew (c.1200-59)/Private Collection/Peter Newark Pictures/Bridgeman Images, (b/r) Illustration by John Graziano; **9** (t/l) © Jan Faukner–Shutterstock.com, (t/r) Illustration by John Graziano, (b) © WENN; **10** (b/l) Illustration by John Graziano, (b/r) © Seregam–Shutterstock.com; **10–11** (bgd) © Jozef Sowa–Shutterstock.com, © Fedor Selivanov–Shutterstock.com, © Picsfive–Shutterstock.com; **11** (t/r) Photo by Mohammed Talatene/Anadolu Agency/Getty Images, (b/r) © peachroomtom–iStock.com; **12** (t) © User: Jorge in Brazil/Wikimedia Commons/CC-BY-SA-3.0; **12–13** (b) Illustrations by John Graziano; **13** (t/l) Courtesy of a private collector, (t/r) © PlanForYou–Shutterstock.com, (r) © Seregam–Shutterstock.com; **14** Illustration by John Graziano; **14–15** (bgd) © www.BillionPhotos.com–Shutterstock.com; **15** (t/r) Illustrations by John Graziano, (c/r) Richard Young/Rex/REX USA, (b/l) Zubova Zhanna; **16** (c) P.PLAILLY/E.DAYNES/SCIENCE SOURCE; **16–17** (b) © JDawnInk–Getty Images; **17** (b) © kontur-vid–Shutterstock.com; **18** © SuriyaPhoto–Shutterstock.com; **19** (t) Photo by David L Ryan/The Boston Globe via Getty Images, (c) Brigantine *Mary Celeste*, commanded by Benjamin Briggs, found without crew, drifting towards Strait of Gibraltar in 1872, print, 19th century/De Agostini Picture Library/Bridgeman Images, (b) Illustration by John Graziano; **20** (c) © Shutterwolf–iStock.com, (b) © Peter Lange/Laird McGillicuddy; **20–21** (bgd) © Jose Angel Astor Rocha–Shutterstock.com; **21** (t) © Seregam–Shutterstock.com, (b) © Signed model release filed with Shutterstock, Inc–Shutterstock.com, (r) Courtesy of Juan Cabana; **22** (t) © Andrew Price/Rex/REX USA, (b) Illustration by John Graziano; **23** (t) © Elite Home Theater Seating/Rex/REX USA, (b/l) Illustration by John Graziano, (b/r) © Eddie Mulholland/Rex/REX USA; **24** (t) *Madame Ching, legendary Chinese Pirate Queen* (engraving), American School, (18th century)/Private Collection/Peter Newark Historical Pictures/Bridgeman Images, (b) Illustration by John Graziano; **24–25** (bgd) © kanate–Shutterstock.com, © Picsfive–Shutterstock.com; **25** (c) Illustration by John Graziano; **26** Illustration by John Graziano; **27** (t, t/l, c, c/l, b/l) 826 Valencia, 826valencia.org/store, (t/r) © Chris Mattison/FLPA/Science Source, (c/r) Illustration by John Graziano, (r) © Seregam–Shutterstock.com; **28** (t) Illustration by John Graziano, (c) *Mary Read, female pirate* (coloured engraving), American School, (19th century)/Private Collection /Peter Newark Historical Picture/Bridgeman Images, (b) Illustrations by John Graziano; **29** (t) © REX USA, (c/l) © Scott Rothstein–Shutterstock.com, (c/r) © SchubPhoto–Shutterstock.com, (b) Dr. Roland Schultz, (r) © Landysh–Shutterstock.com; **30** (b/c) © Fablok–Shutterstock.com, (b/r) Illustration by John Graziano; **30–31** (bgd) © Peshkova–Shutterstock .com; **31** (bgd) © Xial Images, © daksun–Shutterstock.com, (t/l) © mj007–Shutterstock.com, (t/r) © andrewburgess–iStock.com, (c/l) © XiaImages–iStock.com, (c/r) Illustration by John Graziano, (b/l) © sharpner–Shutterstock.com, (b/r) Illustration by John Graziano; **32** (t, b) Illustrations by John Graziano; **32–33** (bgd) © Picsfive–Shutterstock.com; **33** (t) PHOTOGRAPHY BY GAVIN BERNARD/ BARCROFT MEDIA LTD, (c) © Price Family/Rex/REX USA, (b) Illustration by John Graziano; **34** (c) Illustration by John Graziano, (b) © Harry H Marsh–Shutterstock.com; **35** (t) © Melkor3D–Shutterstock.com, (c) By Ehkastning (Own work) [CC BY-SA 3.0 (http://creativecommons.org/licenses/by-sa/3.0)], via Wikimedia Commons, (b/l) © Peter Riss, (b/r) © joshblake–iStock.com; **36** (c/l) © topshotUK–iStock.com, (c/r) Mary Evans Picture Library, (b) © JOE CICAK–iStock.com; **36–37** (bgd) © val lawless–Shutterstock.com; **37** (t/l) BILL KEOUGH/AFP/Getty Images, (t/r) © Seregam–Shutterstock.com, (b/r) © thanakritphoto–Shutterstock.com; **38** (l) *The Capture of the Pirate Blackbeard, 1718*, Ferris, Jean Leon Gerome (1863-1930)/Private Collection/Bridgeman Images, (b/r) © Maksim Shmeljov–Shutterstock.com; **38–39** (bgd) © theromb–Shutterstock.com; **39** (t/l) Public domain, via Wikimedia Commons, (t/r) © Gary Roberts/REX USA; **40** Illustrations by John Graziano; **40–41** (bgd) © Phiseksit–Shutterstock.com, © Eky Studio–Shutterstock.com; **41** (l) Sculpture by Art of Steel/Photo courtesy of Steve Campbell, (t/r) *Queen Elizabeth I knighting Francis Drake*, Matania, Fortunino (1881-1963)/Private Collection/© Look and Learn/Bridgeman Images, (c/r) Illustration by John Graziano, (b/r) Photo by Steve Granitz/WireImage/Getty; **42** (l) © Apriori1–iStock.com, (b) © timhughes–iStock.com; **43** (t/l) © Seregam–Shutterstock.com, (t/r) © Rex/REX USA, (b) *Dead men tell no tales*, 1899 (oil on canvas en grisaille), Pyle, Howard (1853-1911)/© American Illustrators Gallery, NYC/www.asapworldwide.com/Bridgeman Images; **44** (t) Photo by Jonas Gratzer/LightRocket via Getty Images, (c) © Featureflash–Shutterstock.com, (b) © pushlama–iStock.com; **45** (t/l) Today Calendar for Android/Developer: Jack Underwood/Visual Design: Liam Spradlin, (t/r) © jiawangkun–Shutterstock.com, (b/l) AFP/Getty Images, (b/r) Mary Evans Picture Library

Key: t = top, b = bottom, c = center, l = left, r = right, sp = single page, bgd = background

All other photos are from Ripley Entertainment Inc.

Every attempt has been made to acknowledge correctly and contact copyright holders, and we apologize in advance for any unintentional errors or omissions, which will be corrected in future editions.

Ripley's MIGHTY MACHINES
Believe *It* or Not!®

PUBLISHING
a Jim Pattison Company

TWISTS

Written by Ian Graham

Consultant Chris Oxlade

PUBLISHING

Publisher Anne Marshall

Managing Editor Rebecca Miles
Picture Researcher James Proud
Editors Lisa Regan, Rosie Alexander
Assistant Editor Amy Harrison
Proofreader Judy Barratt
Indexer Hilary Bird

Art Director Sam South
Design Rocket Design (East Anglia) Ltd
Reprographics Stephan Davis

www.ripleys.com/books

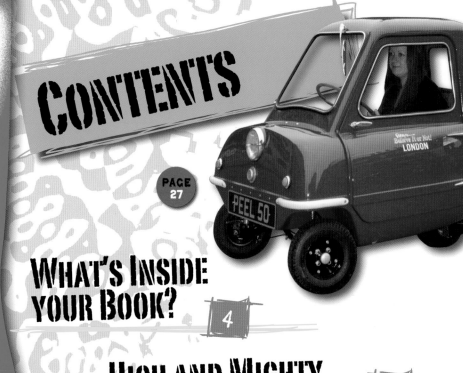

CONTENTS

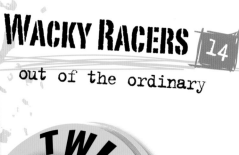

TWISTS

MEAN MACHINES

on the move

Feeling the need for speed? Wish your dad's car was bigger than anyone else's? Or perhaps robots are more your thing? Humans have invented some mighty machines that let us go faster than ever before, reach other planets, soar through the skies, or simply attract attention from unsuspecting passers-by.

Take a trip around your favourite mechanical and moving things with this fun but factual book. Learn about the science of flight, put some wind in your sails, and boost your va-va-voom with special Ripley's fascinating facts and amazing 'Believe It or Not!' stories from around the world. What are you waiting for? Off you go!

WHAT'S INSIDE YOUR BOOK?

Monster Trucks first became popular in the 1970s. The Monster Truck Racing Association, formed in 1988, set down standard rules about safety and construction. These days, Monster Truck shows make millions of dollars.

Learn fab fast facts to go with the cool pictures.

In 1974 a Monster Truck called Bigfoot (see page 6) was the first Monster Truck to drive over cars and crush them.

Big as they are, Monster Trucks can perform cool stunts such as wheelstands, jumps and doughnuts.

TWISTS

Don't forget to look out for the 'twist it!' column on some pages. Twist the book to find out more fast facts about mighty machines.

A small boat is fun to sail, but a big racing yacht is one of the most exciting ways to travel. Racing yachts can slice through the waves at 55 km/h. Super yachts more than 30 m long can go even faster. A few of the 50,000 ships that carry goods and materials around the world have been built with sails too. Using wind power instead of engines saves fuel.

our boat doesn't have engine, you could roll your sleeves and row , or you could hoist a sail and let the wind do the work.

ind power

>> PLAIN SAILING >>

French vet Raphaela Le Gouvello crossed the Indian Ocean on a sailboard just 8 m long and 1.2 m wide. The 6,300-km journey took 60 days. Raphaela spent eight hours a day at the sail. She has also crossed the Atlantic and Pacific Oceans and the Mediterranean Sea by sailboard.

Each mast is 50 m tall.

The sails are made from a strong synthetic fabric and cover an area of 2,500 sq m.

The ship is 187 m long, 20 m wide and weighs nearly 15,000 tonnes.

can carry 308 passengers and has seven decks.

WATER WAYS

Japanese sailor Kenichi Horie spent three months sailing alone across the Pacific Ocean on a yacht made from beer barrels.

British woman Hilary Lister sailed across the English Channel between England and France in August 2005, even though she could not move her arms or legs. She steered her yacht by sucking and blowing through tubes that operated the rudder and sails.

During a round-the-world voyage in 1997, British yachtsman Tony Bullimore survived for five days underneath his capsized yacht in the icy Southern Ocean until help arrived. When a Russian yacht lost its rudder in the Southern Ocean in 2005, the crew replaced it with a cabin door.

twist it!

Even enormous cargo ships can be wind powered. SkySails are huge computer-controlled kites that give extra power and help save fuel.

CLOSE TO THE WIND

The Wind Surf is a cruise liner that can be powered by either computer-controlled sails or engines. Its sails unfurl automatically from the 50-m-tall masts within two minutes of pushing a button on the ship's bridge. Using only sails, its top speed is about 24 km/h, about the same as its maximum speed on engine power.

Ripley's Believe It or Not!

BRICK BOAT

It took Peter Lange from New Zealand three months to build his 6-m-long brick boat using 676 bricks. Amazingly, it didn't sink!

BIG WORD ALERT!

CAPSIZED

Upturned. A capsized boat is one that has rolled upside-down.

Ripley explains...

Low pressure

Thrust

Sail

BOAT

Wind direction

High pressure

A yacht sail works like an aircraft wing. When a sail fills with air, it forms the same curved shape as a wing. This changes the flow of air to create low pressure. The low pressure pulls the boat along. It can move a yacht in a different direction from the wind by setting the sails at the correct angle.

FASCINATING FACT!

Do the twist

This book is packed with amazing mechanical devices. It will teach you cool things about all kinds of machines, but like all Twists books, it shines a spotlight on things that are unbelievable but true. Turn the pages and find out more...

Look for the Ripley R to find out even more than you knew before!

Twists are all about Believe It or Not: amazing facts, feats and things that will make you go 'Wow!'.

Found a new word? Big word alerts will explain it for you.

HIGH AND MIGHTY

monster trucks

They're massive and mean. They leap in the air and flatten cars. No, they're not flying elephants, they're Monster Trucks. These mechanical giants are the stars of stunt-driving shows that never fail to wow the crowds. A roaring 2,000-horsepower engine gives them a top speed of 160 km/h.

In the hands of an expert driver, they can spin on the spot, rear up on their back wheels and jump nearly 8 m off the ground. But don't get in their way. They weigh more than 4 tonnes and they can crush a car so that it's as flat as a pancake.

MEET BIGFOOT 5

Bigfoot 5's giant tyres were originally made for the US Army for use on an Arctic snow train. The tyres ended up in a junkyard where builder Bob Chandler found them and transformed them into Bigfoot 5's weapons of destruction. At 3 m high, the tyres are the largest on any truck. Monster Trucks get to crush about 3,000 junkyard cars in shows every year.

it's home!

Sheikh Hamad Bin Hamdan Al Nahyan, from the United Arab Emirates, is a collector of awesome automobiles, including this towering power wagon, the biggest in the world, complete with air-conditioned bedrooms, lounge, bathroom, kitchen, and patio area in the back.

A harness holds the driver safely in the driving seat.

The body is from a 1996 pick-up truck.

It is powered by a monster 7.5-litre engine.

Each of the wheels weighs more than a tonne.

CRAZY

Monster Trucks can jump nearly 8 m high and a distance of 40 m – about the same as 14 cars parked side by side.

If you want to buy your own Monster Truck, it will cost you about £100,000.

It costs about £165,000 a year to run a Monster Truck team.

Don't get a puncture – a new tyre will cost you £1,700.

Monster Trucks are thirsty. They burn 9.5 litres of fuel in each run of about 76 m – that's 1,000 times faster than a car would burn the same amount of fuel.

TWIST it!

FAST TRACKERS

magnificent motorcycles

Millions of bikers can't be wrong. Two wheels and an engine mean lots of fun. Motorbikes have been around for more than 120 years and they're still as popular as ever. There are motorbikes for riding to work, motorbikes for dirt tracks, motorbikes for looking cool and motorbikes for racing. They're all different.

The strangest are the motorbikes that are specially made for setting speed records. They look like two-wheeled rockets. On 26 September 2008, Rocky Robinson rode one of these crazy machines, called Ack Attack, at a speed of 580.833 km/h. That's nearly twice as fast as a Formula 1 racing car.

power machine!

The Dodge Tomahawk has a huge 8.3-litre engine from a Dodge Viper supercar – that's four or five times bigger than most car engines. The designers think it has a top speed of about 480 km/h, but no one has ever been brave enough to try riding it that fast. Only ten Tomahawks have been built and, if you want one, it will cost about £375,000. Even then you won't be able to ride it on public roads.

A BARGAIN, ONLY £375,000!

8.3 litre engine is also used in supercars.

CUTTING EDGE

Why stop at one engine? This motorbike is powered by no less than 24 chainsaw engines. It's nearly 4 m long and can reach a top speed of 255 km/h.

Dead cool

Gordon Fitch has created a fitting last ride for keen bikers in Britain. They can have their coffins drawn by a Harley Davidson motorbike.

BIKER BEDLAM

In 2004, Indian magician O.P. Sharma rode a motorcycle down a busy street in the city of Patna with a black bag over his head. Don't try this at home!

German tightrope artist Johann Traber rode a motorcycle on a high-wire 160 m above the Rhine River in 2003. His father, also called Johann, sat on a trapeze hanging below the bike during the 579-m crossing.

Gregory Frazier of Fort Smith, Montana, has ridden around the world on a motorcycle five times. He's covered over 1.6 million km.

In 2004, U.S. motorcycle stuntman Robbie Knievel (son of the famous daredevil Evel Knievel) made a spectacular 55-m jump over two helicopters and five aeroplanes parked on the deck of the Intrepid Museum, an aircraft-carrier-turned-museum in Manhattan, New York.

twist it!

Engine air intake.

Double wheels front and back spread the massive weight.

Special rim brakes.

SOMETHING'S MISSING

Ben Gulak in Toronto, Canada, sits atop his fast-track invention – Uno, the world's first one-wheeled motorbike. To give the ride more stability, Ben put the wheels side-by-side just 2 cm apart and directly under the rider, who accelerates by leaning forward. When the rider leans into a turn, the inside wheel lifts and the outside wheel lowers, so both stay firmly on the ground. What's even more unusual about the bike is that it's all-electric, emitting no fumes.

PEDAL POWER
on your bike!

Bicycles aren't very big or fast, but they are mighty machines. A bike's diamond-shaped frame is so strong that it can carry more than ten times its own weight. It has no engine, but can keep going for thousands of kilometres – as long as you keep pushing the pedals.

It's sometimes hard enough to ride a bike with two wheels without falling over, but could you balance on just one wheel? Some people actually enjoy riding a one-wheeled machine called a unicycle. You need a really good sense of balance.

FASCINATING FACT! FASCINATING FACT! FASCINATING FACT!

Chris Hoy from Scotland is surely the most successful sprint cyclist of all time. At the age of 37, he has accumulated the following titles (among others):

🔔 Six Olympic Gold Medals
🔔 Olympic Silver
🔔 Olympic Team Sprint Record
🔔 World Record 500 m
🔔 European Champion
🔔 11 times World Champion
🔔 27 times World Cup Gold

Built for speed

The best track bikes are built for speed. Their weight is cut down as much as possible, because heavier bikes are harder to get moving. Anything that might stick out, catch the air and slow the bike down is smoothed out. The bike's body is made in one piece.

The bars are low to make the rider bend forwards into the right position for good aerodynamics.

The seat is set high to get maximum power from the legs.

Four or five broad spokes stir up less air than thin wire spokes.

Skinny, low-drag tyres.

There are no brakes – they are not needed!

The back wheel is solid, because it slips through the air easily.

PEDAL MEDALS

In 2005, Sam Wakeling rode his unicycle the length of Britain, a distance of 1,406 km.

In May 2007, Quinn Baumberger set out on a nine-month bike journey the length of the Americas, from Alaska to Argentina. He covered 30,600 km and had 50 flat tyres on the way.

The first two-wheeler was built by Baron Karl von Drais in Germany in 1817. It was called a 'draisine' after the Baron. There were no pedals. The rider sat astride it and pushed it along with his feet.

In the 1860s, bikes were called boneshakers because their wooden or metal wheels rattled and bumped over rough cobbled streets.

Twelve cyclists rode 900 km across New Zealand's South Island in 15 days on unicycles.

Frenchman Hughes Richard climbed the 747 steps of the Eiffel Tower on a bicycle in just 19 minutes in April 2002.

Christian Adam of Germany can ride a bicycle backwards while playing a violin.

twist it!

It's hard enough to ride a bike in the usual way, but Dutchman Pieter de Hart can ride a bike while sitting on the handlebars and also facing backwards! In 2002, he cycled 27 km like this.

THINK SMALL!

Bobby Hunt rides this tiny bike in his stage act. It measures only 7.6 cm from the middle of the front wheel to the middle of the back wheel, and it's only 20 cm tall.

Wheely fast!

In 2008, Mark Beaumont became the fastest man to ride around the world, taking just 195 days to pedal 29,446 km and smashing the previous attempt by 81 days.

11

MAGNIFICENT MOTORS

cool cars

It's hard to imagine our world without cars. There are about 700 million of them worldwide – so it's no wonder the roads get jammed sometimes. A few of these millions of cars are special. They are designed to be very fast, or very small, or just very silly.

Cars have been made in all sorts of surprising shapes and sizes. If you fancy driving a car in the shape of an armchair or a hamburger, the chances are that someone, somewhere, has made a car to make your wish come true.

Awesome

The **Bugatti Veyron** is one of the fastest cars in the world. It has a top speed of more than 400 km/h. That's faster than a racing car or an express train.

Ripley explains...

Piston   Cylinder

Suck
intake
stroke

Squeeze
compression
stroke

Bang
power
stroke

Blow
exhaust
stroke

A car engine works by burning fuel. It happens in four steps, called strokes. First, fuel and air are sucked into a cylinder (suck). Then, the mixture is squashed by a piston (squeeze). The fuel burns and the hot gases push the piston down inside the cylinder (bang). Finally, the hot gases are pushed out (blow). Then it all happens again – thousands of times every second. This 'four-stroke cycle' is sometimes called 'suck, squeeze, bang, blow'.

DIVER DRIVER

Frank Rinderknecht loves to go for a drive... in the sea! His submersible car, called 'sQuba', can drive on land or underwater. The car flies through the water at a depth of 10 m, whilst the driver and passenger breathe compressed air. Instead of a four-stroke combustion engine, the car is powered by electric motors.

twist it!

This couch is no slouch! It can reach a speed of 140 km/h, being powered by a 1.3-litre engine. It is steered with a pizza pan!

A single day's consumption of electricity in the USA is enough to power a car more than 36,000 times around the world.

Kenneth L. Moorhouse designed and built a working car only 1.3 m long and 86 cm wide, with a top speed of more than 200 km/h.

Edd China invented the 'office car', an office desk and chair that can be driven like a car. In 2003, it set out from London, England, on a 1,500-km charity road-trip to the south of France.

THE CAR'S THE STAR

The first motor race, from Paris to Rouen in 1894, was won by Count de Dion with an average speed of about 19 km/h. An athlete can run faster than this!

transformers!

Brazilian Olisio da Silva and his two sons, Marco and Marcus, have created a real-life transformer. Their Kia Besta van takes just six minutes to morph into a 3.65-m-high robot, accompanied by thumping music, smoke and flashing lights. It took them nine months and £84,000 to create the 'SuperRoboCar'.

The Bugatti Veyron is one of the world's most expensive cars. Each one costs about a million pounds.

The Veyron's engine is in the middle of the car, behind the driver.

The amazing engine is over six times more powerful than a family car engine.

Two pipes on the roof, called snorkels, lead air down into the engine.

When the car reaches a speed of 220 km/h, a wing-like spoiler unfolds from the back.

13

WACKY RACERS

out of the ordinary

Motor racing is amazingly popular. In the USA, seven million fans watch each NASCAR race. Every Formula 1 race has 55 million people glued to their television screens all over the world.

But 'ordinary' motor racing just isn't enough for some people. They can't look at a lawnmower or a snowmobile without wondering how fast it can go. It isn't long before they're racing each other. You name it, and someone has raced it. Almost anything can have an engine and wheels bolted on for a race. Beds, barrels and even toilets have been turned into wacky racing machines.

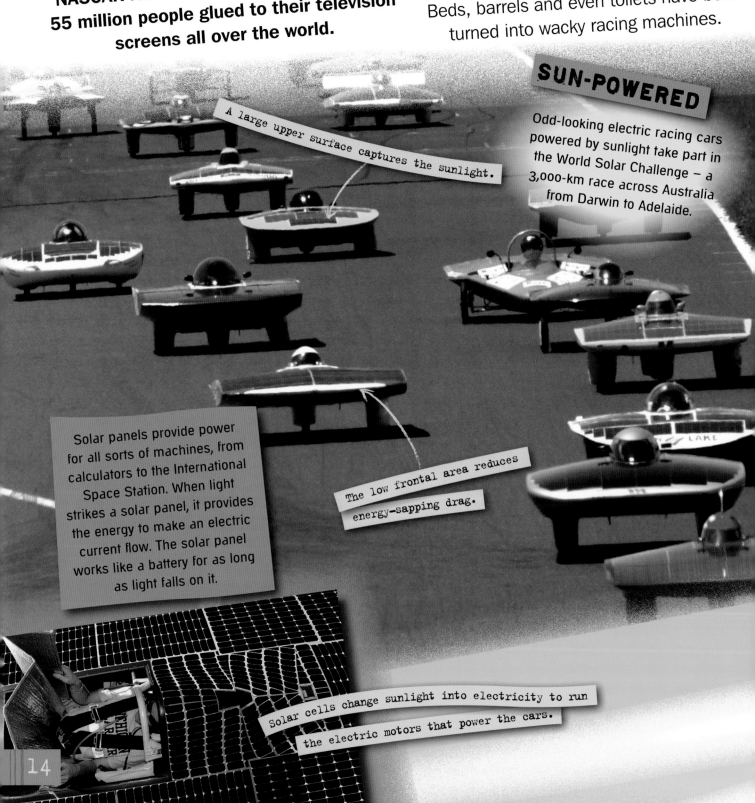

A large upper surface captures the sunlight.

SUN-POWERED

Odd-looking electric racing cars powered by sunlight take part in the World Solar Challenge – a 3,000-km race across Australia from Darwin to Adelaide.

Solar panels provide power for all sorts of machines, from calculators to the International Space Station. When light strikes a solar panel, it provides the energy to make an electric current flow. The solar panel works like a battery for as long as light falls on it.

The low frontal area reduces energy-sapping drag.

Solar cells change sunlight into electricity to run the electric motors that power the cars.

RACING AROUND

The National Lawnmower Racing Championships in Mendota, Illinois, started as an April Fool's joke in 1992, but proved so popular that it became an annual event.

The annual Furniture Race in Whitefish, Montana, involves competitors attaching skis to various items of furniture and racing them down the nearby Big Mountain.

Every year, bed-racing enthusiasts flock to Arizona for the annual Oatman Bed Race. The teams push their beds down the main street, make the beds and then race back to the finish line to the sound of the Chamber Pot Band.

Here's a tale. Emma Crawford was buried on top of Red Mountain, Colorado, in 1891, but her coffin slid down the Canyon in 1929 after heavy rains. Now, as a bizarre form of action replay, every year in nearby Manitou Springs, teams build and race coffins with a living female occupant.

twist it!

These daredevil racers reach 20 km/h on their motorised beer barrels in Windsor, England.

>> chair-raising! >>

Sixty-four participants took part in the Office Chair World Championships, which took place in Olten, Switzerland. Racers sped downhill over 200 m, hurtling over ramps and jumps.

BIG WORD ALERT!

FORMULA 1
A motor-racing championship in single-seat racing cars. Races take place all over the world.

NASCAR
A type of motor racing in the USA.

Joel King's jet-powered street luge board can reach 180 km/h. The board has no brakes – he stops by putting his feet down. Ouch!

PRIVATE TRANSPORTERS

just for one

The robot has eyes made of Ping-Pong™ balls.

It can walk at 2 km/h for up to six hours.

Wu Yulu spent a year building the robot, one of 25 robots he has made.

The robot can talk as well as walk.

If you don't have a bike, there are lots of other personal transporters that you could use instead. You could hop on a hovercraft that is able to fly, or a tiny plane just big enough for one.

In the coldest parts of the world, with thick snow on the ground, a snowmobile is the best way to get around. There are 3 million snowmobiles worldwide, and some of them can scoot across the snow at more than 100 km/h.

Wouldn't it be great to get into a car that in a traffic jam can take off and zoom away in the sky? People have been building flying cars since the 1930s, but you can't buy one – yet.

Sit back and let a robot do the work! This rickshaw is pulled by a robot built by Wu Yulu, a farmer from Mawa Village, near Beijing, in China. Inventor Wu started to build robots in 1986, made from wire, metal, screws and nails found on rubbish sites. Wu was inspired simply by watching people going past his farm, and by thinking about the mechanics of walking.

16

IT'S ELECTRIFYING

This electric engine could change aviation forever. With a battery pack that lets a small, one-person plane fly for about an hour at speeds of up to 210 km/h, it could be a giant step towards eco-friendly flying.

Larry Neal has come up with a solution to being stuck in traffic. Riding his Super Sky Cycle, you can simply unfold the rotors and take off, leaving the traffic behind you. This personal transporter can take off on a 30-m strip of road, fly at motorway speeds, land, and then be driven home as a motorcycle, before being parked in a garage.

Traffic buster

Is it a plane or is it a boat? Neither. It's the invention of Rudy Heeman, from Nelson Haven, New Zealand, who has built a hovercraft that, because of its peculiar aerodynamics, is able to fly.

uplifting!

twist it!

In 1992, US brothers Andre, Carl and Denis Boucher, along with John Outzen, crossed the snow and ice of the North American polar cap, from the Pacific to the Atlantic, on snowmobiles. The 16,500-km journey took 56 days.

In June, 2006, South Africans Adriaan Marais and Marinus Du Plessis travelled 21,000 km by jet ski from Anchorage, Alaska, to Miami, Florida, down the West Coast of the USA and through the Panama Canal.

In 2006, English photographer Roz Gordon travelled the length of Britain, from John O'Groats to Land's End, using 73 different types of transport, including a pogo stick, camel, dog sled, golf cart and stilts.

In 1949, Molt Taylor from Portland, Oregon, invented the Aerocar, a flying four-wheel car with a removable tail and wings, powered by an aircraft engine.

GETTING ABOUT

Millions of tonnes of goods and materials are moved around by trucks every year. But you won't see the biggest trucks of all rumbling past your house, because they're far too big for ordinary roads.

Some carry rock out of mines. These massive trucks are the size of a house. They can carry more than 300 tonnes of rock in one load. Even when they are standing empty, they weigh as much as 190 cars. The massive engine that moves such a heavy machine is as big as 45 car engines and its fuel tank holds enough fuel to fill 20 baths.

In 2004, in Whitehorse, Yukon Territory, a dog managed to put a truck in gear and coast downhill while his owner watched television. A passer-by alerted the police after seeing the truck go by with a dog at the wheel.

06H495 830E KOMA

Each dump truck can cost $2.5 million.

Fully loaded, a dump truck can weigh 592 tonnes.

They work in coal, copper, iron and gold mines all over the world.

KOMATSU

The driver climbs a flight of steps to reach the cab.

Mining dump trucks load up with earth weighing as much as 300 cars.

Each tyre stands around 4 m high.

Don Underwood of Louisville, Kentucky, owns a 1954 fire truck with a built-in swimming pool!

TRAVELLING LIGHT

The 2,000-tonne space shuttle has its own transporter to move it to the launch pad.

The crawler weighs 2,400 tonnes and each side can be raised and lowered independently to keep the shuttle level as it moves up to the launch pad. The crawler travels the 5.6 km from the shuttle depot at a maximum speed of just 1.6 km/h, burning 353 litres of fuel every kilometre. The journey takes an average of about five hours.

>> HUMAN HAULER >>

Krishna Gopal Shrivestava pulled a 270-tonne boat a distance of 15 m in Calcutta harbour using ropes attached to his teeth.

twist it!

A major road in California had to be closed in 2006 after a truck overturned and spilled 10 tonnes of cat litter on the road. It took four hours to clean up.

In May 2006, thieves in Germany stole an entire roller coaster weighing more than 20 tonnes from the back of a parked truck.

At the 2006 Kentucky Art Car Weekend, Lewis Meyer decorated the front of his Nissan truck with a sea monster made from bottle tops.

British sculptor Douglas White created a 4.8-m palm tree from blown-out truck tyres in the middle of a rainforest in Belize.

A locksmith from North Platte, Nebraska, made a truck key by looking at an X-ray of the driver, who had swallowed the key. The new key worked first time.

MOVING HOUSE

Ripley's Believe It or Not!®

This house in Palm Beach, Florida, was donated to a charity and moved to its new location by truck and barge. The owners built a new house on the vacant plot of land.

KEEP ON TRUCKIN'

HOME MADE

art cars and bikes

VEHICLE
A car, bus, truck or other machine for transporting people or cargo.

BIG WORD ALERT!

Some people have to be different. For them, the same car as everyone else just won't do. One popular way to make a car look different is to give it a special paint job. Painted flames, eagle wings or lightning flashes can turn an ordinary vehicle into an amazing work of art.

Another common way to add a personal touch is to cover a car with… well, whatever you like. Owners have customised their cars and, for that matter, motorbikes, by coating them with everything from postage stamps and coins to fur and cartoon characters.

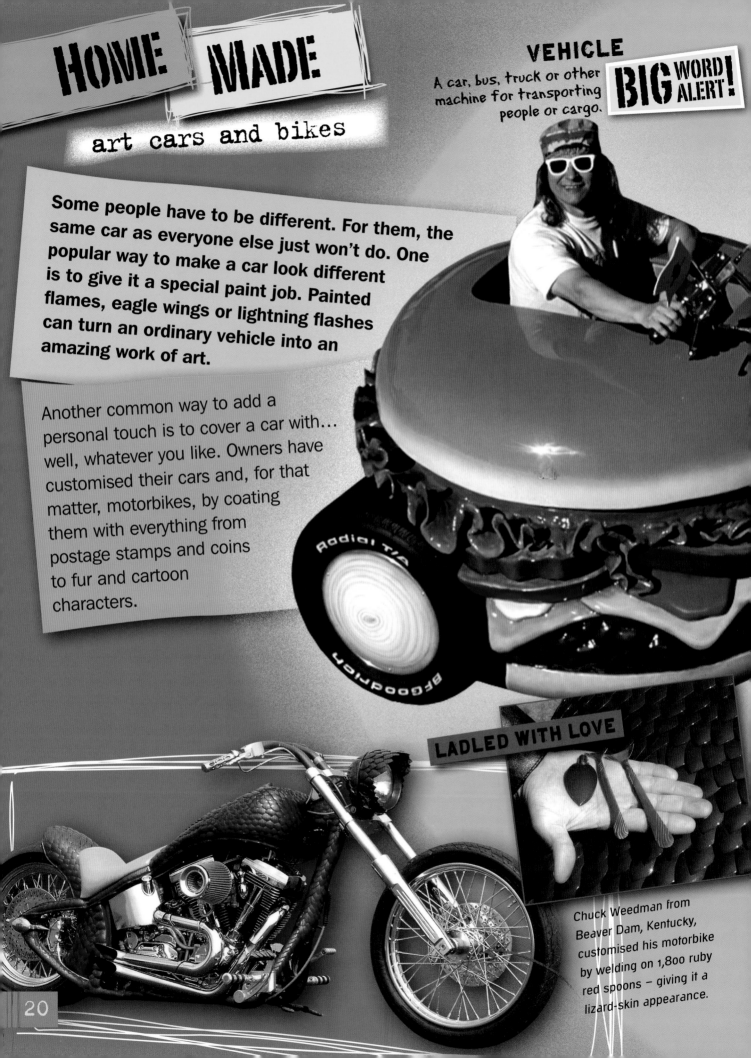

LADLED WITH LOVE

Chuck Weedman from Beaver Dam, Kentucky, customised his motorbike by welding on 1,800 ruby red spoons – giving it a lizard-skin appearance.

>> FULL OF TASTE >>

Complete with lettuce, salad and cheese, Harry Sperl's Hamburger Harley Davidson drives around Daytona Beach, Florida. The bike is just one of thousands of hamburger-related items that Harry has in his home – including a giant hamburger waterbed and a hamburger phone. Each one really is something to relish!

mint condition

Ken Burkitt of Niagara Falls, Ontario, Canada, is obsessed with coins, and has covered several cars with them. Each coin he uses is coated with polyurethane, to stop it discolouring or rusting. This MGB Roadster, which is covered in gold-plated English old pennies, is currently on display at the Ripley's Museum in Mexico. Coins are bent into shape so that they mould to every curve of a car.

ROCK 'N' ROLL MOTOR

School teacher Rebecca Bass from Houston, Texas, and her students created this rock 'n' roll motor that depicts many world-famous musicians – including Jimi Hendrix, ZZ Top, Madonna and Sir Elton John. They covered the car with sculpted Styrofoam, beads, glass, jewellery and albums.

twist it!

IT'S A COVER UP

One of the exhibits at a stamp fair in Germany was a Volkswagen Beetle car covered with more than half a million postage stamps.

Gene Pool not only covered a whole bus in growing grass but also made himself a grass suit. He watered both daily.

Artist James Robert Ford spent three years covering a Ford Capri with 4,500 toy cars.

Torsten Baubach from Wales covered his Mini with tiger-print fur.

Janette Hanson of Macclesfield, England, altered her Mini Cooper so that it matched her handbag.

MUSCLED UP

human-powered machines

A cyclist produces about 200 watts of power by pedalling. This much power could light two or three electric lamps. That's not much, but it's also enough to power a specially designed plane, helicopter, boat or submarine.

Every two years, human-powered submarines race against each other at the International Submarine Races in the USA. In the air, the most famous pedal-powered plane is the Gossamer Albatross. Bryan Allen flew it from England to France, reaching a top speed of 29 km/h.

Amazingly, it's also possible for one strong person to drag a 180-tonne airliner along the ground by muscle power alone.

>> DON'T STOP! >>

Bryan Allen pedalled for nearly three hours to power the Gossamer Albatross plane across the sea between England and France on 12 June 1979. It weighs just 32 kg.

The wings are made from thin plastic film stretched over a plastic frame.

A propeller powers the aircraft through the air.

Pedals turn the propeller.

DEEP THOUGHTS

Students from the University of Quebec, Canada, built a craft that holds the record for the fastest human-powered submarine. Just 4.8 m long, Omer 5 reached 15 km/h in 2007. It has a crew of two. One person turns the propeller by pushing pedals and a second person steers the sub. It's a 'wet' submarine, which means it is full of water. The crew wears diving gear.

Greg Kolodziejzyk has pure pedal power. In 2006, on a racetrack in California, he cycled a mammoth 1,041 km in 24 hours and clocked up the fastest time ever for pedalling 1,000 km – he took just 23 hours 2 minutes. His Critical Power bike is no ordinary two-wheeler. He rides it lying down. It can reach speeds of 100 km/h and has a cruising speed of 50 km/h on a flat road.

Gamini Wasnatha Kumara pulled a 40-tonne railway carriage 25 m in Colombo, Sri Lanka, in 2001, by means of a rope gripped between his teeth.

PHEW!

Eleven-year-old Bruce Khlebnikov towed a plane with a rope attached to his hair on 24 May 2001, in Moscow, Russia.

In 1909, Walter Flexenberger invented the Sea Cycle, a catamaran powered by a paddlewheel turned by pedalling a bicycle.

In 2000, 20 men pulled a dump truck around a car park in Kenosha, Wisconsin, for an hour non-stop, covering a distance of 5 km.

In 2005, Zhang Xingquan from China not only pulled a family car using his ear, he did it while walking on raw eggs – without breaking them.

In 2006, 72-year-old Chinese grandmother Wang Xiaobei pulled a truck loaded with people for 10 m – with her teeth!

FIRST try it!

In Beijing a group of people demonstrate how pedal power can generate electricity that can be stored in portable rechargeable batteries. The batteries are then able to power electrical appliances, such as washing machines.

DID YOU KNOW?

The first submarines were human-powered. In 1620, a Dutchman, Cornelis Drebbel, designed a wooden vehicle encased in leather. It was able to carry 12 rowers and a total of 20 men. Amazingly, the vessel could dive to a depth of 5 m and travel 10 km. The crew turned the propeller by hand.

PUSH HEEL IN

CRAZY TRANSPORT

far out!

If you're bored with travelling in the usual ways, there are some more exciting ways to get around.

Those of you who are really brave could try being fired out of a circus cannon. You could fly 45 m through the air at up to 80 km/h. Or take a leaf out of Felix Baumgartner's book. In 2003, he strapped a 1.8-m wing to his back and jumped out of a plane. He glided 35 km from England to France across the English Channel. You could try fitting rockets to a car, or a jet engine to a boat. Jet-powered racing boats, called hydroplanes, can reach speeds of more than 350 km/h.

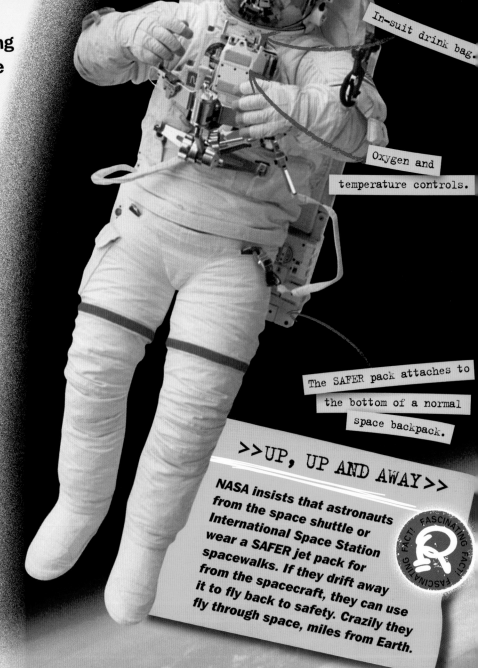

LED

In-suit drink bag.

Oxygen and temperature controls.

The SAFER pack attaches to the bottom of a normal space backpack.

>>UP, UP AND AWAY>>

NASA insists that astronauts from the space shuttle or International Space Station wear a SAFER jet pack for spacewalks. If they drift away from the spacecraft, they can use it to fly back to safety. Crazily they fly through space, miles from Earth.

FASCINATING FACT! FASCINATING FACT!

SAFER JET-PACK

SAFER stands for Simplified Aid For EVA Rescue. It works by sending out jets of nitrogen gas. There are 24 jets pointing in three different directions (up and down, backwards and forwards, and side to side). By choosing which jets to use, the astronaut can vary his or her direction.

BIG WORD ALERT!

NASA

The National Aeronautics and Space Administration - the organisation that carries out space exploration for the USA.

GO FOR IT!

On 5 March 2005, 47 people went surfing on Australia's Gold Coast on a single massive surfboard measuring 12 m long and 3 m wide.

Tim Arfons gets around on a jet-powered bar stool. The stool reached speeds of 64 km/h at a raceway in Norwalk, Ohio.

In 2006, two British women, Antonia Bolingbroke-Kent and Jo Huxster, drove a three-wheel taxi, called a tuk-tuk, 19,000 km from Thailand to England through 12 countries.

WAY TO GO!

This bride and her bridesmaids rode to her wedding in a tractor bucket in China in 2008. The groom arrived in his own tractor bucket, also decorated with balloons.

David Smith, from Missouri, USA, used a cannon to fire himself across the US/Mexican border. He waved his passport as he flew past customs control.

Paul Stender's Port-O-Jet consists of a wooden washroom hut powered by a 50-year-old, 340-kg Boeing jet engine. It travels at 74 km/h and throws 10-m fireballs from the burner at the back. He drives it while seated on the original toilet inside.

25

LITTLE AND LARGE

extreme vehicles

Did you know that you can stretch a car and make it longer? Not like a rubber band – a stretch limo is a luxury car made longer by cutting it in two and putting an extra section in the middle. Whereas an ordinary car is 4 or 5 m long, stretch limos are usually about 8.5 m, but the world's longest is 30.5 m long. However, some people think that small is beautiful. The tiniest cars are less than 1 m high, and the most minuscule planes are just 4 m long. That's about the same length as a car.

Dream Big

Driven mad

Gregory Denham from California, USA, poses at the wheel of his Dream Big motorbike. Rumoured to be the biggest motorbike in the world, it stands a whopping 3.35 m high and 6.2 m long. Denham wanted a bike that could perform like a Monster Truck, so he went ahead and built one!

ROOM FOR EVERYONE

Meet one long, long limo, made by Jay Ohrberg – known as 'The King of Show Cars'. This lengthy motor is 30 m long and has a helicopter landing site at the back. Add some friends... and drive!

26

Room for one

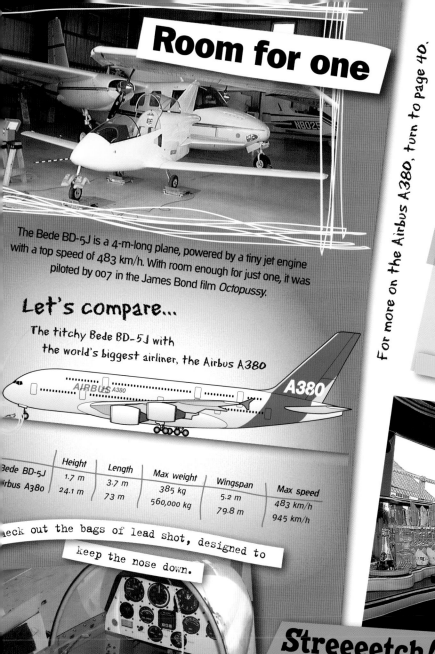

The Bede BD-5J is a 4-m-long plane, powered by a tiny jet engine with a top speed of 483 km/h. With room enough for just one, it was piloted by 007 in the James Bond film *Octopussy*.

Let's compare...

The titchy Bede BD-5J with the world's biggest airliner, the Airbus A380

AIRBUS A380
A380

	Height	Length	Max weight	Wingspan	Max speed
Bede BD-5J	1.7 m	3.7 m	385 kg	5.2 m	483 km/h
Airbus A380	24.1 m	73 m	560,000 kg	79.8 m	945 km/h

Check out the bags of lead shot, designed to keep the nose down.

For more on the Airbus A380, turn to page 40.

twist it!

Benji Ming, at the Edinburgh Festival, Scotland, was so enraged at the small audiences he was attracting for his shows that he transferred his performances from the theatre to the confines of a Smart car. He delivered a comic monologue to a packed house – an audience of one in the passenger seat.

Twenty-one Malaysian students crammed themselves into a Mini Cooper in June 2006.

Jasper, a black Doberman–Labrador owned by Sir Benjamin Slade in England, travels everywhere by stretch limo.

¡EXTREME!

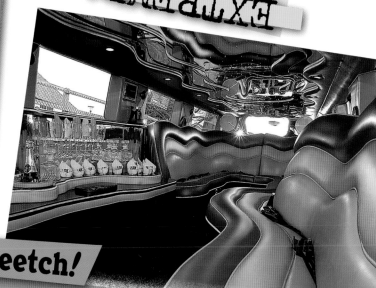

Streeeetch!

There's room to be creative with the interiors in this 12-m-long Hummer, owned by Scott Demaret from Bristol, England.

SMALL IS BEAUTIFUL

Designed to seat one person and a shopping bag, the Peel P50 was a three-wheeled micro-car, first produced in 1963. It had one door, a single windscreen wiper and only one headlight. With vital statistics of just 134 cm by 99 cm, its minuscule frame weighed in at only 59 kg, but could manage a speed of 61 km/h. Handy for slipping into that confined parking space, the Peel had just one drawback – no reverse gear!

ROBOTS ARE REAL!

The robots are coming! Robots in films are often walking, talking machines that look like metal people. Real robots are often not quite so lifelike, but there are more than six million robots in the world today.

man machines

A million of them are industrial robots. These are computer-controlled arms that help to make things in factories. The other five million or so are service robots. These include robot toys, vacuum cleaners and lawnmowers. Honda's ASIMO robot (see far right) is a real walking, talking humanlike robot. ASIMO is 1.3 m tall and weighs 54 kg. It can walk at 2.5 km/h and even run a little faster.

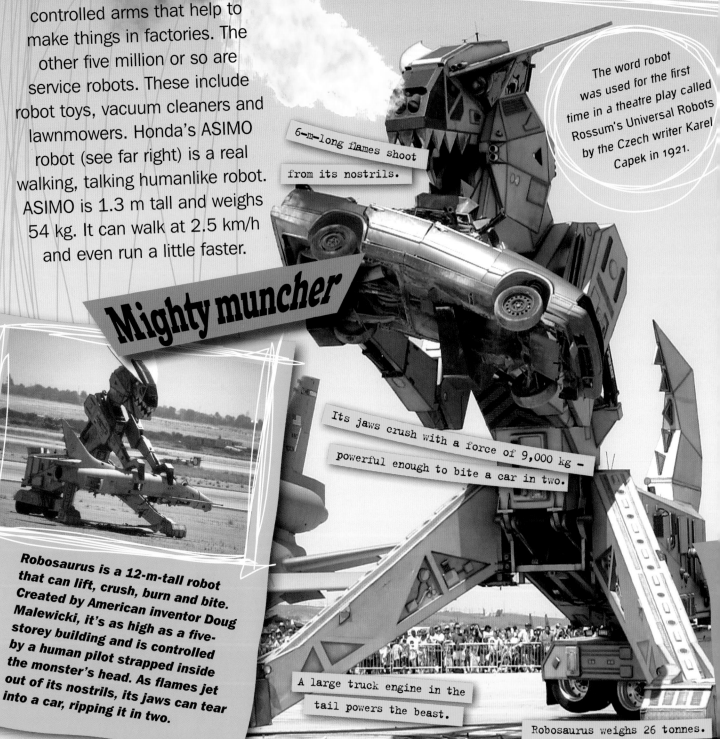

6-m-long flames shoot from its nostrils.

The word robot was used for the first time in a theatre play called Rossum's Universal Robots by the Czech writer Karel Capek in 1921.

Mighty muncher

Its jaws crush with a force of 9,000 kg – powerful enough to bite a car in two.

Robosaurus is a 12-m-tall robot that can lift, crush, burn and bite. Created by American inventor Doug Malewicki, it's as high as a five-storey building and is controlled by a human pilot strapped inside the monster's head. As flames jet out of its nostrils, its jaws can tear into a car, ripping it in two.

A large truck engine in the tail powers the beast.

Robosaurus weighs 26 tonnes.

28

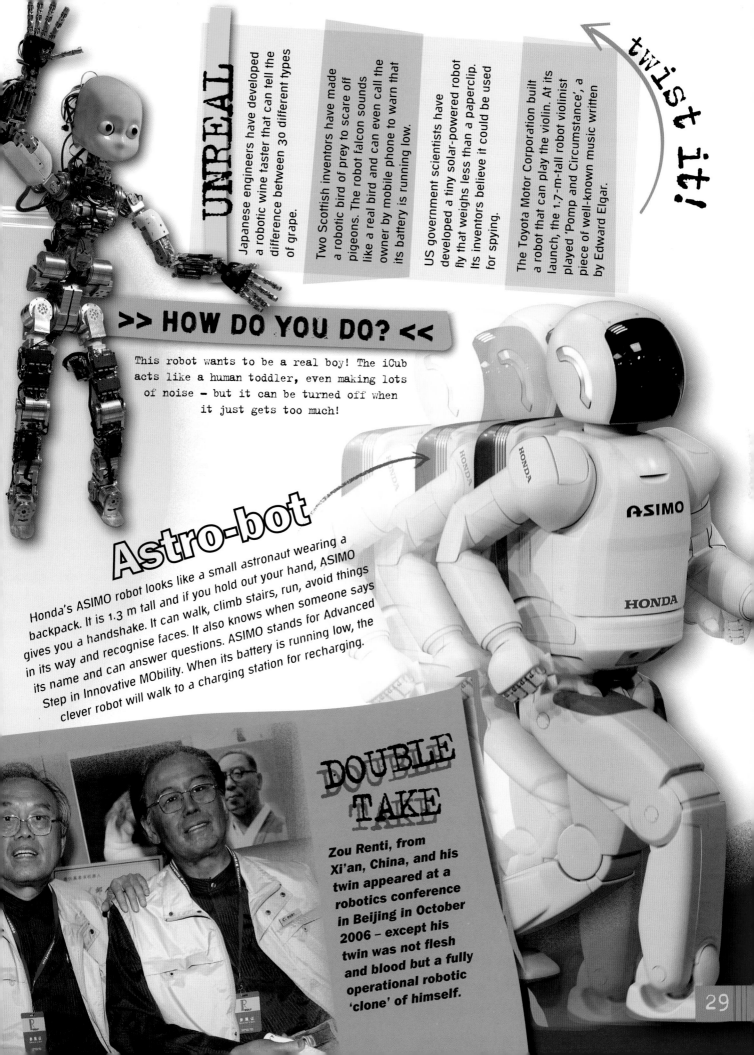

UNREAL

Japanese engineers have developed a robotic wine taster that can tell the difference between 30 different types of grape.

Two Scottish inventors have made a robotic bird of prey to scare off pigeons. The robot falcon sounds like a real bird and can even call the owner by mobile phone to warn that its battery is running low.

US government scientists have developed a tiny solar-powered robot fly that weighs less than a paperclip. Its inventors believe it could be used for spying.

The Toyota Motor Corporation built a robot that can play the violin. At its launch, the 1.7-m-tall robot violinist played 'Pomp and Circumstance', a piece of well-known music written by Edward Elgar.

>> HOW DO YOU DO? <<

This robot wants to be a real boy! The iCub acts like a human toddler, even making lots of noise – but it can be turned off when it just gets too much!

Astro-bot

Honda's ASIMO robot looks like a small astronaut wearing a backpack. It is 1.3 m tall and if you hold out your hand, ASIMO gives you a handshake. It can walk, climb stairs, run, avoid things in its way and recognise faces. It also knows when someone says its name and can answer questions. ASIMO stands for Advanced Step in Innovative MObility. When its battery is running low, the clever robot will walk to a charging station for recharging.

ASIMO

HONDA

DOUBLE TAKE

Zou Renti, from Xi'an, China, and his twin appeared at a robotics conference in Beijing in October 2006 – except his twin was not flesh and blood but a fully operational robotic 'clone' of himself.

FOR SAIL.

If your boat doesn't have an engine, you could roll up your sleeves and row it, or you could hoist a sail and let the wind do the work.

wind power

A small boat is fun to sail, but a big racing yacht is one of the most exciting ways to travel. Racing yachts can slice through the waves at 55 km/h. Super yachts more than 30 m long can go even faster. A few of the 50,000 ships that carry goods and materials around the world have been built with sails too. Using wind power instead of engines saves fuel.

Each mast is 50 m tall.

The sails are made from a strong synthetic fabric and cover an area of 2,500 sq m.

The ship can carry 308 passengers and has seven decks.

Even enormous cargo ships can be wind powered. SkySails are huge computer-controlled kites that give extra power and help save fuel.

BELUGA PROJECTS

powered by SkySails

CLOSE TO THE WIND

The Wind Surf is a cruise liner that can be powered by either computer-controlled sails or engines. Its sails unfurl automatically from the 50-m-tall masts within two minutes of pushing a button on the ship's bridge. Using only sails, its top speed is about 24 km/h, about the same as its maximum speed on engine power.

>> PLAIN SAILING >>

French vet Raphaela Le Gouvello crossed the Indian Ocean on a sailboard just 8 m long and 1.2 m wide. The 6,300-km journey took 60 days. Raphaela spent eight hours a day at the sail. She has also crossed the Atlantic and Pacific Oceans and the Mediterranean Sea by sailboard.

The ship is 187 m long, 20 m wide and weighs nearly 15,000 tonnes.

twist it!

WATER WAYS

Japanese sailor Kenichi Horie spent three months sailing alone across the Pacific Ocean on a yacht made from beer barrels.

British woman Hilary Lister sailed across the English Channel between England and France in August 2005, even though she could not move her arms or legs. She steered her yacht by sucking and blowing through tubes that operated the rudder and sails.

During a round-the-world voyage in 1997, British yachtsman Tony Bullimore survived for five days underneath his capsized yacht in the icy Southern Ocean until help arrived.

When a Russian yacht lost its rudder in the Southern Ocean in 2005, the crew replaced it with a cabin door.

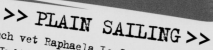

BIG WORD ALERT!

CAPSIZED

Upturned. A capsized boat is one that has rolled upside-down.

WIND SURF

Ripley's Believe It or Not!®

BRICK BOAT

It took Peter Lange from New Zealand three months to build his 6-m-long brick boat using 676 bricks. Amazingly, it didn't sink!

Ripley explains...

Thrust

Low pressure

Sail

BOAT

Wind direction

High pressure

A yacht sail works like an aircraft wing. When a sail fills with air, it forms the same curved shape as a wing. This changes the flow of air to create low pressure. The low pressure pulls the boat along. It can move a yacht in a different direction from the wind by setting the sails at the correct angle.

WATER BABIES

boats and ships

The biggest and heaviest machines that have ever moved across Earth's surface are ships. Large ships are usually made from steel, while smaller boats are made from wood or plastic.

People have tried building boats from different materials. In 1970, the materials. In 1970, the Norwegian Thor Heyerdahl sailed across the Atlantic Ocean in a boat made from bundles of grass-like reeds tied together!

The carrier produces its own electricity — enough for 100,000 people.

The carrier extracts salt from sea water to make its own fresh water — more than 1.5 million litres every day.

PLANE AMAZING!

The US Navy's Nimitz class warships are nuclear-powered floating airports. Each of these ten aircraft carriers is 332 m long, weighs 88,000 tonnes and carries more than 80 aircraft.

One aircraft carrier costs about £3.2 billion.

MILK FLOAT

Inspired by the milk cartons on his breakfast table, Frank Bölter folded some Tetrapack paper – which is what cartons are often made from – and made a 9-m-long boat. He launched it on the River Elbe in Germany in 2007.

UP AND OVER

One minute it's a ship, the next it's a floating platform for scientists at the Scripps Institute of Oceanography in San Diego, California. Most of the 108-m-long FLIP (Floating Instrument Platform) can be flooded with water to make the stern sink and flip the bow into the air.

BY THE WAY...

During World War II, a British scientist came up with the idea of using icebergs as aircraft carriers. Although a model was built on a lake in Canada in 1943, the plan was scrapped because the ice split too easily.

twist it!

FLOAT YOUR BOAT

In 1991, archaeologists in Egypt found a fleet of wooden boats, each 18 m long, built nearly 5,000 years ago.

James Castrission and Justin Jones rowed their kayak 3,300 km across the Tasman Sea between Australia and New Zealand. Their voyage took 62 days of paddling up to 18 hours a day.

In March 2003, comedian Tim Fitzhigham rowed a kayak made of paper 257 km down the River Thames. When it leaked during the eight-day journey, he sealed the holes with sticky tape.

In 2003, Robert McDonald from Emmeloord in the Netherlands stayed afloat for 19 minutes in a boat made from 370,000 lollipop sticks.

A regatta held on the Mohawk River near Canajoharie, New York, involves boats made from recycled materials, including plastic milk cartons and bottles.

Up, Up AND AWAY

balloons

Balloons and airships are actually lighter than air. They contain a gas that weighs less than the air around them. Airships are filled with helium, whereas most balloons are filled with hot air. Hot air is lighter than cold air – that's why smoke floats upwards from a fire.

Airships are powered by engines and propellers, and they can be steered, but balloons drift wherever the wind blows them. Every year, more than 700 balloons take part in the world's biggest balloon festival in Albuquerque, New Mexico.

The first creatures to fly in a hot-air balloon were a rooster, a duck and a sheep in 1783 in France.

MAN POWER

The 46-m-long Action Man that moved through the skies over London claimed to be the world's biggest parachutist balloon.

Ripley explains...

Envelope

Hot air inside balloon

Burners

Basket

Burners above a balloon pilot's head burn propane gas from cylinders in the basket, where the pilot stands. The roaring flame heats the air above it inside the balloon's envelope. The lighter air rises and carries the balloon up with it. The pilot can turn the flame on and off to change the balloon's height above the ground.

BIG BIRD

Balloons can be built in all sorts of shapes, like this eagle. When air is heated by the balloon's gas burners, it expands and fills every part of the eagle.

A LOT OF HOT AIR

At an air base in Chambley, France in 2005, 261 balloons lined up to float into the air at the same time.

World flight

In 1999, Bertrand Piccard and Brian Jones flew the part air-, part helium-filled Breitling Orbiter 3 balloon all the way round the world in one non-stop flight – the first time it had ever been done. The balloon took off in Switzerland, and landed in Egypt.

Helium

Hot air

Gondola

The balloon was in the air for 19 days 21 hours 55 minutes and flew a total distance of 46,814 km.

When fully inflated, the balloon stood 55 m tall.

Propane gas fuelled six burners that heated air in the balloon.

The crew travelled inside a sealed capsule, called a gondola, hanging underneath the balloon.

The gondola had flying controls and instruments at one end, a bed in the middle and a toilet at the other end.

Winds blew the balloon along at up to 176 km/h.

Frenchman Henri Giffard built the first airship and flew it 25 km from Paris to Trappe on 24 September 1852.

Ripley's — Believe It or Not!®

CHAIR LIFT

Balloon pilot Pete Dalby floated over Bristol, England, sitting comfortably in an armchair hanging under a hot-air balloon!

COUCH LIFT

Kent Couch made a 322-km flight over the state of Orgeon, USA, in 2007 while sitting on a lawn chair. The chair was held aloft by 105 balloons filled with helium. Couch reached a height of 4,267 m and controlled his height by dropping water to go higher or popping balloons to go down. As the wind blew him towards mountains, he popped some balloons and landed in a field near Union, Oregon. The flight lasted 8 hours 45 minutes.

105 balloons

4,267 m up!

SLOW DOWN!

parachutes

When mighty machines get going, it takes a lot of force to stop them. The fastest vehicles sometimes use parachutes to help them slow down. The space shuttle lands at 350 km/h. That's as fast as a racing car at top speed, but the space shuttle weighs a lot more, about 100 tonnes. To help it slow down, a huge 12-m-wide parachute pops out of its tail. It catches so much air that it acts like a brake. Parachutes ease the speed of falling things, too.

The bigger a parachute is – the larger its surface area – the more drag it creates.

Whoa!
The space shuttle orbiter stops with a little help from air resistance, or drag.

Ripley explains...

Canopy

Cells

Lines

A simple round parachute floats straight down, slowed down by air caught underneath it. Most parachutists now use a ram-air canopy that acts a bit like a paraglider. When a ram-air canopy opens, air rushes into pockets called cells sewn into it. The cells filled with air give the parachute the shape of a wing. Instead of coming straight down, it flies like a glider.

HIGH FLIERS

French kitesurfer Sebastien Garat competes in the finals of the Kiteboarding World Championship in Sotavento, Fuerteventura, Spain. Using a wind-filled kite, competitors use the short time between uplift and landing to perform breathtaking acrobatics.

36

ground control

Safely down, and the parachutes are cut free. The Apollo 11 crew await pickup in their Command Module.

The Apollo 15 Command Module 'Kitty Hawk', with astronauts David R. Scott, Alfred M. Worden and James B. Irwin aboard, nears a safe touchdown in the mid-Pacific Ocean to end their Moon landing mission in 1971. Although causing no harm to the crewmen, one of the three main parachutes failed to function properly.

Don't Let Go!

Skydiver Greg Gasson hangs by just one hand from his parachute strap, high above Eloy, Arizona.

twist it!

WHAT A DRAG

The jet-powered cars that set speed records are so fast that they use a braking parachute to slow down until they reach a speed slow enough for the car's wheel brakes to be used.

DOWNFALL

The Chinese Shenzhou manned spacecraft lands under a parachute big enough to park 100 cars on – 1,200 sq m.

On 16 August 1960, Colonel Joseph W. Kittinger Jr jumped from a balloon at a height of 31,150 m. He fell for 4 minutes 36 seconds before opening his parachute, taking 13 minutes 45 seconds in total to reach the ground.

When Shayna West of Joplin, Missouri, made a parachute jump in 2005, her main and reserve chutes both failed. She fell 3,050 m and landed in a car park, breaking her pelvis, five teeth and several bones in her face. She survived, along with the unborn baby she did not know she was carrying.

When a skydiver in Pittsburgh, USA, caught his foot on the way out of an aircraft door, he dangled from the plane for 30 minutes until it could land. He was unhurt.

Don Kellner from Hazleton, Pennsylvania, has made more than 36,000 skydives. His wife Darlene has made 13,000. They were even married in mid-air by a skydiving minister, Rev. Dave Sangley.

37

FULL SPEED AHEAD

jet thrust

A jet engine is a big air blower. It blows out a jet of air like a hairdryer, but it blows a lot faster than any hairdryer you've ever used. Air shoots out of a jet engine more than ten times faster than a hurricane and as hot as a blowtorch, so don't ever stand behind a jet engine!

Four of these engines can push a 500-tonne airliner through the air at 900 km/h. Planes aren't the only machines to be powered by jet engines. People have fitted jet engines to boats, cars and even themselves. Jet thrust can also be supplied using water, steam or certain gases.

ENGINE AT THE BACK

Allan Herridge has attached a Viper jet engine to the back of his Volkswagen Beetle. The car has its original 90-horsepower engine at the front, with the 900-kg thrust jet engine at the back. The jet engine can boost the car's speed from 130 km/h to 225 km/h in less than four seconds.

SOLO FLIGHT

This 300 horsepower jet pack enables the wearer to fly at up to 100 km/h and perform tight turns and swoops, soar 9 m up into the air, or hover on the spot. Shooting out two strong jets of water, which provide the thrust, a jet pack flight can last for up to 2 hours.

Sound of mind?

On 15 October 1997, British pilot Andy Green drove a jet-powered car called Thrust SSC faster than the speed of sound. He reached a speed of 1,228 km/h.

38

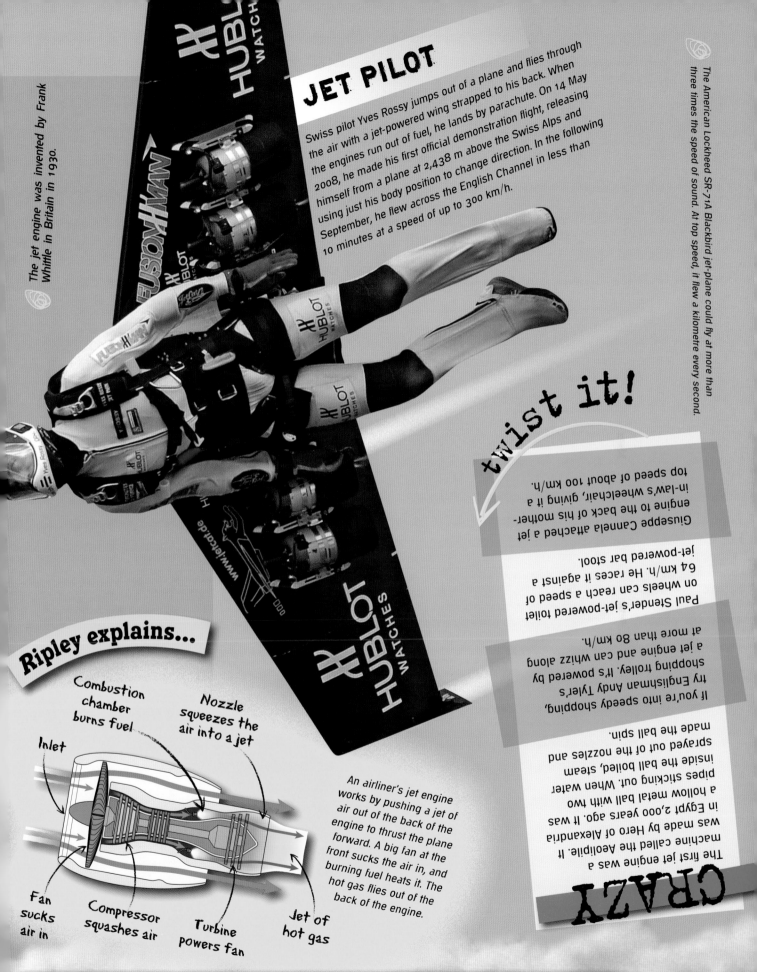

JET PILOT

Swiss pilot Yves Rossy jumps out of a plane and flies through the air with a jet-powered wing strapped to his back. When the engines run out of fuel, he lands by parachute. On 14 May 2008, he made his first official demonstration flight, releasing himself from a plane at 2,438 m above the Swiss Alps and using just his body position to change direction. In the following September, he flew across the English Channel in less than 10 minutes at a speed of up to 300 km/h.

The American Lockheed SR-71A Blackbird jet-plane could fly at more than three times the speed of sound. At top speed, it flew a kilometre every second.

twist it!

Giuseppe Cannela attached a jet engine to the back of his mother-in-law's wheelchair, giving it a top speed of about 100 km/h.

Paul Stender's jet-powered toilet on wheels can reach a speed of 64 km/h. He races it against a jet-powered bar stool.

If you're into speedy shopping, try Englishman Andy Tyler's shopping trolley. It's powered by a jet engine and can whizz along at more than 80 km/h.

CRAZY

The first jet engine was a machine called the Aeolipile. It was made by Hero of Alexandria in Egypt 2,000 years ago. It was a hollow metal ball with two pipes sticking out. When water inside the ball boiled, steam sprayed out of the nozzles and made the ball spin.

Ripley explains...

Combustion chamber burns fuel

Nozzle squeezes the air into a jet

Inlet

An airliner's jet engine works by pushing a jet of air out of the back of the engine to thrust the plane forward. A big fan at the front sucks the air in, and burning fuel heats it. The hot gas flies out of the back of the engine.

Fan sucks air in

Compressor squashes air

Turbine powers fan

Jet of hot gas

IN FULL FLIGHT

airliners

In 2003, Charles McKinley flew from Newark, New Jersey, to Dallas, Texas, in a crate packed in a plane's cargo hold to save money. He was charged so much in fees and fines for doing this that he could have flown first class for the same cost!

Sit back and enjoy the view. You're in an airliner cruising through the sky 10 km above the ground. The clouds are laid out below you like a fluffy white field. They hardly seem to be moving, but you're hurtling through the air at 900 km/h, just below the speed of sound. It's sunny outside, but it's also colder than a deep freeze.

An African airline bought a Gulfstream jet for US$4.9 million on the Internet auction site eBay.

The temperature on the other side of your window could be as low as –60°C, and the air is too thin to breathe. Every year, about 12,000 airliners make more than 15 million flights, carrying more than 2 billion passengers.

Its giant wings measure 79.8 m from tip to tip. They're big enough to park 70 cars on them.

MIGHTY BEAST!

The Airbus A380 'super-jumbo' is the first airliner to have two passenger decks, one above the other, running the whole length of the aircraft. It made its first flight on 27 April 2005, taking off from Toulouse, France, then spending four hours circling over the Bay of Biscay while engineers carried out tests. It can carry as many as 840 passengers, although most airlines will fit about 525 seats inside it.

FLIGHT OF FANCY

Yes, this really is the inside of a plane. The Airbus A380 is more hotel than aircraft.

Four massive jet engines have to propel a plane that can weigh as much as 560 tonnes.

CLEARED FOR TAKE-OFF

John Davis spent eight years building an exact copy of a Boeing 747 airliner cockpit in his spare bedroom in his modest home. A 1.8-m screen in front of the cockpit shows views of places from the Alps to New York.

Winglets The Airbus A380 has massive wings – its wingspan is the same as the length of a football pitch. If the wings were the same construction as on other airliners, in order to get the massive Airbus off the ground, they would have to be incredibly long: too long for airports, which all have a maximum wingspan of just 80 m. Designers of the Airbus A380 looked to the wings of an eagle for a solution to the problem.

Here's the science

The tip of an airliner's wing stirs up the air it is moving through. The spinning air stops the wing from working at its best, so the wing has to be made even longer. Designers noticed how an eagle's wingtips curl upwards as it flies. It gave them an idea. They made turned-up wingtips, called winglets for the A380. Each winglet blocks the spinning air and so the wingspan can be kept to 79.8 m.

If five giraffes stood like a tall tower, each one on the head of the one below, they would be the same height as the new Airbus.

The two decks of the 72.75-m-long aircraft cover a surface area of 500 sq m, the equivalent of ten squash courts.

5,600 people could stand under the shelter of its wings.

Fuselage

The heavier an aircraft, the more fuel used. The Airbus A380 is longer, wider and has more passengers than any other aircraft, but scientists constructed the outside of the aircraft from an aluminium and fibreglass blend, which is strong yet light.

41

IN A SPIN

vertical take-off

Hoverflies are little flies that can stay in the same spot in mid-air as if hanging at the end of an invisible thread. Some aircraft can do the same thing. They can take off straight up into the air and hover in one spot. Most of them are helicopters.

Long thin blades on top of a helicopter whirl around hundreds of times a minute, blowing air down like a big fan. The whirling blades blow hard enough to lift a helicopter weighing several tonnes off the ground. There are about 45,000 helicopters in service all over the world. Helicopters have saved more than 3 million lives since the first helicopter rescue in 1944.

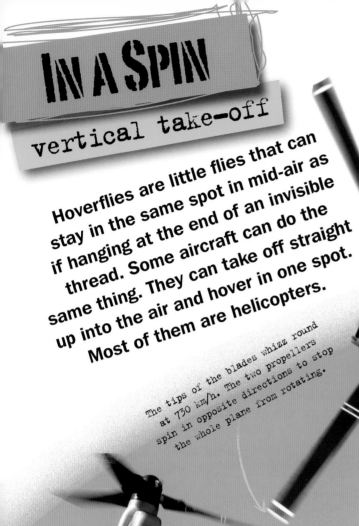

The tips of the blades whizz round at 730 km/h. The two propellers spin in opposite directions to stop the whole plane from rotating.

Refuelling Probe. The Osprey uses this to fill its tanks with fuel from a flying tanker-plane.

The Osprey can carry 24 passengers.

A tail fin provides stability.

MASTER STROKE

Leonardo da Vinci (1452–1519) made a sketch of a flying machine that seems to anticipate the helicopter, though it's not clear how he thought it would work.

WHAT A CHOPPER! OR IS IT?

The V-22 Osprey takes off like a helicopter. Then its engines and propellers tilt forwards and it flies like a plane. This means it can take off and land almost anywhere, even in remote parts of the world where there is no runway. Built for the military and perfect for use on aircraft carriers, each V-22 Osprey costs about £65 million.

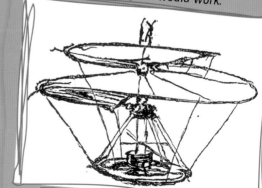

Frenchman Gustave de Ponton d'Amécourt invented the word helicopter in 1861.

The Russian Mil Mi-26 is a giant among helicopters. It can carry more than 80 people or 20 tonnes of cargo.

Drive shaft runs through both wings, connecting rotors together, so that if one of the engines breaks down, the other engine will power both propellers.

At speeds of up to 507 km/h, the V-22 Osprey flies twice as fast as a helicopter.

twist it!

In March 2007, a moose that had been shot with a tranquiliser dart near Gustavus, Alaska, charged the hovering helicopter it had been shot from, and brought it down!

In 2005, Frenchman Didier Delsalle landed his helicopter on top of the world's highest mountain, Mount Everest, at a height of 8,848 m.

In 2003, Jonathan Strickland from Inglewood, California, made his first solo flights in a plane and a helicopter on the same day when he was only 14 years of age. He had to go to Canada to do it, because US pilots have to be at least 16 years old.

Alexander van de Rostyne created a tiny helicopter called the Pixelito, weighing only 6.9 grams.

SPIN IT!

uplifting!

Helicopters usually land with ease, but this one had strongman Franz Muellner to contend with. When the 1,800-kg aircraft landed on his shoulders, he managed to hold it off the ground for nearly a minute in Vienna in 2006.

43

BLAST OFF!

rocket power

Three... two... one... lift off. If you want to be an astronaut, you'll need a rocket. It's the only way to get into space and it's the boldest, fastest journey you will ever make. The mighty *Saturn V* rocket launched astronauts on their way to the Moon. Today, rocket power takes astronauts to the International Space Station. By the end of 2008, nearly 500 people from 39 countries had hitched a ride on a rocket into space. Rockets blast satellites into orbit too, and they send probes to the Moon and planets. Back here on Earth, smaller firework rockets light up the sky at special events and celebrations.

Ariane 5 can launch satellites weighing up to 10 tonnes.

Each of the two booster rockets weighs 260 tonnes.

Upper stage

Ariane 5 made its first flight in 1996.

ARIANE 5

euteisat

ariane space
service & solutions

Payload

An Ariane 5 rocket stands 52 m high and at lift-off weighs 780 tonnes.

Ariane 5 rockets launch satellites for the European Space Agency (ESA). They blast off from ESA's spaceport in French Guiana, South America. Ariane 5 is massive. It stands as tall as a 14-story building and weighs as much as 600 cars. It is actually four rockets linked together. The core stage and two booster rockets fire first. When their fuel is used up, they fall away and the upper stage fires to place the cargo in orbit around Earth.

High point

SpaceShipOne rocketed into history in 2004, when it became the first private, manned spacecraft to reach a height of 100 km. In doing this, its team members won the $10-million Ansari X Prize in a competition to encourage civilian spaceflight.

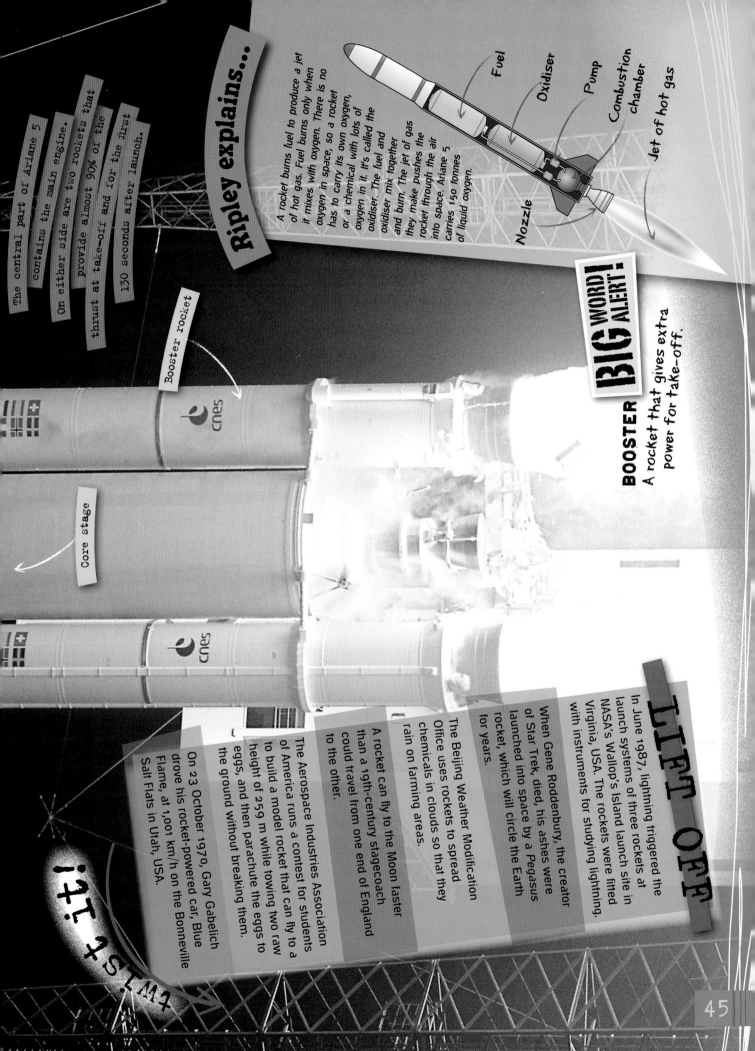

The central part of Ariane 5 contains the main engine. On either side are two rockets that provide almost 90% of the thrust at take-off and for the first 130 seconds after launch.

Ripley explains...

A rocket burns fuel to produce a jet of hot gas. Fuel burns only when it mixes with oxygen. There is no oxygen in space, so a rocket has to carry its own oxygen, or a chemical with lots of oxygen in it. It's called the oxidiser. The fuel and oxidiser mix together and burn. The jet of gas they make pushes the rocket through the air into space. Ariane 5 carries 150 tonnes of liquid oxygen.

Fuel

Oxidiser

Pump

Combustion chamber

Jet of hot gas

Nozzle

BIG WORD ALERT!

BOOSTER
A rocket that gives extra power for take-off.

Booster rocket

Core stage

LIFT OFF

In June 1987, lightning triggered the launch systems of three rockets at NASA's Wallop's Island launch site in Virginia, USA. The rockets were fitted with instruments for studying lightning.

When Gene Roddenbury, the creator of Star Trek, died, his ashes were launched into space by a Pegasus rocket, which will circle the Earth for years.

The Beijing Weather Modification Office uses rockets to spread chemicals in clouds so that they rain on farming areas.

A rocket can fly to the Moon faster than a 19th-century stagecoach could travel from one end of England to the other.

The Aerospace Industries Association of America runs a contest for students to build a model rocket that can fly to a height of 259 m while towing two raw eggs, and then parachute the eggs to the ground without breaking them.

On 23 October 1970, Gary Gabelich drove his rocket-powered car, Blue Flame, at 1,001 km/h on the Bonneville Salt Flats in Utah, USA.

LIFT OFF!

ACKNOWLEDGEMENTS

COVER (l) © Kirill Alperovich – istockphoto.com, (r) Reuters/Ali Jareki; **2** (b) Michael J. Gallagher; **3** (r) Bobby Hunt; **4** (c) Sipa Press/Rex Features; **5** (t/l) © Kirill Alperovich – istockphoto.com; **6** (b/l) Andy Wilman/Rex Features; **6–7** (sp) Photo courtesy of BigFoot 4x4, Inc. © All rights reserved, (bgd) © Eric Gevaert – istockphoto.com; **7** (t/r) Reuters/Ali Jarekji, (b/r) Mike Derer/AP/PA Photos; **8** (b) Rex Features; **8–9** (c) Rex Features; **9** (t/r) Doug Hall/Rex Features, (b) Glenn Roberts, Motorcycle Mojo Magazine/www.motorcyclemojo.com; **10** (c) Reuters/David Mercado; **11** (c) Sean Dempsey/PA Archive/PA Photos, (b) Tina Norris/Rex Features, (r) Bobby Hunt; **12** (sp) Barcroft Media; **13** (r, c/r, b/r) Barcroft Media, (t/l) Patrick Barth/Rex Features, (t/r) Rinspeed; **14** (c) Reuters/Ho New, (b/l) Reuters/ Toshiyuki Aizawa; **15** (c) Greg Williams/Rex Features, (b) Joel King/Wrigley's Airwaves ®, (r) Reuters/Sebastian Derungs; **16** Reuters/Reinhard Krause; **17** (t/l) Camera Press, (l) Gavin Bernard/Barcroft Media, (t/c, t/r) Barcroft Media, (b) BP/Barcroft Media; **18** (b/l, sp) Reuters/Tim Wimborne; **19** (l) Courtesy NASA, (b) Jennifer Podis/Rex Features, (t/r) Arko Datta/AFP/Getty Images; **20** (sp) Photo © Harrod Blank; **21** (t) © Duncan Walker – istockphoto.com; **22** (c, t/r) © Bettmann/Corbis; **22–23** (b) Official ISR Photo; **23** (t, t/r) Greg Kolodziejzyk/www.human-power.com, (c/r) Reuters/Anuruddha Lokuhapuarachchi, (b/r) Reuters/Reinhard Krause; **24** (sp/r) Courtesy NASA; **25** (l) Michel Redondo/AP/PA Photos, (c) Michael.J.Gallagher, (t/r) ChinaFotoPress/Photocome/PA Photos; **26** (b/l) Built by Jay Ohrberg/www.jayohrberg.com, (c) Volker Hartmann/AFP/Getty Images; **27** (t/l, l) Copyright © 2006 by Juan Jimenez – Reprinted with permission, (r) Rex Features; **28** (sp) TSGT Joe Zuccaro/AP/PA Photos, (b/r) © John H. Clark/Corbis; **29** (t/l) WENN/Newscom, (b/l) Reuters/Jason Lee, (r) Reuters/Toshiyuki Aizawa; **30** (b/l) Copyright SkySails, (sp) Windstar Cruises; **31** (t/r) Richard Bouhet/AFP/Getty Images, (b) © Photos by Wally Hirsh, corrugated iron sails by Jeff Thomson; **32** (sp) © UPPA/Photoshot; **33** (t/l) Reuters/Christian Charisius, (sp) Bill Call, Scripps Institution of Oceanography, (b/l, b/r) GoldenStateImages.com © Randy Morse; **34** (l) Reuters/Ian Waldie, (r) Reuters/Denis Balibouse; **35** (l) Reuters/Stringer France, (c) © Fabrice Coffrini/epa/Corbis, (b/l) South West News/Rex Features, (b/r) Pete Erickson/AP/PA Photos; **36** (t) Rex Features, (b/r) © Carlos De Saa/epa/Corbis; **37** (t/l) Joe Jennings/Barcroft Media, (b) Reuters/Dan Chung, (t/c, t/r) Courtesy NASA; **38–39** (b) Michael Sohn/AP/PA Photos; **38** (r) Jetlev-flyer.com/ Solent News/Rex Features, (r) Harry How/Allsport/Getty Images; **39** (c) Fabrice Coffrini/AFP/Getty Images; **40–41** (dp) Reuters/Charles Pertwee; **40** (b/l) Camera Press/David Dyson, (b/c, b/r) ©Airbus 2004 Camera Press/ ED/RA; **41** (t, t/r) David Burner/Rex Features; **42** (r) Mary Evans Picture Library, (l) David Jones/PA Archive/PA Photos, (r) Gerry Bromme/AP/PA Photos; **43** (r) Vladimir Kmet/AFP/Getty Images; **44–45** (dp) ESA/CNES/Arianespace/Service Optique Video du CSG; **44** (l, r) Reuters/Mike Blake

Key: t = top, b = bottom, c = centre, l = left, r = right, sp = single page, dp = double page,
bgd = background

All other photos are from Ripley Entertainment Inc.

All artwork by Dynamo Design

Every attempt has been made to acknowledge correctly and contact copyright holders and we apologise
in advance for any unintentional errors or omissions, which will be corrected in future editions.

Ripley's OCEANS

Believe It or Not!

Ripley
PUBLISHING

a Jim Pattison Company

TWISTS

Written by Camilla de la Bedoyere
Consultant Barbara Taylor

PUBLISHING

Publisher Anne Marshall

Editorial Director Rebecca Miles
Project Editor Lisa Regan
Assistant Editor Charlotte Howell
Picture Researchers James Proud, Charlotte Howell
Proofreader Judy Barratt
Indexer Hilary Bird

Art Director Sam South
Senior Designer Michelle Cannatella
Design Rocket Design (East Anglia) Ltd
Reprographics Juice Creative Ltd

www.ripleys.com/books

CONTENTS

PAGE 19

PAGE 24

TWISTS

MAKING A SPLASH

Have you ever gazed out at the ocean and wondered what lies beneath? Well, wonder no more. Take an ocean trip without getting your hair wet, and dip a toe into the great sea of knowledge!

Two-thirds of our planet is water, and the five great oceans are full of more creatures than any other place on Earth. From the sunny shallows to the dark and dingy depths, this book will bring you face to face with marine mammals, deep-sea divers, and lots and lots of fish. Come on…dive in!

WHAT'S INSIDE YOUR BOOK?

ALL CHANGE

This octopus is called the 'day octopus' because it hunts in the day. As such it needs to be a camouflage expert, so it can hunt successfully, and not be hunted. It is usually brown but can change colour as it swims from sand and rocks to coral. One marine biologist reported seeing an individual day octopus changing colour and patterns 1,000 times in seven hours.

It is one of the largest octopus species, with tentacles 70 cm long.

Learn fab facts to go with the cool pictures.

The day octopus is sometimes called the big blue octopus.

Some colours allow 'false eye' spots to be seen in its pattern, near its tentacles.

TWISTS

BLUE WHALE
The world's largest ever creature, a blue whale eats about 4 tonnes of krill (a tiny shrimplike sea creature) every day.
Size: 25–30 m

THRESHER SHARK
A thresher shark can leap right out of the water. Its tail is often half the length of its body.
Size: 3–5 m

SEA LION
A California sea lion dives for up to five minutes, but can hunt non-stop for up to 30 hours.
Size: 1.6–2.2

Ripley explains....

Ripley explains some of the science and know-how from oceanic experts.

GOOD REEF

COOL CORALS

Coral reefs lie in the shimmering blue waters of coastal areas. They make up just one per cent of all ocean habitats, but these natural places are home to ...er cent of all marine animals and plants.

...ou may think of a coral reef as a rocky place underwater, but it is much more ...han that. Inside each reef there are ...llions of mini-builders called polyps. ...e soft-bodied animals build rocky cups ...nd their soft bodies. Over thousands ...rs, the cups create an enormous, ...structure — the reef itself — and this ...es a giant ecosystem where a huge ...y of living things exist together.

BIG WORD ALERT

ECOSYSTEM
This is a place, such as a rainforest or coral reef, and includes all the animals and plants that live in it and interact with each other.

STAGHORN CORAL

CORAL

STAR CORAL

BRAIN CORAL

...are many
...rent types of
..., and some of
... have names
... describe their
...earance perfectly!

FASCINATING FACT! FASCINATING FACT! FASCINATING FACT!

MUSHROOM CORAL

FAN CORAL

twist it!

Some types of coral can survive in deep, dark, and cold water. There may be more coldwater coral reefs than warm ones.

The most famous reef is the Great Barrier Reef in Australia's waters. It isn't actually just one reef, but a group of around 3,000 reefs and 1,000 small islands that spread over 2,000 km.

Most coral polyps are colonial animals, which means they live together in big groups. They don't always get on, and if there is not much space one polyp might lean over and kill its next-door neighbour!

REEF RICHES

The Coral Triangle is a huge area of sea around Indonesia and Malaysia with many coral islands and reefs. More than 3,000 types of fish live there.

Ripley's Believe It or Not!

Coral kids

These figures are part of an underwater sculpture museum created by a London artist named Jason de Caires Taylor. Jason's artwork is designed to encourage the growth of new corals.

15

Look for the Ripley 'R' to find out even more than you knew before!

These books are all about 'Believe It or Not!' — amazing facts, feats, and things that will make you go 'Wow!'

PELICAN

Pelicans can eat 1 kg of fish each day and can swallow a fish that is 0.5 m long.

Size: 1–1.8 m

LOBSTER

The biggest lobster ever caught was nearly 1.2 m long. It was caught in Nova Scotia, Canada, and was probably over 100 years old.

Size: up to 1 m

SEAHORSE

Seahorses need to eat nearly all the time to stay alive. They have no teeth and no stomach.

Size: 1.5–35 cm

WILD WIND AND WAVES

WORLD WEATHER

Ever wondered where weather comes from, and if the weather, wind, waves and warm air are all connected? The answer is yes! The world's weather is all down to the ways that the Sun, the Earth, its oceans and the atmosphere work together.

The way that ocean water can move closer to or farther away from a coastline is called a tide. Tides happen twice a day in most places and are caused by the way the Moon's gravity pulls on the Earth. In Nova Scotia, Canada, the difference between the ocean's depth at low tides and high tides can reach over 15 m – that's the height of eight men standing on top of one another!

Oceans are giant weather-makers and climate-shakers. They control the planet's atmosphere and temperature, and our seasons, winds and rains. Ocean water collects heat around the Equator, and moves it as far as the Poles – keeping most of the world warm enough for living things to exist. Warm wet air collects over the oceans as clouds and travels to land, where it falls as rain.

BIG WORD ALERT

ATMOSPHERE
The thick layer of gases, including the oxygen we breathe, that surrounds the Earth. The atmosphere plays a big part in the world's weather.

ALL AT SEA

- Waves are caused by wind moving the surface of the ocean. As they approach land, where the water gets shallow, waves move more slowly, but they can become taller.

- A wave at sea is called a swell and the largest ones ever measured reached over 30 m from their troughs (bottoms) to their crests (tops).

- Broken wave patterns might mean deadly rip currents. These currents can pull even the strongest swimmers out to sea, so never swim without an adult's supervision.

Icebergs are giant blocks of floating ice that form in the cold polar regions. Oil companies use boats and ropes to move them when they want to explore the seafloor below!

<< Spiral storm >>

Warm ocean water creates hurricanes by heating air. The warm air starts to swirl, creating winds that become giant storms. When they move onto land, hurricane winds, heavy rain, and a rapid rise in sea level (a storm surge) cause devastation in coastal areas. Hurricanes are also called tropical cyclones or typhoons in the western Pacific Ocean.

The middle of a hurricane is fairly calm and is called 'the eye'.

Ripley explains...

Cloud formation

Rain

Water vapour

Water runs back to the ocean

Ocean

THE WATER CYCLE

Oceans are a major part of the whole world's water system, which is called the global water cycle. Rainwater flows from land to the oceans, and when ocean water is heated it evaporates to form clouds.

OCEAN MOTION

OUT OF SIGHT

Beneath the gently slurping, swelling surface of the oceans, there is a whole other world waiting to be explored. Imagine you are about to dive all the way to the bottom of the sea...you're embarking on a perilous journey.

You travel through the light zones, where sunlight still reaches, and shoals of fish swim past. As you dive deeper, you notice the darkness, and the deathly cold and quiet around you. There are few signs of life. On the ocean floor, your feet sink into deep squashy mud and sludge.

BIG WORD ALERT

MARINE
This word is used to describe anything to do with seas and oceans.

Deep diver

William Trubridge is a top free-diver. In this extreme sport, people descend as far as they can below the surface of the sea on a single breath of air. In 2009, William reached a lung-crunching depth of 88 m.

Normal level

Water recedes

Tsunami hits

Tsunami power

These images show the movement of water during the 2004 Indian Ocean tsunami, at Kalutara in Sri Lanka. The top picture shows the normal level of the ocean. Then, just before the tsunami hit, the water pulled back from the shoreline, and then swirled across roads and houses. This tsunami killed over 200,000 people in 14 countries.

Upward wave

Crust

FAULT LINE

Mantle

The Earth's surface is broken into tectonic plates, which move all the time. When they move suddenly they can cause an earthquake, which pushes a surge of water (a tsunami) onto land. Tsunamis can wipe out entire towns and villages.

Where plates move against one another, mountains and volcanoes can form. The peak of Mauna Kea in Hawaii is the top of an underwater mountain, which is higher than Everest.

WATER WORLD

Rivers of water, called currents, flow within oceans. The global conveyor is an enormous system of currents that travels around all the oceans. It takes about 1,000 years for one part of seawater to move around the Earth.

Ocean water contains 'marine snow', which is made of bits of dead animals, plants and poo. Living things feed on marine snow, which floats down to the seabed at a rate of 200 m a day.

The strongest current in the world is in the Southern Ocean, between South America and Antarctica. Water flows here at an incredible rate of over 130,000 cubic metres per second.

Twist it!

Seawater is packed with minerals, including salts. Salt makes seawater very dense (see page 17). Just one bathtub of seawater contains about 2.8 kg of salt!

Small amounts of gold and copper are also found in the oceans.

Ocean water contains gases, such as oxygen and carbon dioxide, that have dissolved into it. Marine animals and plants need these gases to survive.

A helping flipper

Sea lions are so smart that the US Navy has trained them to do deep-diving. These sea lions and bombs. The underwater and bombs. The underwater mammals can learn how to spot mines and attach marine rescue lines to them, so they can be pulled to the surface.

GROW ZONE

As oceans are the world's biggest habitat it's no wonder they teem with life. There are more living things in ocean waters than anywhere else, and the biggest variety live near the surface.

The reasons for this are simple: in the top 200 m of water (known as the Sunlight Zone) there is light, warmth, and plenty of food – what more could anyone ask for? This region is like the farms or rainforests of the oceans, where food for ocean animals grows. Shallow areas around land are called coasts and they are particularly busy places.

BIG WORD ALERT

HABITAT
The place where a plant or animal naturally lives and grows.

Marvellous mussels!

Rivers flow into the coastal areas, bringing lots of fresh water and food, making these places especially good habitats. Some coastal plants and animals, such as these mussels, have to be able to survive underwater, when the tide is in, and in air when the tide goes out.

First swim of the day, lovely!

Played hide and seek in the water

Met up with the gang. More swimming...

A DAY IN THE LIFE...

Sea otters like to snooze in coastal kelp forests because the seaweed stops them from floating away in their sleep. These marine animals are smart – they lie on their backs and use stones to smash open crabs and shells they have balanced on their bellies!

A shellfish snack while swimming.

Coast

Ocean

Continental shelf

Continental slope

TAKING A DIP

The continental shelf is where land slopes gently into the sea. Light can pass through the water here, right down to the seabed. That's why shallow areas in the sea are called the Sunlight Zone.

Ripley's Believe It or Not!®

Little archer fish catch flying insects by spitting at them! When a stunned insect falls into the water, the smart fish gobbles it up.

GOTCHA!

Sea trees

In some warm places, mangrove trees grow along coasts to create mangrove swamps. Strangely, these trees don't mind salty seawater and they make unique habitats. More than half the world's mangrove swamps have been destroyed in recent times, to make room for fish and shrimp farms.

FEELING WEEDY

Seaweeds are not like other plants – they're slimy! The slime stops other animals from settling on them, and keeps them from drying out at low tide.

Tiny animals and plants, called plankton, drift along in the ocean's Sunlight Zone. They are the food of many other animals. A large whale can eat nearly 2,300 kg of plankton in a day.

We use seaweed as food and to make medicines, cosmetics (make-up), paint, glue and paper.

Brown seaweeds are called kelp and they used to be burned to make soap. Kelp can grow as enormous underwater forests and some types can grow 30–60 cm a day.

twist it!

COASTAL CROCS

Gharials are slender-jawed relatives of crocodiles. They live in coastal waters around India, but they will probably be extinct in the wild soon. There are only about 200 left.

ANIMALS IN ARMOUR

SAFETY SUITS

If you've got a soft, spongy body, what's the best way to protect yourself from predators? Many small marine animals have got the perfect answer – they wear armour. This armour is like a super-strong skin and it's packed with tough minerals that make it hard. A crustacean's armour is called a carapace, but molluscs grow shells.

Sea urchins and starfish hide their armour under a thin layer of colourful skin. They have skeletons made up of interlocking plates of calcium – the strong mineral that's in our bones and teeth. The animals in this group have their mouth on their bottom and tiny suckers called feet!

COCONUT SHY

This veined octopus doesn't grow tough armour, so he made his own out of a coconut shell. He can close the shell when he wants to hide, but when it's time to make a quick getaway he grabs it with his eight tentacles, and runs for it!

Japanese giant

This colossal crustacean's Japanese name means 'tall-leg'. No prizes for guessing why! The largest Japanese spider crab ever recorded measured an enormous 3.7 m from the tip of one leg to another. And some fishermen swear they've seen crabs that are nearly double that size!

ARMY OF ARMS

Three five-armed starfish devour a dead fish. Like heavily armoured tanks, the animals can munch away, protected from predators by their tough outer skins.

CRAB RACING

Meet the elite sports stars of the crab world. These hermit crabs have undergone thorough fitness training to reach their peak, and are primed and ready to race. These little athletes compete for the National Crab Racing Association, based in Florida, and after six months they retire in style, to spend their remaining days in the lap of luxury as pampered pets.

Watch out!

Sea urchins don't have eyes, which might be why this little guy didn't spot the giant sea snail approaching! Sea urchins have spiky spines, but they are still no match for this mighty mollusc.

SO SHELLFISH

Scaly-foot snails have ultra-tough armour. Their shells are so strong that scientists are studying them to find out how to make better armour for soldiers and vehicles. The secret lies in the snails' three-layer shells, which are strengthened with iron.

When Paul Westlake lost his wallet in the ocean, he thought he'd seen the last of it. A few days later, however, a deep-sea diver found the missing wallet in the clutches of a large lobster!

Razor clams can dig themselves into the seabed at a super-speedy rate of 2.5 cm every second. Scientists have copied their technique, and built a digging robot called RoboClam.

13

GOOD REEF

COOL CORALS

Coral reefs lie in the shimmering blue waters of coastal areas. They make up just one per cent of all ocean habitats, but these natural places are home to 25 per cent of all marine animals and plants.

You may think of a coral reef as a rocky place underwater, but it is much more than that. Inside each reef there are millions of mini-builders called polyps. These soft-bodied animals build rocky cups around their soft bodies. Over thousands of years, the cups create an enormous, solid structure – the reef itself – and this becomes a giant ecosystem where a huge variety of living things exist together.

BIG WORD ALERT

ECOSYSTEM
This is a place, such as a rainforest or coral reef, and includes all the animals and plants that live in it and interact with each other.

STAR CORAL

FINGER CORAL

BRAIN CORAL

There are many different types of coral, and some of them have names that describe their appearance perfectly!

STAGHORN CORAL

twist it!

REEF RICHES

The Coral Triangle is a huge area of sea around Indonesia and Malaysia with many coral islands and reefs. More than 3,000 types of fish live there.

Most coral polyps are colonial animals, which means they live together in big groups. They don't always get on, and if there is not much space one polyp might lean over and kill its next-door neighbour!

The most famous reef is the Great Barrier Reef in Australia's waters. It isn't actually just one reef, but a group of around 3,000 reefs and 1,000 small islands that spread over 2,000 km.

Some types of coral can survive in deep, dark, and cold water. There may be more coldwater coral reefs than warm ones.

FAN CORAL

MUSHROOM CORAL

Ripley's Believe It or Not!®

Coral kids

These figures are part of an underwater sculpture museum created by a London artist named Jason de Caires Taylor. Jason's artwork is designed to encourage the growth of new corals.

15

SUPERSIZE SEA

BIG IT UP

Enormous eye

The colossal squid of the Southern Ocean has the biggest eyes of any living animal. Each eyeball can measure nearly 25 cm across and — no surprises here — it has fantastic eyesight, even though it can't see anything in colour.

In 2007, fishermen in the Antarctic seas caught a colossal squid that was 10 m long and weighed over 450 kg. That's more than twice the weight of a large male gorilla.

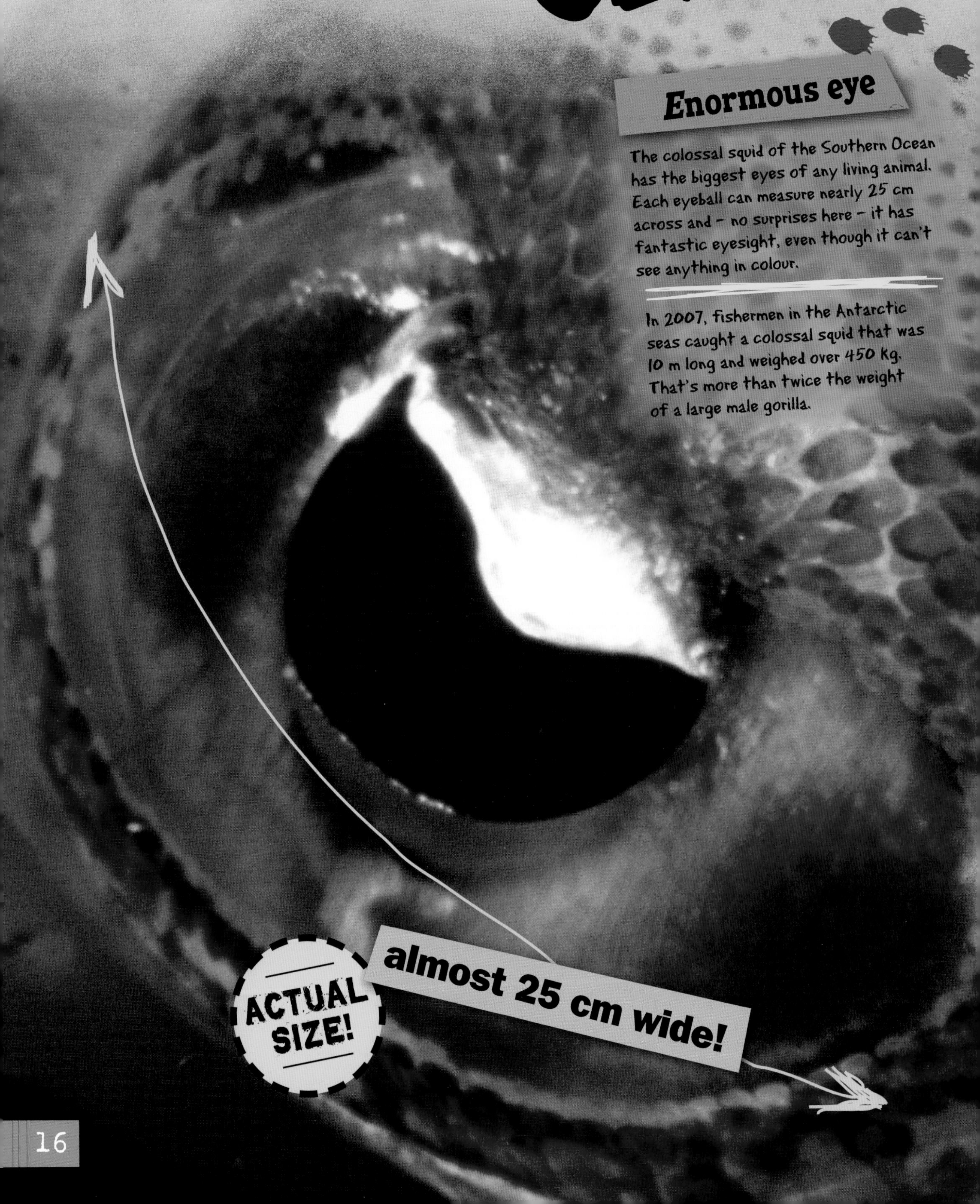

ACTUAL SIZE!

almost 25 cm wide!

When it comes to surviving undersea, size really matters. Being big has one major advantage – it's much harder for other things to catch and eat you!

Seawater is denser than freshwater, or air. That means the particles, or molecules, inside it are packed tightly together, and can hold up objects in it. That's why we can float quite easily in seawater. Things feel lighter in seawater than they do in air, because the water pushes up underneath them and supports their weight. That means ocean animals can grow much bigger than those on land. Floating in seawater may be easy, but moving through it takes lots of energy. So, marine monsters often travel with ocean currents.

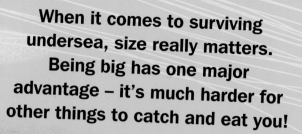

Ripley's Believe It or Not!®

Mega yuck!

The oceans are full of worms that burrow into the seafloor, or live inside another animal. The longest in the world are boot-lace worms, which live in the North Sea. They can grow to 30 m long!

Giant clam

Giant clams can measure more than 1 m across. They live around coral reefs and get food from the water, or from tiny algae that live on the edges of their shells. It is thought they can live to 100 years of age, or even longer.

BIG BLUE BABY

A blue whale calf is one-and-a-half times the length of an average-sized car when it is born. Blue whales are the world's largest animals, so it's no wonder they have big bouncing babies! They weigh up to 3 tonnes at birth: that's the same as 882 human newborns. Once born, the baby (which is known as a calf) drinks over 200 litres of its mother's milk every day.

Blue whales produce monster-sized pink poo! Each poo is about 25 cm wide and several metres long! The strange colour comes from krill, the little shrimp-like animals the whales eat.

FASCINATING FACT! FASCINATING FACT! FASCINATING FACT!

17

What's in a name?

Some fish get their names from the way they look. Would you kiss one of these – even if it was called 'sweetlips'?

ANGEL FISH

HARLEQUIN SWEETLIPS

MASKED BUTTERFLY FISH

SOMETHING FISHY

MASTERS*OF THE SEA**

Fish have been around for a very long time: more than 500 million years! The oceans and seas are now home to zillions of them, and there are more fish in the world than any other type of vertebrate.

Fish are the masters of the sea, but what's the secret to their success? Being able to breathe underwater has got to be one big advantage! A backbone helps, too – it gives an animal something to build its muscles and organs around, and connects the brain to all the other body bits. Fish were the first creatures on Earth to develop a backbone, and it was so successful that all of us other vertebrates then copied this brilliant design.

BIG WORD ALERT

VERTEBRATE
An animal with a backbone. Fish, birds, reptiles, amphibians and mammals are vertebrates.

School meals

The super-talented sailfish has an amazing way of dining out. Several of smaller fish, like sardines or anchovies, into a 'baitball', and then use their high fins to create a wall to stop their prey from escaping.

PARROT FISH

PINEAPPLE FISH

TRUMPETFISH

Ripley's Believe It or Not!®

FAT FISH

The small fish at the top is an aptly named 'great swallower' fish. It was found in the Cayman Islands having somehow eaten a snake mackerel five times bigger!

A fish's body is suited for life underwater. That usually means a body shape that is streamlined (the best shape for swimming), with fins and tails.

Clowning around

All fish, including these clownfish, can breathe because they have special organs called gills, which take dissolved oxygen out of the water.

TOO COOL FOR SCHOOL

A group of fish is called a school or shoal. Millions of herrings get together to make giant, swarming shoals when it is time to spawn (lay their eggs). It's often safer to travel in a group!

Orange roughies don't look remarkable, but these deep-sea swimmers have been known to live to well over 100 years old — making them one of the longest-lived of all fish.

A group of eels is called a seething, a group of herrings is called an army, and a group of sharks is called a shiver.

Many fish have swim bladders that stop them from sinking. When gas goes into a swim bladder, the fish can move up in the water; when gas passes out of it, the fish can sink deeper.

TWIST IT!

19

FAST, FURIOUS, FREAKY

BIODIVERSITY RULES OK

From flesh-sucking lampreys to four-eyed ghostly spookfish, there is an enormous range of fish in our oceans.

There are fish to suit almost every habitat, from rock pools at the seaside to the dark depths, and every way of life. There are hiders and fighters, swimmers and flyers, flat fish and fat fish, angry fish and clown fish – there are even fish with giant fangs, enormous mouths, or poisonous spines. There are also some frankly weird fish out there, too.

Fast!

What a sucker!

This lovely lamprey is like a long, bendy hosepipe, with a scrubbing brush at the end. It attaches itself to its prey with a sucker-mouth while rows of tiny rasping teeth scrape away at the flesh. This hungry fella then sucks it up, with a side order of oozing blood. Yum!

Hey, suckers!

WATCH OUT!

Barracudas are big (up to 2 m in length) and they are smart. They chase their prey into shallow water and start to feed. Once they are full, the barracudas save the rest for later. They work together to guard their prey and stop them escaping!

Eating barracudas is a risky business, because they eat fish that feed on poisonous algae. If you feast on an affected fish you could suffer deadly food poisoning.

WHO YOU LOOKING AT?

Male garibaldis are furious little fish, with bad tempers. They grind their teeth and have been known to attack divers! If there are too many males in a group, some of them change into females.

Furious!

WEIRD AND WONDERFUL

Titan triggerfish don't like people one bit. These large fish attack divers and have a poisonous bite. They've even walloped divers so hard they've passed out!

Tuna fish never stop swimming. They keep moving at a rate of around 6 km an hour for their entire lives. A 15-year-old tuna has probably swum about 800,000 km!

When a female jawfish has laid her eggs, she scoots off and leaves the dad to take over. He keeps them in his mouth until they are ready to hatch.

Baby halibut look perfectly normal, but they morph into freaky flatfish as they grow. One eye moves across its head and joins the other one on the right-hand side, which becomes the top. The mouth twists round to the fish's left side, which turns into its underbelly.

Twist it!

MR BLOBBY

Meet the blobfish: blob by name and slob by nature! These soft and squidgy creatures live in the deep waters around Australia, and they like a lazy life. Females sit on the ocean floor when protecting their eggs, but the rest of the time blobfish hover just above the seabed, mooching around and waiting for lunch to pass by.

Freaky!

Ripley's Believe It or Not!®

Up, up, and away!

Flying fish escape predators by leaping out of the water and gliding just above the waves. They can travel through the air for up to 40 seconds and cover around 45 m.

MEGAMOUTHS

SHARK ATTACK!

Of all the world's creatures, sharks are among the most feared. Their incredible speed, cold black eyes and rows of killer teeth set in enormous jaws have these sleek swimmers marked out as terrifying predators.

SOME-FIN SPECIAL

The megamouth is really a type of shark. It has a huge mouth, but eats tiny creatures such as plankton and jellyfish.

The smallest sharks are dwarf lantern sharks, which are usually around 15 cm long.

A shark's body is covered in teeth rather than scales! Denticles are growths from the skin that are made of enamel (the same hard substance that's in teeth).

Tiger sharks eat almost anything: fish, squid, sea snakes, seals, birds and stingrays...they have also been found with old tyres, rubbish, and car licence plates in their stomach!

twist it!

Ripley explains...

Sharks usually have dark backs. This camouflages them against the dark water when seen from above. They are pale underneath, which helps them to remain invisible when viewed from below, against a pale sky. The same type of colouring is used in fighter planes.

Whale shark

Whale sharks are the largest fish in the world and can grow to over 12 m long. They feed on tiny animals by opening their enormous mouth and sucking in water and food. This means that, if one swims near you, it's safe to stop and enjoy the view! In fact, as far as most sharks are concerned, you wouldn't make good grub. Nearly all sharks have no interest in attacking and eating humans.

We may fear sharks, but the truth is we know very little about them. There could be more than 500 different types of shark, with many of those still waiting to be discovered in the depths of the ocean. Lots of sharks are hunters, but the largest ones actually feed on shoals of tiny krill and other small animals. While some lay eggs, a few sharks are able to give birth to live young.

TOP 3 SURVIVAL TIPS

Fight back: punch the shark on the snout — hard!

Stick your fingers in its eyes and gills.

Get out of the water!

Sharks, skates and rays don't have bones — their skeletons are made of cartilage instead. Cartilage is more flexible than bone, and it's the same stuff that makes your nose and ears stiff.

Ripley's Believe It or Not!®

Life saver

Free diver Craig Clasen had to wrestle with a 3.6-m tiger shark to save the life of his friend Ryan. An experienced diver, he recognised that the shark was hungry and dangerous. It took him two hours to fight off the shark, and he even tried to drown it.

Great white shark

- Baby great whites measure about 1.5 m when they're born.
- A baby must leave its mother straightaway or it might get eaten!
- An adult can swim up to 40 km/h.
- Great white sharks can vomit up their entire stomach. It's a good way to clear out rubbish and bones and avoid an upset tummy!

23

WATER WINGS

BIRDBRAINS

Some birds swoop and soar over the oceans for months at a time. Others prefer to paddle at the seaside, pecking at tasty worms and shellfish. Penguins, however, are supreme marine birds – they are so well suited to ocean life that they have even lost the power of flight, and use their wings like flippers instead.

BLUE SHOES

This little fella is a little blue penguin called Elvis – and he's got blue shoes! He lives at the International Antarctic Centre in Christchurch, New Zealand, with several of his friends, who all wear shoes to protect their feet. They have developed sore feet after standing around much more than they would do in the wild, where they swim almost constantly.

SUN SUIT

Pierre the African penguin has his own wet suit! His friends at the California Academy of Sciences in San Francisco gradually lose their feathers to grow shiny new ones, but Pierre loses so many that he needs his suit to keep him warm, and to stop him from getting sunburn.

Watch the birdie

Marine birds have bodies suited for swimming and diving. Many have webbed feet, waterproof feathers and special glands that help them deal with salt. Some birds fly over water, diving into the oceans to grab food. Others live on the coasts and feed on animals living in muddy seashores.

Male blue-footed boobies strut around in front of females, showing off their lovely webbed toes. The brighter the blue, the more the females are impressed!

Common guillemots lay eggs with very pointed ends. This shape stops the eggs from rolling off the cliff edges where the birds nest.

Herring gulls can be aggressive, and have been known to attack people and dogs.

BLUE-FOOTED BOOBIE

COMMON GUILLEMOT

HERRING GULL

The oceans contain fish, so it's no wonder that birds have adapted to be able to pluck these protein-packed snacks out of the salty water. No birds, however, have been able to become totally marine animals, because they all have to return to land to lay their eggs.

Big bird

MASSIVE WINGSPAN — AS LONG AS A SMALL CAR.......WOW!

Wandering albatrosses have the biggest wingspan of any bird: 3.5 m — that's longer than two adult bikes! They live at sea, snatching squid from the water, and can fly for several weeks at a time without ever landing.

CATCH A WAVE

Surfing is a real action sport, and it's even better when you don't need a board! Gentoo penguins in the Falkland Islands know just where to go to get the best waves, and surf barefoot into shore. They even swim back out again to have another turn!

Pelicans have enormous throat pouches, which they use to scoop up water: as much as 13 litres at a time. They tip their head back to drain out the water, and gobble up any fish.

Puffins are sometimes called sea parrots, because of their startling appearance. They spend most of their time at sea, occasionally diving to grab small fish.

Skuas have gross eating habits. They chase other sea birds and scare them into vomiting up their food – which the skuas then gobble up!

PUFFIN

SKUA

PELICAN

Ripley's **Believe It or Not!**

MARINE MAMMALS

ALL AT SEA

When life on land got too tough, some mammals headed back to the water. Whales, dolphins, seals, walruses and dugongs are all descended from land-living beasts that decided, millions of years ago, that swimming is more fun than walking!

This devotion to the ocean was handy, because it meant marine mammals were able to escape from their predators, and find new sources of food: fish, krill or seagrass. There were some major downsides though – they still had to breathe air, and life in water required new body shapes, less fur, and better ways to keep warm in the icy depths.

Polar bears

Polar bears have super-sensitive hearing and can detect seals swimming below ice that is 1 m thick! Their sense of smell is impressive, too – these giant bears can sniff rotting meat 5 km away. They dive into the water and bear-paddle their way to find lunch. They can swim for 100 km without stopping!

KEY FACTS

- All marine mammals breathe air, but they have evolved (changed over time) to spend a long time underwater before needing to breathe again.

- Whales, dolphins and porpoises belong to a group of mammals called cetaceans (say: set-aysh-uns). They give birth underwater and usually have just one baby at a time.

- The skeletons of marine mammals show they are descended from land-living animals that had four limbs.

Walrus

Male walruses can grow enormous teeth (called tusks) of 50 cm or more. They use the tusks to pull themselves up onto slabs of ice and as lethal weapons when they fight one another.

Marine mammals may not be covered in fur, but they do have some sprouts of hair, such as whiskers. Young marine mammals usually have more hair than adults.

DOLPHINS

Dolphins play bubble hoopla! These clever creatures can create bubbles with air from their blowhole and swim through them. They like to make different shapes and sizes, just for fun!

Swimmers are sometimes surprised to find themselves surrounded by dolphins slapping their tails and circling. The dolphins aren't just being friendly – they are keeping prowling sharks away. No one knows why dolphins protect humans in this way.

twist it!

A blue whale's tongue weighs as much as a whole elephant!

Beluga whales are called sea canaries because they sing so sweetly.

Cetaceans are smart and can talk to each other. Humpback whales make the longest, most complicated sounds of any animal. They sing by forcing air through their nose.

Cetaceans and seals swim with their muscular tail, while sea lions use their front flippers.

IN THE SWIM

Elephant seals

Elephant seals can dive to depths of 10,000 m and can wait for two hours between breaths. Their heart beats very slowly when they dive, to save energy.

BIG WORD ALERT

MAMMAL
These animals have hair or fur and give birth to live young, which they feed with their own milk.

LOOK AT ME

There's an underwater beauty parade of animals that like to razzle, dazzle, dance and display. Animals living in the Sunlight Zone (see page 10) get the full benefit of being in the spotlight, so they are more likely to show off with extraordinary colours and patterns than those who live in deeper, darker water. Light rays dance off their shimmering scales, patterned skins and coloured shells – what a sight!

Attention-seekers use their good looks to impress mates, or to warn predators to stay away. The shy and retiring types prefer to dress down and use colours and patterns to hide in dappled, shallow waters.

Harlequin shrimp

Some shrimps can change colour to blend in with their surroundings, but harlequin shrimps are already perfec. Their brightly coloured patches may not look like an ideal type of camouflage, but when they are hidden i. the shadows, the patterns help disguise the shrimp's outline. The harlequin shrimps then emerge to attac. starfish, which they catch and eat alive, arm by arr.

Mandarin fish are among the most beautiful of all reef fish, but their glorious neon colours aren't there to impress. They warn potential predators of a foul-tasting slime that covers the fish's body.

MANDARIN FISH

Seafood salad

What would you call a crab that looks like a strawberry? A strawberry crab, of course! This tasty-looking fella has only been recently discovered, off the coast of Taiwan. Scientists are trying to find out why a crab would want to look like a strawberry. If they can find others that look like grapes, bananas and oranges they plan to make a delicious crab fruit salad!

Ripley's Believe It or Not!®

CANDY FLATWORM

Some sea creatures like bold and brash looks, while others prefer the delicate and dainty approach. Candy flatworms hide their gentle beauty under rocks, until it's time to brave the waters and seek food. They glide smoothly along the seabed, or swim just above it.

Isn't this jellyfish gorgeous, with its lovely floaty body, pretty colour and little spots? At night these mauve stingers become even more attractive, because their bodies pulse with light as they are carried along by the currents. They may be good-looking, but these are jellyfish you wouldn't want to bump into – they are covered in stinging cells!

Colour is created by pigments, which are in the outer layer of the animal's body. This outer layer may be skin, scales or tough shells. Some deep-sea marine animals have colourful bacteria on their skin, or bacteria that produce light, for an extra-special spectacle.

I can't believe you're wearing the same as me tonight!

Dragon moray eels may have splendid colours, stripes and spots, but they like to keep their beauty well hidden. They lurk in the shadows, and come out only at night.

BIG WORD ALERT

CAMOUFLAGE
The way an animal uses colour and patterns to hide.

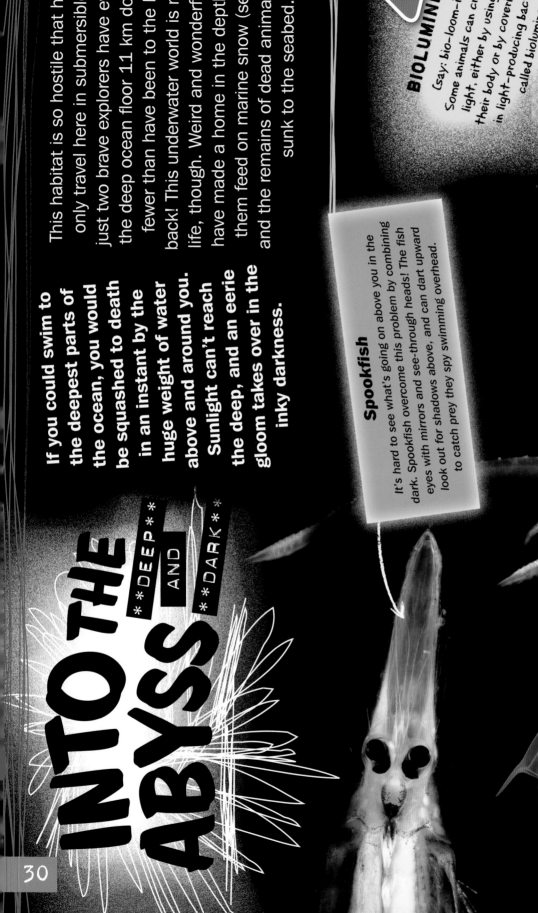

INTO THE ABYSS
DEEP AND **DARK**

If you could swim to the deepest parts of the ocean, you would be squashed to death in an instant by the huge weight of water above and around you. Sunlight can't reach the deep, and an eerie gloom takes over in the inky darkness.

This habitat is so hostile that humans can only travel here in submersibles. So far, just two brave explorers have ever reached the deep ocean floor 11 km down – that's fewer than have been to the Moon and back! This underwater world is not empty of life, though. Weird and wonderful creatures have made a home in the depths. Many of them feed on marine snow (see page 9) and the remains of dead animals that have sunk to the seabed.

BIG WORD ALERT

BIOLUMINESCENCE
(say: bio-loom-in-ess-ence)
Some animals can create their own light, either by using chemicals in their body or by covering themselves in light-producing bacteria. This is called bioluminescence.

Ooh, what big eyes you have... all the better to see you with!

Spookfish
It's hard to see what's going on above you in the dark. Spookfish overcome this problem by combining see-through heads! The fish eyes with mirrors and see-through eyes with mirrors and see-through eyes with mirrors and can dart upward look out for shadows above, and can dart upward to catch prey they spy swimming overhead.

Red shrimp
Most deep-sea animals cannot see the colour red, so this shrimp is actually invisible to them!

Colossal squid are so big their eyes are as large as dinner plates (see page 16). Big eyes are handy in the Twilight Zone, where a little light still reaches.

Ugly hagfish are covered in slime that sometimes gets up their nose and makes them sneeze! To stop this happening, they tie a knot in their own body and force the body downward, squeezing the slime away!

Hot water gushes out of the ocean floor in some places, and living things thrive in the warmth. These hydrothermal vents are home to giant tube worms nearly 2 m long.

Sperm whales have ribs that fold and collapse when they dive. Their lungs scrunch up, too. They can store oxygen in their muscles for more than 30 minutes and can swim to depths of more than 1,500 m.

Comb jelly

Comb jellies are covered in rows of tiny hairs called cilia. When their cilia move, they shimmer with bright colours. They trap their prey with sticky slime on their tentacles.

twist it!

A bit of wind helps a cockatoo squid to float. They use gas-filled organs to move up and swim and down.

Cockatoo squid

The curious-looking cockatoo squid swims with its tentacles delicately arranged above its head — it's a good look!

Anglerfish

An anglerfish hides its dark body in the deep, but suspends a tantalising lure in front of its head. The lure lights up, attracting prey towards the angler's snapping jaws.

HUNT HIDE OR

FEEDING **TIME**

HIDE

Food is energy – energy to grow, move, mate and have young, and to eat even more food! Marine animals, just like those on land, have to spend lots of their time finding food. They also have to try their best not to become someone else's meal!

Animals that hunt others are called predators. They mostly need strength, speed and great senses to find food. The lunch-bunch that get eaten are called prey, and their job is to hide, fight back, or fool predators into thinking they are something else completely. These crafty creatures have got some clever strategies up their sleeves!

Power puff

When a porcupine fish is scared, it hides in caves. If there's nowhere to hide, it fills its body up with water and swells to the size of a prickly football.

HIDE

Wolf fish

This ferocious-looking fish is called a wolf fish, because of its dog-like teeth. It lurks in dark corners and emerges only when it is hungry. Wolf fish like to exercise their jaws on crunchy shellfish, crabs and sea urchins. Every year they grow new teeth to replace the ones destroyed by all that munching.

HUNT

Leaf me alone

Leafy seadragons are masters of disguise. These freaky-looking fish have frills that fool other animals into thinking they are seaweed. They move slowly, sucking prey into their straw-like mouths.

PICK UP A PENGUIN

Look who's come for tea! A killer whale has dropped by for a feast: a tasty penguin snack! These mighty mammals can flip blocks of ice over, so penguins and seals are caught unawares and fall off!

32

twist it!

Sargassum fish look just like seaweed. They lie in wait for crustaceans and small fish, although they have been known to eat fish as big as themselves!

Peculiar-looking cuttlefish can create flashes of colour to dazzle their predators, or change colour to blend in with their surroundings. If all that fails, these molluscs can disappear in a cloud of ink.

A saltwater crocodile can swim far out to sea. It grabs its prey with teeth that grow up to 13 cm long, and holds it underwater until it drowns.

HIDE AND SEEK

Shoals of mackerel fish dart, twist and turn together in a group. Their scales reflect light so that confused predators can't pick out a victim among the swirling, twinkling bodies.

Ripley's —— Believe It or Not!®

Fighting friends

Boxer crabs are the ocean's tough guys with a secret weapon that keeps them safe from predators: poisonous boxing gloves! These smart crustaceans grab hold of sea anemones in their claws and wave them around threateningly. Sea anemones have nasty stings, so predators keep clear of their tentacles. The sea anemones benefit from this strange friendship, too: crabs are such messy eaters they can collect crumbs and other bits of debris that fall out of the crab's mouth!

HIDE

Razor sharp

Razorfish swim in groups, upside down, with their heads pointing toward the seafloor. They look more like plants than predators.

Killer whales have teeth that are up to 10 cm long.

HUNT

Killer whales are smart. They hunt in family groups and can talk to one another in high-pitched sounds.

33

TOXIC SHOCK

A single taste of vile venom could be enough to kill you. Venom is poison that many animals have inside their body. It's a handy weapon in the fight to stay alive, but only if potential predators know you're carrying it around.

That's why many venomous animals like to advertise their highly toxic state with strong signals. Bright and bold colours, patterns and spines all tell predators to keep a safe distance. Some predators, however, use venom to kill their prey. They like to keep their weapon of fast destruction under wraps until the last moment…

DEADLY ANEMONE

Sea anemones are related to jellyfish and, like their swimming cousins, they have stinging tentacles that contain venom. The venom is mostly used to stun or kill prey, but these animals also sting in self-defence.

POISON EATERS

Smart **sea slugs**, called nudibranchs, get their venom from the food they eat. They munch on poisonous corals, sponges and sea anemones, and keep the venom or stings for themselves. Sea slugs wear bright colours to advertise their toxic skin.

STONY GROUND

Watch where you put your foot if you paddle in the warm clear waters of Southeast Asia. **Stonefish** lurk, hidden from view, on the seabed. They have venomous spines on their dorsal fins and they are the world's deadliest venomous fish.

TOXINS

Toxins, like poisons or venoms, are harmful. Something that contains toxins is described as toxic.

VENOMOUS SNAKE

A **beaked sea snake** is twice as deadly as any land snakes and has enough venom to kill 50 people. These swimming slitherers live in shallow water and are camouflaged, so humans often disturb them by accident.

GROUP OF KILLERS

A **Portuguese man o' war** may look like just one animal, but actually it's a whole colony of tiny stinging creatures that hang beneath a gas-filled balloon.

ROAR!

Don't ever square up to a **lionfish**. These brave animals have been known to attack humans, although they usually hunt small fish at night. One smack with a venomous spine is enough to stun the prey, so the lionfish can devour it.

SMART MOVES

Seawater is 830 times denser than air, and that makes moving through it quite an achievement. It's an effort that's worth making, though, as swimmers can go to new ocean locations, in search of food and mates.

Swimmers need lots of energy to get anywhere, which is why lots of marine animals just hang about instead! Many sea creatures are able to float in the ocean, or move up and down by controlling the amount of gas in their body. Others just go with the flow, and allow the sea currents to carry them to new places.

Slow motion

Maned seahorses are named after their lion-like mane of spines, but these fish don't have the big cat's speed. Seahorses have so little muscle power that they can scarcely swim at all and have to wrap their tail around seaweed, to stop any small current from carrying them away.

BIG WORD ALERT

DENSITY

The way that particles are packed inside a substance is called its density, and it is similar to weight. Water is denser, and heavier, than air.

The world's largest movement of animals (a migration) happens twice a day, every day, in the oceans. Under the cover of darkness, billions and billions of plankton swim up to the Sunlight Zone to feast on the tiny plants that grow there. When the sun rises, they swim back down to the Twilight or Dark Zones, and hide from predators.

Hold on!

Every year, thousands of spiny lobsters grab hold of their friends in front to make one enormous line of marching crustaceans on the seabed. Each winter they migrate to deeper water — which is warmer and calmer than the shallow water near the shore at this time — to lay their eggs.

Sailfish can grow to 3.4 metres long.

Sailfish are the fastest swimmers in the world.

They eat squid, octopus, and smaller fish such as sardines and anchovies.

They reach speeds of 109 km/h.

twist it!

WHAT A DRAG!

When an animal moves through water, the water particles push against it. This is called drag, and it slows movement right down.

Most sharks are slow swimmers, but the ferocious mako shark reaches top speeds of 88 km/h.

Leatherback turtles are amazing long-distance swimmers. Using satellite-tracking systems, scientists discovered that one turtle had swum 20,557 km in a single migration!

Coconuts that fall in the sea can travel thousands of kilometres before coming to shore, where they might grow into new palm trees.

Deep sea lantern fish swim more than 1 km every night in a journey to the Sunlight Zone and back. That's like us running one-and-a-half marathons!

MOVE IT

SPEED LIMITS

Killer whale
55 km/h

These enormous mammals can chase and kill animals even bigger than themselves.

California sea lion
40 km/h

Fish swim fast, so sea lions need to be speedy to keep up with their lunch.

Gentoo penguins
36 km/h

These birds almost fly underwater in short bursts when they are chasing their fishy prey.

MARINE MYSTERIES

Sailors, fishermen, swimmers and explorers have all had good reason to fear the deep oceans. Far beneath the twinkling, rippling surface there could be all sorts of dangers, demons or monsters lurking!

For thousands of years, people have reported spooky sounds, unexplained shipwrecks and unrecognisable giant beasts at sea. Until recent times, it has been almost impossible to explore the underwater world, so people made up stories to explain any strange phenomena they encountered. There are usually good explanations for marine mysteries, but this huge habitat still holds many secrets.

MERMAIDS

The myth of mermaids has existed for thousands of years. Even the great explorer Christopher Columbus believed he had seen several of them during his voyages. A mermaid is said to have the upper body of a woman, and the lower body of a fish. It's possible that this myth arose after people saw marine mammals, such as dugongs and manatees, from a distance.

HOAX

Dr J Griffin pretended he got this small 'mermaid' from Japanese fishermen when he brought it to New York in 1842. Crowds of curious visitors paid 25 cents each to see the marvel. Is it real or a fake?

UNSOLVED

INVESTIGATOR'S REPORT
Date: April 1918

Despite extensive searches, we are unable to find any sign of the USS Cyclops. This US Navy boat was lost at sea last month in a region known as the Bermuda Triangle, where other craft have mysteriously disappeared.

LOSSES: The whole crew (309 souls) is presumed lost at sea.

CAUSE: We are unable to establish cause of the disappearance of the ship. There is no wreckage and no distress signals were made.

CONCLUSION: The ship may have been bombed by wartime enemies, or sunk during a storm. However, there is no evidence to support either conclusion.

INVESTIGATOR'S REPORT
Date: January 1948

A Douglas DC-3 aircraft disappeared en route from Puerto Rico to Miami, passing through the Bermuda Triangle.

LOSSES: All 32 people on board are missing, presumed dead.

CAUSE: With no wreckage, and no survivors, it is impossible to say what caused the disappearance of the aircraft.

CONCLUSION: The pilot may not have received radio messages about a change in wind direction, causing him to get lost. Maybe he landed somewhere else safely? We will have to wait and see...

BIG
WORD ALERT

CRYPTOZOOLOGIST
(say: krip-toe-zoo-olo-jist)
People who study stories of mysterious animals, such as krakens (huge mythical sea monsters), and hope to find the truth behind the tales.

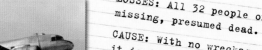

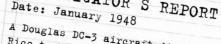

BLISTERING BARNACLES!

Something resembling a giant tentacled sea worm, nearly 2 m in length, alarmed locals when it washed ashore in Wales, UK, in 2009. Was it a mysterious marine monster that had been thrown up from the depths?

No, it actually turned out to be an unusually large colony of goose barnacles attached to an old ship's mast.

SEA MONSTER

The following excerpt is taken from the diary of Jim Harris, a cabin boy on board HMS *Poseidon* in 1827. Does it prove the existence of sea monsters?

"Today we survived a most fearsome attack. The waves were billowing and the ship was pitching from side to side, when the Captain called all hands to deck. What a sight met our sorry eyes! A giant beast, the like of which I've never seen before, had grasped our vessel in its enormous tentacles, and threw us about like a leaf on a pond. We thought we were all done for. Suddenly, the heavens opened and a sheet of lightning ripped through the sky. The monster, which was most surely a kraken, took fright and fell beneath the waves. The Captain called us altogether for prayers of thanksgiving, but I'm too frightened to sleep tonight."

49

Ones to watch

Kraken (noun, mythological)
Said to be enormous sea monsters that resemble squid or octopuses and live in the seas near Norway and Iceland

Longman's beaked whale (noun)
Regarded as the world's most mysterious whale – until recently, no living ones had ever been seen, and scientists only knew they existed because two skulls had been found

bloop (noun)
Noise made by an unknown marine animal, first recorded underwater in 1997; no one has ever discovered what made them

globster (noun)
Dead body of an unidentified monster-like animal washed up on the shore; most globsters are big, jelly-like lumps and some are said to have shaggy hair

Red Devils (noun)
Once believed to be evil sea monsters by Mexican fishermen; have since been shown to be jumbo squid that dart through the water at lightning speed, and instantly change colour from white to red when chased

39

DEEP-SEA EXPLORERS

THAT SINKING FEELING

For many explorers, the deep oceans present the world's last – and greatest – challenge. Every year, more people scale Mount Everest than climb into submarines to descend into the Abyss (see page 30).

Braving the depths is tough. Divers and explorers have to overcome a lack of oxygen, cold currents, and the weight of water bearing down on them. Anyone wanting to go beyond a few hundred metres down needs to climb aboard an underwater vessel. It's a dangerous journey, but one that is rewarded by sights of incredible creatures. Are you ready to take the plunge?

In the 1940s, French diver Jacques Cousteau invented a way that divers could carry compressed air, in tanks on their backs. The system is known as SCUBA: Self-Contained Underwater Breathing Apparatus.

DEEP THOUGHTS

Musician Katie Melua has played at 300 m below sea level with a band, on a platform oil rig in the North Sea.

The first diving suits were used in the 1830s. They were made of watertight rubber and canvas. Air was pumped from a boat above, through long tubes that were connected to the diver's metal helmet.

Robotic submersibles can explore the deep without putting any humans in danger. They are called Remotely Operated Vehicles, or ROVs for short.

The greatest undersea journey took place in 1960, when two explorers dived to 10,911 m in a submersible called the *Trieste*. It took them five hours to reach the bottom of the Mariana Trench in the Pacific Ocean.

The deepest any scuba diver has been able to go is 318 m.

SUPERSUB!

Are you looking for an all-round vehicle with an extra thrill factor? Try the Dolphin and Seabreacher subs designed by Innespace of the USA. The fully enclosed vehicles can dive, jump and roll, and travel over 60 km/h on the surface and 30 km/h underwater.

People first began to explore the ocean depths just 200 years ago. They mostly went in search of valuable cargo, such as gold, which had sunk with shipwrecks.

Diving can be a deadly pastime. If divers return to the surface too quickly, the change in water pressure can give them the bends, a potentially fatal condition.

Ripley's Believe It or Not!®

Man's breath friend

Shadow is a scuba-diving dog that enjoys exploring underwater. He accompanies his owner, Dwane Folsom of the US, on scuba trips. Shadow wears his own special helmet and diving suit, and shares a breathing tube with Dwane.

Room with a view

If you're feeling rich and want to splash out on a hotel with a difference, check in at the Poseidon Underwater Hotel. Rooms will cost about £20,000 a week, but all guests get their own personal submarine to explore the underwater resort, and a luxury room that sits 12 m underwater, on the floor of a lagoon, with a view of the Fijian ocean life swimming by.

UP ANCHOR!

WAVE GOODBYE

Travelling across oceans sometimes requires great courage to combat the combined forces of wind, waves, currents, and the planet's fiercest weather.

Long ago, mariners sailed or rowed across the oceans in search of new lands and opportunities. They found their way by following the stars, but many of them lost their lives in storms and shipwrecks. Most modern journeys make use of the latest technology, including boats that are equipped with communication and satellite navigation systems. Some ocean journeys are even made in the lap of luxury, such as on the *Oasis of the Seas*!

The ship is 360 m long and 65 m wide.

It has 2,706 guest rooms, 16 decks, 24 elevators, and nearly 2,000 balconies.

FUN FEATURES

- Water and light show with 20-m high fountains
- A zipwire stretched between nine decks
- An ice rink
- Diving platforms and a trapeze
- Carousels and funfair activities

SEA MONSTER

The world's largest passenger ship has been described as a holiday village in the ocean – but with 8,000 people on board it's more like a town! The *Oasis of the Seas* is so big it even has room for tropical gardens with 56 growing trees, a science lab, and basketball courts.

AQUALANDS

CENTRAL PARK

ROYAL PROMENADE

Guests on the Oasis enjoy the chilling effects of 50,000 kg of ice cubes every day.

CAROUSEL

BIG WORD ALERT

CIRCUMNAVIGATION

A circumnavigation is a journey all the way around something. It usually refers to a sea voyage all the way around the world.

twist it!

A motor yacht named Dubai was built for one of the world's richest men. It is so large there's room for a helicopter pad, cinema, gym and squash court. It even has its own submarine!

When Ellen MacArthur broke the record for the fastest solo circumnavigation of the globe in 2005, she showed true powers of endurance. The feat took Ellen 71 days and 14 hours, and during that time she never slept for longer than 20 minutes at a time.

The first people to row across the Atlantic Ocean were George Harbo and Frank Samuelson of Norway. It took them nearly two months to row 5,262 km in 1896.

SEAFARERS

TREASURE TROVE

The oceans and seas cover most of the Earth's surface. They are home to billions of living things, and contribute to the planet's health in many different ways. People have been relying on the oceans' rich produce for thousands of years.

Oceans provide food for billions of people around the world, as well as jobs for the people who catch fish. Long ago, people fished for just the food they needed, but now too many fish are being taken from the sea. Too little is being done to protect marine habitats, and too much rubbish is being thrown into the oceans. There is some good news though: people all over the world are working hard to save our seas and create special places where ocean wildlife is safe.

SEAFOOD SHORTAGE

Tuna is one of the world's favourite fish to eat. In recent years, 95 per cent of all bluefin tuna have been removed from the sea, and they could disappear completely soon.

Nearly half of all known types of animals and plants live in oceans.

FOOD FOR THOUGHT

The Inuit people of the Arctic enjoy a type of walrus meat called *igunaaq*. It is stored under a pile of stones and, over the course of one year, it freezes and thaws so many times it becomes a rotting, stinking mass. Yum!

Most countries of the world have agreed not to hunt whales for meat any more, but seven species of great whales are still in danger of dying out forever.

Ermis and Androniki Nicholas love fish and chips so much they travel nearly 100 km every day to the coast for a fish lunch; and they have been making this trip for ten years!

A high-energy drink on sale in Japan is made from...eels! It's yellow, fizzy, and still has the fish heads and bones in it.

twist it!

Pretty wasteful

Pieces of coral, seashells and sea creatures are used to make souvenirs and sold to tourists all over the world. Pearls and sponges are also harvested from the sea. Many animals are killed and their habitats destroyed for this trade.

ANTARCTIC ANTIFREEZE

Fish that live in the icy Antarctic are able to survive thanks to special antifreeze chemicals in their bodies. They work by locking up ice crystals, to stop them from spreading. Scientists hope to copy the chemicals and make antifreeze paint for aircraft wings.

Doctors are using zebrafish and horseshoe crabs in an attempt to discover new medicines and repair damaged human hearts.

Some wind farms are located offshore so they can get maximum benefit from the strong gales that blow over the surface of the oceans.

JELLYFISH NOODLES

Scientists believe that the best way to make sure we don't use up all of the fish in the sea for food is to create marine reserves – areas in the oceans where no one is allowed to fish. Then, the endangered fish would be able to breed in these areas and increase their numbers once more. If we don't do this, some people believe that the only creatures left in the sea in large numbers for us to eat will be jellyfish! Jellyfish noodles, anyone?

RICH RESOURCES

The world's oceans provide a great deal of the energy we use in our everyday lives. Offshore platforms extract oil and natural gas from beneath the seabed, but one day these fuels, which are used to make power, will run out. New technology can harness the power of the wind and the waves to make electricity. These wind and wave farms provide a renewable, or never-ending, source of power that could give the world some of its energy in the future. Phew!

45

ACKNOWLEDGEMENTS

COVER David Fleetham/Taxi/Getty Images, (b/r) Greenpeace/Rex Features

2 (t) © nata_rass – Fotolia.com, (b) © javarman – Fotolia.com; **3** (t) Jim Morgan jmorgan8@cfl.rr.com, (r) Robert Innes; **4** (c) David Fleetham/Taxi/Getty Images; **4–5** (b) © aleksander1 – Fotolia.com; **6** (t, t/r) © Stephen Rees – iStock.com; **6–7** © Ramon Purcell – iStock.com; **7** (t/r) NASA/GSFC, MODIS Rapid Response; **8** (t/l, t/c, t/r) NASA/GSFC, MODIS Rapid Response; **8–9** Igor Liberti www.apnea.ch; **9** (t/r, b/r, b) U.S. Navy Photo; **10** (l) © Paul Allen – Fotolia.com, (b/c) Suzi Eszterhas/Minden Pictures/FLPA, (b/cl) Matthias Breiter/Minden Pictures/FLPA, (b/cr) © Lynn M. Stone, (b/l) © Oceans Image/Photoshot, (c/l) © NHPA/Photoshot; **11** (b/r, t/r) © NHPA/Photoshot (sp) © Alberto Pomares – iStock.com; **12–13** (c) Constantinos Petrinos/Nature Picture Library/Rex Features; **13** (t/r) Jeff Rotman/Naturepl.com, (c/r) Jim Morgan jmorgan8@cfl.rr.com, (b/r) David Fleetham/Bluegreenpictures.com; **14** (c) © Oceans Image/Photoshot, (b/l) © Monty Chandler – Fotolia.com; **14–15** (dp) © John Anderson – iStock.com, (b) David Espin – Fotolia.com; **15** (t/r) © Piero Malaer – iStock.com, (c/r) © Richard Carey – Fotolia.com, (b/r) Barcroft Media via Getty Images; **16–17** (dp) Jim Edds/Science Photo Library; **17** (c) Marlin.ac.uk/stevetrewhella@hotmail.com, (c/r) © David Fleetham/Bluegreenpictures.com, (b/r) © a_elmo – Fotolia.com, (b) © Mark Carwadine/naturepl.com; **18** (t/l) © pipehorse – Fotolia.com, (t/c) Georgette Douwma/Science Photo Library, (t/r) © Richard Carey – Fotolia.com; **18–19** Doug Perrine/Bluegreenpictures.com; **19** (t/l) © Richard Carey – Fotolia.com, (t/c) © nata_rass – Fotolia.com, (t/r) Birgit Koch/Imagebroker/FLPA, (c) P. Bush/Barcroft Media Ltd (b/r) Tommy Schultz – Fotolia.com; **20** (b/l) ImageBroker/Imagebroker/FLPA; **20–21** Gary Meszaros/Science Photo Library; **21** (t/r) © Oceans Image/Photoshot, (c) Michael Nolan/Splashdowndirect/Rex Features, (b/r) Greenpeace/Rex Features; **22** © Reinhard Dirscherl/FLPA; **23** (c) Brandon Cole/Bluegreenimages.com, (b/l) D.J. Struntz/Barcroft Media Ltd; **24** (t/r) International Antartic Centre, (t/c) California Academy of Sciences, (b/l) © javarman – Fotolia.com, (b/c) © Sergey Korotkov – iStock.com, (b/r) © Eric Isselée – Fotolia.com; **25** (c) Andy Rouse/Rex Features, (r) Ingo Arndt/Minden Pictures/FLPA, (b/l) iStock.com, (b/c) © Paul Tessier – iStock.com, (b/r) © Iain Sarjeant – iStock.com; **26** (t, b/l) © NHPA/Photoshot; **27** (t) Barry Bland/Barcroft Media Ltd, (b/r) © Nancy Nehring – iStock.com; **28** (t/r) Dreamstime.com, (c) © idy – Fotolia.com, (b/l) Quirky China/Rex Features; **28–29** (dp) © Ferran Traite Soler – iStock.com; **29** (t) © Alan James/Naturepl.com, (c) © Francesca Rizzo – iStock.com, (b) David Fleetham/Bluegreenpictures.com; **30** (b/l, b/r) David Shale/Bluegreenpictures.com; **30–31** (t) © Frans Lanting/Corbis, (c) © NHPA/Photoshot; **31** (b/r) David Shale/Bluegreenpictures.com; **32** (t) © Oceans-Image/Photoshot, (l) © Scott McCabe – iStock.com, (c/l) © Florian Graner/Naturepl.com; **32–33** (b) Norbert Wu/Minden Pictures/FLPA; **33** (t/r) David B Fleetham/PhotoLibrary, (c) © Markus Koller – Fotolia.com; **34** (t) © Kerry Werry – iStock.com, (b/l) © Achim Prill – iStock.com, (b/r) © John Anderson – iStock.com; **34–35** (dp) pablo del rio sotelo – iStock.com; **35** (t, c/r) © NHPA/Photoshot, (b) © Jacob Wackerhausen – iStock.com; **36** (t) © NHPA/Photoshot, (b) © Doug Perrine/naturepl.com; **37** (t) © Doug Perrine/Bluegreenpictures.com, (b/r) © aleksander1 – Fotolia.com; **38** (b) Rex Features (r) United States Naval History and Heritage Command photograph; **38–39** (dp) © Kevin Russ – iStock.com; **39** (t/l) iStock.com, (t/r) Professor Paul Brain/Wenn.com, (c) Time & Life Pictures/Getty Images, (b) © Stefanie Leuker – Fotolia.com; **40** (t) Robert Innes; **40–41** (c) © Robert Nu/FLPA; **41** (t/r, c/r) Rex Features, (b) Palm Beach Post/Rex Features; **42–43** KPA/Zuma/Rex Features; **44** Wild Wonders of Europe/Zankl/Bluegreenpictures.com; **45** (t) Norbert Wu/Minden Pictures/FLPA, (t/r) © Sean Gladwell – Fotolia.com, (b) Photolibrary.com/photofactory, (b/r) © Francesca Rizzo – iStock.com, (r) Woodfall Wild Images/Photoshot

Key: t = top, b = bottom, c = centre, l = left, r = right, sp = single page, dp = double page, bgd = background
All other photos are from Ripley Entertainment Inc. All artwork by Rocket Design (East Anglia) Ltd.

Every attempt has been made to acknowledge correctly and contact copyright holders and we apologise in advance for any unintentional errors or omissions, which will be corrected in future editions.

Ripley's BRUTAL BEASTS Believe It or Not!

RIPLEY
PUBLISHING

a Jim Pattison Company

Written by Camilla de la Bedoyere
Consultant Barbara Taylor

RIPLEY
PUBLISHING

Publisher **Anne Marshall**

Editorial Director **Rebecca Miles**
Project Editor **Charlotte Howell**
Picture Researchers **Michelle Foster, Charlotte Howell**
Proofreader **Lisa Regan**
Indexer **Hilary Bird**

Art Director **Sam South**
Senior Designer **Michelle Foster**
Design **Rocket Design (East Anglia) Ltd**
Reprographics **Juice Creative Ltd**

www.ripleys.com/books

ISBN 978-1-60991-226-0 (USA)

10 9 8 7 6 5 4 3 2 1

Library of Congress Cataloging-in-Publication Data is available.

Printed in China
in January 2018
2nd Printing

PUBLISHER'S NOTE
While every effort has been made to verify the accuracy of the entries in this book, the Publishers cannot be held responsible for any errors contained in the work. They would be glad to receive any information from readers.

WARNING
Some of the stunts and activities in this book are undertaken by experts and should not be attempted by anyone without adequate training tand supervision.

PAGE 19

CONTENTS

TWISTS

NATURE'S NASTIES

DEADLY PERILS AND HIDDEN HAZARDS

Nature is mostly nasty, not nice. Every animal on our planet has to fight to survive – and the fight is often to the death. Beasts have to be brutal: that means they need killing skills, lethal weapons, and cruel cunning.

This is no ordinary nature trek. Ripley's will take you through jungles, swamps and creeks. We will explore the dangers that lurk in the deepest seas and in the darkest hideaways, where deadly animals prowl. There are many perils in store, and hidden hazards at every twist and turn. Are you ready for the terrifying trip of a lifetime?

fast on her feet

can live almost anywhere

She-devil

Stand back – this leopard is a prima donna and doesn't like having her photo taken. She's brutal and she knows it – that's one baaaad attitude.

quiet and stealthy

enormous fangs

WHAT'S INSIDE YOUR BOOK?

TWISTS

BEASTLY EXTREMES!

CREEPIEST DESERT CENTIPEDE

PAGE 11

A creepy-crawly with lots of legs and big jaws.

CRUNCHIEST PRAYING MANTIS

PAGE 14

A bug that crunches its prey with penknife claws.

Ripley's Believe It or Not!®

This snake has two heads! Most snakes like this don't live very long — except for one two-headed rat snake with two stomachs and two throats that lived for 20 years!

These books are about 'Believe It or Not!' — amazing facts, feats, and things that make you go 'Wow!'

KEY FACTS

Read more unbelievable facts when you spot a Key Facts box.

Look out for the 'Twist It' column on some pages. Twist the book to find out more amazing facts about brutal beasts.

PACKING PUNCHES

EXPLOSIVE POWER

It's a big, bad, brutal, and savage world out there. Could you ever imagine exploding ants, kangaroos that box, or beetles that squirt chemicals from their butt?

Whether they are packing a powerful punch or mixing up chemicals to make a bomb, these cruel critters are truly awesome. They can use excessive force to get their own way, so stand back and watch these animal antics!

WANNA FIGHT?

Ding ding, round one, and the kangaroo in the blue corner is swinging at the kangaroo in the red corner. Over on the Australian grassland there are two kangaroos battling it out in the boxing ring. It's turning nasty and someone's going to get hurt!

Male kangaroos—boomers— get dirty when they fight over a female. They kick out with their massive feet and box with their sharply clawed paws. They are strong enough to crush bone!

BIG WORD ALERT

MARSUPIAL

say mar-soo-pi-al An animal that looks after its baby in a pouch.

kangaroos are part of the marsupial family

Taking one for the team

This little carpenter ant has given up its life to save the lives of the ants it lives with. When a bigger ant from another nest attacked its home, the carpenter ant exploded its own body, producing toxic yellow glue that killed them both.

Super spit

Spitting cobras can fire blinding venom with a deadly aim. They target their victim's eyes and are accurate 90 percent of the time, even when the victim is moving.

A hot shot

This little beetle fears no one because it knows it can fight back using an explosion in its bottom! It keeps two chemicals stashed away near its tail, and when the moment is right they are allowed to mix. The potion gets really hot and explodes, forcing a foul stinging liquid to spray in the direction of an attacker. Impressive!

TWIST IT!

Jellyfish can fire their poisoned barbs in under one-millionth of a second!

Never anger a llama—these feisty animals have short tempers and are quick to kick, head-butt, and bite. Freaked-out males also shoot out big gobbets of spit at an enemy!

Ural owls hate to see anyone near their chicks and they lash out with their huge talons, delivering a punch that can knock a man off his feet.

TAKE COVER!

Finding clams is tricky when the crunchy-shelled critters hide in soft mud. Walruses solve the problem by squirting a jet of water to remove the mud, leaving the clams exposed and ready to eat!

31

Found a new word? Big Word Alert will explain it for you.

QUICKEST PEREGRINE FALCON

PAGE 23

Swift in the air and the world's fastest killer.

BLOODIEST SHORT-HORNED LIZARD

PAGE 34

A scary face — and it can ooze blood from its eyes.

STINKIEST SKUNK

Squirts a stench bad enough to make you vomit.

PAGE 35

NASTIEST MARINE WOODLOUSE

PAGE 36

So gross we weren't sure we could even show you this one!

PACK POWER

GRUESOME GANGS GRAB THE BIG PRIZES

Hard-working hunters can make life easier by pulling together. One lion may have some success at catching a buffalo, but just imagine how powerful a whole pack of predators can be.

Working as a team isn't easy. Every animal must understand the plan of attack, and know what its job is. Not all animals can pull together like this – it takes cool cunning and brains.

African wild dogs are also known as painted dogs because of their strange multi-coloured fur.

TOP DOGS

Your pet pooch may seem cute and cuddly, but tame dogs are closely related to wild and brutal beasts, such as wolves, coyotes, dingos and African wild dogs. They belong to one big animal family called 'canids'. Canids often live in family groups, and hunt together as a pack. With their incredible sense of smell and great eyesight, canids can detect their prey from far away.

African wild dogs don't waste their time creeping up on their prey. The pack simply chooses a target then chases it until it collapses. They can eat through bone and, when they are full, they regurgitate some food (bring it up from their stomach) to share with relatives that were too weak to take part in the chase.

Hunting hawks

Most birds of prey prefer to go solo when hunting, but Harris hawks have found they get to eat more often when they work together as a family. They surround a rabbit, and when it starts to run the bird closest swoops down for the kill, and the meal is shared between the team.

BIG WORD ALERT

PREDATOR

An animal that kills other animals (prey) to eat.

6

Hunting in a pack, wolves can attack prey that is up to ten times the size of any one member of the team.

TWIST IT!

THE BRAT PACK

Hyenas are dog-like pack hunters of the African grasslands. They look, and act, like dogs but they are more closely related to cats!

Lions often hunt at night, and they are most successful when there's no moon. Like all cats, they can see even when there is very little light, but their prey can't.

A male adult lion can eat 34 kg of meat in one sitting – that's 300 quarter pounders!

Lions have huge teeth for stabbing and slicing food, but they can't chew.

When dolphins spy a group of fish, one dolphin swiftly swims in a big circle around the fish. This stirs up mud and sand so the fish have to turn back – and straight into waiting jaws.

The big bad wolf

There's a reason grey wolves are the bad guys in children's stories – they really are cunning creatures that are happy to see Little Red Riding Hood on the menu! Wolf attacks used to be quite common in parts of Europe and North America. Nowadays, wolves are rare and they hunt deer, oxen and moose instead of humans – phew!

Taking pride in your work

Hunting is a family affair for lions. A pride (family group) is mostly made up of females and their cubs, and it's the ladies who lunch – or at least go and get lunch! These clever cats have different tricks for catching their prey, but one cunning plan is this simple:

1. One female walks up to a grazing buffalo.

2. The buffalo is spooked, and runs away in the opposite direction.

3. Other lionesses are ready and waiting – they are hiding just where the buffalo is heading.

4. The buffalo gets a nasty shock when it sees a handful of lions bounding towards it. There's no escape...

BRUTE STRENGTH

ANIMAL CHAMPS

WITH MIGHTY MUSCLES

It's time to get out the big guns – and show those muscles! Strength can be a top factor in survival so these animals have grown large and strong. When battle begins, there can only be one winner.

Join muscles to bones and you create an impressive bit of engineering – and the power to do some deadly damage to your enemy. Add a fearless attitude, and you've created a killing machine.

BIG WORD ALERT
CANNIBAL
An animal that eats others of its own kind.

BRUTAL BEASTS

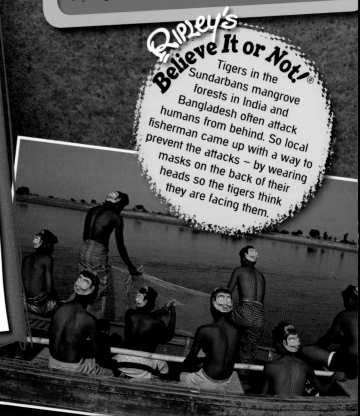

BEWARE OF DRAGONS

Dinosaurs are long-dead, but beware these reminders of a bygone time! A Komodo dragon wouldn't look out of place in a prehistoric forest and it has a furious temper to match that fierce face. In fact, these brutal beasts are so nasty their babies have to hide in trees to keep out of harm's way – the parents sometimes turn cannibal!

Max size: 3 m long

Mega fact: The world's largest lizards, Komodos eat anything they can catch – including humans.

KEY FACTS

MEGA-MONSTERS OF LONG AGO

Enormous beasts ruled the world millions of years ago. Check out some of these super-sized brutes:

Titanoboa
The largest snake that ever lived ruled the rainforests after the dinosaurs died out. It was as long as a *T. rex* and its body was as thick as a human waist.

Pristichampsus
How scary would it be if a crocodile could stand up on its back legs and run after you? Be glad you weren't around about 50 million years ago, with this giant croc-like creature!

Megaspiders
Long ago, giant spiders were common. There was more oxygen in the air, which meant breathing was easier, and all sorts of bugs and spiders could grow bigger.

Brontoscorpio
Scientists have found evidence of a mighty scorpion that lived in the water and grew to 1 m long.

Ripley's Believe It or Not!®
Tigers in the Sundarbans mangrove forests in India and Bangladesh often attack humans from behind. So local fisherman came up with a way to prevent the attacks – by wearing masks on the back of their heads so the tigers think they are facing them.

BRUTAL BEASTS

SILENT BUT DEADLY

This is one of the world's most powerful killers. It may look gorgeous but only a fool would mess with a tiger. With a reputation for attacking grown men, tigers are scared of nothing and no one. They are strong, silent, and very, very deadly.

Max size: 3.3 m nose to tail

Mega fact: About 100 years ago, the Champawat tigress killed more than 400 people in India and Nepal.

BRUTAL BEASTS

OH DEAR, DEER!

Enormous wings, big bills and terrifying talons – golden eagles are North America's largest birds of prey with the killing skills to think big. They mainly hunt rabbits, lizards and even insects – but sometimes their eyes are bigger than their stomach, and eagles swoop to attack deer. This deer had a lucky escape when it dived under a fence.

Max size: 2.3 m wingspan

Mega fact: Golden eagles can dive-bomb their prey, reaching speeds of 240 km/h.

BRUTAL BEASTS

TURNING THE TABLE

Birds love to eat wriggling spiders, swallowing them whole – but this bird got a bit of a shock! Goliath bird-eating spiders are big enough to turn the tables and can catch small birds. Most of the time, they settle for a snack of frogs, lizards, beetles or mice.

Max size: 28 cm legspan

Mega fact: The spider's fangs are longer than a human fingernail and deliver a nasty dose of poison.

BRUTAL BEASTS

BEAR-FACED GREEDY-GUTS

Fruit, berries and roots keep a grizzly bear happy, but their giant cousins, polar bears, are definitely not vegetarians! These meat-lovers live where it's too cold for plants to grow so they have to feast on flesh. Seals are usually on the menu and it takes the bear's huge strength and size, massive paws, and ferocious fangs to kill one.

Max size: 2.6 m nose to tail

Mega fact: A large polar bear was stuffed and put on display at Anchorage Airport in Alaska. It stands over 2.1 m tall.

LETHAL INJECTION

GETTING STRAIGHT TO THE POINT

Is it possible to be brutal and a weakling? These animals may not have large bodies, brute strength or big brains, but they don't need any of those things. They have a super scary secret up their sleeves.

It's VENOM! A poisonous liquid that is injected straight into the body and has a range of nasty effects. Venom can cause severe pain, make flesh rot and die, stop victims from breathing or moving, or make them bleed to death...the list just goes on and on!

Freaky fangs

It is this spider's attitude that makes it so dangerous, not just its venom. When male Sydney funnel web spiders are in the mood for love they leave their burrows and embark on a search for a lady-friend — and they won't let anything get in their way. Anyone in their path is likely to get a nasty nip with those fearsome fangs — and their venom is one of the most deadly known.

KEY FACTS

The world's top five venomous snakes all live in Australia. These snakes have the most deadly venom, but some of them are very shy of humans.

* 1. Inland taipan
* 2. Eastern brown snake
* 3. Coastal taipan
* 4. Tiger snake
* 5. Black tiger snake

Inland taipan snake

Spider slayer

This incredible insect has an unbelievable – and totally revolting – life story. It's a tarantula hawk wasp and it is attacking an enormous tarantula spider, which it grabs with its claws, then stings. The wasp will take the sleepy spider back to its burrow and lay an egg inside its body. When the egg hatches, the larva (young insect) will devour the still-living spider from the inside out!

2 Tail bends over the head.

3 Tip of the tail injects venom into victim's body.

ACTUAL SIZE

A sting in the tail

Scorpions love to hide in small dark places, so wise desert campers always check their shoes in the morning! A scorpion sting can be very painful, and one from a deathstalker scorpion can be fatal to children.

4 Strong jaws mash the victim's body into a pulp.

1 Big claws grab prey.

TWIST IT!

VENOMONSTERS

There are about 3,000 types of snake in the world, and around 300 of these are dangerous to humans.

Venomous lizards, such as gila monsters, use their teeth for injecting venom, chewing, and munching to force the venom deeper into flesh.

There are two types of shark that are known to have venomous spines: Port Jackson sharks and spiny dogfish (also known as spurdogs).

There are no venomous birds, but there are a few birds that have poisonous skin and feathers.

Lethal legs

The giant desert centipede can grow up to 20 cm long! It uses its maxillipeds – which literally means 'jaw-feet' – to grab hold of prey and inject venom into its body.

11

FEARLESS FIENDS

THE RIPLEY HALL OF HEROES

All around the world, nations give medals and awards to people who have shown great courage or skill in battle. We believe there is no reason to leave animals out – many of these creatures show incredible bravery and will fight to the death.

We take great pleasure in announcing the following awards to the brutal beasts of the animal kingdom.

AWARDED FOR:
GREAT SKILL AND DARING DEFENCE OF THE SKIES

RIPLEY'S AWARD FOR FLYING COMBAT

The Award is given to goshawks, secretive birds of prey that defend their nests against all intruders.

Goshawks are fearless fliers and will dive-bomb any animal that enters their own space, or territory. They are plucky birds, and will attack animals much bigger than themselves, including bears and wolves. These raptors don't flinch from danger, and will even launch an attack on humans.

RIPLEY'S STAR OF COURAGE

The Star is awarded to wolverines because they combine all the qualities of great predators.

Wolverines are about as big as a medium-sized dog, but they compete with and hunt for animals that are many times their size. When a wolverine spots an animal it goes in for the kill – it even attacks wolves and black bears with its strong body and clawed-paws.

AWARDED FOR:
FIGHTING BATTLES AGAINST ALL ODDS

AWARDED FOR:
FEARLESS ATTITUDE AND GREAT STRENGTH

Find out even more about this meany on page 40

RIPLEY'S NOBLE ORDER OF THE CLAW

The Order is given to honey badgers, which have a sweet name but are often called 'the meanest animals alive'.

Honey badgers raid beehives to eat the eggs and larvae, and feast on honey, but they will attack almost any animal that takes their fancy. With their enormous claws and teeth, these stout-hearted predators are able to kill small crocodiles and large or poisonous snakes.

RIPLEY'S MEDAL OF HONOUR

The Medal is awarded to all female elephants who have risked life and limb to protect their families.

When a baby elephant is attacked by groups of hyenas or lions, a mother elephant turns her back on fear and faces the pack. Like an out-of-control tank the mother charges the pack, using feet, trunk and tusks to attack. She puts her baby's life, or that of her sisters' babies, above care for her own safety, and is a shining example to us all.

AWARDED FOR:
RISKING OWN LIFE TO SAVE OTHERS

MIGHTY MAULERS

KILLER LIMBS TO TEAR, RIP AND MAUL

Paws, claws, jaws, talons and knife-like limbs – these beasts have got the lot! Serious assassins need the right tools for the job.

When a mighty mauler has its eyes on the prize it needs more than wishful thinking to get lunch in its tum. It has to chase, catch, kill, shred and slash its prey – with limbs that are perfectly adapted for butchery.

Whipped into a frenzy

This miniature monster is a whip spider. It's part of the scorpion and spider family, but it manages to maul its prey without the use of a venomous bite or sting. Instead, it relies on brute force and two huge barbed front limbs, which can touch, grab, stab, crush and mash its victims.

When a mantis attacks, it moves so quickly that it's almost impossible to see the movement with the naked ey

Say a prayer

Male praying mantises treat their female mates with great care, but they still often find themselves on the menu. These super-sized bugs are armed with forelegs that work like penknives with folding blades. Normally, this scissor action is kept for prey, but female mantises often can't resist the urge to kill and eat their unfortunate male mates.

TWIST IT!

TOOLED UP

Mantises can move their head 180 degrees and they have two big eyes, as well as three smaller ones, which means they can spot anything moving nearby.

Vinegaroons (a type of scorpion) carry their babies on their backs until they are ready to look after themselves. The mothers don't eat, and often die of starvation soon after.

A giant anteater can stick its tongue out more than 60 cm to lick up ants. It can use its huge claws to defend itself against big cats, such as pumas.

Talons are made of keratin – the same stuff that your nails and hair are made of. They keep growing, just like nails, all through a bird's life, but they get worn down with use.

Ripley's Believe It or Not!®

This very odd looking animal is actually a frog – known as a hairy frog! This amazing creature has retractable claws made of bone, which it pushes through its skin to defend itself, breaking the bones of its toes as they are forced through.

Digging deep

Anteaters may be toothless, but that doesn't stop them from being one of the world's most effective killers. How many other animals can kill tens of thousands of victims in one day? This anteater is using its claws to dig a hole into a bug nest. It sticks its long tongue into the hole, flicking it three times a second. It can eat up to 30,000 ants in one day.

Mega legs

Secretary birds have very long legs. This bird of prey uses them to stomp through the African grasslands, chasing any little animals that try to run away. The victim is stamped or kicked to death and swallowed whole. Even poisonous snakes are killed this way, as they are too far from the bird's body to get a chance to deliver a deadly bite.

Birds of prey (raptors) use their talons to fight off predators, grasp onto branches and, most importantly, to hold and rip their victims to shreds.

15

SLAUGHTER IN THE WATER

NATURE'S CRUEL RIVERS

Come on board the Ripley's River Cruise of Cruelty. We've collected together some of the world's meanest animals in one place, so let's go on a journey of deadly discovery.

Don't be fooled by the gently rippling surface – rivers and their surroundings are home to plenty of scary critters. They may be hidden from view, but that's the plan. The most effective predators are ones you don't see until it's too late…

Wow, look at that!

Ladies and gentlemen, boys and girls, look to the river bank and, between the plants and the forest shadows, you'll spy a jaguar. A powerful big cat of the Americas, this predator – with a caiman in its jaws – is the heavyweight of the feline family. Look at that vast, broad head and solid shoulders. This prize-fighter is as happy in the river as it is in the forest.

BIG WORD ALERT
CAIMAN
say kay–man
An American member of the crocodilian family.

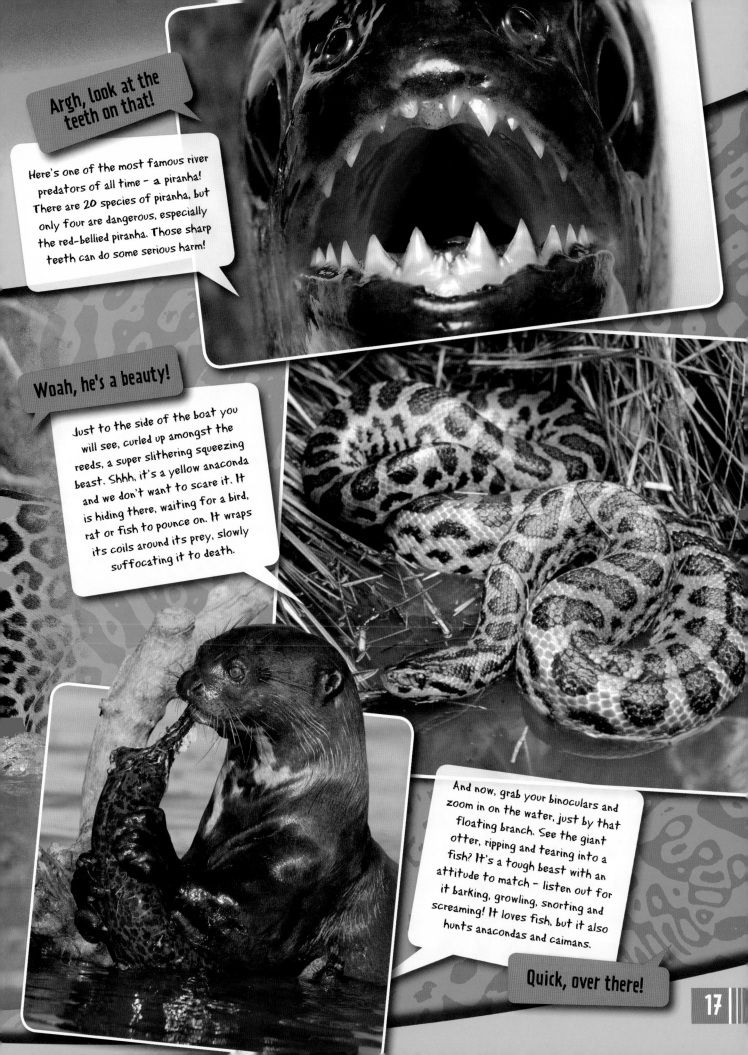

Argh, look at the teeth on that!

Here's one of the most famous river predators of all time – a piranha! There are 20 species of piranha, but only four are dangerous, especially the red-bellied piranha. Those sharp teeth can do some serious harm!

Woah, he's a beauty!

Just to the side of the boat you will see, curled up amongst the reeds, a super slithering squeezing beast. Shhh, it's a yellow anaconda and we don't want to scare it. It is hiding there, waiting for a bird, rat or fish to pounce on. It wraps its coils around its prey, slowly suffocating it to death.

And now, grab your binoculars and zoom in on the water, just by that floating branch. See the giant otter, ripping and tearing into a fish? It's a tough beast with an attitude to match – listen out for it barking, growling, snorting and screaming! It loves fish, but it also hunts anacondas and caimans.

Quick, over there!

KILLER SKILLS

GLADIATORS OF THE ANIMAL WORLD

She's protecting her baby!

The gladiators of Ancient Rome fought in fierce combat – to the death. They had special training, and an impressive range of skills and weapons. Perhaps they got some of their inspiration from looking at these brutal beasts?

The natural world is full of surprises. Who could ever imagine this amazing range of battle skills and strategies? There is a huge variety of living things and life styles on Earth, and this is known as biodiversity.

Lunge and strike

Brutal beast: Pit viper

Weapon: Venomous fangs

Skill: Detects the heat from prey

Pit vipers are master snakes of combat. They can sense the vibration caused by an animal moving and – even more impressive – they can 'see' the heat that it produces. They create 'heat pictures' in their brain, which allow them to judge how far away their prey is, and its size – even in darkness. Their weapons are fangs, which deliver a deadly dose of venom.

Dive-bomb

Brutal beast: *Kestrel*

Weapon: *Talons and beak*

Skill: *Super speed and wee detection*

Kestrels prey on small mammals, such as mice and voles. They find them using their sensitive eyes, which can spot the ultraviolet light reflected from the trails of urine (wee) that the mammals make. Once spotted, the mammal must run at full speed to escape before the kestrel swoops down and grabs it with its talons.

Take aim, fire!

Brutal beast: *Porcupine*

Weapon: *Barbed spears*

Skill: *Rapid attack under pressure*

A porcupine prepares itself for attack by turning its back on its enemy and raising its quills, which are like hundreds of barbed spears. The quills come away at the slightest touch and dig into flesh – they are almost impossible to remove.

Spit and lick

Brutal beast: *African crested rat*

Weapon: *Toxic spit*

Skill: *Being prepared*

African crested rats are always prepared for a fight. They chew the roots and bark of a poisonous tree to make a toxic spit, which they paste over the fur on their back. If a predator gets close enough to bite the rat, the fight is over – even a small dose can kill.

It's a trap

Brutal beast: *Net-casting spider*

Weapon: *Strong, sticky silk*

Skill: *Weaving silk into nets and throwing them*

Net-casting spiders find their prey by sensing its movement, both by touch and sight. Their large eyes can sense light better than those of cats and owls! They weave their silk into webs, and ambush their prey, covering them with a web-net stretched between their legs. Once the victim is under the net, the spider relaxes, and the trap is complete.

RIPLEY'S
Believe It or Not!®

This poor bulldog ended up with more than 500 porcupine quills stuck in her face, after being attacked by a dangerous porcupine. Bella Mae got a little too close to the animal when she was playing near a pond and the porcupine attacked. Bella was fixed up by a vet and made a full recovery.

THE CRUNCH BUNCH

JAWS AND TEETH

There's no ig-gnaw-ing it – sharp teeth and strong jaws can make any animal brutal! Jaws are crushing machines that come with a wide range of sharp daggers, snapping scissors, munching mincers and mashers.

Teeth are very useful! Animals can use them to grab their prey, keep it still, kill it, and then break it up into tasty bite-sized portions. Fangs, or canines, can grow extra long and sharp for a stabbing move, while other top and bottom teeth fit together like scissor blades to tear flesh apart. Bigger molars, at the back of the mouth, help grind meat into a juicy paste.

Brown bears are some of the most deadly of all land mammals. Although known to attack humans, thankfully brown bears prefer to eat fish, roots or berries. When salmon swim upriver to breed, hungry bears lie in wait. The fish have to leap to make it through the cascading water, and that's when the bears get lunch!

KEY FACTS

Scientists compare how hard animals can bite using a measurement of pressure called a Newton. Chew over this list of some of the world's top chomps.

HOW BIG'S YOUR BITE?

★ T-Rex	57,000 Newtons*
★ Saltwater crocodile	16,460 Newtons
★ Lion	3,000 Newtons
★ Hyena	2,000 Newtons
★ Hippopotamus	1,255 Newtons
★ Brown bear	1,000 Newtons

We use about 100 Newtons of pressure to chew a carrot.

*T-Rex is long-dead, of course, so this is an estimate that scientists worked out by looking at its bones.

Bears open their mouth wide and wait for the fish to leap in. A quick snap with those mighty jaws, and the fish's journey is over.

GIGANTIC JAWS

Hippos have a deadly reputation, but just how brutal can a grass-eating, lumbering cousin of a pig be? Very! Hippos attack when they feel threatened. Their teeth, or tusks, can grow up to 50 cm long, and can cut a person in half. Male hippos use their giant jaws and teeth to battle one another at mating time.

Ripley's Believe It or Not!®

Tigers have teeth that are as long as your little finger, so imagine how bad their toothache can get! When Mohan, a white tiger from Dreamland in Brisbane, Australia, began to sulk, his keepers knew something was wrong, and called in a brave dentist. Mohan was put to sleep while Dr Gary Wilson successfully treated the rotten tooth in a two-hour operation.

Hippos don't just attack humans. They will attack any animal that gets too close, including crocodiles, wildebeest and zebras.

ONCE BITTEN

A Titan beetle can snap a pencil in half with its mighty jaws – not impressed? Well, it would be like you biting a tree trunk in half. Bet you're impressed now!

Tuataras are tiny lizardlike reptiles from New Zealand. Although they're small, they can bite off a seagull's head in one snap of the jaws – how gross!

Hyenas have one of the most incredible bites of any animal alive. They can crack bones with one crunch, and eat the bones of their prey – which includes huge beasts such as Cape buffalo.

Scientists have recently discovered a new species of giant wasp called a garuda. Its jaws are longer than its legs!

Giant squid have teeth in their tentacles, but sea urchins have teeth on their bottom!

TWIST IT!

HIGH SPEED CHASE

ANIMAL OLYMPICS

Here in the human world, great athletes and sportspeople pit their skills against one another to achieve glory as supreme champions. We'd like to imagine what it would be like at an Animal Olympics!

These athletes don't need coaches, training or energy drinks. They've already got what it takes – bodies primed for action, a need for speed, and a ruthless attitude.

The triple jump

Sit back and enjoy the spectacle of an all-round sports star as a gentoo penguin does a hop, skip and a jump, then a spot of tobogganing, followed by record-setting underwater swimming – accelerating up to 35 km/h. These athletes also 'fly' above the water, leaping through the air to escape jaws of hungry sharks.

The long jump

While human athletes have struggled to beat the world long jump record of 8.95 m, snow leopards could take it in an easy stride. In fact, one snow leopard was seen running and leaping across a ditch that was 15 m wide!

BIG WORD ALERT

ACCELERATE

When an animal increases its speed it accelerates.

OTHER SPEED FIENDS

Sailfish
109 km/h

Cheetah
105 km/h

22

The sprint

When it comes to running, six legs are better than two! The Australian tiger beetle is the world's fastest running insect, reaching top speeds of 9 km/h; that's the same as a human running at 772 km/h. It uses its speed to chase other insects, which it also devours in a super-speedy time!

The slither

If animals organised the Olympics there would have to be a race for the slithering snakes – and the black mamba would be the clear favourite. It may not be able to keep up with Usain Bolt, but a mamba can achieve an impressive 19 km/h in short bursts.

The swoop

Bats and insects could take part in Olympic flying events – but the birds would probably take a clean sweep of the medals. The champions of speed are peregrine falcons. As they plunge downward in pursuit of prey, falcons can fly at about 200 km/h. No other bird comes close to this incredible feat.

Spiny-tailed iguana
56 km/h

Brown bear
56 km/h

Sea lion
40 km/h

CUNNING KILLERS

KILLERS

NATURE'S BRAINIACS

It has surprised scientists how clever so many animals are. More surprising is how long it has taken the human race to appreciate just what marvellous animals we share our planet with!

In the battle to survive, a big brain is bound to be helpful. Smart animals can make tools, communicate with each other to create a hunting party, plan their actions, and even remember where they have been and what they have done.

Er, ROAR!

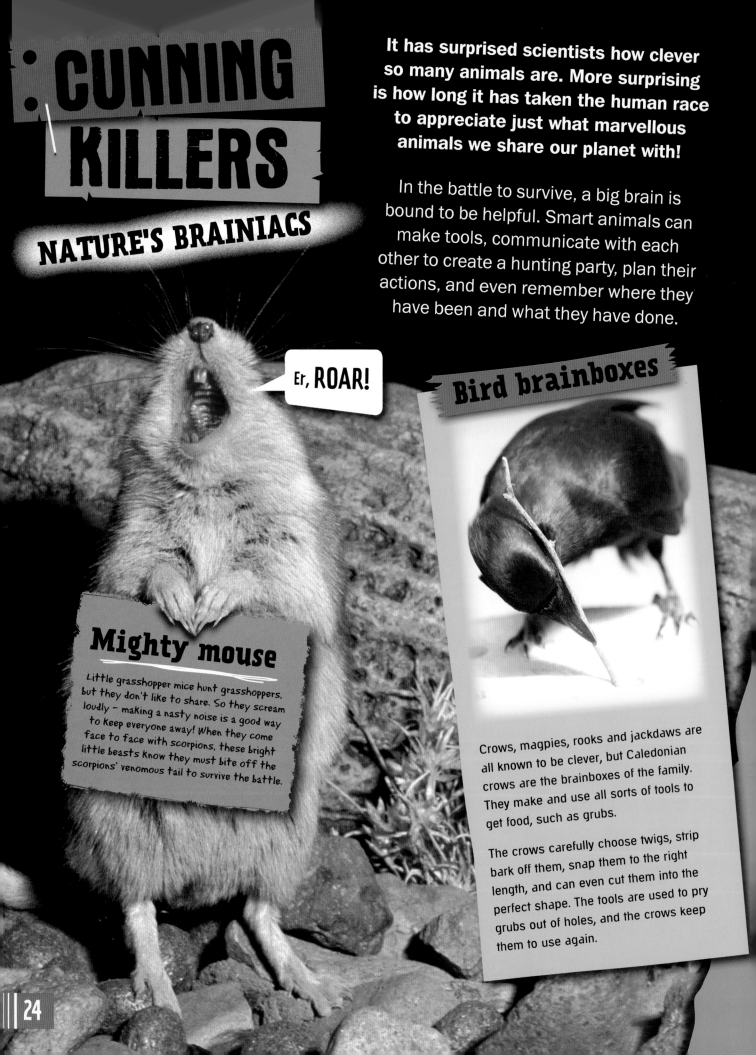

Bird brainboxes

Mighty mouse

Little grasshopper mice hunt grasshoppers, but they don't like to share. So they scream loudly – making a nasty noise is a good way to keep everyone away! When they come face to face with scorpions, these bright little beasts know they must bite off the scorpions' venomous tail to survive the battle.

Crows, magpies, rooks and jackdaws are all known to be clever, but Caledonian crows are the brainboxes of the family. They make and use all sorts of tools to get food, such as grubs.

The crows carefully choose twigs, strip bark off them, snap them to the right length, and can even cut them into the perfect shape. The tools are used to pry grubs out of holes, and the crows keep them to use again.

Chimps are champs, not chumps!

Apes and monkeys are our closest cousins, so it's no wonder they are so clever! Most of them eat plants, but chimps love termites and they hunt, too. Like us, chimps can be caring, friendly and loving but they can sometimes turn violent.

KEY FACTS

DID YOU KNOW?

Chimps can:

- Count, add and subtract numbers
- Learn sign language
- Use leaves to soak up water, then squeeze it into their mouth
- Use nine different types of tool
- Use sticks to get termites out of their nests
- Play tricks on each other
- Work together as a group to hunt
- Use large stones as weapons

You lookin' at me?

TWIST IT!

Tiny tarsiers are primates that scuttle through forests at night, hunting bugs. When they get scared, tarsiers call out and their friends come running to their aid. Together they mob the attacker until it turns tail and leaves. Helping out a buddy is a cunning plan, because the favour may be returned one day.

Spotted hyenas live and work in families, and that takes intelligence. The cubs are ruthless, too – usually they are born as twins but sometimes one will kill its twin to get all of its mother's milk!

Aye-ayes are peculiar little primates that eat burrowing grubs from inside tree trunks. It takes a lot of brainpower to figure out how to reach the grubs, so aye-ayes have huge brains for their little bodies.

Egyptian eagles drop stones onto ostrich eggs to smash them open.

BRAIN WAVES

Angry ape!

Big daddy gorillas are a force to be reckoned with when they are angry. But they would rather not get into a brawl, so they stand tall, beat their chest, and roar. It's a smart move that avoids violence.

SMALL BUT MIGHTY

SIZE DOESN'T MATTER

Insects may be annoying, but are they really deadly? If you take the time to watch insects going about their daily lives you will be amazed by just how surprising – and brutal – many of these little animals are.

Insects have just three pairs of legs, but some unbelievable life stories. There are far more insects than there are people on Earth, and we may share our planet with more than five million different types, from beetles to flies, wasps and butterflies.

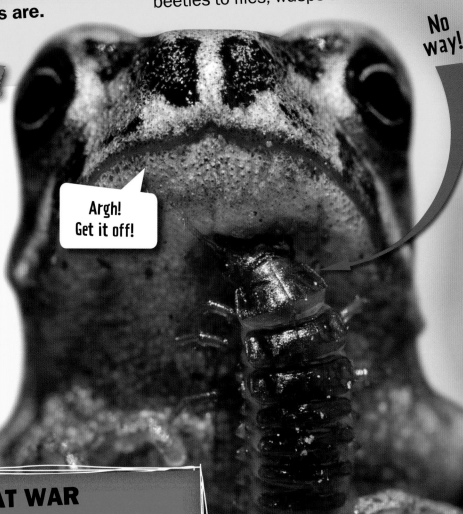

No way!

Argh! Get it off!

Face invaders

This is one of the most disgusting animal stories you are ever likely to read. Prepare yourself for a gross factor of ten!

Frogs eat bugs, but this bug – called an epomis larva – has got its own back. It has massive jaws and it waves them around when it sees a frog. The frog thinks it's spied something tasty, and rushes over to eat it. The larva leaps up to the frog's throat and digs in with its enormous hooked jaws. Then it feeds on the frog, sucking blood and chomping away on flesh.

If the frog gets 'lucky' and manages to eat the larva, it soon regrets its decision and vomits it out – because the larva starts to eat the frog from the inside instead!

KEY FACTS   BUGS AT WAR

Forget bombs, tanks, missiles and big guns – for thousands of years war-makers have been using insects to wage war! Believe it or not...

✳ There are plans to put computer chips into caterpillars so when they turn into butterflies they can be instructed to fly into enemy areas and spy.

✳ The Ancient Romans used catapults to hurl beehives over city walls.

✳ During World War Two, Japanese bombs were packed with fleas that carried bubonic plague – a foul disease that killed millions of people in the Middle Ages.

KILLER ANTS!

One ant is no big deal, but when an army of ants goes on the march it's a different matter. Working together, ants can build giant nests, collect food, and attack prey much bigger than themselves.

FIRE ANTS

Fire ants love to chew on electrical wires, devour crops, and attack creatures such as grasshoppers and birds. Their sting is so painful it's been compared to an electric shock.

DRIVER ANTS

Driver ants march in swarms of up to 22 million and destroy everything in their path, including snakes and rats.

Bullet ants sting with a poison that causes pain that lasts for hours, and reduces a human victim to tears of agony.

Find out even more about this nasty ant on page 41

BULLET ANTS

In the past, human hunters often tipped their spears and arrows with a paste made from poisonous beetles or caterpillars.

Lonomia are killer caterpillars with poisonous spines. If touched, the spines break and inject poisons that can be strong enough to kill a human.

Asian hornets can kill 30,000 honey bees in just a few hours.

Hornets are large stinging wasps that use their stings to kill prey and defend themselves from attack by other animals. A swarm of 30 giant

LITTLE DEVILS

Coo-eee!

These head markings look like two big eyes.

Acid is sprayed from the throat.

Two flashy 'tails' grow out of the last two legs.

Spray that again!

This charming creature gets full marks for its gorgeous looks. It's the caterpillar of a puss moth, and this fancy outfit certainly grabs attention. The weird colours and marks probably tell a predator to stay away, but if the message is missed there's a nasty surprise in store – the caterpillar can spray burning acid at any attacker!

27

SNEAKERS AND CREEPERS

LOOK OUT, THERE'S DANGER ABOUT!

There is a nasty shock in store – predators use some sneaky tricks to get close enough to attack. Their victims happily go about their business with no idea that a deadly danger lurks nearby.

These savage brutes are out to deceive. Their beastly tricks rely on sneaking, creeping, hiding, faking, and tempting their victims to come close.

Crawl and catch

The Amazonian giant centipede can catch and eat bats! An adult centipede can reach up to 35 cm in length – that's as long as a man's forearm – and is able to climb cave walls. This centipede caught a passing bat using some of its 46 legs!

Ripley's Believe It or Not!®

This species of jumping spider can get up close and personal with ants by pretending to be one of the family. This helps the spider get close to prey, and avoids it being eaten by animals that fear a nasty ant sting.

KEY FACTS

SNEAKY TRICKS SPELL SUCCESS

Stealth Animals creep up on their prey in total silence to gain an element of surprise.

Mimicry Pretending to be another animal or a plant is a smart trick if you want to get close to your prey.

Camouflage Using colours and blending into the background makes you invisible to your victims.

Master of disguise

Look closely at this mossy tree trunk and you will see a leaf-tailed gecko – a type of lizard. This reptile is so well camouflaged even his mother wouldn't recognise him!

A tiger's stripes help it to blend into the stripy shadows of its forest home.

Arctic foxes have brown fur in the summer, when there is no snow about, but in the winter their fur turns white so they are perfectly camouflaged.

SEE ME?

Glass frogs are virtually transparent (see-through) so they almost disappear when sitting on a leaf.

Broad and long wings allow the owl to glide, which is quieter than flapping wings.

Swoop and snatch

Snowy owls are white and blend into a white background perfectly. Their feathers are soft and fluffy to deaden the sound as they silently swoop through the air to snatch mice and rats from the ground.

Soft fluffy feathers help to absorb sound.

The ends of these feathers have a special shape. It muffles the noise caused by air passing over them.

Poor mouse doesn't know what's coming!

Stick and slurp

Chameleons are lizards with a long sticky tongue. They can hide amongst the leaves, and shoot out their tongue to grab passing bugs. Chameleons are even able to change the colour of their skin to help them 'disappear', or to show if they're feeling angry!

Awesome tongue!!

29

PACKING PUNCHES

EXPLOSIVE POWER

It's a big, bad, brutal and savage world out there. Could you ever imagine exploding ants, kangaroos that box, or beetles that squirt chemicals from their butt?

Whether they are packing a powerful punch or mixing up chemicals to make a bomb, these cruel critters are truly awesome. They can use excessive force to get their own way, so stand back and watch these animal antics!

WANNA FIGHT?

Ding ding, round one, and the kangaroo in the blue corner is swinging at the kangaroo in the red corner. Over on the Australian grassland there are two kangaroos battling it out in the boxing ring. It's turning nasty and someone's going to get hurt!

Male kangaroos – boomers – get dirty when they fight over a female. They kick out with their massive feet and box with their sharply clawed paws. They are strong enough to crush bone!

BIG WORD ALERT

MARSUPIAL

say mar-soo-pi-al
An animal that looks after its baby in a pouch.

Kangaroos are part of the marsupial family.

Taking one for the team

This little carpenter ant has given up its life to save the lives of the ants it lives with. When a bigger ant from another nest attacked its home, the carpenter ant exploded its own body, producing toxic yellow glue that killed them both.

TWIST IT!

Jellyfish can fire their poisoned barbs in under one-millionth of a second!

Never anger a llama — these feisty animals have short tempers and are quick to kick, head-butt and bite. Freaked-out males also shoot out big gobbets of spit at an enemy!

Ural owls hate to see anyone near their chicks and they lash out with their huge talons, delivering a punch that can knock a man off his feet.

TAKE COVER!

Finding clams is tricky when the crunchy-shelled critters hide in soft mud. Walruses solve the problem by squirting a jet of water to remove the mud, leaving the clams exposed and ready to eat!

Super spit

Spitting cobras can fire blinding venom with a deadly aim. They target their victim's eyes and are accurate 90 percent of the time, even when the victim is moving.

A hot shot

This little beetle fears no one because it knows it can fight back using an explosion in its bottom! It keeps two chemicals stashed away near its tail, and when the moment is right they are allowed to mix. The potion gets really hot and explodes, forcing a foul stinging liquid to spray in the direction of an attacker. Impressive!

31

NIGHT TERRORS

In the moonlight, a beastly battle begins as nocturnal creatures fight to survive. With little light to help, animals rely on superb eyesight, or other senses, to find their way in the dark.

As the sun begins to set, some creatures stir from their sleeping places and prepare for a busy night ahead. Many animals spend the dark time foraging for fruit, berries and seeds to eat. And while they go about their business, deadly night predators prepare to attack.

There are two types of bat: one type mainly hunts insects, while the other type mainly eats fruit.

DANGER IN THE DARK

Going batty

Bats are one of the most common types of mammal in the world, and masters of the night sky. They have good eyesight, but rely on their senses of hearing and smell to hunt (see Key Facts, below). Just one bat can feast on thousands of flies in a single night. Others are able to grab fish or crabs out of water!

TWIST IT!

Big cats are more successful when they hunt at dawn and dusk. It is cool enough for animals to graze, but it's harder for them to spot a tiger or lion lurking in the dim light.

Scientists used to think tarsiers were silent, but now we know they make lots of sound but it is so high-pitched we can't hear it.

Bats have few predators of their own, so they can live to 20 years of age!

AFTER DARK!

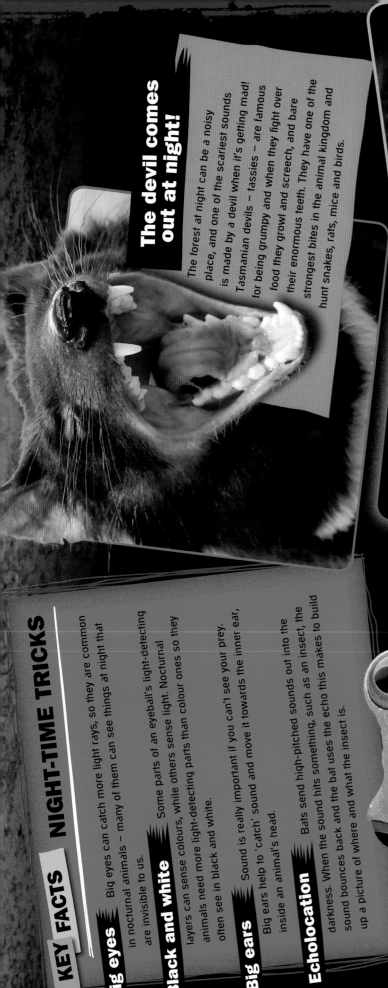

The devil comes out at night!

The forest at night can be a noisy place, and one of the scariest sounds is made by a devil when it's getting mad! Tasmanian devils – tassies – are famous for being grumpy and when they fight over food they growl and screech, and bare their enormous teeth. They have one of the strongest bites in the animal kingdom and hunt snakes, rats, mice and birds.

If you liked leaping around between branches in the dark, you'd need eyes this big! I'm a tarsier and I chase insects, birds and lizards at night. If I didn't have amazing eyesight I'd go hungry, or even worse...I'd fall out of the tree!

How gorgeous am I? I'm a red-eyed tree frog. During the day I hide my lovely colours under a leaf but at night I come out to hunt insects. If I get scared I flash my red feet and make my eyes bulge out of my head. Bet you can't do that!

KEY FACTS NIGHT-TIME TRICKS

Big eyes Big eyes can catch more light rays, so they are common in nocturnal animals – many of them can see things at night that are invisible to us.

Black and white Some parts of an eyeball's light-detecting layers can sense colours, while others sense light. Nocturnal animals need more light-detecting parts than colour ones so they often see in black and white.

Big ears Sound is really important if you can't see your prey. Big ears help to 'catch' sound and move it towards the inner ear, inside an animal's head.

Echolocation Bats send high-pitched sounds out into the darkness. When the sound hits something, such as an insect, the sound bounces back and the bat uses the echo this makes to build up a picture of where and what the insect is.

33

DEFEND OR DIE

WE'RE OFF THE MENU!

In most beastly battles there is an attacker and a defender. These careful critters are determined to keep off the lunch menu, but it takes some smart defence tactics to stay alive.

There are some cool weapons on display here, from multi-coloured froggy jumpsuits to animal acrobatics. And it's amazing what you can do with some spare bottom-gas!

The blood squirt can travel up to 1 m and contains a chemical that is toxic to some dogs, wolves and coyotes.

Squirts blood out of its eyes!

Tears of blood

This short-horned lizard has one of the most bizarre defence mechanisms on Earth – it can shoot blood from its eyes! Some species of short-horned lizard are capable of squirting blood in this way when they feel threatened, by rupturing the tiny blood vessels in their eyelids.

Foaming mess

Grasshoppers can make a perfect snack for birds, but not this one! Foam grasshoppers create clouds of bubbly liquid, which pour out of holes in their skin and become a toxic cloak. The foam smells disgusting and tastes revolting.

Touch me and you'll regret it

Toxic caterpillars have seriously nasty spines.

Some people say I can be a bit prickly at times, but I think my tough outside gives a bad impression. Really, I'm a bit of a softie and I just need to look after myself. My spiny skin helps me hide against a tree trunk but I don't take any chances, and that's why my spines are totally toxic!

TWIST IT!

their bottom to make the foam!
lots of plant sap then blow gases out of
roamy nests, called cuckoo spit. They drink
Their young protect themselves by making
Froghoppers are high-jumping insects.

an attacker!
scared they simply throw up all over
are great at vomiting, so when they get
The caterpillars of large white butterflies

with venomous spurs on their hind legs.
Male duck-billed platypuses can lash out

cocktail. Even leopards are scared of them.
which they mix with spit to make a deadly
They release toxins from their elbows,
Slow lorises are small forest primates.

screams, too.
polecats can produce ear-splitting
that they are rarely attacked. Striped
Polecats spray such a disgusting liquid

STAY AWAY

BELCH!

What a stink

You think you're so big and clever, but look at what I can do! My gorgeous black and white coat is doing a great job of making sure you notice me, which is good because I can put on one impressive show. Watch me doing a handstand – come nice and close...closer...perfect. Now, I'm going to spray a foul and stinky liquid at you!

Spotted skunks have stinky sprays.

Black and white is so last year. We frogs prefer to stay trendy and insist on dressing in the latest must-have jumpsuits in glorious shades. It's not just about fashion of course. Our multi-coloured skin screams 'poison' at any nasty snakes or brutal birds that fancy a dish of frogs' legs for dinner.

Natty dressers

Poison arrow frogs have a poisonous skin that is truly deadly.

MEET THE NASTIES

NATURE'S FOULEST FIVE

Blood-sucker

This marine woodlouse clamps onto the tongue of a fish, then sucks the blood from the fish's tongue until the tongue dies. The creature stays firmly attached in the fish's mouth, working like its original tongue, eating scraps of food, mucus and blood!

Gut-grower

Tapeworms live inside an animal's gut, surviving on semi-digested food. The hooks on the top of its head keep it securely attached. Tapeworms inside human guts have grown to 11.25 m long and can survive for years!

Urgh! This is _TOTALLY_ gross!

Gas attack

This lovely walnut sphinx moth has a nasty habit – when it's scared it passes gas! There's nothing like a bottom burp to keep everyone away!

Baby

Mum!

Woah, gas power!

Monster chick

This chick is not as cute as it looks. It's a young cuckoo and its mother laid her egg in the nest of another bird – dunnocks are common hosts. When the egg hatched, the chick threw the other bird's chicks out of the nest. The poor step-parents then keep feeding the monster chick until it leaves home.

Vile vulture

Turkey vultures usually feast on dying or dead animals. They poop on their own legs to keep cool, and stuff in their poop has the added bonus of killing the nasty bacteria that like to live on their blood-soaked feet.

FAMILY FEUD

FLESH AND BLOOD

Animal battles are not always between predator and prey. Sometimes members of a family or group turn into murderous monsters and attack one another.

Family in-fighting happens when animals want food, to mate, or when bad tempers boil over into brutal behaviour.

BIG WORD ALERT
TERRITORY
An area or space animals call their own.

Get out of my room!

Both male and female cats have territories. They mark their space with smells to tell others to keep out, but if that doesn't work then a fierce fight may follow – these female leopards will settle their score with fangs and claws.

Baboons go berserk

Baboons are monkeys that live in large family groups called troops, and they are famous for their family meltdowns! They solve their problems with violence, and as they are fast, fearsome and fanged they can do a lot of damage.

※ Males often chase and attack females, making a loud 'wahoo' call to scare them and keep other males away.

※ Male baboons sometimes kill baby baboons.

※ Males fight with each other to take over a family group and become the troop's 'top dog'.

Not so gentle giants

Family groups of giraffes are mostly made up of females, but males wander nearby hoping to join the gang at mating time. Sometimes, a fight brews when two males — who may be related — bump into each other. The battle involves head-butting and whacking each other with their necks. It can easily end in death for one of the males.

Watch it!

This looks like a lovely neck-cuddle, but it's actually giraffe-speak for 'Get outta here now, before I wallop you!'

TWIST IT!

These are tough times for polar bears. The ice in their cold Arctic home is melting, and it's harder for the giant carnivores to hunt. As a result, they are becoming more likely to turn cannibal and eat polar bear cubs.

Chimpanzees usually eat plants and bugs, but they sometimes get a taste for meat, and attack chimps from neighbouring groups. They even eat baby chimps.

Lions don't make good step-dads. When a male lion takes over a new pride he may kill all the cubs. This mean streak works well, as all the lionesses are quickly ready to start a new family with him.

BABY BASHERS

Crazy coots

Coots are waterbirds with a short fuse. If the chicks pester mum or dad for food, the exhausted parents may lose their temper and start to peck back at them. If the hungry chicks don't get the hint, they may be pecked to death. It's common for coots to begin with as many as nine chicks, but end up with only two or three.

EIGHT GREAT DINNER DATES

THE MOST BRUTAL BEASTS

They may be short on good conversation but these brutal beasts have got killer skills that will bring any party to life! We've chosen them as our favourites, some you've met before in this book and some are new – but who would be on your invitation list?

We reckon these are some of the most impressive animals in the world.

DINNER INVITATION

T-REX

Possibly the scariest meat-eater that ever lived, the Tyrannosaurus rex – or Terrible Lizard – was a massive dinosaur. His head alone measured 1 m long and just look at those saw-edged teeth!

DINNER INVITATION

HONEY BADGER

Honey badgers have a foul temper and are totally fearless. We admire them because they will attack and kill almost anything – that gives them top scores for brutality!

DINNER INVITATION

GIANT OCTOPUS

This Pacific giant octopus is a phenomenal predator and, for an added bonus, it looks like something from outer space! Its weapons are its sucker-covered tentacles, containing 2,240 suckers in total, and a fierce bite.

Diver

DINNER INVITATION

DEATHSTALKER SCORPION

Deathstalker scorpions have a stinging spray of acid, and huge front limbs for crushing their prey – but we've chosen them because they look like mini-monster car-crushers.

DINNER INVITATION
NILE CROCODILE

More dangerous than a great white shark, more cunning than a cobra – the Nile crocodile snaps and grabs. And how many animals do you know that can spend all day pretending to be a log before springing into action?

DINNER INVITATION
KILLER WHALE

Killer whales, or orcas (their correct name), carefully plan their attacks and can work as part of a deadly team. Killer whales hunt and slaughter their prey with ruthless determination.

DINNER INVITATION
SPOTTED HYENA

Horrible hyenas look as if they are enjoying themselves when they go on a killing spree. They cheerfully rip limbs off a body and can crunch bones with their oversized jaws.

DINNER INVITATION
BULLET ANT

If you had to choose between walking on broken glass or holding a handful of bullet ants, we suggest the glass! These tiny terrors have big jaws and their stings burn like nothing else on earth.

WE WANT BLOOD

SUPER SLURPERS AND SUCKERS

The thought of drinking blood may be repulsive, but it's the world's best power-drink. It's even better than an energy-shot, because it's packed not just with energy, but with life-giving ingredients.

Animals that feed on blood have just one big problem – how do they get to the blood? These brutal beasts have discovered some nifty tricks to reach the red stuff.

Pierce and suck

The deadliest of all blood-suckers is the mosquito, because it passes on the killer disease malaria when it feeds. A mosquito has a needle-like mouthpart which it injects into flesh and uses to suck up blood.

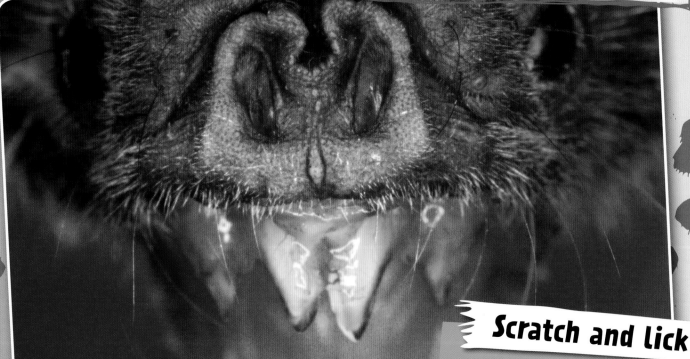

Scratch and lick

Vampire bats scrape the skin away from their victim's feet or ankles with their teeth, then lick up the blood. Vampire bats usually prey on horses and cows, but they do sometimes feed on sleeping humans!

How can blood-feeders feed without being discovered by their prey?

They may inject a painkiller into their feeding spot, so the victim can't feel them break the skin, and they may pour a chemical into the wound that keeps the blood flowing quickly.

The all-in-one meal

Blood contains:
95 percent water

Protein – useful for building muscles

Sugar – useful for instant energy

Vitamins and minerals – useful for growing

Blood doesn't contain much fat, so blood-feeders don't have long-term energy stores. That means they must feed often, or starve to death.

Scrape and swallow

Vampire fish swim into another fish's gills and use their needle-like teeth to scrape at a blood vessel until it breaks open. The fish then simply swallow the blood as it pours out.

Peck and sip

Vampire finches enjoy a booby bloody banquet when there is no other food around. They peck at the skin and feathers of a booby (a type of bird) until they draw blood.

Good guy or bad guy?

Oxpeckers are birds that peck blood-filled ticks off the skin of animals, such as antelopes – and that's great for the antelopes who are then pest-free. But oxpeckers like the flavour of these mini-snacks so much they sometimes go one step further, and peck at the blood-soaked wounds left by the ticks, causing the poor animal even more harm and pain.

BLOOD LUST

A tick can increase in size ten times after it has fed.

Vampire bats find their prey by sensing the heat from their bodies, and also by using heat-detectors to find a blood vessel under the victim's skin.

Only female mosquitoes feed on blood. They need it to be able to lay their eggs.

Blood contains a lot of water, so vampire bats must wee while they are feeding to get rid of some of the water, or they'd be too heavy to fly!

TWIST IT!

WHO'S BRUTAL NOW

People kill Amur leopards because they like their fur and turn it into coats. There are only about 30 Amur leopards left alive in the wild. Their home is now protected from poachers, but their future is bleak.

ENDANGERED!

Orangutans live in trees, and when these are cut down they have nowhere to live. The rainforests of Sumatra are being destroyed to grow palm oil and there are even plans to build a road through their last habitat.

HUNTED TO DEATH

Humans mainly hunt animals for food and fur. Long ago, we only took what we absolutely needed, and we lived in harmony with the ecosystem. In modern times, we have become greedy.

Rhinos used to roam throughout Africa and Asia. Then people decided (wrongly) that their horns were magical and could cure diseases. Rhinos are killed and their horns cut off to be sold. Western black rhinos were declared extinct in 2011.

EXTINCT!

HOMELESS

An animal's home is its habitat, and when that habitat is destroyed by people – often to plant crops or build roads and homes – the animals have nowhere to live or hunt.

There were about 4,000 South China tigers in the 1950s. Then their forest habitat was destroyed and the big cats were killed as 'pests'. By the 1990s there were about 50 tigers left and none have been seen in the wild now for 25 years.

EXTINCT?

IT'S THE END OF THE ROAD...

Animals can be pretty brutal, but maybe the award for the most dangerous product of nature should go to humans.

Since we've been on the planet we have destroyed habitats, hunted entire species to death, and we continue to make our planet a perilous place for the animals we share it with.

ENDANGERED!

The sea lions of the Galapagos Islands live in large groups on rocky shores. Humans have brought new animals, such as dogs, to the islands. These alien invaders carried diseases that killed the sea lions. They can also catch a deadly disease spread by mosquitoes.

LIFE IN THE BALANCE

✳ People who study how animals and plants live together have come up with a handy word to describe the way they need each other: ecosystem [say ee-koh-sist-em].

✳ An ecosystem is a place, and all the living things in it. They all affect each other, and often exist together in a precious balance. When a new animal or plant comes into an ecosystem it can change that balance in a bad way.

✳ Your local park or recreation ground is an ecosystem. Imagine a pride of lions leaving their own ecosystem to live in your park – they would cause havoc!

ENDANGERED!

There are fewer than 2,000 Galapagos penguins left in the wild. They are dying because of pollution in their water, and because they get caught in fishermen's nets. Climate change is also damaging their habitat.

BIG WORD ALERT

CLIMATE CHANGE

A major change in the world's weather patterns.

ALIEN INVADERS

An animal that has moved into a place it doesn't belong is called an alien invader, and it may upset the ecosystem. Often, it is humans that cause the problem by moving animals around.

The dodo was a large flightless bird. When European sailors came to their island home of Mauritius they brought cats, dogs, rats and pigs with them. The dodos could not defend themselves, or their eggs and chicks, from these predators and they became extinct by about 1700.

EXTINCT!

DEATH BY DIRT

Climate change and pollution – which is dirt, dirty air and rubbish – have damaged the habitats of many animals around the world.

The little golden toad used to live in a rainforest in Costa Rica, in Central America. It has not been seen since 1989. Its extinction is thought to be the result of pollution and changes in the climate.

EXTINCT!

ACKNOWLEDGEMENTS

COVER (sp) © NHPA/Photoshot, (b/l) © Eric Isselée - iStock.com; **2** (t) Sipa USA/Rex Features; **3** (t) Gerard Lacz/Rex Features, (b) Dave Beaudette; **4** (sp) © NHPA/Photoshot, (b/l) © Photoshot, (b/r) © Florian Andronache - Shutterstock.com; **5** (t/l) © Eric Isselée - iStock.com, (b/l) Jim Zipp/Science Photo Library, (b/c/l) Dave Beaudette, (b/c/r) © John Downer Productions/naturepl.com, (b/r) Professor Nico Smit; **6** (c) © Tony Heald/naturepl.com, (b/l) © NHPA/Photoshot, (b/r) © Roman Sotola - Fotolia.com; **7** (t) © NHPA/Photoshot, (b) Caters News Agency Ltd/Rex Features, (r) © Anup Shah/naturepl.com; **8** (t) © Sergey Uryadnikov - Shutterstock.com, (b) © Ashok Jain/naturepl.com; **8–9** (bgd) © Rafal Olechowski - Shutterstock.com; **9** (b/r) © Hanne & Jens Eriksen/naturepl.com, (b/l) NHPA/Photoshot, (t/r) Milan Krasula/Solent News/Rex Features, (t/l) © DG Jervis - Shutterstock.com; **10** © NHPA/Photoshot; **11** (t, c) © NHPA/Photoshot, (b) © Photoshot; **12** (t) Gerard Lacz/Rex Features, (b) Alaska Stock Images/National Geographic Stock; **12–13** © Iakov Filimonov - Shutterstock.com, © Kamil Macniak - Shutterstock.com, © Tribalium - Shutterstock.com, © Martan - Shutterstock.com, © stevemart - Shutterstock.com, © Kamil Macniak - Shutterstock.com, © Gary Blakeley - Shutterstock.com, © Aleksei Gurko - Shutterstock.com, © PILart - Shutterstock.com, (bgd) © SongPixels - Shutterstock.com, (l, r) © dencg - Shutterstock.com; **13** (t) Bartlett, Des & Jen/National Geographic Stock, (b) Bournemouth News/Rex Features; **14** (l) © Ryan M. Bolton - Shutterstock.com, (r) © Florian Andronache - Shutterstock.com; **15** (l) Jurgen & Christine Sohns/FLPA, (r) © Tony Heald/naturepl.com, (t/r) Gustavocarra/ Creative Commons License; **16** © Luiz Claudio Marigo/naturepl.com; **17** (t) © Oceans-Image/Photoshot, (c) © NHPA/Photoshot, (b) © David Pattyn/naturepl.com; **18** © Pete Oxford/naturepl.com; **19** (b/l) © Robyn Butler - Shutterstock.com, (c/l) © tratong - Shutterstock.com, (t) Tom Murphy/National Geographic Stock, (b/r) Sipa USA/Rex Features, (t/r) Kevin Deacon; **20** © Sergey Gorshkov/naturepl.com; **21** (t/r) © Herbert Kratky - Shutterstock.com, (c/r) Vaclav Silha/Barcroft USA Ltd., (c/l) Newspix/Rex Features; **22** (c) © NHPA/Photoshot, (t) © Josh Anon - Shutterstock.com, (bgd) © STILLFX - Shutterstock.com, (dp) © Glam - Shutterstock.com; **23** (t) © Alex Hyde/naturepl.com, (c/r) Jim Zipp/Science Photo Library, (b) © NHPA/Photoshot; **24** (sp) © Photoshot, (r) Behavioural Ecology Research Group, Oxford; **25** (t) © DLILLC/Corbis, (b/r) © Andy Rouse/naturepl.com; **26** Gil Wizen; **27** (t) © NHPA/Photoshot, (c) © Martin Dohrn/naturepl.com, (b) Gerard Lacz/Rex Features, (r) © Roger Meerts - Shutterstock.com; **28** (sp) Tim Green; (b/r) Nicky Bay/Science Photo Library; **29** (t) © Alex Hyde/ naturepl.com, (c) © Staffan Widstrand/naturepl.com, (b) © Cathy Keifer - Shutterstock.com; **30** Jurgen & Christine Sohns/FLPA; **30–31** (bgd) © Ghenadie - Shutterstock.com; **31** (c, b) © Michael Richards/John Downer/naturepl.com, (t) Mark Moffett/Minden Pictures/FLPA; **32** © Dietmar Nill/naturepl.com; **33** (l) © Bernhard Richter - Shutterstock.com, (r) © Matej Hudovernik - Shutterstock.com, (b) © Dirk Ercken - Shutterstock.com; **34** (c) Dave Beaudette, (b) Piotr Naskrecki/Minden Pictures/National Geographic Stock; **35** (t) © Cathy Keifer - Shutterstock.com, (b/r) © Dirk Ercken - Shutterstock.com, (c) © John Downer Productions/naturepl.com; **36** (b) Professor Nico Smit, (t) Eye Of Science/Science Photo Library; **36–37** © ririro - Shutterstock.com; **37** (t/r) © Andy Sands/naturepl.com, (c) © Melinda Fawver - Shutterstock.com, (b) © Holly Kuchera - Shutterstock.com; **38** (b) © NHPA/Photoshot; **38–39** (c) © Richard Du Toit/ naturepl.com;**39** © NHPA/Photoshot; **40** (t/l) © DM7 - Shutterstock.com, (c/r) Bartlett, Des & Jen/National Geographic Stock, (b/r) © NHPA/Photoshot, (b/l) © Jeff Rotman/naturepl.com; **40–41** (dp) © idea for life - Shutterstock.com, (dp) © JungleOutThere - Shutterstock. com, (dp) © Matthew Cole - Shutterstock.com, (t) © Green Jo - Shutterstock.com, (t/r) © Taigi - Shutterstock.com, © Alex459 - Shutterstock.com, (t/r, b/l) © Gray wall studio - Shutterstock.com; **41** (c) © Hermann Brehm/naturepl.com, (c/l) © Anup Shah/naturepl. com, (r) © Xavier Marchant - Shutterstock.com, (b/r) Gerard Lacz/Rex Features; **42** (b) Michael & Patricia Fogden/Minden Pictures/FLPA, (t) © Sinclair Stammers/naturepl.com; **43** (t/r) Mark Newman/Science Photo Library, (c) © Villiers Steyn - Shutterstock.com, (b/r) © Jim Clare/naturepl.com; **44** (l) © NHPA/Photoshot, (r) © Kjersti Joergensen - Shutterstock.com; **45** (l) © Kjersti Joergensen - Shutterstock.com, (r) © Alfie Photography - Shutterstock.com

Key: t = top, b = bottom, c = centre, l = left, r = right, sp = single page, dp = double page, bgd = background

RIPLEY's HUMAN BODY

Believe It or Not!®

RIPLEY
PUBLISHING

a Jim Pattison Company

TWISTS

Contents

Written by Camilla de la Bedoyere
Consultant Dr. Irfan Ghani

PUBLISHING

Publisher Anne Marshall

Managing Editor Rebecca Miles Picture Researcher James Proud Editors Lisa Regan, Rosie Alexander Assistant Editor Amy Harrison Proofreader Judy Barratt Indexer Hilary Bird

Art Director Sam South
Design Rocket Design (East Anglia) Ltd
Reprographics Stephan Davis

www.ripleys.com/books

PAGE 8

TWISTS

PAGE 7

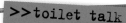

Body Beautiful

>> it's all about you >>

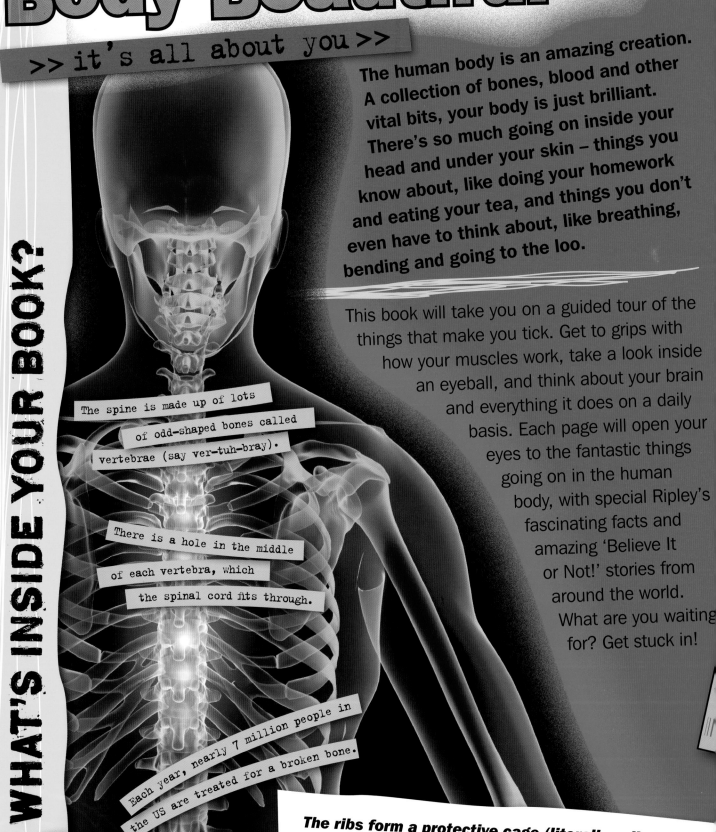

The human body is an amazing creation. A collection of bones, blood and other vital bits, your body is just brilliant. There's so much going on inside your head and under your skin – things you know about, like doing your homework and eating your tea, and things you don't even have to think about, like breathing, bending and going to the loo.

This book will take you on a guided tour of the things that make you tick. Get to grips with how your muscles work, take a look inside an eyeball, and think about your brain and everything it does on a daily basis. Each page will open your eyes to the fantastic things going on in the human body, with special Ripley's fascinating facts and amazing 'Believe It or Not!' stories from around the world. What are you waiting for? Get stuck in!

WHAT'S INSIDE YOUR BOOK?

The spine is made up of lots of odd-shaped bones called vertebrae (say ver-tuh-bray).

There is a hole in the middle of each vertebra, which the spinal cord fits through.

Each year, nearly 7 million people in the US are treated for a broken bone.

The ribs form a protective cage (literally called the ribcage) around vital organs such as the heart and lungs. Most people have 12 pairs of ribs, making 24 altogether, but some people are born with only 11 pairs, and others get an extra rib or two!

TWISTS

BIG WORD ALERT!

EPIDERMIS

The top layer of your skin is called the epidermis. It is made from dead cells that are shed every 27 days.

Found a new word? Big word alerts will explain it for you.

Learn fab fast facts to go with the cool pictures.

It's Alimentary

>>digestion>>

Your digestive system is a fabulous food processor. It pulps and pulverises food before squirting it with burning acids and churning it into a stinking stomach soup that is forced through your gurgling guts (also known as intestines).

Billions of bacteria break the food down into smaller and smaller bits so they can be used to fuel your body and help it grow.

A sandwich's journey through your alimentary canal – from mouth to anus – can take more than 24 hours and covers around 7 m in total.

KEY FACTS

Your **alimentary canal** is packed with chemicals called enzymes. These powerful juices help break food down into useful nutrients.

The **oesophagus** is a tube that leads from your mouth to your stomach. It's made of muscles that force the food downwards.

Your **gall bladder** and **pancreas** store and produce substances that help the body's digestive process.

After a big meal your stomach can stretch to **40 times** the size it was when it was empty.

One type of bacteria – **Heliobacter pylori** – survives in the stomach's burning juices. These mini-bugs infect half of the world's people, and can cause pain and ulcers.

Oesophagus

Stomach

Gall bladder   **Pancreas**

It's big!

The small intestine is lined with tiny, finger-like villi. On the surface of the villi are even tinier folds called microvilli. If you stretched all your villi out they would cover an entire football field!

Believe It or Not!

This rice cracker contains digger wasps! They are a delicacy specially created for the Japanese fan club for wasps.

TASTY!

Appendix

Anus

Small intestine (ileum)

Large intestine (colon)

Do the twist

This book is packed with incredible facts about the human body. It will teach you amazing things about your body, but like all Twists books, it shines a spotlight on things that are unbelievable but true. Turn the pages and find out more...

...ts bicycles, televisions, and even aircraft with no problems! He has to take them apart and slurp down mineral oil before swallowing the smaller bits.

...garbage collection
...Farook, from TirunelvelI,
...d eating nothing but flies.

LIVE TREE FROGS AND RATS

For over 40 years, Jiang Musheng of China has eaten live tree frogs and rats to ward off abdominal pains.

CHICKEN FEED

Jan Csovary, from Prievidza, Slovakia, eats chicken for breakfast, lunch and tea, and has consumed over 12,000 chickens since the early 1970s.

NOTHING BUT CHEESE

Dave Nunley from Cambridgeshire, England, has eaten nothing but grated mild cheddar cheese for more than 25 years and gets through 108 kg of it every year.

DIET OF WORMS

Wayne Fauser from Sydney, Australia, eats live earthworms.

DON'T TRY THIS AT HOME!

twist it!

It takes more brainpower to work your thumb than to control your stomach.

Half a million new stomach cells are made by your body every minute!

Whenever you blush, the lining of your stomach gets redder too.

During the course of your life you will produce enough saliva that's your spit) to fill a swimming pool.

The acids in your stomach are so strong they could dissolve a razor blade!

If you unravelled your oesophagus, stomach and intestines they would reach the height of a three-storey building.

CRAZY

Sonya Thomas is America's competitive eating champion. She weighs just 45 kg, but has managed to put away 46 mince pies in ten minutes and 52 hard-boiled eggs in just five!

EXTREME HEARTBURN FORM...

Twists are all about Believe It or Not: amazing facts, feats, and things that will make you go 'Wow!'.

Don't forget to look out for the 'twist it!' column on some pages. Twist the book to find out more fast facts about the bodies we live in.

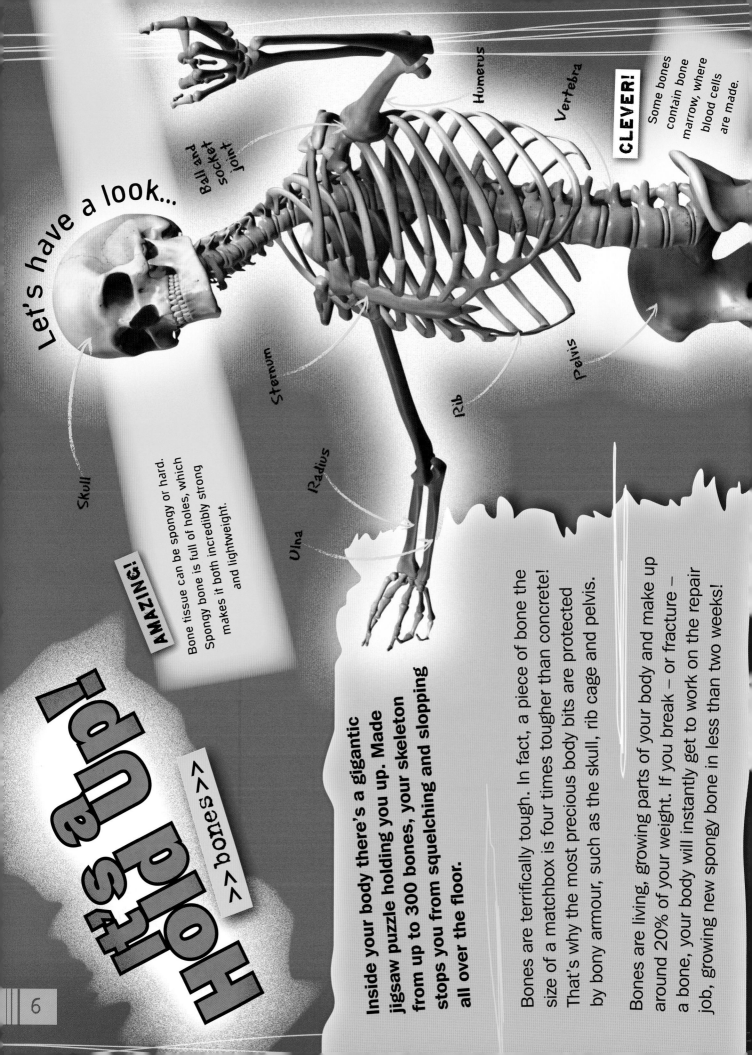

Hold it Up!

>>bones>>

Let's have a look...

Skull

Ball and socket joint

Humerus

Vertebra

Sternum

Radius

Ulna

Rib

Pelvis

AMAZING!

Bone tissue can be spongy or hard. Spongy bone is full of holes, which makes it both incredibly strong and lightweight.

CLEVER!

Some bones contain bone marrow, where blood cells are made.

Inside your body there's a gigantic jigsaw puzzle holding you up. Made from up to 300 bones, your skeleton stops you from squelching and slopping all over the floor.

Bones are terrifically tough. In fact, a piece of bone the size of a matchbox is four times tougher than concrete! That's why the most precious body bits are protected by bony armour, such as the skull, rib cage and pelvis.

Bones are living, growing parts of your body and make up around 20% of your weight. If you break – or fracture – a bone, your body will instantly get to work on the repair job, growing new spongy bone in less than two weeks!

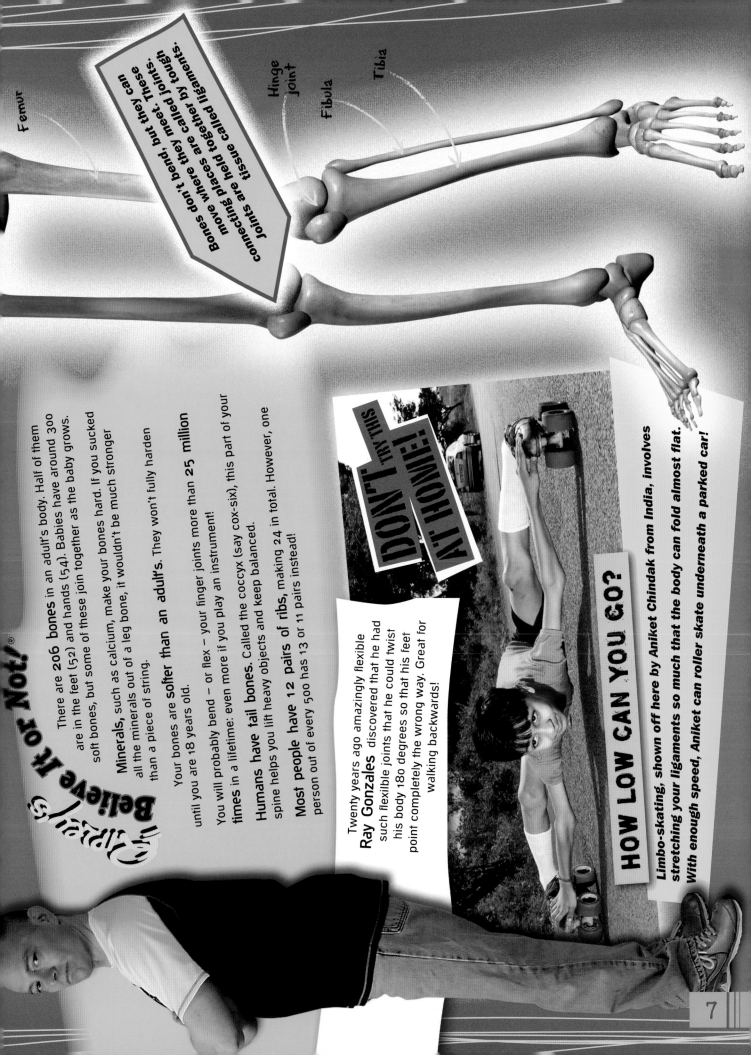

Femur

Fibula

Tibia

Hinge joint

Bones don't bend, but they meet. These places where they meet are called joints. Joints move where... These are held together by tough connecting tissue called ligaments.

Ripley's Believe It or Not!®

There are **206 bones** in an adult's body. Half of them are in the feet (52) and hands (54). Babies have around 300 soft bones, but some of these join together as the baby grows.

Minerals, such as calcium, make your bones hard. If you sucked all the minerals out of a leg bone, it wouldn't be much stronger than a piece of string.

Your bones are **softer than an adult's.** They won't fully harden until you are 18 years old.

You will probably bend – or flex – your finger joints more than **25 million** times in a lifetime: even more if you play an instrument!

Humans have tail bones. Called the coccyx (say cox-six), this part of your spine helps you lift heavy objects and keep balanced.

Most people have 12 pairs of ribs, making 24 in total. However, one person out of every 500 has 13 or 11 pairs instead!

Twenty years ago amazingly flexible **Ray Gonzales** discovered that he had such flexible joints that he could twist his body 180 degrees so that his feet point completely the wrong way. Great for walking backwards!

DON'T TRY THIS AT HOME!

HOW LOW CAN YOU GO?

Limbo-skating, shown off here by Aniket Chindak from India, involves stretching your ligaments so much that the body can fold almost flat. With enough speed, Aniket can roller skate underneath a parked car!

Use the Force

No matter how much you grow, there are parts of your body that shrink – muscles! Thankfully, these bundles of mighty fibres only get smaller to move a bone, before returning to their normal size.

Xie Tianzhuang, an 87 year old from China, lifted 14 bricks with his teeth in 2005. The bricks weighed 35 kg altogether.

Muscles give you power; they make up half your body weight and provide the pulling forces that allow you to bend an arm or lift a foot. Without your muscles – whether they're feeble or fearsome – you simply wouldn't be able to move. You've got 100 just in your head, face and neck!

MOVE IT!

Muscles usually work in pairs. Bend your arm and flex your biceps to see the muscle bulge as it shortens. As you relax your arm the biceps relaxes and the triceps muscle below contracts (becomes shorter).

There are three types of muscle. **Skeletal muscle** helps you move and **smooth muscle** does jobs such as keeping food travelling through your digestive system. **Cardiac muscle** makes your heart pump blood. Skeletal muscles are attached to bones by tough fibres, called tendons.

Bent arm – biceps is contracted.

PUCKER UP!

You use 11 face muscles to frown, 12 to smile and 20 to kiss!

The triceps muscle will contract to straighten the arm again.

Keep on truckin'

The Rev. Jon Bruney, from Indiana, USA, is famous for his strongman achievements, such as bending steel bars and tearing phone directories in half. In 2004 he and two other strongmen joined forces to pull a 15-tonne trailer for 1.5 km.

twist it!

Turn your foot outwards and you will be using 13 different muscles in your leg and 20 in the foot. Taking a simple step forwards uses 54 muscles!

Humans have more than 600 muscles in their bodies, but caterpillars have more than 4,000!

Your body is about two-thirds water, and about half of this is contained in your muscles.

The tiniest muscle in the body is called the stirrup. You have one inside each ear, and it is no bigger than this number 1.

Way back in the 1920s performer Clarence Willard of the USA amazed audiences by growing 15 cm in height, just by stretching the muscles of his knees, hips and throat.

BIG WORD ALERT!

GLUTEUS MAXIMUS
The biggest muscle in your body is called the gluteus maximus. It's in your bottom.

MEGA MUSCLES

need a lift?

Need a lift? Ask John Evans – he could possibly carry you and your car on his head! His best effort is balancing a car weighing 160 kg for 33 seconds.

9

Under Pressure

Blood: you know it as the oozy red stuff that pours out when you cut yourself. But about 5 litres of this thick liquid is racing around your body, keeping everything in good order. Lose half of your blood and you'll drop dead!

Blood is like a river of life. It carries oxygen and nutrients to every cell, and mops up all the toxic waste. It's also at the front line of your body's defence system. White blood cells track down and kill any nasty bugs that are out to damage, or even destroy, you.

There are five types of white blood cell. They patrol your body on the lookout for bacteria, viruses, cancer cells and other unwanted visitors.

CRUSTY!

Scabs are made up of dried, clotted blood and dead skin cells that stick together making a natural plaster.

Blood is made up of red cells, white cells and fragments of cells called platelets.

Red blood cells use iron to transport oxygen. That's why you need this mineral - found in meat and some vegetables - in your diet.

Ripley's Believe It or Not!®

Long ago it was believed that people suffering from some illnesses had 'too much blood'. Blood-sucking leeches were used on the skin to suck out the excess!

BLOOD SUCKERS!

Surgeons operating on a man in Vancouver, Canada, in 2007, were used to the sight of blood – but not dark green in colour! Doctors think it turned that colour because of medication the patient was taking.

Artery wall

Red blood cell

Plasma

blood is brilliant

* **Bone marrow** makes around 2 million red blood cells every second.

* A single red blood cell can carry about one billion packets of oxygen around your body. You have **25 trillion red blood cells**...so that's a lot of oxygen!

* **One drop** of blood contains around 5 million red blood cells.

* **Blood** can be taken from one human body and put into another, in a life-saving procedure called a transfusion. Frank Loose of Germany has donated some of his own blood more than 800 times, and has saved dozens of lives with his gift.

Blood cells float in a fluid called plasma. Blood makes up about 8% of your body weight.

11

Take Heart

In the centre of your chest is your heart. It's a powerful, pumping organ that sends blood whizzing around a network of blood vessels at speeds of 270 km a day!

When your heart beats it pumps blood from inside the heart around your body, through blood vessels. In between beats your heart fills with blood again. Your blood carries oxygen to all parts of your body to make them work.

It gets this oxygen from your lungs when you breathe in. This oxygen-rich blood is taken to your heart to be pumped around the body.

When the blood has delivered the oxygen to your body it comes back to the heart to be pumped out again to collect more oxygen from the lungs.

BODY PUMP

aorta
carries oxygen-rich blood to the body

pulmonary artery
takes blood to the lungs, to collect oxygen

right atrium
blood from the body enters the heart here

left atrium
receives oxygen-rich blood from the lungs

left ventricle
pumps blood to the body through the aorta

right ventricle
pumps the blood to the lungs

A boy called Goga Diasamidze from Tbilisi in Georgia was born with two hearts. The second of them is near his stomach and works perfectly well.

Your heart beats around 60–80 times a minute, but doing exercise can increase this rate to 200 times a minute!

blood vessels

There are two types of large blood vessel. Arteries (shown in red) carry blood away from the heart. Veins (shown in blue) carry blood towards the heart. There are both veins and arteries in all parts of the body.

BEAT IT! Your heart will beat more than 3 billion times if you live to old age and will have pumped enough blood to fill an oil tanker 46 times over!

BRRR!

Capillaries are tiny blood vessels. They connect arteries to veins, and make up 98% of the total length of all blood vessels.

Many of 'Ice Man' Wim Hof's amazing feats take place in icy conditions. Here, he stood in 703 kg of ice cubes for an incredible 1 hour 12 minutes! He has mastered the ability to increase his heart rate and the blood flow to his extremities (like his fingers and toes) to stop the cold affecting him as badly.

FASCINATING FACT! FASCINATING FACT!

HEART OF THE MATTER

Blood vessels connect your heart with all your body bits. If you could lay these tubes out in one long line, they would measure 100,000 km and would circle the world more than twice!

At any moment, about 75% of your blood is in your veins, but only 5% is in your capillaries. The remaining 20% is in your arteries.

CORONARY
To do with the heart.

CIRCULATORY

The network of blood vessels and heart – and the way they send blood round and round the body – is called a circulatory system.

BIG WORD ALERT!

13

Seeing is Believing
>> eyes >>

Eyes are jelly-filled cameras and your body's number-one sense organs. All day long your eyes keep your brain busy, passing it masses of information about the world around you.

Rays of light pour into your eyes, where clear lenses focus them to make a crisp, clean image. Nerves zap info about the image to the brain, which has the tricky task of turning those nerve signals into vision. It can even combine the images from both eyes to make a single 3-D picture.

It takes six muscles to move each eyeball, so you can get a good view all around. If you spy something sad, your tears drain into tiny holes in the corner of your eyes, and flow into your nose. That's why your nose runs when you cry!

Lens

Aqueous humour

Ligaments

Pupil

Iris

Cornea

EYE SPY

Human eye muscles move around 10,000 times a day!

Student Jalisa Mae Thompson can pop her eyeballs so far out of their sockets they hardly look real!

14

Vitreous humour

Retina

Optic nerve

The retina has about 130 million cells for seeing black and white, but only 7 million for seeing colours. Humans can detect 500 shades of grey!

A newborn baby can't make tears until it is around three weeks old!

It's impossible to sneeze with your eyes open.

You lose around 1,600 of your eyelashes each year. Thankfully, new ones are always growing.

The muscles you use to blink are the fastest in your body – moving your eyelids at a super speedy 35 cm a second around 84 million times every year!

FOR YOUR EYES ONLY

BIG WORD ALERT!

HUMOURS
The <u>aqueous</u> and <u>vitreous humours</u> are clear substances (either watery or like jelly) in the eyeball.

Eyes are delicate organs, so we have eyelids, eyelashes, and tears to protect them.

WOOOOAHHH!

A visual (or optical) illusion tricks us into seeing something that isn't real.
Look at this picture, let your eyes roam from circle to circle, and it will appear
to have moving parts. Of course, it doesn't, but sometimes your brain can't
quite keep up with messages sent by your eyes.

The coloured part of your eye is called the iris. It controls how much light enters the pupil, to produce perfect images, and protects your eyes from sun damage.

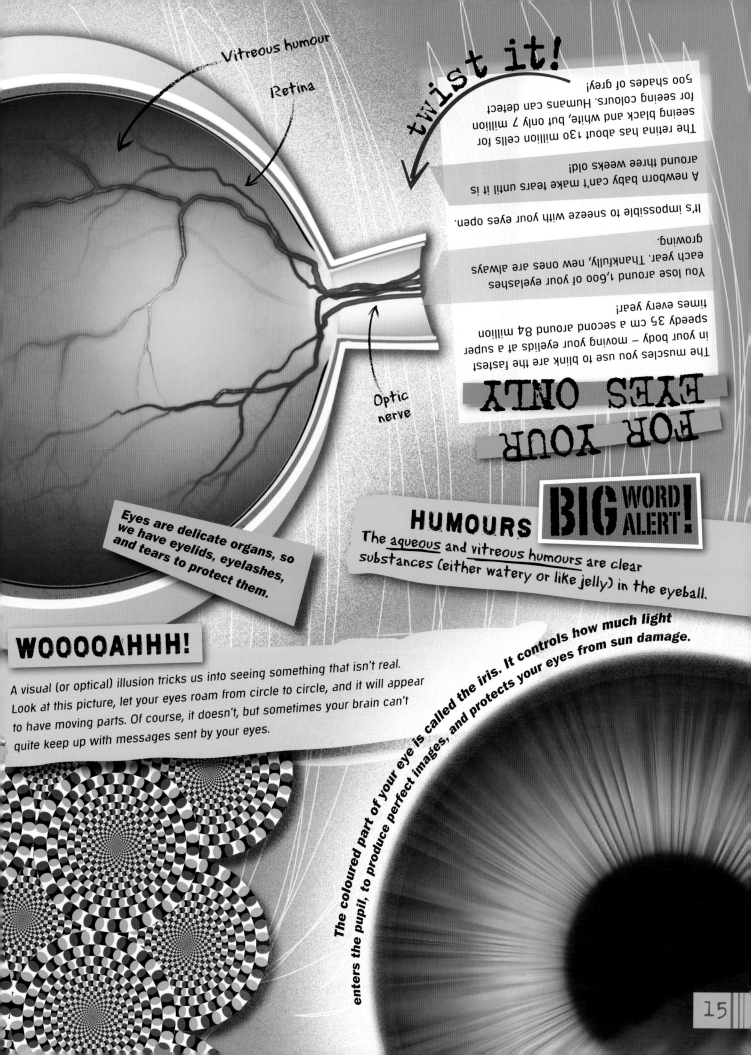

Surround Sound

GET THE BALANCE RIGHT

Listen carefully – it's time to find out how ears hear. These auditory organs don't just help you to sense sound: they stop you from falling over, every time you take a step!

That fleshy flap stuck to the side of your head is just one part of an ear. Each flap, or pinna, sends sound down your ear canal to the eardrum, which vibrates. Those vibrations shimmy through the tiny hammer, anvil and stirrup bones into a shell-shaped organ, called the cochlea.

Squashed next to the cochlea is an organ of balance. It is made up of three tubes, all filled with liquid. If you spin round, that liquid swishes about, making you dizzy!

The cochlea is where the real business of hearing happens. Sound is turned into nerve impulses and sent at lightning speed to the brain. And hey presto – you can hear!

Your smallest bones – stirrups – are in your ears. They measure 2.6 mm long and weigh 0.004 g.

Hammer

Semicircular canals

Anvil

Auditory nerve

To the brain

Here-hear!

Pinna

Ear canal

Eardrum

Stirrup

Cochlea

OUCH!

Playing a personal music player (MP3) on full volume could permanently damage your hearing after just 1 minute 29 seconds.

The cochlea contains millions of tiny hairs. When vibrations make them move, they send messages to the brain along the auditory nerve.

SOUNDS AMAZING

Beethoven was a famous composer of classical music. He continued to write and perform great music even when he lost his hearing!

Wei Mingtang from China has leaky ears. He attaches a hose to them, and then blows out candles or inflates balloons!

Earwax and ear hair protect your ears, and even prevent insects from nesting in the ear canal!

Earwax can be yellow, orange or brown and gross old bits drop out of your ears all the time.

People used to believe that earwigs would climb into ears while people slept, and burrow into their brains to lay their eggs. It's not true, honestly!

twist it!

STEADY AS YOU GO

Balancing on a high wire is tricky enough, but this guy managed to pedal his bike 30 m above the ground without falling off!

BIG WORD ALERT!

AUDITORY
To do with hearing.

It may sound strange (ha ha!) but many people around the world enjoy performing feats of 'ear strength'. This man, celebrating Chinese New Year in Beijing, is just one of several choosing to pull vehicles along with his ear. Ouch!

Hey, you've got something in your ear! Narayan Rasad Pal of India proudly shows off the long strands of hair that grow from his ears. They measure an incredible 10 cm!

17

Staggering Senses

>> taste, touch and more! >>

Close your eyes and touch the tip of your nose with a finger. Easy isn't it? But how did you know where your nose is? Thanks to your staggering senses you've got up-to-date nuggets of info whizzing to your brain all of the time.

How many senses do you have? People used to say we have five: we can see, hear, touch, smell and taste. But now we know there are loads more. Feelings such as cold and hunger are all part of your body's sensory world.

RUMBLE!

Got tummy rumbles and pain in your belly? Your body is telling you to eat – now! You could make like Japan's Takeru Kobayashi, international champion hot-dog eater. In 2005 he retained his title by eating 49 hot dogs in 12 minutes. His personal best is an unbelievable 53·5 hot dogs in that time!

BRRR!

Getting so cold it hurts? Time to put on your winter woollies or go somewhere warm, before you freeze to death. Ice swimmer Lewis Pugh swam 1 km in the Antarctic wearing only a swimming cap, goggles and trunks, in a temperature of 0°C. He was in the water for 18 minutes 10 seconds and described the feeling as a 'screaming pain all over his body'.

FASCINATING FACT
The makers of Stilton cheese have launched their own perfume with the same smell!

Your brain collects sensory information from the rest of your body – and tells you how to react to it all.

FASCINATING FACT

It takes just 0.02 of a second for your brain to realise when you've dropped a book on your toe.

YUM!

Taste is an important sense – it can warn you that something isn't good for you to put in your mouth.

FASCINATING FACT

An ice-cream parlour in Nice, France, offers its customers up to 70 different flavours of ice cream, including tomato and basil, black olive, and chewing gum!

Some pains keep you from harm or tell you it's time to visit the doctor. Not so for Miss Electra, who had 2 million volts of electricity passed through her body and out of her fingertips for a TV show in Hollywood. She doesn't feel any pain when this takes place!

KEY FACTS

Your senses are there to tell your brain what is going on inside, and outside, the body.

Your brain then knows if things are changing, and can decide when to make your body react – perhaps to keep you safe, or get some food or drink, for example.

The information is sent to your brain along nerves.

OUCH!

SNIFF!

Pongs and stenches tell us to stay away – whiffy food might be covered in nasty bacteria. Mind you, blue cheese such as Stilton smells strong but is safe to eat. The blue veins are caused by bacteria, and if you think they smell like stinky feet, you'd be right – it can be the same bacteria.

OOPS!

Stumbling, tripping and falling over – it happens to us all, but most of the time your body is great at keeping your limbs in the right place, and balanced. Shame it only goes wrong when everyone is looking!

Open Up!

>>mighty mouth!>>

Your mouth is home to 10,000 taste buds, up to 32 teeth and billions of bacteria. In fact, there are more bacteria in your mouth than there are people on the planet!

A mouth is a dark hole with lots of jobs to do, from chewing and crunching to coughing, swallowing, tasting and talking. Food begins its digestive journey in your mouth, where teeth grind it into little pieces and morsels get juiced up with sloppy saliva. Thanks to the taste buds on your tongue you can sense flavours – such as salty, sour, sweet and bitter – and either enjoy your snack-attack, or choose to spit out yukky bits.

Dentine

Tough white enamel

Pulp (contains nerves and blood vessels)

Gum

Root

INSIDE A TOOTH

Lips

Incisor

BABY TEETH

Your teeth started growing about six months before you were born!

Gum

Uvula

Tonsil

Tongue

Molar

Premolar

Canine

KEY FACTS

There are more than **500 types of bacteria** in your mouth. Most of them are helpful bugs, but the bad ones can rot your teeth or give you stinky breath.

You use your jaws, lips and tongue to speak. Babies' first sounds include **'coo', 'ba ba' and 'da da'**.

Girls are usually better at identifying flavours than boys, but boys prefer stronger flavours than girls. Teenagers don't like sour-tasting food!

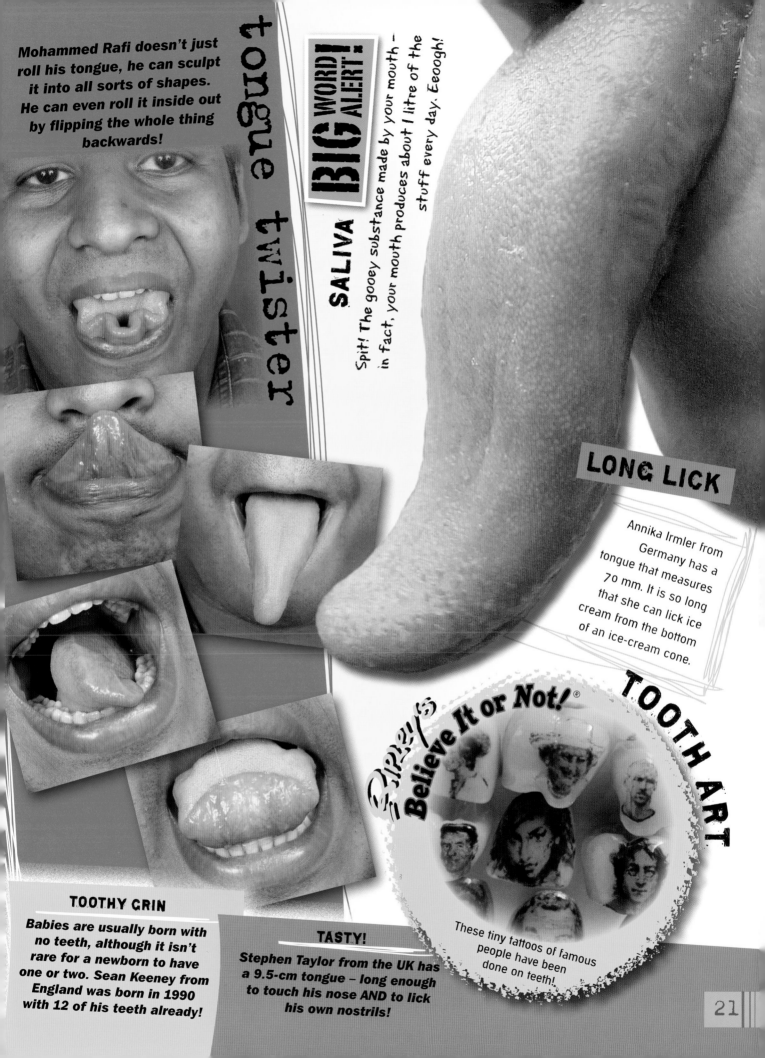

Mohammed Rafi doesn't just roll his tongue, he can sculpt it into all sorts of shapes. He can even roll it inside out by flipping the whole thing backwards!

tongue twister

BIG WORD! ALERT ✱

BIG WORD! ALERT ✱

SALIVA

Spit! The gooey substance made by your mouth – in fact, your mouth produces about 1 litre of the stuff every day. Eeoogh!

LONG LICK

Annika Irmler from Germany has a tongue that measures 70 mm. It is so long that she can lick ice cream from the bottom of an ice-cream cone.

TOOTH ART

Ripley's Believe It or Not!®

These tiny tattoos of famous people have been done on teeth!

TOOTHY GRIN

Babies are usually born with no teeth, although it isn't rare for a newborn to have one or two. Sean Keeney from England was born in 1990 with 12 of his teeth already!

TASTY!

Stephen Taylor from the UK has a 9.5-cm tongue – long enough to touch his nose AND to lick his own nostrils!

21

It's Alimentary

>>digestion>>

Your digestive system is a fabulous food processor. It pulps and pulverises food before squirting it with burning acids and churning it into a stinking stomach soup that is forced through your gurgling guts (also known as intestines).

Billions of bacteria break the food down into smaller and smaller bits so they can be used to fuel your body and help it grow.

A sandwich's journey through your alimentary canal – from mouth to anus – can take more than 24 hours and covers around 7 m in total.

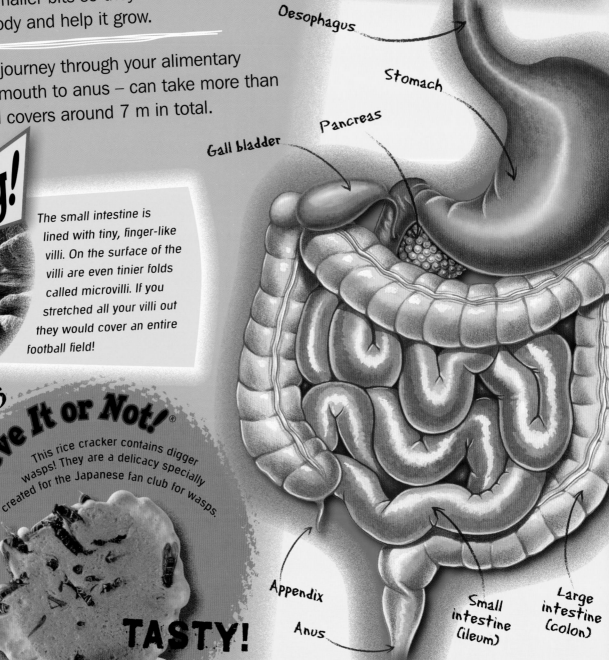

Oesophagus

Stomach

Pancreas

Gall bladder

Appendix

Anus

Small intestine (ileum)

Large intestine (colon)

It's big!

The small intestine is lined with tiny, finger-like villi. On the surface of the villi are even tinier folds called microvilli. If you stretched all your villi out they would cover an entire football field!

Ripley's Believe It or Not!®

This rice cracker contains digger wasps! They are a delicacy specially created for the Japanese fan club for wasps.

TASTY!

LIVE SCORPIONS

Father-of-two Hasip Kaya of Turkey has been addicted to eating live scorpions since he was a boy.

FLY FEAST

In protest at his town's garbage collection service, a man named Farook, from Tirunelveli, India, started eating nothing but flies.

LIVE TREE FROGS AND RATS

For over 40 years, Jiang Musheng of China has eaten live tree frogs and rats to ward off abdominal pains.

CHICKEN FEED

Jan Csovary, from Prievidza, Slovakia, eats chicken for breakfast, lunch and tea, and has consumed over 12,000 chickens since the early 1970s.

NOTHING BUT CHEESE

Dave Nunley from Cambridgeshire, England, has eaten nothing but grated mild cheddar cheese for more than 25 years and gets through 108 kg of it every year.

DIET OF WORMS

Wayne Fauser from Sydney, Australia, eats live earthworms.

Michel Lotito

ate bicycles, televisions, and even aircraft with no problems! He had to take them apart and slurp down mineral oil before swallowing the smaller bits.

DON'T TRY THIS AT HOME!

Sonya Thomas is America's competitive eating champion. She weighs just 45 kg, but has managed to put away 46 mince pies in ten minutes and 52 hard-boiled eggs in just five!

twist it!

It takes more brainpower to work your thumb than to control your stomach.

Half a million new stomach cells are made by your body every minute!

Whenever you blush, the lining of your stomach gets redder too.

During the course of your life you will produce enough saliva (that's your spit) to fill a swimming pool.

The acids in your stomach are so strong they could dissolve a razor blade!

If you unravelled your oesophagus, stomach and intestines they would reach the height of a three-storey building.

CRAZY

what a Waste

As your food makes its way through your digestive system, your body makes sure that nothing it needs goes to waste. A team of friendly organs slogs away, like a recycling plant, to suck out every last bit of goodness.

Blood vessels carry the nutrients from your food to the liver, where they are sorted, processed, recycled or stored. The rubbish bits are sent packing back to your guts where they join the leftovers to make the solid stuff that leaves your body. It's called faeces (say fee-sees).

Faeces is made up of old blood cells, bits of undigested food, bacteria and water. The liquid waste is called urine and it's actually 96% water.

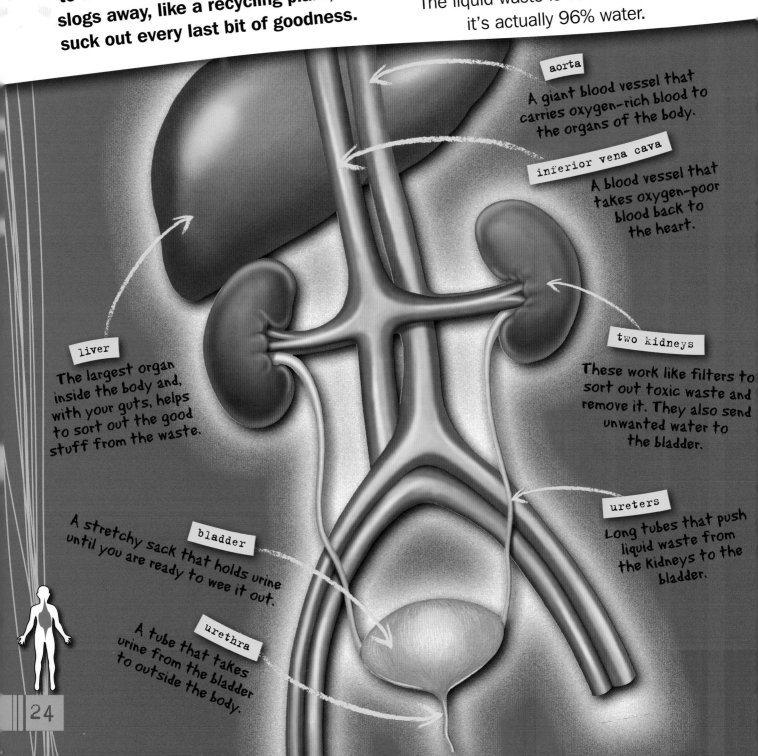

aorta
A giant blood vessel that carries oxygen-rich blood to the organs of the body.

inferior vena cava
A blood vessel that takes oxygen-poor blood back to the heart.

two kidneys
These work like filters to sort out toxic waste and remove it. They also send unwanted water to the bladder.

liver
The largest organ inside the body and, with your guts, helps to sort out the good stuff from the waste.

ureters
Long tubes that push liquid waste from the kidneys to the bladder.

bladder
A stretchy sack that holds urine until you are ready to wee it out.

urethra
A tube that takes urine from the bladder to outside the body.

24

TOILET TALK

TIME FOR TEA

A restaurant in Kaohsiung, China, is totally toilet themed – diners sit on toilets, eat at basin-style tables, and have their food served in bowls shaped like toilets or waste pots.

CLEAN MACHINE!

This wacky flying machine was part of a 2003 flying demonstration in France. Don't flush while you're up there!

FEELING FLUSHED!

Fancy finding a snake in your toilet! A 3-m-long boa constrictor appeared in a loo in Manchester, England, and then again in a neighbour's toilet bowl after moving through the sewage system of a block of apartments.

twist it!

FUNNY TUMMY

Sloppy poo is called diarrhoea (say die-ar-ee-ah). It's often caused by nasty bugs – so wash your hands before eating and after using the loo!

Your liver is the second largest organ of your body and it can continue to work if 80% of it is removed. It will even grow back to its previous size!

One person produces enough urine to fill about 270 bathtubs during a lifetime.

Many ancient people believed that drinking their own urine would cure tummy troubles or other digestive disorders. Romans used it in their toothpaste.

Even waste is recycled. Faeces and urine travel from toilets through sewage pipes to sewage plants, where waste matter can be turned into fabulous fertilizer to be spread on farmers' fields.

WASTE PRODUCTS

There are more than one million tiny tubes, or filters, in the kidneys. They are called nephrons and measure around 65 km in total length!

KEY FACTS

→ The liver has more than 500 different jobs, including cleaning blood, storing vitamins and preparing nutrients to be used by the body.

→ If you don't drink enough water your kidneys stop water going into your bladder. That makes your wee look darker.

→ Minerals in urine can turn into solid stones, called bladder stones, which have to be removed by a doctor.

25

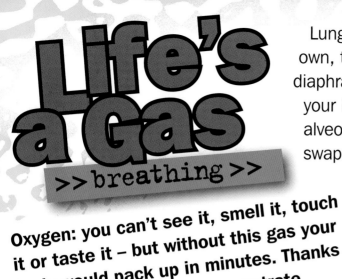

Life's a Gas

>> breathing >>

Oxygen: you can't see it, smell it, touch it or taste it – but without this gas your body would pack up in minutes. Thanks to your lungs you can concentrate on other stuff while you breathe in oxygen – more than 10 million times every year!

Lungs are lazy life-savers. With no muscles of their own, these air-filled puffers rely on rib muscles and a diaphragm to work. Every breath you take draws air into your lungs, which are each packed with 300 million alveoli. These thin-skinned sacs are swap shops, where oxygen is traded for carbon dioxide, the waste gas you breathe out.

Phew!

With six billion people breathing in oxygen you may expect we'd run out one day. Fortunately, when green plants respire they use up carbon dioxide, and produce oxygen. Phew!

Air-mazing

Air contains 21% oxygen. Breathing pure oxygen is actually dangerous.

look inside your lungs!

BREATHE OUT

BREATHE IN

Trachea

Bronchi

Bronchus

Bronchioles

At the top of the trachea is a voice box, or larynx. Passing air through the larynx as you breathe out makes your vocal cords vibrate, creating sound. Breathing in and talking at the same time is almost impossible – try it!

Left lung

Right lung

Bronchiole

Artery from heart

RESPIRATION

Breathing in and out. All the body bits that get oxygen from the air, and pass it into the blood stream, are called the respiratory system.

BIG WORD ALERT!

Deoxygenated blood from heart

Oxygenated blood to heart

Alveoli

twist it!

DEEP BREATH

You breathe around 20 times a minute – that's 700 million times during an average lifetime.

Every day you breathe in enough air to fill 1,000 party balloons. (But we don't recommend it!)

Your lungs contain around 300,000 capillaries (tiny blood vessels). If they were stretched out they would measure 2,400 km!

The loudest scream ever measured was 129 decibels – that's loud enough to make your ears hurt.

In June 2008, freediver Herbert Nitsch from Austria used just the air in his lungs to sink to a record-breaking 214 m in the ocean. During the dive, which took 4 minutes 24 seconds, his lungs shrank to the size of a fist and filled with blood, returning to normal at the surface.

David Merlini spent 10 minutes 17 seconds chained and handcuffed underwater in 2007, without air. He escaped from the five sets of handcuffs and 27 kg of chains all without taking a single breath.

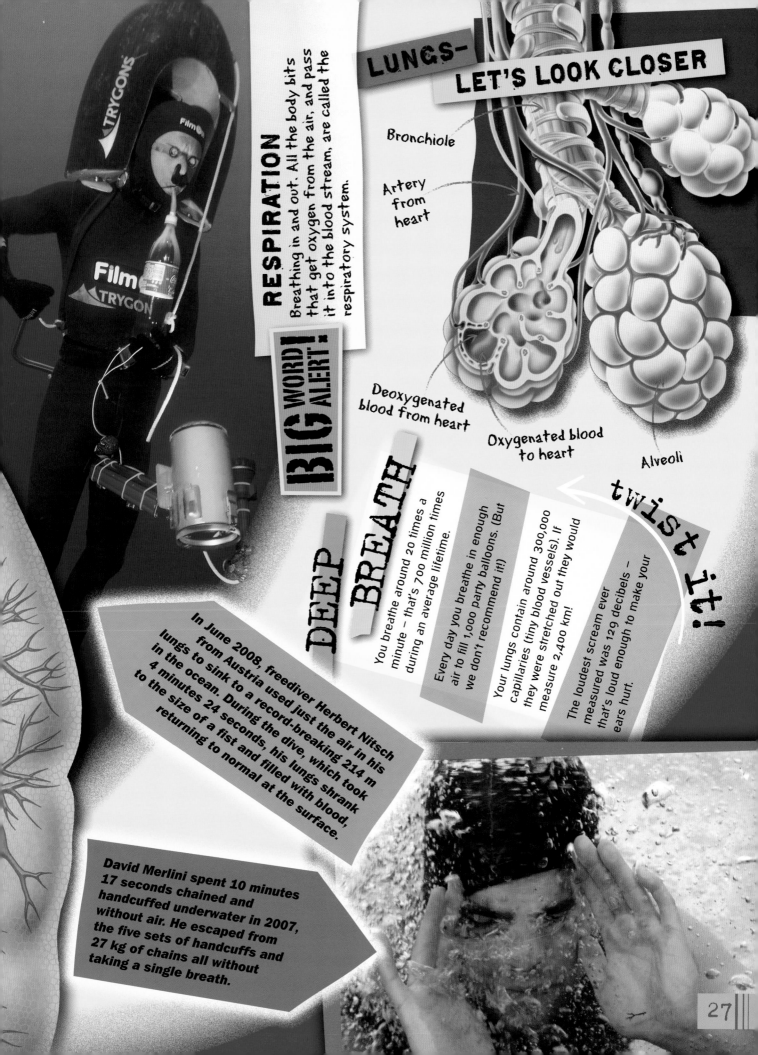

Under Command

Electrical messages buzz around your body at speeds of 100 m/second – that's ten times faster than the fastest human has ever run, and about one-third of the speed of sound.

These speedy signals whizz backwards and forwards on the body's super-highways – your nerves – and are controlled by the brain. You've got a lot of nerve: if all of your body's nerves were spread end to end they would measure more than 150,000 km!

Nerves instruct muscles to move, and send back messages to the brain about what's happening to your body. Like a bossy headteacher, they have everything under their command.

Axon

nervous twitch?

A thick nerve cable – the spinal cord – runs up through the centre of your spine to your brain. It's kept safe and snug inside a column of backbones.

Muscle fibre

Nerve cell

Junction between nerve cell and muscle

Nerves are like long cables of electrical wire. They are made up of nerve cells, called neurons.

Your brain and all your nerves together make up the nervous system. This is your body's main command and control centre.

LOOK OUT!

Catch! Entertainer Nathan Zorchak lives on his nerves, juggling with three chainsaws whizzing past his nose!

STEADY!

You want quick reactions? Look no further than Australian Anthony Kelly, who can catch flying arrows and – wearing a blindfold – speeding paintballs!

SNAKE KISSER

In Malaysia in 2006, Shahimi Abdul Hamid kissed a wild, venomous king cobra 51 times in three minutes, using his quick reflexes to dodge bites from the 5-m snake.

ON YOUR NERVES

If you burn your hand, your nerves swing into action, instructing your muscles to move it to safety in just 0.01 seconds.

The longest cells in your body are found in your brain. Stretched out, each one would measure up to 10 m long.

Professor Kevin Warwick studies robot technology. He has had silicon chips inserted into his body, which connect his nervous system to a computer. Now he can control doors and lights without lifting a finger!

twist it!

NOT FUNNY

The nerves in your elbow run close to the skin, which is why a knock to your 'funny bone' feels so weird.

29

Uncover your Cover

No thicker than 20 pages of this book, yet making up 16% of your weight, your skin works hard for your body!

Here are just some of its jobs: it stops your body soaking up water like a sponge, prevents your blood from boiling or freezing, keeps bugs and bacteria out of your insides, and even senses pain and touch. But that's not all: 50 million bacteria call your skin home!

Skin is the body's largest organ and a piece no larger than a postage stamp holds 650 sweat glands, 20 blood vessels and 1,000 nerve endings.

DON'T BE BLUE!

Except Paul Karason can't help it. His skin has turned blue after treating a skin complaint with an ointment containing silver. He has also been drinking 'colloidal silver' for about 15 years, which may have helped with his colour change. It might even have turned his insides blue, too!

GROSS!

A million dust mites live in your mattress and pillow. They feed on the dead skin cells that fall off your body at night.

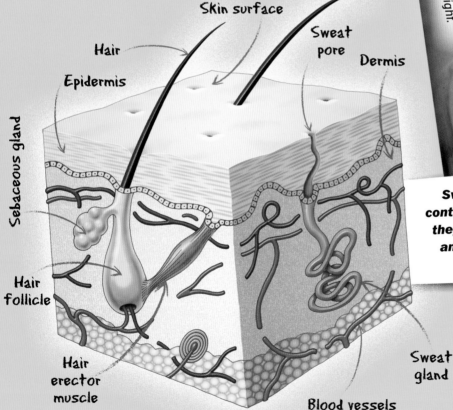

Skin surface
Sweat pore
Dermis
Hair
Epidermis
Sebaceous gland
Hair follicle
Hair erector muscle
Blood vessels
Sweat gland

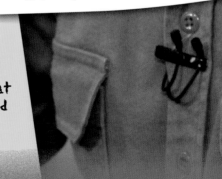

Sweat glands in your skin help to control temperature. When you are hot they ooze sweat, which is 99% water and 1% salt. As sweat evaporates, or dries, it cools your skin.

Meet the Leopard Man of Skye! The skin of Tom Leppard from Scotland has been tattooed with the markings of the big cat; over 99% of his skin is tattooed, with only the insides of his ears and the bits between his toes having no artwork.

BIG WORD ALERT!

EPIDERMIS

The top layer of your skin is called the epidermis. It is made from dead cells that are shed every 27 days.

Stretch it!

Gary Stretch has a rare skin condition that allows him to stretch it – and stretch it – and stretch it some more. His skin cells are affected so they don't hold together as tightly as they should, and his skin appears very loose on parts of his body.

twist it!

Lady Gray Rosemary Jacobs of the USA has grey skin. She thinks the change of colour happened after she used nose drops, which contained tiny amounts of the metal silver.

A computer mouse has been invented that can sense people's emotions. By measuring changes in the user's skin, such as sweat and temperature, the mouse can tell if he or she is feeling sad, angry or tired.

If you could peel off an adult's skin and stretch it out on the floor it would measure around 1.5 to 2 sq m and weigh as much as 4 kg.

Feet sweat because there are 250,000 pores (tiny holes) in the soles. Each squirts about 12 teaspoons of sweat a day.

SKINNY FACTS

31

Hair-raising Tales

>>hair and nails>>

Hair today, gone tomorrow! Most of your body is covered in strands of hair, which grow at a snail's pace of just 8 mm a month. After a few years, each strand of hair falls out.

Thankfully, new hairs grow from special cells in your skin, called follicles, all the time. Each follicle can make about 20 new hairs in a lifetime. Hair grows fastest in the summer, but those dozy follicles like to slow down during the night and catch some zzzz. Both hair and nails are made from dead cells that are toughened with a protein called keratin, which is surprisingly stretchy.

Testing 1-2-3
Scientists can use one strand of hair to find out a person's age, sex and race.

BIG HAIR!
Aaron Studham sports a magnificent Mohawk hairstyle that reaches 53 cm in height. It takes him an hour – and lots of hairspray – to get the look.

ITCHY
Tran van Hay from Vietnam has not cut his hair for 38 years and it now measures a staggering 6.2 m. He wears it coiled around his head, which keeps the hair neat and tidy, and his head warm.

→ You could live without hair or nails, but they are useful. Hair helps to keep you warm, and nails protect your delicate fingertips from damage – and are dead handy when you have an itch!

→ You have hair all over your body except on the palms of your hands, the soles of your feet and your lips. Humans have as many hairs as chimpanzees!

→ Blonde, brunette, raven-haired or redhead? You get your hair colour thanks to the skin pigment, melanin.

snip-its and cuttings

🔵 Human hair was used to make soy sauce in some Chinese barber shops, until the government banned it!

🔵 Your toenails contain traces of gold!

🔵 Mats made from human hair were used in San Francisco to mop up oil that had leaked into the San Francisco Bay.

🔵 Blonde people have about 130,000 hairs on their heads. People with red, black or brown hair have up to 40,000 fewer.

HAIR FACE

Larry Gomez was born with a very rare medical condition, which causes thick, dark hair to grow all over his face and body.

SCRATCHY!

Lee Redmond has been growing her fingernails since 1979. She said it was tough trying to open doors or get dressed, but was very proud when her talons reached 84 cm! Sadly, Lee was involved in a car crash in 2009 and her nails all broke off.

Speedy
Fingernails grow about four times faster than toenails.

Grow Up!

>> from birth onwards >>

In about 270 days, or 38 weeks, a single cell can grow into a perfect human baby!

At birth the baby weighs around 3.4 kg and measures a mere 50 cm from head to toe – but will increase in weight a massive ten times by the age of ten. From ten to 20 this blooming baby will double in weight and should reach around 1.7 m tall.

ALL CHANGE

The time of growth, when kids develop into adults, is called puberty.

TINY TOT

Babies are supposed to develop inside their mother's womb for 37 to 40 weeks, but tiny Amillia Sonja Taylor was born after only 21 weeks and 6 days. She was only 24 cm long.

Heave!

Two-year-old Salvador Quini, from Argentina, could lift weights heavier than himself – not so much a strongman as a strongboy!

SUPER BABY!

Mexican newborn Antonio Cruz weighed a massive 6.4 kg when he was born – about twice the weight of many new babies. Look how big he is compared to the average-sized baby lying next to him!

MARVELOUS MIRACLE!

day 1

Size of a fullstop

6 weeks

Size of a lentil

10 weeks

Size of a strawberry

16 weeks

Size of a pear

Ageing is a one-way road, which eventually leads to death. Most people can expect to live into their seventies, although there are some supercentenarians (aged over 110 years) alive today.

ALL AGES

Three babies are born into the world every second.

Babies born on the island of Bali are not normally named until they are three months old. Before then, they are all called 'mouse'!

Souleymane Mamam of Toga was just 13 years old when he played a World Cup qualifier match against Zambia.

Thanks to the body's amazing ability to heal and grow, doctors are able to stitch new body parts on to people, including arms and faces. Hearts, lungs and kidneys can also be transplanted.

'Red' Rountree was 80 years old when he first decided to rob a bank in the USA. He carried on with his life of crime until he was 92, when he was finally locked up in prison!

twist it!

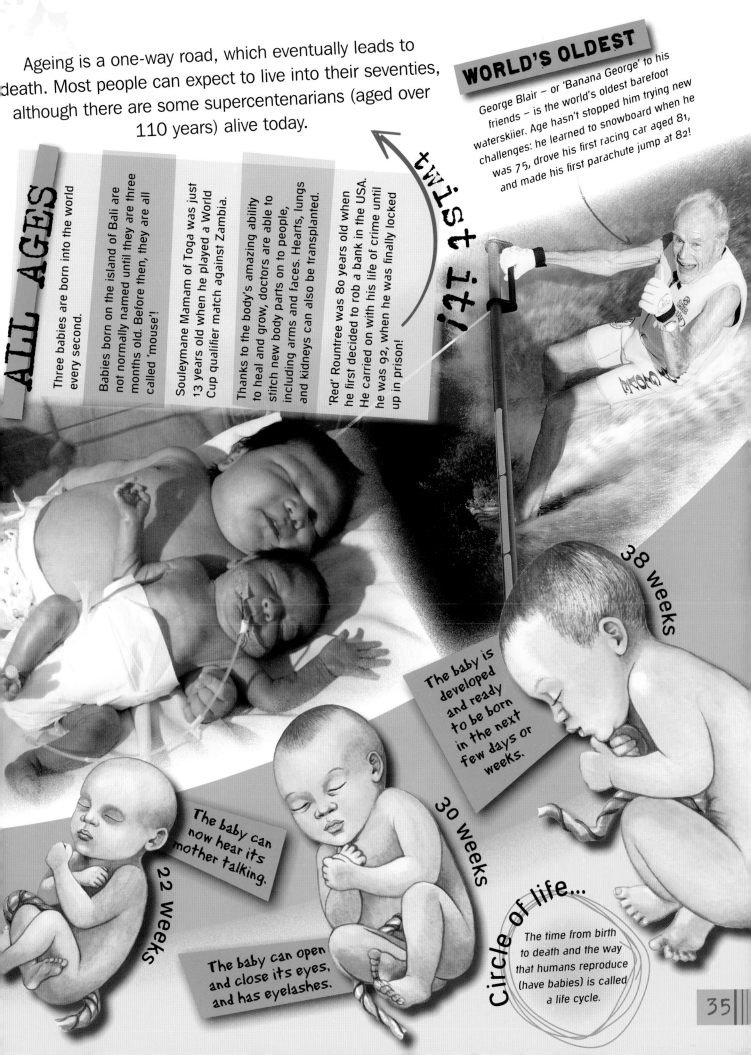

38 weeks

The baby is developed and ready to be born in the next few days or weeks.

30 weeks

22 weeks

The baby can now hear its mother talking.

The baby can open and close its eyes, and has eyelashes.

Circle of life...

The time from birth to death and the way that humans reproduce (have babies) is called a life cycle.

35

Believe It or Not!® Ripley's

Do people with big noses smell more? Better ask Mehmet Ozyurek – his huge honker from Turkey – an impressive measures 8.8 cm.

No way!

The Long and Short of it

>>all shapes and sizes>>

Breaking news! When it comes to bodies, none of us is 100% 'normal'. The simple fact is every one of us is unique – different and totally special.

From big noses to big toes and bulgy brains to bulgy biceps, your body grows by following a set of rules laid down by your DNA. Found in every cell of your body, DNA is a code for life that's packed with between 20,000 and 30,000 instructions, called genes.

How you turn out isn't just down to DNA though; it's about environment too. That means that the way you choose to live your life will affect your body, mind and health.

Bao Xishun looks down on everyone he meets, because he is one of the tallest men in the world, reaching 2.36 m. Bao had a growth spurt when he was 16, which lasted for seven years. Each of Bao's legs is about 1.5 m long!

He Pingping was unusually small, reaching just 74.61 cm in height. From Mongolia, he was the size of an adult's palm when born. His condition was caused by a change in the genes that control growth.

DOWNSIZING

When humans lose weight their fat cells don't disappear, they just get smaller.

Guddi from India is just 97 cm tall. Despite her tiny size, Guddi gave birth to a baby measuring 50 cm.

SUPER SPIRAL

- There is so much DNA in one human-body cell that, if you could stretch it out, it would measure 2 m.

- Everyone gets two lots of DNA, one from their mother and one from their father.

- You can inherit features, such as the colour of your hair or eyes, from your parents. The information is carried in the DNA. That's why people usually look like other members of their family.

- Unusually tall or short people may have DNA that has been damaged, or changed. Sometimes, they just inherit their height from their parents.

Mind Reading

>> inside your head>>

Your brain is like a lump of warm jelly to touch, but don't be fooled by its cunning disguise. This unbelievable organ contains the very essence of you: your thoughts, dreams, memories, hopes and desires. It's home to your amazing, incredible, magical mind!

Every brain is wrapped in a bony case called a skull, which protects its 100+ billion cells. These cells can handle more than 86 million bits of information a day and your memory can hold at least 100 trillion facts during your lifetime – which is the same as a 1,000 gigabyte computer!

This bit deals with movement.

The front of the brain is in charge of personality, thinking and behaviour.

The brain is divided into different areas with different jobs to do. For example, there are particular areas that control speech, movement, vision and hearing.

This is where the brain works on sight and hearing.

This bit controls sleep and growth.

This area controls balance and coordination.

This is where the brain identifies sounds.

Spinal cord

Stephen Wiltshire has an incredible talent for drawing and can produce remarkably accurate and detailed pictures solely from memory. In 2001, after flying in a helicopter over London, he drew in three hours an aerial illustration of a ten-square-km area of the city, featuring 12 landmarks and 200 other buildings, all in perfect perspective and scale.

These brain cells help to feed and repair the brain. They are shaped like stars.

Everybody can boost their brain's brilliance by reading, learning, playing and exercising. Eating a healthy diet helps too.

Dominic O'Brien has won the World Memory Championships eight times. In 2002 he memorised 54 packs of shuffled cards and remembered each card – all 2,808 of them – in almost perfect order. It took more than four hours to recite them, and he made just eight mistakes!

Ripley's Believe It or Not!®
A bit mental!

A brain weighs about 1.4 kg but if all the water it contains were squeezed out, it would weigh just 283 g!

Unborn babies grow new brain cells at the rate of 250,000 every minute!

For its size, a brain needs up to ten times more energy to work than any other organ.

The brain is one of the few body parts that cannot carry out any movements at all, since it has no muscle tissue.

There is no feeling in the human brain, only in the membrane surrounding it, which contains veins, arteries, and nerves. So a person would feel no pain from an injury to the brain alone.

At the age of 60 a person's brain holds four times more information than it did at the age of 21.

Lights Out

Your eyelids are drooping, your arms and legs feel heavy, and you know it's time to get some shut-eye. Sleep is nature's way of giving all those hard-working body bits of yours some well-earned rest.

The good news is that when the thinking part of your brain hits the snooze button, the other parts that control important jobs – like breathing – stay wide awake!

Most people spend around one third of their lives asleep. Some of that time is spent in a deep sleep, but some of it is also spent dreaming. If you're unlucky, a few of those dreams may turn to nightmares!

LIGHT ON YOUR FEET

Shh! Don't wake your family when you need to get up in the middle of the night – wear these slippers with torches in the toes and you can see where you're going without banging into things!

You've been sitting still, doing very little, when the urge to yawn suddenly takes over. It's your body's way of getting more oxygen into your lungs, so you are ready for action.

twist it!

NAP ATTACK

The longest anyone has survived without sleep is 18 days, 21 hours and 40 minutes. The woeful wide awaker suffered from memory loss and hallucinations (that means seeing imaginary things).

New parents lose between 400 and 750 hours of sleep in the first year of their baby's life.

Teenagers and young children need about ten hours of sleep a night.

Snails can sleep for long periods of time – up to three years!

Stephen Hearn crashed his car at 113 km/h when he was sleepwalking near Birmingham, England. When he was found, he was in his pyjamas and still snoring.

Sleepwalker Lee Hadwin of North Wales is a good artist when he is asleep, but when awake he struggles to draw at all! Wandering round the house in his sleep he draws everywhere – even on walls and tables!

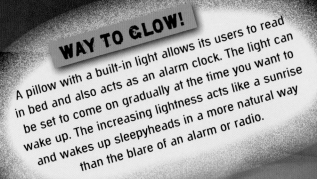

WAY TO GLOW!

A pillow with a built-in light allows its users to read in bed and also acts as an alarm clock. The light can be set to come on gradually at the time you want to wake up. The increasing lightness acts like a sunrise and wakes up sleepyheads in a more natural way than the blare of an alarm or radio.

Your brain needs sleep to be able to work properly. Without sleep you'd find it hard to think clearly, remember anything or keep yourself safe.

BIG WORD ALERT!

SOMNAMBULISTS

It's not unusual for people – especially children – to walk or talk in their sleep. Sleepwalkers are called somnambulists.

ANIMALS SLEEP TOO

Pythons sleep for around 18 hours out of 24, but sheep only need about four hours of sleep.

ICE HOTEL!!

Fancy sleeping on an ice bed? You can do this in Shimukappu, Japan, where an ice hotel caters for sleeping, eating and bathing – all on ice.

Zzzz

SHUT-EYE!

Your eyelids close when you are feeling drowsy. When you dream your eyeballs flick from side to side.

SNORE!

The back of your mouth and throat relax and may partly block your airways, leading to that pig-snuffle snoring sound!

GROW!

While you snooze your body can repair itself and put spare energy into growing.

DREAM!

No one really knows why we dream, but it may help us to organise our thoughts and remember stuff.

RELAX!

Your muscles relax. When you dream, the ability to move your limbs is (usually) switched off – which stops you from acting out your dreams. If this doesn't happen you may find yourself sleepwalking.

Under Attack

You may not know it, but your body is engaged in a deadly battle with the world, right now! It's true – there are plenty of bugs, bacteria and other baddies out there, just waiting to do you harm.

Thankfully, the human body has evolved over millions of years to repel most invaders. Your body has an amazing ability to defend itself, and even repair damage done to it. Without this ability even a simple cold could spell the end of you. Of course, we can't always do it alone, so it's time to say a big 'thank you' to doctors!

Your body fights attackers 24/7. From your tough outer layer – skin – to spit, strong stomach juices, bacteria in your gut, hair in your nose and tears in your eyes, there are lots of clever defence systems in place.

BIG WORD ALERT!

IMMUNE SYSTEM

Your body has an immune system, which makes white blood cells that attack and kill invaders, such as the virus that causes flu.

BUG ALERT!

A VIRUS ATTACKS THE BLOOD STREAM

Vomiting, sneezing, crying, spitting, coughing and diarrhoea (runny faeces) are all ways of chucking out stuff your body doesn't like.

TASTY!

These tiny fish nibble at dead skin on customers' feet at a spa resort in Japan – and leave the feet clean and refreshed!

TOASTY!

Stand back! This fire treatment is popular in China to help prevent colds and flu.

MUDDY!

It's a mucky business in these mud baths, which are meant to ease pain and diseases.

KILL OR CURE

In ancient times, headaches and other medical problems were sometimes cured by drilling holes into the skull. Known as 'trepanation' this operation is still carried out in some parts of the world today.

Maggots are sometimes used to treat infected skin and tissues, which they eat. Because they don't eat healthy flesh, these greedy grubs help wounds to heal before life-threatening infections, such as gangrene, can set in.

A pair of spiders set up home inside the ear canal of nine-year-old Jesse Courtney from America. Thankfully, doctors were able to extract the eight-legged invaders, and no harm was done.

Over 2,000 years ago, Hippocrates, a doctor, told his patients to chew on bark from a willow tree when they were in pain. We now use an ingredient found in willow bark to make aspirin!

twist it!

OLD BONES

In some Chinese villages, dinosaur bones are ground up to make a paste. It's used to treat dizziness and leg cramps!

in the olden days

Before modern medical science took over, people invented some weird ways to get better.

CATCH THAT SHREW!

Aching bones were treated with the help of a dead shrew. Sufferers were told to keep the furry little creatures in their pockets.

DON'T BE AN ASS!

Passing a child under the belly of a donkey three times was said to cure whooping cough.

HOT AND STEAMING!

If you had TB – a deadly chest disease – you'd be told to kill a cow, stick your head into its warm body, and breathe in deeply.

TOM FOR YOUR TUM!

One of the first types of tomato ketchup was used to cure diarrhoea in the 1800s.

Muntoyib, an Indonesian bee-sting therapist, covers himself with hundreds of live honeybees in India. Some people think that bee venom injected from live stinging bees helps treat chronic pain.

Fit for Life

>>take care>>

There's no such thing as a perfect human, but keeping your body bits in tip-top shape has got to make good sense.

The human body is like a mighty machine with lots of working parts. It needs to be taken care of – and that means exercise and a good diet. There are around six billion humans on the planet, and many of them, from super-sized sumo wrestlers to bendy-bodied yogis, keep the power switch turned to maximum.

For kids, it's easy to keep it fun. All you've got to do is play, eat well and sleep. But for some groaning grown-ups, it's a hard, sweaty slog keeping those muscles and bones in peak condition.

GULP!

Water makes up 60% of your body weight. It's the liquid of life, so drink up. Your bones and teeth are packed with calcium – there's loads of this mighty mineral in milk.

GRUB!

Veggies and fruit are great grub. At least one-third of a human's diet should be made up of these super foods.

GO FOR IT!

Squash – the hard-hitting racquet and ball game – has been voted the healthiest sport ever, beating running, swimming and basketball into first place.

FITNESS FUN

Hula hooping is a hu-lotta fun! Alesya Goulevich spun 100 hula hoops at the same time, at the Big Apple Circus in Boston in 2004.

SURF'S UP!

Surfers are super-fit because they use almost every muscle in their bodies to stay balanced and upright on their boards.

PUSHING IT

Ashrita Furman, a health-food store manager from New York City, is super fit. Amongst his amazing feats are climbing Mount Fuji on a pogo stick, hula hooping with a 4.46-m hoop, and doing 9,628 sit ups in an hour. Here, he's pushing an orange along for one mile using his nose!

twist it!

You're never too young to get fit! In 2006 1,100 babies took part in a crawling marathon. The mini racers had to crawl along a 5-m track, and the young winner was rewarded with a bag of baby goodies!

Aged 91, Erwin Ashley of the USA climbed 2,000 steps every day to keep in shape!

Cycling backwards is a popular sport in some parts of the world. Riders sit on the handlebars and pedal in reverse.

Tirtha Kumar Phani from India ran more than 60 km every day, for one year. He clocked up a blistering 22,581 km in total!

Kids should be exercising for at least 60 minutes every day. Running, walking, cycling and playing sports all keep you fit for life.

FITNESS FANATICS

stick with it!

Kyle Nolte from Arkansas has got so good at jumping on his pogo stick, he can also play baseball, hula hoop or skip whilst pogoing!

ACKNOWLEDGEMENTS

COVER (l) © Sebastian Kaulitzki – istockphoto.com, (r) Lilli Strauss/AP/PA Photos; **2** (r) Raymond w. Gonzales, (t/l) © Peter Galbraith – fotolia.com; **4** © Sebastian Kaulitzki – istockphoto.com; **5** (t/r) Lilli Strauss/AP/PA Photos; **6–7** (dp) © AlienCat – fotolia.com; **7** (b/l) Raymond W Gonzales, (b/r) Simon De Trey-White/ Barcroft Media; **8** (r) © Peter Galbraith – fotolia.com, (l) © AlienCat – fotolia.com; **9** (l, b) ChinaFotoPress/Photocome/PA Photos; **10** (sp) © V. Yakobchuk – fotolia.com; **11** (c) © Sebastian Kaulitzki – istockphoto.com, (r) © Wong Sze Fei – fotolia.com; **13** (l) © Roman Dekan – fotolia.com, (t/r) AP Photo/Rubin Museum of Art, Diane Bondareff, (b/r) Jeff Chen/Trigger images; **15** (b/r) © saginbay – fotolia.com; **14–15** (b) © Xtremer – fotolia.com, (c) © saginbay – fotolia.com; **17** (l) Patrick Hertzog/AFP/Getty Images, (c) Prakash Hatvalne/AP/PA Photos, (r) Reuters/Christina Hu; **18** (t/l) Reuters/ Seth Wenig, (b/l) Camera Press/Terje Eggum/Scanpix; **18–19** (b/c) © ktsdesign – fotolia.com; **21** (l) Manichi Rafi, (b) Steven Heward/toothartist.com, (t/r) Fabian Bimmer/AP/PA Photos; **22** (l) Dr. Kessel & Dr. Kardon/Tissues & Organs/ Getty Images, (b) Reuters/Staff Photographer; **23** (t/r) Nils Jorgensen/Rex Features, (b) Matt Cardy/Getty Images, (b/r) Stan Honda/AFP/Getty Images; **24–25** (c) © Mark Kostich – istockphoto.com; **25** (c/r) Sipa Press/Rex Features, (b/r) Phil Noble/PA Archive/PA Photos, (t/r) Reuters/STR New; **27** (l) Dan Burton/underwaterimages.co.uk, (t/r) John Bavosi/Science Photo Library, (b/r) Gabriel Bouys/AFP/Getty Images; **28** (l) © Sebastian Kaulitzki – fotolia.com; **29** (l) Roger Bamber/Rex Features, (r) Tim Barnsley/Armidale Express; **30** (r) NBCUPhotobank/Rex Features; **31** (t) Ian Waldie/Rex Features, (r) Scott Barbour/Getty Images; **32** (l) Jean/Empics Entertainment, (r) Thanh Nien Newspaper/AP/PA Photos; **33** (l) Rex Features, (r) Tao-Chuan Yeh/AFP/Getty Images; **34** (r) Reuters/Ho New; **35** (l) Reuters/Victor Ruiz, (r) George A. Blair; **36–37** (dp) Reuters/China Daily China Daily Information Corp; **36** (t/l) IHA/UPPA/Photoshot; **37** (l) © Dmitry Sunagatov – fotolia.com, (t) © Sasha Radosavljevic – istockphoto.com; **39** (t) Gary Bishop/Rex Features, (b) Greg Williams/Rex Features, (r) © Sebastian Kaulitzki – fotolia.com; **40–41** (dp) © Veronika Vasilyuk – fotolia.com; **40** (c) Rex Features; **41** (t/r) Solent News/Rex Features, (b) Reuters/ Kim Kyung Hoon; **42** (sp) © David Marchal – istockphoto.com; **43** (t/l) Reuters/Larry Downing, (t/c) Chu Yongzhi/ ChinaFotoPress/GettyImages, (t/r) Reuters/China Daily China Daily Information Corp – CDIC, (b) Reuters/Beawiharta Beawiharta; **44–45** (b) Reuters/Sergio Moraes; **44** (t) Boston Herald/Rex Features; **45** (l) Reuters/Shannon Stapleton

Key: t = top, b = bottom, c = centre, l = left, r = right, sp = single page, dp = double page, bgd = background

All other photos are from Ripley Entertainment Inc.

All artwork by Janet Baker & Julian Baker (JB Illustrations)

Every attempt has been made to acknowledge correctly and contact copyright holders and we apologise in advance for any unintentional errors or omissions, which will be corrected in future editions.

RIPLEY's
WHALES AND DOLPHINS

Believe It or Not!®

TWISTS

RIPLEY
PUBLISHING

a Jim Pattison Company

Written by Camilla de la Bedoyere
Consultants Barbara Taylor, Joe Choromanski

PUBLISHING

Publisher Anne Marshall

Editorial Director Rebecca Miles
Project Editor Charlotte Howell
Picture Researchers Michelle Foster, Charlotte Howell
Proofreader Lisa Regan
Indexer Hilary Bird

Art Director Sam South
Senior Designer Michelle Foster
Design Dynamo Design
Reprographics Juice Creative Ltd

www.ripleys.com/books

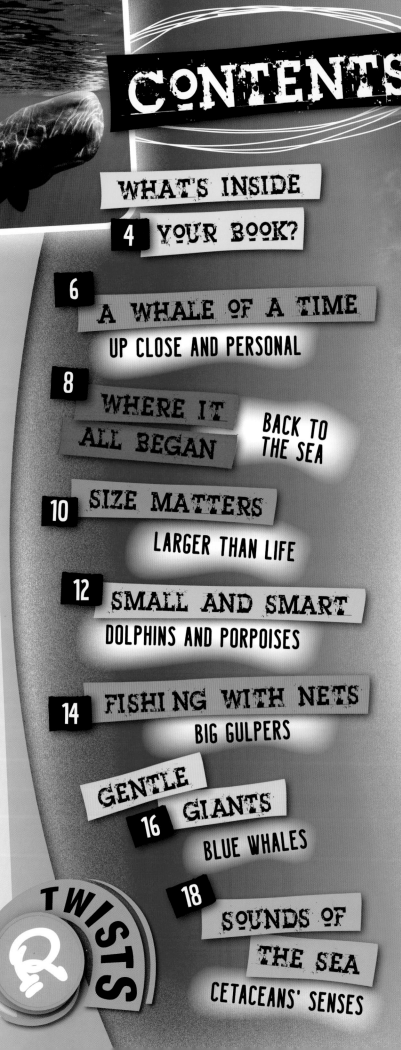

PAGE 33

CONTENTS

TWISTS

GIANTS OF THE SEA

Orcas—also known as killer whales—come from fearsome families. A mother orca and her children prowl through the ocean, seeking other animals to hunt and eat. They are fast, agile, intelligent predators—and full of surprises.

BRILLIANT BEASTS

Orcas are a type of toothed whale—with up to 52 teeth!

They can grow to 30 feet long.

Orcas can be found in all of the oceans in the world.

WHAT'S INSIDE YOUR BOOK?

TWISTS

Our planet's deep blue oceans are home to an extraordinary group of animals. Whales and dolphins roam through the seas on incredible journeys to explore new places, meet up with old friends, and forge new families.

If you think that whales and dolphins are closely related to fish, you'd be wrong. It's hard to believe, but they have more in common with hippos and humans than they do with sharks or salmon. There are lots more amazing things to discover about these magnificent, massive, and majestic beasts.

Ripley explains...
See the "Ripley explains" panels for extra info from our whale and dolphin experts.

Read more unbelievable facts when you spot a Key Facts box.

Look out for the "Twist It" column on some pages. Twist the book to find out more amazing facts about whales and dolphins.

These books are about "Believe It or Not!"—amazing facts, feats, and things that make you go "Wow!"

...LL AND SMART

...S AND PORPOISES

...porpoises are small toothed ...look pretty similar, but dolphins ...eak-shaped mouths.

...hins have a reputation as kind, ...s, they are ruthless predators of the ...or killer whales, are members of this ...hey are some of the planet's most ...savage hunters.

KEY FACTS

- Dolphins have a lump of fatty tissue under the skin of the forehead called a melon.
- Dolphins have lots of cone-shaped teeth in their mouth.
- A dolphin does not have ears on the outside of its head. It only has inner ears, which take sound and turn it into messages for the brain.

On the move

...hins and porpoises are fast swimmers, and some can reach top ...more than 34 mph. Moving quickly takes a lot of energy—and ...so these cetaceans often leap out of the water to breathe as ...swimming. As they "fly" through the air, the animals can stay out ...aws of any chasing predators, while getting enough air to help power their getaway.

BIG WORD ALERT
PREDATOR
An animal that hunts other animals to eat.

TWIST IT!

Dolphins have been badly affected by pollution in the oceans and seas. Poisons, especially the deadly metal mercury, are found in the fish they eat, and are then stored in their body.

Dolphins cannot smell. They lost that sense during evolution, when their nostrils moved to the top of their head and became their blowhole.

The shortest dolphins measure less than 60 inches long.

A harbor porpoise has between 86 and 106 teeth. It uses them to grip onto slippery fish.

Dall's porpoises are the most hunted of all cetaceans in the world. Human hunters have killed more than half a million of them for food in the last 50 years.

SMALL STATS

IN A SPIN

Spinner dolphins love to leap out of the water and spin around and around before splashing back into the sea. Some can spin seven times in a single leap. No one really knows why they do this, but it may help them to get rid of little bugs that burrow into their skin, or it may be to do with communication or play.

Ripley's Believe It or Not!
This dolphin takes a leap over an unsuspecting surfer in Australia! Photographer Matt Hutton caught the rare sight on camera when he decided to try out surf-photography.

When a dolphin mother swims at top speed her little calf can keep up but how? The baby swims in its mother's slipstream, a hair's breadth away from her. The slipstream is the area of water close to her body where there is less drag, making it easier for her baby to keep up with her.

The slipstream is created by the mother's body as it moves through the water—helping the baby to swim by her side.

Porpoises have a round head and face. They do not have a dolphin's long "beak." Porpoises have spade-like teeth.

HARBOR PORPOISE

There are six species of porpoise, and the smallest (and the world's smallest cetacea...) is the harbor porpoise. Porpoises usually l... in groups of 12 and they hunt fish togeth... or eat shellfish found on the seab... Harbor porpoises live mostly in ... sea, but have been spotted in riv...

Whales sleep by switching off one half of their brain at a time!

When whales spout water from their blowhole they breathe out—and most of them have stinky breath!

Found a new word? Big Word Alert will explain it for you.

Bowhead whales may live to 200 years of age—or more!

Many whales listen using their jawbones!

One species of whale grows a single tooth up to 10 feet long.

Dolphins can learn to understand and follow simple instructions.

Some whales are nearly blind but can still find their way around underwater.

Turn over to find out more about whales and dolphins.

A WHALE OF A TIME

UP CLOSE AND PERSONAL

If you want to get to know a whale a little better you need to get close, and really check it out. It's a bit tricky to do that when a whale is underwater, so we've done some research for you.

Whales and dolphins belong to a family of animals called cetaceans (say: set-ay-shuns). They are mammals – which means that, like humans, horses and hippos, they have hair and feed their babies with milk. Most mammals live on land, but cetaceans are perfectly adapted for a life in the world's oceans.

Ripley explains... Whale, human, fish

Whales and fish may look quite similar, and even lead fairly similar lives – but they belong to very different groups of animals: whales are mammals, like humans.

	Whale	Human	Fish
Lives in the sea	✓	✗	✓
Has limbs e.g. legs/flippers	✓	✓	✗
Breathes air	✓	✓	✗
Big brain	✓	✓	✗
Feeds young with milk	✓	✓	✗
Has a good body shape for swimming	✓	✗	✓

Invisible legs

Cetaceans may look as if they don't have any limbs (such as legs, arms or wings), but look again, and you will see them.

Shoulder blade.

The back legs are no longer used. Over millions of years they have mostly disappeared.

Tiny bones are all that's left of the back legs and pelvis.

Both front legs have become flippers, which are used for turning left or right when swimming.

TWIST IT!

Whales and dolphins are fighting to survive in our modern world. At least nine species of whales are in real danger of dying out completely.

Cetaceans don't need to drink water because they can get all the water they need from the food they eat.

Female cetaceans are called cows, the males are called bulls, and the babies are called calves.

Not all adult whales have hair on their heads, but they all sprouted some hair when they were babies developing inside their mother's body.

UNDERWATER LIFE

Make no bones about it

Cetaceans' dorsal fins don't have bones inside them – unlike the fins on a fish's back. That's why they sometimes droop, especially in orcas, which have the largest dorsal fins – reaching up to 2 m high. A blue whale's dorsal fin is just 40 cm in height, and some whales, such as belugas, don't have a dorsal fin at all.

Invisible waste gases are forced out of a whale's blowhole, with the water or water vapour, when they breathe out.

Coming up for air

Whales and dolphins cannot breathe underwater. They need to come to the water's surface to breathe air. Their nostrils are on the top of their head, and are called blowholes. Some whales have one blowhole, and some have two.

WHERE IT ALL BEGAN

BACK TO THE SEA

Long ago, the ancestors of whales lived on land. Then they discovered that there was plenty of food in the oceans – and few predators.

So, about 50 million years ago these creatures began a life in the water where their bodies changed and adapted to the new habitat. Now, take a deep breath and discover how whales became the mammal masters of the ocean.

Going back in time

Look closely at a whale's body, and its ways of life, and you will see the secrets of its land-living past.

* Breathes air
* Has hair (not very much though!)
* Feeds its young with milk
* Has a skeleton that gives clues to how it evolved from a land-living animal

Big change

Ancient whale relatives that lived on land breathed air through their mouth and nostrils, just like us. Most animals that live in the sea can take oxygen from the water, but whales and dolphins still get their oxygen from the air. During evolution, their nostrils moved to the top of their head, creating the blowhole. They breathe air through the blowhole at the surface.

Pakicetus

The earliest whale ancestors were called *Pakicetus*. These were furry wolf-like animals that lived by the sea. They did not look much like whales, but their skulls were similar.

When: about 50 million years ago
Length: 1.7 metres

Ambulocetus

Early whales called *Ambulocetus* began to have similarites to today's whales and they lived in water. They had short legs and their hands and feet were shaped like paddles. Their tail was big and powerful.

When: about 48 million years ago
Length: 4 metres

Pakicetus skeleton

Ambulocetus skeleton

Dorudon

Dorudon is a another early whale. It probably swam like a dolphin and hunted fish. The pelvic (hip) bones had almost completely disappeared (see left) along with the back legs.

When: 40–36 million years ago

Length: 4.4 metres

Breathe deep

Whales stay underwater for a long time because they have evolved to be able to hold their breath for a long time. They don't have particularly big lungs, but they are able to use almost every scrap of oxygen they take in. They can also fill their lungs in just two seconds, and take in about 3,000 times as much air as we do when we inhale (breathe in).

Turn over to find out more about toothed and baleen whales...

← Atlantic spotted dolphin

Around 30 million years ago, two types of cetacean (marine mammals) had evolved to become today's modern whales and dolphins.

Toothed whales

Baleen whales

Atlantic spotted dolphin skeleton →

Whoa—the largest mouth of any animal!

Super spray

When whales breathe out they often make a spout of water or mist, which can be seen from far away, and is quite noisy! When a whale swims, muscles close the blowhole so water doesn't get in.

Dorudon skeleton →

Pelvic bones →

BIG WORD ALERT

EVOLUTION

The way an animal changes over time.

← Bowhead whale

Bowhead whale skeleton →

Pelvic bones →

SIZE MATTERS

Bottlenose dolphin

LARGER THAN LIFE

Whales grow bigger than any other animal we know about – even bigger than dinosaurs.

The oceans are dense – that means they can support the weight of heavy things, making it easier for big animals to survive. Big animals need lots of food, but they can travel far and fast to find it. There are 85 species (types) of whales, dolphins and porpoises, but they can be split into just two groups: the **toothed whales** and the **baleen whales.**

TOOTHED WHALES

- **All dolphins are toothed whales.**
- **Toothed whales are also called Odontoceti.**
- **There are 71 species.**
- **They hunt their prey using echolocation.**
- **Most are small to medium sized.**
- **Males are usually bigger than females.**
- **They have one blowhole.**

Vaquita 1.5 m

Dall's porpoise 2 m

Sperm whale 20 m

Bottlenose dolphin 4 m

Beluga 6 m

Short-finned pilot whale 8 m

Orca (killer whale) 9 m

Male orcas (killer whales) have a huge dorsal fin. It can grow to 2 m high.

Male sperm whales can be over twice the size of females.

North Pacific Right whale 17 m

Bowhead whale 18 m

Fin whale 22 m

Blue whale 30 m

Female blue whales are bigger than males.

Grey whale 15 m

The bowhead whale has the largest baleen (hair–like bristles used for feeding) of any cetacean; each one can measure 5 m.

Minke whale 12 m

Humpback whale 14 m

Grey whale

BALEEN WHALES

- Baleen whales are also called Mysticeti.
- There are 14 species.
- They don't have teeth, and feed using special hair-like bristles (baleen) instead.
- Most are really big!
- Females are sometimes larger than males.
- They have two blowholes.

SMALL AND SMART

DOLPHINS AND PORPOISES

Dolphins and porpoises are small toothed whales. They look pretty similar, but dolphins have long, beak-shaped mouths.

Although dolphins have a reputation as kind, caring animals, they are ruthless predators of the sea. Orcas, or killer whales, are members of this family and they are some of the planet's most cunning and savage hunters.

KEY FACTS

- Dolphins have a lump of fatty tissue under the skin of the forehead called a melon.

- Dolphins have lots of cone-shaped teeth in their mouth.

- A dolphin does not have ears on the outside of its head. It only has inner ears, which take sound and turn it into messages for the brain.

On the move

Most dolphins and porpoises are fast swimmers, and some can reach top speeds of more than 55 km/h. Moving quickly takes a lot of energy – and oxygen – so these cetaceans often leap out of the water to breathe as they're swimming. As they 'fly' through the air, the animals can stay out of the jaws of any chasing predators, while getting enough air to help power their getaway.

BIG WORD ALERT

PREDATOR

An animal that hunts other animals to eat.

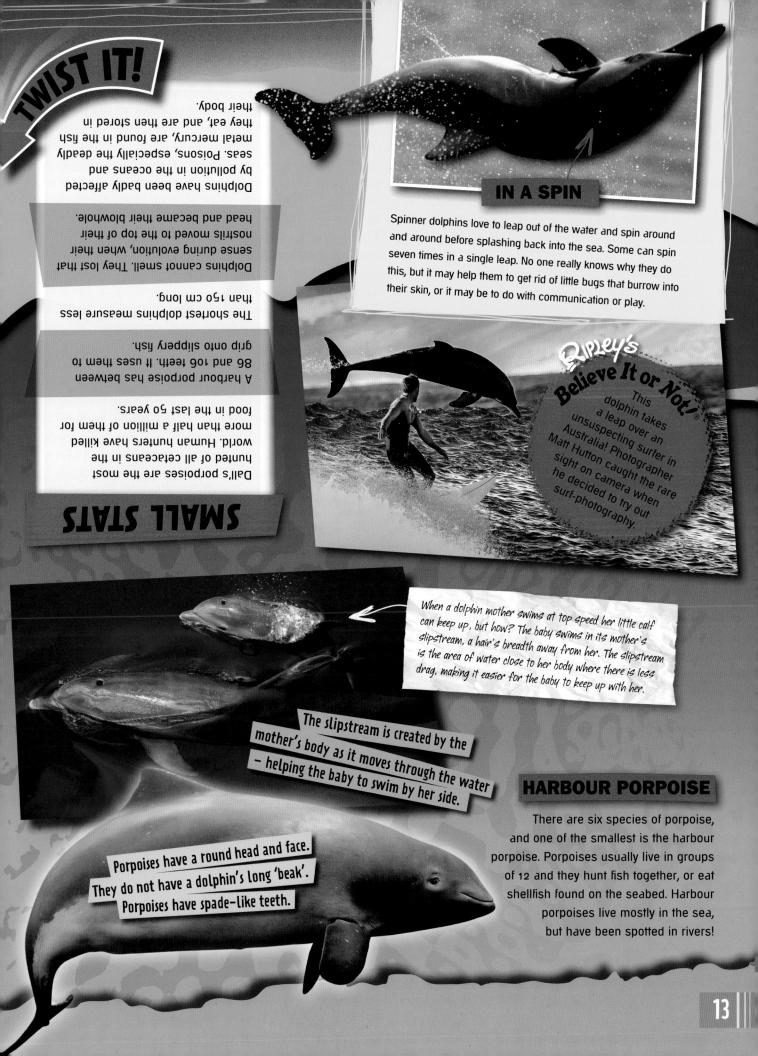

Dolphins have been badly affected by pollution in the oceans and seas. Poisons, especially the deadly metal mercury, are found in the fish they eat, and are then stored in their body.

Dolphins cannot smell. They lost that sense during evolution, when their nostrils moved to the top of their head and became their blowhole.

The shortest dolphins measure less than 150 cm long.

A harbour porpoise has between 86 and 106 teeth. It uses them to grip onto slippery fish.

Dall's porpoises are the most hunted of all cetaceans in the world. Human hunters have killed more than half a million of them for food in the last 50 years.

SMALL STATS

IN A SPIN

Spinner dolphins love to leap out of the water and spin around and around before splashing back into the sea. Some can spin seven times in a single leap. No one really knows why they do this, but it may help them to get rid of little bugs that burrow into their skin, or it may be to do with communication or play.

Ripley's Believe It or Not!®
This dolphin takes a leap over an unsuspecting surfer in Australia! Photographer Matt Hutton caught the rare sight on camera when he decided to try out surf-photography.

When a dolphin mother swims at top speed her little calf can keep up, but how? The baby swims in its mother's slipstream, a hair's breadth away from her. The slipstream is the area of water close to her body where there is less drag, making it easier for the baby to keep up with her.

The slipstream is created by the mother's body as it moves through the water – helping the baby to swim by her side.

HARBOUR PORPOISE

There are six species of porpoise, and one of the smallest is the harbour porpoise. Porpoises usually live in groups of 12 and they hunt fish together, or eat shellfish found on the seabed. Harbour porpoises live mostly in the sea, but have been spotted in rivers!

Porpoises have a round head and face. They do not have a dolphin's long 'beak'. Porpoises have spade-like teeth.

BIG GULPERS

Meet the leviathans. These are the most massive animals that have ever lived on our planet.

Humpback whale

The hairy bristles in a humpback's mouth (the baleen) probably do more than just trap food like a sieve. Scientists think that the 400 baleen plates in a humpback form a shape-shifting net that changes its shape depending on the speed that water flows through it. That would help a hungry humpback trap even more food.

Baleen whales may be big, but they mostly survive on a diet of very small animals – so they have to eat an enormous quantity of them! They feed using special mouthparts called baleen plates that capture little animals, while allowing water to flow through. Most baleen whales go on long journeys, called migrations, in search of food.

BIG WORD ALERT

LEVIATHAN

A 'sea monster' or any gigantic animal of the sea.

To feed, a whale opens its huge mouth and seawater rushes in.

As water passes through the baleen plates, small animals are trapped on the bristles.

Baleen whales have a big tongue, which they use to swallow food, and push water out of their mouth.

The baleen bristles hang down from the roof of a whale's mouth in 'baleen plates'.

Once, all whales had teeth. As baleen whales evolved, they lost their teeth although for some time there were whales that had baleen and teeth.

Scientists find out what whales eat by opening up the stomachs of dead whales that have washed ashore. They can find out even more by examining bits of whale skin.

Baleen whales love to sing, but they probably do not use echolocation (see page 19) to find food.

GIANT GUZZLERS

A Bryde's whale can be identified by three long ridges on its head. It eats about 660 kg of food a day.

Bryde's whale

Bryde's (say: 'Broodah's') whales are large, fast swimmers that live in warm waters throughout the world's oceans, where they are regularly hunted by whaling boats. Bryde's whales usually live alone or in pairs, and eat small fish and crabs as well as plankton.

It's tough being tiny

The small animals and plants that get carried along by the ocean currents are called plankton. Many of them are too small to be seen with the naked eye – and their normal fate is to be eaten by larger animals than themselves.

Southern right whale

Right whales got their name during whaling times, when hunters said they were the 'right' whales to kill. Today, they are the most rare of all marine mammals, but northern right whales are in even greater danger of extinction than southern right whales. Southern right whales eat copepods – animals so tiny that 8,000 of them would fit on a teaspoon!

Baleen is a tough, but slightly bendy substance and it used to be called 'whalebone'. Although it is like bone, baleen is actually more similar to hair and nails.

GENTLE GIANTS

BLUE WHALES

Imagine you are at sea, when the calm blue of the water's gently rippling surface is broken and a supersized, glistening body emerges.

Witnessing a blue whale as it comes up to breathe can be frightening as well as exciting. These creatures are the biggest of all whales – their size alone is breathtaking. It would be easy for a blue whale to tip a boat over. Blue whales are actually the biggest animals on the planet, but despite their size they are peaceful giants.

A blue whale is a baleen whale and, like other baleen whales, the skin of a blue whale's enormous throat is pleated, with lots of folds and grooves. This makes its skin super-stretchy so it can expand when it fills up with water and food.

When a blue whale prepares to dive it does a 'headstand' and its wide tail appears above the water.

Blue whales surface briefly to release a fountain of air and water and take in a big breath through their blowholes.

TWIST IT!

The part of a blue whale's brain that works out the meaning of sounds (the 'acoustic' part) is ten times bigger than ours.

Scientists don't know when blue whales are old enough to give birth, and they don't know where they give birth!

Whipped cream is 30 per cent fat and whale milk is up to 50 per cent fat – that's as thick as toothpaste!

A blue whale mother is the size of a Boeing 737 airplane, and her newborn baby is the size of a fully-grown hippo.

SUPER-SIZED

BLUE WHALE
Weighs 180 tonnes

=

40 ELEPHANTS
Weigh 4.5 tonnes each

FINDING KRILL

Blue whales use hair-like bristles (baleen) to catch their food. They mostly eat krill (tiny shrimp-like creatures), managing to gulp up to 3.5 tonnes a day – that's about 1.5 million krill! To catch krill, the whales dive beneath a swarm of them, then swiftly turn and lunge upwards, filling their mouth with food and water.

Blue whales are the loudest animals alive.

Blue whales feed in the Antarctic in the summer, where billions of krill live. In the winter they move to warmer areas, but they eat very little.

Scientists think that blue whales may sing to tell other blue whales where to find the best supplies of krill.

Side swipe

Lunging deep into water to find swarms of krill takes a lot of energy, but scooping them up at the surface of the sea is much easier! Blue whales often swim sideways to get a big mouthful of krill.

SOUNDS OF THE SEA

CETACEANS' SENSES

Animals use their senses to find food and to locate other animals. In the deep, dark sea, sound is more important than sight.

Cetaceans (whales, dolphins and porpoises) are masters of the marine environment, with special super senses that help them to find their way – and their prey – in the murky darkness of the ocean. Light does not travel very well under the sea because water absorbs light rays. That is why whales, and many other marine animals, use other senses more than sight to find out what's going on around them.

Sight

Whales and dolphins can see about 9 m ahead when they are underwater. They probably can't see in colour, and don't rely on their sight, although they do have special light-reflecting layers in their eyes that are good at picking up even small amounts of light. Dolphins have better vision than most cetaceans. Their eyes can look in different directions at the same time, which is great for checking for nearby predators!

Small fish swarm together for protection forming a 'bait ball'.

Smell

Scientists have long believed that whales and dolphins do not have a sense of smell, but they have recently discovered that some baleen whales may be able to smell swarms of krill.

Dolphins communicate with each other to take turns herding the bait ball and feeding from it.

TWIST IT!

Sound waves travel nearly five times faster in sea than in the air.

Submarines use the same system of echolocation as whales and bats to find objects underwater.

Dolphins have the most advanced detection system of any animal and by hunting in a group they are extremely skilled at finding and chasing shoals of fast-moving fish.

Bats also use echolocation to hunt prey in the dark.

SEA SOUNDS

Sound

Dolphins don't have ears on the outside of their head. Sound travels through their jaws and other bones in their head. These animals have a superb sense of hearing. This helps them to use their special sense of echolocation (see below). They make sounds – called clicks – that travel through the water and bounce off objects. The sound is 'echoed' back to the animal, allowing them to work out the shape, size and distance of the object.

Ripley explains... Echolocation

All toothed whales use echolocation to locate objects around them. Dolphins produce clicking sounds from their phonic lips just below their blowhole. They use their nasal sacs to move air over the lips to make the sounds. These sounds go out through the front of the dolphin's head. When they hit an object, such as a fish, the sounds bounce back to the dolphin enabling their brain to work out where it is coming from and how big it is.

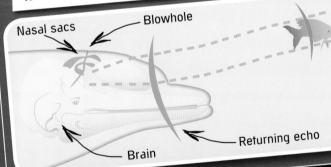

Nasal sacs Blowhole

Brain Returning echo

Taste

Dolphins appear to have a sense of taste, and prefer to eat some fish over others. They also use their sense of taste to find out about other animals. Cetaceans can taste the seawater to detect chemicals (such as wee) that other animals make, so they can get a flavour of what's out there!

HUNTING WHALES

TOOTHED KILLERS

Ocean hunters are among the most impressive predators on the planet, with their sleek bodies, super speed and killer instincts.

There are few places to hide in the ocean, but finding prey – animals to hunt and eat – is still difficult because the seas are wide, deep and dark. Toothed whales have developed incredible hunting skills to help them find, chase and kill animals.

LEARNING TO KILL

Toothed whales are taught how to find and capture their prey by their mother. Every year, orca mums take their young to Monterey Bay in the United States, where there are many grey whales and their calves. This is where the orcas learn how to kill. The young orcas attack the grey whale calves, while orca mothers watch and help out if needed. It can take the orcas six hours to kill one calf, even when they gang up on it.

A torpedo shaped body is the right shape for moving through water at high speed.

Even though grey whale calves are much larger than adult orcas, orcas use their power and strength to win the fight.

An orca must get a grey whale calf away from its mother before it can attack.

GRAB AND GRIP

Many mammals have different types of teeth, for cutting or grinding. Toothed whales, such as this bottlenose dolphin, however, have just one set of teeth that must last their whole lifetime. The teeth of a toothed whale are all simple and cone-shaped. It is a good shape for grabbing onto slippery fish.

TWIST IT!

Dolphins and other toothed whales are such good hunters that other predators often swim behind them, and feast on their leftovers.

Sometimes hundreds, even thousands, of dolphins gather and travel together. These massive groups are made up of many different families.

Toothed whales can use their echolocation (see page 19) to find prey when the water is too dark to see in.

Whales are warm-blooded, like us, and can keep their bodies warm when the water is cold, so they can still swim fast in cold water.

A large group of dolphins is called a herd.

TOUGH TEETH

TOP TEAMWORK

These bottlenose dolphins hunt shoals of fish where the water is shallow, working together to force the fish towards the shore. The dolphins even create waves to push the fish out of the water, where they are stranded. The dolphins join the fish on land and eat – this is called strand feeding.

DEATH BY STEALTH

Toothed whales often hunt in groups, but orcas take the strategy to a whole new level. Scientists know that they 'click' to each other to communicate, but when they begin a hunt orcas switch to silent mode. The seas stay quiet as the orcas come together to co-ordinate and launch their attack, only clicking again to call other orcas to join the feast.

NOWHERE'S SAFE

KILLER WHALES

Orcas (killer whales) are daring, clever predators who attack in the sea and on land.

They are very resourceful, and can even snatch their dinner from beaches! They throw themselves onto the shore in high tide and, unbelievably, manage to grab seal pups. Then, with the catch in their mouth, they use the waves to carry them back out to sea.

Lessons for lunch

If you were a young orca your mum would have to teach you how to get lunch. Here are an orca mother's top tips:

* Whack a group of fish with your strong tail to knock them out.

* Swim under a seal, then use your head to flip it into the air. Have your jaws open wide, and be ready to wolf it down.

* Try a head-butt: simply swim head first at your prey and smash into it with your big strong head.

Killer waves

Orcas sometimes hunt seals that are resting on ice floes. One orca pokes its head above water to look for seals. The other orcas swim at, and under, the floe, creating a wave that tips over the floe and the seal falls into the water. Another orca is waiting to catch the seal.

Ripley's Believe It or Not!®

This lucky gentoo penguin escaped from a pod of hungry orcas off the coast of Antarctica when it jumped onto a boat full of tourists! It then swam away, but returned again later to escape the whales for a second time.

TWIST IT!

Orcas can see just as well out of water as they can underwater. That is useful for an animal that hunts seals, which often rest on ice.

Not all orcas are the same. Scientists think there may be many different types of orca, possibly up to four different species.

A big group of orcas live in the Eastern Pacific Ocean. They are unusual because the males live with their mothers all their lives. We don't know of any other mammals that do this.

In 1978, a pod of orcas was seen chasing a young blue whale. The orcas kept biting the blue whale, which managed to escape but probably died of its injuries soon afterwards.

AWESOME ORCAS

DOLPHIN WORLD

DANCERS OF THE DEEP

Dolphins and porpoises are small toothed whales that live in the sea. There are about 33 types of marine dolphin, six types of porpoise and four types of river dolphin.

Here are some of our favourites...

Finless and friendly

Finless porpoises are small grey cetaceans and are very friendly. They look rather like their cousins, beluga whales. They live near the coast and even swim some distance up rivers. Finless porpoises have a ridge on their back instead of fins, and it's thought that the ridge provides a non-slip surface so calves can grip onto their mum's back and ride along!

Timid hunters

Melon-headed whales, also known as little killer whales, are marine dolphins that have a grey, torpedo-shaped body and can change direction at full speed. These shy creatures hunt in the deep seas and usually stay in warm ocean waters, far from the shore.

Ripley's Believe It or Not!®
Pinky, a rare albino dolphin, was spotted in Lake Calcasieu, Louisiana! It is thought to be the world's only pink bottlenose dolphin.

Friends for life

The shape of a dolphin's face and mouth makes it look as if it's smiling. Scientists can't be sure if a dolphin is happy or not, but these smart animals do often seem to do things just for fun, such as jumping out of the water! Maybe this bottlenose dolphin has found something funny, but the risso dolphin on the right doesn't get the joke!

Show-offs!

Many dolphins like to leap out of the water as they swim – and Pacific white-sided dolphins are especially graceful when they perform these displays. They often swim alongside boats, and even do somersaults! These are very sociable animals, and sometimes swim in schools of thousands.

Wise workers

Better watch out! When Irrawaddy dolphins pop their head above the surface they often spit water to herd fish! In an astonishing display of intelligence, a group of these animals in Burma work with local fishermen, herding fish into their nets in return for being able to feast on the leftovers. No one taught the dolphins to do this – they worked it out for themselves.

SLEEK SWIMMERS

OCEAN MOTION

Whales are too weighty to live on land, but an ocean is the perfect place for a big-bodied beast to swim with all the grace of a ballet dancer.

If a whale had legs, they would snap under its enormous weight if it tried to walk on land. Even its internal organs, such as the lungs and heart, would be crushed. Water can support heavy animals, making it easier for them to float because it is denser than air. As a result, whales move slowly but gracefully through water.

1st A Dall's porpoise in action!

Speedy swimmer

Dall's porpoises are not just fast, they are agile and super-flexible too. They zigzag, take sharp turns and roll – including a special 'rooster-tailing roll', which is named after the cone of water this movement makes – it looks like a rooster, or cockerel, tail!

Into the sea

Fish swim by moving their tail from side-to-side, but whales move their tail up and down. That's because they are descended from four-legged animals that walked on land, using muscles that moved the spine up and down, not from side-to-side.

Sperm whale

A whale's body is packed with strong muscles to power it forwards.

Speedy cetaceans

The fastest members of the whale family include Dall's porpoises, orcas and sei whales, but none of them comes close to the speed of the world's fastest fish – a sailfish, which has a top speed of 110 km/h. Maybe that's why whales usually target slower swimmers, such as squid!

⭐		
1st	Dall's porpoise	55 km/h
2nd	Orca	54 km/h
3rd	Sei whale	48 km/h
4th	Fin whale	46 km/h

STREAMLINED SHAPE

Look at this sperm whale's body. It is shaped like a submarine and can move through water easily. This sperm whale is swimming upside down. They sometimes do this when hunting, or just for fun!

TWIST IT!

Humpback whales can leap clear of the water (breach), up to 200 times in a row without tiring.

Blue whales have flippers that are up to 4 m long!

Some whales have blowholes that are big enough for a baby to crawl into!

BIG MOVERS

Big swimmers need big tails. A blue whale's tail is as wide as a football goal – that's about 8 m.

Whale skin is rubbery and smooth (although sperm whales are a little wrinkly), keeping them sleek and streamlined.

Like most whales, the sperm whale has flippers that are small compared to the rest of their body. A whale uses its flippers for changing direction, stopping and balancing.

DEEP DIVERS

Whales breathe at the surface, but they dive down head first to eat. Their tail fins – called flukes – create forward motion, propelling the animal onward and downward in the water.

27

ANCIENT MARINERS

LIFE STORIES

Whales are born big, and growing up takes a long time. These are some of the longest-living animals on Earth.

No one knows for sure exactly how long some of these huge creatures can live for in the wild, because we haven't been watching them for long enough. However, we do know that humpback whales can live for up to 100 years, blue whales can live for more than 100 years and bowhead whales might reach 200 years of age!

Big babies

Whale and dolphin calves feed on milk made by their mother's body.

Whale babies are called calves. Mothers grow their calves inside their body for a long time. It takes about 16 months for a sperm whale calf to grow before it is born – in comparison humans are pregnant for about nine months. A calf is born underwater, but the mother stays near the surface so she can nudge her baby up to the air to take its first breath.

Mother knows best

Newborn calves stay close to their mother. Some whales live together in families, and all the females help to look after the calves. Sperm whale and grey whale females often feed other females' babies, so the mothers can have a break and go hunting!

Fast learners

Calves, such as this humpback swimming with its mum, copy their mother to learn how to hunt. They stay with their mother for several years, and not all calves leave, even once they are adults.

Great grannies

Grandmothers are also very good at looking after the whole family. They can remember the best places to find food, they lead the family to safe places, and protect the little calves from predators, such as sharks.

A natural end

Many cetaceans live a long life, and die of old age. Others are killed by human and animal hunters. Young cetaceans are preyed on by other whales and sharks.

Believe It or Not!®

This very unusual-looking calf, below, is a rare albino humpback whale. It is thought to be the offspring of a famous albino humpback named 'Migaloo', featured on page 43.

FAMILY TIME

A giant bowhead whale caught in 2007 was found to have part of an old harpoon stuck in its side. The harpoon was fired in 1880, so that whale was at least 130 years old.

Sperm whales have been known to attack boats if they think their calves might be in danger.

When a grey whale calf is scared, its mother gently touches it with her fin to reassure it.

Some cetaceans cannot start producing calves until they are in their twenties, but most start their families younger than that.

Female cetaceans usually have just one calf at a time. They can still make milk and feed other calves in the pod even when they are too old to have calves of their own.

Very few people have ever seen a whale give birth in the wild. Even when scientists are lucky enough to see the beginning of a birth, they often move far away, so they don't disturb the mother and her calf.

TWIST IT!

29

IN DEEP WATER

SPERM WHALES

Sperm whales are the largest toothed whales, and one of the world's biggest predators.

Sperm whales can dive down to around 300 m, where there is no light and few animals can survive. They can stay underwater for nearly two hours, although most dives last less time than this. The sperm whale's deepsea dives are necessary, because its favourite food, the giant squid, is found in the dark ocean depths.

Big head

Sperm whales have a large head that contains a big brain and a strange, waxy substance called spermaceti. This may help a sperm whale to control its buoyancy (how it floats and moves up and down in water). Scientists now think the spermaceti may also help the whale to transmit the clicks and sounds used in echolocation (see page 19).

The whale has small eyes, but it does not need to see well to hunt successfully.

Sperm whales have smooth heads but wrinkly bodies.

The lower jaw is long and narrow with up to 56 teeth. There are no teeth on the top jaw.

The head is huge and box-shaped.

Hungry hunters

Sperm whales eat squid, octopus and fish and they need to eat about 1,000 small squid a day. They are one of the few animals big enough to fight a giant squid – and win.

Underwater battle

Giant squid and sperm whales sometimes get involved in colossal combats. No one has witnessed such a struggle, but models have been built to show what it might look like. The largest squid ever seen to battle with a sperm whale measured 14 m long.

Sperm whales sleep vertically in the water.

TWIST IT!

Sperm whales can live to 75 years of age and a mother can suckle each calf for up to 12 years!

Sperm whales are the biggest predators that hunt single prey (unlike baleen whales that hunt lots of little animals).

A sperm whale's single blowhole is on the left side of its head rather than the top.

Sperm whales have the largest brain of any creature that has ever lived on Earth.

Male sperm whales are more than twice as heavy as females.

OVER-SIZED

Do whales dream?

Sperm whales snatch about 12 minutes of breathless sleep at a time, hanging in the water to enjoy a quick nap. When they sleep, their eyes move backwards and forwards quickly, just like ours do when we dream. Maybe they dream too, but no one knows.

THE PERFECT PLACE

WHALES IN PARADISE

Welcome to paradise! The Gulf of California is a magical place that makes an ideal home for many whales.

It is a narrow strip of water that separates mainland Mexico and a long finger of land, called the Baja Peninsula. The idyllic conditions here create a unique ocean habitat where millions of animals can thrive. Marine biologists – scientists who study life in the oceans – come here to watch whales.

Vaquita porpoise

The vaquita porpoise only lives in the Gulf of California, but it probably won't even be living there for much longer. It is the world's smallest (measuring just 1.4 m long) and most endangered cetacean. There are only about 200 vaquitas left in the world, which is why we do not have a picture of one here. They are dying out because they get caught in fishing nets.

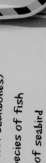
KEY FACTS

THE GULF OF CALIFORNIA IS HOME TO:

- ☑ 32 species of cetacean (marine mammals)
- ☑ 3,000 species of invertebrates (animals without backbones)
- ☑ over 900 species of fish
- ☑ 170 species of seabird

Short-finned pilot whale

A lovely place to live

The Gulf of California is an area of ocean that is welcoming to many animals because it isn't too hot, and it isn't too cold. In the winter, it is cold at the mouth of the gulf, but stays warm near the top. There are huge tides, and plenty of clean water rushing in. Not many people live on the land nearby, which means not too much pollution gets into the sea and spoils it. All of these things mean that many animals find it a good place to live.

United States of America

MEXICO

SONORA

● HERMOSILLO

California

SUR

BAJA

CALIFORNIA

LA PAZ

Gulf

of

California

BAJA

CALIFORNIA

PACIFIC

OCEAN

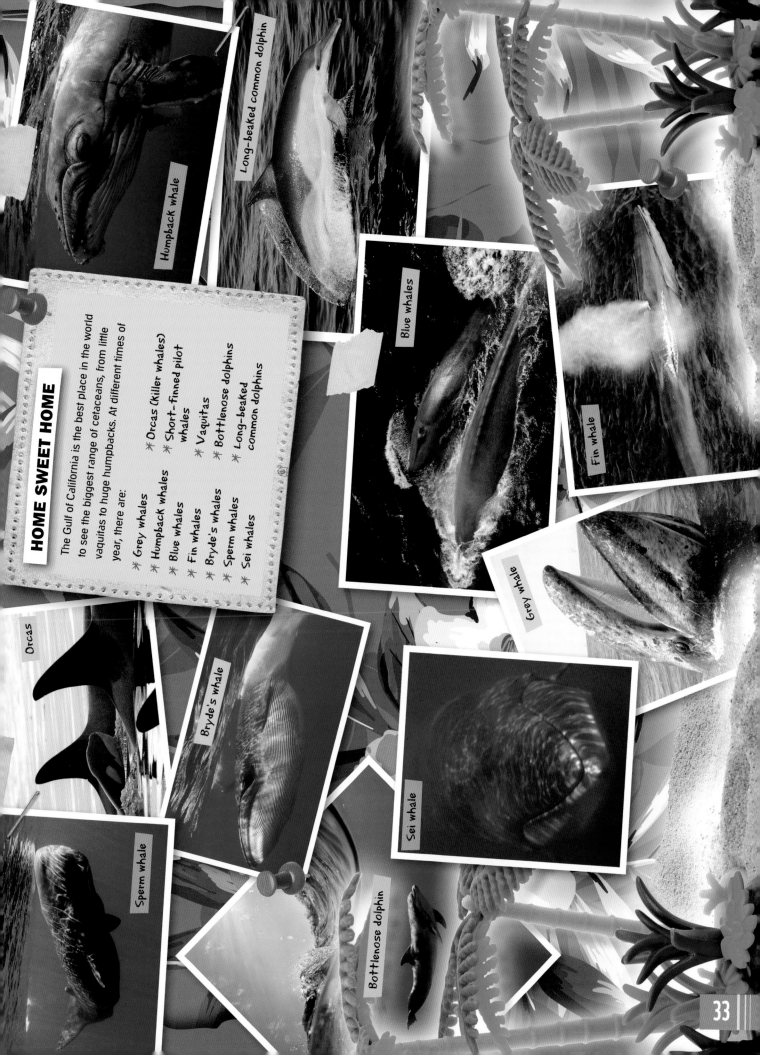

HOME SWEET HOME

The Gulf of California is the best place in the world to see the biggest range of cetaceans, from little vaquitas to huge humpbacks. At different times of year, there are:

* Grey whales
* Humpback whales
* Blue whales
* Fin whales
* Bryde's whales
* Sperm whales
* Sei whales
* Orcas (killer whales)
* Short-finned pilot whales
* Vaquitas
* Bottlenose dolphins
* Long-beaked common dolphins

Humpback whale

Long-beaked common dolphin

Blue whales

Fin whale

Grey whale

Orcas

Bryde's whale

Sei whale

Sperm whale

Bottlenose dolphin

COOL CUSTOMERS

LIFE AT THE COLD POLES

The world's coldest places may look lifeless, but many animals thrive there.

The oceans around the North and South Poles may be chilly, windy, and covered with vast expanses of ice but they are home to many cetaceans. There is enough food here to feed the large populations of dolphins and porpoises, and the biggest whales.

Beluga whales live in groups, or pods, around the Arctic Ocean and 'talk' to each other by making clicking sounds.

The polar regions are extreme places. During the summer, days last for 24 hours, while in winter there is no daylight at all!

The cold waters of the Arctic and Antarctic are home to billions and billions of krill. Seals and penguins eat the krill, and orcas come to feast on the seals and penguins! Baleen whales eat the krill, too.

The white whale

Belugas are small whales that can grow up to 6 m long and live around the Arctic Ocean. Belugas are sometimes called sea canaries because they 'sing' underwater and can make many different sounds. They can also copy the sounds made by other animals. Some divers insist that belugas have copied them when they have called out!

The skin is brown at birth, but gets whiter as the whale ages.

Narwhals mostly swim upside down, on their back. This might be to protect their tusk when they are close to the seabed.

Unicorn whales

Narwhals are the strangest looking whales, with a long spear-like tooth called a tusk. Usually only males have a tusk but sometimes females grow one, and occasionally males grow two. They may use them to fight, or to show off. A good-sized tusk means the narwhal is healthy.

Bowhead whales

The bowhead whale is also known as the Greenland right whale. It holds the record for having the world's biggest mouth, which can be 3 m wide and 6 m deep! It also has a layer of blubber (fat) to help it cope with the Arctic cold that can measure up to 50 cm thick!

No dorsal fin.

A bowhead uses its huge mouth to gulp millions of krill.

White patches around chin.

SMART CETACEANS

All cetaceans, especially dolphins, are smart animals with big brains.

You can teach a dog how to do tricks, but when you show a dolphin how to do a trick, it can change the trick and come up with an even better one! If you play ball with a dolphin it might start to dribble the ball along the seabed, or hold it underwater, then release it suddenly so it shoots up, or blow bubble rings and roll the ball through them.

These artworks represent songs sung by whales and dolphins! Engineer Mark Fischer used special underwater microphones to capture their sounds, even ones we can't hear, and transformed them into images. His work revealed that dolphins have a high level of communication, and even use grammar!

BIG THINKERS

Using tools

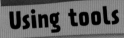

Dolphins belong to a special group of animals that can use tools, like humans do. In the 1980s, a female dolphin was seen using a sea sponge on the end of her snout to protect the tip while she dug for food on the seabed. Now, she has taught all the females in her family to use sea sponges!

Talking matters

Being able to communicate, or talk, with each other is a good sign of being smart, and many cetaceans are great talkers. Humpback whales sing to each other, while dolphins call to each other by name. Young calves begin to make their own whistles, which the other dolphins copy and use whenever they want to get that dolphin's attention. Every dolphin has a different whistle-name.

TWIST IT!

Whale songs have a low frequency, which means they can travel undersea for hundreds – maybe even thousands – of kilometres.

Scientists think that they can probably recognize numbers, but may not be able to count.

Dolphins are able to think, know, and remember in similar ways to humans and apes, but their brains are built in a different way.

Bottlenose dolphins recognize themselves in mirrors.

Male fin whales sing when they feast on krill.

Toothed whales hunt and often live in groups, which means they need to be smart and good at communicating with each other.

Whales speak in dialects – that means their languages are different depending on which area they come from!

WISE WHALES

BEYOND THE SEA

RIVER DOLPHINS

Most cetaceans live in salty ocean water, but these little dolphins have found a new home.

Most river dolphins tend to be small, measuring about 2 m long. They live in muddy rivers where the water is murky and it is difficult to see. They have small eyes, but eyesight is not very important to them. They use their sense of echolocation (see page 19) to find prey instead.

Pink river dolphin

The pink, or Amazon, river dolphin is also known as a 'boto'. Most toothed whales have teeth that are all alike, but botos have two different types of teeth. Peg-like teeth catch fish, but molars at the back of their mouth are perfect for crushing crunchy crabs and turtles. Botos sometimes hunt in packs with tucuxis – grey river dolphins – and giant otters.

Habitat: Amazon River and other rivers nearby
Diet: Fish, crabs and turtles
Features: The largest of the river dolphins

ENDANGERED

Most river dolphins share their habitat with people, which is why they are in danger of dying out.

KEY FACTS

River dolphins can grow to a maximum of 2.7 m but most are smaller, and weigh less than 50 kg. They also have:

- ☑ Long, slender beak
- ☑ Bulging forehead
- ☑ Small eyes
- ☑ Neck
- ☑ Broad fins

Pink river dolphins start their life with black skin, but as they age they get pinker.

Irrawaddy dolphins

These small dolphins are hard to see because their freshwater homes are often filthy with pollution. Irrawaddy dolphins are honoured in parts of Cambodia and Laos where they are believed to carry the souls of people who have died. However, they often get trapped in fishing nets.

Habitat: Rivers, coasts and mangrove swamps in Indo-Pacific region

Diet: Fish, squid and crustaceans

Features: Small, rounded head and no 'beak'

VULNERABLE

NOT VULNERABLE

Tucuxi dolphin

Tucuxi (say: too-koo-shi) dolphins can live in the ocean as well as rivers, and they look and behave more like bottlenose dolphins than other river dolphins. Tucuxis often leap out of the water and play in the ripples and waves created by passing boats.

Habitat: Rivers and coasts in South America and eastern Central America

Diet: Mostly fish

Features: A long beak and grey or pinkish skin

ENDANGERED

ENDANGERED

Blind river dolphins

Ganges river dolphins have terrible eyesight. Their eyes only let in a tiny pinprick of light, but it doesn't matter. Also known as blind river dolphins, these cetaceans use echoes to build up a 'sound picture' of their environment. They also swim on their side, with one flipper touching the riverbed, to help them find food.

Habitat: In and around the Ganges and Brahmaputra Rivers in India and Bangladesh

Diet: Fish, especially carp and catfish

Features: Long fins and large tail fins (flukes)

Indus river dolphins

Indus river dolphins are mysterious animals and little is known about how they live and breed. They prefer to swim in deep water rivers, where they hunt large fish. These river dolphins are hunted by local people for food.

Habitat: In and around the Indus River in Pakistan

Diet: Fish, clams and prawns

Features: Live in groups of up to three

MEGA MIGRATIONS

WHALES ON THE MOVE

Grey whales embark on incredible journeys to be in the right place to feed and breed.

Many whales migrate – they go on long journeys. They have big appetites and travel to the places where there is most food. They also migrate to have their babies because they prefer to look after their calves in warm, sheltered waters away from predators. Whales can make these massive migrations because they are big animals and powerful swimmers.

As grey whales migrate along the North American coastline they stay in shallow water to avoid the attention of hungry orcas.

Big barnacles

A single grey whale may carry more than 450 kg of barnacles. These are crustaceans that glue themselves to the whale's skin and grab food out of the water as the whale swims.

Look at the size of these barnacles!

These shell-like barnacles were once attached to a whale. The shells are sharp and act like a suit of armour if the whale is attacked.

ACTUAL SIZE!

JULY–OCTOBER

The whales are at their northern homes in the Bering and Chuckchi seas. They feast on little sea creatures, their calves learn how to eat solid food and they store blubber for their journey south.

Grey whale migration route

FEBRUARY–JUNE

The whales leave their southern home and start the long journey back up north. The young calves stay with their mothers, because they are still dependent on their mother's milk. Most of the whales will be back in the food-filled Arctic waters by June.

BIG WORD ALERT

MIGRATION

A long journey made by an animal in order to mate, have young or find food.

NOVEMBER–JANUARY

There is little food about as the Arctic seas begin to freeze over, so the long journey south to Mexico's warm waters must begin. Whales swim for 24 hours a day. The females are pregnant, and soon start to give birth in the warm seas.

Grey whale mothers can cover 26,000 km in just six months.

Hitchhikers

It is common for little animals to cling on to a whale and hitch a ride as it travels through the oceans. Barnacles do not harm the whale, but some animals, such as whale lice, can cause skin damage. Animals that live on another and cause harm are called parasites.

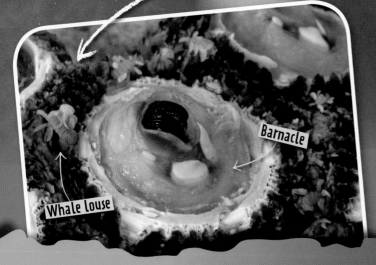

Barnacle

Whale louse

TWIST IT!

No one knows for sure how whales find their way along their migration routes. Scientists think they use both the Sun's position and the Earth's magnetism as a guide.

Female blue whales begin their migration before the males and the oldest whales go the farthest, into the coldest Arctic or Antarctic waters.

Beluga whales live around the Arctic in the summer, but in the winter the seas freeze over, so they usually migrate south to warmer places.

Whale muscles are packed with a protein that is really good at storing oxygen, so whales can make long, deep dives without taking a breath.

Fin whales travel to the poles in summer to gorge on krill. Fin whales are called greyhounds of the sea because they can swim so fast. They can reach speeds of 46 km/h and cover 290 km in a day.

A grey whale female can cover 145 km in just 24 hours. She can do this for six months – that's more than 26,000 km – and scarcely eats during all that time.

MAKING A MOVE

41

SONGS OF THE SEA

HUMPBACK WHALES

Humpback whales may be as big as a bus, but they are gentle giants with very impressive acrobatic skills.

Humpbacks are baleen whales (see page 11) and they are famous for their beautiful songs, their long migrations and the amazing way that they catch their food. These energetic whales may be large, but they can flip out of the water, twist in midair and land on their side with a bang.

White markings on long flippers

Throat grooves, or pleats

Blue-black body

TWIST IT!

It takes ten years for a humpback calf to grow to full size.

Humpbacks that live in the Earth's southern oceans eat lots of krill (tiny animals), but those that live in northern places eat much more fish.

Humpback whales have the same special brain cells that humans have to help them live and work in families and groups.

Humpback whales have the world's longest flippers. They can grow to 5 m, which is about one-third of the whale's body length. They use their flippers to swim, gather fish and stroke their young.

THE HUMP

Singing sensations

Male humpbacks love to make regular patterns of sound – called singing. They are some of the noisiest animals in the ocean and their 'songs' can last for several hours. When they sing, the males hang in the water, with their head pointing downwards.

42

KEY FACTS

Humpback whales

Length: Up to 14 m

Weight: Up to 27 tonnes

Range: Worldwide except the coldest waters

Status: Endangered

Mega migration

Humpback whales gorge on food in the cold oceans near the North and South Poles in the summer, but travel to warm tropical seas to give birth in the winter. During the winter, they eat very little and survive on their stores of fat. Humpbacks in the Indian Ocean may not migrate at all.

Ripley's Believe It or Not!®

Migaloo, as he is known, is thought to be one of the only completely albino whales in the world. Photographer Jenny Dean spotted the white humpback whale while on a whale-watching trip in Australia.

Open wide!

Bubble nets

Humpbacks have developed an amazing way to eat. They swim in circles around a school of fish, breathing out lots of bubbles. The bubbles make a 'curtain of foam' that traps the fish. The whale then swims up through the trap, gulping down large numbers of fish that are caught in the 'bubble net'.

WHALE WATCHING

GETTING TO KNOW YOU

For a long time, people did not understand how special whales and dolphins are. Now we are a much wiser species!

When people discovered that they could use whales for meat, oil (made from whale blubber) and other products they began to hunt some species close to extinction. Most countries of the world now respect a ban on whale hunting, and many populations of whales and dolphins are recovering. Other problems include pollution and over-fishing.

Colossal collision

This blue whale fatally crashed into a ship in the Santa Barbara Channel, California. Blue whales feed in the shipping lane, and as a result there have been dozens of collisions here over the last decade.

STOP PRESS...STOP PRESS...STO

Every day amazing new facts are being discovered about whales and dolphins...

SCIENCE CRACKS THE MYSTERY QUACK

For decades, sailors and submariners have been mystified by strange quacking noises around the Antarctic. The noise – called 'bio-duck' – has now been revealed as the song of Antarctic minke whales.

WONDER WHALE WOWS WORLD WITH NEW RECORD

Extreme divers plunge into the ocean and hold their breath in a dangerous sport called 'free-diving'. The champion 'free-diver' of the world, however, is not a human but a Cuvier's beaked whale. These record-breakers reach depths of nearly 3 km and can stay underwater for up to 137 minutes.

Scientists used satellite tags to follow Cuvier's beaked whales as they dived deeper, and longer, than any other marine mammal.

44

Tagging whales

It's not easy to follow whales underwater! The best way for scientists to find out where they go and what they do is to tag them. Each tag is a mini-computer that sends messages about a whale's movements to a satellite in space. The tag also measures the water temperature, pressure, amount of salt in it and sunlight. The information gathered by doing this helps scientists to make new discoveries about these amazing creatures.

TWIST IT!

About two million whales in total died when whaling was allowed.

The world's largest remaining group of blue whales spends summers on the western coast of the United States and Mexico. There are just 3,000 of them left.

Cetaceans need clean, quiet water to live in. The oceans are dirtier, noisier and busier places than they used to be, and this has made survival difficult for whales and dolphins around the world.

Whales and dolphins breed slowly. They often have only one baby in a year, and sometimes one baby every two years.

A WHALE WARNING

PLAY TIME FOR TALKING DOLPHINS

Dolphin researchers have even taught some of their finned friends to whistle out sounds such as 'scarf' and 'rope' when they want to play with these objects!

WHISTLING DOLPHINS GIVE EACH OTHER NAMES

Scientists have discovered that when a dolphin wants to get hold of one of its pals it grabs its attention by calling out its name! That's right, a group of dolphins uses a different whistle to call each member of the family.

PRESS...STOP PRESS...STOP PRESS

A brighter future

Today, people want to learn more about these big, beautiful beasts. Scientists and wildlife-lovers sail across the ocean to watch and photograph them, rather than hunt them.

ACKNOWLEDGEMENTS

COVER (sp) © Chua Han Hsiung - shutterstock.com, (t) © Natali Glado - shutterstock.com; **2** © Shane Gross - shutterstock.com; **3** (t) Rex/Masa Ushioda/SplashdownDirect, (b) © anyamuse - shutterstock.com; **4** © Monika Wieland - shutterstock.com; **6** © David Herraez Calzada - shutterstock.com; **7** (t) © Karoline Cullen - shutterstock.com, (b) Rex/Masa Ushioda/SplashdownDirect; **8–9** Leonardo Meschini; **10** (t/l) Jurgen & Christine Sohns/FLPA, (b/l) © Thumbelina - shutterstock.com, (t/r, b/r) © laschi - shutterstock.com, (c/l) © dkvektor - shutterstock.com, (t/c) © Ilya Akinshin - shutterstock.com; **11** (t/c/l, t/l, b/l) © Thumbelina - shutterstock.com, (t/c/r, c/l) © Nebojsa Kontic - shutterstock.com, (b/c, t/r) © laschi - shutterstock.com, (b/r) © Biosphoto, Christopher Swann/Biosphoto/FLPA; **12** (sp) © Juniors Tierbildarchiv/Photoshot, (t) © anyamuse - shutterstock.com; **13** (t) Flip Nicklin/Minden Pictures/FLPA, (c/r) Caters News Agency Ltd., (c/l) Konrad Wothe/Minden Pictures/FLPA, (b) Solvin Zankl/Visuals Unlimited, Inc. /Science Photo Library; **14** Jill M Perry; **15** (t) © Doc White/seapics.com, (b) Hiroya Minakuchi/Minden Pictures/FLPA; **16** (b/l) © aleksander1 - fotolia.com, (b/r) © a_elmo - fotolia.com; **16–17** (dp) Matthew Stewart Coutts; **17** (t) © Doug Perrine/seapics.com, (b) © Doc White/naturepl.com; **18–19** (bgd) Alexander Safonov/Getty Images; **19** (t) © Aflo/naturepl.com, (c) Dynamo Design, (b) Rex/FLPA/Dickie Duckett; **20** Brandon Cole; **21** (t) © Pedro Narra/naturepl.com, (c) © Todd Pusser/naturepl.com, (b) FLPA/Rex; **22** Sylvain Cordier/Biosphoto/FLPA; **23** (t) Alain Bidart/Biosphoto/FLPA, (b) R. Roscoe (photovolcanica.com); **24** (t) © Masa Ushioda/seapics.com, (c) Caters News Agency Ltd., (b) © Doug Perrine/naturepl.com; **25** (t) © A. L. Stanzani/ardea.com, (c) © Brandon Cole/naturepl.com, (b) EPA/Barbara Walton; **26** (t) Minden Pictures/Getty Images; **26–27** (b) © Brandon Cole/naturepl.com; **27** (r) © Dan Bach Kristensen - shutterstock.com; **28** (t/r) © Franco Banfi/naturepl.com; **28–29** (dp) © Amos Nachoum/seapics.com; **29** (b/r) Sam Ruttyn/Newspix/Rex; **30** (t) © Nature Production/naturepl.com; **30–31** (dp) © Nature Production/naturepl.com; **31** (t/r) © Susan Dabritz/seapics.com; **32** (c) Sam South, (b) © Rainer Lesniewski - shutterstock.com; **32–33** (bgd) © SalomeNJ - shutterstock.com; **33** (t/c) © Sergey Uryadnikov - shutterstock.com, (t/l) © Joost van Uffelen - shutterstock.com, (t/r) © Juan Gracia - shutterstock.com, (c) © Doug Perrine/naturepl.com, (c/l) © Monika Wieland - shutterstock.com, (c/r) Hiroya Minakuchi/Minden Pictures/FLPA, (b/c) © Willyam Bradberry - shutterstock.com, (b/l) © Shane Gross - shutterstock.com, (b/r) Mammal Fund Earthviews/FLPA, (b/c/r) © James Michael Dorsey - shutterstock.com; **34** (sp) © Doug Allan/naturepl.com; **35** (t) © Franco Banfi/naturepl.com, (c) © Doc White/ardea.com, (b) © Martha Holmes/naturepl.com; **36** (t, b/r) Aguasonic Acoustics/Science Photo Library, (b/l) © Hugh Pearson/naturepl.com; **37** (t) © KateChris - shutterstock.com, (b) Rex/KPA/Zuma; **38** Kevin Schafer/Minden Pictures/FLPA; **39** (t) © Roland Seitre/naturepl.com, (b) © Andrea Florence/ardea.com; **40** (c) © Todd Pusser/naturepl.com, (b) © Michael S. Nolan/seapics.com; **40–41** (dp) Rex/Gerard Lacz; **41** (t) Dynamo Design, (b) Frans Lanting/FLPA; **42** © Biosphoto, Christopher Swann/Biosphoto/FLPA; **43** (t) Jenny Dean/Rex Features, (b) © Brandon Cole/naturepl.com; **44** (t) Flip Nicklin/Minden Pictures/FLPA, (b/l) Norbert Wu/Minden Pictures/FLPA, (b/r) © Todd Pusser/naturepl.com; **45** (t) Flip Nicklin/Minden Pictures/FLPA, (b) Rex/SplashdownDirect/Michael Nolan

Key: t = top, b = bottom, c = centre, l = left, r = right, sp = single page, dp = double page, bgd = background

All other photos are from Ripley's Entertainment Inc. All other artwork by Dynamo Design Ltd.

Every attempt has been made to acknowledge correctly and contact copyright holders and we apologise in advance for any unintentional errors or omissions, which will be corrected in future editions.

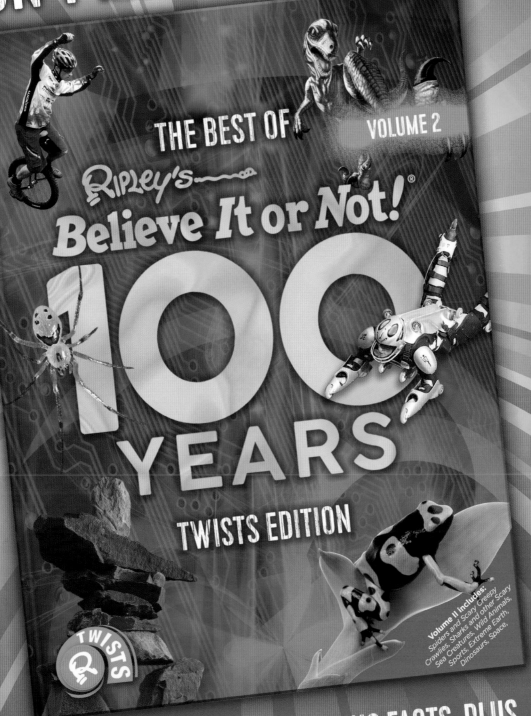

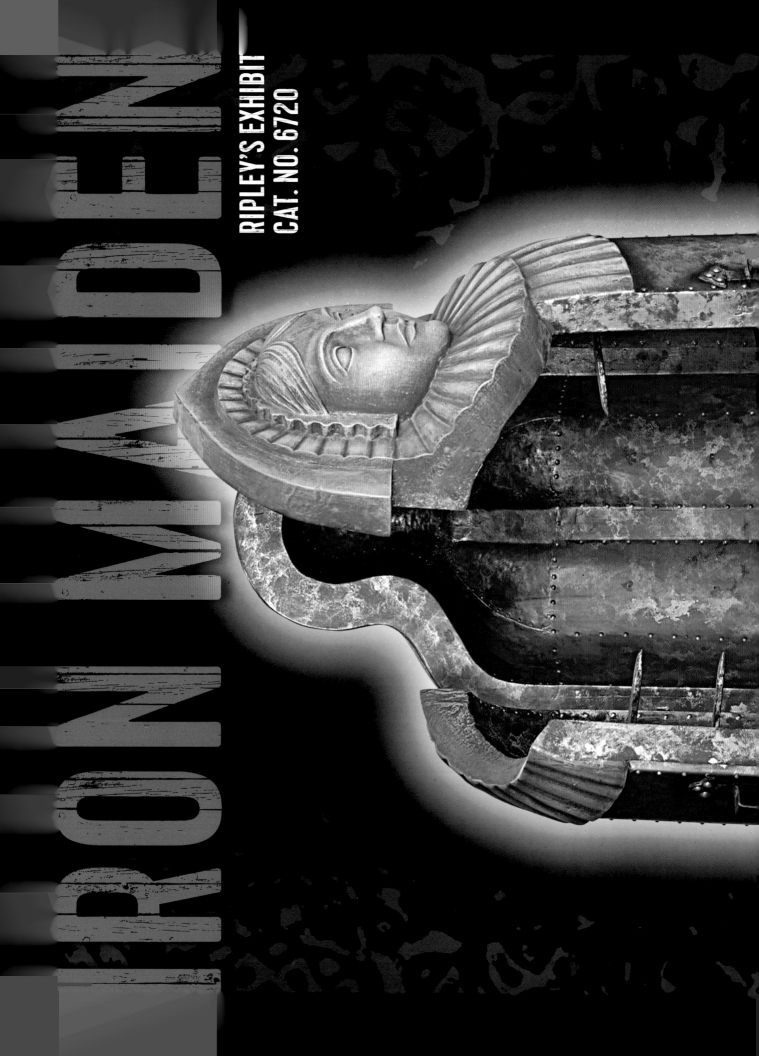

IRON MAIDEN

RIPLEY'S EXHIBIT
CAT. NO. 6720

ADORNED WITH SPIKES ALIGNED TO PIERCE THE EYES, THROAT, AND HEART.

ORIGIN: NUREMBERG, GERMANY

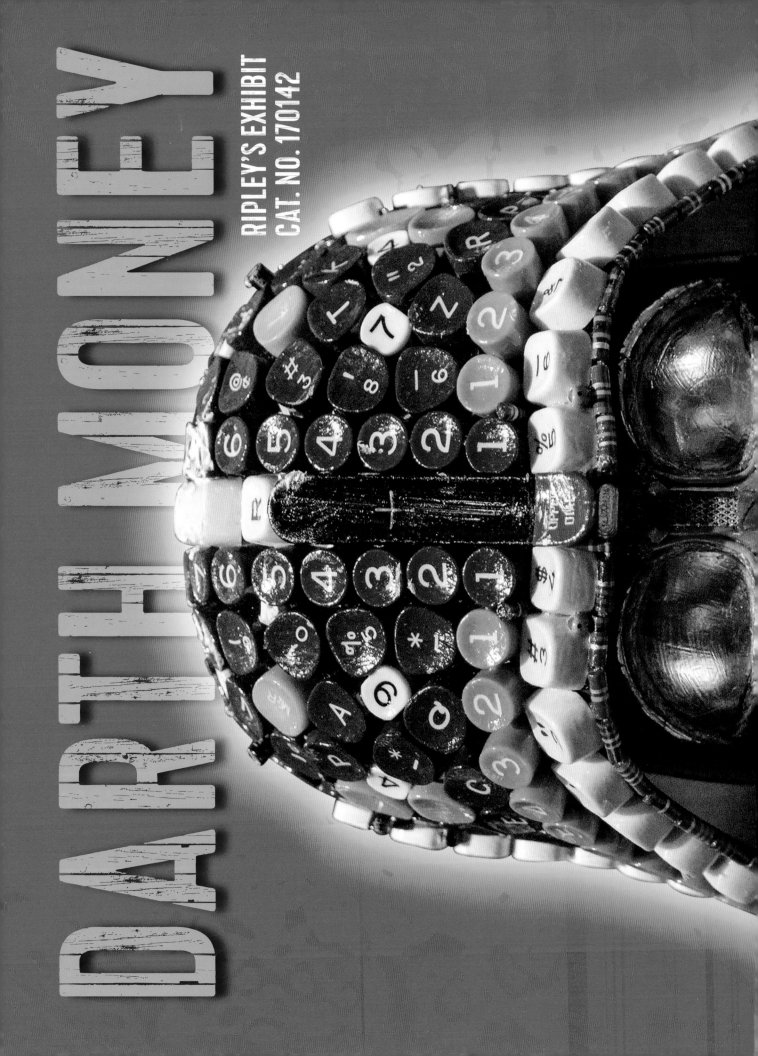

DARTH MONEY

RIPLEY'S EXHIBIT
CAT. NO. 170142

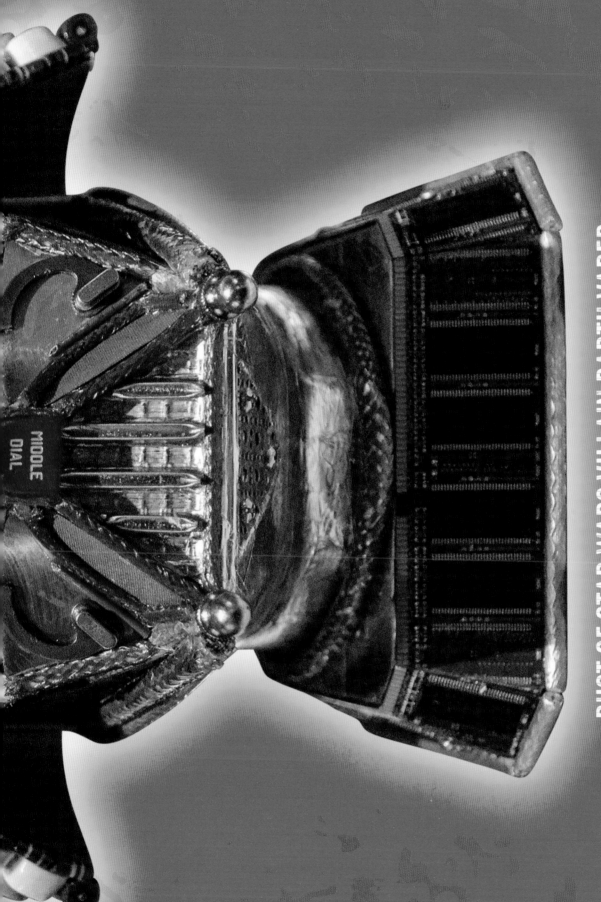

BUST OF STAR WARS VILLAIN DARTH VADER MADE FROM RECYCLED COMPUTER PARTS, ADDING MACHINES, AND TYPEWRITERS.

MIDDLE DIAL

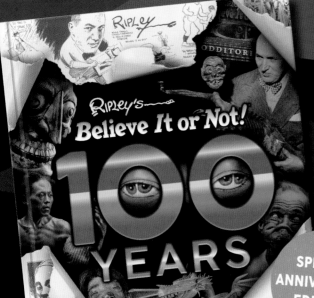

COLORS AND SHAPES

Learning colors and shapes has never been so much fun with these two new board books featuring easy-to-understand, real-life examples, silly characters, and colorful, engaging illustrations!

SHARKEE AND BREMNER

Captivating new picture books feature two favorite Ripley's Aquarium mascots—Sharkee the sand tiger shark and Bremner the puffer fish. Filled with expressive illustrations, silly situations, and lovable characters, kids and parents alike will be enchanted by each of these charming "tails"!

Carrie Bolin and Jessica Firpi • Illustrated by John Graziano

PLAY IT LOUD!

The newest edition to the best-selling Fun Facts & Silly Stories series is packed with amazing stories, unbelievable facts, eye-catching photos, and wacky games and puzzles.

UNBELIEVABLE!

SILLY!

RIPLEY'S BELIEVE IT OR NOT! ODDITORIUMS

Ripley's legacy lives on today with 30 Ripley's Odditoriums all around the world, the greatest collection of oddities ever assembled. The Ripley's team continue to search the globe, hunting for the oddest, most unusual, and the most unbelievable artifacts ever seen.

JEJU ISLAND, KOREA

GATLINBURG, TENNESSEE

NIAGARA FALLS, CANADA

BALTIMORE, MARYLAND

NEW YORK CITY, NEW YORK

Connect with *Ripley's* Online or in Person

30 ZANY LOCATIONS

There are 30 incredible Ripley's Believe It or Not! Odditoriums all around the world, where you can experience our spectacular collection during our century of strange!

Amsterdam
THE NETHERLANDS

Atlantic City
NEW JERSEY

Baltimore
MARYLAND

Blackpool
ENGLAND

Branson
MISSOURI

Cavendish
P.E.I., CANADA

Copenhagen
DENMARK

Gatlinburg
TENNESSEE

Genting Highlands
MALAYSIA

Grand Prairie
TEXAS

Guadalajara
MEXICO

Hollywood
CALIFORNIA

Jeju Island
KOREA

Key West
FLORIDA

Mexico City
MEXICO

Myrtle Beach
SOUTH CAROLINA

New York City
NEW YORK

Newport
OREGON

Niagara Falls
ONTARIO, CANADA

Ocean City
MARYLAND

Orlando
FLORIDA

Panama City Beach
FLORIDA

Pattaya
THAILAND

San Antonio
TEXAS

San Francisco
CALIFORNIA

St. Augustine
FLORIDA

Surfers Paradise
AUSTRALIA

Veracruz
MEXICO

Williamsburg
VIRGINIA

Wisconsin Dells
WISCONSIN

Stop by our website daily for new stories, photos, contests, and more! **www.ripleys.com**
Don't forget to connect with us on social media for a daily dose of the weird and the wonderful.

 /RipleysBelieveItOrNot

 @Ripleys

 youtube.com/Ripleys

 @RipleysBelieveItorNot

Ripley's Believe It or Not!®